GONE PRO
FLORIDA
Gator Athletes Who Became Pros

GONE PRO
FLORIDA
Gator Athletes Who Became Pros

Steve Rajtar
and
Gayle Prince Rajtar

CLERISY PRESS

Gone Pro Florida: Gator Athletes Who Became Pros
COPYRIGHT © 2014 by Steve Rajtar and Gayle Prince Rajtar

ALL RIGHTS RESERVED. No portion of this book may be reproduced in any fashion, print, facsimile, or electronic, or by any method yet to be developed, without express permission of the copyright holder.

For further information,Contact the publisher at:

Clerisy Press
306 Greenup Street
Covington, KY 41011
clerisypress.com

a division of Keen Communications, Birmingham, Alabama

CATALOGING-IN-PUBLICATION DATA IS AVAILABLE FROM THE LIBRARY OF CONGRESS

ISBN-978-1-57860-542-2; eISBN 978-1-57860-543-9

Distributed by Publishers Group West
Printed in the United States of America
First edition, first printing
Editor: Matthew Solan
Cover design: Scott McGrew
Interior design: Annie Long and Donna Collingwood

TABLE of CONTENTS

Acknowledgments vii
About Gone Pro viii
Introduction 1

FOOTBALL 20

BASEBALL AND SOFTBALL 190
    Baseball 191
    Softball 237

BASKETBALL 246
    Men 247
    Women 281

GOLF 295
    Men 296
    Women 319

TENNIS 326
    Men 327
    Women 333

SOCCER 340

MARTIAL ARTS **350**

NASCAR **355**

OLYMPIC SPORTS **357**

    Swimming and Diving 365

    Track and Field 367

    Gymnastics 369

    Soccer 370

    Tennis 370

    Basketball 370

    Baseball 371

    Handball 371

    Cycling 371

    Volleyball 371

    Bobsledding 372

Appendix—Gator Players and Head Coaches
in Halls of Fame 414

Bibliography 420

About the Photographs .425

Index 434

About the Authors 446

Acknowledgments

First, thank you to Sandra Friend, who thought of us when her publisher asked for Gator fans who could write a book about alumni who went on to the pros and the Olympics.

Thanks to Steve Millburg, the "father" of the Gone Pro series, both for the series concept and for being involved in the editing process of this volume, along with Matthew Solan and Tim Jackson.

Thanks to Norm Carlson, Carl Van Ness, and others at the University of Florida for their recommendations of sources of information and photos.

Thanks to all of the photographers who have donated their work to the Florida Photographic Collection and other collections, available to all for use in publications such as this.

Thanks to the other photographers who had limited the use of their work, ordinarily prohibiting its publication, but when approached with the Gone Pro concept eagerly agreed to share their photos.

Thanks to all the football players, swimmers, golfers, baseball players, and everyone else who responded to our requests for photos and information so enthusiastically and wished us well on this endeavor.

Thanks to everyone who gave their recommendations as to which Gators should be on our mythical all-star teams . . . even though they didn't always agree.

Thanks to our kids, Jason and Kelly; their spouses, Karen and Will; and grandkids Nate, Jax, Alex, Gillian, and Elleri for enriching our lives so much.

And thanks to each other for having mutual interests in sports, the Gators, writing, and making life so much fun.

About Gone Pro

The Gone Pro series celebrates college athletes who have continued to compete beyond their college careers as professional athletes or Olympians. This volume focuses on more than a century of sports involving members of the Gator Nation from the University of Florida.

We salute each UF athlete, man or woman, who has participated in a major-league professional sport or the Olympic Games. You will see facts and figures about these former students, many whose names you will recognize (and some you won't remember or never knew), presented according to their level of achievement.

The authors are Gator fans, one who received a couple of degrees from the university and one who worked in an academic office in the stadium. We lived on campus, attended games, and decades later still cheer "Go Gators!" So do our kids, even though they went to other universities. So do our grandkids, even though their choices for higher education are years in the future.

This is your opportunity to find out what happened to the athletes we Gator fans watched in the past, to learn about those who came before or after, or to discover who participated in sports other than those we avidly followed. This is not just a book of statistics. Sure, there are numbers thrown in, but more important are the athletes' stories. This is not merely a "rah-rah" book, but it's also one about real people who have had successes, made mistakes, and experienced the ups and downs of life.

We expect you'll find some of the information to be surprising. We sure did. We thought many of these Gator greats would have gone into coaching after their competition days were over, but many moved from athlete to doctor, lawyer, acupuncturist, chef, minister, teacher, and even professional wrestler. And then others simply disappeared from public life.

Don't take our word for it—keep reading. Welcome to an opportunity to "meet" some of the most accomplished members of the Gator Nation.

WEBSITE

Your Gone Pro experience doesn't have to end when you've finished the book. You can extend it indefinitely by hanging out at the Gone Pro website, GoneProBooks.com. Click on over for regular updates about the Gators in the pro ranks, advance excerpts from other books in the series, and plenty of fun stuff for the Gone Pro community.

TELL US MORE

We hope this book stirs warm memories and tells you some things you didn't know about the University of Florida's athletic heroes. But there's always more to learn and more to tell. If we missed something about one of your favorites, we'd like to know about it. Please contact us at:

Gone Pro
PO Box 43673
Birmingham, AL 35243

You can also reach us through the website, **GoneProBooks.com,** or follow us on Twitter: **@GoneProBks.**

Introduction

When it comes to college sports, most people think only of football and basketball, and with the recent success of the University of Florida's teams, it may appear UF is just a two-sport school. But that couldn't be further from the truth. Florida is one of the most successful schools across a broad range of sports, and its alumni have gone on to great achievements in many areas of athletic competition. Heck, Florida even boasts an Olympic gold medalist in bobsledding!

Sports at Florida go back even further than the establishment of its present campus in Gainesville in 1906. The first official professional from the university was Lance Richbourg (see page 222), who played baseball with the Philadelphia Phillies in 1921. In the years since then, there have been 672 athletes who have gone on to play professional sports and/or compete in the Olympics, and they are included in this book. In addition, we have included three men (two broadcasters and a cheerleader), who, while not collegiate or professional athletes, are so entwined in the history of UF they cannot be ignored.

Before we get to the honored alumni, we need to explain what "Gone Pro" means. Quite simply, these are the athletes who have gone on to compete either in the top professional leagues or in the Olympic Games—basically, the cream of the crop.

SO WHO'S INCLUDED?

This book includes the following athletes and other athletic figures (some may be included in more than one category):

305	Football players (all men)	7	Soccer players (all women)
59	Baseball players (all men)	5	Martial artists (4 men, 1 woman)
7	Softball players (all women)	1	NASCAR racer (a man)
41	Basketball players (28 men, 13 women)	2	Broadcasters (both men)
80	Golfers (55 men, 25 women)	1	Cheerleader (a man)
15	Tennis players (4 men, 11 women)		

and the following Olympians:

105	Swimmers and divers (57 men, 48 women)	3	Basketball players (all women)
41	Track and field competitors (28 men, 13 women)	2	Baseball players (all men)

4	Gymnasts (all women)	1	Handball player (a man)
4	Soccer players (all women)	2	Cyclists (1 man, 1 woman)
1	Judoka (a woman)	1	Beach volleyball player (a woman)
4	Tennis players (1 man, 3 women)	3	Bobsledders (all men)

The majority of these athletes participated in these sports as undergraduates at Florida and then went on to compete on the professional level, but that's not the only way to get honored in this book. Some experienced Olympic glory while in high school, then came to Florida to participate on a college team or perhaps not even play a sport. Some were students at the University of Florida who didn't compete in a sport there, but they either transferred to another college or left school altogether to "go pro." Some exhausted their college sports eligibility elsewhere and came to Gainesville so they could continue to compete in amateur (but not college) competitions while they took classes.

It's also not necessary to have competed in the same sport both at Florida and as a pro or in the Olympics. We've included a Gator basketball player who went to the Olympics as a handball player, an Olympic judoka who was on the Florida track and field team, and, of course, the bobsledders didn't compete at the undergraduate level in their eventual Olympic sport. To get into this book, you had to be a student at the University of Florida and you had to "go pro," but not in any particular order or in any particular sport.

SPORTS AND SEASONS

Florida competes against other schools on a varsity level in nine men's and 12 women's sports. They are listed below, along with the years they began and the seasons they cover:

Baseball (men)
BEGAN: 1912. Baseball is Florida's second intercollegiate sport that is still in existence but the first to have an alumnus "go pro."
SEASON: February through May, followed by Southeastern Conference (SEC) and NCAA tournaments, which end with the College World Series in the middle of June.

Basketball (men and women)
BEGAN: 1915 for men, 1973 for women.

SEASON: Early November through early March, followed by SEC tournament and "March Madness"—the NCAA tournament and National Invitational Tournament (NIT), both of which conclude in early April.

Cross-Country (men and women)

BEGAN: 1935 for men, 1980 for women. The 1935 date reflects the earliest available records, but it's likely that intercollegiate competition predates that.
SEASON: September through November.

Football (men)

BEGAN: 1906. However, see the discussion in the Football chapter regarding earlier games.
SEASON: September through late November/early December, with a possible appearance in the SEC championship game in December and a bowl game in December or January.

Golf (men and women)

BEGAN: 1925 for men, 1971 for women.
SEASON: September through October and February through April, followed by conference and NCAA tournaments into early June.

Gymnastics (women)

BEGAN: 1973.
SEASON: January through mid-March, followed by SEC and NCAA tournaments through April.

Lacrosse (women)

BEGAN: 2010.
SEASON: October; February through April, followed by the ALC and NCAA tournaments in May.

Soccer (women)

BEGAN: 1995.
SEASON: August through October–early November, followed by conference and NCAA tournaments in November.

Softball (women)
BEGAN: 1997.
SEASON: February into early May, followed by SEC and NCAA tournaments ending with the Women's College World Series in early June.

Swimming and Diving (men and women)
BEGAN: 1930 for men, 1972 for women.
SEASON: October through January, followed by SEC and NCAA meets ending in March.

Tennis (men and women)
BEGAN: 1932 for men, 1972 for women.
SEASON: September through November and January through April, followed by SEC and NCAA tournaments in April and May.

Track and Field (men and women)
BEGAN: 1923 for men, 1973 for women.
SEASON: For outdoor competition, March through April, followed by SEC and NCAA meets in late May to early June. The indoor season runs from January through February, followed by SEC and NCAA championship meets winding up in mid-March.

Volleyball (women)
BEGAN: 1984.
SEASON: August through November, followed by the NCAA tournament in December.

WOMEN'S SPORTS

You will notice that while the men's sports may date back more than a century, women's sports are relatively new. That can be explained by the fact that (except for a few individuals in limited situations) there were no female students at Florida until 1946. But it still took another quarter century before there was a big push for women's sports on campus, with a little help from Congress.

The pertinent portion of the Educational Amendments Act of 1972, known as Title IX, reads: "No person of the United States shall, on the basis of sex, be excluded from participation in, be denied the benefits of, or be subjected to discrimination under any education program or activity receiving Federal funding assistance." Because nearly every university receives some sort of federal funding, that meant schools across the country had to ensure there were athletic opportunities for both men and women. If the student body was one-half female, then the varsity sports program had to make sure approximately one-half its athletes were female. Women's sports were established to help balance the large number of male athletes participating in football, and other sports (such as basketball) were opened to both men's and women's teams.

To bring about a balance of sheer numbers, some schools cut men's sports. Others, such as Florida, added sports for women or elevated some sports from club status to the varsity level. It takes several teams in such sports as tennis, golf, and basketball to balance a 100-plus member football team. Some fans praise Title IX for creating opportunities for women, such as the establishment of a women's soccer program. Others criticize the law as limiting opportunities for men. For example, the school couldn't add a men's soccer program because it would have to establish another women's sport to balance it, without adequate funding to do both.

Perhaps Title IX made possible the six national championships in women's tennis. Or perhaps it made impossible championships in men's gymnastics. What we do know is that, thanks to Title IX, UF has more varsity sports for women than for men.

SUCCESS IN SPORTS

There are two annual awards that compare universities' overall intercollegiate sports programs based on national finishes in a number of sports: the NACDA Learfield Sports Directors' Cup (formerly called the Sears Cup) and the Capital One Cup. Both assign a point value for each first-place finish, second-place finish, and so on. The points are totaled, and then the cup is presented to the school with the most points . . . or shall we just say, in the case of the Directors' Cup, to Stanford University.

The first Directors' Cup was awarded to the University of North Carolina for the school year of 1993–94. Since then, all 19 Directors' Cups for Division I sports have gone to Stanford. Each university counts its 10 best finishes in men's sports and its 10 best finishes in women's sports. Florida does not even have 10 men's sports, and Stanford has enough of both to score plenty of points to win each year. However, Florida has done quite well, as shown below:

YEAR	PLACE	YEAR	PLACE	YEAR	PLACE
1993–94	4th	2000–01	7th	2007–08	6th
1994–95	5th	2001–02	3rd	2008–09	3rd
1995–96	3rd	2002–03	7th	2009–10	2nd
1996–97	5th	2003–04	6th	2010–11	4th
1997–98	T2nd	2004–05	6th	2011–12	2nd
1998–99	4th	2005–06	5th	2012–13	2nd
1999–2000	7th	2006–07	6th		

Sometimes, the difference between first and second is out of a school's control. For example, for 2012–13, Stanford edged Florida with the help of points from women's water polo, a sport not offered in the SEC.

The Capital One Cup confers separate awards for men's and women's sports programs. It has a different scoring procedure, with two lists of sports, Group A (generally non-major sports) and Group B (major sports). Within each list, all sports are worth the same number of points. For example, in Group B, the national champion in football scores the same number of points, 60, as the national champion in women's lacrosse. In Group A, the runner-up in swimming and diving scores 12 points, the same as the runner-up in rifle shooting.

For 2012–13, the final results were:

Men's Cup	Points	Women's Cup	Points
1. UCLA	92	1. North Carolina	140
2. Indiana	88	2. Stanford	129.5
2. Texas A&M	88	3. Oregon	112
4. **Florida**	86	4. Texas	92
5. Duke	82	5. Penn State	89
6. Alabama	80	6. **Florida**	85
7. Michigan	76	7. Oklahoma	74
8. Louisville	75	8. Kansas	72
9. North Carolina	66	9. Southern California	72
9. Syracuse	66	10. Connecticut	71

If the same scoring procedures were used, but limited only to sports contested in the SEC, Florida would have won the Directors' Cup for 2012–13. In the Capital One Cup competition, the men's program would have finished second (to fellow SEC member Texas A&M), and the women's program would have still finished sixth.

Within the SEC, there is a similar award, based on sports available to all conference members. From 1973 through 1994, the winner was determined by the SEC. From 1994 through 2011, it was presented by the *New York Times* Regional Newspaper Group; beginning in 2011, it was taken over by the Halifax Media Group. For 2012–13, the All-Sports Title standings were as follows:

	OVERALL	MEN'S TITLE	WOMEN'S TITLE
1.	**Florida**	**Florida**	**Florida**
2.	Georgia	Alabama	Tennessee
3.	Texas A&M	Georgia	Texas A&M
4.	Tennessee	Texas A&M	Georgia
5.	Arkansas	Arkansas	Kentucky
6.	LSU	LSU	Arkansas
7.	Alabama	South Carolina	LSU
8.	South Carolina	Mississippi	South Carolina
9.	Kentucky	Vanderbilt	Alabama
10.	Vanderbilt	Missouri	Missouri
11.	Missouri	Mississippi State	Vanderbilt
12.	Auburn	Tennessee	Auburn
13.	Mississippi	Auburn	Mississippi State
14.	Mississippi State	Kentucky	Mississippi

Florida is the only school in the SEC to earn the overall, men's, and women's titles in the same year. During 2012–13, the university accomplished that feat for the 13th time. Throughout the history of the All-Sports Titles, the Gators have dominated:

YEAR	MEN'S	WOMEN'S	OVERALL
1973–74	3rd	n/a	n/a
1974–75	3rd	n/a	n/a
1975–76	4th	n/a	n/a
1976–77	2nd	n/a	n/a
1977–78	2nd	n/a	n/a
1978–79	3rd	n/a	n/a
1979–80	7th	n/a	n/a

YEAR	MEN'S	WOMEN'S	OVERALL
1980–81	4th	n/a	n/a
1981–82	4th	n/a	n/a
1982–83	4th	n/a	n/a
1983–84	3rd	2nd	2nd
1984–85	4th	1st	2nd
1985–86	6th	2nd	3rd
1986–87	3rd	2nd	3rd
1987–88	2nd	1st	T1st
1988–89	2nd	1st	1st
1989–90	6th	3rd	4th
1990–91	2nd	2nd	2nd
1991–92	1st	1st	1st
1992–93	1st	1st	1st
1993–94	1st	2nd	1st
1994–95	2nd	1st	1st
1995–96	1st	1st	1st
1996–97	3rd	1st	1st
1997–98	1st	1st	1st
1998–99	1st	2nd	1st
1999–2000	1st	1st	1st
2000–01	3rd	1st	1st
2001–02	1st	1st	1st
2002–03	1st	1st	1st
2003–04	1st	2nd	1st
2004–05	1st	3rd	1st
2005–06	2nd	3rd	2nd
2006–07	1st	1st	1st
2007–08	2nd	1st	1st
2008–09	1st	1st	1st
2009–10	1st	1st	1st
2010–11	1st	1st	1st
2011–12	1st	1st	1st
2012–13	1st	1st	1st

FLORIDA CLUB SPORTS

In addition to the above list of varsity intercollegiate sports, numerous other sports are allowed to use the university's name and some of its facilities. These activities are not officially sponsored or funded by the university and are led by students, so the list varies from year to year depending, on current students' interest. For 2013, here are the Florida club sports:

❯ Badminton	❯ Kickboxing	❯ Swimming and Diving
❯ Baseball	❯ Lacrosse (men)	❯ Synchronized Swimming
❯ Bowling	❯ Lacrosse (women)	❯ Table Tennis
❯ Competitive Cheerleading	❯ Paintball	❯ Tae Kwon Do
❯ Crew	❯ Racquetball	❯ Tennis
❯ Cricket	❯ Rock Climbing	❯ Triathlon
❯ Cross-Country and Track	❯ Roller Hockey (men)	❯ Ultimate (men)
❯ Cuong Nhu Martial Arts	❯ Rugby (men)	❯ Ultimate (women)
❯ Cycling	❯ Rugby (women)	❯ Underwater Hockey
❯ Equestrian	❯ Sailing	❯ Volleyball (men)
❯ Fencing	❯ Skimboarding	❯ Volleyball (women)
❯ Gymnastics	❯ Soccer (men)	❯ Wakeboarding
❯ Handball	❯ Soccer (women)	❯ Water Polo (men)
❯ Ice Hockey (men)	❯ Softball	❯ Water Polo (women)
❯ Kendo	❯ Surfing	❯ Wrestling

ALL-SOMETHING

Most sports fans have heard of the title "All-American," which means that an athlete has been selected as the best in the nation at his or her position. Over the years, the process of naming All-Americans has evolved into multiple lists (first team, second team, honorable mentions, etc.), named by a multitude of entities, including the following just for football:

- American Football Coaches Association
- Associated Press
- Football Writers Association of America
- *Sporting News*
- Walter Camp Football Foundation

The NCAA recognizes each of the above. A football player who is selected to the first team by three of the above is labeled a "Consensus" pick, and one who is chosen by all five is a deemed a "Unanimous" pick. Other sports have similar ways of choosing the best athletes, and All-American teams are named by many newspapers, magazines, and websites. Nothing limits how many All-American teams there may be, and no rules regulate the picking of its members.

That's why we don't go overboard in mentioning All-American honors in this book. When we do, we say who picked the team ("He was an AP All-American first team selection . . ."). Otherwise, we don't list the All-American honors. We expect most of the athletes in this book have been on someone's All-American team at some time. The same goes for the vague titles like Player of the Year or Coach of the Year.

That doesn't apply to official selections made by the Southeastern Conference or the NCAA or other applicable organizations. If athletes are choosen as an All-Tournament team for a particular year, we'll include that. If they are named the Freshman of the Year, we'll include that too.

ALL-STAR TEAMS

In the chapters on Baseball, Basketball, and Football, we've picked all-star teams based on who we feel are or were the best pros at each position. It's important to understand that we based the selections solely on their professional careers—and not how they did in competition on behalf of the Gators.

An athlete's performance on the college level is not necessarily a good predictor of success at the professional level. If it were, one of Florida's four Heisman Trophy winners (yes, four!) would have been one of our football all-stars (none of them were). If we were selecting based on Saturday performances at Florida Field, Carlos Alvarez would likely be our all-star wide receiver (he's not). Al Rosen was at Florida for a short time, not long enough to rack up a full college career's worth of statistics. But what he did afterward with the Cleveland Indians should qualify him for serious consideration for enshrinement in the National Baseball Hall of Fame. As a pro, he's easily an all-star.

The all-star selections are also based on the athletes' performance in competition without regard to their personal lives. One of our all-stars was kicked off his college team because of repeated drug use. Another was kicked off his professional team because he was accused of murder. Of course, we don't endorse all of the off-field or off-court actions of these athletes, but we applaud their accomplishments while they participated in their particular sports.

SPORTS FACILITIES
Florida Field (Football)
OPENED: 1930   **SEATING CAPACITY:** 88,458   **SURFACE:** Grass

The 22,000-seat stadium was completed in time for the 1930 homecoming game against the University of Alabama. It was dedicated to the Florida men who died in World War I, and a bronze plaque bearing their names was attached to the north wall. Lights were installed later, paid for through a donation by Jacksonville, Florida, businesswoman Georgia Seagle. After another contributor, Ben Hill Griffin, gave funds toward a $17 million expansion in 1990, the stadium was renamed Ben Hill Griffin Stadium at Florida Field. Former football coach Steve Spurrier nicknamed the stadium "The Swamp" in the early 1990s, and it has been adopted as the unofficial name by fans, players, and even the media.

The stadium is on the south side of University Avenue at the intersection with Gale Lamerand Drive. Between the stadium and the avenue is a large, grassy open area that used to be Fleming Field, named for the state's 15th governor, and was the home venue for Gator football and baseball games prior to the completion of the stadium.

Ben Hill Griffin Stadium at Florida Field

Football Stadiums in the Southeastern Conference

(Ranked by Seating Capacity)

CAPACITY	STADIUM	UNIVERSITY	CITY
102,455	Neyland Stadium	University of Tennessee	Knoxville
101,821	Bryant-Denny Stadium	University of Alabama	Tuscaloosa
92,746	Sanford Stadium	University of Georgia	Athens
92,542	Tiger Stadium	Louisiana State University	Baton Rouge
88,548	Ben Hill Griffin Stadium	University of Florida	Gainesville
87,451	Jordan-Hare Stadium	Auburn University	Auburn, AL
82,600	Kyle Field	Texas A&M University	College Station
80,250	Williams-Brice Stadium	University of South Carolina	Columbia
72,000	Donald W. Reynolds Razorback Stadium	University of Arkansas	Fayetteville
71,004	Farout Field	University of Missouri	Columbia
67,606	Commonwealth Stadium	University of Kentucky	Lexington
60,580	Vaught-Hemingway Stadium	University of Mississippi	Oxford
55,082	Davis Wade Stadium	Mississippi State University	Starkville
40,550	Vanderbilt Stadium	Vanderbilt University	Nashville

Stephen C. O'Connell Student Activity Center
(Basketball, Gymnastics, Swimming and Diving, Indoor Track and Field, Volleyball)

OPENED: 1981   **SEATING CAPACITY:** 11,548 (3,000+ for swimming)

The O'Connell Center, or "O-Dome," is named for the sixth president of the University of Florida, Stephen C. O'Connell. It replaced the Florida Gymnasium, home of the basketball team beginning in 1949.

The roof of the O'Connell Center is made from a waterproof fabric supported by concrete beams and arches and is inflated to keep its shape. Enough sunlight filters through to allow trees and other plants to grow indoors. Inside are weight rooms and the eight-lane Natatorium, a swimming pool that (for competition) replaced the 50-yard outdoor Florida Pool located near the old Florida Gymnasium.

O'Connell Center

Basketball Arenas in the Southeastern Conference
(Ranked by Seating Capacity)

CAPACITY	STADIUM	UNIVERSITY	CITY
23,500	Rupp Arena (men)	University of Kentucky	Lexington
21,678	Thompson-Boling Arena	University of Tennessee	Knoxville
19,368	Bud Walton Arena	University of Arkansas	Fayetteville
18,000	Colonial Life Arena	University of South Carolina	Columbia
15,383	Coleman Coliseum (men)	University of Alabama	Tuscaloosa
15,061	Mizzou Arena	University of Missouri	Columbia
14,316	Memorial Gymnasium	Vanderbilt University	Nashville
13,215	Pete Maravich Assembly Center	Louisiana State University	Baton Rouge
12,989	Reed Arena	Texas A&M University	College Station

CAPACITY	STADIUM	UNIVERSITY	CITY
11,548	O'Connell Center	University of Florida	Gainesville
10,523	Tegeman Coliseum	University of Georgia	Athens
10,500	Humphrey Coliseum	Mississippi State University	Starkville
9,121	Auburn Arena	Auburn University	Auburn, AL
9,061	Tad Smith Coliseum	University of Mississippi	Oxford
8,000	Memorial Coliseum (women)	University of Kentucky	Lexington
3,800	Foster Auditorium (women)	University of Alabama	Tuscaloosa

James G. Pressly Stadium at Percy Beard Track (Soccer)

OPENED (FOR SOCCER): 1995   **SEATING CAPACITY:** 4,500

The soccer stadium is adjacent to Woodlawn Drive, between Southwest Second Avenue and Fraternity Drive. In 1995, the old 1959 stadium for track and field was renovated at a cost of $750,000 to accommodate the new women's soccer team. It is named for Florida alumnus and renowed attorney James G. Pressly, who has consistently been listed in The Best Lawyers in America and has served as past president of the Palm Beach County Bar Association. Soccer practice fields are at the Lacrosse/Soccer Complex near the intersection of Hull Road and Natural Area Drive.

James G. Pressly Stadium

Bostick Golf Course (Golf)

OPENED: 1921

This was once the Gainesville Golf and Country Club, and it was designed by famed golf course architect Donald Ross in 1921. The course, at the northwest corner of the campus, was acquired by UF in 1962. Named for Mark Bostick, an alumnus and benefactor, the course underwent a major renovation in 2001. Located there is the Guy Bostick Clubhouse, named for Mark's father. It is a 6,701-yard, par 70 course on 116 acres.

Mark Bostick Golf Course

Linder Stadium at Ring Tennis Complex (Tennis)

OPENED: 1987   **SEATING CAPACITY:** 1,000   **SURFACE:** Hard

Because of a donation by Dr. Alfred A. Ring, former business and real estate professor and noted philanthropist, the university's tennis complex includes a 5,620-square-foot building housing the men's and women's teams. In addition to the 12 tennis courts outdoors, there are three inside the Charles R. and Nancy V. Perry Indoor Facility, named for alumus Charles Perry and his wife. Perry founded Charles Perry Construction and built many of Gainesville's

Ring Tennis Complex

popular landmarks. The grandstand overlooking six of the lighted outdoor courts is named for Dr. R. Scott Linder, alumnus and longtime UF contributor.

Donald R. Dizney Stadium at the Florida Lacrosse Facility (Lacrosse)

OPENED: 2009   **SEATING CAPACITY:** 1,500

Included are the main playing field and the Rob Gidel Family Practice Field, both at Hull Road and Natural Area Drive. Both have access to the 12,000-square-foot locker facility.

McKethan Stadium at Perry Field (Baseball)

OPENED: 1988   **SEATING CAPACITY:** 5,500   **SURFACE:** Grass

The baseball stadium is named for Alfred A. McKethan, a donor, banker, and baseball fan. The lights were added in 1977 and paid for by a contribution from New York Yankees owner George Steinbrenner. The grass playing field is named for Carl "Tootie" Perry, who captained the 1921 football team. Because he volunteered as water boy for later teams, he acquired the nickname of "All-American Water Boy."

Alfred A. McKethan Stadium at Perry Field

Baseball Stadiums in the Southeastern Conference

(Ranked by Seating Capacity)

CAPACITY	STADIUM	UNIVERSITY	CITY
15,000	Dudy Noble Field	Mississippi State University	Starkville
11,462	Baum Stadium	University of Arkansas	Fayetteville
10,326	Alex Box Stadium	Louisiana State University	Baton Rouge
8,500	Swayze Field	University of Mississippi	Oxford
8,200	Carolina Stadium	University of South Carolina	Columbia
6,571	Sewell-Thomas Stadium	University of Alabama	Tuscaloosa
5,500	McKethan Stadium	University of Florida	Gainesville
5,400	Olsen Field	Texas A&M University	College Station
4,096	Plainsman Park	Auburn University	Auburn, AL

CAPACITY	STADIUM	UNIVERSITY	CITY
3,700	Hawkins Field	Vanderbilt University	Nashville
3,291	Foley Field	University of Georgia	Athens
3,031	Taylor Stadium	University of Missouri	Columbia
3,000	Cliff Hagan Stadium	University of Kentucky	Lexington

Katie Seashole Pressly Softball Stadium (Softball)

OPENED: 1996   **SEATING CAPACITY:** 1,200   **SURFACE:** Grass

The original cost of the softball stadium was $2.6 million, and the facility has since been upgraded to make it one of the finest in the nation. It includes training rooms, team meeting rooms, a 2,300-square-foot locker room, and other amenities. It was named after a major donation by Gator boosters Jamie and Katie Pressly.

Katie Seashole Pressly Softball Stadium

Percy Beard Track and Field Complex (Outdoor Track and Field)

OPENED: 1959   **SEATING CAPACITY:** 4,000

The venue for track and field is named for Percy Beard, who coached the Florida track and field teams from 1937 until 1963 and who held the world record in the high hurdles. The surface of the track was patterned after the one at the 1984 Olympics in Los Angeles and was installed in 1985. The track and field team is headquartered in the adjacent Gale Lamerand Athletic

Center, completed in 1995. In its 46,000 square feet are three practice volleyball courts, plus training and locker rooms and team meeting space.

HALLS OF FAME

Over the years, many Gators have been recognized by sports organizations, colleges, high schools, coaches' associations, and other institutions for inclusion into their halls of fame. Some are actual facilities you can visit, with exhibits honoring their inductees and their sports, while some are simply lists. What they have in common is the recognition of athletes who have excelled, and they have endeavored to preserve the athletes' memory.

We have compiled a list of many of the halls of fame that include University of Florida alumni, from Jack Youngblood and Emmitt Smith in the Pro Football Hall of Fame, down to many smaller ones, such as the Greater Peoria Sports Hall of Fame and the Kent State University Varsity "K" Hall of Fame. By no means is it a complete list. And many of the best athletes who are enshrined in one or more halls of fame are not included in this book. One example is Carlos Alvarez, one of the best UF wide receivers of all time, who did not "go pro." Another is NCAA national champion diver Megan Neyer, who likely would have medaled in the Olympics but was shut out because of the U.S. boycott of the 1980 games.

As we researched the various halls of fame and eliminated some of the minor ones, we still found more than 65 halls that include Gator athletes or head coaches. That list is included in the Appendix.

Now, it's time to meet the athletes themselves, beginning with the largest contingent of Gators: football players.

FOOTBALL

Most Gator fans know their football team plays in "The Swamp," but where did that name come from? It can be traced to the coach who forever changed the legacy of football at the University of Florida during the 1990s, the quotable Ol' Ball Coach Steve Spurrier: "The Swamp is where Gators live. We feel comfortable there, but we hope our opponents feel tentative. A swamp is hot and sticky and can be dangerous." And once Spurrier took over, it was.

In recent years, Florida has been one of the powers in college football—winning three national championships, getting invited to top bowl games, appearing on national television, and having many players drafted into the National Football League. However, it was not always so. One could easily divide the history of Florida football into two eras: before and after the arrival of The Ol' Ball Coach.

During Florida's early years, they and most other colleges played whoever was available. Local rivalries developed, and many games were played against semipro clubs, military units, and whomever else they could find. In 1912, the Gators joined the Southern Intercollegiate Athletic Association, which consisted of several colleges in the Southeast in a confederation without much formal conference championship competition. In 1922, Florida moved to the Southern Conference, which had been formed the year before by Alabama, Georgia Tech, and a dozen other universities. At the urging of UF President John J. Tigert, Florida and 12 other schools west and south of the Applachian Mountains formed the Southeastern Conference in December 1932, and ten of those schools are still competing in the SEC (Georgia Tech, Sewanee, and Tulane have since departed). No longer was the goal merely to compete and strive for a winning season; it was to win the SEC championship, which eventually brought with it the honor of representing the conference on New Year's Day in the prestigious Sugar Bowl game in New Orleans.

And, over the decades, oh, how the Gators have tried. Every year, hopes were high that this would be "The Year of the Gator," but a loss or two during the season to Alabama or Georgia (or any other SEC school for that matter) would derail the team's hopes, and they would wait for "The NEXT Year of the Gator." And the wait lasted for years and years and years.

After 84 years without an SEC championship, Florida hired former Gator quarterback and Heisman Trophy winner Steve Spurrier as its head coach, following his professional playing career in the National Football League and head-coaching stints with the Tampa Bay Bandits, of the short-lived United States Football League, and Duke University. Spurrier confidently predicted he would bring the university its first SEC championship. He almost made good on that promise during his first year as the Gator head coach in 1990. Florida had the best record in the conference, but the program was on probation due to the misdeeds of a prior head coach, and the title was withheld. Still, some (including Spurrier) believed that 1990 was the actual first SEC championship year for Florida.

The SEC title drought officially ended the next year in 1991, and the Gator Nation finally had its "Year of the Gator." In the years that followed, expectations were that Florida would contend annually for the conference championship and even the national championship. The change in Florida's football program from collegiate entertainment to national powerhouse began with Steve Spurrier's teams and continues today. The University of Florida has produced at least 305 athletes who went on to play professional football for 94 major league franchises in the NFL and elsewhere. They can be found on the rosters of the college, pro, and Canadian football halls of fame, and on television in most NFL games from the preseason through the Super Bowl.

At the beginning of every football season, each college team aspires to win its conference championship, which, hopefully, will lead to a shot at the national championship . . . which didn't actually exist for schools in what's known as the Division 1 Football Bowl Subdivision. Before 1992, the unofficial champion was often recognized as the school ranked No. 1 in the Associated Press poll of sportswriters, and/or by the top-ranked team in the Coaches' Poll, conducted first by United Press/United Press International and then by *USA Today* and various partners. When the polls didn't agree, more than one school could lay claim to the title without the NCAA officially identifying anyone as the national champion, which led to much-heated debate in sports bars around the country.

An NCAA rule caps the number of games a school can play, and conference championships are determined by the school with the best record within its conference. Another rule provides that if a conference has at least 12 teams, it can split into two divisions and have a championship game between the two division champs. This was intended to benefit smaller schools with smaller travel budgets by dividing conference territories into halves. Until that final matchup, no one would have to travel far to play conference games, with the exception of a few traditional rivalries.

The major conferences liked the idea and soon figured out they could also benefit from this rule. A championship game not only could keep interest strong throughout the season, because no team could clinch a championship early, but it also could generate substantial revenues for all conference members from an extra nationally televised game. The SEC quickly attracted enough schools to qualify for a playoff; in 1992, the first SEC championship game was held in Birmingham between Florida and Alabama. Florida's seven SEC championship game victories, and 10 total appearances, are the most in the SEC.

The year 1992 also marked a change in the recognition of the national champion. An alliance of several major conferences and independent Notre Dame devised a method using human votes and computer analysis to determine the top two teams, who would then play for the national championship. Over the years, organizers have tweaked the formulae for ranking the teams, and the Bowl Championship Series is moving toward a modified tournament to pick a champion. Beginning with the 2014 season, four teams will be chosen by a committee of 13 (initially chaired by Arkansas athletic director Jeff Long) for the aptly named College Football Playoff.

In the Beginning . . .

When did Florida football begin? Before tackling that question, let's establish when the university actually began. According to the date on the official university seal, the University of Florida was founded in 1853, but that's not technically correct. In 1851, the Florida Legislature passed a law making state funding available for two institutions of higher education, one on each side of the Suwannee River.

Cities, counties, and individuals set out to take advantage of those funds and began competing to establish a school in each location that would earn legislative approval. One opened in 1853 in Ocala and was known as the East Florida Seminary. The following year, the West Florida Seminary opened in Tallahassee. The Tallahassee school went through several names (including the University of Florida for a time!) and around 1900 was a coed university.

The school in Ocala eventually merged with a coed college in Gainesville, which was north of the city's current downtown. Another, the Florida Agricultural College, was founded in Lake City.

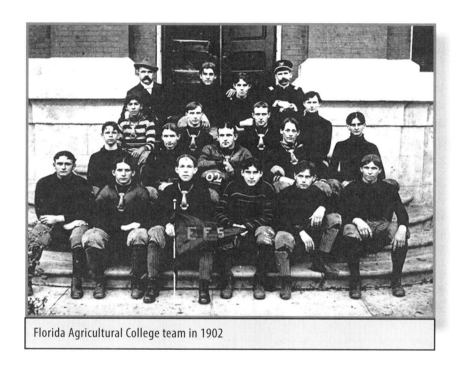

Florida Agricultural College team in 1902

In addition to the foregoing schools for white students, 1887 saw the founding in Tallahassee of the State Normal College for Colored Students. It was renamed in 1909 as the Florida Agricultural and Mechanical College for Negroes; since 1953, it has been known as Florida A&M University.

All of these schools operated independently of each other without shared standards and with some duplication. The Legislature, disappointed at the lack of organization and uniformity, passed the 1905 Buchman Act, which dissolved them all (except for what is now Florida A&M University). It also re-established new universities from the remnants of what had existed, resulting in an all-female school in Tallahassee and an all-male school in Gainesville. The school in Lake City (which had already changed its name to the University of Florida) packed up everything in wagons and set off for the new campus west of downtown Gainesville. It and other institutions were consolidated into today's University of Florida.

According to UF, the school began intercollegiate football in 1906. However, in 1899, it organized a team of 19 players coached by N. H. Cox. But the sole game scheduled that year, against Stetson University, was canceled and the team disbanded. UF also had an informal club that played other schools,

Postcard promoting the upcoming 1904 game against Georgia, which doesn't (or does) count in the Gators' all-time records

beginning with a 6–0 loss to Stetson on November 22, 1901, but its games are not officially counted by the university. The teams who played against the school in Lake City in 1901–05, when it was known as the Florida Agricultural College, or the University of Florida, with unofficial coaches including James M. Farr and J. D. Jeffrey, may argue that the games should count, especially if Florida wants to claim it began in 1853.

Confused? You are not alone. Every year before the Florida-Georgia game in Jacksonville, the announcers discuss the history of the rivalry and explain that Georgia records show one more Georgia victory than the Florida records. Bulldog fans want to count a 1904 loss to Georgia by Florida Agricultural College (coached or captained by M. O. Bridges) while Florida officially doesn't consider that game a true intercollegiate contest.

The First Official Coach

When Florida decided to hire a football coach for the 1906 season, it looked to the other white state school in Tallahassee. While known as the Florida State College, it beat what is now UF by scores of 12–0 (1903) and 23–0

1907 team, Coach James A. Forsythe Jr., second from left in second row

(1904). With the Buchman Act, that school became the Florida State College for Women, and its football coach needed a new job, so James A. Forsythe Jr. was hired by the University of Florida for $500 a year and moved from Tallahassee to Gainesville.

He recruited 23 players and scheduled eight games against colleges and semipro clubs. The first game was a shutout (6–0) of Rollins College, whose team traveled from Winter Park to Gainesville. Two weeks later, the UF team went to Winter Park and was beaten by the same score. The record for the first year was 5-3, and in Forsythe's three years as head coach, the team compiled a record of 14-6-2. One of the stars was Earle "Dummy" Taylor, who is still the only UF player to letter in football for five years (1908–12).

Now you know how football was born at UF. The next, and maybe most important question, is how did the Gators become the "Gators?" An alligator was first used as the unofficial school mascot in 1908, according to most versions. Austin Miller, a native of Gainesville, was a law student at the University of Virginia. His father, Phillip, operated a store in Gainesville. After visiting his son at the Virginia campus, Phillip came up with the idea to sell school banners and pennants at the Gainesville store

Florida playing Jacksonville's semi-pro Riverside Athletic Club in 1907

to celebrate the UF sports teams. The Millers went to a manufacturer near the Virginia campus. After being shown samples from other universities featuring various school mascots, including the Yale bulldog and the Princeton tiger, they realized that young UF didn't have a mascot. The idea of an alligator appealed to Austin because it was native to Florida and he didn't think any other school had used it. The manufacturer confirmed this, but as he had never seen an alligator, he wasn't sure he could design a representation of one. Austin found a photo at the University of Virginia library, and Phillip returned to Gainesville with pennants and small banners featuring alligators in different poses, or just a gator head featuring the then-unofficial school colors of orange and blue. The items became very popular. During the 1911 football season, the school officially adopted the gator as its mascot.

Another version has the school taking its nickname from student Neal "Bo Gator" Storter and a fabled student organization founded in 1907 called the Bo Gator Club. Storter was the Chief Bo Gator and captain of the 1911 football team. The problem is that Storter first denied this story in 1928, then many years later claimed it "bordered on the truth" and offered another explanation: The name came from a headline on a sports story the day before an away game about a bunch of alligators invading the town. First he said it was a Macon game and later that it was a game in

South Carolina in 1911, which corresponds with the official naming of the team during a road trip in South Carolina that October. And there is still another, simpler version offered by a former university employee—that it was simply a good name for a Florida team, especially considering the large number of alligators that lived in campus landmark Lake Alice. Wherever the name came from, it has been the official nickname for more than 100 years and counting, so GO GATORS!

Pre-World War II

Prior to 1940, Florida had 10 head coaches, none of whom stayed for more than five years. In 1909–13, head coach G. E. Pyle ran up a record of 26-7-3, not only because he had star Dummy Taylor, but also because his team played less than stellar opponents like the Gainesville Guards and Georgia A&M. However, Pyle began to schedule tougher opponents, including Auburn, Georgia Tech, and South Carolina. He lost to all three schools in 1913, which likely led to him losing his job, despite a 144–0 shutout win over Florida Southern College (which never even got a first down). That point total is still the highest score by a Gator football team.

Coach G. E. Pyle in about 1913

Pyle also took the Gators to their first, albeit unofficial, bowl game, which took place in Havana, Cuba, on Christmas Day 1912. They beat the Vedado Athletic Club in the Bacardi Bowl game, 27–0. The university was supposed to then play the Cuban Athletic Club, but there was a disagreement over which rules the officials were to enforce and a fight broke out. Pyle led his team off the field, claiming the officials were incompetent and likely biased against Florida—not a good idea for a visiting team. He was briefly jailed before he and the Gators returned home as "fugitives from justice" with each side claiming it won a 1–0 forfeit. Unofficially known as the "Cuban Crisis," the game isn't included in most record books.

Next in charge was Charles J. McCoy, who continued to strengthen the schedule, traveling to schools like Georgia, Alabama, and Tennessee. Over three seasons, he posted a record of 9-10. Next up was Al L. Buser, who fared no better and coached the Gators to a 7-8 record from 1917–19. Fans and the administration, who fondly remembered the 144–0 crushing of Florida Southern College, couldn't take it when Buser's Gators were shut out by the same school, 7–0. So it was time to find another head coach. In 1920, Florida President Albert A. Murphree decided to gamble on the inexperienced, but extremely talented, William G. Kline.

The gamble paid off with the beginning of a decade of Gator football excellence. Kline's teams were well-coached and well-recruited, and he compiled a record of 19-8-2 in 1920–22. Two standout players were Carl "Tootie" Perry, a lineman and two-time team captain who often played the entire 60 minutes and was named to the All-Southern teams in 1920 and 1921 (according to the F Club, the university's lettermen's association), and end Bob Swanson, perhaps better known for his musical skills.

Swanson played trumpet in the university jazz band and co-authored "We Are the Boys from Old Florida," a dance tune played at fraternity parties and other gatherings before being performed as a pep song at the homecoming game in 1924. By the 1930s, legions of swaying fans were singing the song at the end of the third quarter, a Gator tradition that continues today.

In 1921, R. D. "Ark" Newton was visiting from Arkansas and was persuaded to join the team. That same year, Major James A. Van Fleet, a Florida military science professor, became an assistant coach. Both men were excellent choices by Kline and contributed to the team's first-ever win over Alabama in 1921, as did Perry, who dominated the line of scrimmage and was described in a newspaper article as "Dixie's greatest guard."

Florida joined the 2-year-old Southern Conference in 1922, and Kline departed for a coaching job at the University of Nebraska at season's end. He was succeeded by former Gator assistant coach Van Fleet, whose military mentality, combined with his remarkable grasp of the game, helped the Gators continue their winning ways. He had a record of 12-3-4 during his two-year stint as head coach. Road games farther away were scheduled, including trips by train to play Army and the University of Texas, which gave the Gators their first true national schedule. A 1923 victory over Alabama thrust Florida into the spotlight nationwide, knocking the team previously described as "the finest team in Dixie" out of the conference championship and Rose Bowl consideration. It was by far Van Fleet's greatest victory.

After his military assignment changed and he was no longer available, Van Fleet was succeeded in 1925 by his friend and assistant coach, H. L. "Tom" Sebring, who coached the Gators while attending law school. Sebring established a more aggressive, wide-open offense, and, as he said during a 1968 radio interview, "told the boys to open up, spread out, throw the ball, quick kick, pitch out." His 17-11-2 record included a victory against Auburn (then known as Alabama Polytechnic Institute) for homecoming in 1927, his final year.

General James A. Van Fleet in 1953

Tom Sebring while he was an undergraduate at Kansas State Agricultural College

Once again, the Gators searched for a new head coach. They followed the recommendation of renowned Notre Dame coach Knute Rockne to hire one of his former students, Charles. W. Bachman Jr. On the strength of Sebring's recruits, Bachman coached the Gators to an impressive 8-1 season in his first year (1928) as they led the nation in scoring. His forward-thinking formations included two quarterbacks in halfback positions— left-handed Clyde "Cannonball" Crabtree, the fastest runner on the team, and right-handed future pro star Carl Brumbaugh, who called the signals.

Both could throw and kick, and Bachman called his team the best he had ever coached during a 1980 interview for an oral history project. He said he would "put that Florida '28 on a fast field against almost anybody but a pro team. . . . We had a right-hander and a left-hander that would drive a team crazy." He also had Florida's first All-American (chosen first team by the Associated Press and the Newspaper Enterprise Association), Dale Van Sickel, an offensive and defensive end who caught a pass and ran for a touchdown to help Florida beat Georgia in 1928 for the first time in seven tries.

Bachman stayed for five seasons (1928–32), which included the difficult years immediately following the 1929 stock market crash and the ensuing Depression. Florida president John J. Tigert managed to build a new football stadium in 1930 without government funding, but scholarship funds were essentially eliminated, and recruiting became difficult. Bachman still managed a solid record of 27-18-3 and was inducted into the College Football Hall of Fame in 1978. When he left Florida, he took over as head coach at Michigan State.

Former Gator player Dennis K. "Dutch" Stanley became head coach in 1933, just as the university was forced to cut most of its athletic funding. He was paid an annual salary of $3,600 and worked as a bricklayer to supplement his income. Over three seasons, Stanley's teams were the first to play in the newly formed Southeastern Conference, but his record of 14-13-2 was disappointing. He was fired but remained at UF as the director of intramurals, director of physical education, and an assistant football coach. Later, he became the dean of the College of Physical Education, Health, and Athletics. After yet another search, the next head coach, Josh Cody, arrived from Vanderbilt University and compiled a mark of 17-24-2 from 1936 to 1939, with one of the few bright spots being a 7-0 upset of Boston College in 1939.

Coach Dutch Stanley, right

The 1940s

The 1940s saw Gators football go through a rough stretch of mediocrity. They first turned to former Olympic discus medalist Thomas J.

1939 Gators

Lieb, who coached Florida to victories over Georgia and Georgia Tech in 1942 but wound up with a less-than-golden record of 20-26-1 from 1940 through 1945. He was hampered by the loss of most of his players to the military during World War II and the cancellation of the 1943 season. Lieb's final game, a 12–0 loss to the U.S. Amphibs, began a 13-game losing streak that sadly lasted well into 1947.

With the war over, 1946 saw the return of many veterans and the hiring of a new head coach, Raymond B. "Bear" Wolf. He had quite a task ahead of him, building a team made up of boys fresh out of high school and soldiers who had not played football in years. He went winless in his first season, but he ended the losing streak four games into the 1947 season. Center Jimmy Kynes inexplicably called the Bear's tenure "The Golden Era," despite its being the worst from a win-loss standpoint, but the name

Coach Thomas J. Lieb, left, after retirement

stuck. Wolf was fired after the 1949 season with a woeful 13-24-2 record. The Gators hoped the beginning of a new decade would return the school to their winning ways.

The Bob Woodruff Era

The 1950s opened with a new coach, Bob Woodruff, who had worked with Tennessee's Robert Neyland (whose name now appears on Tennessee's stadium) and was determined to turn the Gator program around. Following 12 hours of negotiations, Woodruff was signed to a seven-year contract paying $17,000 a year, which was more than was paid to the school's president. He had big plans to strengthen the Gators' position in the SEC. These included increasing the size of the stadium, reorganizing the booster club to raise money for scholarships, and revamping the athletic department by creating a Department of Intercollegiate Athletics that was overseen directly by President J. Hillis Miller instead of the Physical Education College dean.

Woodruff stressed defense and kicking, but his initial year featured the first sophomore quarterback in SEC history to pass for more than 1,000 yards—future Boston Red Sox owner Haywood Sullivan. Defensively, the team gave up 181 points, which was the most of any Gator team during the decade. An upset on the road of previously unbeaten Vanderbilt put Florida

Haywood Sullivan, left, Angus Williams, and Kent Stevens

in the Associated Press Top 20 poll for the first time in history and had fans jamming the streets in celebration. The Gators finished 5-5 and repeated that record in 1951 with an offense led by Sullivan, Buford Long, J. "Papa" Hall, and Rick Casares. Sullivan set records for most yards passing, total offense, completion percentage, and more, records that remained intact until a quarterback named Spurrier arrived in 1964.

The program turned a corner in 1952, despite a major setback before the season. Sullivan left to go pro, not in football, but in baseball. He accepted a $75,000 signing bonus with the Boston Red Sox. The Gators had some big shoes to fill and replaced Sullivan with Casares, who was not comfortable in the quarterback position. After three games, he was replaced by a guy considered to be a strong team player with an astute grasp of football, defensive end Doug Dickey. Dickey later recalled his job "was just to manage the game and mainly hand the ball to Long, Hall, or Casares," calling them "one of the best sets of backs that have ever played together at Florida."

And it showed. With a convincing 30–0 shutout of Georgia on the way to a 7-3 regular season, Florida earned an invitation to its first official bowl game. On January 1, 1953, UF beat Tulsa by a point, 14–13, in the (quite fitting) Gator Bowl. The final 8-3 record was the best since Bachman's 8-2 season in 1929, and Gator fans were excited for the upcoming season and the possibility that UF was on the verge of a major breakthrough.

Everything looked promising during the second game of the 1953 season as the Gators battled third-ranked Georgia Tech to a 0–0 tie during a torrential downpour. Unfortunately, the rest of their season was washed out with the departure of Casares the next week (after having been drafted by the Army) and an upset loss to Kentucky. Woodruff had his worst season at Florida, going 3-5-2, with the lone bright spot being the team's single SEC win—a victory over Georgia for the second year in a row.

Coach Bob Woodruff and four quarterbacks

The rest of the 1950s had few bright spots. An upset in 1954's second game of fifth-ranked Georgia Tech, the highest-ranked team Woodruff would beat, moved the Gators to number 14 in the AP Poll, their highest ranking ever to that point. But even a 14–0 win in Knoxville at Tennessee's homecoming—the Gators' first-ever victory over Tennessee in 11 tries—couldn't console the fans, who were so upset about the lackluster 5-5 season that they didn't notice the strong 5-2, third-place finish in the SEC, which was the best in the school's history.

After the Gators wound up 4-6 in 1955, they won back their fans in 1956 by winning five games in a row, including big wins over LSU on the road and Georgia. But they lost their last two games and finished 6-3-1. The next season was shortened by one game when a bout of the flu left most of the team too ill to play the season opener. The Gators went on to a respectable 6-2-1 season and likely would have played a bowl game if not for probation imposed due to misconduct by the baseball and basketball programs. The 1958 team went 6-4-1, which was good enough for a Gator Bowl invitation, but they fell to Mississippi, 7–3. The next year, the Gators wound up 5-4-1, and Woodruff's contract was not renewed. After 10 seasons of ups and downs, it was time to move in a new direction. Bob Woodruff departed Florida with a record of 53-42-6, leaving a program that was well-grounded.

Woodruff was known for his great sense of humor. In the late 1950s, three of his players—Vel Heckman, Don Fleming, and Bernie Parrish—caught a five-and-a-half foot alligator one evening and put it in the trunk of the car they were using. They weren't sure what to do with it, so the next morning at breakfast, they asked Woodruff for his thoughts. He suggested they put it in the whirlpool in the training room. The coach had seen the team trainer, Sam Lankford, still at breakfast and knew the training room would be his next stop. With Woodruff's help, the players dragged the poor gator (with its mouth taped shut) into the training room. They managed to get it into the whirlpool and quickly made their exit. They watched as Lankford entered the training room, only to see the gator come out of the whirlpool with a huge growl. Lankford made a beeline out of there.

One highlight of the 1950s was the beginning of one of the greatest rivalries in UF and college football history. The Governor's Cup trophy was created by the Tallahassee Quarterback Club for the winner of the annual game between Florida and Florida State, the first of which took place on November 22, 1958. The victor was to keep it for the following 12 months. On September 30, 1961, the Gators and Seminoles played to a 3-3 tie, and each team wound up keeping the trophy for six months. In the photo on the next page, Florida assistant coach Gene Ellenson (left) and Florida State coach Bill Peterson pretend to fight over the cup.

The Ray Graves Era

With the start of a new decade, many Gator fans wanted to see the team go in a new and more exciting direction, with an emphasis on offense rather than defense. There was criticism when Ray Graves, former Georgia Tech defensive coach, arrived in 1960 and signed a five-year contract as head coach. Even though he was an innovator credited with develop-

The Governor's Cup

ing what was then called the "Monster Defense," featuring a strong safety and a free safety in the backfield, many wondered whether anything was going to change for the Gators in their quest for their elusive first SEC championship if they were led by another defensive-minded coach. Graves' response to inquisitive reporters: "I told them I was going to put in an offense that, as a defensive coach, I would not want to play against."

He soon turned skeptics into believers. The new-look Gators won their first two games, followed by a dramatic come-from-behind victory over 10th-ranked Georgia Tech. Graves' team ended the 1960 season 9-2, including a 13–12 win over Baylor in the Gator Bowl. Its second-place finish in the SEC was the best ever by the Gators and would be one of Graves's most successful during his tenure in Gainesville.

Fired-up Gator fans were let down in 1961, however, with a disappointing 4-5-1 season, Graves's worst year at Florida. But it is hard to blame Graves for the poor record. The university had changed its requirements for students to enter the school's upper division after the first two years, and the team lost 17 players, many who were the nucleus of the team, after they were deemed ineligible under the new rules. The team pulled itself together and improved in 1962 to 7-4, including a Gator Bowl win over ninth-ranked Penn State, thanks in part to the positive motivation of assistant coach Gene Ellenson (likely referencing his experiences under fire at the Battle of the Bulge during World War II). Ellenson was so popular with the players that, even after he left the coaching profession, he was still invited back to Florida to deliver pregame motivational talks.

One of the biggest highlights of Graves's 10 years as Florida coach came in 1963 when the Gators beat the Joe Namath–led Alabama Crimson Tide. This was Bear Bryant's first loss in Tuscaloosa; another inspiring Ellenson pregame speech worked its magic. The Gators finished the season 6-3-1.

Coach Ray Graves in 1972

The next year, 1964, was a major turning point for the program as Steve Spurrier arrived in Gainesville. The Tennessee native sat out his freshman year of 1963 per NCAA rules, and he began the 1964 season sharing quarterback duties with 1962 Gator Bowl MVP Tom Shannon. But he took over in the second game against Mississippi State at Veterans Memorial Stadium in Jackson. With the deafening sound of thousands of cowbells being clanged by rowdy Bulldog fans filling the stadium, the Gators were down with just three minutes left in the game. According to halfback Allen Trammell, "It was so loud you could barely hear the guy next to you. Steve looked at everyone and said, 'Be quiet and just do your job, and we will win this ball game,' and that's exactly what happened." Spurrier marched the Gators down the field for a game-winning field goal and a 16–13 victory on their way to a 7-3 record.

Graves coached the 1965 Gators to a 7-4 record, which included their first major bowl game, the 1966 Sugar Bowl against Missouri. With Florida trailing, 20–0, in the fourth quarter, Spurrier led a valiant rally, throwing for two touchdowns and running for another. However, the Gators failed to convert all three two-point conversions and fell short, losing 20-18. Spurrier's five bowl records (including most passes attempted, most passes completed, most passing yards, and most total offense) made him the first player from a losing team in the Sugar Bowl to earn the MVP award.

That ground-breaking season also featured a development that changed the world of sports forever. Assistant coach Dwayne Douglas was concerned about his players becoming dehydrated in the oppressive Florida heat and consulted with Robert Cade, MD, a kidney disease specialist at the university. Dr. Cade, Jim Free, A. M. deQuesada, and Dana Shires created a drink that they tested on 10 football players. They found that it improved the players' energy levels and stamina and reduced dehydration, while opponents wilted under the Florida sun, and Gatorade was born. However, the first batches were not quite the flavorful beverage we enjoy today. In fact, the first batches tasted so bad that none of the creators could stomach them. Cade's wife suggested the addition of lemon, which improved the taste, but the drink still needed fine-tuning. During the 1965 LSU game, Allen Trammell had a little too much of the stuff and started throwing up as he caught a punt. He made a return of about 25 yards, aided by a defender who essentially let the spewing Gator run past him.

The Gators almost won their first SEC championship in 1966, but a loss to Georgia prevented that honor. However, the season saw several firsts in Gator history: Spurrier became the school's first Heisman Trophy winner; Florida's 9-2 season ended with a 27-12 victory over Georgia Tech in the Orange Bowl for their first victory in a major bowl; and the team finished with a ranking of 11th in the final Coaches Poll, Florida's highest season-ending ranking ever.

For the next two years, the Gators were less successful, finishing 6-4 in 1967 and 6-3-1 in 1968, despite a promising start in the latter year that led to a No. 4 ranking. After winning their first three games, they lost to unranked North Carolina, tied Vanderbilt, and lost their homecoming game to Auburn. Graves tried to shake things up by moving his coaches around, but it didn't help. He decided the next season would be his last as a coach so that he could focus on his other duties as athletics director.

Graves almost changed his mind during the exciting 1969 season. Quarterback John Reaves, tailback Tommy Durrance, wide receiver Carlos Alvarez, defensive back Steve Tannen, defensive end Jack Youngblood, and other talented players provided the team with great all-around depth. A Gator Bowl victory over SEC champion Tennessee gave Graves a 9-1-1 record, the best up to that time for a Gator football team. Graves finally made the official

Dr. Robert Cade, right, and the other creators of Gatorade

decision to retire from coaching two days after the Gator Bowl and finished with a record of 70-31-4 in 10 seasons. His players, a close group known as the Silver Sixties, had a 93 percent graduation rate. Many of them went on to receive law or medical degrees, and the group still meets annually at a reunion that began in 1970. Ray Graves was inducted into the College Football Hall of Fame in 1990.

The Doug Dickey Era

On December 30, 1969, the day after Graves retired, Doug Dickey took over. When Graves raised the issue of retiring, Florida President Stephen C. O'Connell contacted the former Florida quarterback before the 1969 season, while he was still coaching at Tennessee. In his first season, UF had a respectable record of 7-4, thanks to Reaves, Alvarez, Youngblood, and tailback Leonard George. But Dickey realized he needed to build up the players' strength and speed, particularly that of the running backs and receivers, to be more competitive. That strategy was not enough to produce winning records as the Gators dipped to 4-7 in 1971 and 5-5-1 in 1972, despite the addition of talented wide receiver Nat Moore.

Beginning in 1973, it appeared the Gators were turning a corner. The team improved to 7-5 and played in the Tangerine Bowl. Two top stars, quarterback Don Gaffney and tailback Jimmy DuBose, joined the fleet-footed Moore to produce a "November to Remember" with victories over Georgia, Kentucky, Miami, and Florida State. The Gator Nation was excited as the team began to show great promise.

Coach Doug Dickey with quarterback John Brantley III

The following year, Dickey made changes to the offense and instituted the popular run-oriented wishbone, and the Gators were 8-4, including an appearance in the Sugar Bowl, but they fell to Nebraska in a close contest, 13-10 after leading 10-0. Dickey's comment after that game was, "We're close. We just have to learn how to close the deal." That sentiment essentially summed up Dickey's career at Florida.

The Gators almost won the SEC in 1975. They began 4-0 and ranked number 11 as they took on Georgia and were up, 7–3, with three minutes to go. But they lost a heartbreaker, 10–7, and tied for second in the conference. The team finished on a positive note with a win in the Gator Bowl against 17th-ranked Maryland, which gave Dickey his best season at Florida with a record of 9-3. The next year, the Gators were again 4-0 in conference play when they faced Georgia. This time, they held a second-half lead until Georgia took advantage of a failed fourth-down conversion in the third quarter and beat Florida, 41–27, knocking them out of the SEC race again. In postgame interviews, Dickey commented, "I made some dumb calls," which led to the failed play being known as "Fourth and Dumb" and Florida wound up 8-4.

The following season, the Gators were determined to break their three-year losing streak with Georgia. Wide receiver Wes Chandler led the 1977 Gators to a 22–17 victory by scoring all three UF touchdowns, one receiving and two rushing. Linebacker Scot Brantley and the defense held the Bulldog offense to just six yards in the second half. But it turned out to be the high point of an overall disappointing season as the Gators finished 6-4-1 and without a bowl invitation.

In 1978, Dickey's ninth (and final) season, the team slumped to 4-7, including losses to Georgia and Florida State. Dickey was fired by UF President Dr. Robert Marston a few days before the last game, which the Gators lost at home to Miami, 22–21. Dickey's record as Florida's head coach was a solid 58-43-2, and his place in Gator history is tied to his recruitment of some of the greatest players in UF history. But he just couldn't "close the deal" when it came to the SEC conference title.

Pell and Hall

While Doug Dickey was coaching his final season at Florida, Charley Pell was winning the Atlantic Coast Conference championship with his 10-1 Clemson Tigers. University President Dr. Robert Marston hired Pell as the next Florida coach on December 4, 1978, at the airport in Greenville, South Carolina, about three weeks before the Tigers beat Ohio State in the Gator Bowl.

Pell's first task was to change how the Gators trained. He arrived on campus, took one look at the team's facilities, and found them lacking. He immediately pushed for improvements to the training room, weight room, and locker rooms, and spent the spring of 1979 agressively raising funds and recruiting and organizing boosters to help improve the program. All of Pell's hard work paid off, but the time away from his players in the preseason was evident in UF's dismal 0-10-1 record.

After that embrassing season, Pell evaluated the team and decided that for the Gators to compete in the SEC, they needed to bring in more talented and explosive athletes. He increased his efforts to recruit the best players, especially from high schools in Florida. He and his coaching staff had terrific results. Freshmen Wilber Marshall, Lorenzo Hampton, Wayne Peace, and others helped the 1980 team rebound to an 8-4 record, including a victory in the Tangerine Bowl. Pell's Gators were the first college team in history to follow a winless season with a bowl game appearance the next year, and Pell was named SEC Coach of the Year.

The team went 7-5 in 1981, including a win over Florida State after losses in the previous four years, but lost badly to West Virginia in the Peach Bowl. Pell used that defeat as a motivational tool. He buried the game film at a corner of the practice field, placed a massive rock over the hole, and had his players touch the rock daily as a reminder of the embarrassing loss. It seemed to work. The 1982 season began with a hard-fought 17–14 home win over the University of Miami, featuring Marshall's three sacks of future Buffalo Bills quarterback Jim Kelly and an amazing one-handed catch by James Jones to win the game. That was followed by another stunning win over 10th-ranked Southern California on national television. The Gators finished 8-4, including another win over Florida State and a loss to number 14 Arkansas in the Astro-Bluebonnet Bowl. In 1983, the record improved to 9-2-1, and the Gators were ranked as high as number five. The season included an opening-game trampling of eventual national champion Miami, 28–3, and ended with Florida securing a number six ranking.

Coach Charley Pell after beating Florida State in 1981

Gator fans were fired up for the 1984 season as the idea of a first-ever SEC championship appeared realistic, and—dare they hope?—a national title. The season looked glum after an opening loss to Miami, despite a valiant effort by freshman walk-on quarterback Kerwin Bell, and a tie in the next game, against LSU. The Gators then pounded Tulane, and it looked like the season was back on track. But two days later, Pell was ousted by UF President Marshall Criser because of 59 NCAA rules violations (reduced from a list of 107) dating back to 1982. The school also lost scholarships and was banned from postseason games and television appearances for two years. The remaining eight games that season were coached by offensive coordinator Galen Hall. Even though the season appeared lost, the Gators pulled together and ran off eight straight wins to finish 9-1-1 and claim the elusive SEC championship. However, as the Gator Nation painfully knows, the celebration was short-lived. The title was vacated several months later by the 10 SEC university presidents.

Even though the 1985 Gators were on probation, the faithful Gator fans continued to show their support of now–head coach Hall. Home attendance

Coach Galen Hall, right, holding the SEC championship trophy; Florida President Marshall Criser carries the 1984 *New York Times* National Championship trophy

was the highest in school history as the team again finished 9-1-1 in 1985. The highlight was the team's first-ever number one ranking after beating Auburn and holding the nation's leading rusher, Bo Jackson, to a mere 48 yards. (However, they only held the top spot for one week.) Florida had the best record in the SEC and would have won another conference title if not for the SEC-imposed sanctions. But the record books showed that the Gators still had not captured any SEC championships.

The next year, 1986, hurt by the probation's reduced number of scholarships, the Gators limped to a 6-5 record. Yet there was good news as future college and pro hall of fame running back Emmitt Smith accepted one of the few scholarships and began his stellar three-year career in 1987. During this time, Florida's offense revolved around the powerful, workman-like Smith. As one reporter put it, "Florida's offense was Emmitt left, Emmitt right, and Emmitt up the middle." In only his third game, Smith helped the Gators beat 11th-ranked Alabama with a school-record 224 yards rushing. However, even Smith could not do everything, and the team struggled to a 6-6 season, which included a loss in the Aloha Bowl against Troy Aikman and UCLA.

After a 5-0 start in 1988, the Gators then lost their next four games and ended the season 7-5, but they did capture the All-American Bowl, 14-10 over Illinois. The 1989 season started off with great promise and a 4-1 record, including a dramatic last-second 16–13 win over LSU. But the next day, Hall resigned as head coach, following allegations that he made improper payments to a pair of assistant coaches and gave a player money to help make the player's child-support payment. Gary Darnell finished the season as interim head coach and coaxed the team to a mediocre 7-5 record, which included an embarrassing 34-7 loss to Washington in the Freedom Bowl. The program had hit perhaps its lowest point in terms of morale and fan support. But the Gators were about to embark on a remarkable turnaround.

The Steve Spurrier Era

After suffering through two coaches who had apparently broken many NCAA rules, and set the program back through years of probation, Florida President Dr. Robert Bryan turned to a man who was well known and respected in Gainesville and throughout college football, Steve Spurrier. The first University of Florida Heisman Trophy winner was hired on December 31, 1989. He brought an impressive resume of coaching accomplishments, having led the Tampa Bay Bandits during the short-lived United States Football League, followed by a successful tenure as head coach of Duke where he led the Blue Devils to their first-ever Atlantic Coast Conference championship in 1989. Spurrier wasted no time changing how the Gators looked and played. He ripped out the decades-old astroturf field in favor of natural grass and retired the Gators' orange home jerseys for blue in order to re-establish some tradition. (The Gators wore blue during Spurrier's years as quarterback.) He set a goal of winning the SEC championship within five years, adopted a "no excuses for losing" philosophy, and dubbed Florida's home field "The Swamp." With Shane Matthews as quarterback in his newly minted "Fun 'n' Gun" offense, Spurrier's first season in charge ended with a record of 9-2, including an impressive 17–13 win over Alabama on its home field. It should have included the conference title, but again the SEC did not officially recognize Florida as the champion because of the previous probation. In 1991, with a defense led by tackle Brad Culpepper, and the Fun 'n' Gun piling up points, the Gators finally won their first official SEC title and capped a 10-2 season (7-0 in the conference) with a trip to the Sugar Bowl, where they lost to Notre Dame, 39–29.

The next year, the Gators won the newly formed Eastern Division of the SEC and played Alabama in the first SEC championship game, despite a young, inexperienced offensive line. They lost to Alabama, 28-21, but beat North Carolina State in the Gator Bowl to finish 9-4. The next season, however, Spurrier's Gators began an impressive four-year run of domination in the SEC. The team rebounded in 1993 with an 11-2 season, which included its second official SEC championship, this time with a victory over Alabama in the title game. The season also featured a future Heisman Trophy winner, redshirt freshman quarterback Danny Wuerffel, who showed great promise. Wuerffel took over the offense midway through the 1994 season and led the team to another SEC title with an exciting come-from-behind victory over Alabama in the championship. The team lost to seventh-ranked Florida State in the Sugar Bowl in a rematch of the infamous 31-31 tie in Tallahassee in November and finished 10-2-1.

Coach Steve Spurrier at a fan meeting in 1999

Spurrier's innovative offense, built around speed and precision, began to run at high-octane levels. The game day strategy was the same: Score fast and score often. And they did. In 1995, the Gators again won the SEC by beating Arkansas and completed their first-ever regular undefeated season, earning a chance to play for the national championship against top-ranked Nebraska. The Gators fell to the Cornhuskers, but the school enjoyed its most successful season to date: a 12-1 record and number 2 national ranking. Despite falling short, Spurrier and the Gator Nation felt that the ultimate prize of a national championship was within their grasp.

The next year, 1996, finally became The Year of the Gator. After an early season win against Peyton Manning and Tennessee, the Gators secured a number one ranking and marched through the SEC schedule undefeated, with only rival Florida State standing in their way of another perfect regular season. In a tough battle, FSU held on to win a close contest, 24-21. It looked like the Gators' dreams of a possible national championship were over. But after defeating Alabama again for the SEC championship, the Gators earned a trip to the Sugar Bowl for a rematch with the now top-ranked Seminoles. UF was ranked number three entering the contest, but an upset of second-ranked Arizona State in the Rose Bowl opened the door for the Gators. This time, the Gators' offense dominated like it had all year. Led by Wuerffel, who had just won the Heisman Trophy, and a sufficating defense that held FSU to just 42 running yards, Florida cruised to an easy victory, 52–20. In the celebration aftermath on the Super Dome field, Spurrier and the entire Gator Nation could finally relish their first national championship in football. Yes, it was great to be a Florida Gator!

The winning ways continued as Spurrier coached the Gators to a 10-2 season in 1997 that included a victory over Penn State in the Citrus Bowl and another 10-2 season in 1998 that ended with a dominating win over Syracuse in the Orange Bowl. But Spurrier suffered a different kind of loss: His defensive coordinator, Bob Stoops, accepted the head coaching position at Oklahoma. The Florida defense had many times kept the Gators in close games they ultimately won, and his departure was a big loss. The Gators made another appearance in the SEC championship game in 1999, only to lose to Alabama; then they played Michigan State in the Citrus Bowl, on their way to a 9-4 finish. They came back to win the SEC in 2000, beating Auburn, 28-6, but the season ended with a loss to Miami in the Sugar Bowl and a 10-3 record.

The Gators had an impressive start to the 2001 season, winning their first five games. They were ranked number one heading into the Auburn game on the road, which they lost by a field goal with 10 seconds left. They came back to win their next four games, only to lose to Tennessee by two points when they failed to convert a game-tying two-point conversion with 1:10 left. (The game had been rescheduled to later in the year because of the terrorist attacks of September 11). Their dream of another national championship opportunity over, they finished the season on a high note at 10-2 with a convincing win over Maryland in the Orange Bowl. But the celebration was short-lived. Two days later, on January 4, 2002, Spurrier announced that "12 years was long enough" and that both he and the university needed a change. He resigned to try his hand at coaching in the National Football League. Spurrier left a lasting impact on the university. He compiled an incredible record of 122-27-1 in 12 years, the best of any Florida head coach, which included six SEC championships (or seven according to Spurrier who still counts the probation 1990 title) and one national championship. But perhaps his greatest accomplishment was elevating the Gators from longtime mid-level SEC status to national prominence. For the Gator faithful, UF football history will forever be split into two eras: before Spurrier arrived and after Spurrier arrived.

The Ron Zook Years

Steve Spurrier left big shoes to fill. Anything less than top national rankings, victories over key rivals, SEC championships, and a chance at another national championship would be considered unacceptable by Gator fans who had gotten used to winning with The Ol' Ball Coach at the helm. Florida's athletic director, Jeremy Foley, publicly met with big-name coaches like Bob Stoops at Oklahoma and Mike Shanahan from the Denver Broncos, fueling media speculation about who would emerge as the next Gator head coach. After all, the program had reached the big time and deserved a coach of equal stature. That is why many were shocked when the announcement came that Ron Zook, a Florida assistant coach from 1991 to 1995 and the defensive coordinator for the New Orleans Saints, had accepted the position. Students and fans were vocal in their criticism; of particular concern was Zook's lack of experience as a head coach.

While Zook was regarded as a great recruiter of talent, his teams often struggled on the field. In his first two seasons, Zook had identical records of 8-5, including appearances in the Outback Bowl, but lost both games—to Michigan in 2002 and Iowa in 2003. He had some surprising wins, along with more than his share of painful losses, in those first two years. But the 2004 season provided the most shocking loss of all: Mississippi State, which came into the game with five losses in a row. The Bulldogs beat the 19th-ranked Gators, 38–31, and Zook was fired shortly after that game, although he coached the

Ron Zook as head coach at the University of Illinois

rest of the regular season and finished 7-4. The Gators went on to the Peach Bowl led by assistant coach Charlie Strong and lost to Miami.

Zook's record at Florida was a lackluster 23-14. He beat some good teams on the road, such as Georgia, LSU, and Arkansas, but never beat a ranked opponent in The Swamp. In fact, Florida lost more home games during Zook's three years than in the 12 seasons under Spurrier. In his last game, his Gators beat Florida State in Tallahassee, something that even Spurrier did not do. In a statement he read after his firing, Zook expressed how he felt about his team: "I take a lot of pride in the fact that we leave this program in very good shape, with a lot of good young talent and good people." His successor would reap the benefits of his recruiting skills.

The Urban Meyer Era

Now it was athletic director Jeremy Foley's turn to do some recruiting, and this time he kept a lower profile in his search for a new head coach. With Zook agreeing to finish the season, Foley had more time to find the right candidate to lead the Gators back to their winning ways. On December 4, 2004, Urban Meyer was announced as the new head coach. He had turned around troubled football programs at Bowling Green and Utah and compiled a record of 39-8, including leading Utah to an undefeated season and a Fiesta Bowl victory. The question was, could he do the same for Florida?

Meyer proved to be just what the Gator Nation needed. In his first year with the Gators, the team's record was 9-3, better than in any of the Ron Zook seasons, and featured wins over Georgia and Florida State and an Outback Bowl victory over Iowa. But there was no SEC championship . . . yet.

The 2006 season found the Gators with, according to the NCAA, the toughest schedule in the country. Meyer decided that, in order for his players to win, he had to teach them to be champions. He had them watch a video of championship moments featuring a variety of teams and individuals, including Florida's 2006 championship by the men's basketball team, and had that team's coach, Billy Donovan, deliver a 30-minute speech before the season. Meyer also worked with senior quarterback Chris Leak in his final season as a Gator to take a more active role as the team leader—and the team won its first six games. Florida entered the Auburn game ranked number two in the country, but the 11th-ranked Tigers proved hard to tame at home, and the Gators lost, 27–17.

Urban Meyer in 2008

Meyer took advantage of the following bye week to inspire his team and refocus it on winning, giving the players business cards showing championship rings of past years, plus a Danny Wuerffel quote about refocusing following Florida's 1996 loss to Florida State. The Gators responded by winning the rest of their regular season games and then beating Arkansas to win their seventh SEC championship. Meyer did a brilliant job throughout the season of keeping his players motivated, including having his players watch videos of past Gator SEC title game victories the week before the Arkansas game. He had an amazing quarterback in the soft-spoken Leak. Meyer used Leak to full advantage, rotating him occasionally with touted freshman Tim Tebow, a quarterback with the size of a linebacker, who provided the offense with a needed spark by smashing through defenses to pick up key first downs and keep drives alive. The Gators also boasted one of the top defenses and routinely shut down or contained many of the SEC's top offenses.

When it came time to pick the two teams for the BCS National Championship Game, Ohio State, ranked number one, was waiting for the outcome of the UCLA-USC game. It was a foregone conclusion that number two USC was just one win away from taking on the Buckeyes in the final game that everyone wanted to see. But as Lee Corso of ESPN's College GameDay might say: NOT SO FAST! The Bruins upset the Trojans, and the debate began over which of several highly ranked teams would play against Ohio State: one-loss Florida or Michigan, which had lost a close contest to the Buckeyes.

Despite criticism by many who did not believe the Gators deserved to be there, because of their close wins and lack of domination, they were invited to the BCS Championship Game against The Ohio State University. The Gators were huge underdogs against undefeated Ohio State, led by Heisman

Trophy-winning quarterback Troy Smith. Once again, master motivator Meyer used the criticism to his advantage. On January 8, 2007, Florida proved that it was more than a worthy opponent for the Big Ten champions when it dominated the Buckeyes and won, 41–14. The Gators held the Buckeyes to just 82 yards of total offense and allowed only four completions by Smith, while the Gator offense gained 370 yards. Leak was the main quarterback, completing 25 of 36 passes, and Tebow threw for a touchdown and ran 10 times for 39 yards and one touchdown. The Gators had their second national championship in school history in Meyer's second season at the helm.

The next season was a bit of a letdown with a record of 9-4, including a loss in the Citrus Bowl to Michigan, but it also featured the school's third Heisman Trophy winner. Tebow took over for Leak and became the first sophomore in history to win the award and set many records that still stand. The 2008 season saw the Gators winning their eighth SEC title, beating number one–ranked Alabama in the championship game, and Meyer guided them to their third national championship, marred only by a 31–30 loss to Mississippi in the fourth game. They ended the season with a BCS Championship Game victory over top-ranked and undefeated Oklahoma, 24–14.

Meyer had his third one-loss season in 2009, but, unlike the previous such years, it did not end with a championship. The team went into the SEC championship game ranked number one with a record of 12-0 and its sights set on back-to-back championships but lost to number two Alabama, 33–13, and had to settle for a victory over Cincinnati in the Sugar Bowl. It was the last year for Tebow in a Gator uniform. He and Meyer made a formidable duo and had been part of two national title teams.

But Meyer's success seemed to come at a price. In a surprise move shortly after the loss to Alabama, Meyer announced he would retire after the Sugar Bowl due to health reasons. However, he changed his mind, and said he would instead take a leave of absence for several months. He rejoined the team in the spring of 2010, but he seemed to have lost some of his zeal, and the Gators slumped to an 8-5 record, but they did finish on a high note with an Outback Bowl win over Penn State. Meyer soon resigned again for health reasons, this time for real, following a crushing loss to Florida State, saying, "I know it is time to put my focus on my family and life away from the field." One has to wonder if coaching at Florida just wasn't as much fun without Tebow as his quarterback.

Meyer left Florida with a lasting legacy, as well as a record that matches Spurrier in many ways. He finished with an impressive record of 65-15, two conference championships, two national titles, and one Heisman winner in Tebow. He became an announcer for ESPN the following January; however, just ten months later, the Ohio native returned home and accepted the head coaching job at Ohio State.

And Now, Coach Muschamp

When Meyer left, Florida again searched for a coach to carry the torch. They hired away the Texas defensive coordinator, William "Will" Muschamp, a former assistant coach in the SEC who was in line to become the next head coach of the Longhorns when Mack Brown moved on. Muschamp had grown up in Gainesville but graduated from high school in Rome, Georgia. He played football at Georgia and was the defensive coordinator at LSU and Auburn as well as Texas. He was also a defensive coach for the Miami Dolphins.

In his first year, Muschamp led the Gators to a record of 7-6. Although lacking a regular season winning record, the Gators were invited to the TaxSlayer.com Gator Bowl, where they beat Ohio State, 24–17. That preserved Florida's streaks of 24 winning seasons and 32 seasons of a .500 record or better, the longest such in the nation.

In 2012, the team improved to a surprising 11-2, with a solid 7-1 record in the SEC. It tied Georgia for the best record in the SEC East and earned a trip to the Sugar Bowl, where the Gators lost to Louisville—not bad for a team that figured to be in a rebuilding year, especially after the NCAA again determined that Florida had the toughest schedule in

Coach Will Muschamp as a spectator at a Gator basketball game

the nation. For the 2013 season, Florida slipped to 4-8 and missed playing in a bowl game for the first time in more than 20 years, fueling speculation by the media and the Gator Nation as to Muschamp's future. But Florida Athletic

Director Jeremy Foley has continued to support his head coach, and loyal Gator fans are rooting for Muschamp to return the team to its winning ways and are hopeful for the future.

Although the undergrads ended their year uncharacteristically early, Gator alumni did well in the professional post season. The Pro Bowl, held January 26, 2014, included Joe Haden, Mike Pouncey, and Cam Newton. A week later, Percy Harvin of the Seattle Seahawks and Jeremy Mincey of the Denver Broncos played against each other in Super Bowl XLVIII.

Head Coaching Records

WINNING YEARS	COACH	RECORD	PCT.
1906–08	James Forsythe	14-6-2	.682
1909–13	G. E. Pyle	26-7-3	.764
1914–16	Charles McCoy	9-10-0	.474
1917–19	Al L. Buser	7-8-0	.467
1920–22	William Kline	19-8-2	.690
1923–24	J. A. Van Fleet	12-3-4	.737
1925–27	Tom Sebring	17-11-2	.600
1928–32	Charles Bachman	27-18-3	.594
1933–35	D. K. Stanley	14-13-2	.517
1936–39	Josh Cody	17-24-2	.419
1940–42, '44–45	Thomas J. Lieb	20-26-1	.436
1946–49	Raymond B. Wolf	13-24-2	.359
1950–59	Bob Woodruff	53-42-6	.554
1960–69	Ray Graves	70-31-4	.686
1970–78	Doug Dickey	58-43-2	.573
1979–84	Charley Pell	33-26-3	.556
1984–89	Galen Hall (1985 SEC Championship)	40-18-1	.686
1989	Gary Darnell	3-4-0	.429
1990–2001	Steve Spurrier (SEC Championship 1990 (unofficial), '91, '93, '94, '95, '96, 2000; 1996 National Championship	122-27-1	.817
2002–04	Ron Zook	23-14-0	.622

WINNING YEARS	COACH	RECORD	PCT.
2004	Charlie Strong	0-1-0	.000
2005–10	Urban Meyer (2006, '08 SEC & National Championships)	65-15-0	.813
2011–13	Will Muschamp	22-16-0	.579

National Titles Since 1990
(Through 2013 season)

TEAM	YEARS	TITLES
Alabama	1992, 2009, 2011, 2012	4
Florida	1996, 2006, 2008	3
Florida State	1993, 1999, 2013	3
Nebraska	1994, 1995, 1997 (split)	3
LSU	2003 (split), 2007	2
Miami (Florida)	1991 (split), 2001	2
Southern Cal	2003 (split), 2004	2
Nine others		1

Major College Leaders Since 1990
(Through 2013 season)

TEAM	WINS	TOP 10 FINISHES		HOME WINNING PERCENTAGE
Ohio State	235	**Florida**	14	**Florida** 132-19 .874
Florida	232	Florida State	13	Nebraska 140-22 .864
Nebraska	230	Ohio State	12	Florida State 116-20-1 .853
Florida State	224	Alabama	10	Kansas State 128-26-1 .832
Boise State	221	Five others	8	Texas A&M 116-33-1 .779

Florida Bowl History

DATE	GAME	CITY	FINAL SCORE
1/1/1953	Gator Bowl	Jacksonville	Florida 14, Tulsa 13
12/17/1958	Gator Bowl	Jacksonville	Mississippi 7, Florida 3

DATE	GAME	CITY	FINAL SCORE
12/31/1960	Gator Bowl	Jacksonville	Florida 13, Baylor 12
12/30/1962	Gator Bowl	Jacksonville	Florida 17, Penn State 7
1/1/1966	Sugar Bowl	New Orleans	Missouri 20, Florida 18
1/1/1967	Orange Bowl	Miami	Florida 27, Georgia Tech 12
12/27/1969	Gator Bowl	Jacksonville	Florida 14, Tennessee 13
12/22/1973	Tangerine Bowl	Gainesville	Miami (Ohio) 16, Florida 7
12/31/1974	Sugar Bowl	New Orleans	Nebraska 13, Florida 10
12/29/1975	Gator Bowl	Jacksonville	Maryland 13, Florida 0
1/2/1977	Sun Bowl	El Paso, TX	Texas A&M 37, Florida 14
12/20/1980	Tangerine Bowl	Orlando	Florida 35, Maryland 20
12/31/1981	Peach Bowl	Atlanta	West Virginia 26, Florida 6
12/31/1982	Astro-Bluebonnet Bowl	Houston	Arkansas 28, Florida 24
12/30/1983	Gator Bowl	Jacksonville	Florida 14, Iowa 6
12/25/1987	Aloha Bowl	Honolulu	UCLA 20, Florida 16
12/29/1988	All-American Bowl	Birmingham	Florida 14, Illinois 10
12/30/1989	Freedom Bowl	Anaheim, CA	Washington 34, Florida 7
1/1/1992	Sugar Bowl	New Orleans	Notre Dame 39, Florida 28
12/31/1992	Gator Bowl	Jacksonville	Florida 27, NC State 10
1/1/1994	Sugar Bowl	New Orleans	Florida 41, West Virginia 7
1/2/1995	Sugar Bowl	New Orleans	Florida State 23, Florida 17
1/2/1996	Fiesta Bowl	Tempe, AZ	Nebraska 62, Florida 24
1/2/1997	Sugar Bowl	New Orleans	Florida 52, Florida State 20

DATE	GAME	CITY	FINAL SCORE
1/1/1998	Florida Citrus Bowl	Orlando	Florida 21, Penn State 6
1/2/1999	Orange Bowl	Miami	Florida 31, Syracuse 10
1/1/2000	Florida Citrus Bowl	Orlando	Michigan State 37, Florida 34
1/2/2001	Sugar Bowl	New Orleans	Miami (Florida) 37, Florida 20
1/2/2002	Orange Bowl	Miami	Florida 56, Maryland 23
1/1/2003	Outback Bowl	Tampa	Michigan 38, Florida 30
1/1/2004	Outback Bowl	Tampa	Iowa 37, Florida 17
12/31/2004	Chick-fil-A Peach Bowl	Atlanta	Miami (Florida) 27, Florida 10
1/2/2006	Outback Bowl	Tampa	Florida 31, Iowa 24
1/8/2007	Tostitos BCS National Championship	Glendale, AZ	Florida 41, Ohio State 14
1/1/2008	Capital One Bowl	Orlando	Michigan 41, Florida 35
1/8/2009	FedEx BCS National Championship	Miami	Florida 24, Oklahoma 14
1/1/2010	Allstate Sugar Bowl	New Orleans	Florida 51, Cincinnati 24
1/1/2011	Outback Bowl	Tampa	Florida 37, Penn State 24
1/2/2012	TaxSlayer.com Gator Bowl	Jacksonville	Florida 24, Ohio State 17
1/2/2013	Allstate Sugar Bowl	New Orleans	Louisville 33, Florida 23

All-Time Florida Bowl Game Records
(Through January 2014)

All-American Bowl	1-0
Aloha Bowl	0-1

Astro-Bluebonnet Bowl	0-1
BCS National Championship	2-0
Fiesta Bowl	0-1
Freedom Bowl	0-1
Gator/TaxSlayer.com Gator Bowl	7-2
Orange Bowl	3-0
Outback Bowl	2-2
Peach/Chick-fil-A Peach Bowl	0-2
Sugar/Allstate Sugar Bowl	3-6
Sun Bowl	0-1
Tangerine/Florida Citrus/Capital One Bowl	2-3

Top 20 Schools by Bowls Played
(Through January 2014)

61*	Alabama	45	LSU	39	Arkansas
52	Texas	44	Michigan	38	Auburn
50	Nebraska	44***	Ohio State	36	Clemson
50**	Southern California	44	Penn State	36	Texas Tech
49	Georgia	43	Florida State	35	Miami (Florida)
49	Tennessee	42	Georgia Tech	35	Mississippi
46	Oklahoma	40	**Florida**	35	Texas A&M

* Total includes 2006 Cotton Bowl win vacated by NCAA ruling.
** Total includes 2005 Orange Bowl and 2006 Rose Bowl wins vacated by BCS ruling.
*** Total includes 2011 Sugar Bowl win vacated by NCAA ruling.

Top 20 Schools By Bowl Wins
(Through January 2014)

36-22-3*	Alabama	25-24-0	Tennessee
33-17-0**	Southern California	23-19-0	Georgia Tech
28-18-1	Oklahoma	23-21-1	LSU
27-14-2	Florida State	23-12-0	Mississippi
27-19-3	Georgia	22-14-2	Auburn
27-15-2	Penn State	20-20-0	**Florida**
27-23-2	Texas	20-23-0	Michigan
25-25-0	Nebraska	20-24-0***	Ohio State

| 18-18-0 | Clemson | 16-16-1 | Washington |
| 18-17-0 | Miami (Florida) | 16-17-0 | Notre Dame |

* Totals include 2006 Cotton Bowl win vacated by NCAA ruling.

** Totals include 2005 Orange Bowl and 2006 Rose Bowl wins vacated by BCS ruling.

*** Totals include 2011 Sugar Bowl win vacated by NCAA ruling.

SEC Championship Game Records (Began 1992)
(Through January 2014)

TEAM	APPEARANCES	WINS	TEAM	APPEARANCES	WINS
Florida	10	7	Mississippi State	1	0
Alabama	9	4	South Carolina	1	0
LSU	5	4	Kentucky	0	0
Auburn	5	3	Mississippi	0	0
Georgia	5	2	Missouri	0	0
Tennessee	5	2	Texas A&M	0	0
Arkansas	3	0	Vanderbilt	0	0

Our Florida All-Stars: Football
(Based solely on their pro careers)

OFFENSE:		DEFENSE:	
Quarterback:	**Rex Grossman**	Safety:	**Bruce Bennett**
Running Back:	**Emmitt Smith**	Safety:	**Louis Oliver**
Running Back:	**Neal Anderson**	Cornerback:	**Lito Sheppard**
Wide Receiver:	**Nat Moore**	Cornerback:	**Bernie Parrish**
Wide Receiver:	**Ike Hilliard**	Linebacker:	**Wilber Marshall**
Tight End:	**Aaron Hernandez**	Linebacker:	**David Little**
Guard:	**Cooper Carlisle**	Linebacker:	**Mike Peterson**
Guard:	**Burton Lawless**	End:	**Jack Youngblood**
Tackle:	**Lomas Brown**	End:	**Jevon Kearse**
Tackle:	**John Barrow**	Tackle:	**Ellis Johnson**
Center:	**Maurkice Pouncey**	Tackle:	**David Galloway**
Placekicker:	**Don Chandler**	Punter:	**Bobby Joe Green**
Kick Returner:	**Wes Chandler**	Coach:	**Chan Gailey**
Best Overall:	**Jack Youngblood**		

Athlete Bios

College years are those during which the athlete was awarded a letter for football. Pro years are those for which the athlete was active for at least one game.

For the leagues listed below (except the ArFL, NFLE, UFL, WLAF, and XFL), all Gators who played at least one regular season game are listed. If their careers happen to have included time in a minor league (ArFL, NFLE, UFL, WLAF, and XFL), that is also included. If their only play was in one or more of those leagues, they are not included.

AAFC:	All-America Football Conference
AFL:	American Football League
AFLG:	American Football League (Grange)
ArFL:	Arena Football League
CFL:	Canadian Football League
NFL:	National Football League
NFLE:	NFL Europe
UFL:	United Football League
USFL:	United States Football League
WFL:	World Football League
WLAF:	World League of American Football
XFL:	XFL

CHARLES NEAL ANDERSON (1964–) ■ *Running Back*

COLLEGE: 1982–85   5-11, 210 lbs.   **NFL:** 1986–93

A native of Graceville, Florida, Neal Anderson was a formidable Gator running back whose highlight games include a 197-yard effort against Kentucky as a freshman and 178 yards against Tennessee as a junior. He had 14 games in which he gained more than 100 yards, and his rushing total for his four years was an impressive 3,234 (on 639 carries), placing him third all-time for UF behind Errict Rhett and Emmitt Smith—not bad company. He also caught 49 passes for 525 yards in his college career.

The Associated Press gave him an honorable mention for All-American in 1984 and 1985, when he also received the Fergie Ferguson Award, given by the Florida coaches to the "senior football player who displays outstanding leadership, character, and courage." Anderson joined other great players in the University of Florida Athletic Hall of Fame in 1995, and the Southeastern Conference named him to its list of Legends in 1994. In 2013, the *Orlando Sentinel* ranked him 12th on its list of the 50 Greatest Gators.

Anderson was selected in the first round of the 1986 NFL draft by the Chicago Bears, where he remained for his entire eight-year career. After the retirement of

Walter Payton in 1987, Anderson became the Bears' starting running back and proved to be a worthy replacement. He had three consecutive years of more than 1,000 yards rushing and at least 10 touchdowns (1988–90). His career stats were impressive: 2,763 yards receiving and 6,166 rushing yards, placing him behind only Payton on Chicago's all-time rushing list. He was named to four consecutive Pro Bowls beginning in 1988.

Injuries and lessened playing time led Anderson to retire after the 1993 season. He went into business in Williston, a small town near Gainesville, establishing a bank and buying a peanut farm. Fans will remember his incredible bursts of speed and dramatic leaps into the end zone.

Neal Anderson as a Gator

REIDEL CLARENCE ANTHONY (1976–) ■ *Wide Receiver*
COLLEGE: 1994–96   5-11, 178 lbs.   **NFL:** 1997–2001

After playing at Glades Central High School in Belle Glade, Florida, Reidel Anthony joined the Gators, who won the Southeastern Conference championship in each of his three years, beginning in 1994. As a junior in 1996, he led the conference with 1,293 receiving yards on 72 catches and scored 18 touchdowns, which is still the Florida and SEC single-season record. He was a major factor in Florida's 12-1 season and national championship, and later was inducted into the University of Florida Athletic Hall of Fame. Anthony skipped his senior year and was drafted in the first round by the Tampa Bay Buccaneers.

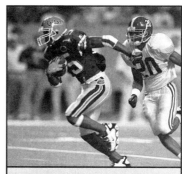
Reidel Anthony eluding an Alabama defender

In Anthony's first professional game in 1997, his touchdown catch put him in the record books as the youngest NFL player with a scoring reception. He spent his entire career with the Buccaneers. In his best game, he had 126 receiving yards and two touchdowns against the Jacksonville Jaguars in 1998. In his five-year pro career, he totaled 144 pass receptions for 1,846 yards.

After retiring, Anthony coached at Trinity Catholic High School in Ocala, Florida, and at Glades Central. In 2009, the Southeastern Conference named him an SEC Legend. In 2013, the *Orlando Sentinel* ranked him 20th on its list of the 50 Greatest Gators. He is a 2014 inductee of the Palm Beach County Sports Hall of Fame.

RAYMOND L. "TRACE" ARMSTRONG III (1965–)
■ *Defensive End-Tackle*

COLLEGE: 1988   6-4, 275 lbs.   **NFL:** 1989–2003

It wasn't how Raymond "Trace" Armstrong had planned it, but he wound up at Florida for his senior year. After an all-state high school career in Alabama, he enrolled at Arizona State and was redshirted his first year in 1984. During 1985, he played in 10 games. He worked his way up to starting defensive tackle by his junior year in 1987. Both United Press International and the Associated Press gave him an All-American honorable mention.

Trace Armstrong (93) of the Miami Dolphins

The NCAA, however, denied him another year of eligibility at Arizona State due to a clerical error, but allowed him to play in 1988 if he transferred to another university. Rather than go right to the NFL, Armstrong joined the Gators and had his best year. In addition to recording seven sacks, he set the Gators' season record for the most tackles for a loss (19).

Armstrong was a first-round pick of the Chicago Bears in the 1989 draft and was selected as All-Rookie by UPI after making five sacks in his first season. After six years with the Bears, he was traded to the Miami Dolphins, where he became a pass-rushing specialist. In 2000, he led the conference with 16.5 sacks and was named to the Pro Bowl—an amazing feat considering he was not a starter but was brought in on specific plays just to get the quarterback. The following year, Armstrong became an Oakland Raider. He saw limited action in 2001–03 because of injuries. His final career stats include 619 tackles and 106 sacks.

Armstrong received his bachelor's degree in liberal arts from Florida in 1989, and he returned to earn his master's in business administration in 2006. From 1996 to 2003, he was president of the NFL Players Association. He was inducted into the University of Florida Athletic Hall of Fame in 2000 and in 2005 was named by the Southeastern Conference as an SEC Legend. Armstrong lives in Gainesville and is an agent for several broadcasters and NFL coaches.

JOHN B. BARROW (1935–) ■ *Offensive-Defensive Tackle*

COLLEGE: 1953–56   6-2, 255 lbs.   **CFL:** 1957–70

During his senior year at UF, John Barrow was team captain and was a first-team Associated Press and United Press International All-Southeastern Conference lineman.

The Football Writers Association of America also named him a first-team All-American. The National Football League's Detroit Lions picked him in the fifth round of the 1957 draft, but Barrow opted to play north of the border instead. He signed with the Hamilton Tiger-Cats of what is now the Canadian Football League. In his first year, they won the Grey Cup (the league championship), the first of four during his 14 years on the team.

Barrow received many individual honors, being named an Eastern Conference All-Star 12 years, a CFL All-Star each year from 1962 through 1967, and All-Canadian in 1964 through 1967. In 1967, he was named the CFL Lineman of the Century.

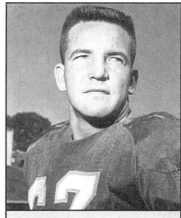

Canadian Football League All-Star John Barrow

After his playing days, he was the general manager of the CFL's Toronto Argonauts from 1971 to 1975. He is a member of the University of Florida Athletic Hall of Fame. Since 1976, he has been a member of the Canadian Football Hall of Fame, and he was inducted in 1991 into the Palm Beach County Sports Hall of Fame. In a poll by a Canadian sports network in 2006, Barrow was voted 17th on the list of the top 50 CFL players of all time.

KERWIN DOUGLAS BELL (1965–) ■ *Quarterback*

COLLEGE: 1984–87   6-3, 207 lbs.   **NFL:** 1996; **WLAF:** 1991–92; **CFL:** 1993–95, 1998–2001

Kerwin Bell was a walk-on at the University of Florida. The Gators already had several quarterback recruits—in fact, Bell was eighth on the depth chart—but Bell wanted to be a Gator even if he never played a down. Although he made the team as a freshman in 1983, he was redshirted. Luckily for him, everyone ahead of him before the 1984 season either transferred to other schools or incurred injuries, so Bell was made the starting quarterback. That season resulted in a 9-1-1 record and a Southeastern Conference championship (which was later vacated for rule violations under a previous head coach). The *Nashville Banner* newspaper named him its SEC Player of the Year.

Bell was granted a scholarship and led the team to another 9-1-1 record in 1985. For a time, the Gators were ranked No. 1 by the Associated Press, for the first time in their history. In his junior and senior years, the team posted 6-5 records. As a senior, Bell was the team captain and was presented the Fergie Ferguson Award as the senior who displays outstanding leadership, character, and courage. He received his bachelor's degree in psychology in 1987. For his four years, Bell completed 549 passes for 7,585 yards and 56 touchdowns.

His NFL career was frustrating. Bell was selected in the seventh round of the 1988 draft by the Miami Dolphins, but did not make it onto their active roster. For part of the season, he was a member of the Atlanta Falcons but still saw no action. The next year, he was the third-string quarterback for the Tampa Bay Buccaneers, and he once again saw no game action. Bell finally got into a professional game when he moved to the World League of American Football's Orlando Thunder for the 1991 and 1992 seasons. During the next three years, he played in the Canadian Football League for the Sacramento Gold Miners (1993–94) and Edmonton Oilers (1995).

Bell came back to the NFL in 1996 and finally got into a game as a member of the Indianapolis [the Colts moved from Baltimore in 1984] Colts. In his only appearance, he completed all five of the passes he attempted, including one for a touchdown. He remained with the Colts through 1997, but he never played another down with them. He went back to the CFL and played for the Toronto Argonauts in 1998 and the Winnipeg Blue Bombers in 1999 and part of 2000, then finished his playing career with the Argonauts for the rest of 2000 and 2001.

Kerwin Bell (12) with Coach Galen Hall

While recovering from an injury in 1990, Bell had his first taste of coaching as a graduate assistant at UF. After his playing days with the Argonauts ended in 2001, he became the team's offensive coordinator. Later, he was the head coach at Trinity Catholic High School in Ocala, Florida, and then, beginning in 2007, Jacksonville University.

Bell was inducted into the University of Florida Athletic Hall of Fame in 1997. Nine years later, *The Gainesville Sun* ranked him 26th on its list of the best all-time Gator football players. The Southeastern Conference named him to its list of SEC Legends in 1999.

LAMAR BRUCE BENNETT JR. (c.1944–) ■ *Safety*
COLLEGE: 1963–65   5-10, 175 lbs.   **CFL:** 1966–72

Bruce Bennett played quarterback for the Georgia state champion Valdosta High School Wildcats and switched to safety when he joined the Gators in 1963. During his years in Gainesville, he intercepted 13 passes (a Gator career record that stood for 27 years), including three in one game in 1963 against Georgia. During 1965, he served as the senior defensive captain of the team, and its 7-3 regular season record earned the Gators a trip to the Sugar Bowl. It was only the second time UF played in a game on New Year's Day.

During 1964 and 1965, Bennett was named first-team All-Southeastern Conference (by Associated Press in both years, also by United Press International in 1965), and UPI listed him as an All-American in 1965. According to his coach, Ray Graves, Bennett was Florida's best free safety of the decade. He received his bachelor's degree from the university in 1968.

Bennett signed with the Saskatchewan Roughriders of the Canadian Football League in 1966. That year, the team won the Grey Cup league championship game. He ranked with the CFL's top safeties, and his reputation for good hands got him on the field for onside kicks as well. During his 112 games, he intercepted 35 passes, which put him third on the all-time Saskatchewan list. Bennett was named a Western Conference All-Star during the last six of his seven seasons, and in 1969 was a CFL All-Star. He is a member of the University of Florida Athletic Hall of Fame.

AHMAD BLACK (1989–) ■ *Safety*
COLLEGE: 2007–10   5-9, 185 lbs.   **NFL:** 2011–13

Ahmad Black of Lakeland, Florida, played for the Gators from 2007 through 2010, making 244 tackles and picking off 13 passes. His seven interceptions in 2008 led the NCAA, with the last one coming in the BCS national championship game victory over Oklahoma. In 2010, his teammates chose him for the Ray Graves Award as the Gators' MVP, and he was named the Player of the Game in the Outback Bowl against Penn State.

Ahmad Black's 80-yard touchdown return in the 2011 Outback Bowl

The Tampa Bay Buccaneers selected Black in the fifth round of the 2011 NFL draft. He was signed, cut, re-signed, placed on the practice squad, and was finally activated in time to make it into four games that season. During the 2012 season, he played in all 16 regular-season games, making 37 tackles and intercepting two passes. After making eight tackles in four games during the 2013 season, Black was waived by the Buccaneers on October 1, 2013, and it remains to be seen if he will sign as a free agent with another team in 2014.

SCOT EUGENE BRANTLEY (1958–) ■ *Linebacker*
COLLEGE: 1976–79   6-1, 230 lbs.   **NFL:** 1980–87

As a linebacker for Forest High School in Ocala, Florida, Scot Brantley was a member of two state championship teams (1974–75). He was considered one of the top college recruits, not only for football but also as an outfielder (the New York Mets drafted him right after high school). More than three decades later, when the Florida High School Athletic Association listed its 100 Greatest Players of the First 100 Years of Florida high school football, Brantley was included.

As a true freshman, Brantley led the Gators with 145 tackles. His career total of 467 ranks second on the Gators' all-time list. His senior season in 1979 ended early when he was knocked unconscious during a game and suffered a brain injury. He recovered and, during the 1980 NFL draft, was selected in the third round by the Tampa Bay Buccaneers. By 1982, he had become a starter. In his eight NFL years, all with the

Scot Brantley, right, with linebacker Charles Williams and defensive coordinator Doug Knotts

Buccaneers, he played in 114 games and registered 622 tackles. *Buccaneer Magazine* ranked him as one of the top 50 Buccaneers of all time.

Gator fans of later years likely know Brantley from his broadcasting career. After his years as a player, he was a commentator on the Buccaneers Radio Network. He also was an analyst for the Gator Radio Network. Brantley is a member of the University of Florida Athletic Hall of Fame. In 2006, *The Gainesville Sun* newspaper listed him 25th among the 100 greatest Gators from the university's first 100 football seasons. He ranked 37th on the 2013 *Orlando Sentinel* list of the 50 Greatest Gators.

LAWRENCE SYLVESTA BRINSON (1954–)
■ *Running Back-Kick Returner*

COLLEGE: 1973–76   6-2, 214 lbs.   **NFL:** 1977–80

After playing for Miami Northwestern High School, running back Larry Brinson played four years for the University of Florida under coach Doug Dickey. In 1977, he received his bachelor's degree from Florida and began a brief professional career.

The Dallas Cowboys signed him as a free agent and used him as a running back and kick returner. He appeared in 38 games over three years as a Cowboy, always as a backup, and compiled 172 yards rushing and nine receiving, plus 25 kick returns averaging 21 yards each. Brinson spent his final NFL year playing in seven games for the Seattle Seahawks as a backup running back.

Following his retirement as a player, Brinson was the running backs coach for Air Force (1983), Arkansas (1984–89), Clemson (1990–93), Rice (1994–2005), and Kentucky (2007–12).

ALEX JAMES BROWN (1979–) ■ *Defensive End*
COLLEGE: 1998–2001   6-3, 262 lbs.   **NFL:** 2002–10

Alex Brown of Jasper, Florida, was an all-state linebacker for the Hamilton County High School Trojans before coming to the University of Florida. He was also the state champ in the discus throw and a basketball star. At UF, he was redshirted his first year, played as a backup linebacker in 1998, and by 1999 was a starter. That year, he registered 7.5 sacks, including five in one game against number two-ranked Tennessee. Brown was named All-Southeastern Conference by the Associated Press and the conference's coaches and was listed as a first-team All-American by the *Football News* and the Walter Camp Football Foundation. Overall, he made 161 tackles, 47 of them for a loss of yardage. With 33 quarterback sacks, he ranks first on the all-time Gator list.

During 2001, Brown was the Associated Press SEC Defensive Player of the Year. Brown was drafted in the fourth round of the 2002 NFL draft by the Chicago Bears and played right defensive end. During 2005, *Sports Illustrated* named him to its All-Pro team. Following the 2009 season, he moved to the New Orleans Saints and started all 16 games at left defensive end during what turned out to be his final year as a player.

After retiring, his activities have included hosting a sports radio talk show in Chicago. In 2012, he was named to the University of Florida Athletic Hall of Fame. In 2013, he was ranked 29th on the *Orlando Sentinel* list of the 50 Greatest Gators.

Alex Brown at the Chicago Bears training camp in 2008

JOSEPH BARRY BROWN (1943–) ■ *Linebacker-Tight End*

COLLEGE: 1964–65   6-3, 230 lbs.   **NFL:** 1966–68; **AFL:** 1969–70

Barry Brown played both offense and defense for the Gators under head coach Ray Graves. One of his highlight games was the 1966 Sugar Bowl, in which as a tight end he caught nine of quarterback Steve Spurrier's passes for 88 yards. Brown graduated in 1965 with a bachelor's degree in health and human performance.

The Baltimore Colts chose him in the 19th round of the 1965 NFL draft, and he made the team as a linebacker. During the 1966–67 seasons, he played as a backup in 24 regular-season games. He moved to the New York Giants in 1968 and appeared in a dozen games at linebacker.

In 1969, Brown moved to the American Football League to play for the Boston Patriots, where he played tight end for two years. He started 12 of the 21 games in which he played, catching 21 passes for a total of 214 yards. As of 2011, Brown was living in Rockville, Maryland, with his wife, Jean. Due to multiple concussions he suffered in NFL games, the couple was part of a plaintiff group suing the league and others for failing to warn players of the risks of long-term brain injuries, and for equipment failing to protect players. According to Brown, "When you know you've got a concussion, and they put you back in the game, it's abuse." It was just one of ten such lawsuits filed over a six-month period, and it will likely be some time before player injuries cease to be a controversial topic.

LOMAS BROWN JR. (1963–) ■ *Offensive Tackle*

COLLEGE: 1981–84   6-4, 282 lbs.   **NFL:** 1985–2002

In 2007, the Florida High School Athletic Association named Lomas Brown of the Miami Springs Golden Hawks to its All-Century Team of high school football

Continued on next page

Gator Growl

If you were a student at UF, you probably have great memories of one of the oldest and most enjoyable traditions in the history of Florida football—Gator Growl, which began in 1923. Each year on the eve of the homecoming game, Ben Hill Griffin Stadium is packed with students, alumni, and others from the Gator Nation to experience the event that has been called "the world's largest student-run pep rally."

The Florida Blue Key organization, a local student honor and service society, stages the huge party. It was an outgrowth of "Dad's Day," a pre–World War I pep rally attended by the (all male) student body and their visiting fathers. Each freshman brought his weight in firewood for a huge bonfire to "fire up" the team for the following day's game.

In recent decades, the more than 500 student workers at each Gator Growl have put on memorable shows featuring the University of Florida cheerleaders, fireworks, and the school's marching band. Hosts and entertainers who have appeared over the years include Bob Hope, Robin Williams, Bill Cosby, Billy Crystal, Jay Leno, Lynyrd Skynyrd, Jerry Seinfeld, Tracy Morgan, and Larry the Cable Guy.

Fireworks at Gator Growl 2011

players. At UF, he played 34 games at tackle and as a senior in 1984 was a team captain. That year, he earned the Jacobs Blocking Trophy as the Southeastern Conference's best blocker and anchored "The Great Wall of Florida," the offensive line that protected the Gator backfield in a 9-1-1 season.

Brown was a first-round selection of the Detroit Lions in the 1985 NFL draft. He remained with the team for 11 years, spending a lot of time blocking for running back Barry Sanders. He played 164 regular-season games for the Lions, starting all but one. His Lions made the playoffs four times. Brown was considered one of the best offensive tackles in the league. He took classes in the off-season and earned his UF bachelor's degree in health and human performance in 1996.

Lomas Brown taking calls for United Way in Detroit in 2006

He also played for the Arizona Cardinals (1996–98), Cleveland Browns (1999), New York Giants (2000–01), and Tampa Bay Buccaneers (2002), bringing his total of games played to 263. After earning a Super Bowl championship ring with Tampa Bay, he retired and became a television football analyst for the NFL Network and ESPN. He has also served as an assistant coach at Andover High School in Bloomfield Hills, Michigan.

Brown was ranked eighth on the all-time list of Gator greats by *The Gainesville Sun* in 2006 and is enshrined in the University of Florida Athletic Hall of Fame. The *Orlando Sentinel* in 2013 named him 11th on its list of the 50 Greatest Gators. In 2004, the SEC added him to its list of SEC Legends. Brown made several All-Pro teams during his NFL career and was named to the Pro Bowl roster each year from 1990 through 1996.

CARL LOWRY BRUMBAUGH (1906–69) ■ *Quarterback-Halfback*
COLLEGE: 1927–28   5-10, 170 lbs.   **NFL:** 1930–34, 1936–38

Ohioan Carl Brumbaugh played football for Ohio State, then transferred to Florida for his final two years. In 1928, he was part of the "Phantom Four" Gator backfield that helped set a national record of 336 points in a season. The Gators won eight of their nine games that year, losing by only one point to Tennessee. Brumbaugh is a member of the University of Florida Athletic Hall of Fame.

His professional career began in 1930 with the Chicago Bears, where he won NFL championships in 1932 and 1933. After sitting out 1935 in a salary dispute with the Bears, he split 1937 among the Cleveland Rams, Brooklyn Dodgers, and the Bears. He wound up his playing career with the Bears in 1938. He also was an assistant backfield coach, instructing future Bears stars in the complex new T formation, including quarterback Sid Luckman. Later, he was a busy man—coaching and consulting for teams with an emphasis on the T, including Boston College; Holy Cross; the University of Cincinnati; the high school in West Milton, Massachusetts; and the NFL Chicago Cardinals. Some believe he also consulted for Notre Dame and

Northwestern University, but those might only be local legends. Other post-football endeavors included working at the Fore River Shipyard in Weymouth, Massachusetts, and working with his father running a frozen food locker in West Milton in the 1940s; doing radio play-by-play for University of Dayton football games in 1953; real estate and construction ventures in the 1950s; and an unsuccessful attempt to interest the American Broadcasting Company in the 1960s to televise football games with Brumbaugh as part of the broadcast team, utilizing instant replay with isolated cameras. He also copyrighted the name of "Yesterday, Today and Tomorrow in Sports" for a proposed television program featuring athletes of the past and present comparing their careers in sport, but it never progressed beyond the concept stage.

Prior to Brumbaugh, the Bears employed a simple T formation, with a fullback standing behind the quarterback and between two halfbacks. In 1930, assistant coach Ralph Jones introduced the concept of sending a halfback in motion before the snap, opening up many more scoring options. Brumbaugh devised a play that head coach George Halas claimed would turn football into an "aerial circus." Brumbaugh handed the ball off to fullback Bronko Nagurski, who ran toward the line of scrimmage, then backpedaled and passed to halfback Red Grange.

Chicago Bears quarterback Carl Brumbaugh

The Bears had several formations that left defenses scrambling. In 1933, one formation was designed with options allowing everyone in the backfield to throw passes (confusing defenses, which had previously had to deal with only one or two likely passers), and Chicago won its division that year with the halfback throwing more passes than quarterback Brumbaugh. Halas characterized Brumbaugh as a smart quarterback and an ideal experimenter. Brumbaugh died on October 24, 1969, in his hometown of West Milton, Ohio.

ANDRE JEROME CALDWELL (1985–) ■ *Wide Receiver-Kick Returner*
COLLEGE: 2003–04, 2006–07   6-1, 207 lbs.   **NFL:** 2008–13

At Jefferson High School in Tampa, Florida, Andre "Bubba" Caldwell played wide receiver as a junior. The next year, as starting quarterback, he led his team to the state championship. He was named the Hillsborough County Player of the Year by the *Tampa Tribune. Parade* magazine, SuperPrep, and *USA Today* listed him as a high school All-American.

During his freshman year at Florida in 2003, he caught 19 passes for 174 yards. His sophomore numbers were much better, with 43 receptions (three for touchdowns) for 689 yards, plus 66 yards rushing. His third year ended early because of a leg fracture,

Andre Caldwell as a 2011 Cincinnati Bengal

and a medical redshirt allowed him to come back for his junior season in 2006. That year, Caldwell was the team's second-leading receiver, and he completed a touchdown pass in the 2006 Southeastern Conference championship game win over Arkansas.

The Gators won the BCS National Championship at the end of the 2006 season, and Caldwell opted to come back for a fifth year rather than enter the NFL draft. As a senior in 2007, he was a team captain and caught 56 passes for 761 yards. That gave him a total of 185 receptions for his career, a Gator record. He was awarded the Fergie Ferguson Award for his leadership, character, and courage and graduated with a bachelor's degree in sociology.

In the 2008 NFL draft, the Cincinnati Bengals chose Caldwell in the third round. He played four seasons for the Bengals as a wide receiver and kick returner, making it into 51 regular season games and catching 124 balls for 1,172 yards. He also returned 45 kickoffs for an average of 21.2 yards each. In 2012, he left the Bengals as a free agent and played in eight games for the Denver Broncos in the first half of a two-year contract. In 2013, he made it into all 16 games as a backup, catching an average of one pass per game. He was then re-signed by Denver to a second two-year contract.

DONALD RECHE CALDWELL JR. (1979–) ■ *Wide Receiver*
COLLEGE: 1999–2001   6-0, 210 lbs.   **NFL:** 2002–07

Reche Caldwell starred in three sports at Tampa's Jefferson High School and was chosen by the Cincinnati Reds in the 1998 Major League Baseball draft. But he wanted to play college football and instead was a wide receiver for coach Steve Spurrier. His 2001 junior year stats included 65 catches for 1,059 yards, which made him the ninth player in UF history to have more than 1,000 yards receiving in a single season.

His sure hands made him a second-round draft pick in 2002 by the National Football League's San Diego Chargers. As a rookie, he caught 22 passes for 208 yards and three touchdowns and appeared in all 16 regular season games. He played in nine games during 2003 and started the first six games in 2004, but a knee injury ended his season. Caldwell played for the Chargers in 16 games during 2005, but when they failed to re-sign him after that year he moved to the New England Patriots.

New England Patriot Reche Caldwell

His first year with the Patriots was by far his best in the NFL. He started 14 of the 16 games he played in and caught 61 passes for 760 yards. The Patriots released him just before the 2007 season, which he spent as a member of the Washington Redskins. He signed with the St. Louis Rams for 2008 but was cut before the season began. Reche's overall NFL stats include 152 receptions for 1,851 yards.

After his playing career, Caldwell got into the public eye for run-ins with the law. In 2011, he was pulled over for a suspended driver's license, then after a search of his car was arrested for marijuana possession. In January 2014, Caldwell was one of several men arrested in Tampa as one of the three ringleaders of an illegal gambling operation. Charged with running a gambling house and bookmaking business, he was released on bond awaiting an eventual resolution of the case.

GLENN SCOTT CAMERON (1953–) ■ *Linebacker*
COLLEGE: 1972–74   6-2, 225 lbs.   **NFL:** 1975–85

Glenn Cameron was a star for the Coral Gables High School Cavaliers before attending the University of Florida. During 1974, he was first-team Associated Press All–Southeastern Conference and third-team on the AP All-American list. He graduated from Florida with a bachelor's degree in management in 1976. *The Gainesville Sun* in 2006 ranked him 43rd among the 100 top Gators from the team's first 100 years. Cameron made the University of Florida Athletic Hall of Fame in 1984.

As the 14th pick in the first round of the 1975 NFL draft, he became a Cincinnati Bengal. He remained a member of that team for his entire pro career, which included playing in Super Bowl XVI. After retiring from football, Cameron earned a law degree at UF in 1987. He entered the practice of law in West Palm Beach, Florida, with the firm of Cameron, Davis & Gonzalez PA, and is now the head of the litigation department of Cameron, Gonzalez & Marroney, PA. The Southeastern Conference named him to its list of SEC Legends in 1998.

COOPER MORRISON CARLISLE (1977–) ■ *Offensive Guard-Tackle*
COLLEGE: 1996–99   6-5, 295 lbs.   **NFL:** 2000–12

After being a first-team All-State member (as selected by *The Clarion-Ledger* newspaper of Jackson, Mississippi) of the McComb High School Tigers, Cooper Carlisle enrolled at Florida in 1995 but was redshirted. He was an instrumental part of the Gators' 1996 national championship team. As a senior in 1999, he captained the team and was named first-team All-Southeastern Conference by the SEC coaches. Carlisle was the 1997 recipient of the James W. Kynes Award given by UF for "toughness and determination." He also was on the SEC Academic Honor Roll for four years and received his bachelor's degree in finance in 1999.

Chosen in the fourth round of the 2000 NFL draft by Denver, he played for the Broncos for seven years and started his last 30 games there. Carlisle became a free agent and signed with the Oakland Raiders in 2007; he was their starting right guard through 2012. He played in 190 regular season games as a professional. Carlisle remains an unrestricted free agent and may someday return to the game.

KEVIN LOUIS CARTER (1973–) ■ *Defensive End-Tackle*

COLLEGE: 1991–94   6-5, 290 lbs.   **NFL:** 1995–2008

Kevin Carter lettered for four years at Florida, and the school won Southeastern Conference championships in three of them (1991, 1993, and 1994). As a sophomore, he was named to the All-Southeastern Conference second team by the Associated Press.

During 1994, Carter was named first-team All-SEC (both the AP and the conference coaches) and was a consensus first-team All-American. He had 11.5 sacks that year, then the third best total all-time for UF. He became a member of the University of Florida Athletic Hall of Fame in 2004. Carter is 42nd on the *Orlando Sentinel* ranking of the 50 Greatest Gators. His 1995 bachelor's degree was in zoology.

Kevin Carter returning a fumble in 2000

The St. Louis Rams picked him sixth in the first round of the NFL draft in 1995. With his 37 tackles and six sacks, Carter was an obvious choice for the Carroll Rosenbloom Memorial Award, selected by the Rams' players and coaches as their rookie of the year. During 1998, he led the team with a dozen sacks and received the Daniel F. Reeves Memorial Award, presented by the team to the Rams' season MVP. He was even better in 1999, when he registered 17 sacks to lead the NFL and made the Pro Bowl, as well as the All-Madden and Phil Simms All-Iron teams. The Rams ended that year with a 13-3 record and won the Super Bowl.

During 2000, Carter moved from defensive end to tackle. He was traded the following year to the Tennessee Titans, where he made the Pro Bowl in 2002 and led the team's linemen with 79 tackles in 2003. After 2005, he signed with the Miami Dolphins. He played for them for two years, then spent his final two years with the Tampa Bay Buccaneers. Never missing an NFL game, he played in 224 and started 219 of them.

After football, Carter and his wife continued to be active with the community organizations he had participated in while he was a player, including the Kevin Carter Foundation and the Make-A-Wish Foundation. He also established the Kevin Carter Football Endowment to provide scholarships to athletes at Florida. He has served as a sports analyst for Fox and ESPN. In 2010, he was named by the Southeastern Conference as an SEC Legend.

RICARDO JOSE CASARES (1931–2013) ■ *Fullback-Punter-Kicker*
COLLEGE: 1951–53   6-2, 226 lbs.   **NFL:** 1955–65; **AFL:** 1966

At age 15, Rick Casares was a Golden Gloves boxing champion, but his mother made him turn down a professional boxing contract. At Tampa's Thomas Jefferson High School, he turned to other sports, including football, track and field, baseball, and basketball. He was named by the Florida High School Athletic Association as one of the 33 best high school football players of the first 100 years of the sport in the state.

Casares played fullback (and placekicker and punter and sometimes quarterback) for the Gators and also led the basketball team in scoring and rebounds as a sophomore and junior. He missed his senior year in 1953 because he was drafted, not by a professional football team, but by the U.S. Army during the Korean War. He was stationed at Fort Jackson, South Carolina, and was discharged with the rank of private. In 2006, *The Gainesville Sun* ranked him 37th among the top all-time 100 Gators.

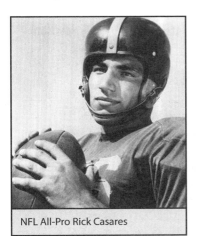

NFL All-Pro Rick Casares

In 1954, he was drafted by the Chicago Bears. While on leave from the military, he met with Bears owner George Halas and negotiated a salary, opting not to accept a larger offer made by the Toronto Argonauts. After he left the Army, he played for the Bears from 1955 through 1964. During the first six of those years, he led the team in rushing, and in 1956 led the NFL with 1,126 yards. He is still the Bears' third-leading rusher, just behind fellow Gator alumnus Neal Anderson. He completed his professional career with one season each for the Washington Redskins and the Miami Dolphins while the latter team was still in the American Football League.

Rick Casares was first-team All-Pro in 1956 and made the Pro Bowl roster each year from 1955 through 1959. He is a member of the University of Florida Athletic Hall of Fame and the National Italian American Sports Hall of Fame and, according to his teammate Mike Ditka, was "the toughest man to have ever played for the Chicago Bears." After his playing days, Casares was involved in real estate, including ownership of a lounge club (the Huddle Lounge, before the location was turned into a strip club by a later owner) and the music recording industry. He died September 13, 2013, at his home in Tampa.

DONALD GENE CHANDLER (1934–2011) ■ *Kicker-Punter*
COLLEGE: 1954–55   6-2, 215 lbs.   **NFL:** 1956–67

Don Chandler began college at Bacone College in Oklahoma, then transferred to UF and played halfback, placekicker, and punter. During his senior year in 1955, he had the best average among major-college punters of 44.3 yards per kick, his longest being 76 yards (second-longest in UF history). He received a UF bachelor's degree in 1956 and is a member of the University of Florida Athletic Hall of Fame and the Oklahoma Sports Hall of Fame.

The 1956 NFL draft saw Chandler become a New York Giant. In 1957, he led the NFL with an average of 44.6 yards per punt and once had a punt of 90 yards. His 1962 field goal percentage of 67.9% also led the league. After the 1964 season, he asked to practice only half weeks to take care of his business in Oklahoma, but team management refused.

Don Chandler's official Oklahoma Sports Hall of Fame portrait

Instead, he was traded to the Green Bay Packers, who needed him because their part-time kickers, guard Jerry Kramer and halfback Paul Hornung, had become ineffective. He was a part of three championship Packer teams: the 1965 NFL championship and the first two Super Bowls. His four field goals in 1968's Super Bowl II are tied for the most in Super Bowl history.

When he started in the NFL, there were few true kicking specialists. Chandler was one of the first to bring three shoes to every game, one for his left foot and two for his right. When he was punting, he wore a low-cut shoe; when he was placekicking, he used a high-top shoe with a squared-off toe. He often changed the right shoe at least 10 times a game.

He kicked the Packers to victory over the Baltimore Colts in a 1965 playoff game—first with a field goal to tie the game at 10-10 and then the winner in overtime. But it came with some controversy that resulted in a change at every NFL stadium. No one could be sure if Chandler's game-tying kick was good because the uprights were short and the ball sailed far above them. Starting the following season, the uprights were made 20 feet taller. The extra footage was nicknamed the Chandler Extension.

Don Chandler played in the 1967 Pro Bowl and was named the punter on the NFL 1960s All-Decade Team. He is a member of the Green Bay Packers Hall of Fame and the New York Giants Wall of Fame. Chandler died August 11, 2011, at his Tulsa, Oklahoma, home.

JEFFREY ROBIN CHANDLER (1979–) ■ *Kicker*

COLLEGE: 1998–2001   6-2, 218 lbs.   **NFL:** 2002–04

Jeff Chandler was a walk-on as a UF placekicker in 1997. After making the only extra point he tried, he was redshirted for the rest of the year. He made the team in 1998 and was granted a scholarship at the end of the season. In 1999, Chandler was voted the team's MVP (the Ray Graves Award). He set team career records that stood until 2012 for field goals attempted—80, of which he made 67—and extra points kicked—167 of 180 tries. He is the second-leading all-time scorer in Southeastern Conference history with 368 points. Chandler received his bachelor's degree in telecommunications in 2001.

He was picked by the San Francisco 49ers in the fourth round of the NFL draft in 2002. In two years there, he made 14 of 19 field goals and 21 of 22 extra points. In 2004, Chandler appeared in two games for the Carolina Panthers and three for the Washington Redskins. His NFL totals were 19 field goals made on 27 attempts and 35 of 36 extra points made.

WESLEY SANDY CHANDLER (1956–) ■ *Wide Receiver*
COLLEGE: 1974–77   6-0, 196 lbs.   **NFL:** 1978–88

Wes Chandler starred for the Barracudas of New Smyrna Beach High School in Florida before becoming a Gator. The Florida High School Athletic Association lists him as one of the 100 greatest players of the first 100 years of Florida high school football. Under run-focused head coach Doug Dickey, he still caught 92 passes (a school record 22 for touchdowns) for 1,963 yards, leading the team in receiving in 1975–77. He was first-team All-Southeastern Conference (1976 and 1977 Associated Press, 1977 United Press International) and All-American (1976 by the Newspaper Enterprise Association, 1977 by the NEA, UPI, *The Sporting News,* and *Football News*), and in 1977 received the Fergie Ferguson Award (given by his coaches, for his leadership, character, and courage) and was named a first-team Academic All-American by the College Sports Information Directors of America. Chandler was inducted into the University of Florida Athletic Hall of Fame in 1989. According to the *Orlando Sentinel* in 2013, he is eighth on the list of the 50 Greatest Gators.

During the 1978 NFL draft, the New Orleans Saints used the third overall pick to draft Chandler. He played for the Saints for four years. In 1979, he had more than 1,000 receiving yards and was named to the Pro Bowl. During the 1981 season, he was traded to the San Diego Chargers and totaled 1,142 yards for that year. The 1982 season was shortened by a strike, but Chandler's 1,032 yards gave him an average of 129 per game, still a league record. During his years in San Diego, the sure-handed receiver made three more Pro Bowl teams. He is a member of the San Diego Chargers Hall of Fame. He played his final year for the San Francisco 49ers.

Wes Chandler at Florida Field

After his years as a player, Chandler was a busy man. He was an assistant coach for the Orlando Thunder (World League of American Football), the University of Central Florida, Father Lopez High School (Daytona Beach, Florida), the Rhein Fire (NFL Europe), the Frankfurt Galaxy (NFLE), the Berlin Thunder (NFLE), the Dallas Cowboys (NFL), the Minnesota Vikings (NFL), the Cleveland Browns (NFL), the New York Sentinels (United Football League), and the University of California.

HAGOOD CLARKE III (1942–) ■ *Safety-Punt Returner*
COLLEGE: 1961–63   5-11, 217 lbs.   **AFL:** 1964–68

Hagood Clarke tried out for the Gators as a walk-on in 1961. The multitalented athlete made it onto the offense and defense, at halfback and safety. He was also the main

Penalty on . . . a Bird?

Players get whistled for penalties on a routine basis. Sometimes coaches do, too, and occasionally students in mascot costumes get flagged for overexuberant activity, such as beating up the other team's mascot. But there are few (if any) instances of a member of another species causing a penalty, except for one instance involving Florida.

On the day before Halloween in 1976, the Gators hosted the Auburn Tigers . . . who, confusingly, also claim the battle cry of "War Eagle." They brought to the game a real eagle, tethered to a handler on the sidelines near the goal line Auburn was defending. During a close game (UF won, 24–19), Florida quarterback Jimmy Fisher threw a pass of less than five yards to wide receiver Wes Chandler. Chandler eluded all the Auburn tacklers, running back and forth, almost from sideline to sideline, and sped through the end zone. As he did, the Auburn eagle took flight and bit Chandler in the back of his shoulder pads.

The play resulted in six points, 15 yards against Auburn for unsportsmanlike conduct, and no injury to the man who made the play thereafter known as "Chandler's Run." Fortunately for Chandler, the Auburn offender on the play was "Tiger" (their aptly named eagle) and not a real tiger.

Auburn's eagle in later years

punter in 1962 and, in 1961 and 1962, led the team in punt return yardage. Clarke was awarded the Fergie Ferguson Award for leadership, character, and courage as a senior and in 1965 received his bachelor's degree in business administration.

The San Francisco 49ers picked him in the seventh round of the 1964 NFL draft, but Clarke instead joined the Buffalo Bills of the American Football League, who chose him in the 18th round of the AFL draft. In his first three years, the Bills reached the AFL championship game, winning it in 1964 and 1965. At the end of the 1965 season, in which he made seven interceptions, he played in the AFL All-Star Game as a member of the league champion Bills. The following year, he intercepted five passes and was named to the All-AFL second teams of the Associated Press and the *New York Daily News*. He appeared in 67 games during his five-year career. Clarke is a member of the University of Florida Athletic Hall of Fame. After football, he worked as a financial consultant for UBS Financial Services Inc. in Fort Lauderdale. He serves as the Senior Vice President—Wealth Management.

ANTHONY CRIS COLLINSWORTH (1959–) ■ *Wide Receiver*
COLLEGE: 1977–80   6-5, 192 lbs.   **NFL:** 1981–88

Cris Collinsworth played quarterback in Titusville, Florida, for the Astronaut High School War Eagles and was a state champion in the 100-yard dash. Florida recruited him as a quarterback, and, in his first game, he tied the NCAA record with a 99-yard touchdown pass. As the Gator program moved its focus from rushing to passing, Collinsworth moved to wide receiver.

He was named first-team All-SEC in 1978–80 by both the Associated Press and United Press International; as a senior, he was also a first-team College Sports Information Directors Association Academic All-American and team captain. He was named the MVP of the 1980 Tangerine Bowl. In 1981, he graduated with a degree in accounting. A decade later, he was inducted into the University of Florida Athletic Hall of Fame and was a 2001 inductee into the Academic All-America Hall of Fame. In 2006, *The Gainesville Sun* ranked him 12th on its list of the all-time 100 greatest Gators. Seven years later, the *Orlando Sentinel* ranked him 32nd on a list of the 50 Greatest Gators.

Collinsworth was a second-round draftee of the Cincinnati Bengals in 1981. He had more than 1,000 receiving yards in four of his eight years in Cincinnati and made the Pro Bowl in 1981, 1982, and 1983. While he was there, the Bengals won the AFC championship in 1981 and 1988. Collinsworth caught five passes for 107 yards in Super Bowl XVI and ended his career with three catches for 40 yards in Super Bowl XXIII, both losses for the Bengals against the San Francisco 49ers. He had joined the Tampa Bay Bandits of the United States Football League for the 1985 season, but, after a bad ankle caused him to fail the physical exam, he went back to the Bengals.

After his playing days, Collinsworth went into broadcasting with a talk show on Cincinnati's WLW radio station and was a reporter for *Inside the NFL* on HBO. In

1990, he started doing color commentary for NFL and college games on NBC, and he still found time to graduate with a law degree from the University of Cincinnati in 1991. The industrious Collinsworth also worked for Fox and was on three different networks for part of 2006. He has also done Olympics commentating and provided the voice of the color commentator on some versions of the Madden NFL video game. He has received several Sports Emmy Awards as the Outstanding Sports Personality (Sports Event Analyst). Since 2009, Collinsworth has been the color commentator for NBC's highly rated *Sunday Night Football* telecast.

RILEY THOMAS COOPER (1987–) ■ *Wide Receiver*

COLLEGE: 2006–09   6-3, 222 lbs.   **NFL:** 2010–13

Philadelphia Eagle Riley Cooper in 2011

Ranked by Rivals.com as the country's 10th-best football player coming out of high school in 2006, Riley Cooper signed to play for the Gators under head coach Urban Meyer. The Philadelphia Phillies baseball team drafted him in 2006, but he opted to remain at Florida to play outfielder as well as wide receiver. As a freshman on the football field, most of his action was on special teams. He had four pass receptions (three for touchdowns, all in one game) for 92 yards on the season.

The next year, Cooper spent more time at wide receiver but was limited to 182 yards on eight catches because of an injury. As a junior, he played in every game and made key receptions in the Southeastern Conference and BCS championship games. During his senior year, he caught 51 passes (nine for touchdowns) for 961 yards.

In 2010, Cooper was again drafted by a second Philadelphia team, this time the NFL's Eagles, who took him in the fifth round. His rookie season statistics included 116 yards on seven catches and a touchdown scored against the Tennessee Titans. Those numbers improved in 2011 to 16 receptions, 315 yards, and a touchdown in 16 games. His 2012 season was limited to 11 games because of a broken collarbone, but he still managed 23 receptions for 248 yards and three touchdowns.

Cooper made news both on and off the field in 2013. He was criticized for making alleged racist comments in the offseason. After a couple of days away from the team for counseling, he returned and developed into a starting wide receiver averaging nearly 18 yards for each of his 47 receptions in the 16 regular season games.

RANDOLPH CHANNING CROWDER (1983–) ■ *Linebacker*

COLLEGE: 2003–04   6-2, 247 lbs.   **NFL:** 2005–10

Several organizations ranked Channing Crowder among the best high school linebackers in the country. He was signed by the University of Florida in 2002, but he waited to start school until 2003 to rehab an injured knee. In 2003, Crowder played in 11 games, and his nine starts set the record for the most in Gator history for a freshman linebacker. The *Sporting News* listed him on its All-Freshman team and named him the Southeastern Conference Defensive Freshman of the Year.

In his second year, he was a team captain and made 73 tackles. Against Mississippi State, Crowder made 18 tackles and forced a fumble, and in the LSU game, he sacked the quarterback twice. The Associated Press had him on its second-team All-American list, while ESPN had him on its first team.

Channing Crowder as a Miami Dolphin

The Miami Dolphins selected Crowder in the third round of the 2005 NFL draft, and he made the most of the opportunity. In his rookie season, he played in all 16 regular-season games, starting 13 of them, and had the second-most tackles on the team. In 2006, he had 104 tackles to again finish second. During the next four years with Miami, he was often sidelined because of injuries and fighting with other players, and he retired in August 2011. It just got to the point where, in Crowder's words, "I just woke up and saw my pregnant wife and all the teams that were talking to me and I said, 'I don't want to do it.'" Beginning that season, he began working as a sports commentator on WQAM, the flagship radio station for the University of Miami Hurricanes. He and Adam Kuperstein co-host an afternoon talk segment called the *Kup & Crowder Show*.

JOHN BROWARD CULPEPPER II (1969–) ■ *Defensive Tackle*
COLLEGE: 1988–91   6-1, 275 lbs.   **NFL:** 1992–2000

John Broward "Brad" Culpepper was a star for the Leon High School Lions in Tallahassee, then followed in the steps of his father, uncle, and grandfather and enrolled at Florida. In 1991, he was named to the All-Southeastern Conference teams of both the Associated Press and the conference coaches and was a captain when the Gators won that year's SEC championship. He also won the National Football Foundation Scholar-Athlete Award and was named to the College Football Association scholar-athlete team. Culpepper was also a first-team Academic All-American, and he received the 1991 Vincent de Paul Draddy Trophy (now known as the William V. Campbell Trophy), annually presented to the college player with the best combination of academics, community service, and on-field performance. In all four of his college years, he was on the SEC Academic Honor Roll. He received three degrees from UF, a bachelor's in history, a master's in exercise and sports sciences, and a law degree.

In the 1992 NFL draft, Culpepper went in the 10th round to the Minnesota Vikings, for whom he played in 1992–93. He then went to the Tampa Bay Buccaneers for 1994–99 and finished his career in 2000 with the Chicago Bears. He started 83 of the 131 games he played in and made 316 tackles and 34 sacks.

Brad Culpepper now practices law in Tampa. He became a member of the University of Florida Athletic Hall of Fame in 2001. *The Gainesville Sun* listed him 47th on its 2006 list of the 100 greatest all-time Gator players, and the *Orlando Sentinel* ranked him 48th on its list of the 50 Greatest Gators. In 2002, the Southeastern Conference named him one of its SEC Legends.

Gator tackle Brad Culpepper

ANDRA RAYNARD DAVIS (1978–) ■ *Linebacker*
COLLEGE: 1998–2001   6-1, 255 lbs.   **NFL:** 2002–11

Andra Davis captained the football team for Suwannee High School in Live Oak, Florida, before coming to Gainesville. He sat out a redshirt year before his four years of college competition. In 2000, he was part of the Gators' Southeastern Conference championship squad. Davis was a team captain in his senior year and started 23 of the 35 games in which he played as a Gator.

The Cleveland Browns picked him in the fifth round of the NFL 2002 draft, and Davis played seven seasons for them. In 2003, he became the starter at middle linebacker and led the team in tackles. In one game, he tied the franchise record with four sacks. In 2005, he had 20 tackles in a game against the Packers.

Davis also played one season (2009) with the Denver Broncos, totaling 90 tackles and 3.5 sacks, then was released in March 2010. He next moved to the Buffalo Bills and, in the first game of the season, injured his shoulder. He continued to play and got into six games, but he was placed on injured reserve for the rest of 2010. Davis came back with limited time in all 16 regular season games in 2011 before ending his playing career. During October of that final season, he lost his starting position to a rookie linebacker, and Davis commented that the Bills were moving to a system utilizing smaller linebackers (perhaps they were also quicker than he was). As a free agent, he did not return to Buffalo or sign on with another team. That year, he was presented with the Ed Block Courage Award, given to a player on each NFL team

Denver Bronco Andra Davis

who exemplifies sportsmanship and courage, as determined by the votes of his teammates. In 2012, he finished his bachelor's degree in social sciences at the University of Nevada, Las Vegas.

JAMES FRANKLIN DEMPSEY (1925–2013) ■ *Linebacker-Lineman*

COLLEGE: 1946–49   6-3, 235 lbs.   **NFL:** 1950–53; **CFL:** 1954–55

Frank Dempsey of Miami played for Gator head coach Frank Wolf during one of the least successful periods of UF football. Although the players called it the "Golden Era," after center Jimmy Kynes referred to it as such (perhaps sarcastically), the season records were 0-9, 4-5-1, 5-5, and 4-5-1.

Dempsey was a lineman, playing on both offense and defense, but was known more for his pranks and off-field activities, often involving his war surplus jeep even without him behind the wheel. At one point, Dempsey had several hundred parking tickets due to his teammates and other students putting his jeep in as many different places as possible, including the university president's front porch and the top of the steps leading to the president's office. Dempsey managed to graduate (in spite of all the parking violations) with a bachelor's degree in physical education in 1950 and is a member of the University of Florida Athletic Hall of Fame.

NFL and CFL lineman Frank Dempsey

In the 1950 NFL draft, the Chicago Bears selected him in the 13th round. Over the next four seasons, he played for the Bears on offense and defense, at guard, tackle, and linebacker. After his years in Chicago, he moved to what is now the Canadian Football League. He played for the Hamilton Tiger-Cats for 1954 and part of 1955, and the Ottawa Rough Riders for the rest of 1955, before retiring. The first league all-star game, known as the Shrine Game, was played in 1955, and Dempsey was chosen as an East All-Star.

After football, he owned a gun and sporting goods store in Peterborough, Ontario, for about 25 years. He and his wife moved to Vero Beach, Florida, in the mid-1990s, then relocated to the Kensington Retirement Home in Oakville, a city not far from Toronto, Ontario. He died there on June 1, 2013.

GUY DURELL DENNIS JR. (1947–) ■ *Guard-Center-Tackle*

COLLEGE: 1966–68   6-2, 255 lbs.   **NFL:** 1969–75

A native of Davisville, Florida, Guy Dennis played on the offensive line for the Gators. During his senior year, the team presented him with the Fergie Ferguson Award to recognize his leadership, character, and courage, and later he was inducted into the

University of Florida Athletic Hall of Fame. Dennis played in the 1969 North-South All-Star Game. He received his bachelor's degree from UF in 1970.

During the 1969 NFL draft, the Cincinnati Bengals picked him in the fifth round, and he played for them for four years at three different positions (center, guard, and tackle). His last three years were with the Detroit Lions. Dennis played in a total of 89 games during his professional career.

After his playing days, he returned to Gainesville to be a coach, then worked for a company that sold paper supplies. He launched his own business in 1981, the Hillman Supply Company, which sells janitorial supplies from Alachua, Florida. Dennis is still involved as its CEO. In 2013, he was ranked #41 on the *Orlando Sentinel* list of the 50 Greatest Gators.

CALVERT ROY DIXON III (1969–) ■ *Center-Guard*
COLLEGE: 1988–91   6-4, 302 lbs.   **NFL:** 1992–96; **XFL:** 2001

Cal Dixon began his years at the University of Florida under head coach Galen Hall and finished under Steve Spurrier. His senior year in 1991 was special for both Dixon and the Gators: He served as a team captain, the school won its first Southeastern Conference championship in football, and Dixon was named by the Associated Press as a second-team All-American. The coaching staff honored him by presenting him with the Fergie Ferguson Award, which goes to one senior each season who displays outstanding leadership, character, and courage, and he received the Jacobs Blocking Trophy for being the best blocker in the SEC. Dixon was also recognized for his accomplishments off the field, was named to the College Football Association's scholar-athlete team in his senior year, and for all four years was on the SEC Academic Honor Roll.

Dixon was drafted in the fifth round in 1992 by the New York Jets, and played center and guard for them through the 1995 season in 55 games. He played for the Miami Dolphins in 1996 and went to Dolphins' preseason camp in 1997, but retired before the season because of back injuries. His 66-game NFL career came to a close, but he made one more attempt at playing professional football.

When the XFL advertised a more exciting brand of football, and Dixon's former college coach, Galen Hall, signed to lead the Orlando Rage, Dixon tried out and made the team at the center position. The end of the 2001 season marked the end of football for Dixon, the Rage, and the XFL. In the years since, he has hosted celebrity fishing and golf tournaments to benefit charitable organizations. Dixon was inducted into the Space Coast Sports Hall of Fame in 2014.

CHRISTOPHER PAUL DOERING (1973–) ■ *Wide Receiver*
COLLEGE: 1993–95   6-4, 202 lbs.   **NFL:** 1996–97, 1999, 2002–04

Gainesville resident Chris Doering played three sports for P.K. Yonge High School, then tried out as a walk-on for the Gator football team. After he was redshirted in 1991, he was offered a scholarship. He played on three Southeastern Conference championship teams (1993–95) and set a Gator and SEC record for making 31 touchdown catches during his career, with a total of 2,107 passing yards. Doering was a team captain in his senior year.

He received his bachelor's degree in telecommunications in 1995 and later was inducted into the University of Florida Athletic Hall of Fame. *The Gainesville Sun* ranked Doering #19 on its 2006 list of the 100 all-time best Gator players, and the *Orlando Sentinel* in 2013 put him at #47 on its list of the 50 Greatest Gators.

In the 1996 NFL draft, Doering was picked in the sixth round by the Jacksonville Jaguars and was then traded to the Indianapolis Colts before the start of the season. He was a Colt for two years but only played in three games. In 1998, he was waived, then signed by the Cincinnati Bengals, but was waived again before the beginning of the season.

Wide receiver Chris Doering

Doering became a Denver Bronco in 1999 and played in three games that year. Prior to the next season, he suffered a ruptured Achilles tendon and worked his way back to the Denver practice squad for 2001. In 2002, the Washington Redskins (led by his former Gator coach, Steve Spurrier), signed Doering, and he had his best year as a pro, playing in 15 games with 18 receptions, followed by two years with the Pittsburgh Steelers in 2003 and 2004. He wound up with a career total of 42 catches for 476 yards.

After his football career ended, Doering co-hosted a sports talk show in Gainesville and Ocala, and he operated a Gainesville home loan mortgage brokerage.

JIMMY DUWAYNE DUBOSE (1954–) ■ *Running Back*
COLLEGE: 1973–75   5-11, 217 lbs.   **NFL:** 1976–78

Gator fullback Jimmy DuBose

A "picture perfect fullback" is how head coach Doug Dickey described Jimmy DuBose, who could run through or around potential tacklers. Offensive coordinator Jimmy Dunn thought DuBose was the most complete player he ever coached. DuBose put on quite a display during his senior year in 1975, rushing for 180 yards against Vanderbilt and 204 yards against FSU, while averaging almost seven yards per carry for a total of 1,307 rushing yards (third best in UF history). The Gators had nine regular season wins (a 9-2 record overall) for the first time. As a senior, DuBose was presented by the team with the Fergie Ferguson Award for his leadership, character, and courage and was later inducted into the University of Florida Athletic Hall of Fame. The *Nashville Banner* named him its Southeastern Conference Player of the Year for 1975.

In the 1976 NFL draft, DuBose was selected in the second round by the expansion team Tampa Bay Buccaneers. He suffered through the Bucs' initial 26-game losing streak, which lasted almost to the end of their second season, and personally had difficulty playing on an injured ankle. During 1978, he became the first Tampa Bay running back to rush for more than 100 yards in a game, but later in that same game he tore ligaments in his knee, which kept him out for the rest of 1978 and all of 1979. DuBose was traded to the Miami Dolphins but was cut from the team because the coach felt he wasn't large enough to fill the position. DuBose retired after playing in a total of 33 games and compiling 704 rushing yards. He received his bachelor's degree from UF in public relations in 1980. In 2013, he was ranked #34 on the *Orlando Sentinel* list of the 50 Greatest Gators.

DAN CLEMENT FIKE JR. (1961–) ■ *Guard-Tackle*
COLLEGE: 1979–82   6-7, 280 lbs.   **USFL:** 1984–85; **NFL:** 1985–93

Dan Fike of Pensacola arrived at the University of Florida just before the school experienced its worst football record in history (0-10-1). He and his teammates turned things around, more than any major college in previous years, to finish the 1980 season with an 8-4 record, including a victory over the University of Maryland in the Tangerine Bowl. Fike's performance during his senior year put him on the All-Southeastern Conference list (second-team) chosen by the Associated Press.

During the 1983 NFL draft, Fike was selected in the 10th round by the New York Jets, but was assigned only to the practice squad. He played in 1984–85 for the USFL Tampa Bay Bandits, but when that league folded in 1985, he signed with the Cleveland Browns. For the next eight years, he played at right guard or right tackle, mostly as a starter. He started for the Browns during their five consecutive playoff runs from 1985–89, including three American Football Conference championship games.

Fike was traded by the Browns to the Green Bay Packers in 1993 but was waived before the start of the season. In October, he joined the Pittsburgh Steelers and played three more games, bringing his NFL career total to 115 (of which he started 102). The *Plain Dealer* newspaper in 2012 ranked him #73 on its all-time list of the best Browns players.

DONALD DENVER FLEMING (1937–63) ■ *Safety*
COLLEGE: 1956–58   6-0, 188 lbs.   **NFL:** 1960–62

According to UF head coach Bob Woodruff, Don Fleming was the best Gator receiver of the 1950s. He served as team captain during his senior year in 1958 and was drafted by the NFL Chicago Cardinals, but Fleming decided to stay in school because he still had

Gator Walk

An extremely popular yet young tradition for home game days is the Gator Walk, which was begun by Coach Urban Meyer in 2005 prior to his first game at UF. The team arrives by bus, and the players and coaches, dressed in coats and ties, disembark along University Avenue, just north of Ben Hill Griffin Stadium. The players slowly make their way toward the stadium on a narrow path through a throng of Gator fans. The walk takes place two hours and fifteen minutes before game time, but the fans get there much earlier to try and find a spot close to the ropes so they can photograph or "high-five" their favorite players as they go by.

Coach Muschamp leads his team on the Gator Walk before the 2011 game against Florida Atlantic

The path they take is along a bricked walkway, also known as the Gator Walk, leading to the north end of the stadium. The Gator Walk crosses the site of the first University of Florida football field, Fleming Field, where the Gators played long before the construction of Florida Field.

---

years of eligibility left for baseball. He played for three years and led UF in home runs and stolen bases.

In 1959, the Chicago Cardinals again drafted Fleming (28th round), but he wasn't done with baseball and continued to play in Gainesville for another year. Also, he wanted to play for the Cleveland Browns, where fellow Gator Bernie Parrish was playing. Chicago agreed to the trade, and Fleming played for the Browns from 1960 through 1962. His career stats show 10 interceptions returned for 160 yards.

Fleming signed a contract to play another year for the Browns for the 1963 season but never played. He was a foreman for a construction company in the off-season to both keep in shape and build a career after football. In June 1963, while working on a site

Don Fleming at Shadyside High School

near Orlando, Fleming and a co-worker were electrocuted when a crane they were operating touched a 12,000-volt electrical line.

Fleming was inducted into the University of Florida Athletic Hall of Fame and the Florida Sports Hall of Fame. The Cleveland Browns retired his jersey #46, and his high school, Shadyside High in Shadyside, Ohio, named its football field after him.

DERRICK TYRONE GAFFNEY (1955–) ■ *Wide Receiver*
COLLEGE: 1975–77   6-1, 181 lbs.   **NFL:** 1978–84, 1987

Derrick Gaffney played football at William M. Raines High School in Jacksonville before coming to the University of Florida. He made it into the record book by being on the receiving end of a 99-yard touchdown pass thrown by Chris Collinsworth in 1977 against Rice University, which set a record for the longest in the Southeastern Conference and tying the NCAA record.

In the eighth round of the 1978 NFL draft, Gaffney was chosen by the New York Jets, for whom he played eight seasons. As a rookie in 1978, he caught 38 passes (three for touchdowns) for 691 yards. That turned out to be his best statistical season. Over his professional career, he caught 156 passes for 2,613 yards in 100 games.

Gator wide receiver Derrick Gaffney

Gaffney's participation as a Gator football player is part of a family tradition. Older brother Don played quarterback, nephew Lito Sheppard played cornerback, and son Jabar Gaffney followed in Derrick's footsteps as a wide receiver. In 2011, Derrick Gaffney became the new head coach of Team USA American Football Stars & Stripes, an organization promoting the play of American Football worldwide.

DERRICK JABAR GAFFNEY (1980–) ■ *Wide Receiver*
COLLEGE: 2000–01   6-1, 205 lbs.   **NFL:** 2002–12

Jabar Gaffney followed the same path as his father, playing football at William M. Raines High School in Jacksonville, then becoming a wide receiver for the Gators. He was redshirted his first year and was a starter in 2000 and 2001. During his first year, *Street and Smith* named him their National Freshman Player of the Year, and the Southeastern Conference coaches chose him as their SEC Freshman of the Year. He was honored with the Ray Graves Award as the team's MVP for 2000.

Despite only wearing a Gator uniform for two years, Gaffney had a lasting impact. He caught 138 passes (27 for touchdowns) for a total of 2,375 yards, and he had 14 100-yard games (still a Florida receiving record). In 2001, the Touchdown Club of

Jabar Gaffney at 2011 Redskins training camp

Columbus presented Gaffney with the Paul Warfield Award, recognizing him as the country's top college wide receiver. In 2013, he was ranked #16 on the *Orlando Sentinel* list of the 50 Greatest Gators.

In the 2002 NFL draft, he was chosen by the Houston Texans in the second round. Over the next four years with Houston he averaged more than 500 receiving yards per season. Gaffney then signed with the Philadelphia Eagles but was released before the 2006 season. In October that year, he joined the New England Patriots, and, during that season's playoffs, he contributed greatly with a pair of 100-plus yard games.

After playing a second season with the Patriots, Gaffney moved to the Denver Broncos for two years, amassing 732 and 875 yards. After being traded to the Washington Redskins for 2011, he had his best year with 947 yards on 68 catches, but in mid-2012, he was released by the Redskins. Gaffney re-signed with the Patriots but was released at the end of the summer. Part way into the 2012 season, he joined the Miami Dolphins and played in three games before being released just days before the NFL announced that he was suspended for two games for having failed to timely report an arrest that occurred about two years before. Gaffney had resisted arrest after a traffic stop in 2010 and completed a pre-trial diversion program while a member of the Broncos. His pro career numbers included 447 catches for 5,690 yards with 24 touchdowns.

LAWRENCE JOSEPH GAGNER (1943–) ■ *Guard*
COLLEGE: 1963–65   6-3, 240 lbs.   **NFL:** 1966–69,1972; **WFL:** 1974–75

A member of the state champion Seabreeze High School Sandcrabs in Daytona Beach, Larry Gagner was named by the Florida High School Athletic Association to the list of the 33 all-time greatest Florida high school football players. He played for the Gators mostly at offensive guard, but he also appeared as linebacker, defensive tackle, and center. One of the highlights of Gagner's college career was his final game as a Gator, the 1966 Sugar Bowl, which was the school's first ever bowl appearance outside of Jacksonville. As a UF student, he studied advertising design.

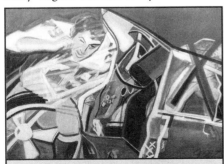

"Career Crash" painted by Larry Gagner, including the artist as a Steeler

Gagner was picked in the second round of the 1966 NFL draft by the Pittsburgh Steelers. The same year, he was selected in the third round of the

American Football League draft by the Miami Dolphins. He decided not to pass up the $150,000 offered by the Steelers, and he played in 52 games for that team over four seasons. A broken hip suffered in a traffic accident kept him out of football in 1970–71, and he was traded to the New York Giants, and then to the Denver Broncos, but never got on the field for either team.

His 1972 season was spent with the Kansas City Chiefs, playing in seven games in a backup role. During preseason camp the following year, he decided to retire. However, when the World Football League was founded, he attempted a comeback. He played a little for the WFL team in Jacksonville when it was called the Sharks (1974) and the Express (1975), before retiring for good. His post-football activities have included teaching, driving a taxi, serving as a security guard, and painting fine art in Tampa.

THOMAS CHANDLER GAILEY JR. (1952–) ■ *Coach*

COLLEGE: 1971–73   **NFL:** 1985–90, 1994–2001, 2008, 2010–12; **WLAF:** 1991-92 (all as a coach)

Chan Gailey played quarterback at the University of Florida under run-oriented head coach Doug Dickey. Gailey received his bachelor's degree in physical education in 1974, then worked for the university as a graduate assistant for the next two years before taking his first job elsewhere as a football coach. His career path followed that of a Ping-Pong ball, bouncing back and forth between college and pro football.

Chan Gailey when he was the head coach of the Dallas Cowboys

He began at Troy State University where he coached defensive backs (1976–78). He had the same position with the Air Force Academy (1979–80) before becoming its defensive coordinator (1981–82). Gailey then returned to Troy State and served as head coach (1983–84).

Moving up to the pros, he started with the Denver Broncos, where he coached the tight ends (1985–87), special teams (1986), wide receivers (1987 and 1989–90), and quarterbacks (1988). He was the offensive coordinator for 1989–90, and while Gailey was there the Broncos went to three Super Bowls. The Birmingham Fire of the World League of American Football also went to the playoffs both of the years he was at the helm (1991–92).

After a year as head coach of Samford University (1993), Gailey moved to the Pittsburgh Steelers where he coached wide receivers (1994–96) and served as offensive coordinator (1996–97), and all four years the Steelers made it to the playoffs. In both of his seasons as the head coach of the Dallas Cowboys (1998–99), they reached the playoffs. Gailey then moved to the Miami Dolphins, where he was the offensive coordinator.

In 2002, college football again beckoned, and he became the head coach of Georgia Tech, where the Yellow Jackets posted a record of 44-32 during his six-year tenure. After that, it was back to the pros to be the offensive coordinator of the Kansas City Chiefs (2008) and then head coach of the Buffalo Bills (2010–12), where he was fired at the end of the season and decided to take a break from coaching. Gailey's overall record as head coach was 68-41 in college, 34-46 in the NFL, and 12-7 in the WLAF.

WILLIAM ALBERT GAINES (1971–) ■ *Defensive Tackle*

COLLEGE: 1990–91, 1993   6-5, 310 lbs.   **NFL:** 1994–97; **ARFL:** 1999–2004

William Gaines played defensive tackle for the Steve Spurrier–led Gator teams that won the Southeastern Conference championship when he was a sophomore (1991) and a team captain and senior (1993). He was the Gators' 1993 recipient of the Fergie Ferguson Award to recognize his leadership, character, and courage.

In the fifth round of the 1994 NFL draft, Gaines was selected by the Miami Dolphins. In his only season in Miami, he played in half of the Dolphins' games in a backup role. The next year, he moved to Washington and played three seasons for the Redskins. Gaines then moved to the Arena Football League and played for the Nashville Kats (1999–2001), Georgia Force (2002), Detroit Fury (2003), and Orlando Predators (2004).

DAVID LAWRENCE GALLOWAY SR. (1959–)
■ *Tackle-End-Nose Tackle*

COLLEGE: 1977–81   6-3, 277 lbs.   **NFL:** 1982–91

A three-sport athlete at Brandon High School near Tampa, David Galloway attended the University of Florida and played the defensive end and tackle positions. As a senior, he served as a team captain and was an Associated Press and United Press International first-team All-Southeastern Conference, and he was named a first-team All-American by the Football Writers Association of America.

He was selected in the second round of the 1982 NFL draft by the St. Louis (later, Phoenix) Cardinals. After nine years with them, he played one year for the Denver Broncos. Over his career, he played in 99 professional games and started 76 of them, recovering five fumbles and recording 38 sacks.

Galloway, a member of the University of Florida Athletic Hall of Fame, was ranked as #48 on *The Gainesville Sun* 2006 list of the 100 all-time greatest Florida Gator football players. After his playing days, he and his wife established a marriage ministry through a church located in North Miami Beach.

TIMOTHY GEORGE GOLDEN (1959–) ■ *Linebacker-Defensive End*
COLLEGE: 1978–80   6-1, 220 lbs.   **NFL:** 1982–85

Before becoming a Gator, Tim Golden was a Boyd H. Anderson High School Cobra in Lauderdale Lakes, Florida. He experienced some of the worst and the best of Florida football as a part of the squad that had a record of 0-10-1 in 1979, then produced an NCAA-record turnaround to an 8-4 season and a win over the University of Maryland in the Tangerine Bowl. Golden received his bachelor's degree in broadcasting from UF in 1981.

He was not chosen by any team in the 1982 NFL draft but instead signed as a free agent with the New England Patriots. As a backup in 1982–84, he played in 40 games, one as a starting linebacker. Golden finished his professional football career with the Philadelphia Eagles, playing in two games during the 1985 season.

EARNEST GRAHAM JR. (1980–) ■ *Running Back-Fullback*
COLLEGE: 1999–2002   5-9, 215 lbs.   **NFL:** 2004–11

As a running back for Mariner High School in Cape Coral, Earnest Graham set Florida state records for rushing yards and touchdowns. *Parade* magazine named him a high school All-American, and he was given the title of Florida's "Mr. Football" for 1997. The Florida High School Athletic Association named him as one of Florida's 100 best players in its first 100 years of high school football.

Earnest Graham on the Tampa Bay Buccaneers

Barely into his first year at UF, Graham suffered a foot injury and was redshirted for the rest of the season. The following year in 1999, he started in seven games, and his 654 rushing yards and five touchdowns landed him a spot on the Southeastern Conference All-Freshman team chosen by the conference's coaches. For the next two years, Graham and Robert Gillespie shared the position, with Graham earning second-team All-SEC honors in 2001. Finally, in his senior year as a team captain, he was the starting running back and rushed for 1,085 yards and scored 11 touchdowns. He wound up with 3,065 yards on 603 carries during his college career.

He was not drafted by any NFL team, but he signed with the Tampa Bay Buccaneers as a free agent in 2003. After many months on the practice squad, he was activated during the 2004 season. He did not carry the ball much during his first

Continued on next page

The Three (Newark) Bears

ERVING MAX GOLDSTEIN (1904–48) ■ **COLLEGE: 1923–25**

ROBERT D. NEWTON (1903–74) ■ **COLLEGE: 1921–24**

BERTON CASWELL WILLIAMS (1903–65) ■ **COLLEGE: 1923–25**

Once upon a time, there were three Gators: guard Erving Max "Goldy" (a.k.a. Izzy) Goldstein, named All-Southern in 1923, 1924, and 1925; halfback Robert D. "Ark" Newton (All-Southern 1923), who also played on the UF basketball team in 1922–23 and 1925–26 and earned a total of 14 sports letters; and tackle Berton Caswell "Cy" Williams. This is the story of how they became Bears.

The year 1926 saw the creation of the American Football League as a rival to the National Football League. Because it was not the only league with that name, it is often referred to as AFLG or the Grange League, since it featured Hall of Famer Red Grange. One of its original teams was the Newark Bears, owned by the president of the New Jersey Athletic Association. The trio of Gators headed north to become Bears for the 1926 season, which turned out to be the only one before the team folded.

In 1919, Dan Blaine had acquired an independent semi-pro team, the Staten Island Stapletons, and on November 14, 1926, the Newark Bears arrived for a game on the Stapletons' home turf at Thompson's Stadium. The Bears were winless in five league games and had scored only once, so Blaine was shocked by the 33–0 drubbing his players suffered. His solution to his team's ineptitude was to buy the Bears and merge them with his team. Goldstein left the former Bears as quickly as Goldilocks left her bears.

The following year, the Stapletons entered the NFL, and Newton played for them until 1928, scoring on a 50-yard touchdown run early in the 1927 opening game against the Atlantic City Roses. Williams stayed until 1930, then played one more season, 1932, for the NFL's Brooklyn Dodgers. During his last days as a football player, he was also in training as a professional wrestler (see page 353), and he eventually held a version of the World Heavyweight Championship. Goldstein and Newton are members of the University of Florida Athletic Hall of Fame.

EARNEST GRAHAM JR. *Continued from previous page*

three years in Tampa but led the Bucs in special teams tackles in two of them. It took injuries to three other Buccaneer running backs in 2007 for Graham to become a starter, and he took advantage of the opportunity by rushing for 898 yards and ten touchdowns, and he became only the second-ever Buccaneer running back to have back-to-back 100-yard games. He played four more years for the team, but largely as a fullback or special teams player, often platooning with others. His job as fullback was more as a blocker than a ball carrier.

During 2011, Graham was moved to tailback to replace another injured starter, and in his first game in that role rushed for 109 yards on 17 carries. In the next game, he suffered an injury to his achilles tendon and never played another professional game.

In December 2013, Graham took over as head football coach at North Fort Myers High School. The school is located in Lee County, Florida, where he still ranks number two all-time in high school career rushing yardage.

ANTHONY EDWARD GREEN (1956–) ■ *Running Back-Kick Returner*

COLLEGE: 1974–77   5-9, 185 lbs.   **NFL:** 1978–79

As a freshman with the Gators in 1974, Tony Green had an impressive game against the University of Maryland with 11 carries for 178 yards. In four years at UF, he rushed 445 times for 2,590 yards. He also had pass receptions totaling 287 yards and ran back punts and kickoffs for 775 yards.

Green was drafted by the Washington Redskins in the sixth round in 1978 and only played for that team for one memorable season. He rushed 22 times for 82 yards and caught four passes, but his specialty was returning kicks and punts. He averaged 25.6 yards over 34 kickoff returns, including one for 99 yards and a touchdown. The explosive Green fielded 42 punts and returned them an average of 10.5 yards, and was named to the Pro Bowl as a return specialist. His second season was his final one, divided between four unimpressive games for the New York Giants and 11 for the Seattle Seahawks. He then retired from professional football and dropped out of the headlines.

BOBBY JOE GREEN (1936–93) ■ *Punter*

COLLEGE: 1958–59   5-11, 175 lbs.   **NFL:** 1960–73

After graduating from College High School in Bartlesville, Oklahoma, Bobby Joe Green headed to Gainesville and became a punter and halfback for Florida. His head coach, Bob Woodruff, considered him and Don Chandler to be the team's best kickers of the decade. During his senior year, Green averaged 44.9 yards per punt (the UF record until 2010). His best punt was 82 yards against Georgia in 1958, and it remains the Gators' all-time longest. The athletic Green was also a high jumper and sprinter on the track team in 1959–60. He was inducted into the University of Florida Athletic Hall of Fame.

The San Francisco 49ers chose Green in the ninth round of the 1959 draft, but instead of signing with them, he wound up playing for the Pittsburgh Steelers for two years. He was then traded to the Chicago Bears and was on the 1963 NFL championship team and later made it to the Pro Bowl in 1970. Green spent a dozen years in Chicago and retired after kicking 970 punts in 187 games. He averaged 42.6 yards per kick over his 14 professional years.

After his playing days were over, he established a specialty advertising business in Gainesville. Green also served as a volunteer kicking coach for the university from 1979 to 1989. He died May 28, 1993.

D'TANYIAN JACQUEZ GREEN (1976–) ■ *Wide Receiver*
COLLEGE: 1995–97   5-10, 172 lbs.   **NFL:** 1998–2002

Gator wide receiver Jacquez Green

Before coming to the University of Florida, Jacquez Green was a star in basketball, track, and football, playing quarterback, running back, and wide receiver. When he arrived in Gainesville, he became a wide receiver with great results. His best games included the 1997 Sugar Bowl win over Florida State University (resulting in the Gators' first national football championship for 1996) in which he made seven catches for 79 yards. Green showed his versatility in the 1997 game against Auburn University by scoring three different ways—catching a touchdown pass, throwing a pass for a score, and rushing for one. As a junior, he caught 61 passes (nine for touchdowns) for 1,024 yards, and he then left early for the NFL.

He was taken in the second round of the 1998 NFL draft by the Tampa Bay Buccaneers. Green played there for four years, then moved to the Washington Redskins in 2002, and finished that season with the Detroit Lions. Before retiring, he signed in 2003 with Tampa Bay but did not play in any more games. Overall, in 66 professional games, he caught 162 passes for 2,311 yards and seven touchdowns.

After retiring as a player, Green went into coaching at the prep level. Schools where he has served as an assistant coach include Gibbs High School (St. Petersburg), Lincoln High School (Tallahassee), and Valdosta High School (Valdosta, Georgia).

SAMUEL LEE GREEN (1954–) ■ *Linebacker*
COLLEGE: 1972–75   6-2, 228 lbs.   **NFL:** 1976–80; **USFL:** 1983

Sammy Green played linebacker for head coach Doug Dickey from 1972 through 1975. One of the highlights of his career was his 1973 forcing of a fumble by Auburn University tailback Sullivan Walker, which resulted in a Gator touchdown and an upset victory for Florida, its first at Auburn's Jordan-Hare Stadium.

Green served as a team captain during his senior year. In 2003, he was inducted into Florida's Athletic Hall of Fame and, in 2006, *The Gainesville Sun* ranked him #51 on its list of all-time greatest Gator football players. He is listed at #38 on the *Orlando Sentinel* list of the 50 Greatest Gators compiled in 2013. Green's 202 tackles in 1976 is still a Florida record.

He was chosen in the second round of the 1976 NFL draft by the newly formed Seattle Seahawks. In his four seasons there, Green started in 44 of 60 games. He ended his NFL career with two games for the Houston Oilers during the 1980 season, but he came back to professional football in 1983 to play one more season for the USFL Birmingham Stallions.

Green received his master's degree at Iowa State University and teaches literature and humanities at Washington High School in Cedar Rapids, Iowa.

REX DANIEL GROSSMAN III (1980–) ■ *Quarterback*
COLLEGE: 2000–02   6-1, 222 lbs.   **NFL:** 2003–13

Rex Grossman was named "Mr. Football" for Indiana in 1998, after leading Bloomington High School South to the state championship, and was considered one of the top 15 players in the nation. He came to the University of Florida and was redshirted his first year. In 2000, he had tough competition for the starting quarterback position, but he succeeded and led the Gators to the Southeastern Conference championship and was named the MVP of the championship game.

In 2001, Grossman was the top quarterback in Division I in passing efficiency, was the Associated Press National Player of the Year, the *Nashville Banner*'s SEC Player of the Year, and the runner-up in the voting for the Heisman Trophy. He should be

Rex Grossman at a Washington Redskins practice

nicknamed "Mr. Recordholder" as he holds many Gator passing marks, including attempts and completions in a season (503 and 287 in 2002) and completions in a game (36 against Georgia in 2002). His 3,896 passing yards in 2001 is also a UF record, and Grossman holds the records for the most 300-yard passing games in a season (10 in 2001) and in a career (17), and the most consecutive 300-yard games (9). In both 2001 and 2002, his teammates voted him as the Gator MVP, presenting him with the Ray Graves Award. After his junior season, having accumulated more than 9,000 passing yards in just three years, Grossman opted to go pro.

He was a first round selection of the Chicago Bears in the 2003 draft, and he played for them through the 2008 season. Despite being sidelined by various injuries during 2004 and 2005, Grossman was able to lead the Bears into the 2005 playoffs and to the Super Bowl after the 2006 season (a Chicago loss to the Colts), and was presented with the Ed Block Courage Award from his teammates based on his being a role model of inspiration, sportsmanship, and courage.

In 2007, he moved between starter and backup because of injuries to him and Brian Griese, and the same happened in 2008, with Grossman and Kyle Orton each starting a portion of the season. In 2009, Grossman worked out with the Cincinnati Bengals but signed with the Houston Texans and played in only one game. Beginning in 2010, Grossman has been a quarterback for the Washington Redskins both as a starter and a backup. With the arrival of Robert Griffin III in 2012, Grossman went from starting 13 games (2011) to making zero appearances in 2012–13, while remaining on the Redskins' active roster and mentoring the younger quarterbacks.

He was inducted into the University of Florida Athletic Hall of Fame in the spring of 2013. That same year, the *Orlando Sentinel* named him as #10 on its list of the 50 Greatest Gators.

DARREN HAMBRICK (1975–) ■ *Outside Linebacker*
COLLEGE: 1993–94   6-2, 227 lbs.   **NFL:** 1998–2002

A three-sport star in high school, Darren Hambrick was named by the *St. Petersburg Times* as the best football player in Pasco County. He came to the University of Florida for football and played two seasons, but before the 1995 Sugar Bowl he was removed from the team by head coach Steve Spurrier, after Hambrick hit fellow Gator Anthony Riggins in the face with broken glass during a team dinner. Hambrick transferred to the University of South Carolina and played as a Gamecock.

Hambrick was drafted in the fifth round of the 1998 NFL draft by the Dallas Cowboys and signed a five-year contract, but he didn't last that long. He appeared in 30 games in 1998–99, and during 2000 he was the team's leading tackler. Nevertheless, after failing to attend off-season workouts before the 2001 season, his relationship with the team was strained. (He is probably best known for his reply when he was asked why he failed to report to the voluntary off-season workouts: "What do voluntary mean?") Hambrick played in the first five games, all as a starter, and then was abruptly released from the team. He spent the rest of the year with the Carolina Panthers, but his troubles continued. While a Panther, he reported that one of his paychecks had been stolen, despite his already having cashed it, and Carolina did not re-sign him for another season. He signed with the Cleveland Browns for 2002, but he did not make the team.

After the end of his playing days, Darren Hambrick was involved in a number of criminal incidents, including battery and a parole violation, which in 2010 had him spending time in the Pasco County jail.

MALCOLM EUGENE HAMMACK (1933–2004)
■ *Halfback-Fullback-Linebacker*

COLLEGE: 1953–54   6-2, 205 lbs.   **NFL:** 1955–66

Malcolm "Mal" Hammack played football for the Arlington State Junior College Rebels in Arlington, Texas, before enrolling at the University of Florida for his junior and senior years. In 1954, he was the first to receive the Fergie Ferguson Award, which is presented annually by the coaches to the senior UF football player who displays outstanding leadership, character, and courage. Hammack completed his bachelor's degree from Florida in 1958, and he was later inducted into the University of Florida Athletic Hall of Fame. According to coach Bob Woodruff, Hammack was one of the five best offensive backs of the 1950s.

In 1955, the Chicago Cardinals chose him in the third round of the NFL draft. He began playing with them that season and moved with the team to St. Louis, where he wound up his 12-year career. For most of it, Hammack was a fullback whose main activity was blocking for ball carriers including John David Crow and Joe Childress, but he also rushed for 1,278 yards on 320 carries. In addition, he caught 27 passes for 255 yards.

Albert the Alligator

While the University of Florida adopted the Gator as its official mascot in the early 1900s, the first appearance of the beloved Albert the Alligator came in 1970 when a student was seen in a gator costume. Albert's garb and features have changed over the years, from a large bobble-head cartoon look to the 1979 version with a more ferocious headpiece and costume made of leather and vinyl (not a good combination in the Florida heat) to the 1984 more modern, plush (and much cooler) Albert we know and love today. Alberta joined the Gator family in 1986, and both are regular fixtures in The Swamp on game day in their orange-and-blue outfits. GO GATORS!

Mascots Albert and Alberta enjoy a game in The Swamp in 2004

After his playing days, Hammack worked as a shoe company sales representative and radio color commentator for Cardinals football games. He died July 19, 2004.

LORENZO TIMOTHY HAMPTON (1962–) ■ *Running Back*
COLLEGE: 1981–84   5-11, 205 lbs.   **NFL:** 1985–89

Lorenzo Hampton as a Gator

Lorenzo Hampton played running back for the Gators at a time when the team had several good ones, including John L. Williams and Neal Anderson. As a result, Hampton often was used as a blocking back clearing a path for the others to follow. Over four seasons in Gainesville, he accumulated 1,993 yards on the ground and 655 in the air.

The Miami Dolphins drafted Hampton in the first round of the 1985 NFL draft, and he remained with the Dolphins for five seasons. He was the starting running back in 33 of the 70 games in which he played and gained 1,949 yards on 500 rushing attempts. He also caught 123 passes for nearly a thousand yards.

To reach out to inner-city youth, Hampton founded a charitable foundation known as Lemon-Aid Makers, which runs summer football camps in South Florida for kids aged 7–14.

JAMES CLARENCE HARRELL JR. (1957–) ■ *Linebacker*
COLLEGE: 1977–78   6-1, 224 lbs.   **NFL:** 1979–83, 1985–87; **USFL:** 1984–85

Based on his years playing for the Chamberlain High School Chiefs in Tampa, James Harrell was offered scholarships from smaller colleges, but his dream was to play for a major university. He walked on at UF; although he tried out as a linebacker, he was persuaded by Coach Doug Dickey to play strong safety, a position he had never played, because the team needed more depth at that position. His willingness to adapt led to his earning a scholarship at the end of his freshman year.

As a sophomore, Harrell played defensive end and saw action on special teams. By the time he was a senior, he was getting significant playing time. Later, between NFL seasons, he finished his degree at UF in public relations and graduated in 1984.

In the 1979 NFL draft, he was not selected but was signed as a free agent by the Denver Broncos. They waived him before the start of the season, and Harrell was claimed by the Detroit Lions, for which he played from 1979 through 1983. In 1984 and 1985, he joined the United States Football League's Tampa Bay Bandits, then returned to the Lions for the 1985 and 1986 seasons. His final year in the pros was 1987 with the Kansas City Chiefs. He played 89 games in the NFL.

After his playing days, Harrell became a coach for three Tampa high schools. He was an assistant at Jesuit High School from 1994 to 2004, the defensive coordinator at Plant High School in 2005–08, and the head coach of Freedom High in 2009 before returning to Jesuit as the head coach from 2010 through 2012. For six months in 2013, Harrell was an outside linebackers coach at Kentucky Christian University.

Beginning in August 2013, James Harrell was back at Plant High School as the defensive coordinator and linebacker coach. He also works for All-Pro Lawyer Referral Service in the Tampa area.

DERRICK HARVEY (1986–) ■ *Defensive End*
COLLEGE: 2005–07   6-5, 268 lbs.   **NFL:** 2008–11

Derrick Harvey was the Maryland Gatorade Player of the Year in his senior year at Eleanor Roosevelt High School in Greenbelt, Maryland. What is amazing is that he only began playing in his junior year. After considering several major universities, he picked Florida and was redshirted in 2004. He played in nine games in 2005 as a backup and the next year became a starter for five games, after the regular defensive end was injured, and led the Gators with 11 sacks.

Denver Bronco Derrick Harvey

As a junior, Harvey served as a team captain, started all 13 games, and made 49 tackles (31 unassisted). He is ninth on the Gators' all-time sack list with 20.5 and third on their list of tackles for a loss with 51.5, even though he only played three years before leaving early for the NFL.

Harvey was chosen in the first round of the 2008 NFL draft by the Jacksonville Jaguars and played defensive end there for three seasons, starting 32 games and substituting in 15 more. The Jaguars waived him in July 2011, and he was picked up by the Denver Broncos. He saw limited action in five games for Denver and was not re-signed. In early 2012, Harvey signed with the Cincinnati Bengals, but he was released before the beginning of the season.

WILLIAM PERCY HARVIN III (1988–) ■ *Running Back-Wide Receiver*
COLLEGE: 2006–08   5-11, 200 lbs.   **NFL:** 2009–13

A three-sport star athlete in Virginia Beach, Virginia, Percy Harvin was one of the most sought-after recruits in the nation. He wound up choosing the University of Florida and played football and ran track for the Gators for three years. As a freshman in 2006, he saw limited action because of injuries, but he recovered in time to

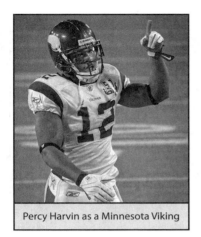
Percy Harvin as a Minnesota Viking

play in the Southeastern Conference championship game, where he was awarded its MVP trophy. Harvin then rushed for 22 yards and caught passes for 60 more in the BCS championship win over Ohio State. The Associated Press named him its SEC Freshman of the Year.

As a sophomore, Harvin caught 59 passes (four for touchdowns) for 858 yards, rushed 83 times for 764 yards, and led the NCAA with 9.2 yards per carry. In only two seasons, he became the first Gator receiver to pass the career 1,000-yard mark in both rushing and receiving and was an Associated Press first-team All-SEC honoree. The next year, he was All-SEC at two positions: AP and SEC coaches named him an all-purpose player, and AP chose him for their second-team as a wide receiver. During his junior year, he was hampered by several injuries but still accumulated 660 yards on the ground and 644 in the air.

Harvin was selected in the first round of the 2009 NFL draft by the Minnesota Vikings and became the first Viking to score a touchdown in each of his first three games. He made the Pro Bowl roster and was named the AP Offensive Rookie of the Year. In four regular seasons with Minnesota, he rushed for 659 yards, caught 278 passes for 3,292 yards, and returned kickoffs for 3,144 yards. Harvin's kick returns included five for touchdowns and the NFL record for the longest non-scoring play (a 104-yard kickoff return against the Atlanta Falcons to the Falcons' 3-yard line).

In March 2013, Harvin was traded to the Seattle Seahawks. That same year, he was ranked by the *Orlando Sentinel* as #5 on its list of 50 Greatest Gators. As a result of hip surgery, he saw action in only one regular season game that year. He came back in time for Super Bowl XLVIII, in which he ran back the opening kickoff 87 yards for a touchdown in the Seattle win over the Denver Broncos.

CHARLES KIMBERLIN HELTON (1948–) ■ *Coach*

COLLEGE: 1967–69 **NFL:** 1983–92, 2002–03; **CFL:** 2004–06 (all as a coach)

Kim Helton played center for the Gators for three years and, in 1970, received his bachelor's degree in physical education. He remained at the University of Florida as a graduate assistant, then moved up to the offensive line coach position under new head coach Doug Dickey from 1973 to 1978. The following year, he began a four-year stint at the University of Miami as its offensive coordinator under head coach Howard Schnellenberger.

Helton moved to the NFL in 1983 and worked as offensive line coach for the Tampa Bay Buccaneers (1983–86), the Houston Oilers (1987–89), and the Los Angeles

Raiders (1990–92). He was about to move to the Miami Dolphins, but he changed his mind when the University of Houston head coaching position was offered to him. There, Helton had a seven-year record of 24-53-1; following the 1999 season, he was fired. He was inducted into the University of Florida Athletic Hall of Fame in 2001.

In 2002, Helton was hired as offensive line coach by Steve Spurrier for the Washington Redskins. When Spurrier left, Helton shifted to running backs coach for the Canadian Football League Toronto Argonauts for 2004–06. That was followed by his next job, offensive coordinator at the University of Alabama-Birmingham, which he began in 2007.

Kim Helton when he coached at the University of Houston

AARON MICHAEL HERNANDEZ (1989–) ■ *Tight End*

COLLEGE: 2007–09   6-2, 245 lbs.   **NFL:** 2010–12

During his senior year of high school, Aaron Hernandez was chosen as the Connecticut Gatorade Football Player of the Year. He initially committed to play for the University of Connecticut but changed his mind and enrolled at Florida. He played in 13 games during his freshman year in 2007, scoring two touchdowns on nine receptions totaling 151 yards. As a starter for 11 of the 13 games in 2008, Hernandez raised his totals to 34 catches for 381 yards, finishing the season with five receptions for 57 yards in the BCS national championship win over the University of Oklahoma.

Aaron Hernandez on the New England Patriots sideline

As a junior, Hernandez was the first Gator recipient of the John Mackey Award presented by the Friends of John Mackey, recognizing him as the top tight end in the country, and he led Florida with 68 receptions for 850 yards. He was a first-team All-American according to each of *College Football News,* the Associated Press, and *The Sporting News.* During his three years as a Gator, Hernandez accumulated 1,382 yards on 111 catches (still a Florida record), scoring a dozen touchdowns. According to the *Orlando Sentinel* in 2013, Hernandez ranked #35 on the list of 50 Greatest Gators.

Hernandez was chosen in the fourth round of the 2010 NFL draft by the New England Patriots and began the 2010 season as the youngest player on any NFL team's active roster. Two weeks into the season, he became the youngest player since 1960 to have a 100-yard receiving game, and he completed the season with 45 catches for 563 yards.

In 2011, Hernandez played in 14 games, sharing tight end duties with Rob Gronkowski. The duo became the first pair at their position in NFL history to score at least five touchdowns each in consecutive seasons for a single team. As a tandem, they also set records for receptions, yardage, and touchdowns for tight ends.

On June 26, 2013, Hernandez was arrested for the murder of semi-pro football player Odin Lloyd. Later in the day, Hernandez was cut from the Patriots. In August 2013, he was indicted for first-degree murder and multiple weapons charges. While awaiting trial, he also has been sued by a man claiming to have been shot by him in February 2013, and by the families of two alleged murder victims from July 2012.

REYNALDO ROMEL HILL (1982–) ■ *Cornerback*
COLLEGE: 2003–04   5-11, 187 lbs.   **NFL:** 2005–08; **UFL:** 2011–13

Reynaldo Hill attended Dodge City Community College in Kansas and led the National Junior College Athletic Association by defending 22 passes, making 57 tackles, three interceptions, and returning two kicks and one punt for touchdowns. He then transferred to the University of Florida in 2003. In two seasons, he played in 25 games, including 12 starts as a senior, and had 57 tackles as a Gator.

Hill was chosen in the seventh round of the 2005 NFL draft by the Tennessee Titans and played for that team for four seasons. During his first year, he intercepted three passes to lead his team and tie for the lead among all NFL rookie defensive backs. He started 14 of the 15 games he played but had a much lesser role in 2007 and 2008, and he finished his NFL career with 48 games played and 127 tackles. In 2011, he returned to professional football by signing with the Omaha Nighthawks of the United Football League.

Reynaldo Hill as a cornerback for the Tennessee Titans

The UFL ran into financial trouble and suspended operations after the 2011 season. They announced intentions to resume games later and entered into guaranteed player contracts prior to what would have been the 2012 season. When games were not played and salary checks were not issued, a lawsuit against the league and others was filed in early 2013 by 78 of the UFL players. Hill was not one of those named plaintiffs.

ISAAC JASON HILLIARD (1976–) ■ *Wide Receiver*
COLLEGE: 1994–96   5-11, 210 lbs.   **NFL:** 1997–2008

Isaac "Ike" Hilliard from Louisiana was a Gator wide receiver from 1994–96, and the team won the Southeastern Conference championship in all three years. In his junior year (1996), he was paired with teammate Reidel Anthony, and both exceeded 1,000 receiving yards. That was also the season the UF football team won its first national

Ike Hilliard as a Buccaneer wide receiver

championship with a win over Florida State University in the 1997 Sugar Bowl. In that game, Hilliard scored three touchdowns and gained 150 yards through the air.

The Gainesville Sun in 2006 ranked him #14 among the 100 all-time greatest Gator football players, and he is a member of the University of Florida Athletic Hall of Fame. During 2011, the conference named Hilliard to its list of SEC Legends. Two years later, he was ranked at #24 on the *Orlando Sentinel* list of the 50 Greatest Gators.

In the 1997 NFL draft, he was chosen in the first round by the New York Giants, and by 1998 he was a Giants starting wide receiver. Hilliard played in the Super Bowl at the end of the 2000 season; during his time with the Giants he caught 368 passes for 4,630 yards and 27 touchdowns. After 2004, he moved to the Tampa Bay Buccaneers and, in four years there, caught 62 passes for 722 yards and returned 42 kickoffs.

Following 12 seasons in pro ball and suffering with a neck injury, Hilliard retired and got into coaching. His first job was a volunteer position where he coached receivers for the United Football League Florida Tuskers in 2009–10. Next, he came back to the NFL to be an assistant wide receivers coach for the Miami Dolphins and, after a year, moved to be the wide receivers coach for the Washington Redskins (2012) and then the Buffalo Bills (2013). Hilliard returned to the Redskins in 2014.

CHARLES RAY HUNSINGER (1925–98) ■ *Halfback*

COLLEGE: 1946–49   6-0, 188 lbs.   **NFL:** 1950–52; **CFL:** 1953–55

Chuck Hunsinger played halfback for Florida right after World War II, at a time the Gators regularly lost more than they won. His play was one of the bright spots on the team, with 2,017 yards on the ground. He was a popular player among the students, and one of the locally sung tunes (the "Humdinger Song") mentioned him in its lyrics ("Hunsinger is a humdinger").

His best season was 1948, which included a 96-yard kickoff return for a touchdown against the University of Alabama, and his rushing total of 842 set a Florida single season record, which stood for 24 years. The highlights of his 1949 season were a 199-yard effort against Furman University and 174 yards (with three touchdowns)

Chuck Hunsinger the humdinger

Work 'em Silly

The interior of Ben Hill Griffin Stadium is painted a bright orange and blue, and signs at the ends declare it to be Gator Country and The Swamp. Fans bring homemade signs to the games often with inspirational messages urging the Gators to victory. Most of those signs likely wind up in the trash at the end of the game, but there is one that has appeared at nearly every home game (and some away games) for the past 20 years.

A familiar sign

In 1993, Pete Calamore was a freshman at the University of Florida who, on the spur of the moment, made a sign from a bedsheet he bought from the Salvation Army. He spray-painted "Work 'em Silly, Gators!" on it and took it to the 1993 home game against Tennessee. Hanging over the bright orange wall, it was easily seen by nearly everyone in the stadium, and he continued to bring it for the rest of the season. Fans approached him to let him know they saw the sign . . . and so did national television audiences.

In 1995, Jeri Spurrier, the wife of the then-head football coach, complimented the sign as it hung at the Fiesta Bowl, telling Calamore that she would look for the sign at every game. He then made another spur-of-the-moment decision—to bring the sign to every game. It has worn out over the years, and he's had to replace it twice. People have tried to steal it. But Calamore, who wound up working for UF in the College of Health and Human Performance, continues the tradition of encouraging the team to "Work 'em Silly." Watch for the sign at the next game.

against the University of Georgia—with an unofficial assist from beloved Gator sportscaster Otis Boggs. Boggs knew Hunsinger loved to hunt with his teammate, Frank Dempsey, and all of them were tired of the Gators' losing streak to Georgia. The week of the game, Boggs told Hunsinger that if he ran for more than 100 yards and two touchdowns, they would beat Georgia, and, if he did, Boggs promised to get the two of them a bird dog. Following the victory, Boggs kept his promise and gave the boys a liver-spotted pointer that turned out to be an excellent hunting dog. Hunsinger received a bachelor's degree from UF in 1950 and later was inducted in the University of Florida Athletic Hall of Fame.

He was the third pick in the first round of the 1950 NFL draft and became a member of the Chicago Bears. In his three years there, he ran for 834 yards, caught 23 passes, and also ran back kickoffs and punts. After his tenure in Chicago, he joined the Canadian Football League Montreal Alouettes in 1953 and played for three seasons, adding 516 yards to his professional total. He tried to retire after the 1954 season, but he decided to return after receiving a 310-foot-long telegram with 21,000 signatures from fans wanting him to play another year. He came back in 1955 but late in the season, broke his ankle and retired from playing for good. He began teaching in 1958 at Harrisburg High School in Illinois, his alma mater, where he remained until his retirement in 1990, although he continued to serve the community as a member of the school board for three years. Hunsinger died on March 23, 1998, and the following August, the Harrisburg Community School District renamed the high school stadium Hunsinger Stadium in his honor.

SCOTT RAWLS HUTCHINSON (1956–) ■ *Defensive End*
COLLEGE: 1974–77   6-4, 246 lbs.   **NFL:** 1978–81, 1983; **USFL:** 1985

Scott Hutchinson of Winter Park played on the defensive line for head coach Doug Dickey for four years. As a senior, he served as a team captain and was named an honorable mention All-American by the Associated Press.

He was chosen in the second round of the NFL draft in 1978 by the Buffalo Bills, and over the next three seasons played in all 48 regular season games, starting eight of them. After the 1980 season, Hutchinson was waived by Buffalo and was picked up by the Tampa Bay Buccaneers. There, he played all 16 games in 1981 and briefly left football.

In 1983, he was back on the Bills and played in five games, giving him a total of 69 games played in the NFL. Buffalo again waived him in August 1984. He also played in 1985 for the Orlando Renegades of the United States Football League.

In 2012, Hutchinson joined with Floyd Little and numerous other NFL players in a lawsuit against the league, resulting from head injuries incurred during his playing years, which were improperly diagnosed and treated. He alleged that he suffered from short-term memory loss, sleeplessness, and depression as a result. Hutchinson and his wife, Sharyn, live in Winter Springs, Florida.

GELINDO INFANTE (1940–) ■ *Halfback-Coach*
COLLEGE: 1960–62   **CFL:** 1963 (player); **WFL:** 1975; **NFL:** 1977–78, 1980–82, 1986–91, 1995–97; **USFL:** 1984–85 (coach)

After playing fullback for Miami Senior High School, Gelindo "Lindy" Infante became a tailback for the University of Florida in 1960. His most memorable games include a pair in which he scored the winning touchdowns—one against Georgia Tech in 1960 and the other against Clemson University in 1961. His senior year in 1962 was cut short because of a broken leg suffered in the LSU game.

Infante played one year as a halfback for the Canadian Football League Hamilton Tiger-Cats, and then returned to Gainesville to receive his bachelor's degree in physical education in 1964. His coaching career began almost accidentally, as an assistant at both his high school and college alma maters, Miami Senior High in 1965 and Florida from 1966–71. He was on the way to a career in architecture, when he was unexpectedly offered his first job as a coach, and he remained in coaching for more than three decades. Infante moved to the pros for a year as an assistant for the World Football League's Charlotte Hornets, but he came back to the college ranks as the offensive coordinator for Tulane University.

Lindy Infante (top) and 3 teammates form a totem pole in 1962

After a brief stint as a receivers coach for the New York Giants, Infante returned to Tulane as its offensive coordinator for 1979. The next stop on his travels was Cincinnati in the NFL, where he coached the Bengals' quarterbacks in 1980 and was the offensive coordinator from 1981–82. He left to become the head coach of the United States Football League Jacksonville Bulls in 1984–85, and, when that league was terminated, Infante returned to the NFL as the offensive coordinator of the Cleveland Browns (1988–91).

He finally became a head coach in the NFL with the Green Bay Packers (1988–91). During his tenure, the Packers had a record of only 24-40, but during their 10-6 season in 1989, Infante was honored as the Associated Press NFL Coach of the Year. He was fired by Green Bay in 1991; three seasons later, he came back to the NFL to coach for one more team. He served as the offensive coordinator for the Indianapolis Colts in 1995, then moved up to head coach for the next two years. There, he posted a record of 12-20 and made it to the first round of the playoffs in 1996.

Infante is a member of the University of Florida Athletic Hall of Fame and is enjoying his retirement with his wife, Stephanie in Crescent Beach, Florida.

CHAD W. JACKSON (1985–) ■ *Wide Receiver*

COLLEGE: 2003–05   6-1, 215 lbs.   **NFL:** 2006–09; **UFL:** 2011

Chad Jackson was a three-sport athlete in high school and a *Parade* magazine All-American. He played for three years at the University of Florida and had an outstanding junior year in 2005. His 88 pass receptions not only led the Southeastern Conference for the season, but also tied the Gators' all-time record. Those catches totaled 900 yards, and nine of them went for touchdowns. Jackson also rushed for two more touchdowns on 16 runs for 89 yards. He skipped his senior year to play in the NFL.

He was chosen in the second round of the 2006 NFL draft by the New England Patriots. A hamstring injury caused him to miss the preseason and limited his production during the season, as did a groin injury. He managed to get into 12 games and catch 13 passes for 152 yards and three touchdowns. In the American Football Conference championship game, he suffered a torn ACL and saw no more action until partway through the 2007 season, and he made only one catch for 19 yards in the regular season.

Chad Jackson while he was on the New England Patriots

Jackson was released by the Patriots in 2008 and joined the Denver Broncos that year, during which he played in four games. He was released by Denver in September 2009 and briefly was a member of the Buffalo Bills (2010) and the Oakland Raiders (2011), but he saw no game action with either team. His professional football career continued as a member of the Omaha Nighthawks of the United Football League (2011). He remains an unsigned free agent.

DARRELL LAMONT JACKSON (1978–) ■ *Wide Receiver*
COLLEGE: 1997–99   6-0, 201 lbs.   NFL: 2000–08

Darrell Jackson (#82) running a pattern for the 49ers

As a senior at Tampa Catholic High School, Darrell Jackson set national records for average yards per catch and total career receiving yards. He was named in 1999 to *The Tampa Tribune* list of the 33 best high school football players in the state's last 100 years.

While he was a part of the Gators team during his freshman and sophomore years, Jackson received little playing time. During his junior year, however, he more than made up for it and caught 67 passes for 1,156 yards in Coach Spurrier's "Fun 'n' Gun" offense. After a three-year college career with 1,501 yards, he skipped his senior year and declared himself eligible for the 2000 NFL draft.

Jackson was selected in the third round by the Seattle Seahawks, where he stayed for seven seasons. During 2004, he set the then franchise record of 87 catches in a season, and, in Super Bowl XL against the Pittsburgh Steelers, he tied the record for most receptions in the first quarter (five). Jackson played in a backup role for the San Francisco 49ers (2007) and the Denver Broncos (2008) before retiring to Tampa.

RANDALL BELFORD JACKSON (1944–) ■ *Tackle*
COLLEGE: 1964–65   6-5, 250 lbs.   **NFL:** 1967–74

A graduate of Lake City High School in Lake City, Florida, Randy Jackson came to the University of Florida and played offensive tackle. His last game as a Gator was the university's first major bowl game in its history—the 1966 Sugar Bowl. In 1968, he received his bachelor's degree in business administration from UF; he is a member of the University of Florida Athletic Hall of Fame.

In the 1966 NFL draft, Jackson was selected in the fourth round by the Chicago Bears and was also picked in the third round of the AFL draft by the Buffalo Bills. He began playing for Chicago in 1967 and started at left tackle for every game for the next two seasons. He remained at that position for the Bears through the 1974 season, although in later years in a backup role. By the time he retired at the end of the 1974 season, Jackson had played in 105 NFL games.

Randy Jackson (88) pursuing Richmond quarterback Bill Silvi

TAYLOR HOUSER JACOBS (1981–) ■ *Wide Receiver*
COLLEGE: 1999–2002   6-1, 210 lbs.   **NFL:** 2003–07

Gator wide receiver Taylor Jacobs

In his 10 games as a true freshman, Taylor Jacobs caught seven passes for 99 yards. He played in all 12 games as a sophomore and increased to 17 catches for 198 yards. By the time he was a senior, he was the team's top wide receiver, with a four-year total of 133 receptions (16 for touchdowns) for 2,097 yards. Jacobs' 246 yards against the University of Alabama-Birmingham is still the UF single-game record. His post-season honors included invitations to the Senior Bowl and Hula Bowl all-star games. He was named the MVP of the Orange Bowl victory over the University of Maryland on January 2, 2002. Jacobs received his bachelor's degree in sociology from UF in 2009.

Continued on next page

The Jackson Family

WILLIE BERNARD JACKSON SR. (c.1950–)
Wide Receiver   WFL: 1975

WILLIE BERNARD JACKSON JR. (1971–)
Wide Receiver   NFL: 1995–2002

TERRANCE BERNARD JACKSON (1976–)
Fullback   NFL: 1999–2005

In some families, it is a tradition to follow in the footsteps of a relative who has played football for the Gators and don the orange and blue for Saturday games. In one family, this tradition even extended to the jersey number, as the father and his two sons wore number 22 while they played for Florida.

It started with Willie Jackson Sr., who accepted his Gator scholarship offer on December 18, 1968. He became one of the first two black football players to appear in an intercollegiate game for UF, and he lettered in 1970–72. During 1970 and 1971, he led the team in all-purpose yards, in spite of escalating racial tension.

In 1971, the Black Student Union staged a protest regarding the treatment of black students, which resulted in 66 students being arrested. When the school president decided to press charges, almost one-third of the black students and several faculty members left the campus. Ten black athletes remained, and Jackson acted as their spokesman, saying they had decided to remain and told the student newspaper, "There's got to be somebody left here to keep the pressure on so changes can be made." He went on to play one year as a professional wide receiver with the World Football League Jacksonville Express (1975).

Willie Jackson Sr.

One of his sons, Willie Jackson Jr., was also a wide receiver at Florida in 1991–93. During his first two years, he was the team's leading receiver, and his 1992 totals of 62 catches and 772 yards made him one of the best in the Southeastern Conference. Overall, he had 162 receptions for 2,172 yards and 24 touchdowns. Jackson also lettered in basketball in 1990 and 1991, and he is a member of the University of Florida Athletic Hall of Fame. He received his bachelor's degree in telecommunications in 1993.

Willie Jr. wore several professional uniforms during his career. He was drafted in the fourth round in 1994 by the Dallas Cowboys but did not play any games there. In 1995, he was one of the unprotected players available during the expansion draft and was chosen by the Jacksonville Jaguars, where he played from 1995 through 1997. He also played for the Cincinnati Bengals (1998–99), the New Orleans Saints (2000–01), the Atlanta Falcons (2002), and the Washington Redskins (2002). His NFL totals were 3,641 yards on 284 receptions.

Willie Sr.'s younger son, Terry Jackson, played for the Gators from 1995 through 1998. After a redshirt year as a strong safety, he switched to fullback. During his freshman and sophomore years, the Gators won the SEC championship. For four years, he was on the SEC Academic Honor Roll and received his bachelor's degree in business administration in 1998. That same year, he was named to the Academic All-America team selected by the College Sports Information Directors of America, and in 1999 he won the NCAA Post-Graduate Scholarship Award.

The San Francisco 49ers selected Terry in the fifth round of the 1999 NFL draft and, unlike his brother, he stayed with one team for his entire seven-year career. Most of the time, he was a blocker or a third-down receiver, and he also played on special teams. His NFL totals were 331 yards rushing and 351 receiving.

TAYLOR HOUSER JACOBS *Continued from previous page*

His first head coach at Florida was Steve Spurrier, and they were reunited when Jacobs was chosen in the second round of the 2003 NFL draft by the Spurrier-led Redskins. Injuries limited his rookie season to three catches in eight games. In 2004, he played in 15, including four starts, and averaged 11.1 yards for each of his 16 receptions.

Jacobs was traded in 2006 to the San Francisco 49ers, and he played eight games that season and four in the next, before he was released. He joined the Denver Broncos and finished his professional career by appearing in six games for them in 2007. He was released from that team on August 26, 2008. Overall, Jacobs had 37 receptions for 384 yards and a pair of touchdowns.

JOHN WILBUR JAMES JR. (1949–) ■ *Punter*
COLLEGE: 1970–71   6-3, 197 lbs.   NFL: 1972–84

John James played golf and basketball (but not football) for Gainesville High School, and he was a walk-on for the Gators in 1969. By the following year, he was the team's regular punter. His average during his senior year was 40.3 yards per punt. James received his bachelor's degree in 1971 and was inducted into the University of Florida Athletic Hall of Fame seven years later.

His first team in the NFL was the Atlanta Falcons in 1972 where James played for ten years and punted 873 times with an average of 40.6 yards. Four times (1974, 1975, 1976, and 1978) he led the NFL in the categories of most punts and total punting yardage; in 1975, he had the league's longest punt (75 yards). He was named to the Pro Bowl in 1975, 1976, and 1977.

He also played in three games for the Detroit Lions (1982) before moving to the Houston Oilers (1982–84). Over his career, he made 1,083 punts and was only blocked six times, for a total of 43,992 yards. In 1986, James became the executive director for Gator Boosters, Inc. at the university, which is a fund-raising organization for athletic scholarships.

DOUG JOHNSON JR. (1977–) ■ *Quarterback*
COLLEGE: 1996–99   6-2, 225 lbs.   NFL: 2000–04

Gainesville native Doug Johnson was selected in the second round of the 1996 Major League Baseball draft by the Tampa Bay Devil Rays and was a minor league infielder for a time. A rotator cuff injury caused him to drop baseball and focus on football.

He played quarterback under head coach Steve Spurrier beginning in 1996. During one game in his sophomore year, Johnson set the Southeastern Conference record for the most touchdown passes in a game and tied the Division I NCAA record for the most in a half, when he threw seven against Central Michigan University (that also tied Terry Dean's UF game record of seven touchdowns). Johnson passed for 460 yards in that game and wound up with more than 7,000 passing yards as a Gator.

Doug Johnson with his final team, the Cincinnati Bengals

In 2000, Johnson was not drafted, but he instead signed as a free agent with the Atlanta Falcons. Over the next four seasons, he played in 23 games, started 11, and threw for 2,532 yards. In 2004, he was on the practice squad of the Jacksonville Jaguars before signing with the Tennessee Titans and playing in his final two NFL games. Over the next two seasons, Johnson was a member of the Cleveland Browns and the Cincinnati Bengals, but he saw no game action.

One of his post-playing activities was his founding and heading the Reeling For Kids Tournament in 2004. Fishermen near Steinhatchee, Florida, compete and raise money for the Boys and Girls Club of Alachua County. Johnson is also active with the Gainesville chapter of the Cystic Fibrosis Foundation. In 2013, he acquired the Perry McGriff, Johnson & Fletcher Insurance Agency in Gainesville.

ELLIS BERNARD JOHNSON (1973–) ■ *Defensive Tackle-End*
COLLEGE: 1991–94   6-2, 288 lbs.   **NFL:** 1995–2004

Ellis Johnson joined the Gator football team in 1991, after playing for Wildwood High School in Wildwood, Florida. As a member of the defensive line, he was part of the team that won the Southeastern Conference championship in 1991, 1993, and 1994. His senior year also saw individual honors for him, including CNN Defensive Player of the Year. Over four years, Johnson registered 26.8 tackles for a loss and 16.3 quarterback sacks. In 1994, he received the Ray Graves Award as the team's MVP.

Johnson was ranked #32 on *The Gainesville Sun* newspaper's list of the top 100 all-time Gators in 2006. The next year, he was inducted into the University of Florida Athletic Hall of Fame.

In the first round of the 1995 NFL draft, Johnson was chosen by the Indianapolis Colts, and he played for them through 2001. His release from the team was reportedly at Johnson's request, so he could find a team where he could play full time. He spent two years with the Atlanta Falcons, and then his final season was with the Denver Broncos. Johnson's NFL career stats show 51 sacks in 149 games, plus three interceptions, and 356 tackles.

TODD EDWARD JOHNSON (1979–) ■ *Safety-Defensive Back*
COLLEGE: 1999–2002   6-1, 200 lbs.   **NFL:** 2004–09

Following a redshirt year, Todd Johnson began playing safety for the Gators in 1999, lettered all four years, and started every game after his freshman year. As a sophomore, he led the team in tackles with 102—his best season total during his career—along with five interceptions and four fumble recoveries (one returned for a touchdown), and was named to the Associated Press All-Southeastern Conference first team for two consecutive years. Johnson was a team captain as a senior and he was named to the All-SEC second team in 2002 by the AP and the conference coaches. As a Gator, he played in 49 games and made 284 tackles and nine interceptions. In 2009, he completed his bachelor's degree in applied physiology and kinesiology.

Chicago's Todd Johnson (#35) tackling Pittsburgh's Jerome "The Bus" Bettis during a snowy game

Johnson was selected in the fourth round of the 2003 draft by the Chicago Bears. He missed the season that year because of a broken jaw from a preseason game, but he spent the next three seasons there and appeared in 42 games with 143 tackles. He played for the St. Louis Rams (2007–08) and the Buffalo Bills (2010) before retiring.

In 2011, Johnson accepted the position of head coach at Riverview High School in Sarasota, where years before he had been an all-state high school football player and hurdler.

JAMES ROOSEVELT JONES (1961–) ■ *Fullback-Running Back*
COLLEGE: 1979–82   6-2, 229 lbs.   **NFL:** 1983–92

While playing football at Blanche Ely High School in Pompano Beach, Florida, James Jones was nicknamed "The Franchise." He was a *Parade* magazine All-American following his senior year. Later, he was named to a list of the 100 greatest Florida high school football players by the Florida High School Athletic Association.

Jones played for the Gators beginning in 1979, when the team posted a dismal record of 0-10-1, and as a sophomore helped the Gators make the biggest one-year turnaround in NCAA history with an 8-4 record. He was a team captain both as a junior and a senior; in his last year, he was the team's Fergie Ferguson Award winner, recognizing him for his leadership, character, and courage. Jones led the team in rushing yardage for three years, from 1980 through 1982, and had a four-year total of 2,026 yards. He also had 593 yards receiving and passed for 48 yards. *The Gainesville Sun* ranked him #45 on its all-time list of greatest Gators in the first century of football, and he is a member of the University of Florida Athletic Hall of Fame.

Jones was a first-round draft pick by the Detroit Lions in 1983. Initially, he served as a fullback blocking for Billy Sims, but he took over as the main running back in 1985 when Sims was injured. In his last three years with Detroit, he was paired in the backfield with Garry James, and they were referred to as the "James Gang."

In 1989, Jones was traded to the Seattle Seahawks, and he remained with them until he retired in 1992. His professional career included 135 games, and he ran for 3,626 yards and caught 318 passes for 2,641. Years after retiring from the NFL, he served as the head coach for his high school alma mater for one season in 2007. Jones also worked for a Tampa insurance agency and the Gator Radio Network.

James Jones (#30) after getting a handoff from Wayne Peace (#15)

JEVON KEARSE (1976–) ■ *Defensive End*
COLLEGE: 1996–98   6-4, 265 lbs.   **NFL:** 1999–2009

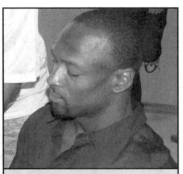

Jevon Kearse signs autographs for the troops in Iraq in 2010

In high school in Fort Myers, Jevon Kearse played tight end and strong safety. *USA Today* named him a prep All-American after his senior year, and he was a member of the National Honor Society.

He enrolled at the University of Florida in 1995 and was redshirted his first season, which gave him time to prepare to play linebacker or defensive back. The next year, he shifted to outside linebacker and caught the attention of his opponents. Kearse was freakishly fast, agile, had a 38-inch vertical leap and a long wingspan, which earned him the nickname of "The Freak." At the end of that season, he helped the Gators win the national championship with a win over Florida State University in the Sugar Bowl.

In 1997 and 1998, he led the team in sacks with 6.5 and 7.5 and made a total of 92 tackles. As a senior, he was named the Associated Press Southeastern Conference Defensive Player of the Year. His four goals in playing for the Gators had been to become a better person, to win a national championship, to get an education, and to have a chance to play in the NFL. Having completed the first three, Kearse opted to enter the NFL draft a year early.

He was selected in the first round in 1999 by the Tennessee Titans. In his first month as a professional player, Kearse was named the NFL Defensive Rookie of the Month. That honor was bestowed on him every month except for one that season, and he was chosen as the NFL Defensive Rookie of the Year. That same year, he was named to the Pro Bowl and played in Super Bowl XXXIV. He again played left defensive end in 2000, then the next year switched to right defensive end and made his third Pro Bowl roster. Kearse missed much of 2002 and part of 2003 because of injuries but still was key in the Titans' march to the playoffs.

Before the 2004 season, he signed with the Philadelphia Eagles for a contract worth more than any previous defensive lineman. He played with Philadelphia through 2007, although 2006 ended early because of injuries. The Eagles released him in early 2008. Soon, he went back to the Titans and started 16 games in 2008 but was a backup for his final year in 2009. During his 11-year career, Kearse made 314 tackles and sacked quarterbacks 74 times.

In 2013, the *Orlando Sentinel* ranked him at #14 on its list of the 50 Greatest Gators. He continues to work with the NFL, making appearances at the Super Bowl and corporate events. Kearse trains regularly to remain in shape and may try his hand at coaching some day.

CRAWFORD FRANCIS KER (1962–) ■ *Guard*
COLLEGE: 1983–84   6-3, 288 lbs.   **NFL:** 1985–91

As a junior at Dunedin High School, despite not having played any prior high school football, Crawford Ker decided to go out for the team and hopefully play in the NFL someday. He worked out to build up his 145-pound body to a more football-worthy 210, and he played on a team that won the county championship during his senior year. Overlooked by recruiters, he spent a year after graduation working out and adding another 50 pounds.

He attended junior college at Arizona Western College in 1981–82 and was honored as a National Junior College Athletic Association All-American. He accepted a scholarship to play at Florida and was on the offensive line for 1983 and

Crawford Ker on the Dallas Cowboys

1984, a part of "The Great Wall of Florida," which included Lomas Brown, Jeff Zimmerman, Phil Bromley, and Billy Hinson. They blocked for quarterback Kerwin Bell and star running backs John L. Williams and Neal Anderson, and helped the team to a 9-1 record in 1984, the first (later vacated) Southeastern Conference football championship for Florida.

In the third round of the 1985 NFL draft, Ker went to the Dallas Cowboys and played in five games as a rookie. The next year, he moved up to starter and stayed there for five seasons until he left as a free agent in 1991. Ker finished his professional football career by playing a dozen games for the Denver Broncos during the 1991 season. After football, he founded a chain of Florida sports bars and restaurants known as Ker's WingHouse Bar & Grill, which he continues to operate.

ERRON QUINCY KINNEY (1977–) ■ *Tight End*
COLLEGE: 1996–99   6-5, 275 lbs.   **NFL:** 2000–05

Erron Kinney was a member of the Patrick Henry High School team, which won the Virginia state championship while he was a senior, and then he came to the University of Florida for a redshirt year while he studied elementary education. His first active year as a player was in 1996, and he was part of the Gators' first national championship team. As a four-year Gator, Kinney caught 39 passes (five for touchdowns) for 507 yards.

Erron Kinney on the Tennessee Titans

The Tennessee Titans drafted Kinney in the third round of the 2000 NFL draft, and he played his entire professional career there. His best year was his final one in 2005, when he caught 55 passes for 543 yards.

During 2008, Kinney become a firefighter in Brentwood, Tennessee. Four years prior to that, he had been appointed to the Tennessee State Firefighting Commission. He later served as a captain with the St. Andrews Fire Department of Charleston, South Carolina, and took over the position of fire chief of Mt. Juliet, Tennessee, in March 2013. Kinney also conducts a summer youth football camp in Nashville at Lipscomb University.

RICHARD BURTON LAWLESS (1953–) ■ *Guard*
COLLEGE: 1972–74   6-4, 253 lbs.   **NFL:** 1975–80

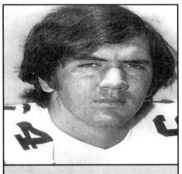

Former Florida guard Burton Lawless

In Punta Gorda, Florida, Burton Lawless was an all-state tight end for the Charlotte High School Fighting Tarpons football team. The Florida High School Athletic Association named him to its team of the 100 greatest high school football players from the first 100 years of football in the state.

Lawless had intended to play at tight end, but in his first practice session he suffered a broken shoulder. When he returned to the team, he was moved to starting offensive tackle and later shifted to offensive guard. Many consider him to be the greatest pulling guard in UF history. He started his last three years, and after his senior year, Lawless was invited to the Chicago College All-Star Game and played against the Pittsburgh Steelers.

He completed his bachelor's degree in exercise and sports sciences in 1977; the following year, he was inducted into the University of Florida Athletic Hall of Fame. *The Gainesville Sun* in 2006 named him #42 on its list of the top 100 all-time Gators.

The Dallas Cowboys chose Lawless in the second round of the 1975 NFL draft. He was one of only two rookies to earn starting positions that year with Dallas, and he wound up starting 10 of the 14 games, all at left guard, and made the United Press International NFL All-Rookie Team. During 1976–79, he platooned at the position with others and played in three Super Bowls (the Cowboys won one of them). Lawless was traded to the Miami Dolphins during the 1980 training camp, was released before the season started, and signed as a free agent with the Detroit Lions, for which he played in nine games and started five.

Lawless was back on the Dolphins roster for the last part of the 1981 season, but he did not play. He signed with the Chicago Bears for 1982, but early that year he was badly injured in a farm accident when a 5,000-pound plow-arm fell on his neck and head, which resulted in 17 days of paralysis and ended his football playing days. After football, Lawless has been involved in faith- and community-based groups, including the Fellowship of Christian Athletes, Ronald McDonald House, Boys and Girls Clubs, and Legacy Outfitters, which endeavors to help men become true leaders of their families. As part of his rehabilitation from his 1982 accident, he was placed in a hospital in Waco, Texas, and he wound up settling there. One of his activities in Waco was spotting for the public address announcer at Baylor University football games.

TERRY JEROME LECOUNT (1956–) ■ *Wide Receiver*
COLLEGE: 1975–77   5-10, 178 lbs.   **NFL:** 1978–84, 1987

Before college, Terry LeCount was a champion, both on the running track and as a quarterback, leading Jacksonville's William M. Raines High School Vikings to the state championship in 1973. He played for the Gators from 1974 through 1977 under head coach Doug Dickey, who generally shunned the aerial barrage preferred by pass-oriented coaches. In those years, the primary attack was on the ground, and LeCount led a variation of the wishbone offense known locally as the Gatorbone. He started out as the second black Gator quarterback (Don Gaffney was the first in 1973) and eventually shifted to wide receiver.

Terry LeCount (left) with Earl Carr, Tony Green, and Willie Wilder

LeCount was chosen in the fourth round of the 1978 NFL draft by the San Francisco 49ers, where he played in three games in 1978 and two in 1979. During the 1979 season, he was traded to the Minnesota Vikings, where he played in 66 games through the 1984 season. An injury prevented him from playing in 1985 and 1986, but in 1987 he returned for one more game in a Viking uniform as a replacement player during a strike.

Over the course of his professional career, LeCount caught 89 passes for 1,354 yards. He also rushed for 90 and returned kickoffs. After football, he spent years as a mentor and educator, including assisting in a kindergarten classroom at Oakhurst Elementary School in Decatur, Georgia. LeCount donated a kidney to his younger brother and considers that and his sobriety to be the biggest accomplishments of his life.

ROBERT ANTHONY LILLY (1962–) ■ *Safety*
COLLEGE: 1980–83   6-0, 199 lbs.   **NFL:** 1984–87

Tony Lilly showed football skills early and was named to the United Press International Virginia All-State football team while he was in high school. He came to Florida and was a backup as a freshman until an injury to Tim Groves late in the season moved him up to the starting position, which he held for his last three years.

The Denver Broncos picked Lilly in the third round of the 1984 NFL draft. For four seasons, he played there, including starting at safety in Super Bowl XXII. Overall, he started in 15 of the 58 games he played, recovered three fumbles, and made nine interceptions.

In recent years, Lilly has been a special education instructor and head football coach. In 2005–09, he coached at Potomac Senior High School in Dumfries, Virginia. His team had an 11-2 record in 2006 and was a regional champion. The following year, his squad improved to 13-1 and was the runner-up in the state finals. Since 2010, Lilly has coached the football team at C.D. Hylton High School in Woodbridge, Virginia. He also teaches television production at the school.

DAVID LAMAR LITTLE SR. (1959–2005) ■ *Linebacker*

COLLEGE: 1977–80 6-1, 232 lbs. **NFL:** 1981–82

After starring for Miami's Andrew Jackson High School Generals, David Little enrolled at the University of Florida and played linebacker. During his senior year in 1980, he helped the team set an NCAA record for the biggest turnaround to date, from a 1979 season record of 0-10-1 to a 1980 record of 8-4 and a trip to a bowl game. That year, Little was the recipient of the Gator's Fergie Ferguson Award for his leadership, character, and courage. His 475 tackles during his Gator career also set the school's all-time record, which still stands.

He was drafted in the seventh round in 1981 by the Pittsburgh Steelers, and remained with that team for his entire 12-year professional career. A standout middle linebacker, Little participated in 179 games, starting 125 of them that included a streak of 89 in a row. He recovered 11 fumbles, made 10 interceptions during his career, and was named to the Pro Bowl in 1990. He was inducted into the University of Florida Athletic Hall of Fame in 1991.

Little suffered from heart disease, and one day he experienced a cardiac flutter. Unfortunately, he was bench-pressing 250 pounds at the time. He dropped the weight, and it rolled onto his neck and suffocated him. He died on March 17, 2005.

In 2006, *The Gainesville Sun* newspaper ranked him #18 on its list of the 100 greatest all-time Gator football players. On the list of the 50 Greatest Gators compiled by the *Orlando Sentinel* in 2013, Little was ranked #17.

BUFORD EUGENE LONG (1931–2006) ■ *Defensive Back-Halfback-End*

COLLEGE: 1950–52 6-1, 195 lbs. **NFL:** 1953–55

Today's football rules permit practically unlimited substitutions, but decades ago it was necessary for many players to be prepared to play on both offense and defense. Buford Long was one of the better ones and starred at both halfback and defensive back. Head coach Bob Woodruff considered him one of the three best Gator backs of the 1950s.

As a senior, he had 14 rushing touchdowns to add to the 11 he had in previous years, which still ranks him tied for seventh all-time for UF. One of his most memorable scores was a hand-off from quarterback Doug Dickey, which resulted in a 77-yard touchdown run as part of the Gators' 30–0 victory over Georgia in 1952. In addition to football, he also lettered in track and baseball. Long received his bachelor's degree in physical education in 1955, and he is a member of the University of Florida Athletic Hall of Fame.

Gator halfback Buford Long

He became a New York Giant after being selected in the fifth round of the 1953 NFL draft. In 23 games over three seasons with New York, he rushed 52 times for 164 yards, caught 33 passes for 462 yards, and returned 23 kickoffs.

After his playing days, he owned Buford Long Equipment and Buford Long Citrus. He also served as the chairman of the board of directors of the First National Bank of Wauchula, Florida. Long died of cancer at the age of 74 on September 1, 2006.

MARQUAND ALEXANDER MANUEL (1979–) ■ *Defensive Back*

COLLEGE: 1998–2001   6-0, 209 lbs.   **NFL:** 2002–09

Marquand Manuel was a high school standout in multiple areas. He ran the 100-meter dash for the Miami Senior High School Stingarees, was on the academic honor roll all four years, and was a top defensive back recruiting prospect, according to the All-American teams compiled by National Recruiting Advisor, SuperPrep, and PrepStar.

Manuel accepted a scholarship to play at the University of Florida and was redshirted in his freshman year in 1997. During the next year, he played in every regular season game, and, in 1999, he made 118 tackles to lead the team. The Gators won the Southeastern Conference championship in 2000 and played in the Sugar Bowl with a 10-3 record, and were 10-2 in 2001 when Manuel was a senior captain. The team was ranked number three in the nation in the final polls that year.

Green Bay Packer Marquand Manuel in 2006

Manuel also excelled in the classroom and made the SEC Academic Honor Roll for all four years. He graduated with a bachelor's degree in criminal justice in 2000, and he played his senior year while he served as a graduate assistant and worked toward a master's degree in counseling education.

The Cincinnati Bengals chose Manuel as their sixth round draft pick in 2002. He played in 18 games for the Bengals over the next two seasons, was waived, and became a member of the Seattle Seahawks in 2004. He played in 15 games that year and made 10 tackles, then in 2005 played in every game. During the National Football Conference championship game, Manuel ran back an interception 32 yards to set up a touchdown to help beat the Carolina Panthers. He was the starting free safety in Super Bowl XL but had to leave the game because of an injury.

In 2006, Manuel played for the Green Bay Packers, spent 2007 with the Panthers, 2008 with the Denver Broncos, and 2009 with the Lions. Over his eight years, he amassed 366 tackles and started in 57 of 116 games played. In 2012, he became an assistant special teams coach for the Seahawks, who moved him to defensive assistant beginning with the 2013 season. Manuel established the Marquand Manuel Foundation in Miami to work with children.

WILBER BUDDYHIA MARSHALL (1962–) ■ *Linebacker*
COLLEGE: 1980–83   6-1, 231 lbs.   **NFL:** 1984–95

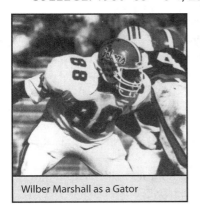

Wilber Marshall as a Gator

After his high school years at Titusville's Astronaut High, *Parade* magazine All-American Wilber Marshall went to Gainesville and embarked on a career that made him one of the Gators' greatest linebackers. In his four years under head coach Charley Pell, he made 343 tackles, recorded 23 quarterback sacks, and was named first-team All-SEC for 3 years beginning in 1981 (all three years by the Associated Press, 1982-83 also by United Press International). In 1982 and 1983, he was a Rotary Lombardi Award finalist (as one of the best college linemen or linebackers) and a consensus first-team All-American, and ABC Sports named him its National Defensive Player of the year for 1983.

The Gainesville Sun honored Marshall three times, beginning in 1999 when it listed him first-team on the Gators' "Team of the Century." They also called him the Defensive Player of the Century. Then in 2006, the newspaper's list of the 100 greatest all-time Gator football players had him ranked as #4 (the same ranking that the *Orlando Sentinel* had for him in 2013 on its list of 50 Greatest Gators). The university honored him by making him the fifth member of its Ring of Honor in 2007 and inducted him into the University of Florida Athletic Hall of Fame. Marshall is also a member of the College Football Hall of Fame, and his career 58 tackles for a loss (27 of them in one season) are still Florida records. He was also listed on the Florida High School Athletic Association's list of the 33 greatest all-time Florida high school football players in 2007.

Marshall was chosen in the first round of the 1984 NFL draft by the Chicago Bears and played there for four years, including the 18-1 1985 season, which resulted in the teams's first Super Bowl victory. One of the highlights of that year was the National Football Conference championship game, in which Marshall picked up a fumble in the snow and ran it back 52 yards for a touchdown.

In 1988, he signed with the Washington Redskins and played for them for five years, including a victory in Super Bowl XXVI. Marshall finished out his career with one year each for the Houston Oilers, Arizona Cardinals, and the New York Jets. In his 12-year career, he made more than 1,000 tackles, intercepted 23 passes, and sacked quarterbacks 45 times. After his playing days, he had years of financial difficulty and declining health from the injuries sustained on the field, but finally he was awarded disability benefits from an NFL retirement plan and now lives in Sterling, Virginia.

MICHAEL SHANE MATTHEWS (1970–) ■ *Quarterback*
COLLEGE: 1990–92   6-3, 196 lbs.   **NFL:** 1996, 1999–2002, 2004

Shane Matthews was honored as the Mississippi Player of the Year after his years quarterbacking Cleveland High School and Pascagoula High School. He became a Gator in 1989 under coach Steve Spurrier and moved up to the starting quarterback position in 1990. During that season, the team posted a record of 9-2, best in the Southeastern Conference, although they were ineligible to win the championship. The next year, they went 10-2 and undefeated in the conference, giving them their first official SEC championship.

Matthews completed 722 passes (74 for touchdowns) in his four years, and his 9,287 passing yards total was for a time the team career record. Three years in a row, he led the SEC in passing yardage, and, in 1990 and 1991, he was named the SEC Player of the Year by the *Nashville Banner*. In 1992, he was presented with the Ray Graves Award as team co-MVP (with Carlton Miles). Matthews graduated with a bachelor's degree in business administration in 1997 and in 2002 was inducted into the University of Florida Athletic Hall of Fame. *The Gainesville Sun*'s 2006 list of the 100 greatest Gator football players ranks him #9, while the list of the 50 Greatest Gators compiled by the *Orlando Sentinel* in 2013 has him at #13.

Matthews was not drafted, but he joined the Chicago Bears in 1993 to serve in a backup role. The first time he played was in 1996, when he appeared in two games. In 1997–98, he was on the roster of the Carolina Panthers as a backup but did not play. Matthews rejoined the Bears in 1999 and played 19 games for Chicago over the next three years, starting in 15 of them. He then went to the Washington Redskins in 2002 and played in eight games under Steve Spurrier.

Chicago Bear quarterback Shane Matthews

In 2003, Matthews was a backup quarterback for the Cincinnati Bengals, but he again saw no game action. In 2004–05, he made it into three games for the Buffalo Bills. He retired at the end of 2005 and attempted a comeback with the Miami Dolphins in late 2006, but he was never used and re-retired in early 2007. Over 14 seasons, Matthews appeared in 32 games, completing 492 passes for 4,756 yards.

Later, he went into coaching at the high school level, working with quarterbacks at Gainesville High School. Early in 2012, he became the head coach of the Allen D. Nease Senior High School Panthers in Ponte Vedra, Florida. He still holds the Florida record for the most consecutive 200-yard passing games (17 over 1990–92).

ANTHONY BERNARD MCCOY (1969–) ■ *Defensive Tackle*
COLLEGE: 1987–88, 1991   6-1, 289 lbs.   **NFL:** 1992–2000

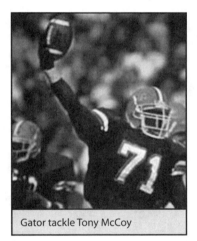

Gator tackle Tony McCoy

Tony McCoy of Orlando began his college football career at Florida under head coach Galen Hall, and he continued under Steve Spurrier to be part of the school's first official Southeastern Conference football championship. That year, the Gator players chose McCoy as their MVP by presenting him with the Ray Graves Award. He graduated with a bachelor's degree in sociology in 2001.

In the fourth round of the 1992 NFL draft, McCoy was chosen by the Indianapolis Colts, and he stayed with that team for eight seasons, most of the time at left defensive tackle. McCoy played his final year for the Arizona Cardinals. His overall career statistics include 114 games played (of which he started 79), 23 quarterback sacks, and a total of 327 tackles.

While he was still with the Colts, he became a minister for the United Christian Church and Ministerial Association. After his playing days, he owned a restaurant named Fish Pro and was a director of McCoy Investments, Inc. In late 2011, McCoy was diagnosed with leukemia and began treatment at Shands Hospital on the University of Florida campus. By late 2012, tests showed that the cancer was gone. He and his wife, Jodie, serve as pastors for Hope International Church in Groveland, Florida.

BOBBY L. MCCRAY JR. (1981–) ■ *Defensive End*
COLLEGE: 2001–03   6-6, 262 lbs.   **NFL:** 2004–10

After playing as a high school All-American in Homestead, Florida, Bobby McCray arrived in Gainesville and was redshirted for his first year. The next season, he played in three games, then moved up to eight in 2001. That year, he made 12 tackles and seven big plays (sacks, tackles for loss, and forced fumbles).

McCray played in all 13 games as a junior and started five of them. In his senior year in 2003, he played in 12 games, eight as a starter, and made the All-Southeastern Conference second teams of the Associated Press and the conference's coaches. During his four years at Florida, McCray played in 36 games and collected 107 tackles.

In the seventh round of the 2004 NFL draft, McCray was chosen by the Jacksonville Jaguars and played in all 16 games during his rookie year. He played three more years for the Jaguars and finished his tenure there with a sack and a forced fumble that won the American Football Conference wild card game at the end of the 2007 season.

New Orleans Saint defensive end Bobby McCray

McCray moved to the New Orleans Saints in 2008 and played 16 games, starting eight of them, and the following year was shifted to a reserve spot for the regular season. He switched to being a starter in the post-season after the 2009 regular season games, including the Saints' win in Super Bowl XLIV. In 2010, New Orleans released McCray, re-signed him, and waived him because he was not living up to the "sack specialist" label he had acquired. He was picked up by the Philadelphia Eagles and played in one game during 2010, a regular season-ending loss to the Dallas Cowboys, before retiring as a free agent. He is married to actress Khadijah Haqq.

RAYMONDO ANTOINE MCDONALD (1984–) ■ *Defensive End*
COLLEGE: 2003–06   6-3, 290 lbs.   **NFL:** 2007–13

Palm Beach County football star Ray McDonald came to Gainesville and was redshirted for his freshman year. He played the following four seasons, two under Ron Zook and two with Urban Meyer, and as a senior in 2006 served as a team captain. McDonald was part of the team that beat The Ohio State University 41–14 in the BCS championship game, the second national title for the Gators. He was named to the All-Southeastern Conference first team by the SEC coaches.

McDonald was drafted by the San Francisco 49ers in the third round of the 2007 NFL draft and, through 2013, has played in 101 games for them, including 40 as a starter. His father, Ray McDonald, Sr., played for the Gators from 1982 to 1985 as a wide receiver.

Ray McDonald (#95) tackling a Southern Mississippi ball carrier

REGINALD GERARD MCGREW (1976–) ■ *Defensive Tackle*
COLLEGE: 1996–98   6-1, 312 lbs.   **NFL:** 2000–02

Reggie McGrew (#92) about to bring down the Tennessee quarterback

After a redshirt year in 1995, Reggie McGrew played defensive tackle for the Gator squad that beat Florida State University 52–20 in the 1997 Sugar Bowl to capture UF's first football national championship. He was recognized by the Associated Press and the conference coaches as first-team All-Southeastern Conference after his junior year in 1998.

Skipping his senior year, McGrew entered the 1999 NFL draft and was chosen in the first round by the San Francisco 49ers. He saw no game action during his rookie season because of injuries, but he played in 22 games in a backup role for the 49ers over the next two years. To wrap up his professional career, he played in two games for the Atlanta Falcons during 2002. He attempted a comeback with the Jacksonville Jaguars in 2003 but was released before the start of the season. McGrew returned to UF in 2010 and received his bachelor's degree in sociology.

WILLIAM TRAVIS MCGRIFF (1976–) ■ *Wide Receiver*
COLLEGE: 1995–98   6-1, 185 lbs.   **NFL:** 1999–2001; **ARFL:** 2003–05

Gator wide receiver Travis McGriff

A third generation Florida athlete, Travis McGriff joined the Gators as a wide receiver in 1995. He was part of the squad that won the Southeastern Conference championship that season and the next, as well as the Gators' first national championship. As a senior, McGriff snagged 70 passes, 13 of which came in a 222-yard effort against the University of South Carolina. His 1,357 yards receiving set a single-season record for the SEC. In 2004, he received his bachelor's degree from UF in exercise and sport sciences.

In the third round of the NFL draft in 1999, McGriff was picked by the Denver Broncos. In three seasons for the Broncos, he played in 34 games and made five receptions for 88 yards. After a short time away from the game, he spent three years in the Arena Football League as a member of the Orlando Predators and the Nashville Kats. He was that league's Rookie of the Year in 2003 and caught 158 passes for 2,290 yards before retiring for good.

The Voice of the Gators

Nothing beats the excitement of watching the Gators play football—at Florida Field in The Swamp, in Jacksonville at the "World's Largest Outdoor Cocktail Party" (as the Florida-Georgia game used to be known), or at an away game in hostile territory. But you may not always be able to make it to a game, and over the years, many of the games were not televised. You had to rely on radio broadcasts to follow the Gators, and luckily, the Voice of the Gators was there to describe all the play-by-play action.

Otis Boggs announcing a game at Florida Field

Otis Boggs was born in South Carolina and attended high school in Auburndale, Florida. He was the valedictorian of his 1937 class, and he headed north to Gainesville to attend the University of Florida to study chemistry. Two years later, the sophomore attended an audition at WRUF, the AM radio station on campus—and all thoughts of being a chemist vanished. In March 1939, Boggs began to announce games in the high school basketball championship tournament. Soon after, he provided color commentary for UF football games for play-by-play man Dave Russell and later shifted to doing play-by-play while still a student. He graduated from UF with a degree combining majors in chemistry, German, English, and history.

After three years in the Army, Boggs spent a year in Texas in broadcasting before returning to Florida, and he later became the Voice of the Gators in 1948. For a time, Boggs was the sports information director at WRUF, while his game broadcasts were heard throughout Central Florida on the Gator Football Network. He co-hosted morning talk shows with Bob Leach (*The Bob and Otis Show*) beginning in 1979 and with Jim Finch (*The OJ Show*) beginning in 1986. For years, Finch served as the Florida Field public address announcer.

From 1960 through 1963, he was honored as Florida's Outstanding Sportscaster. As a tribute to his widespread popularity, sports writer Gary Ledman wrote an article about Boggs in 1980 and mentioned that the last time broadcast rights to UF football and basketball were up for bid, one bidder was asked if he was planning to retain Otis Boggs. His incredulous reply: "Are you kidding? If you have a belching contest at Florida, you get Otis to do the play-by-play."

In 1982, Boggs retired from broadcasting the games, and David Steele took his place, while Boggs remained as the host of a pre-game show. According to *The*

> *Gainesville Sun* newspaper, Boggs broadcast 403 Gator football games and many, many basketball games.
>
> The University of Florida College of Journalism and Communication bestowed upon him its Distinguished Alumnus Award in 1989. That same year, he became a charter member of the WRUF Hall of Fame, and in 1990 he was enshrined in the Florida Sports Hall of Fame. He is also an inductee of the University of Florida Athletic Hall of Fame as an honorary letter winner.
>
> Boggs died August 28, 2002, but is not forgotten. UF Athletic Director Jeremy Foley summed up Boggs' place in Gator history: "Otis was a big part of our program for so many years. There was no better Gator anywhere than Otis. He'll be missed. He loved the Gators, and he loved his job. He was a big part of Florida football."

Travis also had a brief movie career. In the 2006 film *Invincible*, he was the football stunt double for star Mark Wahlberg. Travis and his father, Lee, are one of just two sets of father-son All-SEC first-teamers (Lee 1974 by the Associated Press and United Press International, Travis 1998 AP and the SEC coaches).

DENTER EUGENE MCNABB (1969–) ■ *Fullback*

COLLEGE: 1988–91   6-2, 250 lbs.   **NFL:** 1992–93, 1995

After playing football for Walton High School in DeFuniak Springs, Florida, Dexter McNabb began his Gator career as a fullback, and he was part of the university's first official Southeastern Conference football championship team as a senior. McNabb was selected in the fifth round of the 1992 NFL draft by the Green Bay Packers and played as a backup in all 32 regular season games for them over the next two seasons. He sat out 1994; in 1995 he signed with the Philadelphia Eagles and played in one final NFL game.

When his playing days were over, McNabb went back to the university and completed his degree in sociology in 2003. He then went back to high school, as a coach and administrator, to work with at-risk students at West De Pere High School in Wisconsin while coaching football and girls' track and field. McNabb is currently an associate principal at Pulaski High School in Pulaski, Wisconsin.

DARREN MICKELL (1970–) ■ *Defensive Tackle*

COLLEGE: 1990–91   6-4, 285 lbs.   **NFL:** 1992–98, 1999–2001

Because of his football success for the Miami Senior High School Stingarees, Darren Mickell was highly recruited and accepted a scholarship from head coach Galen Hall. However, he was declared to be academically ineligible as a freshman in 1989. He played in 1990, but new head coach Steve Spurrier required him to sit out the first five games of 1991 as a result of his failure to attend classes.

Once he returned to the active roster, Mickell was a defensive star in the November 1991 14–9 victory over Florida State. His off-field problems were not over, however, and he was suspended for the 1992 season because of violations of team rules. Rather than remain in Gainesville and hope he might be able to play in 1993, Mickell declared himself eligible for the 1992 NFL supplemental draft. He was chosen by the Kansas City Chiefs; and over the next four seasons, he played 45 games for that team.

Mickell was traded to the New Orleans Saints for the 1996 season and moved from backup to starter in 25 of the 26 games he played as a Saint in 1996–97. Unfortunately, his playing time was limited because of a four-game league suspension for violation of the NFL substance-abuse policy. During 1998–99, he only got into one game, and the following year he signed with the San Diego Chargers. There, he started all 16 regular season games and made 35 tackles. Mickell finished his career by playing one game during the 2001 season, his 89th as a pro, for the Oakland Raiders. He had been with the Raiders during the preseason training camp, was cut before the season, then was added to the roster to fill in for injured players. He suited up in a number 98 jersey but participated in no significant action on the field.

ERNEST LEE MILLS III (1968–) ■ *Wide Receiver*
COLLEGE: 1987–90   5-11, 192 lbs.   **NFL:** 1991–99

Ernie Mills of Dunnellon played wide receiver under UF head coaches Galen Hall and Steve Spurrier. One of Mills' most memorable games occurred in 1990 against Alabama when he caught a 70-yard pass from Shane Matthews (from the Gator 2-yard line), which led to a field goal in the 17–13 victory. That year, as a senior, Mills served as captain of the Gators, whose 6-1 record led the Southeastern Conference and finished 9-2. He was the team's co-leader in receiving yardage (with tight end Kirk Kirkpatrick), as well as its touchdown leader with ten. Mills earned his bachelor's degree in 1990 in exercise and sport sciences.

Jacksonville University assistant coach Ernie Mills

After being selected in the third round of the 1991 NFL draft by the Pittsburgh Steelers, Mills played with that team for six seasons. His best year was 1995, during which he caught 39 passes (eight for touchdowns) totaling 679 yards, which helped the team reach Super Bowl XXX. He finished his professional career with the Carolina Panthers (1997) and the Dallas Cowboys (1998–99). His final stats were 196 receptions in 118 games played for 2,934 yards and 20 touchdowns.

Mills was the wide receivers coach for five years for the Jacksonville University Dolphins under former Gator Kerwin Bell. He now coaches the wide receivers for Florida A&M University.

JEREMY LAMAR MINCEY (1983–) ■ *Defensive End*
COLLEGE: 2004-05   6-4, 265 lbs.   **NFL:** 2006–13

After high school in Georgia, Jeremy Mincey attended Butler County Community College in Kansas, where he was first-team all-conference and ranked by Rivals.com as the 18th-best junior college football player in the United States. He transferred to Florida for his junior and senior years, and he completed his bachelor's degree in health and human performance in 2007.

As a senior on the defensive line, Mincey was fourth on the team in number of tackles (62), of which 10.5 were for a loss. He was a starter in each of the 24 games he played for Florida and was named to the All-Southeastern Conference second team by both the Associated Press and the SEC coaches.

Mincey was chosen in the 2006 NFL draft in the sixth round by the New England Patriots. He was on that team's roster for the 2006 season but did not see any action. For the next season, he moved to the Jacksonville Jaguars and played in eight games in 2007 (including two playoff games) and three in 2008. During the summer of 2009, Mincey was injured, waived, put on injured reserve, and sat out the entire 2009 season. He came back in 2010 and played in 15 games, eight as a starter. In 2011 and 2012, he started all 32 regular season games for Jacksonville.

In 2013, he was relegated to being a non-starter, then moved to the Denver Broncos during the season and appeared in two regular season games. He also made it into post-season action, including Super Bowl XLVII.

JEFFREY CLAY MITCHELL (1974–) ■ *Center*
COLLEGE: 1993–96   6-4, 300 lbs.   **NFL:** 1998–2005

As a defensive tackle for Countryside High School in Clearwater, Florida, Jeff Mitchell was honored several times. *USA Today* included him on its high school All-American list with an honorable mention. *The Tampa Tribune* named him the Pinellas County Player of the Year, the *St. Petersburg Times* called him the All-Suncoast Defensive Player of the Year, and he was chosen the MVP of the Pinellas County Athletic Conference.

After a redshirt 1992 year, Mitchell started three of the next four years, during which the Gators won four consecutive Southeastern Conference championships. He was the senior captain for the UF team that won the national championship at the end of the 1996 season. During his four years in a Gator uniform, Mitchell also spent time studying and received academic honors. *The Gainesville Sun* newspaper ranked him #41 in 2006 on its all-time list of the greatest Gator football players.

In 1997, he was selected by the Baltimore Ravens in the fifth round of the NFL draft, but Mitchell didn't play during his rookie year. The following year, he was the starter for all but one game in which he appeared, which was the only one of his 119-game professional career he did not start. In his fourth and final season with Baltimore, he was the starting center in the Super Bowl XXXV win over the New York Giants.

Center Jeff Mitchell (#71) hiking to quarterback Danny Wuerffel (#7)

Mitchell played center for the Carolina Panthers from 2001 through 2005; in 2003, he set a team record for permitting opponents to make only 23 sacks for the season. He was one of only two Carolina offensive linemen to start every game in 2004.

Between seasons, Mitchell was active as the Vice President of Client Relations for the consulting firm of Threadfin Business Solutions. After his playing career ended, he has continued to work for that company.

ALONZO LOQWONE MITZ (1963–) ■ *Linebacker-Defensive End*

COLLEGE: 1982–85   6-3, 275 lbs.   **NFL:** 1986–89, 1991–92

Alonzo Mitz played for the Gators starting in 1982 for head coaches Charley Pell and Galen Hall. He was picked in the eighth round of the 1986 NFL draft by the Seattle Seahawks, where he played for the next four seasons. Mitz appeared in six games in each of his first two seasons, then in 1988 played in all 16 regular season games, four as a starter. That year, he had three quarterback sacks. His last year with the Seahawks was 1989, during which he played in 12 games.

Alonzo Mitz while he was with the Seattle Seahawks

Mitz left Seattle and moved to the Cincinnati Bengals for the 1991 season and started 13 of the 15 games in which he played. His final year, also with the Bengals, was 1992, and he started 14 of the 16 games there. His NFL career consisted of 71 games and included two interceptions and eight sacks.

In his post-playing days, Mitz loves to work with kids and play golf (with an unorthodox one-handed swing). He can often be found participating in youth football camps and celebrity golf tournaments in the Seattle area.

NATHANIEL MOORE (1951–) ■ *Wide Receiver*

COLLEGE: 1972–73   5-9, 184 lbs.   **NFL:** 1974–86

Before coming to the University of Florida, Nat Moore attended Miami Edison Senior High School, Miami-Dade Community College, and the University of Tennessee–Martin. He transferred as a junior; in his first year wearing orange and blue, he was the team's leading rusher with 145 attempts for 845 yards. He also caught 25 passes for 351 yards and scored 13 touchdowns (nine rushing, four receiving). Moore received his bachelor's degree from UF in 1975 in exercise and sport science.

Nat Moore at Florida Field

During the 1974 NFL draft, Moore was chosen in the third round by the Miami Dolphins, where he remained for his entire 13-year career. His best year was 1977, when he led the league with a dozen touchdown receptions and was chosen for the Pro Bowl. That year, the Associated Press also named him to its All-Pro list. His total NFL stats include 510 pass receptions in 183 games for 7,546 yards, 249 yards on 40 rushes, and 1,150 yards on kickoff and punt returns.

Moore is not just known for his athletic prowess, but also for his dedication to charitable causes. He received the NFL Man of the Year Award in 1984 for outstanding service to his community. Two years later, he was honored by the National Football League Players Association with the Byron "Whizzer" White Humanitarian Award. Additional honors include his induction into the University of Florida Athletic Hall of Fame in 1978 and, in 2006, *The Gainesville Sun* ranked him #49 on its list of all-time greatest Gator football players. The Southeastern Conference in 1996 named Moore to its list of SEC Legends. In 1999, he was added to the Miami Dolphins Honor Roll.

He established the Nat Moore Foundation to work with Miami-area disadvantaged youth in 1998. In 2010, he became a Dolphins vice president and senior advisor. He was also a Sun Sports broadcaster for Gator football games until 2011, and he can still be heard on the air providing analysis of preseason Miami Dolphins games. His Nat Moore & Associates, Inc. is a sports promotions firm, and he remains active in the Dolphins administration.

JARVIS JARAY MOSS (1984–) ■ *Defensive End*
COLLEGE: 2003–06   6-7, 260 lbs.   **NFL:** 2007–11

A high school football star in Texas, Jarvis Moss played in the U.S. Army All-American Bowl in 2003 and was named a high school All-American by *Parade* magazine. He then headed to Gainesville to play for Ron Zook and Urban Meyer, but he was sidelined by injuries and saw little playing time in his first two years. His most impressive game was the 2006 win over the University of South Carolina, in which he blocked two kicks with the last one preserving the Gators' chance at a national championship. With the Gamecocks leading 16–10 in the fourth quarter, he blocked an extra point

Jarvis Moss in 2006

to keep the Gators within striking distance. After the Gators made the score 17–16 and the clock ticked down to eight seconds left, Moss blocked what would have been the South Carolina winning field goal. The Gators then won the Southeastern Conference championship and eventually the BCS national championship. Moss was named by *Pro Football Weekly* as a first-team All-American.

Following the Gators' national championship, Moss opted to enter the NFL draft and was chosen in the first round by the Denver Broncos. He played six games that year, before his season ended when he broke his shin. Moss played in a dozen games in 2008 for the Broncos, then for 2009 was moved from defensive end to outside linebacker and played seven games. After nine games for Denver in 2010, Moss was released and joined the Oakland Raiders to finish that season and play one more year. Over his NFL career, he appeared in a total of 53 games.

Moss tried a comeback in 2013 with the Dallas Cowboys, but showed no interest in signing him. He returned to the university to work on his bachelor's degree but soon got into trouble. After being stopped in January 2014 for running a stop sign, Moss was arrested when the police officer saw him attempting to swallow what was believed to be marijuana. He was charged with possession and tampering with evidence. Charges were dropped two weeks later for lack of evidence.

MICHAEL RENE MULARKEY (1961–) ■ *Tight End-Coach*

COLLEGE: 1980–82   6-4, 245 lbs.   **NFL:** 1983–91 (as a player); 1994–2012 (as a coach)

A quarterback in high school in Oakland Park, Florida, Mike Mularkey played tight end for the Gators under head coach Charley Pell from 1980 through 1982. He was picked in the ninth round of the 1983 NFL draft by the San Francisco 49ers but was released before playing a game. He spent the rest of the 1983 season, and the following five, with the Minnesota Vikings. His final three years as a player, 1989 through 1991, were as a member of the Pittsburgh Steelers. Mularkey's final professional statistics include 102 pass receptions in 114 games for 1,222 yards and nine touchdowns.

Mularkey is better known for his coaching career, which he began in 1993 as an assistant for the Concordia College Cobbers in Moorhead, Minnesota. After one year, he moved up to the NFL and became the tight ends coach for the Tampa Bay Buccaneers in 1994–95. With the Steelers, he coached tight ends (1996–2000) and served as the offensive coordinator (2001–03). In 2001, the Pro Football Writers of America named him the Assistant Coach of the Year.

Mike Mularkey as the Jaguar head coach in 2012

His first head coaching job was with the Buffalo Bills. In 2004, the Bills had a record of 9-7 and did not make the playoffs. The following year, their record decreased to 5-11 and Mularkey resigned.

Early in 2006, he became the offensive coordinator for the Miami Dolphins and the following season served as their tight ends coach, but after 2007 produced a record of 1-15, the Dolphins fired all of their coaches. In 2008, Mularkey served his first of four years as the Atlanta Falcons' offensive coordinator, making improvements in the team's offense and getting into the playoffs in three of his four years. For 2010, *The Sporting News* named him the Coordinator of the Year, and Mularkey decided once again to become a head coach.

A position opened with the Jacksonville Jaguars, and on January 11, 2012, he got his second chance at the helm of an NFL team. Unfortunately, the Jaguars posted a record of 2-14, and, after one year, Mularkey was again a coach without a team. In January 2014, he was hired as the tight ends coach of the Tennessee Titans.

LOUIS MORRIS MURPHY JR. (1987–) ■ *Wide Receiver*

COLLEGE: 2005–08   6-2, 200 lbs.   **NFL:** 2009–13

Oakland Raider Louis Murphy in 2010

Louis Murphy was ranked in 2005 by Rivals.com as the 37th-best high school wide receiver in the United States. He was also a basketball power forward, state champion track star, and quarterback for Lakewood High School in St. Petersburg. For the Gators, he played mostly on special teams as a freshman, caught his first touchdown as a sophomore, and became a starting wide receiver as a junior. That year, Murphy caught 36 passes (five for touchdowns) for 544 yards.

During his senior year in 2008, he was a captain and led the team in receiving yards, which gave him more than 1,000 yards for his college career. The talented receiver had a streak of 27 consecutive games in which he caught a pass, and he grabbed his final touchdown as a Gator in their 24–14 BCS championship victory over the University of Oklahoma. He was that year's recipient of the Fergie Ferguson Award, as the senior who best displayed leadership, character, and courage, and received his bachelor's degree.

Continued on next page

Where Did the Gators Go?

After collegiate football careers of varying lengths and measures of success, Gators have departed Gainesville to play for more than 100 different franchises throughout the U.S., Canada, and Europe. Below is a list of the teams for which they played. Because many Florida alumni have played for multiple teams, the totals below exceed the number of individuals listed in this chapter. Although a number of minor league franchises are shown, the numbers for them are for players who also participated in a major league. Those who played professional football solely in one or more minor leagues are not included.

› Tampa Bay Buccaneers (NFL) 42
› Denver Broncos (AFL/NFL) 27
› Boston Braves/Washington Redskins (NFL) 24
› Chicago Bears (NFL) 24
› Pittsburgh Steelers (NFL) 21
› Miami Dolphins (AFL/NFL) 19
› Cincinnati Bengals (AFL/NFL) 18
› Houston Oilers (AFL/NFL)/
 Tennessee Oilers/Titans (NFL) 18
› San Francisco 49ers (AAFC/NFL) 18
› Cleveland/Los Angeles/
 St. Louis Rams (NFL) 16
› Boston/New England Patriots (AFL/NFL) 15
› Atlanta Falcons (NFL) 14
› Baltimore/Indianapolis Colts (AAFC/NFL) 14
› New Orleans Saints (NFL) 14
› Philadelphia Eagles (NFL) 14
› Seattle Seahawks (NFL) 14
› Chicago/St. Louis/Phoenix/
 Arizona Cardinals (NFL) 13
› Minnesota Vikings (NFL) 13
› New York Giants (NFL) 13
› Los Angeles/San Diego Chargers (AFL/NFL) 12
› Cleveland Browns (AAFC/NFL) 12
› Jacksonville Jaguars (NFL) 12

› Portsmouth Spartans/Detroit Lions (NFL) 12
› Toronto Argonauts (CFL) 12
› Green Bay Packers (NFL) 11
› Tampa Bay Bandits (USFL) 11
› Dallas Cowboys (NFL) 10
› Los Angeles/Oakland Raiders (AFL/NFL) 10
› New York Jets (AFL/NFL) 10
› Buffalo Bills (AFL/NFL) 9
› Hamilton Tiger-Cats (CFL) 9
› Kansas City Chiefs (AFL/NFL) 9
› Carolina Panthers (NFL) 7
› Baltimore Ravens (NFL) 6
› Jacksonville Express (WFL) 6
› Jacksonville Sharks (WFL) 6
› Orlando Predators (ArFL) 6
› Regina/Saskatchewan Roughriders (CFL) 6
› Frankfurt Galaxy (WLAF/NFLE) 5
› Rhein Fire (NFLE) 5
› Boston Yanks/Brooklyn Dodgers (NFL) 4
› Montreal Alouettes (CFL) 4
› Sacramento Gold Miners/
 San Antonio Texans (CFL) 4
› Winnipeg Blue Bombers (CFL) 4
› Florida Tuskers/Virginia Destoyers (UFL) 3

- Houston Texans (NFL) 3
- Montreal Alouettes II (CFL) 3
- Newark Bears (NFLG) 3
- Omaha Nighthawks (UFL) 3
- Tampa Bay Storm (ArFL) 3
- Washington Federals/
  Orlando Renegades (USFL) 3
- Amsterdam Admirals (NFLE) 2
- Calgary Stampeders (CFL) 2
- Carolina Cobras (ArFL) 2
- Detroit Drive/Massachusetts Marauders/
  Grand Rapids Rampage (ArFL) 2
- Edmonton Eskimos (CFL) 2
- Frankford Yellow Jackets (NFL) 2
- Jacksonville Bulls (USFL) 2
- Minneapolis Red Jackets (NFL) 2
- Nashville Kats I/Georgia Force (ArFL) 2
- New York Sentinels/Hartford Colonials (UFL) 2
- Ottawa Rough Riders (CFL) 2
- Scottish Claymores (WLAF/NFLE) 2
- Staten Island Stapletons (NFL) 2
- Arizona Wranglers/Outlaws (USFL) 1
- Barcelona Dragons (WLAF/NFLE) 1
- BC Lions (CFL) 1
- Berlin Thunder (NFLE) 1
- Birmingham Fire (WLAF) 1
- Birmingham Stallions (USFL) 1
- Buffalo Bisons (AAFC) 1
- Charlotte Hornets (WFL) 1
- Chicago Blitz (USFL) 1
- Chicago Bruisers (ArFL) 1
- Cleveland Indians (NFL) 1
- Detroit Fury (ArFL) 1
- Florida Blazers/San Antonio Wings (WFL) 1
- Jacksonville Sharks (ArFL) 1
- Las Vegas Gladiators (ArFL) 1
- Las Vegas Locomotives (UFL) 1
- Los Angeles Xtreme (XFL) 1
- Memphis Showboats (USFL) 1
- Miami Seahawks (AAFC) 1
- Michigan Panthers/Oakland Invaders (USFL) 1
- Montreal Machine (WLAF) 1
- Nashville Kats II (ArFL) 1
- NY/NJ Hitmen (XFL) 1
- Orlando Rage (XFL) 1
- Orlando Thunder (WLAF) 1
- Philadelphia Soul (ArFL) 1
- Providence Steam Roller (NFL) 1
- Sacramento Attack/Miami Hooters/
  Florida Bobcats (ArFL) 1
- Shreveport Pirates (CFL) 1
- Utah Blaze (ArFL) 1

LOUIS MORRIS MURPHY JR. *Continued from previous page*

Murphy had knee surgery following his senior year, and, in the 2009 NFL draft, he was selected in the fourth round by the Oakland Raiders. In his three years in the Bay Area, he caught 90 passes for 1,371 yards and seven touchdowns and rushed for 143 yards. Murphy was traded in July 2012 to the Carolina Panthers, where he had 25 receptions in 16 games for 336 yards and a touchdown. In March 2013, he was traded to the New York Giants and saw little game action in a backup role for the season.

GODFREY CLARENCE MYLES (1968–2011) ■ *Linebacker*

COLLEGE: 1988–90   6-1, 240 lbs.   **NFL:** 1991–96

As a junior linebacker at the University of Florida in 1989, Godfrey Myles was named by *The Sporting News* as an honorable mention All-American. The following year, he served as a Gator team captain and made the All-Southeastern Conference first team selected by the SEC coaches.

In the 1991 NFL draft, Myles was chosen in the third round by the Dallas Cowboys, who used him mostly on special teams and as a backup linebacker. In his six years with the Cowboys, he received three Super Bowl rings (XXVII, XXVIII, and XXX). He moved up to the starting position in 1995, but near the end of Super Bowl XXX, Myles suffered an ACL

Godfrey Myles, Dallas Cowboys linebacker

injury. He saw only limited action in a backup role the next year, then signed with the Denver Broncos in 1997. He was waived before the beginning of the season, and Myles retired. During his six NFL seasons, he made 135 tackles and picked off two passes in 76 games. Sadly, Myles suffered a massive stroke and died after being removed from life support on June 10, 2011.

RICKY RENNARD NATTIEL (1966–) ■ *Wide Receiver*

COLLEGE: 1983–86   5-9, 180 lbs.   **NFL:** 1987–92

Ricky Nattiel was a quarterback when he played for Newberry High School near Gainesville, as well as an all-county basketball and track star. He was recruited by Charley Pell to play either defensive back or wide receiver. The decision was made during the middle of his freshman year after senior Dwayne Dixon was injured, and Nattiel took over as starting wide receiver. He became one of the main receivers over the next two years, during which the team had identical 9-1-1 records.

He was incredibly fast and known as "Ricky the Rocket," especially after he scored a touchdown against the University of Georgia on a 96-yard pass

Ricky "the Rocket" Nattiel of the Denver Broncos

from Kerwin Bell in 1984. He served as a team captain; received the Fergie Ferguson Award as a senior for leadership, character, and courage; and was on the Southeastern Conference Academic Honor Roll in his sophomore and senior years, as well as the All-SEC first team in 1986 (as selected by the Associated Press, United Press International, and the SEC coaches). Nattiel received his bachelor's degree from UF in 1987 in public health, and he became a member of the University of Florida Athletic Hall of Fame in 1998. *The Gainesville Sun* ranked him at #46 on its list of all-time greatest Gator football players in 2006.

Nattiel was chosen in the first round by the Denver Broncos in the 1987 NFL draft and played there for his entire six-year professional career. In addition to 70 regular season games, he also played in eight playoff games and two Super Bowls. For all six years, he shared wide receiver duties with Vance Johnson and Mark Jackson, and the small, fast trio was known as "The Three Amigos." Nattiel finished with 121 catches (eight for touchdowns) for 1,972 yards.

After retiring as a player, he coached the junior varsity and wide receivers at Trinity Catholic High School in Ocala. In 2007, he served as varsity head coach for one year and led the team to the regional playoffs.

DAVID ALAN NELSON (1986–) ■ *Wide Receiver*
COLLEGE: 2006–09   6-5, 215 lbs.   **NFL:** 2010–13

David Nelson on the Buffalo Bills in 2011

David Nelson of Wichita Falls, Texas, was redshirted in 2005 after briefly appearing in one game and began playing for the Gators in 2006 as a wide receiver. While he was on the team, UF won a pair of Southeastern Conference championships (2006 and 2008) and two BCS national championships at the ends of those two seasons. As a senior in 2009, Nelson's best game was against the University of Alabama in the SEC championship game, where he had four catches for 53 yards. He graduated in 2009 with a bachelor's degree in sociology.

Nelson was part of an important play in Gator history, which many think of when they recall Tim Tebow. During the BCS championship game on January 8, 2009, against Oklahoma, Tebow threw a "jump pass" into the end zone, catching the Sooner defense by surprise. What few remember is that it was Nelson who caught that pass.

As an undrafted free agent, Nelson signed with the Buffalo Bills in 2010 and played for them for three seasons, appearing in 32 games and catching 94 passes for 1,042 yards. He appeared in only one game in the 2012 season and was released by the Bills. The following April, he signed with the Cleveland Browns, who cut him from the team before the start of the 2013 season. Nelson soon signed as a free agent with the New York Jets and saw action in 12 regular season games in 2013.

REGGIE NELSON (1983–) ■ *Free Safety*
COLLEGE: 2005–06   5-11, 210 lbs.   **NFL:** 2007–13

At Palm Bay High School, Reggie Nelson set a Florida state record for 1,531 yards on kickoff and punt returns. Later, the Florida High School Athletic Association named him one of the 33 best high school football players of the first 100 years of Florida football. He then played football (after a redshirt first year) at Coffeyville Community College in Kansas and earned an associate's degree.

Jaguar safety Reggie Nelson in 2007

Nelson arrived in Gainesville as a sophomore and started at free safety in four games in 2005, and he had seven tackles in each of three games. As a junior, he was a member of the team's Leadership Committee and was voted as the most valuable player by his fellow teammates. That year, Nelson had 51 tackles and six interceptions and helped lead the Gators to the BCS national championship against Ohio State. He was presented with the Jack Tatum Award by the Touchdown Club of Columbus as the country's most outstanding defensive back. Rather than remain at Florida for his senior year, Nelson opted to try for the NFL.

That turned out to be a good decision, as he was a first-round pick by the Jacksonville Jaguars in the 2007 NFL draft. In his first pro game, he led Jacksonville with seven tackles and sacked the Titans' quarterback, forcing a fumble. Nelson played in Jacksonville for three years, then was traded to the Cincinnati Bengals. In his first seven years in the NFL, he has played in 106 games and has had five sacks and 18 interceptions. In 2013, the *Orlando Sentinel* ranked Nelson as #21 of the 50 Greatest Gators.

CAMERON JERRELL NEWTON (1989–) ■ *Quarterback*
COLLEGE: 2007–08   6-5, 245 lbs.   **NFL:** 2011–13

After Cam Newton graduated from high school in Georgia, he enrolled at the University of Florida and joined the football team. He became the backup quarterback, behind Tim Tebow and ahead of John Brantley, and played in five games in 2007. He passed for a total of 40 yards and ran for 103. Newton began the 2008 season with some playing time in the opening game against the University of Hawaii, but because of an ankle injury opted to redshirt the rest of the season.

In November 2008, he was arrested for stealing a laptop computer from another student and was suspended from the team. In January 2009, he transferred to Blinn College in Brenham, Texas, where he threw for 2,833 yards en route to the NJCAA national football championship. For what became the final season of his college career, he attended Auburn University in 2010, where he quarterbacked the team to its first BCS national championship, and he was awarded the Heisman Trophy.

Newton was the first pick in the 2011 NFL draft and became a member of the Carolina Panthers. In his first game, he broke the NFL record for rookie passing yards (422) on opening day, and his total for his first two games (854) was an NFL record for a rookie's first two games. It was actually the record by any quarterback for the first two weeks of the season until later that day, when Tom Brady of New England eclipsed the record with 940 yards. That season, Newton broke the rookie quarterback record for rushing touchdowns and became the first rookie to pass for more than 4,000 yards.

Cam Newton as a Carolina Panther rookie in 2011

Newton played in the 2011 Pro Bowl and was named the Pepsi NFL Rookie of the Year, *The Sporting News* Rookie of the Year, and the Associated Press Offensive Rookie of the Year, despite his team finishing with a record of 6-10. During 2012, he improved his passer rating from 84.5 to 86.2, increased his rushing yardage (to lead the team), and reduced the number of interceptions, but the Panthers' record improved only to 7-9. His rating increased to 88.8 for 2013, and he led Carolina to first place in the National Football Conference South Division. On January 26, 2014, Newton played in his second Pro Bowl.

TIMOTHY REGINALD NEWTON (1963–) ■ *Defensive Tackle*

COLLEGE: 1981–84   6-0, 280 lbs.   **NFL:** 1985–93

Gator linebacker Tim Newton (#51)

Tim Newton played linebacker for Orlando's Jones High School before coming to the University of Florida in 1981. There, he switched to nose tackle. He had both quickness and strength and often required double teaming to keep him out of the offensive backfield. In his senior year, he was honored as a first-team All-Southeastern Conference pick by the Associated Press, United Press International, and the SEC coaches.

In the 1985 NFL draft, Newton was selected in the sixth round by the Minnesota Vikings, where he played for five years. His next team was the Tampa Bay Buccaneers, where he played in 14 games in 1990 and started all 16 regular season games in 1991. He finished up his playing career with the Kansas City Chiefs, for which he played in all 16 games in a backup role in 1993. Overall, Newton appeared in 108 professional games and made 17 quarterback sacks.

JACK EDWARD O'BRIEN (1932–) ■ *End*
COLLEGE: 1951–53   6-2, 213 lbs.   **NFL:** 1954–56

Playing end on both sides of the line of scrimmage, Jack O'Brien (according to head coach Bob Woodruff) was one of the team's best ends and receivers of the 1950s. He played in the 14–13 Gator Bowl win over the University of Tulsa on January 1, 1953, the Gators' first NCAA-sanctioned postseason bowl game. O'Brien was a team captain during his senior year.

In the 1954 NFL draft, the Pittsburgh Steelers selected O'Brien in the seventh round, and he played in 31 games over three seasons. The offense was focused on rushing, so, as a receiver, he didn't get a lot of opportunities to touch the ball, but he still managed to catch 16 passes for 185 yards and a pair of touchdowns. He came back to the university and received his bachelor's degree in physical education in 1958.

After retirement from playing, O'Brien coached football at William R. Boone High School in Orlando, Florida.

JASON BRIAN ODOM (1974–) ■ *Offensive Tackle*
COLLEGE: 1992–95   6-5, 307 lbs.   **NFL:** 1996–99

Offensive lineman Jason Odom started all four years for the Gators during a period in which the team won three Southeastern Conference championships and played in a Bowl Alliance national championship game (which they lost to Nebraska). Individually, Odom was honored twice as the best blocker in the SEC, by being presented with the Jacobs Blocking Trophy in 1994 and 1995. He also made both the Associated Press and the conference coaches' All-SEC rosters in 1994–95 and was a unanimous first-team All-American in 1995. In 1996, he graduated with a bachelor's degree in exercise and sports science.

Tampa Bay Buccaneers tackle Jason Odom

The Gainesville Sun ranked Odom #28 on its list of the 100 greatest Gator football players in 2006; in 2010, he became a member of the University of Florida Athletic Hall of Fame. In 2013, the *Orlando Sentinel* placed him at #23 on its list of the 50 Greatest Gators.

In the 1996 NFL draft, Odom was selected in the fourth round by the Tampa Bay Buccaneers. He played in 46 games over four years and was a starter for all but five games. Odom retired due to a back injury in 2001, and he has worked as a deputy sheriff in Hillsborough County in Tampa since 2008.

LOUIS OLIVER III (1966–) ■ *Safety*

COLLEGE: 1985–88   6-2, 224 lbs.   **NFL:** 1989–96

Safety Louis Oliver

At Glades Central High School in Belle Glade, Florida, Louis Oliver was an outstanding player who blocked two punts in a single game. He was a walk-on at the University of Florida in 1985 and worked his way up to a scholarship. He became the starting free safety and served as team captain and had 11 interceptions as a Gator. Twice, Oliver made it on the Southeastern Conference Academic Honor Roll, and several times he was honored on all-conference and All-American teams.

As a senior, he was presented with the Fergie Ferguson Award for his outstanding leadership, character, and courage. Oliver received his bachelor's degree in criminal justice in 1989 and, in 2000, was inducted into the University of Florida Athletic Hall of Fame. *The Gainesville Sun* in 2006 ranked him #24 on its list of the all-time greatest Gators, and, in 2013, the *Orlando Sentinel* ranked him #15 on its list of the 50 Greatest Gators.

The Miami Dolphins drafted Oliver in the first round of the 1989 NFL draft, and he played the next five years for the 'Fins. A personal highlight was a 1992 interception he made against the Buffalo Bills, which he returned 103 yards for a touchdown. In 1994, Oliver moved to the Cincinnati Bengals and started all 12 games in which he played, then returned to the Dolphins in 1995 to finish his career there with the 1996 season. For his NFL career, Oliver appeared in 117 games, starting 101 of them, made over 500 tackles, and returned 27 interceptions for a total of 605 yards.

In 2006, the Southeastern Conference named him to its list of SEC Legends. After football, he became a party liaison for celebrities and athletes; he later got involved in the Miami-area real estate market with a focus on high-end properties for celebrities. He was inducted into the Broward County Sports Hall of Fame in 2011.

RALPH ORTEGA (1953–) ■ *Linebacker*

COLLEGE: 1972–74   6-2, 220 lbs.   **NFL:** 1975–80

Ralph Ortega, who played football and was a shot putter at Coral Gables High School, was named one of the 100 all-time greatest Florida high school football players by the Florida State High School Athletic Association in 2007. He was part of what was considered one of the greatest moments in Gator football history when the team beat Auburn University on its home turf, Jordan-Hare Stadium, for the first time in 14 games there. Ortega made a hard tackle on the Auburn rusher, forcing a fumble at the end of the first half inside the Florida five-yard line to prevent a touchdown.

Ortega's college statistics include 357 tackles, five interceptions, and a dozen forced fumbles. In 1973 (as selected by the Associated Press and United Press International) and 1974 (by UPI), he was first-team All-Southeastern Conference and, in 1974, was a first-team *Time* and *The Sporting News* All-American. During his senior year, he was a team captain. In 1976, Ortega graduated with a bachelor's degree in management and, two years later, was inducted into the University of Florida Athletic Hall of Fame. *The Gainesville Sun* ranked him as #40 on its 2006 list of the 100 all-time greatest Gator football players; in 2013, the *Orlando Sentinel* ranked him #44 on its list of the 50 Greatest Gators. Ortega was designated by the Southeastern Conference as an SEC Legend in 2007.

He was chosen in the second round of the 1975 NFL draft by the Atlanta Falcons, and he remained with that team for four seasons. He played linebacker, but by 1978 was moved to special teams. The next year, he was traded to the Miami Dolphins, where he stayed until 1980. During his six-year NFL career, Ortega appeared in 81 games. He later became a stockbroker in Miami.

BERNARD PAUL PARRISH (1936–) ■ *Cornerback*
COLLEGE: 1956–57   5-11, 194 lbs.   **NFL:** 1959–66; **AFL:** 1966

Bernie Parrish played football and baseball at Gainesville's P.K. Yonge High School and did the same at Florida. He played halfback and defensive back for the football team. One of his highlight games was a 14–7 victory over Vanderbilt University, in which he rushed for 111 yards, scored both touchdowns, kicked both extra points, made seven tackles, and caught an interception. He was named the Associated Press Back of the Week.

The talented Parrish was also a Gator baseball star, batting .433 in 1958, and he was named first-team All-Southeastern Conference. He was the first Gator to be named a first-team All-American

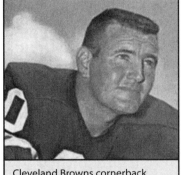

Cleveland Browns cornerback Bernie Parrish

in baseball, an honor bestowed by the American Baseball Coaches Association. He decided to skip his senior year of football eligibility for major league baseball, and he played on a minor league farm team in the Cincinnati Reds organization. In between seasons, he took courses at UF and graduated in 1960 with his bachelor's degree in building construction. In later years, he was honored as a member of the University of Florida Athletic Hall of Fame.

In the 1958 NFL draft, Parrish was picked in the ninth round by the Cleveland Browns. He played for them for seven full years, including their 1964 NFL championship season. During his years there, he caught 29 interceptions and returned three for touchdowns, as well as recovered five fumbles. He was named to the Pro Bowl in 1960 and 1963.

Parrish began the 1966 season with the Browns, but after one game he asked for his release because he did not want to share his cornerback position with another player. Cleveland granted his request, and he spent his last 11 games playing for the American Football League Houston Oilers before retiring.

Football continued to play a prominent roll for Parrish after his playing days. He was involved in league politics and served as his team's representative to the NFL Players Association; later, he was the NFLPA vice president. In his 1971 book, *They Call It a Game,* he explained the politics and economics of professional football and alleged the league had determined in advance the outcome of certain games. Later, Parrish went into business as a hotel developer. He was instrumental in litigation to obtain financial compensation for retired players for image and licensing fees, which resulted in a $28.1 million verdict against the NFLPA.

MICHAEL WAYNE PEARSON (1980–) ■ *Offensive Tackle*

COLLEGE: 1999–2001   6-7, 297 lbs.   **NFL:** 2002–05; **CFL:** 2007

Mike Pearson started out at the University of Florida as a redshirt freshman in 1998. He played three years at offensive tackle and started 33 of the 35 games he played for the Gators, including the 2000 Sugar Bowl and the 2001 Orange Bowl. In 2000, he was presented by the team with the James W. Kynes Award as the lineman who "best exemplified mental and physical toughness and iron-man determination." Pearson was selected by the conference coaches for the All-Southeastern Conference first team in 2000 and 2001, and by the Associated Press for 2001. He was a consensus first-team All-American in 2001, and he was on the SEC Academic Honor Roll for two years. In 2001, he received a bachelor's degree in business administration and has been inducted into the University of Florida Athletic Hall of Fame.

In the 2002 NFL draft, Pearson was selected in the second round by the Jacksonville Jaguars. During his rookie season, he became a starter because of an injury to another player and continued as a starter until he suffered his own injury in October 2004. After knee surgery, he was placed on injured reserve for the rest of the season. Pearson attempted a comeback in 2005 but, after starting in two games, was released. During 2006, he was briefly a Miami Dolphin and a Houston Texan, but he saw no game action with either team. His NFL career was over after appearing in 40 games.

Pearson played for the Canadian Football League Toronto Argonauts in 2007 and made it into nine games, despite having an infected finger. He retired from football after incurring a season-ending ankle injury.

PORTER MICHAEL PETERSON (1976–) ■ *Linebacker*

COLLEGE: 1995–98   6-1, 226 lbs.   **NFL:** 1999–2012

After playing football for the Santa Fe High School Raiders near Gainesville, Mike Peterson played linebacker for the Gators from 1995 through 1998, including the 1996 national championship season. He played in 42 games for UF, starting 24 of them, and had 249 tackles. As a senior, he served as a team captain and was selected by his teammates as their MVP (the Ray Graves Award).

In the 1999 NFL draft, Peterson was chosen by the Indianapolis Colts and he played for that team through the 2002 season. He also was a Jacksonville Jaguar from 2003 through 2008, and played as an Atlanta Falcon from 2009 through 2012, becoming an unsigned free agent in 2013. Peterson played in 196 NFL games, starting 163 of them.

Mike Peterson while he was with the Jacksonville Jaguars

During 2011, he became a member of the University of Florida Athletic Hall of Fame. Two years later, he was ranked at #40 on the *Orlando Sentinel* list of the 50 Greatest Gators. In 2004, he and his wife created the Mike Peterson Foundation, an organization to support underprivileged youth and families of Atlanta, Jacksonville, and Alachua, Florida. In 2013, Peterson returned to UF to complete his degree in sociology while working as an undergraduate assistant coach in the football program.

ZACHARY PAUL PILLER (1976–) ■ *Guard*

COLLEGE: 1996–98   6-5, 315 lbs.   **NFL:** 1999–2006

After quarterbacking for Lincoln High School in Tallahassee, Zach Piller played football for Georgia Tech as a freshman and then transferred to the University of Florida. He spent his sophomore year in 1996 helping the team win its first national championship. In 1997, he won the team's James W. Kynes Award for his mental and physical toughness and "ironman" determination. Piller served as a team captain in his senior year in 1998 and was selected first-team All-Southeastern Conference by its coaches. He later came back to the university and completed his bachelor's degree in exercise and sport sciences in 2006.

Tennessee Titan Zach Piller

In the third round of the 1999 NFL draft, Piller was chosen by the Tennessee Titans. He played there for seven years and started 58 of the 87 games in which he played. In 2007, he was released by the Titans, signed and released by the Detroit Lions, and signed and released by the New York Giants, without playing in a single game. When the United Football League had its first draft in 2009, the Florida Tuskers selected Piller, but he retired before the season began after dislocating his shoulder during practice, and his career as a pro was over.

In 2011, he partnered with Jody Myers and former Tennessee Titans player Donnie Nickey to open Neighbors bar and restaurant in the Sylvan Park area of Nashville.

KEIWAN JEVAR RATLIFF (1981–) ■ *Cornerback*

COLLEGE: 2000–03   5-11, 188 lbs.   **NFL:** 2004–10; **UFL:** 2011–12

Keiwan Ratliff of the Cincinnati Bengals

While a high school football player in Ohio, Keiwan Ratliff was considered an All-American by Super Prep, National Blue Chips, and Prep Star. He chose to play for the Gators and set several records during his four years—for the most interceptions in a game (three) and a season (nine), and most yards on punt returns (860). While he was a senior and served as a team captain, *The Sporting News* and the Associated Press named him the Southeastern Conference Defensive Player of the Year. Ratliff was also chosen first-team All-SEC in 2002 (by AP) and 2003 (by AP and the conference coaches), and he was a consensus choice for first-team All-American in 2003, the same year he received the Gators' 2003 Ray Graves Award as the team's MVP.

Ratliff was chosen by the Cincinnati Bengals in the second round of the 2004 NFL draft. He played in 51 games in a little more than three seasons, then was released in September 2007. He was picked up by the Tampa Bay Buccaneers but was cut before seeing any action. The day after he was waived by Tampa Bay, the Indianapolis Colts grabbed him, and Ratliff finished the 2007 season with them and also played there in 2008, where he was cut and re-signed several times. He scored his first touchdown that year, an interception return against the Jacksonville Jaguars that clinched a playoff berth for the Colts.

In 2009, Ratliff signed with the Pittsburgh Steelers and played in eight games before being released during the 2010 season. That year, he was also on the roster of the United Football League Florida Tuskers, before playing three more NFL games with Cincinnati. He signed with the UFL Virginia Destroyers in September 2011 and was shortly thereafter placed on injured reserve. His career and the league ended in 2012.

After his playing days, Ratliff was an assistant coach for the Orlando Predators of the Arena Football League and the Miami Dolphins, and he was the offensive coordinator for Oak Ridge High School in Orlando. Other activities include working with Citrus Scouting (an NCAA-certified football scouting service in Central Florida) and serving as a trainer at the football camp known as Camp Ratliff. He coaches a 7-on-7 football team in Orlando. Ratliff was inducted in 2014 into the University of Florida Athletic Hall of Fame.

The Pouncey Twins

LESHAWN MAURKICE POUNCEY (1989–)
- Center NFL: 2010–13

JAMES MICHAEL POUNCEY (1989–)
- Center NFL: 2011–13

Maurkice Pouncey and his twin, Mike, were stars on the Lakeland, Florida, High School team that won the Florida state championship during their sophomore through senior years. *USA Today* recognized the team as the national high school champion for the last two of those years. They became Gators in 2007, with Maurkice starting 11 of 13 games at right guard and Mike beginning on the offensive line but moving across the line to fill in a hole caused by injuries to several defensive linemen.

Mike (#55) and Maurkice (#56) Pouncey with Tim Tebow (#15) before the 2009 FSU game

> As sophomores, Maurkice was the starting center and Mike played right guard for the BCS national championship team. As juniors, they were named first-team All-Americans (Maurkice by the Football Writers Association of America, *The Sporting News* and the Walter Camp Football Foundation; Mike by *Pro Football Weekly*). Maurkice was presented with the Rimington Trophy by the Boomer Esiason Foundation as the country's top center. Mike moved to center when his brother opted to enter the NFL draft a year early. Both brothers received the Gators' James W. Kynes Award (Maurkice in 2009, Mike in 2010), presented to the offensive lineman who exemplified the mental and physical toughness and "iron-man" determination shown by the award's namesake. In 2013, the *Orlando Sentinel* named Maurkice as #26 on its list of the 50 Greatest Gators.
>
> Maurkice was chosen in the first round of the 2010 NFL draft by the Pittsburgh Steelers, and in his rookie year he made it to the Pro Bowl roster. Because of an ankle injury, he wasn't able to play in the Super Bowl that year. Through 2012, Maurkice Pouncey had played in 45 games for Pittsburgh, all as a starter. In the first game of the 2013 season, he suffered a torn ACL and MCL, a season-ending injury.
>
> Mike was drafted in 2011 by the Miami Dolphins in the first round, and through the 2013 season, has started at center for that team in 46 of its 48 regular season games, missing two as a result of a gall bladder problem. Mike also was named to the Pro Bowl roster in 2013.

THOMAS JOHNSON REAVES (1950–) ■ *Quarterback*

COLLEGE: 1969–71   6-3, 210 lbs.   **NFL:** 1972–81, 1987

John Reaves quarterbacked Tampa's national champion T.R. Robinson High School Knights, and was later named by the Florida High School Athletic Association as one of the 100 all-time greatest high school players in the state. He enrolled at the University of Florida and, in 1969, was known as one of the "Super Sophs" who led the team to a 9-1-1 record and a victory in the Gator Bowl. In his three years in Gainesville, Reaves set the Southeastern Conference career record of 56 touchdowns and the NCAA record of 7,581 yards. He holds the Florida record for most pass attempts in a game (66 against Auburn University in 1969).

As the country's best college passer, he received the Sammy Baugh Trophy from the Touchdown Club of Columbus. He also was presented with the Fergie Ferguson Award for his leadership, character, and courage, as determined by the Gator coaches.

His most memorable play (the "Florida Flop") allowed him to set the NCAA record for career passing yards. In a blowout win over the University of Miami at the end of the season in 1971, the Gators' Harvin Clark ran a late Miami punt in for a touchdown. Had he just fielded the punt, Reaves would have had an easy opportunity to pass for the record. So when Miami had the ball with about a minute to go near the UF 20-yard line, the Florida defense laid down to allow Miami quarterback John Hornibrook to score a meaningless touchdown and get the ball back into Reaves' hands for one more set of downs before time expired. With a completed pass to Carlos Alvarez, Reaves broke Jim Plunkett's record and then he threw another short one to beat the old total by five yards.

John Reaves is congratulated by Governor Rubin Askew

Reaves received his bachelor's degree in business administration in 1973, and he is a member of the University of Florida Athletic Hall of Fame. In 2000, the Southeastern Conference named Reaves to its list of SEC Legends. *The Gainesville Sun* ranked him #30 on its 2006 list of the all-time greatest Gator football players, while the *Orlando Sentinel* in 2013 had him at #28 of its list of the 50 Greatest Gators.

Reaves was drafted in the first round in 1972 by Philadelphia. He played in 16 games for the Eagles over the next three years, then was traded to the Cincinnati Bengals, where he played in 28 games. After being waived in 1979, he joined the Minnesota Vikings but saw no game action during that year or the next. In 1981, Reaves played in five games for the Houston Oilers. He became a starting quarterback when he joined the United States Football League Tampa Bay Bandits and played for head coach Steve Spurrier in 1983–85. That league went out of business in 1985, and Reaves played one more year (1987) in two games as a backup for the Tampa Bay Buccaneers.

In nine seasons in the NFL, Reaves passed for 3,417 yards. In just three seasons in the USFL, he exceeded 10,000 yards. He worked for the Gators as an assistant coach under Steve Spurrier during 1990–92 and in 1994; he then held the same position in 1995–97 for the University of South Carolina. Reaves is currently involved in real estate, works hard to maintain his sobriety after well-documented drug and alcohol addictions, and hopes to inspire others.

ERRICT UNDRA RHETT (1970–) ■ *Running Back*

COLLEGE: 1990–93   5-11, 210 lbs.   **NFL:** 1994–2000

As a tailback for the University of Florida, Errict Rhett broke the school rushing record previously held by Emmitt Smith. In four years, Rhett gained 4,163 yards on the ground and 1,230 yards on pass receptions. As a senior, he served as a team captain and was named the MVP of the 1994 Sugar Bowl, in which he ran for 105 yards and three touchdowns in a 41-7 victory over the University of West Virginia. Rhett was selected first-team All-Southeastern Conference in 1991 (by the Associated Press) and 1993 (by the AP and the SEC coaches) and was also a 1993 *Football News* first-team All-American. The speedster was known as a prankster and kept an 11-foot-long boa constrictor named Bushwick in his dorm room.

Rhett was given the Ray Graves Award as the team's MVP, as selected by his fellow players, in 1993. He is a member of the University of Florida Athletic Hall of Fame, and, in 2006, *The Gainesville Sun* ranked him #34 on its all-time list of greatest Gator football players. In 2013, the *Orlando Sentinel* ranked him at #22 on its list of the 50 Greatest Gators.

Florida running back Errict Rhett

In the 1994 NFL draft, Rhett was chosen in the second round by the Tampa Bay Buccaneers. As a rookie, he ran for 1,011 yards and seven touchdowns. He improved those numbers during his second year with the Bucs by rushing for 1,207 yards and 11 touchdowns. In 1996, he only participated in nine games, but he still led the team with 539 yards. Rhett saw limited action with Tampa Bay in 1997, his last year with that team.

In 1998 and 1999, he played for the Baltimore Ravens, but he wasn't as productive in those two years as he had been in his best year with Tampa Bay. He finished his career by playing in five games for the Cleveland Browns in 2000. Overall, in 86 NFL games, Rhett ran for 4,143 yards and 29 touchdowns. He caught 89 passes for 552 yards and three touchdowns. In 2008, he was added by the Southeastern Conference to its list of SEC Legends.

His activities after football include operating Errict Rhett Custom Homes and the Errict Rhett Foundation. The foundation aims to help underprivileged children in South Florida, and the construction company builds custom homes for those in need. Rhett was inducted into the Broward County Sports Hall of Fame in 2007.

JAMES W. ROUNTREE (1936–2013) ■ *Defensive Back-Halfback*

COLLEGE: 1955–57   5-10, 187 lbs.   **CFL:** 1958–67

Jim Rountree, as a senior at the University of Florida in 1957, was the recipient of the university's Fergie Ferguson Award for his leadership, character, and courage and was selected first-team All-Southeastern Conference by the Associated Press. When head coach Bob Woodruff was asked to name the best Gators of the decade, he said that Rountree was not only one of the two best defensive backs, but he was also one of the two best running backs. Rountree was inducted into the University of Florida Athletic Hall of Fame in 1971.

During the 1958 NFL draft, he was chosen by the Baltimore Colts, but he decided to head north and become a member of the Toronto Argonauts of the Canadian Football League. During his rookie season in Canada, he played both defensive back and halfback, rushing 26 times for 200 yards. He played for 10 seasons and made 41 interceptions, returning them for 464 yards and a touchdown. He was a CFL All-Star in 1962 and an East All-Star in 1959–64 and 1967. In 2004, Rountree was named by the team as an All-Time Argo.

After his decade as a player in 137 games, he served as an assistant coach for the Argonauts in 1968–72 and 1977–78. He and his wife later operated an insurance agency in Tamarac, Florida. Rountree died there September 30, 2013.

JOHNNY BOYKINS RUTLEDGE III (1977–) ■ *Linebacker*
COLLEGE: 1995–98   6-3, 239 lbs.   **NFL:** 1999–2003

As a sophomore, Johnny Rutledge was part of the Gator team that won the university's first football national championship by beating Florida State University in the Sugar Bowl in 1997. He made the Associated Press second team All-Southeastern Conference list in 1997 and 1998. After his years in the NFL, he returned to Gainesville and completed his bachelor's degree in health and human performance in 2007.

Rutledge was picked in the second round of the 1999 NFL draft by the Arizona Cardinals. He played linebacker for the Cardinals for five years and appeared in 40 games, starting four. For his final season in 2003, he played in six games for the Denver Broncos.

Today, Rutledge serves as the athletics director for the Miami-area World Changers Church International.

JOSEF IAN SCOTT (1981–) ■ *Defensive Tackle-Nose Tackle*
COLLEGE: 2000–02   6-3, 302 lbs.   **NFL:** 2003–06, 2008–09

An industrial engineering major while at UF, Ian Scott played for head coaches Steve Spurrier and Ron Zook for three years and was a starter in 2001 and 2002. He was named by the Associated Press to the All-Southeastern Conference second team for both years and then skipped his senior season to enter the NFL. He was picked in the fourth round of the 2003 NFL draft by the Chicago Bears.

In four years with the Bears, Scott started 33 of the 49 games in which he played. After the 2006

Gator tackle Ian Scott (#89) going after the Tennessee quarterback

Coaches' Trophy

You've probably seen the presentation of the Coaches' Trophy given to the college team that represents the national champion in Division I football for those schools designated as part of the Football Bowl Subdivision. Since 1986, this beautiful piece of crystal has been photographed in the hands of the championship coach and held (and even kissed) by the players before being placed on display. Handmade in Ireland from Waterford crystal and valued at $30,000, the elegant trophy is the size and shape of a football and weighs eight pounds, and is displayed resting on a massive base but can be removed. The American Football Coaches Association hands out the trophy and has strict rules regarding how it can be depicted.

Quarterback Chris Leak hoists the Coaches' Trophy after winning the championship at the end of the 2006 season

It cannot be shown, even in simulation, as being broken, shattered, dropped, thrown, or rolled on the ground. When the Gators received their second trophy by defeating Ohio State on January 8, 2007, the university insured it for $8,000. Considering all this, you would expect any school that has earned this prestigious award to keep it in a prominent, but securely locked, display case worthy of such a beautiful treasure.

Maybe not. In 2008, before the Gators won their second national championship in three years, prospective recruits were shown highlights of the campus, including the beautiful crystal trophy. One of the students on the tour was Orson Charles, who had starred for H.B. Plant High School in Tampa. While viewing the trophy, he accidentally dropped it onto the floor, where it shattered into pieces and reportedly cost the university $4,000 to replace (over and above the insurance proceeds). In addition to being the end of that trophy, it signaled the end of Charles' UF experience, as he went on to play instead for the University of Georgia Bulldogs (who as of yet have not won their own crystal trophy).

season, he was released and signed with the Philadelphia Eagles for 2007, but he wound up on injured reserve and did not play in a game. The following year, he was a Carolina Panther for part of the summer and was then released before the start of the regular season after suffering a sprained knee in practice.

After a two-year hiatus from participating in actual games, Scott joined the San Diego Chargers and (after being released and re-signed) played in four games during 2009. The following season he played in a dozen games, as a starter in seven. In June 2010, he was released by San Diego, bringing an end to an NFL career that included 40 starts in 65 games. Scott was drafted in 2011 by the United Football League Virginia Destroyers, but he did not make it onto the team's roster.

LITO DECORIAN SHEPPARD (1981–) ■ *Cornerback*
COLLEGE: 1999–2001   5-10, 194 lbs.   **NFL:** 2002–11

A high school All-American according to *USA Today* while he attended William M. Raines High School in Jacksonville, Lito Sheppard was named by the Florida High School Athletic Association in 2007 as one of the best 100 Florida high school football players of all time. He then headed to UF for three years and started 22 games at cornerback, returned kickoffs and made eight interceptions. In his sophomore year in 2000, he was a first-team All-American according to the Football Writers Association of America, and he was a first-team selection by the Associated Press and the conference coaches to their All-Southeastern Conference teams in 2000 and 2001. *The Gainesville Sun* newspaper ranked Sheppard #44 on its list of the all-time greatest Gators in 2006. On the 2013 list of the 50 Greatest Gators compiled by the *Orlando Sentinel*, he was ranked at #49.

Eagle Lito Sheppard signing autographs at a 2005 military appreciation day event

Foregoing his senior year, Sheppard entered the 2002 NFL draft and was picked by the Philadelphia Eagles. He played in 2002 and 2003, mostly in a backup role, and blossomed in 2004. He started all 15 games in which he played and, after bringing back two interceptions for touchdowns, he was named November's Defensive Player of the Month. At the end of the season, he was named to the Pro Bowl roster, and he made it again in 2006.

Sheppard holds the distinction of being the first player in the NFL to have two 100+ yard interception returns (in 2004 and 2006). Injuries began to limit his playing time in 2005, and, after the 2008 season, he was traded to the New York Jets. For 2009, he started nine of the 11 games in which he played, then was released by the Jets in March 2010. He was a Minnesota Viking for the 2010 season and played in 13 games and then played nine for the Oakland Raiders in 2011. In his ten years in the NFL, Sheppard appeared in 126 games.

Sheppard's cousin, Jabar Gaffney, played wide receiver for the Gators in 2000-01. His uncle (and Jabar's father) was a Gator wide receiver in the mid-1970s.

BRANDON T. SILER (1985–) ■ *Inside Linebacker*

COLLEGE: 2004–06   6-2, 239 lbs.   **NFL:** 2007–12

Brandon Siler was offered scholarships from the University of Tennessee and the University of Maryland, but luckily for the Gators, he accepted one from the University of Florida. In 2004, he started in six games and was selected by the Southeastern Conference coaches as the SEC Freshman of the Year. In 2005, he set the UF record for fumble recoveries (seven), and his career total (eight) is tied for the most by a Gator. Siler's junior year was capped by a 41–14 victory in the BCS national championship game over The Ohio State University, and his personal honors included All-SEC second-team selections by the Associated Press and the SEC coaches. He decided to skip his senior year and enter the 2007 NFL draft.

Kansas City Chief Brandon Siler in 2012

Siler was drafted in the seventh round by the San Diego Chargers as a linebacker but was also used on special teams and as backup for long snaps. In four years, he played in 58 regular season games for the Chargers. The following year, he joined the Kansas City Chiefs but within weeks was on the injured reserve list with a ruptured Achilles tendon, and he did not play in 2011. He came back in 2012 and appeared in all 16 games for the Chiefs, four in a starting role, but was not resigned for 2013 after his contract expired. Siler is now a real estate agent in Ocoee, Florida.

JOHN MARLIN SIMPSON (1934–) ■ *Defensive Back*

COLLEGE: 1953–56   5-10, 183 lbs.   **NFL:** 1958–62; **CFL:** 1963–66

As a collegian, John "Jackie" Simpson played both halfback and defensive back. Although he wasn't a big athlete, he had some big numbers in college. He set the Southeastern Conference record for the longest interception return for a touchdown (100 yards against Mississippi State University in 1955), and his per-carry average as a halfback was 6.3 yards, ranking him in the top three all-time for UF. The University of Florida Athletic Hall of Fame inducted him in 2001. According to his head coach, Bob Woodruff, Simpson was the best defensive back and one of the three best running backs for the Gators during the 1950s.

In the 1957 NFL draft, Simpson was chosen by the Baltimore Colts and played three seasons with them, but he had to wait 21 months before joining the Colts in order to complete his U.S. Army training. He made it back to the Colts for the last two games of 1958 and then participated in 22 games over the next two years. He was a part of two NFL championship teams (1958 and 1959).

Following the 1960 season, Simpson was traded to the Pittsburgh Steelers, where he played two years and appeared in 21 games, making two interceptions. Not quite done with professional football, he played three more seasons in the Canadian Football League, with the Toronto Argonauts, Hamilton Tiger-Cats, and Montreal Alouettes. After football, Simpson had a number of business interests, including owning a lounge in downtown Miami, working in the roofing business and for a parking company, before retiring to Pensacola.

Jackie Simpson returning a punt for a touchdown against LSU in 1955

CEDRIC DELON SMITH (1968–) ■ *Fullback*

COLLEGE: 1986–89   5-11, 238 lbs.   **NFL:** 1990–91, 1994–97

Cedric Smith was a running back for the Enterprise High School Wildcats in Enterprise, Alabama. He enrolled at the University of Florida and moved to fullback, where he was more of a blocker than a ball carrier. During his last three years, he was clearing the way for another Smith, premier running back Emmitt Smith, buthe also earned a spot on the Southeastern Conference Academic Honor Roll as a sophomore, junior, and senior. He served as a team captain in 1989; the following year, he received his bachelor's degree in public health.

In the fifth round of the 1990 NFL draft, Smith was selected by the Minnesota Vikings. He played one year there, appearing in 15 games but totaled only 19 yards rushing. The next year, he played for the New Orleans Saints and saw some action in six games. Smith then left the NFL for two years.

He made a comeback in 1994 and played two years with the Washington Redskins, making it into 20 games, then joined the Arizona Cardinals for his last 31 games in 1996–97. His NFL career statistics show 40 carries for 100 yards, plus 20 catches for 141. After his playing career ended, Smith became a strength and conditioning coach for the Denver Broncos (2001–06), the Kansas City Chiefs (2007–09), and the Houston Texans (2010–2013). He and the rest of the Houston strength and conditioning staff were fired in January 2014 by new head coach Bill O'Brien.

EMMITT JAMES SMITH III (1969–) ■ *Running Back*

COLLEGE: 1987–89   5-10, 216 lbs.   **NFL:** 1990–2004

In high school, Emmitt Smith ran for 106 touchdowns and 8,804 yards and was later named by the Florida High School Athletic Association as one of the top 100 all-time high school players in Florida. Nevertheless, when it came time for college, some

Emmitt Smith on his way to a Gator touchdown

recruiters felt he was too small and too slow. The amazingly talented runner came to the Gators as a freshman in 1987 and proved the recruiters to be wrong. In his first full game, he rushed for 224 yards to break the university record for a single game, as the Gators upset the University of Alabama on the road. In his seventh game, he passed the 1,000-yard mark earlier than any previous running back in the NCAA. Smith was named the Southeastern Conference Freshman of the Year by the *Knoxville Sentinel* and was named the Touchdown Club of Columbus Freshman Player of the Year. *Street and Smith* declared him to be the National Freshman Player of the Year.

He missed part of his sophomore season with a knee injury (but still managed to gain 988 yards), and came back healthy in 1989 as a junior and wore out the record keepers. Smith set the UF single season rushing record (1,599 yards), single game record (316 yards against the University of New Mexico in 1989), career rushing yards (3,928), most 100-yard games (23), longest rushing play (96 yards), and career rushing touchdowns (36). He was chosen as the SEC Player of the Year by the *Nashville Banner* newspaper and made the All-SEC first-team rosters for all three years for each of the Associated Press, United Press International, and the SEC coaches. Early in 1990, pass-oriented Steve Spurrier became the new head coach at Florida, and it seemed likely that the emphasis would be shifted from the running back to an aerial attack, so Smith skipped his senior year for the NFL.

He was chosen in the first round of the 1990 NFL draft by the Dallas Cowboys, where he continued his record-setting hobby, becoming the first NFL player to rush for at least 1,400 yards in each of his first five seasons and the first to rush for 1,000+ yards in 11 consecutive seasons. Smith is the NFL's all-time rushing touchdowns (164) and rushing yards (18,355) leader, holds numerous other records for the regular season, and has three Super Bowl rings (for XXVII, XXVIII, and XXX). He played for the Cowboys through 2002 then had two seasons with the Arizona Cardinals. He was released by the Cardinals and re-signed by the Cowboys for one day for a one-dollar salary, and he then immediately retired as a member of his former team.

Smith is a member of the University of Florida Athletic Hall of Fame, the College Football Hall of Fame, the Florida Sports Hall of Fame, and the Gator Football Ring of Honor. In 2006, *The Gainesville Sun* ranked him #3 on its all-time list of the greatest Florida football players, while the *Orlando Sentinel* in 2013 had him listed at #6 of the 50 Greatest Gators. In 2010, he was enshrined in the Pro Football Hall of Fame and has worked in sports broadcasting. Smith is also known to many who don't follow professional football as the winner of season three of ABC-TV's "Dancing with the Stars," proving that he can boogie off the football field as well as he did on it.

WILLIAM LAWRENCE SMITH (1947–) ■ *Running Back*
COLLEGE: 1966–68   6-3, 220 lbs.   **NFL:** 1969–74

In high school in Tampa, Larry Smith scored 47 touchdowns and was honored by *Parade* magazine as an All-American. The Florida High School Athletic Association named him one of its 100 greatest Florida high school football players of all time.

At the University of Florida, Smith played tailback for three years. One of his highlight games was the 1967 Orange Bowl when the Gators beat Georgia Tech and Smith had a 94-yard touchdown run (and almost lost his pants!) on his way to becoming the game's MVP. As a senior, he received the team's Fergie Ferguson Award for his leadership, character, and courage, and he was a three-time All-Southeastern Conference selection by United Press International (and twice by the Associated Press). In three years as a starter, Smith gained 2,186 yards on 528 rushes (with 24 touchdowns) and 607 yards on pass receptions. When he left Florida, he held the school's all-time career rushing record.

Smith received his bachelor's degree in business administration in 1970 and was inducted 13 years later into the University of Florida Athletic Hall of Fame. *The Gainesville Sun* in 2006 ranked him #29 on its list of the greatest Gator football players of all time, while the *Orlando Sentinel* in 2013 had him at #43 on its list of the 50 Greatest Gators. The Southeastern Conference in 2003 named him to its list of SEC Legends.

In the first round of the 1969 NFL draft, Smith was selected by the Los Angeles Rams. Over the next five years for the Rams, he appeared in 65 games, starting 35 of them. He spent his last NFL season with the Washington Redskins. For his six-year career, he rushed for 2,057 yards on 528 carries and caught 149 passes for 1,176 yards.

Smith wasn't done with his studies. He returned to UF in 1975 to get his master's degree in business administration, worked in banking and the Tampa Sports Authority, and then earned a law degree from Stetson University in 1982. Smith is a shareholder in the Tampa law firm of Hill, Ward & Henderson.

JAMES ARTHUR SPENCER (1969–) ■ *Cornerback*
COLLEGE: 1988–90   5-9, 188 lbs.   **NFL:** 1992–2003

One of many Gators who played their high school years for the Glades Central High School Raiders in Belle Glade, Florida, Jimmy Spencer arrived in Gainesville in 1988. He was utilized at the cornerback position, and one of his most memorable moments was as a senior, when he blocked a punt late in the game against the University of Alabama. It was picked up by another player and was returned for a touchdown to upset the favored Crimson Tide in their own stadium.

After his junior year at Florida, Spencer left early for the NFL and was drafted in 1991 in the eighth round by the Washington Redskins, but he did not play for them in the upcoming season. He played with four other teams—the New Orleans Saints (1992–95), the Cincinnati Bengals (1996–97), the San Diego Chargers (1998–99), and the Denver Broncos (2000–03). Over a dozen seasons, he appeared in 177 games and made 26 interceptions. During his final year with the Broncos, he did double duty and played in all 16 regular season games while also serving as an assistant defensive backs coach, which made him only the second player to achieve this in the NFL since 1972.

In November 2004, player-coach Spencer became just a coach, working with the Broncos' secondary. He remained with Denver as a defensive backs coach until 2008 and coached that same position in the 2006 Pro Bowl. He now serves on the coaching staff of Breakout Football Academy, a football camp in Pascagoula, Mississippi. Since 2012, Spencer has been a member of the Palm Beach County Sports Hall of Fame.

BRANDON SPIKES (1987–) ■ *Linebacker*
COLLEGE: 2006–09   6-2, 255 lbs.   **NFL:** 2010–13

Before coming to Gainesville, Brandon Spikes already earned a reputation for being an outstanding linebacker. Rivals.com ranked him #1 in North Carolina and Scout.com ranked him #33 on its list of the best players in the United States. He was one of the high school players invited to play in the all-star U.S. Army All-American Bowl.

Coach Meyer and Brandon Spikes congratulating each other after the FSU game in 2009

With several scholarship offers on the table, Spikes chose Florida over Alabama, North Carolina State, and Virginia Tech, which turned out to be a great choice for him and the Gators. He began his freshman year as a backup and appeared in nine games, including the BCS championship victory over The Ohio State University. In 2007, Spikes became a starter at middle linebacker, and he was second in the Southeastern Conference with 131 tackles and named to the All-SEC first team by the Associated Press and the conference coaches.

He led the team with 93 tackles as a junior, including six in the BCS championship win over the University of Oklahoma and eight against Alabama in the SEC championship game. He served as a team captain in both his junior and senior years. As a senior, Spikes had 68 tackles and was listed as a first-team All-American by *The Sporting News* and the Walter Camp Football Foundation. Chevrolet awarded him the title of National Defensive Player of the Year. He was also selected for All-SEC first team (2008 by AP and the SEC coaches, 2009 by the coaches and *The Sporting*

Continued on page 156

The Heisman Trophy

In 1935, the Downtown Athletic Club in New York established the DAC Trophy to recognize the best college football player east of the Mississippi River. When the club's athletic director, who had been an early player and coach, died in 1936, the award was renamed after him; over the years, the Heisman Trophy has become the most prestigious collegiate football honor.

The Downtown Athletic Club, whose headquarters were damaged by the September 11, 2001, terrorist attacks, declared bankruptcy in 2002. The award was picked up by the Yale Club of New York City, which presented the award in 2002 and 2003. Since 2004, the trophy has been awarded by the Heisman Trust.

The winners of the award have come from a long list of colleges, as follows:

7	Notre Dame	2	Texas	1	Minnesota
7	Ohio State	2	Texas A&M	1	Oklahoma State
6*	Southern California	2	Wisconsin	1	Oregon State
5	Oklahoma	2	Yale	1	Penn State
3	Army	1	Alabama	1	Pittsburgh
3	Auburn	1	Baylor	1	Princeton
3	Florida	1	Boston College	1	South Carolina
3	Florida State	1	BYU	1	Southern Methodist
3	Michigan	1	Chicago	1	Stanford
3	Nebraska	1	Colorado	1	Syracuse
2	Georgia	1	Houston	1	Texas Christian
2	Miami (Florida)	1	Iowa	1	UCLA
2	Navy	1	LSU		

* 2005 award vacated, otherwise USC would have 7

Typically, Heisman Trophy winners spend their entire college football career at one school, but those who have gone to the professional leagues have not always had as much success there as they did at the collegiate level. It reinforces the belief that college football and professional football are quite different. Although winning the Heisman Trophy focuses a great deal of attention and fame on the recipient, it doesn't even guarantee being drafted by a professional team.

The books say the University of Florida has had three Heisman winners, all quarterbacks: Steve Spurrier, Danny Wuerffel, and Tim Tebow. An unusual situation occurred when a future winner (Wuerffel) was coached during his Heisman year by a past winner (Spurrier), which was the first time this has happened in college football. In reality, however, Florida has had *four* quarterbacks receive the Heisman Trophy, and in 2007 had two quarterbacks on the roster simultaneously who eventually won the award. That year, Tim Tebow (Heisman 2007) was the starting quarterback, and his backup was Cam Newton (Heisman 2010). However, Newton is listed with Auburn, where he spent his last year in college. If each of his college teams were to be able to claim him as a Heisman winner, then that would give the University of Florida its fourth honoree and Blinn College, where Newton attended after Florida and before Auburn, would be added to the list.

The University of Florida, in addition to its three (or four) winners, has had several other players who received consideration for the award. The complete list:

Year	Gator	Class	Position	Rank
1965	Steve Spurrier	Junior	Quarterback	9th
1966	Steve Spurrier	Senior	Quarterback	1st
1977	Wes Chandler	Senior	Wide Receiver	10th
1987	Emmitt Smith	Freshman	Running Back	9th
1989	Emmitt Smith	Junior	Running Back	7th
1991	Shane Matthews	Junior	Quarterback	5th
1995	Danny Wuerffel	Junior	Quarterback	3rd
1996	Danny Wuerffel	Senior	Quarterback	1st
2001	Rex Grossman	Sophomore	Quarterback	2nd
2007	Tim Tebow	Sophomore	Quarterback	1st
2008	Tim Tebow	Junior	Quarterback	3rd
2009	Tim Tebow	Senior	Quarterback	5th
2010	Cam Newton	Junior	Quarterback	1st

BRANDON SPIKES *Continued from page 153*

News) and was a unanimous first-team All-American. He holds the Florida record for career interceptions for touchdowns (four).

Spikes was chosen by the New England Patriots in the second round of the 2010 NFL draft and soon was a starter at the inside linebacker position. Against the Baltimore Ravens, he made 16 tackles in one game. His first season was cut short because of a suspension resulting from a banned substance detected in his ADHD medication, and he issued a heartfelt apology for not getting clarification on the drug's status.

Through 2013, Spikes has participated in 51 regular season games, starting 39 of them and making 2 interceptions. In 2013, he was ranked #25 on the *Orlando Sentinel* list of the 50 Greatest Gators.

STEVEN ORR SPURRIER (1945–) ■ *Quarterback-Punter-Coach*

COLLEGE: 1964–66   6-2, 204 lbs.   **NFL:** 1967–76 (player) and 2002–03 (coach); **USFL:** 1983–85 (coach)

Under head coach Ray Graves, quarterback Steve Spurrier played 31 games for the Gators, for whom he accumulated 4,848 yards in the air and 442 on the ground with 37 touchdowns. One of his most notable games was in 1966 against Auburn University. Late in the game, the coach sent in the field goal kicker, but Spurrier waved him back to the bench and kicked it himself, resulting in a 30–27 Florida victory. He wasn't known for having the most physical ability, but no one matched him in terms of self-confidence.

As a junior, Spurrier was a first-team All-American selection of the Football Writers Association. In his senior year, he received the Fergie Ferguson Award from UF for his leadership, character, and courage, and he became the first Gator to receive the Heisman Trophy as the nation's top college football player. He was a unanimous choice for first-team All-American, and the *Nashville Banner* newspaper named him its SEC Player of the Year. According to *The Gainesville Sun* newspaper in 2006, Spurrier was the #2 all-time Gator football player. In 2013, the *Orlando Sentinel* ranked him #3 on its list of the 50 Greatest Gators. He is a member of the University of Florida Athletic Hall of Fame and the Gator Ring of Honor.

Steve Spurrier (left) with quarterback Tommy Shannon

He was drafted in 1967 by the San Francisco 49ers and for nine seasons was mostly a punter and a backup quarterback. Spurrier played one more season, for the new Tampa Bay Buccaneers, in 1976. Overall, he played in 106 NFL games and threw for 6,878 yards and 40 touchdowns, and, as a punter, he had an average of 38.3 yards.

After his playing days, Spurrier became a coach, first working with quarterbacks at Florida (1978), then heading to Georgia Tech (1979) and Duke University (1980–82).

His first head coaching opportunity arrived when the United States Football League was formed, and he led the Tampa Bay Bandits for the three years of their existence (1983–85), where he had a record of 35-19. Two years later, he was back at Duke as the head coach, and there he was honored as the Atlantic Coast Conference Coach of the Year in 1988 and 1989 when he led the Blue Devils to the ACC title. But he had always maintained a good relationship with his alma mater, and when UF President Dr. Robert Bryan came calling, Spurrier said yes.

Beginning in 1990, Spurrier was the head coach for the Gators, taking a non-contender school in trouble with the NCAA to its first Southeastern Conference championship in 1991. Under his guidance, the team won five more SEC championships and a national title. Spurrier was named the SEC Coach of the Year five times and was the first major college coach to win 120 or more games in his first 12 seasons at a single school. His pass-oriented, big-play "Fun 'n' Gun" offense resulted in the Gators being the only team to score at least 500 points for four consecutive years (1993–96), at least since the NCAA started keeping such records in 1937.

His decision to leave the Gators came as a shock to many, none more than UF Athletic Director Jeremy Foley, who told reporters at the January 2002 press conference announcing Spurrier's resignation that, "He brought us a program we could only dream about." Spurrier took over the head coaching position for the Washington Redskins ten days later with a lucrative five-year contract. While his "Fun 'n' Gun" offense was successful at the college level, it did not translate well in the pros, and, after his team had a two-year record of 12-20, he resigned and speculation soon began that he would return to coach in the college ranks. After Ron Zook was fired in 2004, Spurrier at first indicated he might consider coming back to Florida, but then changed his mind. The day after South Carolina coach Lou Holtz resigned in November 2004, Spurrier was announced as the new head coach for the University of South Carolina Gamecocks, and The Ol' Ball Coach has continued to do what he does best: produce highly competitive, winning college football teams. In May 2013, Steve Spurrier became the second Gator football pro to be honored as a Great Floridian by the Florida Division of Historical Resources.

MAXIMILLIAN WEISNER STARKS IV (1982–) ■ *Offensive Tackle*
COLLEGE: 2000–03   6-8, 345 lbs.   **NFL:** 2004–13

Orlando native Max Starks was so big in eighth grade that he had trouble finding shoes to fit his size-15 feet—and wound up borrowing some from Shaquille O'Neal while he was a star for the Orlando Magic. After receiving national attention as a high school offensive lineman, Starks began playing for Florida in 2000; during his four-year career, he blocked for quarterbacks Rex Grossman and Chris Leak. As a rookie, Max was part of the squad that won the Southeastern Conference championship, and he was a team captain in his senior year and named first-team All-SEC by the conference coaches. He received his bachelor's degree from UF in sociology in 2007.

Starks was picked in the third round of the 2004 NFL draft by the Pittsburgh Steelers, and, in his rookie pro season, the big man got into ten games and was the starting right tackle in 2005-06. During his first nine years in the NFL, he started 96 of the 123 games in which he played. His strength of character was visible off the field; in 2011, he was chosen by his teammates to receive the Ed Block Courage Award for being a role model of inspiration, sportsmanship, and courage. In May 2013, he signed with the San Diego Chargers but was cut before the start of the 2013 season. He joined the St. Louis Rams, but was released on October 1, 2013, after appearing in two games.

Steeler tackle Max Starks in 2005

Outside of football, Starks worked while a student in Gainesville with Kids Against Drugs, Alcohol, and Tobacco. He presently serves on the board of directors of Cents of Relief, an organization working to provide access to healthcare for vulnerable women, and to prevent human trafficking.

GEORGE KAY STEPHENSON (1944–) ■ *Quarterback-Coach*

COLLEGE: 1964–66   6-1, 210 lbs.   **AFL:** 1967–68; **WFL:** 1974 (player); **NFL:** 1983–85; **WLAF:** 1991–92; **CFL:** 1995, 1998 (coach)

Although Kay Stephenson was a star quarterback in high school, he wound up at the University of Florida in competition with another recruit at that position, Steve Spurrier. Spurrier soon became the starter with Stephenson as his backup all the way through his teammate's Heisman Trophy season as a senior. Stephenson graduated in 1967 with a bachelor's degree in physical education.

He signed with the American Football League's San Diego Chargers and played in seven games during the 1967 season, completing 11 of 26 passes for 117 yards and two touchdowns. The following year, he was on the AFL's Buffalo Bills and made it into ten games, three as a starter, and had 29 completions out of 79 attempts for 364 yards and four touchdowns. Stephenson then retired as a player, but he made a brief comeback with the World Football League's Jacksonville Sharks in 1974. When that league folded, he became the player personnel director of the reorganized WFL's Jacksonville Express; when the WFL went under for a second time in 1975, he joined the staff of Chuck Knox as an assistant with the NFL's Los Angeles Rams.

He moved with Knox to the Buffalo Bills, but when Knox moved to Seattle, Stephenson was made the new Bills head coach and became the first coach to win two of his first three games in charge of that franchise. His team had a record of 10-26 before he was fired during the 1985 season. He served as head coach of three other teams—the World League of American Football Sacramento Surge (1991–92), the

Canadian Football League San Antonio Texans (1995), and the CFL Edmonton Eskimos (1998)—before retiring.

JOHN RICHARD SYMANK (1935–2002) ■ *Defensive Back-Coach*
COLLEGE: 1955–56   5-11, 180 lbs.   **NFL:** 1957–63 (player), 1966–88 and 1979–83 (coach)

John Symank spent his first two years in college football at Arlington State Junior College in Arlington, Texas. He transferred to the University of Florida for his junior and senior years and, according to his coach, Bob Woodruff, he was one of the five best Gator defensive backs of the 1950s. He lettered in both football and track and received his bachelor's degree in business administration in 1957, and he became a member of the University of Florida Athletic Hall of Fame.

In the 1957 NFL draft, Symank was selected in the 23rd round by the Green Bay Packers. Although the team had a disappointing 3-9 record that year, he was a bright spot in setting the league rookie interception record (nine). He is remembered for a particularly hard hit on Baltimore Colts quarterback Johnny Unitas, which broke three of his ribs and punctured a lung, but Unitas came back after missing only two games.

The Packers improved under new coach Vince Lombardi, and, in 1960, Symank led the team in yardage—both in returning interceptions and kickoffs. Green Bay made it to the NFL title game and, helped by a Symank interception in the end zone, nearly came back against the Philadelphia Eagles. The Packers returned in 1961 and 1962 to win the championship, helped by Symank's performance. Lombardi described him as looking more like a baseball player and "the lightest man on the squad," but that he was "serious and intense, and in a game he would just as soon break your leg as not."

He was traded in 1963 to the New York Giants, but before Symank got a chance to play, he was traded again, this time to the St. Louis Cardinals. That turned out to be his final season in a career that lasted seven years and featured 19 interceptions returned for 387 yards in 89 games.

Symank's second football career was in coaching, which began in 1964 as an assistant at Tulane University (along with fellow coach Bill Arnsparger, who later would serve as the athletic director at Florida), followed by the University of Virginia in 1965. With the creation of the Atlanta Falcons, he was lured to the NFL in 1966 and remained with that team through 1968. Then it was back to college coaching at Northern Arizona University for 1969–70, followed by his first head coaching job (University of Texas at Arlington, 1971–73).

In 1974, Symank returned to the NFL for five years as an assistant with the New York Giants coached by Bill Arnsparger and then coached for the Baltimore Colts in 1979–81. When all of the Colts' coaches were terminated, he left the NFL for the last time. When his friend Arnsparger took over as the head coach at Louisiana State University in 1984, he hired Symank to be his defensive coordinator. They turned around a floundering program, and Arnsparger was named the Southeastern Conference Coach of the Year. Symank moved to coaching the LSU linebackers and running the school's recruiting program, and he finally retired for good after the 1986 season. Symank died of cancer on January 23, 2002.

STEVEN OLSON TANNEN (1948–) ■ *Safety-Cornerback*
COLLEGE: 1967–69   6-1, 194 lbs.   **NFL:** 1970–74

Gator safety Steve Tannen

According to the Florida High School Athletic Association, Steve Tannen was one of the 100 greatest high school football players in Florida during the first century of the sport. After playing for Southwest Miami High School, he came to Gainesville and played defensive back for the Gators and was known as a tough player. He was named first-team All-SEC by the United Press International in 1968 and was a *Time* and *The Sporting News* first-team All-American in 1969. As a senior that year, Tannen led the team in punt return yardage and was presented with the school's Fergie Ferguson Award for his leadership, character, and courage.

Probably his most noteworthy play was the punt he blocked during the 1969 Gator Bowl, which was returned for a touchdown in the Gators' 14–13 upset victory over the University of Tennessee. That win brought the Gators to a season record of 9-1-1, which was their best ever to that point. Tannen received his bachelor's degree in business administration in 1972 while playing professional football. *The Gainesville Sun* in 2006 ranked him #15 all-time on its list of the greatest Gator football players, and he is a member of the University of Florida Athletic Hall of Fame. He was added to the Southeastern Conference's list of SEC Legends in 2012. The following year, the *Orlando Sentinel* listed him at #18 of the 50 Greatest Gators.

In the first round of the 1970 NFL draft, Tannen was selected by the New York Jets, and he played five seasons for that team. A high point of his rookie year, in which he played in all 14 regular season games, was his block of a Buffalo Bills punt, which he picked up and ran in for a touchdown. During 1972, he missed three games, but he still led the team with seven interceptions; in his five-year career, Tannen appeared in 61 games and made a dozen interceptions.

After retiring from football, Tannen worked in California for about 40 years, then moved back to Gainesville in 2012. One of his jobs in California was as an actor, and he appeared in several television series including The *A-Team* (1984–86) and *Lou Grant* (1979). He had small parts in movies including *Capricorn One* (1977) and *She's Having a Baby* (1988) and portrayed quarterback Terry Hanratty in 1980's *Fighting Back*, a made-for-television movie about Pittsburgh Steeler running back Rocky Bleier.

FREDERICK ANTWON TAYLOR (1976–) ■ *Running Back*
COLLEGE: 1994–97   6-1, 228 lbs.   **NFL:** 1998–2010

Fred Taylor started out at Glades Central High School in Belle Glade, Florida, as a linebacker, then switched to running back. He became a star at that position and was named one of the 100 all-time Florida high school football players by the Florida High School Athletic Association. He rushed for the Gators for four years, beginning as a true freshman, and gained 3,075 yards with 31 touchdowns during his career. Taylor's yardage total is fourth-best all time for the University of Florida.

As team captain in his senior year, he led the Gators with 1,292 yards, scored 12 touchdowns, and won the Ray Graves Award as the Gators' MVP. He also made the Associated Press and coaches' first-team All-Southeastern Conference list and the Walter Camp Football Foundation All-American squad. Taylor was ranked #36 on *The Gainesville Sun*'s 2006 list of the all-time greatest Gator football players, and he was inducted into both the University of Florida Athletic Hall of Fame and the Palm Beach County Sports Hall of Fame in 2010. In 2013, the *Orlando Sentinel* put him at #31 on its list of the 50 Greatest Gators.

The Jacksonville Jaguars selected Taylor in the first round of the 1998 NFL draft. As a rookie, he started 12 of 15 games and rushed 264 times for 1,223 yards and 14 touchdowns. The following year, he had the longest run from scrimmage in playoff history, a 90-yard touchdown against the Miami Dolphins. Several injuries kept him out of 23 of the 48 regular season games in his first three seasons, which led to the nickname "Fragile Fred" by critical members of the media. Taylor only made it into two games in 2001 and did not care for the descriptive title. He also had to deal with financial losses by his agent, who allegedly stole millions from his clients, primarily Florida alumni, and Taylor later admitted that he considered retiring at that point.

Jacksonville running back Fred Taylor in 2008

Then in 2002, the events of the past year faded as Taylor started all 16 games and set a Jacksonville record of 1,722 combined yards for rushing and receiving. In 2003, he again started 16 games and increased his season rushing best to 1,572 yards. He had a streak of 46 consecutive starts snapped by a knee injury late in 2004, but he continued to post impressive stats in 2005 and 2006. In 2007, he passed the 10,000-yard career rushing mark with 1,202 yards for the season. Taylor was named to the Pro Bowl as an injury replacement, then played one more season for the Jaguars and started in 13 games before being sidelined by another injury, which this time resulted in his being placed for the first time on injured reserve.

Early in 2009, he was released by Jacksonville and was signed by the New England Patriots. Again plagued by injuries, he played in only six games, and in his final season in 2010, he played in seven games as a reserve. Taylor went back to Jacksonville in September 2011 with a one-day contract to formally announce his retirement as a Jaguar. Over a 13-year career, Taylor played in 153 games and started in 137 of them. His 2,534 rushing attempts resulted in 11,695 yards (15th on the NFL's all-time list) and 66 touchdowns. In 2012, he was the second player inducted into the Pride of the Jaguars.

After retiring as a player, Taylor went into consulting to guide other players as they transition to being ex-players. He helps find companies that will benefit them and not take advantage of their wealth, and he gives advice on time and money management. He is also active with charitable organizations, including the Fred Taylor Foundation, which works with physically disabled children. In mid-2013, Taylor accepted the position of director of client relations with the Law Offices of Berman & Berman Law Firm in Florida.

TRAVIS LAMONT TAYLOR (1978–) ■ *Wide Receiver*
COLLEGE: 1997–99   6-1, 210 lbs.   **NFL:** 2000–07

Travis Taylor was a high school star in Jacksonville before coming to the University of Florida. During a three-year college career under head coach Steve Spurrier, Taylor started 11 games and caught 72 passes for 1,150 yards and 15 touchdowns. Two of his best games were the 1999 Orange Bowl, when he caught seven for 159 yards and two touchdowns against Syracuse University and was named the game's MVP, and the 2000 Florida Citrus Bowl, where his 11 catches went for 156 yards and three touchdowns in a losing effort against Michigan State University.

Wide receiver Travis Taylor as a Minnesota Viking

During his junior year of 1999, Taylor served as a team captain and then made himself eligible for the NFL draft. He was selected in the first round in 2000 by the Baltimore Ravens, and he impressed his new team when he scored two touchdowns in the second game that season. Although they celebrated winning Super Bowl XXXV at the end of the season, Taylor's statistics were not as strong as predicted, with 28 catches for 276 yards over nine games. He continued with Baltimore for four more seasons, then was released.

Taylor played for the Minnesota Vikings in 2005–06 and then appeared in one game for the Oakland Raiders in 2007. That same season, he tried out for the St. Louis Rams and played in one game, where he caught a pass for four yards. The Carolina Panthers signed him before the end of the 2007 season and kept him until August 2008, but he played in no games for them. His final team was the Detroit Lions, which he was a part of from December 2008 until May 2009, but he saw no game action. During his eight seasons in the NFL, Taylor started 90 of the 101 games in which he played, and he had 4,017 yards receiving and 232 rushing.

While a member of the Vikings, Taylor made the news as part of the group of players accused in the "Minnesota Vikings party boat scandal." In October 2005, a sex party allegedly took place on a pair of houseboats rented by 17 players on Lake Minnetonka. Taylor refused to comment on the incident and, unlike some of his teammates, avoided criminal prosecution. In 2007, Travis was arrested in Minneapolis after being tasered by police outside of a nightclub when he pushed an officer who was trying to disperse a large crowd to allow an ambulance to pass through the area. After pleading guilty, he paid a fine and performed community service.

TIMOTHY RICHARD TEBOW (1987–) ■ *Quarterback*

COLLEGE: 2006–09   6-3, 236 lbs.   **NFL:** 2010–12

Although homeschooled, Tim Tebow played quarterback at Allen D. Nease High School in Ponte Vedra. He was a *Parade* magazine All-American and Florida's Mr. Football as a senior. When he arrived at UF, he was made a backup quarterback behind Chris Leak and was used mostly in short-yardage situations, where he often ran the ball himself, and scored eight touchdowns. In the BCS national championship win over The Ohio State University, Tebow ran for one touchdown and threw for another.

He moved up to starter at the beginning of his sophomore year. For the regular season, he had the country's second-highest passing efficiency rating (177.8) and on the ground averaged 4.3 yards per carry. He set Florida's single-game rushing record for a quarterback (166 yards), the Southeastern Conference's single-season rushing touchdown record (20), and the SEC's single season total touchdown record (55). Tebow was awarded the Davey O'Brien Award as the country's best quarterback and the Heisman Trophy as the most outstanding player (the first sophomore to win that award). Also recognized in the classroom, he was a first-teamer on the Academic All-America team during 2007–09 and was named the *ESPN the Magazine* Academic All-American

Tim Tebow when he was a Denver Bronco in 2010

of the Year in 2008 and 2009. As a sophomore (and then again as a junior), Tebow received the Sullivan Award as the country's top amateur athlete. CBSSportsline.com and Rivals.com named him their National Offensive Player of the Year. As a sophomore and junior, the Associated Press named him its SEC Offensive Player of the Year.

As a junior, Tebow broke Emmitt Smith's Gator career rushing touchdown record and led the team to a 12-1 record, including a victory over the University of Alabama in the SEC championship game. The team then went on to win its third national championship with a win over the University of Oklahoma. Tebow finished third in the Heisman Trophy balloting that season, but he received the Maxwell Award (as he also had done in 2007) and the Manning Award (as the nation's best quarterback). He continued to rack up awards and honors as he was named the National Player of the Year by the Associated Press, which also designated him as the National Offensive Player of the Year for both 2008 and 2009. Tebow also received the Wuerffel Trophy, which goes to the national player who best exemplifies community service and academic excellence, and the Wooden Cup for his positive impact upon the lives of others. He was presented with an Espy Award as the best male college athlete and Disney's Wide World of Sports Spirit Award, and the U.S. Sports Academy named him its Athlete of the Year.

After announcing that he would continue to play for the Gators for his 2009 senior year, Tebow broke Herschel Walker's SEC career rushing touchdown record (51) and led the team to the SEC championship game. In his 55 college games, he threw for 9,286 yards on 661 completions, and he ran for 2,947 yards on 692 attempts. He scored a total of 112 touchdowns, and his 482 passing yards against the University of Cincinnati in the 2010 Sugar Bowl is a UF record, as is his career completion percentage of 66.4%.

Tebow received his bachelor's degree in December 2009. That year, he was presented with the National Football Foundation Scholar-Athlete Award, the NCAA Today Top Eight Award, and the Draddy Trophy. He was selected by his teammates as the winner of the Ray Graves Award three times as the team's MVP (2007, 2008, and, in 2009, he shared it with Joe Haden). He holds the UF record for lowest career interception percentage (1.61%), and for a time in 2007–08 he had a streak of 203 consecutive passes without an interception (also a Gator record).

Going into the 2010 NFL draft, there was doubt about Tebow's ability to play in the NFL. Experts from several teams and the media felt that he lacked the passing ability it takes to be successful. The Denver Broncos picked him in the first round and intended to use him as a backup. He performed in that role in his rookie season in six games, then started the last three games of the season. He became the first NFL quarterback to run for a touchdown in each of his first three starts.

In 2011, with the Broncos falling to a 1-4 record and losing the sixth game to the San Diego Chargers, Tebow was brought in to replace Kyle Orton. He nearly won that game and was installed as the starter. For the rest of the season, he played well, often in come-from-behind situations in the fourth quarter or overtime. The Broncos made it to the playoffs and won their first post-season game over the Pittsburgh Steelers, with Tebow setting the Denver franchise record for quarterback rating (125.6) in a playoff game, in addition to the NFL record for yards per completion (31.6) in a playoff game.

In early 2012, he was traded to the New York Jets and was used on special teams and as a tight end and backup quarterback in limited action. In April 2013, Tebow was designated as a Great Floridian by the Florida Division of Historical Resources in recognition of his contributions to the progress and welfare of the state. During the following month, the Jets released him; in June 2013, he signed with the New England Patriots but was cut before the start of the regular season.

In 2013, the *Orlando Sentinel* ranked him #1 on its list of the 50 Greatest Gators. He is the co-author of *Through My Eyes: A Quarterback's Journey*. At the end of the year, he was hired to be a college football analyst by ESPN, chiefly to co-host *SEC Nation*, a pre-game show on the SEC Network. In addition to starring in commercials, Tebow is active in charitable activities, including First and 15 (which raises funds for Uncle Dick's Orphanage in the Philippines), Shands Hospital Pediatric Cancer Center, and The Tebow CURE Hospital in Davao City, Philippines.

MARCUS THOMAS (1985–) ■ *Nose Tackle*

COLLEGE: 2003–06   6-3, 316 lbs.   **NFL:** 2007–11; **CFL:** 2013

Denver defensive tackle Marcus Thomas in 2009

After an all-state prep career at Mandarin High School in Jacksonville, Marcus Thomas came to the University of Florida to play football and major in anthropology. He played nose tackle and likely would have been part of the squad, which went on to win the BCS championship over The Ohio State University at the end of the 2006 season. However, Thomas was removed from the team in November 2006 for violation of team rules following his reinstatement from a suspension.

In the 2007 NFL draft, Thomas was selected in the fourth round by the Denver Broncos. In his five years in Denver, he played in 76 games (starting 34 of them), made 150 tackles, and recovered a fumble. He also returned two interceptions for a total of nine yards. During 2012, he signed with the New York Giants but was released 15 days later before the start of the season. In October 2013, Thomas joined the Canadian Football League's Toronto Argonauts and played in a pair of games against Winnipeg and Hamilton.

BENJAMIN LASHAUN TROUPE (1982-) ■ *Tight End*
COLLEGE: 2003-06   6-4, 260 lbs.   **NFL:** 2004-08

Gator tight end Ben Troupe

According to the Atlanta Constitution newspaper, Ben Troupe was one of the top four prospects in the Southeast coming out of high school at the tight end position. He came to Florida and played for coaches Steve Spurrier and Ron Zook. Over his four years, he caught 64 passes (seven for touchdowns) for 958 yards. He served as a team captain as a senior, received first-team All-Southeastern Conference honors as a freshman from the Associated Press and the SEC coaches, and was named a first-team All-American by *Sports Illustrated*, ESPN, and Rivals.Com. Troupe was one of the three finalists for the 2003 John Mackey award, presented to the nation's best tight end. An agile player, he earned the nickname of "The Leaping Lizard" by jumping over defenders.

In the 2004 NFL draft, Troupe was chosen by the Tennessee Titans in the second round. Called "Troupe Scadoup " by his teammates, he played tight end for the Titans for four seasons and gained 1,056 yards on 106 receptions, seven for touchdowns. In 2008, he leapt onto the Tampa Bay Buccaneers roster and played two games in place of a starter out on suspension, then was released. Three days later, Troupe signed with the Oakland Raiders, but he was placed on injured reserve in October and was released the next month.

He currently is a regular guest on an afternoon radio talk show on ESPN Radio. On his website, Troupe claims that he will do any charity event that benefits people of all ages, sizes, shapes, and colors. Those include banquets, sports camps, game nights, sports tournaments, silent auctions, and serving as a guest speaker. His motto is WEAWEN (We All We Got, We All We Need).

HARMON LEON WAGES (1946-) ■ *Running Back*
COLLEGE: 1965-67   6-1, 215 lbs.   **NFL:** 1968-71, 1973

Harmon Wages was a high school quarterback in Jacksonville before coming to the University of Florida. As a sophomore and junior, he was a backup behind Steve Spurrier and was occasionally a starter during his senior year in 1967. He completed his bachelor's degree in business administration in 1969.

Wages was not chosen in the 1968 NFL draft and instead signed as a free agent with the Atlanta Falcons. He played five seasons for them, listed on the depth chart both at halfback (#2) and quarterback (#3). When the starting halfback was injured,

Wages was given increased playing time. One of his highlight games was against the New Orleans Saints in 1969, when he ran 66 yards for a touchdown, caught a touchdown pass for 88 yards, and threw a 16-yard pass for a touchdown. Only seven times in NFL history has a player scored three touchdowns in a single game by running, passing, and receiving. Wages's final NFL stats show 332 rushing attempts for 1,321 yards and 85 pass receptions for 765 yards.

After retiring as a player, he went into sports broadcasting with WAGA-TV (CBS) and then WXIA-TV (NBC), both in Atlanta. After a three-month prison sentence for cocaine possession in 1985, he returned to broadcasting with WTLV-TV (NBC) in Jacksonville and WGNX-TV (CBS) in Atlanta. Wages serves as an advisory member of the board of directors of Jacksonville's Police Athletic League.

AARON SCOTT WALKER (1980–) ■ *Tight End*

COLLEGE: 1999–2002   6-6, 270 lbs.   **NFL:** 2003–07

Aaron Walker losing his helmet while being tackled by two Miami Hurricane players

In high school in Titusville, Aaron Walker was a two-position standout, at tight and defensive end. Prep-Star considered him to be an All-American, as did Super Prep. He came to the University of Florida and focused on the offensive side of the line. For his college career of 47 games, he gained 716 yards with 56 receptions (nine of them for touchdowns), and he was named second-team All-Southeastern Conference in 2002 by the Associated Press and the SEC coaches.

During the 2003 NFL draft, Walker was selected in the fifth round by the San Francisco 49ers. He played in all 32 regular season games over the next two seasons, starting six of them. Beginning in 2006, he was a St. Louis Ram for two seasons, seeing action in 23 games. His NFL statistics include 25 catches for 312 yards and a single touchdown. Walker was also a member of the Baltimore Ravens (2008) and the Cleveland Browns (2009), but he remained on their practice squads.

After his playing days, Walker became involved in NASCAR auto racing. For three years, he worked on a pit crew for Hendrick Motorsports and JR Motorsports. He moved in 2012 to Penske Racing's Nationwide Series team and the No. 7 Cup team of Tommy Baldwin Racing, serving as a jackman.

IDREES KENYATTA WALKER (1979–) ■ *Offensive Tackle*

COLLEGE: 1998–2000   6-5, 302 lbs.   **NFL:** 2001–06

Kenyatta Walker was a football standout in Meridian, Mississippi, before coming to Gainesville, where he was redshirted for the 1997 season. In 1998, he was named an All-American by the *Knoxville News-Sentinel* newspaper and a freshman All-American by *Football News*. In 1999, he made the All-Southeastern Conference second teams of the Associated Press and the SEC coaches, and, as a junior, he was a semi-finalist for the Outland Trophy and the winner of the Jacobs Blocking Trophy. Walker was named an All-American by AP, *Football News*, *Sporting News*, and Sports Xchange.

Skipping his senior year, Walker was chosen in the first round of the 2001 NFL draft by the Tampa Bay Buccaneers. During his 2001 season, he played left tackle, then was moved the following year to right tackle. He earned a championship ring for playing in Super Bowl XXXVII, which Tampa Bay won over the Oakland Raiders. During his six years with the Bucs, he played in 75 games and started 73 of them, despite being hospitalized for a time in 2003 because of an MRSA infection.

After the 2006 season, Walker was released by Tampa Bay and was signed by the Carolina Panthers, but he was cut from that team before seeing any playing time. A week later, he became a Canadian Football League Toronto Argonaut but only made it to the team's practice roster. During that time, he came back to UF and completed his bachelor's degree in sociology in 2007 and officially retired in 2008.

Walker's charitable activities included work with the Boys and Girls Clubs (supported by his Kenyatta Walker Foundation) and the Kenyatta Walker Foundation Golf Tournament. For his accomplishments and serving as a fine example for young Mississippians, Walker was officially commended and congratulated by the legislators with Resolution No. 17, adopted by the Mississippi House of Representatives in 2003.

GERARD THURSTON WARREN (1978–) ■ *Defensive Tackle*

COLLEGE: 1998–2000   6-4, 330 lbs.   **NFL:** 2001–11

After a high school career, which included three Florida state championships and All-American honors by Prep Stars and *USA Today*, Gerard Warren headed to the University of Florida. A decade after graduation from Union County High School, the Florida High School Athletic Association honored him as one of the state's best 100 players during the first 100 years of high school football.

Warren played for the Gators for three years through his junior year, during which he served as a team captain and was twice a second-team All-Southeastern Conference selection of the Associated Press and the SEC coaches, as well as a 2000 first-team All-American, according to *Pro Football*

Denver Broncos tackle Gerard Warren

Weekly. During his college career, he had 159 tackles (30 for a loss), 9.5 sacks, and started 22 of the 35 games in which he played. Warren skipped his senior year so he could enter the 2001 NFL draft.

He was chosen in the first round by the Cleveland Browns and played for them for four years, starting 59 of the 60 games he played, and registered 16.5 sacks. In early 2005, Warren was traded to the Denver Broncos. There, he played for two seasons and had 5.5 sacks, starting all 31 games in which he played.

During the summer of 2007, Warren was traded to the Oakland Raiders, and he played in a dozen games that season. In 2008 and 2009, the durable tackle was a starter in all 32 regular season games. Early in 2010, he was released by Oakland and was picked up by the New England Patriots. He started at defensive end, and in week 6 moved to nose tackle and began to get reduced playing time. Warren played in 11 games in 2011, all in a backup role, and then was released during the summer prior to the 2012 season.

In May 2013, a Fort Lauderdale securities broker was barred from the securities business by the Financial Industry Regulatory Authority for recommending an unsuitable investment, an Alabama casino project that resulted in $43 million of losses. One of the 31 NFL players that the broker had gotten into the deal between 2008 and 2011 was Gerard Warren. Other Gator alumni included Fred Taylor and Jevon Kearse.

DALE BARNARD WATERS (1909–2001) ■ *Lineman*
COLLEGE: 1928–30   6-2, 212 lbs.   **NFL:** 1931–33

On both sides of the line, Dale Waters of Indiana played for Gator head coach Charlie Bachman in the best season to that date, 1928, when the team's record was 8-1. The only loss was to the University of Tennessee by a score of 13–12. He also played in 1929 and 1930, and he lettered for the Gator basketball team in 1929–31.

Waters started his professional career with the NFL Cleveland Indians in 1931 and played in six games, four as a starter. During that year, he moved to the NFL Portsmouth Spartans and got into one more game. After the season, he moved to the NFL Boston Braves (which turned into the Boston Redskins) and played for them in 1932–33. Overall, his NFL career lasted 27 games, of which he started 12.

After his professional football career, Waters returned to Gainesville and completed his bachelor's degree in physical education in 1935. He died December 19, 2001, and the age of 92.

Dale Waters practicing on the beach

JOSEPH FREDERICK WEARY (1974–) ■ *Cornerback*
COLLEGE: 1994–97 5-10, 181 lbs. **NFL:** 1998–2003

After playing for the Mandarin High School Mustangs in Jacksonville, Fred Weary started playing as a Gator cornerback in 1994. He was part of the squad that won Florida's first football national championship, beating Florida State University 52-20 in the 1997 Sugar Bowl. As a senior, he was a team captain and made six interceptions for a total of 15 in his college career, which set a new Florida record. Weary was named first-team All-Southeastern Conference in 1996 (by the SEC coaches) and 1997 (by the coaches and the Associated Press), was a consensus first-team All-American as a senior, and blocked 35 passes as a Gator.

Cornerback Fred Weary (#24) eluding offensive would-be tacklers

In the fourth round of the 1998 NFL draft, Weary was chosen by the New Orleans Saints. He was a backup defensive back his rookie season and played in 14 games. During the next two years, he was a starting right cornerback for most of the regular season. In his last year with the Saints (2001), he played in 14 games but started only one.

As a backup, Weary played two more years for the Atlanta Falcons (2002) and the St. Louis Rams (2003). His final NFL stats show that he started in 25 of 83 games and is credited with two sacks, seven interceptions, and two fumble recoveries. After retiring, he went back to UF and completed his bachelor's degree in exercise and sports science in 2005.

Weary has been involved in legal disputes with former Gator teammate Anthone Lott dating back to 2006 involving joint construction ventures. He works as a football evaluator for Athletes for College, LLC, an organization that verifies and evaluates high school prospects considering playing football at the collegiate level.

ADRIAN DARNELL WHITE (1964–) ■ *Cornerback–Safety–Coach*
COLLEGE: 1984–86, 1988 6-0, 200 lbs. **NFL:** 1987–89, 1991–93 (player) and 2008–12 (coach); **NFLE:** 2001–02, 2003–07 (coach)

Adrian White played high school football for the Orange Park High School Raiders in Orange Park, Florida. He left the state and spent the 1983 season playing for Southern Illinois University; however, after one year there, he returned to Florida and was a walk-on at UF. He impressed Galen Hall enough to be a starter all three years for the Gators, and he also lettered in track as a sprinter. In 1986, the senior earned a first-team All-Southeastern Conference honor from the Associated Press and the SEC coaches.

In the second round of the 1987 NFL draft, White was picked by the New York Giants. After five years in New York, he played in 1992 for the Green Bay Packers and in 1993 for the New England Patriots. Overall, he started five games and served as a backup in 65. After his professional playing days ended, White returned to Florida and finished his bachelor's degree in criminal justice (1993) and later obtained a master's degree in education from Fairleigh Dickinson University in New Jersey.

Football was still in his blood, and White went into coaching, initially for Southern Illinois University (1999–2000), where he worked with the defensive backs. Next, he moved on to the National Football League Europe Rhein Fire (2001–02) as an assistant coach and then to Indiana State University (2002) and back to the Rhein Fire (2003–06).

After another year in Europe with the NFLE Berlin Thunder (2007), White made his way back to the NFL with the Buffalo Bills. He was the defensive quality control coach in 2008–11 and the assistant defensive backs coach through the end of 2012.

DAVID WAYNE WILLIAMS (1966–) ■ *Offensive Tackle*
COLLEGE: 1985–88   6-5, 294 lbs.   **NFL:** 1989–97

Gator running back Elijah Williams

As a result of his success playing for the Lakeland High School Dreadnaughts, David Williams was named an All-American by *Parade* magazine and *USA Today*, and the Florida High School Athletic Association called him one of the state's greatest 100 players of the first 100 years of Florida high school football.

Williams arrived in Gainesville and was one of the few players who became a starter as a freshman, a status he never relinquished. He was honored by the Associated Press, the United Press International, and the conference coaches as a first-team All-Southeastern Conference player while he was a senior team captain in 1988. He was inducted into the University of Florida Athletic Hall of Fame in 1999, and *The Gainesville Sun* in 2006 ranked him #27 on its list of the all-time greatest Gator football players. In 2013, the *Orlando Sentinel* had him at #30 on its list of the 50 Greatest Gators.

In 1986, Williams was the first recipient of the James W. Kynes Award presented to the Gator offensive lineman who displayed mental and physical toughness and "iron-man" determination, and he received the same award again in 1988.

The Houston Oilers chose him in the first round of the 1989 NFL draft, and Williams played there for seven years, becoming a starter by his third year at right tackle. After his tenure with the Oilers, he played two years for the New York Jets before retiring. He started 106 of the 128 games in which he played.

Williams also was in the middle of a media storm while playing for Houston in 1993 when he missed an away game because he was with his wife in Houston. She had a miscarriage the year before, and Williams wanted to be with her for the birth of their child. He called the team on Saturday and was excused from the following day's game. However, the baby was born on Saturday night and Williams got into trouble by not leaving for New England for the Sunday afternoon game. The Oilers were criticized by fans and media alike for docking Williams' pay and publicly criticizing him for putting family ahead of his team, especially owner Bud Adams, who described him as having misplaced priorities. The episode was dubbed "Babygate" and likely led to teams handling family matters with more sensitivity and understanding.

ELIJAH ELGEBRA WILLIAMS (1975–) ■ *Defensive Back-Running Back*
COLLEGE: 1994–97   5-10, 181 lbs.   **NFL:** 1998–2001

While he played for Florida, Elijah Williams was a running back and the team's leading rusher in 1995 and 1996. His highlight games include 109 yards against Louisiana State University and 116 against Auburn University, both in 1996. He accumulated 3,023 all-purpose yards over his four years with UF, 842 on pass receptions and 2,181 rushing, on the way to the Gators' three consecutive Southeastern Conference championships (1994–96) and a national title (1996).

The Atlanta Falcons made Williams their sixth-round pick of the 1998 NFL draft. He saw limited action as a running back in his rookie year, and then he became a kick return specialist and backup defensive back, appearing in 50 games over four seasons for the Falcons. After retiring, Williams went back to Florida and completed his bachelor's degree in health science education in 2003.

He returned to football in 2005 as a defensive coordinator at Titusville's Astronaut High School for three years and spent one year as an assistant coach at Orlando's Oak Ridge High School before becoming its head coach in 2009. Williams ran a successful program there and, in 2013, accepted a position with Florida A&M University as a recruiting coordinator and running back coach. That same year, he returned in October to be the head coach at Oak Ridge.

JARVIS ERIC WILLIAMS SR. (1965–2010) ■ *Safety*
COLLEGE: 1984–87   5-11, 200 lbs.   **NFL:** 1988–94

After being part of the state champion Palatka High School Panthers, Jarvis Williams enrolled at the University of Florida and continued his winning ways. During his first two years, the Gators had identical records of 9-1-1 and were (over the two years) 10-1-1 against other teams in the Southeastern Conference. The hard-hitting Williams was a starter in 45 consecutive games as a Gator (second-highest all-time for UF), and as a senior he led UF in punt returns and tackles. He was selected to

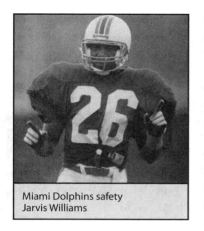

Miami Dolphins safety Jarvis Williams

the first-team All-SEC by the United Press International and the SEC coaches in 1986, was a first-team Walter Camp Foundation All-American in 1987, and in 2001 was inducted into the University of Florida Athletic Hall of Fame. In 2013, he was ranked #45 on the *Orlando Sentinel* list of the 50 Greatest Gators.

The 1988 NFL draft saw Williams chosen in the second round by the Miami Dolphins. For five of the six seasons he played for Miami, he and fellow Gator alumnus Louis Oliver were the starting safeties. After he left the Dolphins, he played one more year for the New York Giants in 1994. He appeared in 104 games (of which he started 95) during his seven years in the NFL.

When his playing days ended, Williams kept active in the sport he loved as an assistant coach at Ocala's Trinity Catholic High School and at Interlachen High School. He died unexpectedly from an acute attack of asthma on May 25, 2010.

JOHN L. WILLIAMS (1964–) ■ *Fullback*

COLLEGE: 1982–85   5-11, 231 lbs.   **NFL:** 1986–95

Chosen by the Florida High School Athletic Association as one of the 100 greatest high school players in the first century of football in Florida, John L. Williams played fullback for the Gators, often in the same backfield as Neal Anderson. They ran behind the offensive line known as "The Great Wall of Florida" and were major factors in the team finishing with a record of 9-1-1 in both 1984 and 1985.

Williams was the first Gator to have more than 2,000 yards (2,409) on the ground and at least 700 (863) in the air during his college career. He was selected second-team All-SEC in 1984 and 1985 by the Associated Press. *The Gainesville Sun* in 2006 ranked Williams as #31 on its list of all-time greatest Gator football players, and in 2013 the *Orlando Sentinel* put him at #36 on its list of the 50 Greatest Gators. He became a member of the University of Florida Athletic Hall of Fame in 1997.

In the 1986 NFL draft, Williams was chosen in the first round by the Seattle Seahawks, where he spent eight years and made the Pro Bowl twice (1990 and 1991). After the 1993 season, he signed with the Pittsburgh Steelers and played two more years, with his final game being the Super Bowl XXX loss to the Dallas Cowboys. In 10 years, Williams started 135 of the 149 games that he played and gained 5,006 yards on 1,245 rushes (18 touchdowns). He also caught 546 passes for 19 touchdowns and 4,656 yards.

After his playing days, Williams moved back to Palatka, Florida, and opened John L's Club Remy, a nightclub he kept for six years. In 2005, he became an assistant coach at Trinity Catholic High School in Ocala, Florida, on the same staff with former Gator player Kerwin Bell, who was the following year succeeded by Gator alumnus Ricky Nattiel.

MAJOR WRIGHT (1988–) ■ *Strong Safety*

COLLEGE: 2007–09   5-11, 204 lbs.   **NFL:** 2010–13

Major Wright was a high school football star in Fort Lauderdale and, as a senior, was a finalist for the National U.S. Army Player of the Year Award. He picked the University of Florida and began playing as a true freshman in 2007. He was the starting free safety in seven of that year's 13 games, and he made 67 tackles, forced four fumbles, and caught one interception. He was placed on the first-team All-American list of CollegeFootballNews.com and the second-team list of Rivals.com.

Major Wright in the BCS championship game in 2009 against Oklahoma

During his sophomore year, Wright started every game and made 66 tackles and returned one of his four interceptions for a touchdown. In the BCS championship win over the University of Oklahoma, he had nine tackles and one interception. He decided it was time to start his pro career, and Wright skipped his senior year for the 2010 NFL draft.

He was chosen in the third round by the Chicago Bears and played in 11 games during his rookie season. In 2011, he became the starter and made three interceptions during 2011, four during 2012, and two in 2013, and returned one for a touchdown in each of those years. Wright left the Bears after the 2013 season as a free agent and followed his coach, Lovie Smith, to his new head coaching job with the Tampa Bay Buccaneers. He signed a one-year contract with the Bucs on April 7, 2014.

DANIEL CARL WUERFFEL (1974–) ■ *Quarterback*

COLLEGE: 1993–96   6-1, 212 lbs.   **NFL:** 1997–2002; **NFLE:** 2000

As a senior in high school, Danny Wuerffel was considered by many to be the top football recruit in the state of Florida. He enrolled at Florida and led the team to three consecutive Southeastern Conference championships, after playing backup to quarterback Terry Dean during the 1993 SEC championship season. The player known as "Danny Wonderful" for his actions both on and off the field took the team to two consecutive national championship games, winning the second (his final game as a Gator) over Florida State University by a score of 52–20.

Danny Wuerffel speaking to air commandos at Eglin Air Force Base in 2009

In his first year, Wuerffel was named the SEC Freshman of the Year by the *Knoxville Sentinel*. As a junior in 1995, he was presented the Sammy Baugh Trophy (as the nation's top passer), the Davey O'Brien Award (as the top quarterback), and was the SEC Most Valuable Player. In both his junior and senior years, Wuerffel was on the Academic All-America Team, the CFA Scholar-Athlete Team, was named the National Offensive Player of the Year by *Football News,* and the SEC Player of the Year by the *Nashville Banner*. In 1995 and 1996, his fellow players voted him their MVP, naming him the recipient of the Ray Graves Award.

As a senior, Wuerffel again was the conference MVP and the recipient of the Davey O'Brien Award, plus the winner of the Heisman Trophy (most outstanding player), the Draddy Trophy (best combination of academics, community service, and on-field performance), the Johnny Unitas Golden Arm Award (outstanding senior quarterback), the Maxwell Award (best football player), the National Football Foundation Scholar-Athlete Award, the NCAA Today Top Eight Award, and the Quarterback of the Year Award. *The Sporting News* named him its National Offensive Player of the Year.

He also would have been on the *Playboy* All-American team and its Scholar-Athlete of the Year, but Wuerffel declined to be included in the magazine with the comment, "That's not the type of person I am or would like to portray myself as." He also garnered several All-American honors and was included on many all-time (or teams of the century) squads. He twice was named the National Player of the Year (1995 by the College Football Foundation and 1996 by the Walter Camp National Football Foundation).

His amazing career at Florida included 708 pass completions for 10,875 yards and 114 touchdowns, both of which set SEC records. His percentage of passes that were touchdowns was a national record, as was his pass efficiency rating (163.56). Wuerffel was the first college quarterback to have two consecutive years with a rating of 170 or more. He is a member of the University of Florida Athletic Hall of Fame and has a UF bachelor's degree in public relations. In 1997, he won the NCAA Post-Graduate Scholarship Award.

In the fourth round of the 1997 NFL draft, Wuerffel was chosen by the New Orleans Saints. He played for three years for the Saints, mostly in a backup role and then was a backup for the Green Bay Packers (2000), Chicago Bears (2001), and Washington Redskins (2002). In his NFL career, he started 10 of the 25 games in which he played, and he completed 184 passes for 2,123 yards and a dozen touchdowns. Between his time with the Saints and the Packers, he quarterbacked the National Football League

Europe Rhein Fire, leading them to the league championship while also winning the NFLE MVP trophy.

Wuerffel has worked for community and spiritual concerns, particularly the Desire Street Ministries in New Orleans. When its headquarters and the Wuerffel home were destroyed by Hurricane Katrina, Wuerffel made public appearances to support the reconstruction of the city and the ministry. He has lectured on college campuses on the subject of character, and in 2005 the All Sports Association of Fort Walton Beach established the Wuerffel Trophy to be presented annually to a player who shows the type of character Wuerffel did when he played.

He is a member of the Gator Football Ring of Honor and was ranked #1 by *The Gainesville Sun* on its 2006 all-time list of the greatest Gator football players and #2 by the *Orlando Sentinel* in 2013 on its list of the 50 Greatest Gators. In 2013, he was inducted into the College Football Hall of Fame. Perhaps the best description of Wuerffel was provided by his coach, Steve Spurrier, who said, "Danny is a better person than he is a quarterback, and Danny is a great, great quarterback." Wuerffel is the co-author of the 2004 book, *Danny Wuerffel's Tales from the Gator Swamp: Reflections of Faith and Football*.

DESHAWN WYNN (1983–) ■ *Running Back*
COLLEGE: 2003–06   5-10, 232 lbs.   **NFL:** 2007–10

Ohio native DeShawn Wynn was named a *Parade* magazine high school All-American, and headed south to play for the Gators. He had been a running back, linebacker, and safety, but at Florida focused on running with the ball out of the backfield, with an occasional pass reception. A highlight of his career was his final game, in which he was the starting running back in the BCS national championship game win over The Ohio State University. In four years, he totaled 2,077 yards on the ground and 376 through pass receptions and scored 25 touchdowns.

DeShawn Wynn (#21) just after scoring a touchdown

In the 2007 NFL draft, Wynn was selected in the seventh round by the Green Bay Packers. He played three years for the Packers and began his rookie year with a season-ending shoulder injury in the game against the Denver Broncos in late October 2007. It still turned out to be his best year, with appearances in 11 games for 203 yards on 50 rushing attempts and nine receptions for 73 yards.

Wynn played two more years for the Packers with limited action as a backup in nine games. Most of his 129 yards rushing for that period came on a single touchdown run against the Detroit Lions. In 2010, he became a member of the New Orleans Saints, who treated him a bit like a yo-yo—he was released, re-signed, was on the active roster for three games and then was waived. He was picked up by the San Francisco 49ers, who had him on their active roster for four games and waived him just after Christmas.

New Orleans re-signed him, but he did not see any game action and he wound up with the Canadian Football League Saskatchewan Roughriders in 2012. He was signed to a contract with that team in March but was released in July of the same year.

JAMES KELLEY YARBROUGH (1946–) ■ *Offensive Tackle*

COLLEGE: 1966–68   6-5, 265 lbs.   **NFL:** 1969–77

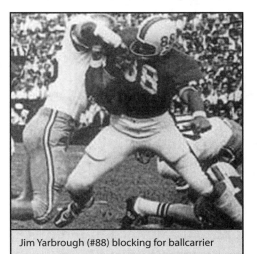

Jim Yarbrough (#88) blocking for ballcarrier

During high school in Arcadia, Florida, Jim Yarbrough played both offense and defense on the football team, was a shot-putter, and played center on the basketball team. When he came to UF, he focused on football and the offense, where he played tight end for three years.

Yarbrough, a sophomore starter, was part of the squad that played in the 1967 Orange Bowl, beating Georgia Tech by a score of 27 to 12. He is a member of the University of Florida Athletic Hall of Fame, and, in 2006, *The Gainesville Sun* ranked him #98 on its list of all-time greatest Gator football players.

In the 1969 NFL draft, Yarbrough was selected by the Detroit Lions in the second round, where he stayed for his entire nine-year professional career. He started out as a backup at left tackle and moved up to the starting position for most of his final four years. He played in 112 NFL games, starting 41 of them. Yarbrough came back during the off-season and earned his bachelor's degree in marketing in 1971.

After retiring from football, Yarbrough became a financial advisor at Money Concepts Capital Corp. in Winter Park, Florida.

HERBERT JACKSON YOUNGBLOOD III (1950–) ■ *Defensive End*

COLLEGE: 1968–70   6-4, 245 lbs.   **NFL:** 1971–84

After a year on the freshman team, sophomore Jack Youngblood played on the Gator defensive line at end and tackle, as well as placekicker. At the end of his junior year, he was a key player in the upset of the University of Tennessee, making nine tackles and forcing a fumble in Florida's win in the Gator Bowl. He had a five-sack game against Florida State University and set the UF season record with 14 sacks.

Continued on next page

Nicknames of Gator Players and Head Coaches

- *Ark* (Robert D. Newton)
- *Babe* (Donald Gene Chandler)
- *The Baby Snake* (Robert Todd Hewko)
- *Bam* (Byron Bernard Hardmon)
- *Bear* (Raymond B. Wolf)
- *Beeflegs* (Bob Woodruff)
- *Big Daddy* (Crawford Francis Ker)
- *Big Money* (Gerard Thurston Warren)
- *Blade* (Ralph Lawrence Rentz)
- *Brad* (John Broward Culpepper)
- *Brummie* (Carl L. Brumbaugh)
- *Bubba* (Andre Jerome Caldwell)
- *Buck* (Sheddrick Tobias Gurley)
- *Bull* (David Lawrence Galloway Sr.)
- *Cadillac* (Anthony Cris Collinsworth)
- *Cannonball* (Clyde Crabtree)
- *Catfish* (Fred Abbott)
- *The Comeback Kid* (Steven Orr Spurrier)
- *Cy* (Berton Caswell Williams)
- *Danny Wonderful* (Daniel Carl Wuerffel)
- *Dee* (Demetrice A. Webb)
- *Del* (Delfonico Arnese Speer)
- *Dutch* (Dennis K. Stanley)
- *Fragile Fred* (Frederick Antwon Taylor)
- *The Franchise* (James Roosevelt Jones)
- *Friendly Frank* (James Franklin Dempsey)
- *The Freak* (Jevon Kearse)
- *The Genial Irishman* (Thomas J. Lieb)
- *Goldy* and *Izzy* (Erving Max Goldstein)
- *The Great Wall of Florida* (Crawford Ker, Phil Bromley, Lomas Brown, Billy Hinson, and Jeffrey Alan Zimmerman)
- *Humdinger* (Charles Ray Hunsinger)
- *The Icebox* (Timothy Reginald Newton)
- *Ike* (Isaac Jason Hilliard)

HERBERT JACKSON YOUNGBLOOD III *Continued from previous page*

After his senior year, he was on the Associated Press and United Press International All-Southeastern Conference squads, was voted the SEC Lineman of the Year, and received the university's Fergie Ferguson Award for his leadership, character, and courage. Youngblood was named a first-team All-American by *Time* magazine, and *The Gainesville Sun* ranked him #5 on its list of all-time greatest Gator football players. In 2013, the *Orlando Sentinel* put him at #7 on its list of the 50 Greatest Gators. In 1972, he completed his UF bachelor's degree in business administration.

Youngblood recounted one of his funniest memories of his years as a Gator in *Tales from the Gator Swamp* involving an attempted panty raid during his

Jack Youngblood as a member of the Los Angeles Rams

- *Inspector Gadget* (Michael Rene Mularkey)
- *Jack* (Herbert Jackson Youngblood III)
- *Jack* (Elliott Cornelius Jackson Jr.)
- *Jackie* (Joseph Marlin Simpson)
- *Joel* (Joseph Lee Parker)
- *Josh* (Ioosa Taotaoi)
- *Kim* (Charles Kimberlin Helton)
- *L.A.* (for *Lower Alabama*) (Nathaniel Moore)
- *Lazy Jack* (Jack Ridley Harper)
- *Leaping Lizard* (Benjamin LaShaun Troupe)
- *Lindy* (Gelindo Infante)
- *Mo* (Damon Jamal Collins)
- *Mo* (Sparrow Maurice Hurt Jr.)
- *Mr. Inside* (Jimmy DuWayne DuBose)
- *Mr. Outside* (Anthony Edward Green)
- *Muddy* (Dale Barnard Waters)
- *O.J.* (Ozell Jermaine Small)
- *The Ol' Ball Coach* and *The Head Ball Coach* (Steven Orr Spurrier)
- *The Old Gray Fox* (Thomas J. Lieb)
- *Pee Wee* (James A. Forsythe Jr.)
- *Phantom Four* (Carl Lowry Brumbaugh, Royce Ethelbert Goodbread, Clyde Crabtree, and Rainey Cawthon)
- *Ran* (Arandic Kornell Carthon)
- *The Rocket* (Ricky Rennard Nattiel)
- *Sexy Rexy* (Rex Daniel Grossman III)
- *Slick Rick* (Ricky Rennard Nattiel)
- *Snake* (Robert S. Davis)
- *Steve Superior* (Steven Orr Spurrier)
- *The Three Amigos* (UF's Ricky Rennard Nattiel; Broncos' Vance Johnson and Mark Jackson)
- *The Throwin' Mayoan* (Kerwin Douglas Bell)
- *Tom* (H.L. Sebring)
- *Touchdown Tommy* (Thomas L. Durrance)
- *Trace* (Raymond L. Armstrong III)
- *Troupe Scadoup* (Benjamin LaShaun Troupe)
- *Val* (Varoly Agusta Brown)
- *Vito* (Juan DeVito McKeever)
- *The Whip* (Bob Woodruff)

freshman year. He and his cohorts were arrested and taken to the university police station. Youngblood hated to call the freshman coach, Jimmy Haynes, because he knew how tough the coach was, but the bad experience turned out to be good for Youngblood. The coach made him get up early and run every morning for a month, and, in Youngblood's words, "When he got through with me, I was in the best shape of my life, and after that I was a lot better football player."

In the 1971 NFL draft, Youngblood was chosen in the first round by the Los Angeles Rams, and in his first season was named All-Rookie by *Football Digest*. He played backup at left defensive end, but, by 1972, he was the starter there. His 70 tackles led the Rams defensive lineman that season. He was their lineman of the year in 1973, and in 1974 he led the team with 15 quarterback sacks.

In 1975, UPI named him its National Football Conference Defensive Player of the Year, and he was named NFL Defensive Lineman of the Year by *Pro Football Weekly*. He went to the Pro Bowl seven consecutive years (1973–79) and consistently was a team and league leader in defensive categories.

Youngblood was tough and ran up a consecutive games streak of 201, ended only when he ruptured a disk in his lower back in 1984, but that only caused him to miss one game. Even a fibula broken in a game against the Dallas Cowboys (confirmed by an X-ray in the locker room) didn't stop him, and he played with it in pain through the entire 1979 playoffs, Super Bowl XIV, and the Pro Bowl. The NFL Network series *NFL Top Ten* chose Youngblood's painful play during those playoffs as number one on their "Gutsiest Performances" of all time list, and he was also dubbed the "John Wayne of football" by head coaches Jim Hanifan and John Madden. Youngblood retired in 1985 with a career total of 151.5 sacks, and led the Rams for nine seasons.

He didn't let retirement slow him down. After playing football, Youngblood appeared in a pair of made-for-television movies and was nominated for an Emmy as best supporting actor. He was a co-host and reporter for ESPN's *NFL GameDay* show, and was the host of ESPN's weekly Wal-Mart's *Great Outdoors* in 2000–03. His autobiography, entitled *Blood,* was published in 1988.

His connection with the Rams continued as Youngblood worked in player relations and marketing (1985–90), and he provided color commentary on radio broadcasts (1986–91). The busy man became the director of marketing for the World League of American Football Sacramento Surge in 1991; then in 1993, he added color analysis for the Canadian Football League Sacramento Gold Miners. In 1995, Youngblood was an executive with the Arena Football League's Orlando Predators, and he became a liaison between that league and the NFL in 1999. Other businesses in which he has been involved include a company that produces an octane-boosting additive for cars, a cattle and pine tree farm, a western clothing store, and several for which he modeled or acted as a spokesman.

Youngblood is in the St. Louis Rams Ring of Fame, the Orange County (California) Sports Hall of Fame, and in 2001 he was inducted into the Pro Football Hall of Fame. NFL Films in 1996 named him to its list of the 100 Toughest Players of All Time, and four years later *Sports Illustrated* listed him as the fourth-greatest pass rusher of all time. He has been involved in a long list of charitable activities (in his "spare" time), including fundraising for retired NFL players and numerous youth organizations.

After the SEC's 50th season in 1982, the SEC Skywriters (a media group which covered football in the Southeastern Conference), named Youngblood to its All-Time SEC Team. The conference itself named him to its list of SEC Legends in 1995.

JEFFREY ALAN ZIMMERMAN (1963–) ■ *Offensive Tackle-Guard*

COLLEGE: 1983–86   6-3, 320 lbs.   **NFL:** 1987–90

During the mid-1980s, the Gator backfield was protected by an offensive line known as The Great Wall of Florida, which included Jeff Zimmerman. Together, the five linemen protected quarterback Kerwin Bell and running backs John L. Williams and

Neal Anderson, for a Gator team that posted identical 9-1-1 records for two straight years, as well as the best team records in the Southeastern Conference. Zimmerman was chosen as first-team for both All-SEC (by the Associated Press and the conference coaches in 1985 and 1986 and also by United Press International in 1986), and All-American honors in 1985 (*The Sporting News* and the Walter Camp Foundation) and 1986 (*The Sporting News* and Scripps-Howard).

In the 1987 NFL draft, Zimmerman was chosen by the Dallas Cowboys in the third round. He played in four seasons as a backup, largely at guard, through 1990. In his four years with the Cowboys, he appeared in 34 games, twice as a starter.

Other Florida Athletes Who Went Into Pro Football

Pro Career Started in the 1930s

NAME	POSITION	COLLEGE	PRO	TEAMS
Clyde Crabtree	B	1927–29	NFL 1930	Frankford Yellow Jackets, Minneapolis Red Jackets
Royce Ethelbert Goodbread	WB/HB	1927–29	NFL 1930–31	Frankford Yellow Jackets, Minneapolis Red Jackets, Providence Steam Roller

Pro Career Started in the 1940s

NAME	POSITION	COLLEGE	PRO	TEAMS
Douglas Ray Belden Sr.	QB	1946–48	CFL 1949, 1951–52	Saskatchewan Roughriders
Paul Albert Duhart	B	1942	NFL 1944–45	Green Bay Packers, Boston Yanks, Pittsburgh Steelers
Clark William Goff	T	1937–39	NFL 1940	Pittsburgh Steelers
Nicholas Klutka	E	1940–42	AAFC 1946	Buffalo Bisons
Floyd Walter Konetsky	E	1940–42	NFL 1944–45; AAFC 1947	Cleveland Rams, Baltimore Colts
Eugene Orson Lee	C	1942	NFL 1946	Boston Yanks
Fondren Lack Mitchell	HB	1940–42	AAFC 1946	Miami Seahawks
John G. Smith Jr.	T	1938–39	NFL 1945	Philadelphia Eagles

Pro Career Started in the 1950s

NAME	POSITION	COLLEGE	PRO	TEAMS
Everett Dewayne Douglas	T	1951–52	NFL 1953	New York Giants
James W. Kynes	C	1946–49	CFL 1950	Saskatchewan Roughriders

Pro Career Started in the 1960s

NAME	POSITION	COLLEGE	PRO	TEAMS
James Edward Beaver	DT	1959–61	NFL 1962	Philadelphia Eagles
Thomas Floyd Dean	LB	1960–61	NFL 1964–65	San Francisco 49ers
Jack Ridley Harper	RB	1964–66	NFL 1967–68	Miami Dolphins
Joseph Martin Hergert	LB/K	1956–58	CFL 1960; AFL 1960–61	Montreal Alouettes, Buffalo Bills
James Andrew Jordan	RB	1964	NFL 1967	New Orleans Saints
Francis Joseph Lasky	T	1962–63	NFL 1964–65; CFL 1969	New York Giants, Montreal Alouettes
Alvin Dennis Murphy	DT	1962–64	NFL 1965	Chicago Bears
Anton Berdette Peters Jr.	DT	1961–62	AFL 1963	Denver Broncos
Ralph Lawrence Rentz	DB	1966–68	NFL 1969	San Diego Chargers
Allen Raymond Trammel Jr.	DB	1963–65	AFL 1966	Houston Oilers
Richard Earl Trapp	FL/WR	1965–67	AFL 1968–69; WFL 1974	Buffalo Bills, San Diego Chargers, Florida Blazers
James Melvin Yeats	TE	1955–57	AFL 1960	Houston Oilers

Pro Career Started in the 1970s

NAME	POSITION	COLLEGE	PRO	TEAMS
Frederic M. Abbott	LB	1970–72	WFL 1974–75	Jacksonville Sharks, Jacksonville Express
Ricky Browne	LB	1971–73	WFL 1975	Jacksonville Express
Earl W. Carr	RB	1975–77	NFL 1978–79	San Francisco 49ers, Philadelphia Eagles
Alvis Russell Darby	TE	1973–75	NFL 1976, 1978	Houston Oilers, Seattle Seahawks, Tampa Bay Buccaneers
Robert S. Davis	QB	1973	WFL 1975	Jacksonville Express
Thomas L. Durrance	TB	1969–71	WFL 1974	Jacksonville Sharks
Lewis Howe Gilbert Jr.	TE	1975–77	NFL 1978, 1980–81; USFL 1983–84	Atlanta Falcons, Philadelphia Eagles, San Francisco 49ers, Los Angeles Rams, Tampa Bay Bandits
Clinton D. Griffith Jr.	DT	1972–74	WFL 1975	Jacksonville Express
Vincent Kendrick	RB	1971–73	NFL 1974, 1976	Atlanta Falcons, Tampa Bay Buccaneers
Lee Colson McGriff	WR	1972–74	WFL 1975; NFL 1976	Charlotte Hornets, Tampa Bay Buccaneers

NAME	POSITION	COLLEGE	PRO	TEAMS
Joseph Lee Parker	WR	1971–73	NFL 1974–75, 1977	New Orleans Saints
David Ellsworth Posey	K	1973–76	NFL 1978	New England Patriots
Willie B. Wilder	FB	1975–77	CFL 1979; USFL 1983	Saskatchewan Roughriders, Tampa Bay Bandits

Pro Career Started in the 1980s

NAME	POSITION	COLLEGE	PRO	TEAMS
Greg Barrow	OL	1980	CFL 1981	Hamilton Tiger-Cats
Varoly Agusta Brown	LB	1979–82	USFL 1984–85	Jacksonville Bulls, Orlando Renegades
Clifford Tyrone Charlton	LB	1984–87	NFL 1988–89	Cleveland Browns
Brian Matthew Clark	K	1979–81	NFL 1982	Tampa Bay Buccaneers
Michael Hugh Clark	DE	1978, 1980	NFL 1981–82, 1987; USFL 1984–85; ArFL 1988	Washington Redskins, San Francisco 49ers, Tampa Bay Bandits, Tampa Bay Buccaneers, Chicago Bruisers
Randall Charles Clark	DB	1981–83	NFL 1984	Tampa Bay Buccaneers
Gregory Leon Cleveland	NT	1982–83, 1985	NFL 1987	Miami Dolphins
Raymond Alan Criswell	P	1982–85	NFL 1987–88	Tampa Bay Buccaneers
Derrick L. Crudup	DB/RB	1983 (DNC)	NFL 1989, 1991	Los Angeles Raiders
Ivory Curry	DB	1980–82	NFL 1987	Tampa Bay Buccaneers
Dwayne Keith Dixon	WR	1980–83	NFL 1984, 1987; ArFL 1988–91	Tampa Bay Buccaneers, Washington Commandos, Detroit Drive
Willie Charles Richard Easmon	DB	1981–84	NFL 1985–86	Dallas Cowboys, Tampa Bay Buccaneers
Christopher Alan Faulkner	TE	1979–82	NFL 1984–85	Los Angeles Rams, San Diego Chargers
Robin Lynn Fisher	LB	1979–81	USFL 1983–84	Arizona Wranglers, Chicago Blitz
Russell Alvin Gallon	DE	1981–82	USFL 1985	Tampa Bay Bandits
Cecil Timothy Groves	S	1978–79	USFL 1983	Tampa Bay Bandits, Memphis Showboats
Roy Elliott Harris	DE/DT	1981–83	NFL 1984–85, 1987	Atlanta Falcons, Tampa Bay Buccaneers
Robert Todd Hewko	QB	1980–82	NFL 1983	Tampa Bay Buccaneers

NAME	POSITION	COLLEGE	PRO	TEAMS
Eric Neal Hodges	WR	1985–86	NFL 1987	Kansas City Chiefs
John Stephen Hunt	T/G	1981–83	NFL 1984, 1987	Dallas Cowboys, Tampa Bay Buccaneers
Fernando C. Jackson	LB	1980–82	USFL 1984	Jacksonville Bulls
Spencer Jackson	WR	1979–82	USFL 1984–85; CFL 1985	Tampa Bay Bandits, Calgary Stampeders
Alonzo Johnson	LB	1981, 1983–85	NFL 1986–87	Philadelphia Eagles
Mark Curtis Korff	LB	1983–84	NFL 1987; CFL 1988	San Francisco 49ers, Ottawa Rough Riders
Frederick Milton McCallister	LB	1980–83	USFL 1984–85; NFL 1987	Tampa Bay Bandits, Orlando Renegades, Tampa Bay Buccaneers
Juan DeVito McKeever	DB	1980–83	USFL 1984; NFL 1986–87	Michigan Panthers, Tampa Bay Buccaneers
Leon Patrick Miller	LB	1982–85	NFL 1987–88	San Diego Chargers
Frankie Leon Neal	WR	1983–85	NFL 1987	Green Bay Packers
Leon Tyrone Pennington	LB	1982–85	NFL 1987	Tampa Bay Buccaneers
Willis L. Snead III	WR	1987–88	CFL 1989; WLAF 1991	Toronto Argonauts, Montreal Machine
Anthony R. Stephens	WR	1976–78	USFL 1983	Tampa Bay Bandits
Donald L. Swafford	OT	1976–78	CFL 1980–83	Saskatchewan Roughriders, BC Lions
Ronald John Tilton	G	1981–82	NFL 1986	Washington Redskins
Bruce Allen Vaughan	CB	1980–83	USFL 1984–85	Tampa Bay Bandits
Rhondy Weston	DE	1985–88	NFL 1989	Tampa Bay Buccaneers
Tyrone Donnive Young	WR	1979–82	NFL 1983–84	New Orleans Saints

Pro Career Started in the 1990s

NAME	POSITION	COLLEGE	PRO	TEAMS
Tremayne Allen	TE	1995–96	NFL 1997–98; NFLE 2000; WFL 2001	Chicago Bears, Scottish Claymores, Los Angeles Xtreme
Ephesians Alexander Bartley Jr.	LB	1988–91	NFL 1992; CFL1995	Philadelphia Eagles, San Antonio Texans
Michael Breon Brandon	DE	1989–91	NFL 1993–94, 1995–96; CFL1995	Indianapolis Colts, Arizona Cardinals, Scottish Claymores, San Francisco 49ers
Mark Anthony Campbell	DT	1992–95	NFL 1997	Arizona Cardinals
Damon Jamal Collins	G/T	1995–97	NFL 1998–2003	Oakland Raiders

NAME	POSITION	COLLEGE	PRO	TEAMS
Dexter Lavista Daniels	LB	1992–95	NFL 1996	Baltimore Ravens
Terry Dean	QB	1991–94	CFL 1995; ArFL 1996; NFLE 1996	Winnipeg Blue Bombers, Florida Bobcats, Rhein Fire
Randall Shayne Edge	P	1991–94	NFL 1996; WLAF 1996	Pittsburgh Steelers, Barcelona Dragons
Tre Everett	WR	1990–92	CFL 1994	Sacramento Gold Miners, San Antonio Texans
Richard Alexander Fain	DB	1987–90	NFL 1991–92	Phoenix Cardinals, Cincinnati Bengals, Chicago Bears
Houston Antonio George Jr.	DB	1995–98	NFL 1999–2000; NFLE 2001	New England Patriots, Frankfurt Galaxy
Monty Roy Grow	DB	1989–90, 1992–93	NFL 1994–95	Kansas City Chiefs, Jacksonville Jaguars
Benjamin Ujean Hanks	LB	1992–95	NFL 1996–97; NFLE 1999; XFL 2001	Minnesota Vikings, Detroit Lions, Rhein Fire, NY/NJ Hitmen
Elliott Cornelius Jackson Jr.	WR	1992–94	NFL 1995–96; CFL 1997; ArFL 1999–2000	Chicago Bears, Toronto Argonauts, Orlando Predators, Carolina Cobras, Florida Bobcats
Eric Joel Kresser	QB	1993–95	NFL 1998; NFLE 2000; CFL 2002	Cincinnati Bengals, Berlin Thunder, Montreal Alouettes
Thomas Jerome Lomack	WR	1986–89	NFL 1990–91	Los Angeles Rams, Phoenix Cardinals
Anthone Vouchan Lott	DB	1993–96	NFL 1997	Cincinnati Bengals
Henry James McMillian	DT	1992–94	NFL 1995–96	Seattle Seahawks
Michael Edward Moten	DT	1995–97	NFL 1998	Arizona Cardinals
Mark Allen Murray	LB	1987–90	NFL 1991	Denver Broncos
Huey L. Richardson Jr.	LB/DE	1987–90	NFL 1991–92	Pittsburgh Steelers, Washington Redskins, New York Jets
Edward Robinson III	LB	1990–93	NFL 1994; WLAF 1996	Pittsburgh Steelers, Frankfurt Galaxy
Stacey Andrew Simmons	WR	1986–88	NFL 1990; ArFL 1995	Indianapolis Colts, Tampa Bay Storm
Delfonico Arnese Speer	DB	1989–92	NFL 1993–94	Cleveland Browns, Seattle Seahawks
William D. White	DB	1989–92	CFL 1995	Shreveport Pirates
Lawrence D. Wright III	DB	1993–96	NFL 1997, 1999	Cincinnati Bengals

Pro Career Started in the 2000s

NAME	POSITION	COLLEGE	PRO	TEAMS
Dallas Baker	WR	2003–06	NFL 2008; 2010; ArFL 2010; CFL 2011	Pittsburgh Steelers, Jacksonville Sharks, Montreal Alouettes, Saskatchewan Roughriders

NAME	POSITION	COLLEGE	PRO	TEAMS
Tim Beauchamp	DE	1995–97	CFL 2001	Hamilton Tiger-Cats
Brock Sterling Berlin	QB	2000–01	NFL 2007–08	St. Louis Rams
Travis C. Carroll	LB	2000–01	NFL 2002–03; NFLE 2005	New Orleans Saints, Houston Texans, Amsterdam Admirals, Rhein Fire
Arandic Kornell Carthon	RB	2000–03	NFL 2005–06	Indianapolis Colts
Joe Cohen	DT	2003–06	NFL 2009; CFL 2012	Detroit Lions, Toronto Argonauts
Ciatrick Antione Fason	RB	2002–04	NFL 2005–06	Minnesota Vikings
Robert Nolan Gillespie	RB	1998–2001	NFL 2002–03; NFLE 2003	Washington Redskins, Frankfurt Galaxy, Jacksonville Jaguars
Sheddrick Tobias Gurley	DT	1997–2000	NFL 2002; NFLE 2003; ArFL 2004–07	Tampa Bay Buccaneers, Frankfurt Galaxy, Orlando Predators, Tampa Bay Storm, Grand Rapids Rampage
Steven Harris	DT	2003–06	NFL 2007	Denver Broncos
Kelvin Jerome Kight	WR	2000–03	NFL 2004, 2006; NFLE 2005	Green Bay Packers, Frankfurt Galaxy, New England Patriots
Tron LaFavor	DT	1999–2002	NFL 2003–04	Chicago Bears, Dallas Cowboys
Christopher Patrick Leak	QB	2003–06	CFL 2008–10; ArFL 2012	Hamilton Tiger-Cats, Montreal Alouettes, Jacksonville Sharks, Orlando Predators
Henry Ingle Martin IV	QB	2002–03	NFL 2006; UFL 2009	Green Bay Packers, New York Sentinels
Eugene William McCaslin Jr.	LB	1996–99	NFL 2000	Green Bay Packers
Carlton Kabaka Medder	G	2005–07	UFL 2009; CFL 2010–11	New York Sentinels, Winnipeg Blue Bombers
Michael Dondril Nattiel	LB	1999–2002	NFL 2003–04	Minnesota Vikings
Jesse Palmer	QB	1997–2000	NFL 2002–03	New York Giants
Guss T'Mar Scott	DB	2000–03	NFL 2004–06	New England Patriots, Houston Texans
Ozell Jermaine Small	WR	2001–04	NFL 2005; NFLE 2006	Tennessee Titans, Amsterdam Admirals
Phillip Charles Trautwein	T	2004–06, 2008	NFL 2009–12; UFL 2011–12	St. Louis Rams, Las Vegas Locomotives
Tavares Washington	G/T	2005	NFLE 2007; NFL 2008; UFL 2009–10	Rhein Fire, Kansas City Chiefs, Las Vegas Locomotives
Demetrice A. Webb	DB	2003–05	NFL 2006–07; ArFL 2008, 2010; CFL 2009, 2011–13	Jacksonville Jaguars, Philadelphia Soul, Calgary Stampeders, Jacksonville Sharks, Toronto Argonauts, Hamilton Tiger-Cats

Football 187

Pro Career Started in the 2010s

NAME	POSITION	COLLEGE	PRO	TEAMS
Jonathan Bostic	LB	2009–13	NFL 2013	Chicago Bears
Jermaine Alexander Alfred Cunningham	LB	2006–09	NFL 2010–13	New England Patriots, New York Jets
Jeffrey Demps	RB	2008–13	NFL 2013	Tampa Bay Buccaneers
Dustin Doe	LB	2006–09	CFL 2011–12	Winnipeg Blue Bombers
Carlos Dunlap	DE	2007–09	NFL 2010–13	Cincinnati Bengals
Matt Elam	S	2010–13	NFL 2013	Baltimore Ravens
Josh Evans	S	2009–12	NFL 2013	Jacksonville Jaguars
Sharrif Floyd	DT	2010–12	NFL 2013	Minnesota Vikings
Marcus Christopher Gilbert	OL	2007–10	NFL 2011–13	Pittsburgh Steelers
Mike Gillislee	RB	2009–12	NFL 2013	Miami Dolphins
Joseph Walter Haden III	DB	2007–09	NFL 2010–13	Cleveland Browns
Chas Henry	P	2007–10	NFL 2011–12	Philadelphia Eagles, Tampa Bay Buccaneers
Will Hill	DB	2008–10	NFL 2012–13	New York Giants
Jaye Howard	DL	2008–11	NFL 2012–13	Seattle Seahawks, Kansas City Chiefs
Sparrow Maurice Hurt Jr.	OL	2007–10	NFL 2011–12	Washington Redskins
Brandon Keith James	WR	2006–09	NFL 2010; CFL 2011	Indianapolis Colts, Edmonton Eskimos
Janoris Jenkins	DB	2008–10	NFL 2012-13	St. Louis Rams
Jelani Jenkins	LB	2010–12	NFL 2013	Miami Dolphins
William Latsko	RB	2003–04, 2006	NFL 2010; UFL 2011–12	San Diego Chargers, Virginia Destroyers
Drew Miller	C	2004–07	NFL 2011; ArFL 2012; UFL 2012	St. Louis Rams, Orlando Renegades, Omaha Nighthawks
Xavier Nixon	OT	2013	NFL 2013	Indianapolis Colts
Christopher Arthur Rainey	RB/WR	2008–11	NFL 2012	Pittsburgh Steelers
Jordan Reed	TE	2010–12	NFL 2013	Washington Redskins
Caleb Sturgis	K	2008–12	NFL 2013	Miami Dolphins
Deonte Thompson	WR	2008–11	NFL 2012–13	Baltimore Ravens
Justin Trattou	DE	2007–10	NFL 2011, 2013	New York Giants
Eric Wilbur	P/K	2003–06	CFL 2010–12	Hamilton Tiger-Cats, Toronto Argonauts

Two Bits

The foregoing bios and lists of more than 300 Florida alumni who "went pro," the succession of coaches, and a radio announcer who was heard by fans for more than four decades does a complete job of telling the story of Florida football—or does it? There is one more person who needs to be included . . . someone who is more recognizable to generations of football fans and the Gator Nation than anyone else mentioned in this book, but who never played a down with the Gators: George Edmonson, Jr.

The name may not be familiar, but you no doubt know the look: yellow button-down long-sleeved shirt, saddle oxford shoes, (in later years) white and blue striped pants and an orange-and-blue striped tie, and of course, carrying his trademark homemade sign and whistle. Mr. Two Bits!

The story of Mr. Two Bits goes like this: George Edmonson, an insurance salesman from Tampa, was invited by a friend to the 1949 Florida home opener against The Citadel, his alma mater, and the two friends and their wives made their way to the game. The Gators had wrapped up the 1948 season by losing five of their last six games, and expectations for the new season were not good. As soon as the announcer said, "Heeeeeerrrrrrreeeeee come the Gators!" here came the boos from the fans. They booed the players and coaching staff before the game ever began. That did not sit well with George, who recalled in an interview in 2007, "I thought it was terrible." The team might not have been good, but George told his group, "They're just kids out there, they're doing the best they can, we ought to cheer for them. Every time they make a mistake, we're going to stand up and cheer for them." He recruited a few of the fans around them to yell, on the count of three, an old familiar cheer:

Two Bits!
Four Bits!
Six Bits!
A Dollar!
All for the Gators stand up and holler!

His cheer was so well received that he came back and did it again for the next game. It didn't take long before he spent much of each game moving to different sections in the stadium to lead his cheer. Carrying a sign that said, "Two Bits!" and blowing a whistle to get the fans' attention and begin the cheer, he would quickly whip sections of the stadium into excitement, as well as, or sometimes even better, than the "official" cheerleaders on the field. And he was particular about the timing of his cheer: He chose not to lead it when a play was in progress or there was an announcement over the P.A. or when one of the bands played. But when the team was behind and needed a little boost, Mr. Two Bits was ready.

First-time fans at Florida Field might have been surprised when George would blow his whistle, but everyone quickly caught on and enthusiastically joined in the cheer. Even if he was at one end of the field, people throughout the stadium would cheer and stand. After about 50 years of driving from Tampa, wearing the same outfit, and leading the same cheer many times each game, George Edmondson retired from his role as volunteer cheerleader.

Mr. Two Bits revving up the crowd at a game in 1985

However, the retirement didn't stick, and he came back and continued his beloved cheerleading for another decade. George retired a second time, this time permanently, in a ceremony held in 2008, appropriately before a game against The Citadel, the same Gator opponent that launched his unofficial and unexpected cheerleading career for nearly 60 years.

Throughout the years, George missed a total of only three home games. He was made an honorary alumnus and was inducted into the University of Florida Athletic Hall of Fame in 1992. We have included him in this book because of his essential connection with Florida football, despite the fact that he never participated in the Olympics and never performed professionally, even though he could have.

During the 1970s, the owner of the new Tampa Bay Buccaneers, Hugh Culverhouse, approached George and offered to pay him to lead his cheer at Tampa Bay games. Turning down the paycheck, Mr. Two Bits explained that, "What I do for the Gators is from the heart, not from the pocketbook."

The "Two Bits" tradition is not gone, even though Mr. Two Bits has retired. Coach Will Muschamp decided to revive the cheer for home games starting with the 2013 season, with a guest cheerleader appearing on the field before each kickoff. The first was former Gator running back Errict Rhett who, on August 31, 2013, led the fans in an enthusiastic "Two Bits" cheer before the Gators' win over the University of Toledo, wearing the familiar yellow button-down long-sleeved shirt, orange-and-blue striped tie, sign, and whistle.

BASEBALL
SOFTBALL
BASEBALL
SOFTBALL

BASEBALL

Florida Agricultural College baseball team in 1914

Baseball was played at Florida before it became a university. In the days before consolidation of the several schools into one [see pages 23–25], the boys at the Florida Agricultural College in Lake City played the game against other schools, but there were no conferences and no championships.

Even when the Buckman Act created the University of Florida at its present Gainesville campus, there still was not a great push to underwrite intercollegiate sports other than football. It took until 1912 before the school had its first varsity baseball team, and then it still lacked the financial ability to hire a head coach who could focus solely on the sport. The team was often coached by older students or professors who may have played the sport before they graduated, a practice used by other schools in similar situations.

Top 30 All-Time College Teams
(Ranked by wins through 2013)

RECORD	TEAM	WINNING PCT.	SEASONS PLAYED
4,320-2,164-48	Fordham	.665	153
3,303-1,179-31	Texas	.735	117
2,741-1,550-28	Southern California	.638	119
2,727-1,714-35	Stanford	.613	120
2,725-1,595-36	Michigan	.630	140
2,709-1,311-8	Arizona State	.672	102
2,665-983-11	Florida State	.730	66
2,655-1,408-23	Arizona	.653	108
2,641-1,466-30	Clemson	.642	116
2,635-1,543-37	North Carolina	.630	124
2,587-1,621-6	Washington State	.615	118
2,479-1,404-42	Texas A&M	.637	111
2,467-1,412-25	Minnesota	.619	125
2,460-1,438-27	Mississippi State	.630	124
2,459-1,491-23	Alabama	.622	121
2,450-1,847-21	California	.570	122
2,441-1,586-38	Illinois	.605	134
2,434-1,637-35	Harvard	.597	146
2,432-1,431-8	Fresno State	.630	85
2,427-1,228-4	Oklahoma State	.664	102
2,420-1,572-40	Ohio State	.605	130
2,412-1,385-11	Oklahoma	.635	108
2,412-1,445-17	South Carolina	.625	121
2,392-981-18	Miami (Florida)	.708	69
2,358-1,443-21	Notre Dame	.617	121
2,353-1,499-6	LSU	.611	118
2,325-1,923-23	UCLA	.547	94
2,305-1,480-24	**Florida**	.605	99
2,301-1,538-38	San Diego State	.598	81
2,285-2,052-41	Yale	.527	149

(Ranked By Winning Percentage)

WINNING PCT.	TEAM	RECORD	WINNING PCT.	TEAM	RECORD
.735	Texas	3,303-1,179-31	.672	Arizona State	2,709-1,311-8
.730	Florida State	2,665-983-11	.665	Fordham	4,320-2,164-48
.708	Miami (Florida)	2,392-981-18	.664	Oklahoma State	2,427-1,228-4

WINNING PCT.	TEAM	RECORD	WINNING PCT.	TEAM	RECORD
.653	Arizona	2,655-1,408-23	.617	Notre Dame	2,358-1,443-21
.642	Clemson	2,641-1,466-30	.615	Washington State	2,587-1,621-6
.638	Southern California	2,741-1,550-28	.613	Stanford	2,727-1,714-35
.637	Texas A&M	2,479-1,404-42	.611	LSU	2,353-1,499-6
.635	Oklahoma	2,412-1,385-11	.605	Florida	2,306-1,479-24
.630	Mississippi State	2,460-1,438-27	.605	Illinois	2,441-1,586-38
.630	Michigan	2,725-1,595-36	.605	Ohio State	2,420-1,572-40
.630	North Carolina	2,635-1,543-37	.598	San Diego State	2,301-1,538-38
.630	Fresno State	2,432-1,431-8	.597	Harvard	2,434-1,637-35
.625	South Carolina	2,412-1,445-17	.547	UCLA	2,325-1,923-23
.622	Alabama	2,459-1,491-23	.567	California	2,450-1,847-21
.619	Minnesota	2,467-1,512-25	.527	Yale	2,285-2,052-41

2013 Division I College Baseball Home Attendance Leaders

Team	Conference	Average Per Game Attendance	Total Season
LSU	SEC	11,006	473,298
Arkansas	SEC	8,335	250,055
Mississippi	SEC	7,996	239,909
Mississippi State	SEC	7,617	281,840
South Carolina	SEC	7,445	260,605
Texas	Big 12	5,793	185,400
Clemson	ACC	4,751	147,296
Florida State	ACC	4,594	183,770
Texas A&M	SEC	4,523	149,263
Creighton	Big East	4,041	88,916
TCU	Big 12	3,570	107,117
Florida	SEC	3,511	126,421
Hawaii	Mountain West	3,357	97,355
Rice	Conference USA	3,287	92,043
Alabama	SEC	3,262	101,137
Southern Mississippi	Conference USA	3,147	91,286
Virginia	ACC	3,012	102,410
Arizona	Pac-12	2,691	94,197
Miami (Fla.)	ACC	2,635	97,515
Vanderbilt	SEC	2,563	89,733

Southeastern Conference Championships
(Through 2013, Regular Season)

16 LSU	6 Mississippi	2 Arkansas
14 Alabama	5 Auburn	1 Georgia Tech
12 **Florida**	5 Vanderbilt	1 Kentucky
7 Mississippi State	4 South Carolina	0 Missouri
6 Georgia	3 Tennessee	0 Texas A&M

(Through 2013, Conference Tournament)

10 LSU	3 Tennessee	0 Auburn
7 Alabama	2 Mississippi	0 Kentucky
7 Mississippi State	2 Vanderbilt	0 Missouri
6 **Florida**	1 South Carolina	0 Texas A&M
3 Auburn	0 Arkansas	

The Early Coaches

In 1912, under first official head coach H.D. McLeod, the team posted a 9-4-2 record while playing the Jacksonville Olympics, Stetson University, Rollins College, and Southern College. During the following year, under coach R.P. Hoffman, they reached out geographically to play teams outside of Florida, beginning with Mercer University, Auburn University, and Suwannee.

After having five coaches in the previous eight seasons (and suspending play for 1918), William G. Kline took over the leadership of the team in 1921. He had previously served as the athletic director for Nebraska Wesleyan University (1911–18), then took over as the head coach at the University of Nebraska (1918). Starting in 1919, he taught at the University of Florida Law School, and he coached football (1920–22), baseball (1921), and basketball (1920–22), while also serving as athletic director, a fine example of multitasking. After 1923, he went back to coaching at Nebraska and wrote books on how to coach sports.

The Gators' first student to be recognized as a professional athlete in any major league was Lance Richbourg, who returned to Gainesville after a year with the Philadelphia Phillies to coach the UF baseball team in 1922–23. After playing for the Washington Senators for a year, he again coached the Gators in 1926; he left for good to play for the Boston Braves and Chicago Cubs. While in Gainesville, his teams compiled a good 39-21 record, which included wins against the Key West Town Team, the Pensacola Aviators, and soldiers at Camp Benning.

Coach Farrior and his 1924 Gators

When Richbourg left the first time, the team was next coached by Rex Farrior, a Florida alumnus who had played football (1913–16) and baseball (1915–17) and came back to earn a law degree while he coached the baseball team. For the 1925 season, he was followed by James L. White, who had previously coached at the University of Virginia and Wake Forest University. In addition to coaching the Gators in baseball (1925), basketball (1923–25), and track and field (1924), White was also the athletic director. In those days, Florida got its money's worth from its coaching staff.

Coach Clemons as a student in 1931

The first head coach to remain for more than three years was Brady Cowell (1927–33), who also coached football (1924–32) and basketball (1925–33). In his final year at Gainesville, the Gators played their first season in the Southeastern Conference, managing a conference record of 4-4. After Florida, he moved on to Stetson University, where he coached football and served as athletic director. Ben

Clemons, a star on the baseball, basketball, and football teams around 1930, returned to coach all three, including baseball in 1934–36.

Next was Lew Hardage, who coached in 1937–39 and had his best year in 1938, when the team had a 14-9 overall record and came in second in the SEC with a record of 4-2 against conference opponents. He had previously coached football at Vanderbilt University, the University of Oklahoma, and Furman University, but his only baseball experience was at Florida, where his teams had a 35-24-1 record. Sam McAllister led the team in 1940–42, while he also coached basketball and football.

Florida did not play baseball in 1943–44 because of World War II. When play resumed in 1945, the head coach was Bob Pittman, who had played baseball and basketball for the Gators in the early 1930s. That year, the team suffered through a record of 2-9 while playing against "formidable" opponents—military base teams, one from the state prison, and one called Food Machinery. That was Pittman's only year as coach, as Sam McAllister returned to lead the team once again in 1946–47.

Coach Pittman as a student in 1931

The Dave Fuller Era

Modern UF baseball began in 1948 with the hiring of Dave Fuller, a former three-sport star at Wake Forest University, as the head coach. He compiled a record of 557-354-6 by the time he retired after the 1975 season. Three times (1952, 1956, and 1962), the Gators won the SEC championship, and Fuller was honored by his fellow conference coaches as the SEC Coach of the Year all three times. He took them to the SEC Regional tournament four times.

As did his predecessors, Fuller also coached football at Florida (1948–76), and he remains the assistant coach with the longest career at the university in any sport. Fuller's baseball teams included 47 players named to All-SEC first teams, including Bernie Parrish in 1958 [see page 138], and six of his players went on to play major league baseball.

In addition to being the longest-tenured assistant coach, Fuller holds the Florida record for the most wins in any sport and the longest run as a head coach. He is a member of the University of Florida Athletic Hall of Fame.

The Jay Bergman Era

Following a 28-year coach is never easy, but Jay Bergman managed to make a name for himself in his second season, 1977, by taking the team to the championship of the SEC East and a berth in the NCAA Mideast Regional in Minneapolis. They successfully defended their SEC East title each year through 1981, Bergman's final season at Florida.

Coach Fuller (left) talking with team captain Bobby Barnes in 1958

That year saw the Gators also win the SEC tournament and get into the NCAA South Regional. Bergman left the University of Florida with a record of 216-113, which was the best percentage (.657) of anyone who had coached Gator baseball for more than one season. He moved on to the University of Central Florida, where he continued to coach until 2008.

For 1982 and 1983, the head coach was Jack Rhine, who led the team to a record of 72-39-1. The Gators were SEC East champions both years, and, in 1982, they also won the conference and made it to the NCAA Atlantic Regional, where they were eliminated by losses to the University of South Florida and Stetson University.

The Joe Arnold Era

The next head coach was Joe Arnold, who had previously played in the Houston Astros organization and coached at Florida Southern College. He had led Florida Southern to a pair of Division II national championships, so hopes were high that he could bring a championship to Gainesville.

In his first year of 1984, Arnold took the SEC East champion Gators to the NCAA South I Regional, where they lost to the University of Miami and the University of South Alabama. The next year, they again won the SEC East and had a 3-2 record in the NCAA Atlantic Regional. Following a couple of off years, they came back in 1988 as SEC champions and won the NCAA East Regional in Tallahassee for their first-ever trip to the College World Series

(CWS) in Omaha, Nebraska. There, they lost to Wichita State University, beat the University of California, and lost to Arizona State University.

Arnold coached the team to the NCAA East Regional in 1989 and, in 1991, won the SEC tournament and the NCAA East Regional and returned to the College World Series. The Gators beat Florida State University and Fresno State University, but they lost twice to LSU. They again went to the East Regional in 1992 and the Atlantic Regional in 1994, Arnold's final year at UF, but failed to advance to the CWS. Arnold went on to coach minor league teams in the New York Yankee organization, then Polk State College in Winter Haven.

The Andy Lopez Era

The Gators went to the west coast to find their next coach. Andy Lopez had previously coached at a pair of universities in California and, in 1992, led Pepperdine University to its only national championship in the school's history. The Gators brought him to Florida in 1995, and he guided the Gators to a 32-24 record, but only 12-14 in the SEC. The next year was much better, with a conference championship and a trip to the NCAA East Regional. There, the team went 4-0 and clinched its third trip to the College World Series.

Coach Lopez in 2012 with the University of Arizona

They beat Florida State University twice, but two losses to LSU kept them from their first national championship in the sport.

In 1997, they again won the SEC East and made it to the NCAA Atlantic Regional, but they were eliminated by losses to Arizona State University and the University of Miami. They went further in 1998, winning the SEC and the NCAA South I Regional, but at the College World Series they lost their first two games, to Mississippi State University and to the University of Southern California.

After a year without a tournament, the Gators went to the NCAA Waco Regional in 2000. They posted a record of 3-2, with both losses coming at the hands of San Jose State University. In the NCAA Coral Gables Regional in 2001, they defeated Stetson University, then lost to the University of Miami and the rematch with Stetson.

Lopez, who had been named SEC Coach of the Year in 1996, left after the 2001 season. He is the head coach at the University of Arizona and, in 2012, was named the Pac-12 Coach of the Year and the *Collegiate Baseball* and American Baseball Coaches Association National Coach of the Year after leading the Wildcats to a national championship.

The Pat McMahon Era

Again the Gators searched for a new baseball leader, but this time they didn't go as far. Long-time baseball coach Pat McMahon, whose most recent job had been as head coach at Mississippi State University, took over as the head coach of the Gators in 2002. That year, a respectable record of 46-19 got them to the NCAA Gainesville Regional, but they were eliminated by two losses to the University of Miami. The following year also ended with a loss to Miami in the NCAA Coral Gables Regional. McMahon took them to the NCAA Oklahoma City Regional in 2004, where they won all three games. However, they were stopped at the Coral Gables Super Regional when they dropped both of their games to the University of Miami.

In 2005, it appeared that a national championship might be on the horizon. The Gators had a record of 48-23 and won the SEC East and the conference regular season, then went to the NCAA Gainesville Regional and beat Stetson University, the University of North Carolina, and Notre Dame. At the Super Regional, also in Gainesville, they beat Florida State University to advance to the College World Series. There, they went 3-1 in their first four games (including a finals-clinching 6–3 victory over the University of Arizona, led by former UF head coach Andy Lopez). That was the first time Florida had made it to the finals of the CWS, and the Gators played the University of Texas in a best-two-out-of-three series to determine the winner. Unfortunately, Texas won both, by scores of 4–2 and 6–2, but McMahon was named the SEC Coach of the Year and the 2005 College Baseball Foundation National Coach of the Year.

The 2006 and 2007 seasons, with records of 28-28 and 29-30, were unacceptable, so McMahon was fired on June 7, 2007. He went on to coach minor league affiliates of the New York Yankees.

Kevin O'Sullivan Era

The next head coach had been an assistant coach at Clemson University. Kevin O'Sullivan came to Florida in 2008 and in his first head coaching position, has done very well. The Gators came in second in the SEC East during his first year in charge but went winless in the conference tournament and the NCAA Tallahassee Regional.

The next year was an improvement, as the Gators won the SEC East and the NCAA Gainesville Regional, including a pair of victories over the University of Miami. At the Super Regional, however, they lost both games to the University of Southern Mississippi.

They kept improving under O'Sullivan with a 47-17 record in 2010, and they won both the SEC East and the conference. They went 3-0 in the NCAA Gainesville Regional, beat the University of Miami twice to win the Gainesville Super Regional, and were once again in the College World Series. They played two games, to UCLA and Florida State University, but lost them both.

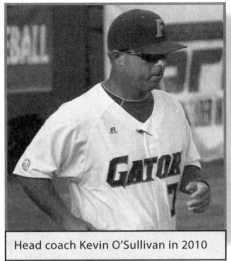

Head coach Kevin O'Sullivan in 2010

Still improving, Florida set a school record for victories in 2011 with 53 (against 19 losses) and tied for first in the SEC East. They won the conference regular season and tournament, then went 3-0 in the NCAA Gainesville Regional. At the Super Regional, also held in Gainesville, they had to play Mississippi State University three times. They beat them twice, earning a trip to the CWS. There, they defeated the University of Texas and Vanderbilt University (twice) to reach the finals for the second time under O'Sullivan. However, they lost to the University of South Carolina 2–1 in an 11-inning game and again 5–2 to finish as runner-up for the second time in school history.

Although the 2012 team did not win the conference or its division, it played in the NCAA Gainesville Regional and beat Bethune-Cookman University and Georgia Tech (twice), then moved on to the Super Regional and posted two victories over North Carolina State University. Once again in the College World Series, the Gators lost both of their games, to the University of South Carolina and Kent State University.

In 2013, the Gators had a record of 29-30, including a loss to Texas A&M University in the single-elimination SEC tournament and losses to Austin Peay State University and Valparaiso University in the double-elimination NCAA Bloomington Regional.

Head Coaching Records

YEARS	NAME	SEASONS	RECORD	WINNING PCT.
\multicolumn{5}{l}{Championships (E=East, S=Season, T=Tournament, R=Regional, SR= Super Regional)}				
1912	H.D. McLeod	1	9-4-2	.667
1913	R.P. Hoffman	1	11-9-1	.548
1914–16	Pat Flaherty	3	15-29-1	.344
1917	Hugh Wicher	1	8-3-0	.727
1919–20	Artie Phelan	2	14-16-1	.468
1921	William Kline	1	4-10-0	.286
1922–23, 26	Lance Richbourg	3	39-21-0	.650
1924	Rex Farrior	1	5-14-0	.263
1925	James White	1	3-6-0	.333
1927–33	Brady Cowell	7	61-65-2	.484
1934–36	Ben Clemons	3	20-29-1	.410
1937–39	Lew Hardage	3	35-24-1	.591
1940–42, 46–47	Sam McAllister	5	40-56-4	.420
1945	Bob Pittman	1	2-9-0	.182
1948–75 SEC(S) 1952, 1956, 1962; SEC(E) 1960, 1962, 1968, 1969	Dave Fuller	28	557-354-6	.611
1976–81 SEC(S) 1981; SEC(T) 1981; SEC(E) 1977, 1978, 1979, 1980	Jay Bergman	6	216-113-0	.656
1982–83 SEC(S) 1982; SEC(T) 1982; SEC(E) 1982, 1983	Jack Rhine	2	72-39-1	.647
1984–94 NCAA(R) 1988, 1991; SEC(S) 1984, 1988; SEC(T) 1984, 1988, 1991; SEC(E) 1984, 1985	Joe Arnold	11	434-244-2	.640
1995–2001 NCAA(R) 1996, 1998; SEC(S) 1996, 1998; SEC(E) 1996, 1997, 1998	Andy Lopez	7	278-159-1	.636
2002–07 NCAA(R) 2004, 2005; NCAA(SR) 2005; SEC(S) 2005; SEC(E) 2005	Pat McMahon	6	231-143-1	.617
2008–13 NCAA(R) 2009, 2010, 2011, 2012; NCAA(SR) 2010, 2011, 2012; SEC(S) 2010, 2011; SEC(T) 2011; SEC(E) 2009, 2010, 2011	Kevin O'Sullivan	6	252-132-0	.656
Total		99	2306-1479-24	.609

Major League Players by School
(Top 25 Colleges through 2013)

107	Southern California	68	LSU	56	**Florida**
102	Arizona State	64	Oklahoma	56	Fordham
102	Texas	63	Alabama	56	Santa Clara
86	Stanford	62	Florida State	53	Pennsylvania
77	Michigan	61	Oklahoma State	53	Texas A&M
76	Holy Cross	60	Notre Dame	52	Cal State Fullerton
72	Illinois	58	St. Mary's of California	52	Ohio State
72	UCLA	58	California		
70	Arizona	57	North Carolina		

(Southeastern Conference through 2013)

68	LSU	45	Mississippi State	39	Missouri
63	Alabama	45	South Carolina	36	Georgia
58	**Florida**	43	Arkansas	29	Kentucky
53	Texas A&M	42	Tennessee	27	Vanderbilt
46	Auburn	40	Mississippi		

Our Florida All-Stars: Baseball
(Based on their pro careers)

CATCHER:	Mike Stanley
FIRST BASEMAN:	Matt LaPorta
SECOND BASEMAN:	Robby Thompson
SHORTSTOP:	David Eckstein
THIRD BASEMAN:	Al Rosen
LEFT FIELDER:	Ryan Raburn
CENTER FIELDER:	Brad Wilkerson
RIGHT FIELDER:	Lance Richbourg
STARTING PITCHER:	Josh Fogg
RELIEF PITCHER:	Doug Corbett
BEST OVERALL:	Al Rosen

Athlete Bios

College years are those during which the athlete was awarded a letter for baseball. Pro years are those for which the athlete was active for at least one game.

Pro years are years actually played through 2013.

Statistics are pro career totals through the 2013 season:

PITCHERS: *win-loss record/earned run average/saves*

NONPITCHERS: *batting average/on-base percentage/slugging percentage*

ROSS BAUMGARTEN (1955–) ■ MLB: 1978–82 ■ *Pitcher*

COLLEGE: 1977   6-1, 180 lbs.   22-36 / 4.00 / 0

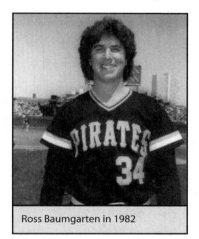

Ross Baumgarten in 1982

Ross Baumgarten attended New Trier High School in Winnetka, Illinois, before coming to Florida to pitch in the 1977 baseball season.

He was drafted in the 20th round that same year by the Chicago White Sox, and he played in his first major league game for them the following year, after setting an ERA of 1.82 at minor league Appleton. Baumgarten was fourth in the balloting for the American League Rookie of the Year for 1979, but, just before the 1982 season, Chicago traded him to the Pittsburgh Pirates, where he pitched in a dozen games and had a record of 0-5. He was released before the 1983 season and never made it back to the majors.

Today, Baumgarten is a financial advisor and first vice president at RBC Wealth Management in Chicago. He also coaches baseball at his alma mater, New Trier High School.

RODNEY LEE BREWER (1966–)
■ MLB: 1990–93 ■ *First Baseman, Pinch Hitter, Outfielder*

COLLEGE: 1985–87   6-3, 210 lbs.   .278 / .336 / .351

After playing for Apopka High School in Apopka, Florida, Rod Brewer was drafted in 1984 in the 25th round by the Toronto Blue Jays, but he chose not to sign with them. Instead, he joined the Gators for three seasons.

Brewer was drafted in the fifth round in 1987 by the St. Louis Cardinals, and he stayed in their organization for four major league seasons. He spent time in the minors with Rookie League Johnson City and Single-A Springfield starting in 1997. He also played for Double-A Arkansas and Triple-A Louisville.

His major league debut was September 5, 1990, and he played in a total of 14 games that year, hitting for a .240 average. The following year, Brewer played in 19 games and his average dropped to 0.077, but, in 1992, he brought it up to .301. He played the majority of his games (110) in his final season of 1993.

Brewer left the country to play in Japan, but he returned in 1995 at the Triple-A level for teams in the Marlins and Giants organizations. In 1996, he played for an independent minor league team in Abilene and began the 1997 season with the Triple-A Buffalo Indians. After they released him, he signed on with Amarillo, where he hit .320. Brewer ended his baseball playing career in the Mexican League in 2000 and 2001.

JOHN CHANDLER BURKE (1970–) ■ MLB: 1996–97 ■ *Pitcher*
COLLEGE: 1990–92   6-4, 220 lbs.   4-6 / 6.75 / 0

John Burke came from Cherry Creek High School in Englewood, Colorado. He had been drafted in the 34th round in 1989 by the Baltimore Orioles, and in the first round in 1991 by the Houston Astros (who offered him a $350,000 signing bonus), but declined to sign with either team. He instead played three seasons for the Gators and broke the Florida records for most career strikeouts and the highest career per-inning strikeout average. In 1991, he threw a no-hitter against Furman University. Burke played in the College World Series in 1991 and, in 1992, was named by *Baseball America* to its All-American first team.

The right-hander was drafted in the first round in 1992 by the Colorado Rockies and eventually played for them for two years. Before that, he spent time in the minors with Single-A-Advanced Central Valley and Triple-A Colorado Springs. The managers in the Pacific Coast League voted Burke the pitcher with the best breaking pitch and the best prospect for the major leagues.

His first game in the major leagues was on August 13, 1996. He pitched in a total of 11 games that year and 17 the next year, then was out of the major leagues. In 2000, Burke went back to the university and completed his bachelor's degree in anthropology.

JOHN HENDERSON BURNETT (1904–59) ■ MLB: 1927–35 ■ *Shortstop, Third Baseman, Second Baseman*
COLLEGE: 1926   5-11, 175 lbs.   .284 / .345 / .366

Johnny Burnett was born in Bartow, Florida, and played for one season at the University of Florida.

After graduating from Florida, Burnett signed with the Cleveland Indians and made his major league debut on May 7, 1927. He played for eight years with the Indians, and, in 1932, he set a major league record, which still stands, by making nine hits in a game. The game went on for 18 innings and Burnett got up to the plate 11 times against the Philadelphia Athletics. With the two hits he had the game before, he

Johnny Burnett in the 1930s

set an American League record of 11 hits over two consecutive games. That game also set the current record for most hits by a team (Cleveland Indians, 33) and most by both teams (58).

After the 1934 season, Burnett was traded to the St. Louis Browns, where he played 70 games in his final major league season and hit .223. He was traded to the Cincinnati Reds just before the 1936 season, but he saw no more major league playing time. Burnett died on August 12, 1959, in Tampa, Florida, from acute leukemia.

JAMES BAILEY CHAPLIN (1905–39)
■ MLB: 1928, 1930–31, 1936 ■ *Pitcher*

COLLEGE: 1925–27   6-1, 195 lbs.   15-23 / 4.25 / 4

James "Tiny" Chaplin was born in Los Angeles and attended high school in Miami. He played football and baseball for three years at the University of Florida, then signed with the New York Giants. He was assigned to minor league teams in Williamsport and Jersey City in 1927 and made his major league debut on April 13, 1928.

In 1929, Chaplin played for minor league Springfield and San Antonio, then went back to the Giants in 1930–31 and had a record of 5-8. Then it was back to the minors for several years.

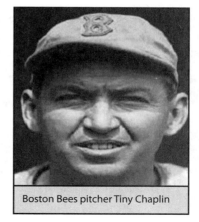

Boston Bees pitcher Tiny Chaplin

His next major league play was in 1936, when he appeared in 40 games for the Boston Bees, who had purchased his contract from the Giants in January of that year. After the season, he was traded to the San Diego Padres of the minor league Pacific Coast League. On March 25, 1939, during spring training, Chaplin died in an auto accident in National City, California, when the car in which he was a passenger hit another while swerving to avoid a machine parked in the road.

KEVIN ALLEN CHAPMAN (1988–) ■ MLB: 2013–14 ■ *Pitcher*

COLLEGE: 2007–10   6-3, 225 lbs.   1-1 / 1.77 / 1

While Kevin Chapman was a student in 2006 at Westminster Academy in Fort Lauderdale, he was drafted in the 42nd round by the Detroit Tigers, but he opted not to sign a contract with them and attended the University of Florida. He was again drafted, this time in 2009 when the Chicago White Sox picked him in the 50th round, and again he chose the Gators over professional baseball.

The third time Chapman was drafted, in 2010's fourth round, he signed with the Kansas City Royals and was assigned to the minor league Wilmington Blue Rocks and Northwest Arkansas Naturals. However, he was traded to the Houston Astros before seeing any major league action. In the Astros' farm system, he pitched for the Corpus Christi Hooks and Oklahoma City RedHawks. On August 8, 2013, he was called up to the majors and played in his first game as an Astro. He appeared in 25 games in 2013, pitching 20 1/3 innings.

DOUGLAS MITCHELL CORBETT (1952–)
■ **MLB: 1980–87** ■ *Pitcher*

COLLEGE: 1971–74   6-1, 185 lbs.   24-30 / 3.32 / 66

After pitching for Sarasota High School, Doug Corbett came to the University of Florida in 1971. In 1974, he was honored as a member of the All-Southeastern Conference team and received his bachelor's degree in exercise and sport science. He became a member of the University of Florida Athletic Hall of Fame in 1996.

Undrafted, Corbett was signed as a free agent in 1974 by the Kansas City Royals. He played with the minor league GCL Royals and was released in 1975. He signed with the Cincinnati Reds and played two seasons with the Tampa club in the Florida State League, then with Trois-Rivieres, Nashville, and Indianapolis. In December 1979, the Minnesota Twins got him from the Reds in a Rule 5 draft, and he made his major league debut for the Twins on April 10, 1980, and pitched for them for a little more than two years, posting a record of 10-14. During his rookie year, Corbett saved 23 games and finished third in the Rookie of the Year balloting. In 1981, he was a member of the American League all-star team and led the league in the number of games finished (45).

Corbett was traded to the California Angels early in the 1982 season, and he pitched in 165 games for that team through 1986, also spending time with Spokane and Edmonton of the Pacific Coast League. He was released by the Angels during the 1987 season and signed with the Baltimore Orioles. In his final season of 1987, he played in 11 games for the Orioles and had a record of 0-2. Baltimore released Corbett in August 1987.

DAVID MARK ECKSTEIN (1975–)   ■ **MLB: 2001-10**
■ *Shortstop, Second Baseman*

COLLEGE: 1994–97   5-6, 170 lbs.   .280 / .345 / .355

David Eckstein played for Seminole High School in Sanford, Florida, before coming to the University of Florida as a walk-on. He became a member of the University of Florida Athletic Hall of Fame in 2007.

David Eckstein at spring training with the San Diego Padres in 2009

The Boston Red Sox drafted Eckstein in the 19th round in 1997, and he played for several minor league teams, including the Harrisonburg Turks of the Valley Baseball League and the Trenton Thunder. He was waived by the Red Sox in August 2000 and was picked up by the Anaheim Angels, making his major league debut on April 3, 2001. In his second season, Eckstein played in the World Series, batting .310 in the Angels' victory in seven games over the San Francisco Giants. That same season, he led the major leagues with three grand slam home runs.

While he was with the Angels, Eckstein led the American League in sacrifice hits (2001 and 2002) and number of times hit by pitches (2001 and 2002). His fielding percentage was the best in the American League for 2004, and he was a fan favorite known for his grit and determination. That was his last season with the Angels, and he then became a free agent and signed with the St. Louis Cardinals.

Eckstein played 2005–07 for the Cardinals, all at shortstop, and made the National League All-Star team in 2005 and 2006. During the 2006 World Series, he hit for an average of .364 and was named the MVP. He moved to the Toronto Blue Jays for the 2008 season, where he played shortstop, second base, and occasionally designated hitter. At the end of August, he was traded to the Arizona Diamondbacks and played 18 games, then to the San Diego Padres and played through the end of the 2010 season, all at second base.

After that, Eckstein took some time to consider his options, and there was speculation as to whether or not he had officially retired from baseball. One of his postplaying activities was making public appearances at professional wrestling events. He remained open to the possibility of signing with a team who would appreciate him, but he never played with another team, He chose instead to work with his wife, Ashley Eckstein, and was part of the staff to help select players for the 2013 USA 18U National Team. Eckstein also represented the Angels during the 2013 Major League Baseball first-year player draft.

DAVID WILLIAM EILAND (1966–)
■ **MLB:** 1988–93, 1995, 1998–2000 ■ *Pitcher*

COLLEGE: 1985   6-3, 210 lbs.   12-27 / 5.74 / 0

Dave Eiland pitched for the University of Florida for the 1985 season, then transferred to the University of South Florida for the rest of his college career.

He was drafted in 1987 by the New York Yankees, and in 1988 played in his first major league game. In 1990, while playing for the Triple-A Columbus Clippers, he was named the International League's Pitcher of the Year. Eiland remained with the Yankees through 1991 and had a record of 6-10, then was released and signed as a free agent with the San Diego Padres. After two seasons and a record of 0-5, he moved to the Cleveland Indians but was traded to the Texas Rangers before appearing in an Indians game.

Kansas City Royals coach Dave Eiland in 2012

The Rangers didn't play him, either, and Eiland left in early 1994 to spend a season with the Yankees. He then went to the St. Louis Cardinals and back to the Yankees (again not playing for either) before he settled in with the Tampa Bay Devil Rays, where he played from 1998–2000 and posted a record of 6-12. After the 2000 season, Eiland signed as a free agent with the Oakland Athletics, but he didn't play another major league game. He has the distinction of being the only major leaguer to both hit a home run in his first at-bat and give up a home run to the first batter he faced as a pitcher.

In addition to his playing career, Eiland had a brief movie career. In 1999's *For the Love of the Game*, he played the body double for Kevin Costner. He served as a minor league pitching coach in the Yankee organization, for the Gulf Coast Yankees (2003), Staten Island Yankees (2004), Trenton Thunder (2005–06), and Scranton/Wilkes-Barre Yankees (2007). In 2008, he was promoted to pitching coach for the New York Yankees and served until 2010. Eiland became an advisor for the Tampa Bay Rays after the 2010 season and, starting after the 2011 season, has been the pitching coach for the Kansas City Royals.

MARK WILLIAM ELLIS (1977–)
■ **MLB: 2002–03, 2005–14** ■ *Second Baseman*

COLLEGE: 1996–99   5-10, 190 lbs.   .265 / .330 / .390

After graduating from Stevens High School in Rapid City, South Dakota, and being named the South Dakota American League Player of the Year in 1994 and 1995, Mark Ellis headed south to play for the Gators. In 1998, in the Gainesville regional leading up to the College World Series, Ellis was named the tournament MVP. Although he was a second baseman as a professional, he played third base for the Gators, which became known as Ellis Island.

He was drafted in the ninth round of the 1999 draft by the Kansas City Royals and was assigned to minor league teams, where he was honored as a Short-Season A All-Star in 1999 and a Carolina League All-Star in 2000. The Royals traded him to the Oakland Athletics in January 2001, and Ellis was assigned to the Triple-A Sacramento River Cats.

He made his major league debut for Oakland in 2002 and played 98 games that year. Ellis remained with Oakland into the 2011 season, despite missing all of 2004 due to a shoulder injury, as well as most of the post-season play in 2006 with an injured hand. As an Athletic, Ellis played a total of 12 games in the playoffs, in 2002, 2003, and 2006. He led Oakland in batting average (.316) for 2005, and, in 2006, he had the best fielding average of all time for second basemen in the American League.

At the end of June 2011, the Athletics traded him to the Colorado Rockies, and he played there through the end of the season. As a free agent, he signed with the Los Angeles Dodgers in November 2011 and played 110 games for them in 2012. Ellis remained the Dodgers' second baseman for 2013 and established himself as a solid defensive player.

Mark Ellis of the Dodgers in 2013

As a free agent, he signed with the St. Louis Cardinals in December 2013. Ellis got into 12 games in the Cardinals' spring training in 2014 and hit for an average of .233, and he began the season on the disabled list because of tendinitis in his knee.

JOSHUA SMITH FOGG (1976–) ■ MLB: 2001–09 ■ *Pitcher*
COLLEGE: 1996–98   6-2, 205 lbs.   62-69 / 4.79 / 0

Josh Fogg in 2007 pitching for the Colorado Rockies

Josh Fogg played baseball for Cardinal Gibbons High School in Fort Lauderdale, then began pitching for the University of Florida in 1996. As a senior, he was named an All-American by the National Collegiate Baseball Writers Association, *Baseball America*, and *Collegiate Baseball*. He is a member of the University of Florida Athletic Hall of Fame.

The Chicago White Sox drafted Fogg in the third round of the 1998 draft. He played his first game as a major leaguer on September 2, 2001, and he pitched in 10 more for the White Sox that season. After that, he was traded to the Pittsburgh Pirates, and Fogg played for them for four years, averaging a little more than 30 appearances in each season. His record with the Pirates was 39-42.

Early in 2006, Fogg signed as a free agent with the Colorado Rockies and in two seasons posted a record of 21-18 and an ERA of 5.05. In the 2007 postseason, he appeared in three games and had a record of 2-1 with no errors, which led all National League pitchers in fielding average.

Oh, Doctor!

UF alumnus Walter Lanier "Red" Barber was one of the best-known sports figures and baseball and football radiomen of the 20th Century. He announced Cincinnati Reds baseball games on radio from 1934 until 1939, when the Brooklyn Dodgers hired him and where he remained until he joined the rival Yankees from 1954 to 1966. He covered 13 World Series and 4 All-Star Games, 5 Army-Navy games, 11 college bowl games, and 4 National Football League Championships. Barber is perhaps best remembered for his "Barberisms," folksy phrases to describe the action on the field. The movement of a graceful fielder was as "easy as a bank of fog," or if the player was unable to nab the ball, it was "slicker than boiled okra." A successful team was "walkin' in the tall cotton" or "sittin' in the catbird seat" and any altercation or on-field dispute was a "rhubarb." "Oh Doctor!" was often exclaimed after a particularly good play.

Barber (1908–92) entered the University of Florida in 1928 and 2 years later, after working as a waiter and a janitor, stumbled onto broadcasting as a better way to support himself. He announced the first Gator football game

Red Barber broadcasting during the 1930s

For 2008, Fogg played a single season with the Cincinnati Reds, then returned to the Rockies for his final season in 2009. He briefly was a member of the New York Mets and then the Philadelphia Phillies in 2010, but he was released from both before seeing any major league playing time and has since retired.

MATTHEW VINCENT LAPORTA (1985–)
■ MLB: 2009–12 ■ *First Baseman, Left Fielder*

COLLEGE: 2004–07   6-2, 215 lbs.   .238 / .301 / .393
OLYMPICS: 2008 bronze medal

Matt LaPorta of Port Charlotte, Florida, played baseball at Charlotte High School in Punta Gorda, Florida, and Port Charlotte High School. He was drafted by the

at Florida Field in 1930 (a 20–0 loss to Alabama's Crimson Tide) and left the university to pursue his newfound career, returning later to accept an honorary degree. He began doing the Reds' play-by-play for the 1934 opening day game, the first major league baseball game he had ever watched. The next year, the 27-year-old announced the 1935 World Series for the Mutual Broadcasting System. He left the Reds in 1938 to become the voice of the Brooklyn Dodgers and announced the first major league game on television—and did the first-ever TV commercial during that game. He moved over to the Yankees' booth in 1954 alongside former rival Mel Allen, where he remained until 1966 when, under new management, attendance at one rescheduled late-season home game, when the Yankees were in last place, totaled just 413 paying fans. Barber, known as much for his honesty as his folksy, Southern style, asked the cameras to show the rows of empty seats in "the house that Ruth built" (the television director nixed that) and talked about the attendance instead of the game, embarrassing the owners, and Barber was fired. He moved back to Florida where he wrote books and appeared on local television.

The Baseball Hall of Fame inducted Barber and Allen as the first two members of its Broadcasters' Wing in 1978, the only time they have chosen two in the same year. Barber joined National Public Radio in 1981 for a weekly conversation with host Bob Edwards about sports and life in general, which continued until 17 days before his death in 1992. He received UF's Distinguished Alumni Award in addition to many other honors, and is a member of the Florida Sports Hall of Fame. In 2009, the American Sportscasters Association ranked Barber number 3 on its list of the top 50 sportscasters of all time.

Chicago Cubs in 2003, but he instead opted to go to UF for the 2004 season. In 2005, he led the NCAA with 26 home runs and played in the finals of the College World Series. The Boston Red Sox drafted him in 2006, but he decided to remain with the Gators, and, as both a sophomore and a senior, he was the Southeastern Conference Player of the Year as determined by the SEC head coaches.

LaPorta was drafted in 2007 by the Milwaukee Brewers as the seventh overall pick and was sent to the Rookie League Helena Brewers. After seven games, he was promoted to the Single-A West Virginia Power and, during the fall, he played for the Mesa Solar Sox. In 2008, LaPorta hit a grand slam homer on opening day for the Huntsville Stars, and he was traded in the middle of that season to the Cleveland Indians, who assigned him to Double-A Akron. Later in July, he was invited to play in the Futures Game for Team USA and was named to the 2008 U.S. Olympics Team.

Prior to the Olympics, LaPorta played four games against Canada and hit three homers. He played in the Olympics, but a mild concussion he incurred playing against China caused him to miss the rest of the game (and the Chinese pitcher and pitching coach were ejected). LaPorta played in the bronze medal game, and his home run in the final round helped the U.S. beat Japan for third place.

Matt LaPorta playing for Team USA at the 2008 Olympics

In 2009, LaPorta went to spring training with Cleveland and played for a time with the Triple-A Columbus Clippers. In 21 games, he hit five home runs, four doubles, two triples, and had 14 RBIs. He made his major league debut with the Indians on May 3, 2009. That same year, he completed his UF bachelor's degree in health and human performance.

The Indians started the 2010 season with LaPorta in a backup role, and he was soon back in Columbus so he could get more playing time. When Russell Branyan was traded to the Seattle Mariners, LaPorta was called up to be the starting first baseman. He played in 110 games for the Indians in 2010 and 107 in 2011; however, in 2012, he only saw action in 22 for Cleveland, while spending the rest of the season with the Columbus Clippers.

He had hip surgery in November 2012 and was waived by the Indians, but no other team claimed him. LaPorta went to spring training with Cleveland in 2013, and he was again assigned to Columbus to play first base and be the designated hitter. However, his production was limited due to spending time on the disabled list. As a free agent, LaPorta signed with the Baltimore Orioles in February 2014 and had one at-bat in spring training, but he was released on March 21 of that year prior to the regular season.

STEPHEN PAUL LOMBARDOZZI SR. (1960–)
■ **MLB: 1985–90** ■ *Second Baseman*

COLLEGE: 1980–81   6-0, 175 lbs.   .233 / .307 / .347

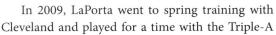

After playing junior college baseball in 1978–79 at Gulf Coast Community College in Panama City, Florida, Steve Lombardozzi Sr. transferred to the University of Florida to play for two more seasons. As a senior, he was All-Southeastern Conference and SEC All-Tournament.

He was drafted by the Minnesota Twins in the ninth round in 1981 and was assigned to the Elizabethton Twins in the Appalachian League, and then he steadily moved up to Single-A Visalia, Double-A Orlando, and Triple-A Toledo. Lombardozzi played his first major league game for the Twins on July 12, 1985, after beginning the season in Toledo.

In four seasons in Minnesota, he appeared in 423 games and had the best fielding percentage (.991) for a second baseman in the American League in 1986. In 1987, he had his one postseason opportunity and made the best of it. Lombardozzi hit .344 in 11 games against the Detroit Tigers and the St. Louis Cardinals, and he is one of the few Gator alumni to earn a World Series championship ring. His .412 average against St. Louis was best on either team. Lombardozzi had the unusual distinction (which lasted for five years) of being the player with the longest last name to homer against any team in the postseason.

Minnesota traded him in 1989 to the Houston Astros; he played 21 games for them that year and two the following year before being released in May 1990. In less than two weeks, he signed with the Detroit Tigers and spent the rest of the season with Triple-A Toledo, but he never made another appearance in a major league game.

Steve Lombardozzi (left) and Tim Laudner (#15) of the Twins

In 2009, Lombardozzi got back into baseball as the Pittsburgh Pirates' minor league fielding coordinator. He is now the baseball coach at Our Lady of Good Counsel High School in Olney, Maryland. Lombardozzi's son, Steve, is a utility infielder with the Baltimore Orioles.

SCOTT EDWARD LUSADER (1964–)
■ **MLB: 1987–91** ■ *Outfielder (mostly a Right Fielder)*

COLLEGE: 1984–85   5-10, 165 lbs.   .246 / .313 / .346

Chicago-born Scott Lusader played two seasons at Florida and graduated with a bachelor's degree in marketing. In 1985, he was drafted in the fifth round by the Detroit Tigers and was assigned to Single-A Lakeland and then Double-A Birmingham. In 1986, he played at Double-A Glens Falls, and the following season he played for Triple-A Toledo.

Lusader made his major league debut with the Tigers on September 1, 1987. Over 23 games, he hit .319, made five extra base hits, and drove in eight runs. He hit his first home run (of five in the majors) to clinch the American League East title for Detroit. In his second year, however, his average dropped to .063, and he was sent back to Toledo for the first part of the season.

On September 8, 1990, Lusader accomplished something that had not been seen in the American League in 65 years—he committed three errors in the outfield in a single inning. He dropped a fly ball, overthrew home plate, and let a hit ball get by him for an extra base.

After playing in 135 games for the Tigers over four seasons, Lusader was waived. The New York Yankees picked him up for the 1991 season, where he only managed a .143 batting average in 11 games, and that finished his career in the major leagues. After baseball, Lusader was a vice president of Diversified Solutions Group and served as a youth baseball coach.

JOHN NICHOLAS MARONDE (1989–) ■ MLB: 2012–14 ■ *Pitcher*
COLLEGE: 2009–11   6-3, 205 lbs.   0-0 / 3.97 / 0

Nick Maronde pitching for the Gators

While a sophomore at Lexington Catholic High School in Lexington, Kentucky, Nick Maronde pitched for the state championship team. After he graduated in 2008, he was drafted by the Oakland Athletics but instead opted to attend the University of Florida. He played in two College World Series tournaments while there, making it to the finals once.

The second team to draft him was the Los Angeles Angels of Anaheim, who took Maronde in the third round in 2011. He skipped his senior season at Florida and was assigned to the Double-A Arkansas Travelers. On September 1, 2012, the organization promoted him to the Angels.

The following day, he made his major league debut by pitching against the Seattle Mariners and throwing three strikes to retire the only batter he faced. Three days later, Maronde pitched one inning against the Oakland Athletics and struck out all three batters. That year, while pitching 6 innings in a total of 12 games, he posted a 1.50 earned run average. He was sent back to the Travelers to begin the 2013 season, and he went back to the Angels on July 29.

Maronde got into ten games for the Angels in 2013, striking out 5 in a total of 5 1/3 innings. He still pitches for the Angels, rarely getting to pitch a whole inning in a game.

JAMES BRIAN MCANDREW (1967–) ■ MLB: 1995, 1997 ■ *Pitcher*
COLLEGE: 1987–89   6-2, 190 lbs.   3-4 / 5.98 / 0

Jamie McAndrew, the son of former major league pitcher Jim McAndrew, played baseball for Ponderosa High School in Parker, Colorado. He was selected in the 23rd round of the 1986 draft, but he decided not to sign a contract. Instead, he came to Florida to pitch and played for three seasons, including the College World Series in 1988. During 1986 and 1987, he was also the starting punter on the UF football team.

The Los Angeles Dodgers drafted McAndrew in the first round in 1989. Before he saw his first major league playing time, he was taken from the Dodgers in the 1992 expansion draft, then wound up in the Florida Marlins organization. They subsequently traded him to the Milwaukee Brewers in April 1993.

McAndrew missed the 1994 season because of injury, and, during the next year's spring training, he was a replacement player for the Brewers, filling in while the regular roster players were on strike (which was settled before the regular season began). Because he served as a replacement player, he was blacklisted and denied membership in the Major League Baseball Players Association.

He finally made his major league debut on July 17, 1995, making him one of the first replacement players to get into a major league game. McAndrew played in ten games that season for the Brewers and had a record of 2-3. He missed 1996 because of injury, went 1-1 in five games for Milwaukee in 1997, and became a free agent after the season ended. The following January, McAndrew signed with the Cleveland Indians, but he saw no major league playing time after July 1997.

ROBERT ALBERT MURPHY (1960–) ■ MLB: 1985–95 ■ *Pitcher*
COLLEGE: 1979–80   6-2, 200 lbs.   32-38 / 3.64 / 30

After playing baseball for Christopher Columbus High School in Miami, Rob Murphy attended the University of Miami. In 1979, he transferred to UF and pitched for two seasons. During his freshman year, he led the team with an ERA of 2.53, and, for his two years as a Gator, he compiled a 6-3 record.

He was drafted by the Milwaukee Brewers in 1978 but did not sign. When he was drafted as the third pick in the first round in 1981 by the Cincinnati Reds, he signed a contract and played for the Tampa Tarpons, Cedar Rapids Reds, Vermont Reds, and Denver Zephyrs. Murphy made his major league debut for the Reds on September 13, 1985. For the 1986 season, he had an ERA of 0.72 and a record of 6-0, and his ERA is still a National League record for pitchers who have completed at least 50 innings in a season. In 1987, he made 87 appearances, breaking the record for left-handed pitchers, and his 76 appearances in 1988 led the National League for that season.

Rob Murphy as a member of the 1989 Boston Red Sox

After four seasons and a cumulative record of 14-11, Murphy was traded to the Boston Red Sox; in 1989, the Boston area sportswriters named him the Red Sox Fireman of the Year. In 1990, he stretched his errorless streak from the start of his career to 332 (the previous major league record had been 175). Two seasons with that team resulted in a record of 5-13 (and his entire postseason experience of 2/3 of an inning in 1990), and he was traded to the Seattle Mariners in April 1991.

Murphy appeared in 57 games for the Mariners in 1991, had a loss in his only decision, and saved four games. He became a free agent and played for the Houston Astros in 1992, the year he broke the major league record of consecutive games without a win (146). He also played for the St. Louis Cardinals (1993 and most of 1994), New York Yankees (part of 1994), Los Angeles Dodgers (part of 1995), and the Florida Marlins (the rest of 1995). He wound up pitching in 597 games for eight different major league teams. Murphy made more than twice as many appearances during his major league career than has the next-busiest Gator alumnus.

Murphy is a member of the Columbus Athletic Hall of Fame. After baseball, he went into raising racehorses through his company, M375 Thoroughbreds, Inc. He is also active in fundraising projects supporting research to fight cystic fibrosis, cancer, muscular dystrophy, and ALS, and coaches local baseball and softball teams.

DARREN CHRISTOPHER O'DAY (1982–)
■ MLB: 2008–14 ■ *Pitcher*

COLLEGE: 2003–06   6-4, 220 lbs.   20-9 / 2.61 / 4

A graduate of Bishop Kenney High School in Jacksonville, Darren O'Day pitched for Florida, but it took him a year to make the team. He was cut as a freshman and spent the year studying with the hope of attending medical school, lifting weights, and being a regular college student. A friend talked him into pitching in a summer "beer league," where he devised his unorthodox sidearm pitching style. His father watched him play and was convinced his son should make another try for the Gator team. O'Day figured he had nothing to lose, and he went for it.

Baltimore Oriole Darren O'Day in 2012

Between the workouts and his unusual style, he threw a lot harder and struck out every batter he faced during his tryout. He made the team, earned a scholarship, and still kept up with his studies. For four consecutive years, O'Day was on the Southeastern Conference Academic Honor Roll and was honored by *ESPN The Magazine* as an Academic All-American for his senior year. In 2006, he received his bachelor's degree in agricultural and life sciences.

The Los Angeles Angels of Anaheim drafted O'Day in 2006, and he made his major league debut with them on March 31, 2008. He posted a 0-1 record after 30 appearances that year, but they lost him in a Rule 5 draft to the New York Mets after the season.

Where Did the Gators Go?

After collegiate baseball careers of varying lengths and measures of success, Gators have gone on to play for every major league franchise, at least two per team. The teams they played for are listed below. Because many Florida alumni have played for multiple teams, the totals below exceed the number of individuals listed in this chapter.

St. Louis Cardinals 8	Philadelphia Phillies 4
Atlanta Braves/Boston Bees/Boston Braves/Milwaukee Braves 7	San Diego Padres 4
Boston Red Sox 7	Texas Rangers 4
San Francisco/New York Giants 7	Washington Nationals/Montreal Expos 4
Cleveland Indians 6	Arizona Diamondbacks 3
Oakland/Philadelphia/Kansas City Athletics 6	Baltimore Orioles/St. Louis Browns 3
Cincinnati Reds 5	Chicago Cubs 3
Colorado Rockies 5	Kansas City Royals 3
Detroit Tigers 5	Minnesota Twins/Washington Senators 3
Houston Astros 5	New York Mets 3
Los Angeles Dodgers 5	Seattle Mariners 3
New York Yankees 5	Toronto Blue Jays 3
Pittsburgh Pirates 5	Miami/Florida Marlins 2
Chicago White Sox 4	Milwaukee Brewers 2
Los Angeles Angels of Anaheim/California Angels/Anaheim Angels 4	Tampa Bay Devil Rays/Tampa Bay Rays 2

During 2009, he pitched three innings over four games for New York, was waived, and was picked up by the Texas Rangers, pitching for them the day he was claimed. (He had to wear someone else's uniform.) O'Day finished the 2009 season by pitching in 64 Rangers games, then had a 6-2 record for them in 2010. In the postseason, he pitched in four games against the Tampa Bay Rays, three against the New York Yankees, and three against the San Francisco Giants.

After one more season with the Rangers, the Frisco RoughRiders, and the Round Rock Express, he was picked up off waivers by the Baltimore Orioles. The 2012 season was his best from a win-loss standpoint, with a record of 7-1. During the postseason, he pitched in one game against the Texas Rangers and four against the New York Yankees. O'Day is still a relief pitcher for the Orioles, one of the few submariners in the major leagues, and often pitches only the seventh inning.

His family's last name was originally Odachowski but was changed decades ago, and he has "D. Odachowski" stitched on the side of his game glove to honor the family name. O'Day is married to his college sweetheart who undoubtedly knows his real identity.

TIMOTHY LANE OLSON (1978–) ■ MLB: 2004-05 ■ *Third Baseman*
COLLEGE: 2000   6-2, 200 lbs.   .182 / .302 / .313

After graduating from St. Mary's Central High School in Bismarck, North Dakota, Tim Olson began college at Hutchinson Community College, also in Bismarck. He later transferred to Florida, where he played baseball in 2000 and set a Gator team record with a 29-game hitting streak.

Tim Olson as a member of the Texas Rangers

Olson had been drafted the first time by the Tampa Bay Devil Rays in 1998, but he declined to sign a contract. He was drafted in the seventh round in 2000 by the Arizona Diamondbacks and made it to the majors with them, playing his first game on May 30, 2004. During that season, he played in 48 games as a Diamondback, then was released in November.

The Colorado Rockies was the next stop for Olson and he played in three games during 2005, getting no hits in two at-bats. After the season, he signed as a free agent with the Texas Rangers, but he saw no playing time with them and was traded in July 2006 to the Toronto Blue Jays. He did not get into any games with that team, nor with the Colorado Rockies, during his final major league season of 2007.

Currently, Olson is a vice president with Arthur J. Gallagher and Co. in the Dallas/Ft. Worth area and is married with three children.

RANDALL JEFFREY O'NEAL (1960–) ■ MLB: 1984-90 ■ *Pitcher*
COLLEGE: 1981   6-2, 195 lbs.   17-19 / .472 / 3

After attending Palm Beach Community College in Lake Worth, Randy O'Neal transferred to the University of Florida, where he played baseball in 1981. Including the games played in the Southeastern Conference and NCAA championship tournaments, O'Neal led the Gators in complete games (nine) and innings pitched (108).

He was drafted in January 1979 by the Montreal Expos and in June 1979 by the Minnesota Twins, but didn't sign with either team. During 1980, he was drafted by the

Milwaukee Brewers and the Cincinnati Reds, but he again did not sign with either team. O'Neal finally joined a team after he was drafted as the 15th pick in the first round by the Detroit Tigers in 1981 and was assigned to the Class-A Advanced Lakeland Tigers.

O'Neal made his major league debut with the Tigers on September 12, 1984, and he remained with them through the 1986 season as a starting pitcher. After a cumulative 10-13 record, Detroit traded him to the Atlanta Braves, where he posted a 4-2 record as a middle reliever through late July, when he was traded to the St. Louis Cardinals. During the rest of the season, O'Neal made one appearance for the Cardinals. He stayed with St. Louis for the 1988 season, then played in 1989 with the Philadelphia Phillies and in 1990 with the San Francisco Giants.

His final season, 1991, was spent with the Double-A Memphis Chicks, a minor league team in the Kansas City Royals organization. O'Neal later taught and coached baseball at Orlando's Olympia High School. After seven seasons there, including two district championships, he took over as the head baseball coach at Lake Highland Preparatory School in Orlando. One of his pitchers there was his son, who has committed to pitch for David Lipscomb University in Tennessee.

JAVIER VICTOR ORTIZ (1963–)
■ **MLB: 1990–91** ■ *Outfielder, Pinch Hitter*

COLLEGE: 1982   6-4, 220 lbs.   .275 / .374 / .394

After playing baseball at Miami-Dade South Community College, Javier Ortiz transferred to the University of Florida for the 1982 season.

In the 1983 amateur draft, he was selected as the fourth pick in the first round by the Texas Rangers and was assigned for that year to the Single-A Burlington Rangers. For 1984, he moved up to Double-A Tulsa. In 1987, he played for Triple-A Burlington.

While still in the minors, Ortiz was traded to the Los Angeles Dodgers in 1987 and to the Houston Astros in 1989. His first major league game was on June 15, 1990, with Houston, and he played with them in 77 games through the end of the 1991 season. He was released and did not return to the major leagues, but he did play with farm teams for the Pittsburgh Pirates, Kansas City Royals, and Chicago White Sox. His last team was the Triple-A Nashville Sounds in 1995.

Later, Ortiz became an agent for other baseball players, including Jose and Ozzie Canseco.

MICHAEL IRVIN PÉREZ ORTEGA (1964–)
■ **MLB: 1990-97** ■ *Pitcher*

COLLEGE: 1985   6-0, 185 lbs.   24-16 / 3.56 / 22

Mike Pérez of Puerto Rico played his college ball at the University of Florida and Troy State University.

He was drafted in the 12th round in 1986 by the St. Louis Cardinals, and he made his major league debut with them on September 5, 1990. He played in St. Louis for five seasons, the best of which was 1992, when he posted a record of 9-3 and had an ERA of 1.82. After the 1994 season, Pérez became a free agent and for 1995 signed with the Chicago Cubs.

Over the next two seasons, he had a record of 3-6 and two saves and then moved to the Kansas City Royals. In his final season of 1997, he made 16 appearances and had a record of 2-0, but in August the Royals released him. During his career, Pérez pitched in 313 games, all in relief.

HERBERT EDWARD PERRY (1969–)
■ **MLB: 1994-96, 1999-2004** ■ *Third Baseman, First Baseman*

COLLEGE: 1988–91   6-2, 210 lbs.   .272 / .335 / .436

After playing football and baseball for Lafayette High School in Mayo, Florida, Herb Perry enrolled at the University of Florida and played quarterback for the football team in 1987–88. He also played baseball in 1988–91 and participated in the 1987 and 1991 College World Series as a Gator. During 1989, he led the team with a batting average of .370. In 1991, he was the co-MVP of the Southeastern Conference championship tournament. That year, Perry graduated with a bachelor's degree in agricultural operations management.

The Cleveland Indians drafted him in the second round and signed him to a contract in 1991. He made his major league debut on May 3, 1994, and appeared in four games for the Indians that season. Perry went on to play in a total of 59 games for the Indians in 1995 and 1996, including the 1995 postseason through the World Series.

The Tampa Bay Devil Rays drafted him in 1997 in the expansion draft, but he missed the 1997 and 1998 seasons because of an injury. He played 66 games for them in 1999 until he was waived. Perry was picked up by the Chicago White Sox and got into his second postseason (2000) and hit .444 against the Seattle Mariners, but, following the season, he was traded to the Texas Rangers. After three years and 192 games with the Rangers, he left the major leagues. Perry, the older brother of fellow Gator and MLB alumnus Chan Perry, is back in Mayo and coaches junior varsity baseball at his old high school.

KEVIN MICHAEL POLCOVICH (1970–)
■ **MLB: 1997–98** ■ *Shortstop, Second Baseman, Third Baseman*

COLLEGE: 1991–92   5-9, 170 lbs.   .234 / .307 / .326

Kevin Polcovich of Auburn, New York, played two seasons for Florida. In 1991, he participated in the College World Series and was named to the All-Tournament team.

He was drafted in the 30th round in 1992 by the Pittsburgh Pirates. Polcovich moved up to the majors in May 1997 and played in 84 games that year for them. With the Pirates in rebuilding mode and having the lowest payroll in the majors, Polcovich helped to support himself during spring training by bagging groceries, and he got his big break when the Pirates' starting shortstop suffered an injury. He made the most of the situation, anchoring the infield as the team became a contender in the NL Central Division until their elimination in the final week of the season. But the story of Polcovich's rise from bagboy to starting shortstop remains a favorite for Pirates' fans.

The following year, he played in 81 more games for Pittsburgh before leaving the major leagues. During his time in professional baseball, he played a total of 10 years in the minors. Today, Polcovich is a personal trainer and nutrition specialist and serves as the CEO of Icanetics Nutrition Network, a company owned by his wife.

RYAN NEIL RABURN (1981–)
■ MLB: 2004, 2007–14 ■ *Leftfielder, Second Baseman*

COLLEGE: 2000   6-0, 185 lbs.   .258 / .317 / .445

Ryan Raburn of the Detroit Tigers in 2011

When Ryan Raburn of Plant City, Florida, was drafted in the 18th round of the 1999 draft by the Toronto Blue Jays, he did not sign. Instead, he went to UF and played for the Gators for one year and then transferred to South Florida Community College. He was drafted in the fifth round in 2001 by the Detroit Tigers and this time signed.

Raburn started out in the minors as a third baseman with the Gulf Coast League Tigers, then moved up to the Oneonta Tigers. When the 2002 season began, he was injured and then played for a time with the West Michigan Whitecaps. He remained with West Michigan for the start of 2003 and, after 16 games, was elevated to the Lakeland Tigers for 95 games. In 2004, he was moved to second base.

Detroit called him up to make his major league debut in September 2004, and Raburn played in 12 games. His 2005 season was spent with Toledo of the International League, and he led the league with the most errors by a second baseman (21). After 2006, he was left unprotected and could have been picked up by any team, but he wasn't. Instead, he remained in the Tigers organization and was assigned to the Triple-A Toledo Mud Hens. His next time in the majors, still with Detroit, came in 2007, and he remained with that team while they bounced him back and forth with the Mud Hens through 2012. Raburn was occasionally used as a starter and played in three games in the divisional playoff series in 2012, as well as six games in the league championship series in which Detroit lost to Texas.

He was released by the Tigers in November 2012 and signed as a free agent with the Cleveland Indians the following January. He made the team's roster and was named the

American League Player of the Week for April 29–May 5. In August 2013, the Indians signed Raburn to a two-year contract. His first post-season opportunity occurred in 2013, when Cleveland became one of the two American League wild card teams.

WILLIAM THRACE RAMSEY (1945–2008) ■ MLB: 1945 ■ *Outfielder*

COLLEGE: 1939–40   6-0, 175 lbs.   .292 / .326 / .372

Former Gator Bill Ramsey as a Boston Brave

Bill Ramsey played baseball for Florida just before World War II. His rights were owned by the St. Louis Cardinals when, on November 1, 1944, under a Rule 5 draft, he was drafted by the Boston Braves. He played his first major league game on April 19, 1945, and appeared in 78 games for the Braves, usually as an outfielder but sometimes as a pinch-hitter. At the end of the 1945 season, Ramsey left the major leagues.

On August 30, 1946, the Braves assigned him to Seattle of the Pacific Coast League, ending his major league career. Ramsey died in Memphis, Tennessee, on January 4, 2008.

LANCE CLAYTON RICHBOURG (1897–1975)
■ MLB: 1921, 1924, 1927–32 ■ *Rightfielder*

COLLEGE: 1919, 1922   5-10, 160 lbs.   .308 / .352 / .400

After playing for DeFuniak Springs High School, Lance Richbourg enrolled at the University of Florida and played on its baseball team. In 1921, he signed with the New York Giants and was traded to the Philadelphia Phillies, with which he played 10 games, making him the first UF student to go professional in any sport. After one year, he was back in school at Florida and received his bachelor's degree in 1922. Richbourg then was the Gators' baseball coach in 1922–23 and also in 1926.

He played again in 1924 in 15 games for the Washington Senators after briefly being the property of the New York Yankees. The Senators sent him to Milwaukee of the American Association, which sold him to the Boston Braves after the 1926 season. Richbourg played for the Braves for five years, then was waived after the 1931 season. During 1927, he set a National League record by playing 18 consecutive innings in right field without a single fielding opportunity. He was picked up by the Chicago Cubs, and Richbourg played 44 games with them in 1932.

Rightfielder Lance Richbourg wearing a Yankees cap

After the 1932 season, the Cubs traded him to the Cincinnati Reds, and, about five weeks later, he was acquired by the St. Louis Cardinals, but Richbourg had already played his final major league game on September 25, 1932. He later managed the Nashville team in the Southern Association for four years.

His high school adopted the Braves nickname because its famous major league alumnus was a member of the Boston Braves during 1926. Under his leadership, Florida compiled a record of 39-21. Richbourg died September 10, 1975, in Crestview, Florida.

PAUL DAVID RIGDON (1975–) ■ MLB: 2000–01 ■ *Pitcher*

COLLEGE: 1996   6-5, 210 lbs.   8-10 / 5.45 / 0

Paul Rigdon played for Trinity Christian Academy in Jacksonville and then played one year for the University of Florida.

He was drafted by the Cincinnati Reds in 1994, but he did not sign, waiting until 1996 when he was drafted in the sixth round by the Cleveland Indians. After appearing in just five games, Cleveland traded him in late July 2000 to the Milwaukee Brewers. He spent the rest of 2000 and all of 2001 with the Brewers and saw action in 27 games.

Milwaukee released Rigdon in 2003, and he again signed with the Cleveland Indians for 2003, followed by the Boston Red Sox for 2004, but saw no major league action with either team.

STEVEN "PACO" FRANCIS RODRIGUEZ (1991–) ■ MLB: 2012–14 ■ *Pitcher*

COLLEGE: 2010–12   6-3, 220 lbs.   3-5 / 2.21 / 2

As a high school pitcher, Paco Rodriguez was named by the *Miami Herald* newspaper to the All-Dade Team. He was drafted after graduation by the Houston Astros, but he instead chose to be a Gator and wound up as the team's closer. In 86 appearances, Rodriguez had an earned run average of 2.19. For three consecutive years, he and his team made it to the College World Series.

The second time he was drafted, it was by the Los Angeles Dodgers, who assigned him to the Great Lakes Loons of the Midwest League. Rodriguez moved up to the Chattanooga Lookouts of the Southern League and had a 1.32 ERA in 15 games. On September 9, 2012, in his major league debut against the San Francisco Giants, he pitched to one batter and got him out. He appeared in ten more games that season and pitched a total of 6 2/3 innings.

Rodriguez saw much more action in 2013, with 54 1/3 innings in 76 games. In 2014, he continued as a relief pitcher for the Dodgers.

ALBERT LEONARD ROSEN (1924–)
■ **MLB: 1947–56** ■ *Third Baseman, First Baseman*

COLLEGE: 1942   5-10, 180 lbs.   .285 / .384 / .495

Al Rosen had asthma as a child, and his family moved from South Carolina to Miami in search of a warmer climate for his health. He graduated from St. Petersburg's Florida Military Academy and then tried out with Single-A Wilkes-Barre in 1941. He was offered $75 a month to play for Class-D Thomasville in the North Carolina State League, but he instead began classes at UF in the fall of 1941 and played for the Gators in the spring of 1942. After that, he attended the University of Miami and played end on the Hurricanes' football team and won the Florida boxing championship. Rosen left school before graduation to play minor league baseball in the Red Sox organization in 1942, but he delayed his playing career by spending four years in the Navy and saw action in the South Pacific.

All-Star Al Rosen of the Cleveland Indians in 1953

After playing in 1946 for the Pittsfield Electrics and leading the Canadian-American League in home runs and RBIs, Rosen moved to the Oklahoma City Indians for 1947 and was chosen as the MVP of the Texas League. He made his major league debut with the Cleveland Indians on September 10, 1947, and played seven games for them that season.

The year 1948 began with Rosen on the Triple-A Kansas City Blues, where he was named the MVP of the American Association. In one stretch, he hit five home runs in five consecutive at-bats. In late 1948, he was back with the Indians, where he remained for his entire career through the end of 1956. He was named to the American League all-star team for four consecutive years, beginning in 1952, and in the 1954 game hit two home runs and had five RBIs. He played in two World Series (1948 and 1954).

In 1953, he was chosen as the American League's Most Valuable Player, and, three years before that, he was the first rookie to win the home run title. Rosen appeared on the cover of *Sports Illustrated* in 1955. He led the American League in several categories, including:

Category		Year		Year
Hit By Pitch	10	1950		
Home Runs	37	1950	43	1953
Games Played	154	1951		

Category		Year		Year
Runs Batted In	105	1952	145	1953
Total Bases	297	1952	367	1953
Extra Base Hits	75	1953		
Runs Scored	115	1953		
Slugging Percentage	.613	1953		
Sacrifice Flies	11	1954		

Rosen just missed hitting for the Triple Crown in 1953. He hit .336, and Mickey Vernon of the Washington Senators was barely ahead of him, going into the last two innings of the last game of the season against another team. Vernon's teammates knew if he came to bat in the ninth inning and made an out, his average would be slightly behind Rosen's. To prevent that, in the eighth inning, Mickey Grasso purposely allowed himself to be picked off. In the ninth, Kite Thomas let himself be tagged out after running past first base toward second on a single. Eddie Yost popped out on a pitch over his head, and Pete Runnels struck out to end the game. Mickey Vernon ended the season in the on-deck circle, the winner of the batting average title.

Rosen was considered to be tough, dating back to his days as an amateur boxer. He broke his nose nine times trying to field ground balls. As one of the majors' few Jewish players at that time, Rosen had to deal with anti-Semitism and was asked how he handled it in a 2010 interview as a documentary entitled *Jews and Baseball: An American Love Story* was being released. He replied, "I have broad shoulders. I took it upon myself. There were times I had to assert myself and other times I just let it roll . . . ." Occasionally, the comments and attitudes were too much, and, in the film, Rosen honestly commented, "There's a time that you let it be known that enough is enough . . . . You flatten [them]."

A broken finger in 1954, combined with other injuries, led to his retirement, and he became a stockbroker with Bache and Company. Rosen partnered with George Steinbrenner to bid on the purchase of the Cleveland Indians in 1972, but it was rejected. After Steinbrenner acquired the Yankees, Rosen was made that club's president and served in 1978 and 1979. For a little more than a year, he was the executive vice president of an Atlantic City hotel and casino. He also led the Houston Astros (1980–85) and served as the general manager of the San Francisco Giants (1985–92). He was Major League Baseball's 1987 Executive of the Year.

Rosen was inducted into the National Jewish Sports Hall of Fame in 1998. He is also a member of the Florida Sports Hall of Fame, the International Jewish Sports Hall of Fame, the Texas League Hall of Fame, and the Cleveland Indians Hall of Fame.

STEVEN ALLEN ROSENBERG (1964–) ■ MLB: 1988–91 ■ *Pitcher*

COLLEGE: 1985–86   6-0, 186 lbs.   6-15 / 4.94 / 1

Brooklyn-born Steve Rosenberg was a left-handed pitcher who played for Coral Springs High School and Broward Community College before transferring to the University of Florida, where he played in 1985 and 1986.

He was drafted by the New York Yankees in the fourth round in 1986, signed with the team, and played in the minors at Oneonta, Single-A Fort Lauderdale, Double-A Albany, and Triple-A Columbus. He was traded in November 1987 to the Chicago White Sox, who assigned him to Triple-A Vancouver. Over the next three seasons, Rosenberg appeared in 77 games for Chicago and posted a record of 5-14. Just before the 1991 season, he was traded to the San Diego Padres and pitched in 10 games that year.

The Padres traded him in December 1991 to the New York Mets, but he saw no further action in the majors. Rosenberg last pitched for Single-A Riverside and appeared in six games, but a previous shoulder injury resulted in his retirement. After his years as a player, Rosenberg coached baseball at Coral Springs Christian Academy.

DAVID WADE ROSS (1977–) ■ MLB: 2002–14 ■ *Catcher*

COLLEGE: 1998   6-2, 205 lbs.   .237 / .323 / .441

David Ross went to high school in Tallahassee and played college baseball with Auburn University (1996–97) and the University of Florida (1998), and he played in the College World Series with each.

The Los Angeles Dodgers drafted Ross in 1995, but he didn't sign, and they again drafted him in the seventh round in 1998. He made his debut with the Dodgers in 2002 and played with them through 2004, including two playoff games. The Pittsburgh Pirates purchased his contract just before the 2005 season, and he played in 40 games before being traded to the San Diego Padres. Ross played 11 games for them, and, after the season, was traded to the Cincinnati Reds.

Catcher David Ross of the Atlanta Braves in 2012

In more than two seasons for Cincinnati, he hit for an average of .227 and was subsequently released. Three days later, he signed with the Boston Red Sox and appeared in eight games in the regular season and one in the playoffs. After the 2008 season, Ross signed as a free agent with the Atlanta Braves and played through the end of 2012. He then signed a contract with the Boston Red Sox extending through the 2014 season. Ross is considered to be one of the best backup catchers playing today and is also well liked by his teammates.

SCOTT DREW RUSKIN (1963–) ■ MLB: 1990–93 ■ *Pitcher*

COLLEGE: 1982–85   6-2, 185 lbs.   11-9 / 3.95 / 8

Before he was a Gator, Scott Ruskin played his high school ball at Sandalwood High School in Jacksonville. He then played for UF in 1982–85.

He was drafted by the Cincinnati Reds (1981, 14th round), Texas Rangers (1984, 4th round), Cleveland Indians (1985, 3th round), and Montreal Expos (1986, 1st round), but he signed with none of those teams. Instead, he signed with the Pittsburgh Pirates, who drafted him in the 3rd round of the second 1986 draft.

Ruskin made his major league debut in 1990 and played for the Pirates in 44 games, earning a 2-2 record. Before the end of the season, he was traded to the Montreal Expos, and he appeared in 23 games that season and 64 games in 1991. He was then traded to the Cincinnati Reds and played in 1992 and 1993 and then signed in the off-season with the Kansas City Royals (but appeared in no games for that club). In 2003, Ruskin completed his bachelor's degree at Florida in computer and information science.

According to his high school coach, Ruskin was one of the most natural athletes ever to attend Sandalwood and was special because he could both hit and pitch so well. Following his playing days, he settled near Jacksonville and operated a tanning salon in Jacksonville Beach.

STEPHEN RUSSELL MALLORY SCARRITT (1903–94) ■ MLB: 1929–32 ■ *Left Fielder*

COLLEGE: 1922–28   5-10, 165 lbs.   .285 / .320 / .385

Russ Scarritt of Pensacola attended the University of Florida during the 1920s and played in the minor Sally League, hitting .377 in 1926. Scarritt made his major league debut on April 18, 1929, with the Boston Red Sox, played in 151 games that year, and hit 17 triples, which is still the Red Sox rookie record. After three years with the Red Sox, he played 11 games in 1932 for the Philadelphia Phillies.

He went back to the minors and played until 1937, compiling a batting average of .321, quite a bit better than in his 285 games in the majors. Scarritt died December 4, 1994, in Pensacola, Florida, at the age of 91.

Boston Red Sox left fielder Russ Scarritt

RYAN NELSON SHEALY (1979–)
■ MLB: 2005–08, 2010   ■ *First Baseman*

COLLEGE: 1999–2002   6-5, 240 lbs.   .268 / .331 / .424

Fort Lauderdale native Ryan Shealy played baseball for the University of Florida and graduated with a bachelor's degree in advertising in 2002. He was drafted by the Colorado Rockies that same year and was assigned to the advanced rookie team, the Casper Rockies. In 2005, Shealy was a member of the team that played for USA Baseball in the Olympic qualifying tournament. That year, he was presented with the Richard W. "Dick" Case Award as the top USA Baseball player.

Shealy made his major league debut with the Colorado Rockies in 2005 and split the season with that club and Triple-A Colorado Springs.

Kansas City Royals player Ryan Shealy in 2007

Partway through the 2006 season, He was traded to the Kansas City Royals and played with them through 2008. In 2010, Shealy appeared in five games with the Boston Red Sox and then was a member of the Toronto Blue Jays organization for the 2011 season, but he saw no action for them on the field.

ROBERT MICHAEL STANLEY (1963–)
■ MLB: 1986–2000   ■ *Catcher, First Baseman*

COLLEGE: 1982–85   6-1, 185 lbs.   .270 / .370 / .458

Boston Red Sox catcher Mike Stanley

Mike Stanley played baseball for the Gators in 1982 through 1985, and was honored as Southeastern Conference All-Tournament in 1982, 1984, and 1985. He also was NCAA Regional All-Tournament in 1985.

Stanley was drafted in 1985 by the Texas Rangers and made his major league debut for them the following year. He played six seasons for the Rangers, became a free agent, signed with the New York Yankees, and played for four years, including four games in the 1995 playoffs. That same year, he made it to the American League all-star team. Stanley had received the Silver Slugger Award in 1993. After the 1995 season, he signed with the Boston Red Sox, who in August 1997 traded him back to the Yankees. At the end of that season, he played in two playoff games against the Cleveland Indians.

In December 1997, Stanley joined the Toronto Blue Jays, but, before the 1998 season ended, he was back on the Red Sox and in the playoffs. The next year, he and Boston again made it to the playoffs, winning the first round against Cleveland, but losing to the Yankees in the American League Championship Series. Stanley started 2000 with the Red Sox but was released in July. He finished the season with the Oakland Athletics and retired as a player at the end of the season.

Stanley served as the Boston bench coach in 2002 but resigned to spend more time with his wife and four children. They live in Maitland, Florida, and Stanley is a volunteer assistant coach for Lake Highland Preparatory School in Orlando. He was inducted into the Broward County Sports Hall of Fame in 2003 and the University of Florida Athletic Hall of Fame in 2014.

HAYWOOD COOPER SULLIVAN (1930-2003)
■ MLB: 1955, 1957-1963   ■ *Catcher, First Baseman, Manager*

COLLEGE: 1950–51   6-4, 210 lbs.   .226 / .312 / .318

Dothan, Alabama, was the home of Haywood Sullivan, who was the starting Florida quarterback in 1950 and 1951, as well as a catcher on the Gators baseball team. After his junior year, he signed a contract with the Boston Red Sox that provided a $45,000 bonus. The next two years were spent in military service, and Sullivan made his major league debut in 1955 by catching two games for the Sox.

He played in two more games in 1957 and then missed the entire 1958 season because of back surgery. In and out of the minor leagues, Sullivan made it into only four games for Boston in 1959, but, in 1960, he finally moved up to backup catcher. That year, major league baseball expanded, and he was drafted by the Washington Senators, who two weeks later traded him to the Kansas City Athletics. He played 252 games for the Athletics in 1961–63 before retiring as a player.

Haywood Sullivan when he played quarterback for the Gators

In 1964, Sullivan began coaching for the Double-A Birmingham Barons; the following year, he moved to the Triple-A Vancouver Mounties. After 25 games, he was promoted to manager of the Kansas City Athletics. For the 1965 season, the team was in last place when Sullivan took over as manager, and that's also where they wound up at the end of the season, his only one in that position.

Later in 1965, he moved to the Boston Red Sox front office and, after about two years, became more active in scouting amateur players. In 1977, after the death of owner Tom Yawkey, Sullivan was part of a group that purchased the club. The new ownership group included Yawkey's widow, who installed Sullivan as the general manager. The Red Sox briefly showed improvement, but, after 1978, several of Sullivan's trade decisions were being questioned, as star players were being traded but the team was getting little in return. In 1979, he was criticized for drafting his son, Marc, who wound up batting only .186 over five seasons.

By missing a mailing deadline, Sullivan lost some of the team's stars in 1980, including Carlton Fisk. He refused to be involved with acquiring free agents, preferring to obtain younger players through the Boston farm system, and he drafted poorly. In 1983, he was ousted by his partners, but Sullivan and Mrs. Yawkey successfully sued to regain control, with Sullivan stepping down as general manager the following year. In 1993, he sold his interest in the club for $33 million.

Sullivan retired from baseball and moved to Naples, Florida, where he operated a marina and became a successful real estate investor. He died after suffering a stroke in 2003 in Fort Myers, Florida, at age 72. Sullivan is a member of the Boston Red Sox Hall of Fame and the University of Florida Athletic Hall of Fame.

MARC COOPER SULLIVAN (1958–)
■ MLB: 1982, 1984–87 ■ *Catcher*

COLLEGE: 1977–79   6-4, 205 lbs.   .186 / .236 / .258

The son of Florida quarterback and Boston Red Sox general manager Haywood Sullivan, Marc Sullivan was drafted by his father in the second round in 1979 and made his major league debut with the Red Sox in 1982, appearing in two games that year and two more in 1984. In 1985–87, he played in 133 more for the Sox. Although his minor league batting average was only .222, it was far better than the .186 he hit for the Red Sox.

Sullivan was considered to be more of a defensive specialist, but he also occasionally hit for power. In December 1987, he was traded to the Houston Astros for a minor league player and saw no more action in the big leagues.

His post-major league activities included running a fantasy baseball camp in Fort Myers, Florida.

ROBERT RANDALL THOMPSON (1962–)
■ MLB: 1986–96 ■ *Second Baseman*

COLLEGE: 1983   5-11, 165 lbs.   .257 / .329 / .403

After playing baseball for Forest Hill Community High School in West Palm Beach, Robby Thompson went to Gainesville to play a year for the Gators.

Thompson was drafted in January 1982 by the Oakland Athletics and in June 1982 by the Seattle Mariners, but he did not sign. When he was drafted and signed in 1983 by the San Francisco Giants as the second overall pick, he played for the Shreveport Captains of the Texas League, where he was named to its all-star team in 1985.

San Francisco Giant second baseman Robby Thompson

In 1986, Thompson made his major league debut with the Giants; that June, he set a major league record of being caught stealing four times in one game. He was *The Sporting News* Rookie of the Year and runner-up in the race for official National League Rookie of the Year honors. During the National League Championship Series in 1987, he set a record by turning ten double plays.

Thompson was named as a reserve on the all-star team in 1988, but he missed the game because of injury. The following year, he led the National League with 11 triples, although his strikeout total increased and his batting average decreased. He hit two home runs in the 1989 National League Championship Series but made only one hit in the World Series, which the Giants lost. In 1991, Thompson received the Willie Mac Award (voted by Giants' players and coaches) to recognize his spirit and leadership.

He was named to his second all-star team in 1993 and again missed it because of injury. In August of that year, he hit home runs in five consecutive games to help San Francisco challenge for the pennant, but he had to miss eight games in September because of a cheekbone broken by a pitched ball. Wearing a protective mask, Thompson played in the final game, but the Giants just missed winning another trip to the playoffs. He was honored with Gold Glove and Silver Slugger Awards.

Thompson played 11 seasons, all with San Francisco. In 1997, he signed as a free agent with the Cleveland Indians but did not get into any games. He became the Giants' first base coach in 2000 and stayed there for two seasons, then moved to the Indians and served as the first base coach, special assistant to the general manager, and bench coach. From 2010 through 2013, he was the bench coach for the Seattle Mariners. Thompson filled in for about a month in 2013 as the Mariners' interim manager while their manager was recovering from a mild stroke.

During his playing years, he was known to use a well-worn glove for most of his career. After an article was written about the glove, Rich Aurilia, one of his teammates toward the end of his career, commented, "I think by the time Robby was done, the glove mainly consisted of pine tar and chew spit. I don't even know how much leather was left in it. I know for a fact Robby still has that glove."

MARC CHRISTOPHER VALDES (1971–)
■ MLB: 1995–98, 2000–01 ■ *Pitcher*

COLLEGE: 1991–93   6-0, 170 lbs.   12-15 / .444 / 4

Marc Valdes was born in Dayton, Ohio, and played high school baseball in Tampa. In 1991, he enrolled at UF and played for three seasons and had 31 wins with 351 strikeouts.

Valdes was drafted by the Cincinnati Reds in 1990, but he did not sign. After college, he was drafted in the first round by the Florida Marlins and signed with them, making his major league debut in 1995 and appearing in three games for the Marlins. After the 1996 season, he was waived by the Marlins and picked up by the Montreal Expos. He pitched for Montreal in 68 games in 1997–98 and then, in 1999, signed with the Tampa Bay Devil Rays. Valdes saw no action for the Rays and, in 2000, was traded to the Houston Astros.

He played in 2001 for the Atlanta Braves, then went to Japan and played for the Hanshin Tigers (2002) and Chunichi Dragons (2003–04). Valdes attempted to get back into the major leagues in 2005 with the New York Yankees, but he saw no game action with them before being released in July. He then went into coaching at the minor league level with the Mets organization, where he has spent six years. Valdes has worked with the Kingsport Mets, Savannah Sand Gnats, and the Binghamton Mets, and since 2013 has been the pitching coach for the Brooklyn Cyclones.

STEPHEN BRADLEY WILKERSON (1977–)
■ **MLB: 2001–08** ■ *Outfielder, First Basemen*

COLLEGE: 1996–98   6-0, 200 lbs.   .247 / .350 / .440;
OLYMPICS: 2000 gold medal

In 1995, Brad Wilkerson played on the U.S. national junior baseball team. During the World Junior Baseball Championship, he batted .360, hit three home runs, and pitched a three-hit shutout of Taiwan in the gold medal game and was named the MVP of the tournament. In his first and last years at Florida, his hitting and pitching helped the team to reach the College World Series. A high point was his grand slam home run against Florida State University in the 1996 CWS. In his junior year of 1998, he became the first college player to win 10 games as a pitcher, hit 20 home runs, and steal 20 bases. Wilkerson was named the College Player of the Year by the National Collegiate Baseball Writers' Association and was presented with the Rotary Smith Award by the Greater Houston Sports Association to recognize the country's top collegiate player.

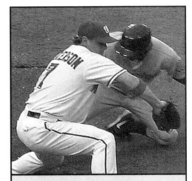

Brad Wilkerson as a Washington National in 2005

He was drafted by the Los Angeles Dodgers in the 1995 draft but opted not to sign. After college in 1998, he was chosen by the Montreal Expos in the first round, signed with them, and played for Double-A Harrisburg and Triple-A Ottawa. In 2000, as part of the U.S. national team, he received a gold medal at the Sydney Olympics when they defeated Cuba in the final game, which was a huge upset.

> **Nicknames of Gators**
>
> › *Casey* (Kendall Cole Wise)
> › *Dragon Slayer* (Joshua Smith Fogg)
> › *Eck* and *X Factor* (David Mark Eckstein)
> › *Flip* (Albert Leonard Rosen)
> › *Hank* and *Haney* (Henry Tate Boney)
> › *Hebrew Hammer* (Albert Leonard Rosen)
> › *The Last Expo* (Stephen Bradley Wilkerson)
> › *Lefty* (Witt Orison Guise)
> › *Paco* (Steven F. Rodriguez)
> › *Red* (Walter Lanier Barber)
> › *Square Jaw* (William Thrace Ramsey Jr.)
> › *Tiny* (James Bailey Chaplin)

Wilkerson made his major league debut with the Expos in 2001 and was still with the team when it became the Washington Nationals beginning in 2005. He was named *The Sporting News* National League Rookie of the Year in 2002. At the end of the 2004 season, he hit the last home run for the team known as the Expos; he later wore his Montreal uniform at an all-star series in Japan, earning him the nickname of "The Last Expo." With the team renamed as the Washington Nationals, Wilkerson hit its first grand slam home run.

Next came the Texas Rangers in 2006, and, in 2007, Wilkerson hit three home runs in a single game there. He began the 2008 season as a Seattle Mariner and finished it as a Toronto Blue Jay. In 2010, after a time in the minors and a brief retirement, he attempted a comeback. Wilkerson was a member of the Boston Red Sox and then the Philadelphia Phillies, but he was released before the start of the season.

Wilkerson became a member of the University of Florida Athletic Hall of Fame in 2010 and, in 2012, became the first Gator inducted into the College Baseball Hall of Fame. He is married and has three children.

KENDALL COLE WISE (1932–2007)
■ **MLB: 1957–60** ■ *Second Baseman, Shortstop*

COLLEGE: 1952–53   6-0, 170 lbs.   .174 / .243 / .240

Kendall Cole "Casey" Wise (whose nickname came from the initials of his first and middle names) was born in West Lafayette, Indiana, and played for Florida for two years. He graduated in 1956 with a bachelor's degree in mechanical engineering. Thereafter, he played a total of 126 games over four seasons in the major leagues, winding up with one of the lower batting averages of all time.

Wise made the most appearances (43) in his first year (1956) with the Chicago Cubs, then spent two years with the Milwaukee Braves and finished with 30 games played in 1960 with the Detroit Tigers. Most of his time was spent at second base, but he also was used at shortstop. His World Series experience consisted of playing in two games for the Braves in 1958 against the New York Yankees. In his only official at-bat, he struck out.

After retiring from baseball, Wise went to the University of Tennessee, earned degrees in dentistry and orthodontics, and opened the first orthodontics practice in Naples, Florida, in 1968. He retired from his practice in 1991 and, following complications from heart surgery, died February 20, 2007.

MICHAEL ACCORSI ZUNINO (1991–) ■ MLB: 2013–14 ■ *Catcher*
COLLEGE: 2010–12   6-2, 220 lbs.   .214 / .290 / .329

Mike Zunino was a graduate of Mariner High School in Cape Coral, Florida, when he was drafted by the Oakland Athletics in the 29th round of the MLB draft in 2009, but he did not sign. Instead, he played the next three years with the Gators. As a sophomore, he was a *Baseball America* All-American and the Gators' second Southeastern Conference Player of the Year. As a senior, Zunino won the Golden Spikes Award (USA Baseball's selection of the top amateur player in the country), the Dick Howser Trophy (National Collegiate Baseball Writers Association's national college baseball player of the year), and the Johnny Bench Award (as determined by the Greater Wichita Area Sports Commission, college baseball's top Division I catcher). He also played in the College World Series all three years.

Mike Zunino catching for Florida in 2011

In the 2012 draft, Zunino was chosen as the 3rd pick of the 1st round by the Seattle Mariners. He signed a contract with them on July 2, 2012, and was assigned to the Double-A Everett AquaSox. Late in the season, he moved to the Double-A Jackson Generals.

The 2013 season began with Zunino on the Tacoma Rainiers. He was added to the Mariners' MLB roster on June 11 and played in his first major league game on June 12, 2013. He broke his hand in July and did not return until September, but he ended the season hitting .214 with five homeruns and 14 RBIs in 52 games.

Other Florida Athletes Who Went Into Pro Baseball

Pro Career Started in the 1920s

NAME	POSITION	COLLEGE	MLB	STATS	TEAMS
Henry Tate Boney	P	1926–27	1927	0-0/2.25/0	New York Giants
Ned Swindell Porter	P	1924–26	1926–27	0-0/2.25/0	New York Giants

Pro Career Started in the 1930s

NAME	POSITION	COLLEGE	MLB	STATS	TEAMS
William Joseph Ferrazzi	P	1933–35	1935	1-2/5.14/0	Philadelphia Athletics

Pro Career Started in the 1940s

NAME	POSITION	COLLEGE	MLB	STATS	TEAMS
Witt Orison Guise	P	1930	1940	0-0/1.17/0	Cincinnati Reds

Pro Career Started in the 1950s

NAME	POSITION	COLLEGE	MLB	STATS	TEAMS
Nicholas Testa	C, PR	1946	1958	.000/.000/.000	San Francisco Giants

Pro Career Started in the 1960s

NAME	POSITION	COLLEGE	MLB	STATS	TEAMS
Dennis Kay Aust	P	1960–61	1965–66	0-1/5.82/2	St. Louis Cardinals
William Albert Graham	P	1955–56	1966–67	1-2/2.45/0	Detroit Tigers, New York Mets
Dale Jerome Willis	P	1955–56	1963	0-2/5.04/1	Kansas City Athletics

Pro Career Started in the 1980s

NAME	POSITION	COLLEGE	MLB	STATS	TEAMS
Jeffrey Thomas	P	1984–85	1987, 1989	0-1/9.53/0	Montreal Expos, Los Angeles Dodgers
Roger Holt	2B	1975–77	1980	.167/.286/.167	New York Yankees

Pro Career Started in the 1990s

NAME	POSITION	COLLEGE	MLB	STATS	TEAMS
Robert Wayne Dodd	P	1994	1998	1-0/7.20/0	Philadelphia Phillies

Pro Career Started in the 2000s

NAME	POSITION	COLLEGE	MLB	STATS	TEAMS
Brian Christopher Augenstein	P	2005–07	2009, 2011	0-2/8.34/0	Arizona Diamondbacks, St. Louis Cardinals
Mark Winston Kiger	INF	2000–02	2006	.000/.000/.000	Oakland Athletics
Chan Perry	RF, 1B, PH	1993–94	2000–01	.080/.080/.080	Cleveland Indians, Kansas City Royals
Ryan Sadowski	P	2002	2009	2-4/4.45/0	San Francisco Giants

Pro Career Started in the 2010s

NAME	POSITION	COLLEGE	MLB	STATS	TEAMS
Matthew G. den Dekker	OF	2007–10	2013	.207/.270/.276	New York Mets

SOFTBALL

A version of baseball played with a larger ball on a smaller field, what we now call softball, was invented in the late 19th century as a game that could be played indoors when the weather was harsh. Over the years, it evolved into its own sport and has been played by women in collegiate and international programs, including the Olympics.

Florida fielded its first women's softball team in 1997 under head coach Larry Ray, a graduate of Idaho State University. A respectable 42-25 first season moved the Gators into third place in the Eastern Division of the Southeastern Conference. The following year, they improved to 47-22 and were the regular season conference champions. Ray was named the SEC Coach of the Year, and the team was ranked #25 in the nation.

Coach Walton (left) exchanges words with an umpire

The second coach, Karen Johns, took over in 2001 after playing at the University of South Carolina and coaching at the University of Alabama. During her five years in Gainesville, the Gators finished second in the Eastern Division once and third four times.

The present coach took over prior to the start of the 2006 season and has brought the program into the national limelight. Tim Walton, a graduate of the University of Oklahoma, has reached 500 coaching victories faster than any previous SEC coach, and Florida became the first team in the conference to play in four consecutive Women's College World Series. Walton was named as the SEC Coach of the Year in 2008, 2009, and 2011.

The Gators captured their first softball national championship in 2014. From the beginning of the NCAA regional tournament through the title-clinching victory over Alabama, Florida posted a record of 10-1 and outscored its opponents 81-10. The scoring differential could have been much higher but for five of the games being stopped early under the "mercy rule" to prevent embarrassment of teams without a reasonable hope of coming back.

Florida Softball Coaching Records

Coach	Years	SEC Wins	SEC Losses	SEC Pct.	Overall Wins	Overall Losses	Overall Pct.
Larry Ray	1997–2000	65	42	.647	169	106	.615
Karen Johns	2001–05	79	69	.534	192	131	.594
Tim Walton	2006–14	187	60	.757	492	114	.812
Total		331	171	.659	853	351	.708

Women's College World Series Appearances
(Through 2014)

YEARS	#1	TEAM	YEARS	#1	TEAM
25	12	UCLA	4	0	DePaul
22	8	Arizona	4	0	Iowa
12	1	California	3	0	Baylor
12	1	Fresno State	3	0	LSU
11	2	Arizona State	3	0	Louisiana Tech
11	1	Washington	3	0	Massachusetts
10	1	Michigan	3	0	Nevada-Las Vegas
9	1	Alabama	3	0	Oregon
9	2	Oklahoma	3	0	South Carolina
8	0	Florida State	3	0	Utah
8	0	Nebraska	2	0	Adelphi
7	0	Oklahoma State	2	0	Cal State Northridge
7	2	Texas A&M	2	0	Creighton
6	1	Cal State Fullerton	2	0	Georgia
6	1	**Florida**	2	0	Indiana
6	0	Missouri	2	0	Princeton
6	0	SW Louisiana/LA-Lafayette	2	0	Southern Mississippi
5	0	Long Beach State	2	0	Stanford
5	0	Northwestern	1	0	Central Michigan
5	0	Tennessee	1	0	Connecticut
5	0	Texas	1	0	Hawaii
4	0	Cal Poly Pomona	1	0	Illinois-Chicago

YEARS	#1	TEAM	YEARS	#1	TEAM
1	0	Kansas	1	0	South Florida
1	0	Kent State	1	0	Toledo
1	0	Northern Illinois	1	0	Utah State
1	0	Oregon State	1	0	Virginia Tech
1	0	Pacific	1	0	Western Michigan

Southeastern Conference Championships

YEAR	REGULAR SEASON	TOURNAMENT
1997	South Carolina	South Carolina
1998	**Florida**	Alabama
1999	LSU	LSU
2000	LSU	South Carolina
2001	LSU	LSU
2002	LSU	LSU
2003	Georgia	Alabama
2004	LSU	LSU
2005	Georgia	Alabama
2006	Alabama	Tennessee
2007	Tennessee	LSU
2008	**Florida**	**Florida**
2009	**Florida**	**Florida**
2010	Alabama	Alabama
2011	Alabama	Tennessee
2012	Alabama	Alabama
2013	**Florida**	**Florida**
2014	Alabama	Georgia

SEC Championships by Team
(Through 2014)

TEAM	REGULAR SEASON	TOURNAMENT
LSU	5	5
Alabama	5	5
Florida	4	3
Georgia	2	1

TEAM	REGULAR SEASON	TOURNAMENT
South Carolina	1	2
Tennessee	1	2
Arkansas	0	0
Auburn	0	0
Kentucky	0	0
Mississippi	0	0
Mississippi State	0	0
Missouri	0	0
Texas A&M	0	0

Athlete Bios

College years are those during which the athlete was awarded a letter for softball. Pro years are those for which the athlete was active for at least one game.

Pro years are years actually played through 2013.

KELSEY BRUDER (c. 1989–) ■ *Outfielder*

COLLEGE: 2008–11   5-5   **PRO:** 2008–13

Kelsey Bruder in her home run trot

Kelsey Bruder played softball for Santiago High School in Corona, California, while graduating with a 4.0 grade-point average. She arrived in Gainesville as a freshman in 2008 and played in 37 games that season, including six appearances as a pitcher. As a sophomore, she played in all 68 games, batted .369, and hit 16 home runs. Her 139 bases led the team and was the second highest in the SEC. Bruder set the all-time Gator slugging percentage record for a season that year (.713), and then broke it as a senior (.764). She was named by Easton as a first-team All-American and by NFCA/Louisville Slugger to its second team. In the Southeastern Conference, she made the All-Tournament team, the All-Defensive team, and was named a first-team All-SEC and All-Southeast Region first-team player.

During her junior year, Bruder hit for an average of .367 and had 66 hits, both the second-best on the team. She hit .565 in the NCAA tournament to lead the Gators in hitting. Her season included 131 total bases, which again led UF and tied for second-most in the SEC. She was named to the *ESPN The Magazine* Academic All-District 3 first team and the second team of *ESPN The Magazine* Academic All-Americans.

In 2011, Bruder was part of the team that posted a record of 56-13 and was runner-up in the NCAA tournament to Arizona State University, and her batting average of .387 was the best of her college years. She was named the SEC Player of the Year and set Florida records for total bases in a season (152) and runs (79), as well as being named to the SEC Academic Honor Roll her last three years.

In June 2011, Bruder was named the winner of the Honda Award, honoring her as the top college female softball player. She is the first from the University of Florida to receive the award and the second from the SEC. She was also presented with the NCAA Today Top VIII Award, given to eight student-athletes to recognize their success in both sports and the community. Bruder received her bachelor's degree from UF in health and behavior in December 2011. She was also a Capital One Academic All-American.

In the 2011 National Pro Fastpitch senior draft, she was chosen fifth by the USSSA Florida Pride and had 39 at-bats, driving in 3 runs and hitting for an average of .205. In 2012, she increased to 65 at-bats, 13 RBIs (one home run), and an average of .231.

Bruder played left field for the Pride and served as a volunteer assistant coach for Murray State University in 2012. Since 2013, she has coached at Florida and works in sports ministry.

MEGAN BUSH (1989–) ■ *Utility Infielder*
COLLEGE: 2008–11 5-7 **PRO:** 2011–12

As a member of her high school softball team in Anaheim, California, Megan Bush was named the 2007 Canyon High School Female Athlete of the Year and the Century League Player of the Year. She arrived in Gainesville and played in 74 games for the Gators during her freshman year. Bush was second on the team that year in home runs (13), one of which was in her first at-bat as a college player, and she hit the game-winning home run against the University of California in the NCAA Super Regional.

As a sophomore, she was named to the NFCA/Louisville Slugger All-Southeast Region team and the All-Southeastern Conference second team. Bush played in 67 games, starting 66 of them at shortstop and, at the Women's College World Series, she was named to the WCWS All-Tournament team. In her junior year, she hit .362 while starting 58 of 59 games, at shortstop and first base, while setting a new Florida career record for sacrifice flies (12). Her accolades included first-team honors for the NBCA/Louisville Slugger All-Southeast Region and the SEC All-Tournament. She was named first-team All-SEC and was on the SEC Academic Honor Roll.

As a senior, Bush started all of the 69 games in which she played and hit 21 home runs, which brought her career total to 65 and broke the previous SEC record. She had her best fielding percentage (.985) and wound up with a four-year batting average of .318. Bush was busy off the field as well. She was named a top-20 finalist for the NCAA Senior CLASS Award for her accomplishments in her community, classroom, character, and competition.

In the 2011 college draft, Bush was chosen in the second round (sixth pick overall) by the Akron Racers of National Pro Fastpitch, and that same year she was one of four Gators selected to compete for a spot on the USA National Team. She tried out but was not chosen for the team.

Bush played with Akron through the 2012 season and, in 52 games batted, for an average of .195. Megan was on a touring NPF all-star team, which played university teams in the fall of 2012 that included a game against the University of Florida. She did not return to the Racers for 2013. Bush has served as a radio color commentator for Gator softball games.

KRISTEN BUTLER (1984–) ■ *Catcher*

COLLEGE: 2003–06   5-6   **PRO:** 2006–09

Kristen Butler (left) just after receiving the ceremonial first pitch from a Navy ensign during Chicago Navy Week 2012

As a student at Central Florida Christian Academy, Kristen Butler was honored as the *Orlando Sentinel* High School Sports Athlete of the Year. She was also the Orange County Player of the Year and the All-Central Florida Player of the Year. She played varsity softball for six years, and her high school batting average was over .500.

Butler was a four-year starter for the Gators and made it on the Southeastern Conference Academic Honor Roll for her last three years. She set UF records for her position, including lowest stolen base percentage by a catcher, runners caught stealing, and pick-offs. During her senior year, she led the team in home runs, slugging, and on-base percentages, and RBIs. Butler was named the SEC Player of the Year for 2006 and was honored by CoSIDA/ *ESPN The Magazine* as an Academic All-American (District 3). She served as a student assistant, helping with the coaching staff, for part of 2007 and graduated that spring with a bachelor's degree in sports management.

Later in 2007, Butler joined the National Pro Fastpitch Akron Racers and played through 2009, twice being named to the All-National Fastpitch League team, and was the Defensive Player of the Year in 2008. In 2009–10, she was one of the six Americans who accepted invitations to play in the Japan National League. Butler played catcher, third baseman, and designated player, and set the Japanese record for home runs in one game (three). She returned to the United States and played in the PFX professional softball tour during 2010–11, which had a little less demanding schedule, giving her time to focus on her upcoming marriage and to prepare to enter coaching.

Butler became an assistant coach at Mississippi Valley State University, where the team in 2011–12 won the SWAC Conference title and participated in the NCAA

Regional tournament. For the 2012 professional season, she played for the Chicago Bandits as a catcher and designated player, and she finished with the second-highest totals of home runs and RBIs (7 and 29) in the league. In September 2012, Butler joined the coaching staff of Charleston Southern University, where she works with pitchers and catchers.

LINDSEY CAMERON (1984–) ■ *Outfielder*

COLLEGE: 2003–06   5-6   **PRO:** 2006

Lindsey Cameron graduated from Palm Beach Gardens High School after being its best hitter for three years. She was named its MVP as a freshman and junior and its Offensive MVP as a sophomore. During the summer, she played for the Florida Lady Gators.

In her freshman year at Florida, Cameron led the team with 35 runs scored and was second in batting average with .316. She set a team freshman record for slugging percentage in conference games (.614) and was also named to the Regional All-Tournament team.

As a sophomore, she was on the Southeastern Conference Academic Honor Roll and was named to the All-SEC first team; she started 52 of the 56 games in which she played (mostly in the outfield). In 2005 as a junior, Cameron missed 13 games as a result of an injury to her wrist but still managed to lead the Gators in home runs, hits, RBIs, batting average, and slugging percentage. She was a first team NFCA/Louisville Slugger All-American.

Cameron was on the All-SEC first team as a junior and a senior. She played one year as a pro, as an outfielder for the NPF Philadelphia Force. In 2008, she played for the Macerata team in the Italian Softball League.

FRANCESCA ENEA (1988–) ■ *Outfielder*

COLLEGE: 2007–10   5-8   **PRO:** 2010–13

In her freshman year in 2007, Francesca Enea was named to the All-Southeastern Conference second team and the SEC All-Freshman team. She was listed on the SEC Freshman Honor Roll and, the next three years, she was on the SEC Academic Honor Roll. As a sophomore, she started all of the team's 74 games and, despite a torn anterior cruciate ligament, played in all 68 games as a junior (starting 62 in left field after beginning the year as a catcher).

At the university, Enea was named to the NFCA/Louisville Slugger All-American second team in both 2008 and 2009, plus the Easton

Francesca Enea in the 2009 Women's College World Series

All-American first team those same years. In 2008, she was listed on the Women's College World Series All-Tournament team, and, in 2009, she was on the All-Southeastern Conference second team (and moved up to the first team in 2010). Enea held the Gator record in season slugging percentage (.713 until broken by Kelsey Bruder), and she has records in season home runs (18), season RBIs (70), season sacrifice flies (six), career home runs (41), and career RBIs (156). She was an NFCA/Louisville Slugger All-American in 2008, 2009, and 2010 (second team).

Enea majored in youth, family and community services with the goal of becoming a speech pathologist. She was honored by being named a top-10 finalist for the NCAA Senior CLASS Award for her attributes in the community, classroom, character, and competition.

In 2010, she joined the USSSA Pride, which that year won its first National Pro Fastpitch championship. Out of the team's 57 games that year, she played in 25, plus three exhibition games and two in the playoffs. In her second year, she had a batting average of .315, a .407 on-base percentage, and a slugging percentage of .452. During 2012, Enea hit four home runs and had 15 RBIs.

She has served as a coach in the Central Florida area and has served as a featured clinician for the Midwest Sports Productions softball camp. Enea is the Marketing Manager for Easton Fastpitch, a manufacturer of softball equipment.

AJA PACULBA (1989–) ■ *Second Baseman*

COLLEGE: 2008–11   5-3   **PRO:** 2011–13

A three-time All-Academic Athlete at Elsinore High School in Wildomar, California, Aja Paculba batted for an average of .336 in her freshman year at Florida. She started all 75 games at second base and scored the third-most runs (61) in the Southeastern Conference. Paculba was honored as a second-team NFCA/Louisville Slugger All-American and a first-team Easton All-American. She was named to the SEC All-Defensive and All-Freshman teams, plus the All-SEC second team.

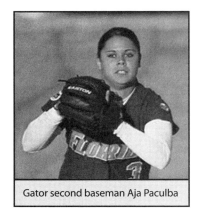
Gator second baseman Aja Paculba

In her sophomore year of 2009, she started all 68 games and hit for an average of .368. Paculba led Florida in several categories: at-bats, runs, hits, triples, stolen bases, walks, multi-hit games, batting average in games against SEC opponents, and game-winning runs. Her 27 stolen bases set a new Gator record. Paculba repeated on the All-American teams from her freshman year and the SEC All-Defensive team, and she was named to the All-SEC first team.

As a junior, she again was on the All-SEC Defensive first team and the second team of the NFCA/Louisville Slugger All-Southeast Region. Her 16-game hitting streak tied the longest ever for a player at Florida. Paculba wound up her four years at UF with a batting average of .340 and 35 home runs and holds the school career records for runs scored (188) on-base percentage (.459), runs (69), walks (49), and stolen bases (27) in a season.

In 2011, she signed with the NPF Diamonds after being drafted 17th by them, but she could only play 18 games that year because she could not join until the Gators finished their run in the Women's College World Series.

In February 2012, Paculba was traded to the Akron Racers and presently is their shortstop. During her first season with the team, she hit for an average of .250 and had 15 RBIs. For the week of June 10, 2012, she was named the National Pro Fastpitch Offensive Player of the Week for hitting .416 in four games.

In addition to being a professional softball player, Paculba was an assistant softball coach at Florida International University in 2012 and, in 2013, joined the coaching staff of Western Kentucky University.

STACIE PESTRAK (1983–) ■ *Outfielder*

COLLEGE: 2005–06   5-5   **PRO:** 2006–07

After graduating from Gainesville's Buchholz High School, Stacie Pestrak attended Santa Fe Community College and earned the Florida Community College Activities Association's Jean Williams Scholar-Athlete Award. In 2003, she batted .354 and was named her school's rookie of the year. The next year, she was a junior college All-American, being named to the second team by the NJCAA and the third team by the National Fastpitch Coaches Association. She set school records for career runs (92), career steals (92), and season steals (52) and was the recipient of the Leadership and Drive Award.

As a member of the softball team at UF, Pestrak played as an infielder. She graduated in 2007 after batting .283 and starting 108 of the 126 games in which she played. In both of her years as a Lady Gator, the team went to the NCAA tournament, and she made the Southeastern Conference Academic Honor Roll in 2006.

Pestrak turned professional that same year and played mostly in the outfield and, the following year, as a member of the Philadelphia Force, was selected to represent her team and the National Pro Fastpitch league at the Major League Baseball All-Star Game Fan Fest in San Francisco. For two years, she served as assistant coach with Santa Fe Community College in Gainesville.

From 2010 to 2012, Pestrak was an assistant coach for the Lady Demons of the Northwestern State University in Natchitoches, Louisiana. During 2012, she was a member of the inaugural class of inductees of the Santa Fe College Hall of Fame.

BASKETBALL
BASKETBALL
BASKETBALL

MEN

GO GATORS! GO GATORS! You are probably thinking the editors of this book made a mistake—why else would the phrase "GO GATORS!" be back-to-back? Ah, perhaps now you see why. This represents what the Florida men's basketball team did in 2006 and 2007 when they won the NCAA Championship Tournament two years in a row. The Gators are only the second team in the last 30 years to do this. Of course, this is nowhere near the staggering record held by UCLA of seven in a row (plus a total of 11 titles, ten of them between 1964 and 1975). But the Gators had two unprecedented accomplishments: They won the basketball championship two years in a row with the same starting lineup, and they remain the only team in NCAA Division I history to simultaneously hold championship titles in both football and men's basketball for the same season.

If you look at the overall picture of the two basketball titles with the football championship in the middle, you could say the Gators were back-to-back-to-back champs—as illustrated on one of our T-shirts that has two basketballs with a football in the middle! And we would be remiss if we didn't mention that, in the 2006 BCS Football Championship game that took place in January of 2007 and the final game in the 2007 NCAA Tournament held in April, the Gators beat the same school in both finals, The Ohio State University. We're not trying to rub it in . . . okay, maybe just a little. But it was a pretty amazing coincidence.

The Early Coaches

The University of Florida sponsored its first official intercollegiate basketball team during the 1915–16 academic year. There had been a team in 1913, but it was unofficial and a record of scores does not exist. C.J. McCoy, who also coached the football team, served as the basketball head coach in 1915–16. The first game was a 30–14 victory over the Jacksonville YMCA, and the second game was an "away" game at Columbia College in Lake City, Florida. That game must have brought back memories for some of the fans because Columbia was the college that took over the Florida Agricultural College campus when the institution was merged into the University of Florida and moved from Lake City to Gainesville. The team's first-year record was 5-1, with all being away games.

From 1916 to 19, there was no team because of World War I. The postwar team came back in 1919 without a coach for the year, was captained by C.A. Coxe, and had a record of 2-5. The next year, the Gators opened with their first home game, a 36–18 loss to Stetson University, under head coach William G. Kline, who remained with the basketball team for one more year while coaching the football team. In 1923, Kline left Florida to coach basketball and baseball at the University of Nebraska.

The Gators next turned to J.L. White in 1923, who took over as head coach for two years and had a record of 7-17. Brady Cowell followed in 1925 and, over eight seasons, had a record of 62-76. In the early part of his tenure, the Gators played some interesting teams, including Seminole Canoe, Ralph's Cleaners, the Masked Marvels, Olson's Swedes, and other non-universities. In 1927, home games were moved from the 1919 building that was known for many years as the Women's Gymnasium (and more recently as Ustler Hall), to the New Gym (Building R). Cowell's last season, 1932–33, was Florida's first in the Southeastern Conference, and the schedule took on a more respectable look with teams that included the University of Georgia, Vanderbilt University, Auburn University, and the University of Kentucky. Florida's all-time record before the formation of the SEC was 79-120 and included only three winning seasons. It was time for Cowell to move on, and he left Gainesville to head a little south to DeLand to be the Stetson University football coach.

Coach Clemons when he was a student-athlete

He was followed by recent Gator player Ben Clemons, who was in charge for three years, and former Vanderbilt University football standout Josh Cody, who coached Gator basketball for just one year but stayed for three more seasons to coach the football team.

Sam McAllister, who was an assistant coach for UF football and head coach for baseball and basketball, took over from 1937 to 1942 and had a record of 56-36 and then left in 1943 to join the Navy. Assistant football coach Spurgeon Cherry succeeded him, and that year under his leadership, the team was 0-6 against SEC competition and 8-1 against a slate mostly comprised of military bases. There was no team for the 1943–44 season because of World War II.

Coach McAllister in 1941

Cherry was back in 1944 for two more losing seasons, followed by the return of Sam McAllister for a second shot as head coach from 1946 through 1951. Beginning with 1944, the Gators had a streak of seven seasons in which they lost their first (and only) game in the annual single-elimination SEC Tournament. However, they had something to look forward to in 1949 when home games were moved to the new Florida Gymnasium, which was nicknamed Alligator Alley.

The next coach was John Mauer, who had previously coached basketball at the University of Kentucky, Miami University, the University of Tennessee, and Army. Before that, he had been an All-Big Ten player at the University of Illinois in both basketball and football, and his Tennessee teams won the SEC regular season and tournament championships in 1941 and 1943. Everyone had high hopes for the exciting new coach, also an assistant for the Florida football team, who thought he might be able to bring a title to Gainesville. Mauer coached the Gators from 1951 until 1960, and, unfortunately, the closest he got was in 1952–53, when an 8-5 conference record was only good enough for third place. His basketball coaching records at Tennessee and Kentucky are still near the top in the history of those schools, but, at Florida, Mauer was unable to win more than he lost.

The First Norm Sloan Era

The Gators desperately wanted to be a force in the conference in basketball and hired Norm Sloan as head coach in 1960. He had become the head coach of Presbyterian College just two years after playing guard for North Carolina State University. In 1957, he coached the first of his three seasons at The Citadel and was named the SoCon Coach of the Year, and the team received the George Mikan Award for Most Improved Team in the Nation.

Norm Sloan (center) in 1962

Sloan was Florida's first full-time basketball head coach who, unlike his predecessors, didn't have to concern himself with football or baseball or serve as the university's athletic director. He was named SEC Coach of the Year in 1961 and had a winning record in five out of six seasons, but the best his teams could do in the conference were three fourth-place finishes. The program under Norm Sloan was elevated from a club team-like status to a real major college competitor, but it still didn't make it to the postseason or challenge for an SEC title, and Sloan returned to North Carolina State in 1966.

Three More Coaches

Sloan's successor was Tommy Bartlett, who starred at the University of Tennessee in basketball and tennis. He coached both sports, more years in tennis than in basketball, at the University of Tennessee and the University of Tennessee-Chattanooga. In his first year at Florida, the team went 21-4 and came in second in the conference, but over the next six seasons the best it could manage was third place. UF was Bartlett's last college basketball coaching job, but he continued as a tennis coach.

The next leader was John Lotz, who played basketball for Baylor University and then became an assistant coach at the University of North Carolina for eight years, including four trips to the NCAA Final Four. At Florida, he went 83-88 over less than seven seasons, and he was named the SEC Coach of the Year in 1977 when the Gators went 17-9. He left midway through the 1979–80 season to become the assistant athletic director at North Carolina, while Ed Visscher stepped in as interim head coach for the last 17 games in 1980.

The Second Norm Sloan Era

Meanwhile, Norm Sloan was winning at North Carolina State, even though he had earned the nickname "Stormin' Norman" as much for his battles with other ACC coaches as for the garish plaid sports coat he favored. His teams won a pair of ACC regular season championships, three ACC tournament championships, and the 1974 NCAA national championship. The Gators decided a do-over was in order, and Sloan was rehired for the 1980 season to lead the program in a new direction in the brand-new O'Connell Center.

His second stint in Gainesville did not begin well, with records of 12-16, 5-22, and 13-18, and Stormin' Norman began new feuds in the SEC. In 1983–84, the team improved to 16-13, a third-place finish in the SEC, and a trip to the National Invitational Tournament (back when the NIT was a prestigious post-season tournament, not a consolation tournament for those who missed the NCAA tournament, as it is viewed today).

Momentum continued to build as the Gators had winning records in each of the next five seasons and made it to the NIT in two years and the NCAA tournament in three straight seasons, including a Sweet Sixteen appearance in 1987. The Gators finally won their first-ever SEC regular season title in 1988–89. Under Sloan, the Gators beat Florida State University seven out of eight years, had their first win at the University of Tennessee, and posted their first regular season win over the University of Kentucky. However, the decade's success was tarnished by a drug scandal and alleged NCAA rule violations, which resulted in the vacating of some of the Gators' wins and losses, as well as a two-year probation, and Sloan was forced to resign.

Former Gator coach Don DeVoe

He was replaced by interim head coach Don DeVoe, formerly the coach at the University of Tennessee. He clashed with some of his players and wound up with a record of 3-15 before leaving in 1990 to become the head basketball coach at Navy.

The Lon Kruger Era

Once again, the Gators found themselves looking for a coach, this time under less-than-desirable circumstances, and they turned to a former player at Kansas State University, Lon Kruger. He had coached at Pittsburg State University, Kansas State, and Texas-Pan American when he took over at Florida in 1990. The team was still under probation; in his first year, they managed a record of only 11-17, but Kruger turned it around in 1991–92 as the Gators went 19-14 and made it to the NIT, and Kruger was named the SEC Coach of the Year. The following season also included an NIT berth, and the program peaked under Kruger as he received his second Coach of the Year honor in 1993–94.

Former Gator coach Lon Kruger

That season turned out to be a breakthrough for the program. The team had an overall record of 29-8, including 12-4 in the SEC to tie for the best conference regular season record. The Gators went to the NCAA tournament and made it to the Final Four, their first-ever appearance, by beating James Madison University, the University of Pennsylvania, the University of Connecticut, and Boston College. In the Final Four, the Gators lost to Duke University in the national semi-final.

After two more seasons at Florida with one trip to the NCAA tournament that ended with their losing the first game, Kruger left in 1996 to coach at the University of Illinois. He went into the NBA for three years as head coach of the Atlanta Hawks and one as an assistant with the New York Knicks, before returning to the college ranks. Kruger spent seven years as the head coach at the University of Nevada-Las Vegas and, since 2011, has served as the head coach at the University of Oklahoma.

The Billy Donovan Era

Kruger was replaced by Florida's present coach, Billy Donovan. He had played for Providence College (where he received the nickname "Billy the

Kid" and was the starting point guard on the team that made it to the 1987 Final Four) and the New York Knicks, then served as a graduate assistant at the University of Kentucky. He moved up to assistant coach, and then took over as head coach of Marshall University in 1994. That year, he was named the *Basketball Times* Rookie Coach of the Year, the West Virginia College Coach of the Year, and the Southern Conference Coach of the Year. After two years there, Donovan became the Gator head coach in 1996.

During his first year in Gainesville (1996–97), the Gators finished with a record of 13-17 and missed the postseason. That is the last time they did, and through 2014 under Donovan, Florida has played in the NCAA tournament 14 times and the NIT three times. His 2000 Gators made a deep run into the NCAA tournament and reached the Final Four for the second time in school history. The Gators defeated North Carolina to reach the national title game against Michigan State University, but they fell to the Spartans 89-76. They were getting close to a national championship.

And then came the 2005–06 season, which was special right from the first tip-off. Florida won its first 17 games, the best start in school history, and was 23-0 against non-conference opponents. A 10-6 record against conference teams gave it a second-place regular season finish in the SEC East. But the best was still yet to come. At the SEC tournament, the Gators beat the University of Arkansas, LSU, and the University of South Carolina to take the conference title. The Gators went into the NCAA tournament seeded No. 3 and proceeded to knock off the University of South Alabama, the University of Wisconsin-Milwaukee, Georgetown University, and Villanova University to reach the Final Four in Indianapolis. They beat the Cinderella George Mason University by a score of 73 to 58 to make it to the final game, where they beat UCLA 73–57 for their first national championship. The Gators wound up with an unusual souvenir of their win—the university purchased the basketball floor on which the final games were played and

Billy Donovan coaching in 2013

installed it in the O'Connell Center so present and future Gators could play on the same floor where the school won their first national championship.

The core of the team, then four juniors and one senior, all decided to forego the NBA draft with an ambitious goal in mind—to win two national championships in a row. For the first time in school history, Florida began the basketball season ranked No. 1 in both major polls. At one point in the season, Donovan's Gators had a record of 24-2 and early on clinched the SEC regular season championship. After winning the SEC tournament for the second year in a row, the team entered the NCAA tournament as a No. 1 overall seed with a record of 29-5. After victories over Butler University, the University of Oregon and UCLA, Florida beat The Ohio State University in the final game by a score of 84 to 75 to become the first team in the history of the NCAA to win the championship in consecutive years with the same starting lineup. They were the first team since Duke University in 1991 and 1992 to capture back-to-back titles and the seventh school overall to repeat as champions.

In the next college draft, four UF starters and the "sixth man" were selected by NBA teams, and the university went into rebuilding mode. The next two years, the Gators were not invited to the NCAA tournament and instead went to the NIT, where they were eliminated early. In 2010, they were back in the NCAA tournament but lost in the first round.

The 2010–11 season kicked off a series of three consecutive Elite Eight appearances—the only school in the country to make it that far in all three years. They also won the SEC regular season in 2010–11 and 2012–13. In 2013–14, they did even better by becoming the first SEC basketball team to finish the season with an 18-0 record against conference teams (and the first NCAA team to do so in any major conference). At the NCAA tournament (where they were the number one seed overall), they beat the University at Albany, the University of Pittsburgh, UCLA, and the University of Dayton, but seemed to finally run out of steam and lost to the University of Connecticut in the Final Four.

In spite of that loss, the Gators had an incredible season. Donovan received his second consecutive SEC Coach of the Year honor. The players also received awards, as voted by the conference coaches: Scottie Wilbekin (SEC Player of the Year), Patric Young (SEC Defensive Player of the Year and SEC Scholar-Athlete of the Year), and Dorian Finney-Smith (SEC Sixth Man of the Year).

Florida Coaching Records

Years	Head Coach	Seasons	All Games Wins	All Games Losses	All Games Pct.	SEC Wins	SEC Losses	SEC Pct.
1915–16	C.J. McCoy	1	5	1	.833			
1919–20	No Coach	1	2	5	.286			
1920–22	W.G. Kline	2	10	11	.476			
1922–23	C.Y. Byrd	1	2	5	.286			
1923–25	J.L. White	2	7	17	.292			
1925–33	Brady Cowell	8	62	86	.419	4	4	.500
1933–36	Ben Clemons	3	23	25	.479	10	13	.434
1936–37	Josh Cody	1	5	13	.278	1	9	.111
1937–42, 1946–51	Sam McAllister	10	119	96	.553	45	62	.421
1942–43, 1944–46	Spurgeon Cherry	3	22	33	.400	6	14	.300
1951–60	John Mauer	9	98	102	.490	43	82	.344
1960–66, 1980–89	Norm Sloan	15	232	192	.547	126	124	.504
1966–73	Tommy Bartlett	7	95	85	.528	62	64	.492
1973–80	John Lotz	6+	83	88	.487	46	66	.412
1980	Ed Visscher	1-	3	14	.176	1	13	.071
1989–90	Don DeVoe	1	7	21	.250	3	15	.166
1991–96	Lon Kruger	6	104	80	.565	51	47	.520
1997–2014	Billy Donovan	18	451	169	.727	192	100	.658

Southeastern Conference Teams
(All-time Wins through 2014)

RECORD	TEAM	WINNING PCT.	SEASONS
2,140-672	Kentucky	.761	111
1,581-968	Alabama	.620	101
1,578-862	Arkansas	.647	91
1,578-1,066	Missouri	.597	108
1,552-985	Tennessee	.612	105
1,526-1,079	Vanderbilt	.586	112

RECORD	TEAM	WINNING PCT.	SEASONS
1,465-1,118	LSU	.567	106
1,334-1,123	Mississippi State	.543	102
1,332-1,201	Georgia	.526	109
1,331-1,050	**Florida**	.559	95
1,325-1,187	South Carolina	.527	106
1,325-1,211	Texas A&M	.522	102
1,264-1,130	Auburn	.528	108
1,218-1,243	Mississippi	.495	104

Southeastern Conference Championships
(Regular Season through 2014)

45	Kentucky	3	Vanderbilt	1	South Carolina
11	LSU	2	Arkansas	1	Tulane
8	Alabama	2	Auburn	0	Mississippi
8	Tennessee	2	Georgia Tech	0	Missouri
7	**Florida**	1	Georgia	0	Texas A&M
6	Mississippi State				

(Conference Tournament)

28	Kentucky	2	Georgia	1	Georgia Tech
6	Alabama	2	Mississippi	1	LSU
4	**Florida**	2	Vanderbilt	0	Missouri
4	Tennessee	1	Arkansas	0	Texas A&M
3	Mississippi State	1	Auburn		

Florida in the NCAA Tournament

1987	Sweet Sixteen*		2004	First Round
1988	Second Round*		2005	Second Round
1989	First Round		2006	National Champ
1994	Final Four		2007	National Champ
1995	First Round		2010	First Round
1999	Sweet Sixteen		2011	Elite Eight
2000	National Runner-up		2012	Elite Eight
2001	Second Round		2013	Elite Eight
2002	First Round		2014	Final Four
2003	Second Round			

* Vacated by NCAA

Florida in the Postseason NIT

1969	First Round	1986	Fourth Place	1998	First Round
1984	First Round	1992	Fourth Place	2008	Semifinals
1985	First Round	1993	First Round	2009	Quarterfinals

NCAA Championships
(Through 2014)

11	UCLA	2	Oklahoma State	1	Michigan
8	Kentucky	2	San Francisco	1	Nevada-Las Vegas
5	Indiana	1	Atlanta	1	Ohio State
5	North Carolina	1	Arkansas	1	Oregon
4	Connecticut	1	California	1	Stanford
4	Duke	1	CCNY	1	Syracuse
3	Kansas	1	Georgetown	1	Texas-El Paso (Texas Western)
3	Louisville	1	Holy Cross	1	Utah
2	Cincinnati	1	La Salle	1	Villanova
2	**Florida**	1	Loyola (Illinois)	1	Wisconsin
2	Michigan State	1	Marquette	1	Wyoming
2	North Carolina State	1	Maryland		

Our Florida All-Stars: Basketball
(Based solely on their pro careers)

Point Guard:	Jason Williams
Shooting Guard:	Vernon Maxwell
Center:	Joakim Noah
Power Forward:	David Lee
Small Forward:	Mike Miller
Best Overall:	Joakim Noah

Athlete Bios

College years are those during which the athlete was awarded a letter for basketball. Pro years are those for which the athlete was active for at least one game.

Pro years are years actually played through the 2013–14 regular season.

Statistics are pro career (per game) averages through the 2013–14 regular season: **Points / Rebounds / Assists / Blocks / Steals**

BRADLEY EMMANUEL BEAL (1993–)
■ **NBA: 2012–14** ■ *Shooting Guard*

COLLEGE: 2011–12   6-5, 207 lbs.   15.7 / 3.8 / 2.9 / 0.4 / 0.9

Bradley Beal was a high school basketball star in Missouri, being named Mr. Show-Me Basketball and the Gatorade National Player of the Year in 2011 as a senior. Playing for USA Basketball in the International Basketball Federation (FIBA) World Championships (under 17) the year before, he and his teammates won the gold medal. He had already committed to play for Florida in November 2009 and had his first season in Gainesville in 2011–12.

Bradley Beal as a Washington Wizard in 2013

Beal, whose motto is "humble and hungry," started strong, and was named Southeastern Conference Freshman of the Week by the Southeastern Conference coaches in November. That was the first of five such honors, in addition to making the coaches' SEC All-Freshman team. He also was recognized as a first-team coaches' All-SEC player and averaged 14.8 points per game his freshman year, which was his only year as a Gator.

In the 2012 draft, Beal was selected in the first round by the Washington Wizards. During his rookie season, he was Eastern Conference Rookie of the Month for December and January, and at the end of the year was named as a first-team All-Rookie and was chosen to play in the Rising Stars game held during the NBA All-Star Game weekend. During his first 56 regular season games, Beal averaged more than 13 points a game, but, because of a leg injury, his 2012–13 season ended on April 3, 2013. He came back the following year and increased his scoring average to more than 17 points a game.

MATTHEW ROBERT BONNER (1980–)
■ **NBA: 2004–14** ■ *Power Forward*

COLLEGE: 2000–03   6-10, 240 lbs.   6.2 / 3.2 / 0.7 / 0.3 / 0.4

Matt Bonner played for three-time state champion Concord High School in New Hampshire and graduated at the top of his class. He played four years for Florida and wound up in the Gator all-time record books in the top 10 in six statistical categories. Bonner was named an Associated Press All-American honorable mention in 2001–02 and 2002–03 and was presented with the Ben Hill Griffin Award in 2003, as the top University of Florida student-athlete for all sports.

He graduated with a 3.96 grade point average and was a three-year recipient of the Southeastern Conference Good Works/Community Service team designation. He was a two-time College Sports Information Directors of America Academic All-American and for the 2002–03 season was honored as the Creamland Dairies College Basketball Student-Athlete of the Year. Bonner is one of only four basketball lettermen in Florida history to receive an NCAA postgraduate scholarship.

San Antonio Spur Matt Bonner in 2010

In the second round in 2003, Bonner was drafted by the Chicago Bulls and then was traded to the Toronto Raptors. Because there was no immediate spot on the Toronto team for him, he played in 2003–04 for a team in Messina, Italy. During the season, the team declared bankruptcy and stopped paying its players, but Bonner was a member of the half of the team that remained to finish the season, and he averaged 19.2 points and 9.3 rebounds per game.

For the next season, he was a member of the Raptors and played in all 82 regular season games and picked up the nickname "Red Rocket" because of his red hair and his frequent use of the city's transit system that has red cars and uses the slogan "Ride the Rocket." Bonner played one more season in Toronto and was one of the team's main three-point shooters.

He was traded in 2006 to the San Antonio Spurs and continues to play for them. Despite having the size of a center, he led the NBA in three-point percentage (.457) in 2010–11, usually an honor going to a guard. Bonner participated in the Foot Locker Three-Point Shootout as part of the 2013 NBA All-Star festivities and made it to the final round of competition. *The Sporting News* named Bonner the 19th-smartest athlete in 2010.

COREY WAYNE BREWER (1986–) ■ NBA: 2007–14 ■ *Small Forward*
COLLEGE: 2004–07   6-9, 188 lbs.   10.0 / 3.0 / 1.6 / 0.3 / 1.4

While in high school in Portland, Tennessee, Corey Brewer was named the Tennessee Secondary School Athletic Association Class 2A Mr. Basketball and was a McDonald's All-American. He came to Florida and, as a sophomore, posted the first triple-double in Gator history, with 15 points, 10 rebounds, and 13 assists in December 2005.

Brewer was a starter on the 2005–06 NCAA National Championship team and was a co-Southeastern Conference Defensive Player of the Year, as selected by the

SEC coaches. Although projected to be drafted high if he went to the NBA at that point, he and his Gator teammates decided to stay for another year and try for a second championship. They not only won that in 2007, but Brewer was also named the MVP of the Final Four. He was also an honorable mention on the Associated Press All-American team in 2007.

In the 2007 draft, the Minnesota Timberwolves selected him as the seventh pick in the first round, and he played for them in 301 regular season games over the next three-plus seasons. During the 2010–11 season, Brewer was traded to the New York Knicks and a week later (without seeing any playing time as a Knick) was put on waivers. Just two days later, he signed a three-year contract with the Dallas Mavericks, which turned out to be a good place for him.

Corey Brewer of the Minnesota Timberwolves in 2007

Three months later, he and his Dallas teammates won the NBA championship. Brewer got into 13 regular season games and six in the playoffs. That was his only experience with the Mavericks, as he was traded before the end of 2011 to the Denver Nuggets. In his two seasons with Denver, he averaged about 14 minutes per game in a backup role at small forward. On July 12, 2013, Brewer returned to the Timberwolves and signed a three-year contract. He started all 81 games in which he played and averaged 12.3 points per game for Minnesota.

NICHOLAS WILLIAM CALATHES (1989–)
■ **NBA: 2013–14** ■ *Shooting Guard*

COLLEGE: 2007-09   6-6, 213 lbs.   4.9 / 1.9 / 2.9 / 0.1 / 0.9

When Nick Calathes graduated from Lake Howell High School in Winter Park, Florida, he was the all-time leading scorer for Seminole County. Because of his size and ability, he played point guard, shooting guard, and small forward during his two years at the University of Florida.

As a freshman, he led UF in scoring and was named by the coaches as the Southeastern Conference Newcomer of the Year and co-SEC Freshman of the Year. As both a freshman and a sophomore, he broke the Florida record for assists per season and, after only two years, had the Gators' third-most career assists. The SEC coaches chose him as a first-team All-SEC member in 2009.

Nick Calathes scoring a field goal against an Israeli team in Eurobasket 2009

Rather than going to the NBA in 2009, Calathes opted to play for the Greek team Panathinaikos Athens. That same year, he was drafted by the Minnesota Timberwolves, who traded his rights in 2010 to the Dallas Mavericks. In 2011, he was honored as the Eurobasket.com first-team for the All-Greek A1 League, a member of the All-Defensive Team, and the Most Improved Player.

Calathes moved in 2012 to the Russian team Lokomotiv Kuban Krasnodar and was chosen as the season MVP of the league. As a free agent, he finally became an NBA player on August 14, 2013, when he signed with the Memphis Grizzlies, where he remains a frequent substitute shooting guard.

BEN JEROME DAVIS (1972–) ■ NBA: 1996–2000 ■ *Power Forward*

COLLEGE: DNC   6-9, 242 lbs.   1.4 / 1.3 / 0.1 / 0.1 / 0.2

Ben Davis played his high school basketball for Oak Hill Academy in Mouth of Wilson, Virginia, and was named a McDonald's High School All-American in 1991. His first college-level play was at the University of Kansas, which he attended in 1991–92. He was a student at the University of Florida in 1992–93, but he did not play for the basketball team. Davis tested positive for a banned substance and left Florida.

His third college was Hutchinson Community College in Hutchinson, Kansas, where he was the leading scorer on the Blue Dragons in the National Junior College Athletic Aassociation national championship game in 1994. Next, he played for the University of Arizona from 1994 until 1996.

Ben Davis (left) at the Lute Olson (Arizona's head coach) Celebrity Auction 25th Anniversary

Davis was drafted in the second round in 1996 by the Phoenix Suns and played in 20 games for that team during the 1996–97 season, averaging 1.5 points per game. Before the start of the next season, he signed with the Miami Heat but was waived a month later without seeing any regular season game time. He joined the Grand Rapids Hoops of the Continental Basketball Association and then was called up by the New York Knicks in February 1998. After playing seven games for the Knicks, Davis played for three teams—Capitanes de Arecibo (Puerto Rico 1998), Grand Rapids again (1998–99), and Tau Cerámica (Spain 1998)—before making it back to New York for eight more games as a Knick.

In 1999, he also played for the Idaho Stampede (CBA) and signed with the Dallas Mavericks, but he was waived before the start of the fall season. In January 2000, the well-traveled Davis made it back to the NBA for five games with the Phoenix Suns, then left the league for good and played for Brujos de Guayama (Puerto Rico 2000), Kansas City Knights (ABA 2000), Madedonikos (Greece 2000–01), Trotamundos de

Carabobo (Venezuela 2001), Cantabria Lobos (Spain 2001–02), Roseto Sharks (Italy 2002–03), Westchester Wildfire (USBL 2004), Benfica (Portugal 2005–06), Paysandu BB (Uruguay 2006–07), and Lechugueros de León (Mexico 2008–09).

ANDREW DONALD DECLERQ (1973–)
■ NBA: 1996–2005 ■ *Center*

COLLEGE: 1992–95   6-10, 255 lbs.   10.3 / 9.1 / 1.2 / 1.1 / 1.4

Former Gator Andrew DeClerq visiting a UF basketball game in 2009

After graduating from Countryside High School in Clearwater, Florida, Andrew DeClerq played center at Florida for four years. During 1994, he was part of the team that made it to the NCAA Final Four for the first time in Gator history. That year, he also played for the U.S. national team in the Goodwill Games in St. Petersburg and came home with a bronze medal. He received his bachelor's degree in history from UF in 1995; in 2007, he was honored as a Legend of SEC Basketball.

In the 1995 NBA draft, DeClerq was selected in the second round by the Golden State Warriors and played for them for two seasons. As a free agent, he signed with the Boston Celtics and played one full season and part of the next, then was traded to the Cleveland Cavaliers. DeClerq played the rest of 1998–99 and all of 1999–2000, appearing in 115 games as a Cavalier. In the off-season, he was traded to the Orlando Magic, where he played from 2000 through 2005.

After that season, he left the NBA and, in 2009, became an assistant coach at the high school level for Montverde Academy in Montverde, Florida. DeClerq moved in 2010 to Foundation Academy in Winter Garden, Florida, and serves as a physical education teacher and the head coach of the boys' varsity team. He is also the owner and operator of DeClerq Basketball, which teaches youth basketball in Central Florida.

JAMES THOMAS GRANDHOLM (1960–)
■ NBA: 1990–91 ■ *Power Forward*

COLLEGE: 1979–80   7-0, 235 lbs.   3.0 / 1.9 / 0.3 / 0.3 / 0.1

After graduating from Elkhart Central High School in Indiana, Jim Grandholm came to the University of Florida and played center for one year, appearing in 26 games and averaging 3.6 points and 3 rebounds. He had been recruited by John Lotz; when Norm Sloan became the new head coach, Grandholm was unhappy with the change and transferred to the University of South Florida, where he played from 1981 to 1984.

Grandholm was drafted in the fourth round in 1984 by the Washington Bullets, but, before he saw any NBA playing time, he played in Europe for Saint-Étienne

Nicknames of Gator Players and Head Coaches

- *A.D.* (Andrew Donald DeClerq)
- *Billy the Kid* (Billy Donovan)
- *Brady* (Warren C. Cowell)
- *Flight* (James William White IV)
- *Hawk* (Vernon Maxwell)
- *The Hawk* (Neal Eugene Walk)
- *J-Dub* (Jason Chandler Williams)
- *J-Will* (Jason Chandler Williams)
- *Mad Max* (Vernon Maxwell)
- *Red Mamba* (Matthew Robert Bonner)
- *Red Rocket* (Matthew Robert Bonner)
- *The Rev* (Ed Visscher)
- *Stormin' Norman* (Norm Sloan)
- *White Chocolate* (Jason Chandler Williams)

Basket (France 1985–86), Vevey-Riviera (Switzerland 1986–87), Dentigomma Rieti (Italy 1987–88), and Corona Cremona (Italy 1990).

In 1988–89, he was traded to the Houston Rockets, was waived, signed as a free agent with the Rockets, was waived again, signed as a free agent with the Orlando Magic, and was waived again. Grandholm signed with the Dallas Mavericks before the 1990–91 season, was waived less than three weeks later, was re-signed by Dallas the following month, and played 26 games that season as a Maverick, for his only NBA game experience. Dallas waived him for the final time in October 1991, and Grandholm went back to France and played with JDA Dijon for the 1991–92 season.

TAUREAN GREEN (1986–) ■ NBA: 2007–08 ■ *Point Guard*
COLLEGE: 2004–07   6-0, 177 lbs.   1.6 / 0.6 / 0.6 / 0.0 / 0.1

Taurean Green, who played basketball for a different high school in each of four years, graduated from Cardinal Gibbons High School in Fort Lauderdale. He played point guard for Florida in its first two national championship seasons and exceeded the 1,000-point mark, as did each of the other four championship starters. Green set an all-time Gator record in 2005–06 for the most assists in a season (184) and led the Southeastern Conference in free throw percentage (.849) in 2006–07.

Taurean Green in 2007

In the 2007 draft, Green was selected in the second round by the Portland Trail Blazers. He started the 2007–08 season with Portland and then was sent to developmental affiliate Idaho Stampede in December. He came back to Portland before the end of the year, and was traded in February to the Denver Nuggets. Green was sent to the Denver developmental affiliate Colorado 14ers. His NBA experience totaled eight games for the Trail Blazers and nine for the Nuggets. Denver traded him in the summer of 2008 to the New York Knicks, but he was released after one day.

Finding little playing time in the United States, Green headed to Europe. His first team there was CAI Zaragoza (Spanish ACB League), where he started each of the 25 games in which he appeared in 2008–09, and for which he averaged 10.7 points per game. In 2009–10, he played for AEK Athens (Greece), and then came back to Spain in 2010 to play for Gran Canaria. Green remained with that team until 2012, when he played for Tofaş Bursa (Turkey). Later in 2012, he was back in Spain as a member of Basket Barcelona; the following year, he moved to Limoges Cercle Saint-Pierre, his current French team. Green trains during the off-season with the Orlando Hoops staff to improve his game and his strength, hoping to eventually get back into the NBA.

ORIEN RANDOLPH GREENE II (1982–)
■ **NBA: 2005–08, 2010–11** ■ *Point Guard, Shooting Guard*

COLLEGE: 2000–02   6-5, 218 lbs.   2.5 / 1.5 / 1.2 / 0.1 / 0.7

Orien Greene of Gainesville began his college career at the University of Florida in 2000, but he did not play as much in his freshman and sophomore years as he wanted to. He transferred to the University of Louisiana-Lafayette and became the Sun Belt Conference Defensive Player of the Year. He appeared in 43 games for them, but when the NCAA found out that he was using correspondence courses from another college to maintain his eligibility (an "obvious error" according to the NCAA), they eliminated Greene's college basketball record. The school had those 43 games vacated and was put on two years' probation.

Orien Greene of the Boston Celtics in 2006

In 2005, Greene was drafted by the Boston Celtics and played backup point guard, appearing in 80 games and averaging 3.2 points per game. After the season, he was waived, then signed as a free agent with the Indiana Pacers, and played in half the games of the 2006–07 season. After being waived, he was picked up by the Sacramento Kings and played in seven games before being waived again in November 2007.

Greene then played three months in 2007–08 with the New Zealand Breakers of the Australian National Basketball League. Next was Hapoel Jerusalem B.C. (Israel), followed by 2008–09 with MyGuide Amsterdam (Netherlands). Back in the U.S., he played 86 games for the Utah Flash of the D-League in 2009–11, interrupted by three games during a 10-day contract for the New Jersey Nets in 2011.

In November, Greene began play for the Halifax Rainmen (National Basketball League of Canada), and, before 2011 ended, he was on the D-League Los Angeles

D-Fenders, where he played 69 games into the year 2013. During that time, he was a member of the Milwaukee Bucks for a month in 2012, but he did not see any NBA playing time. In February 2013, Greene became a member of the D-League Reno Bighorns.

DONNELL EUGENE HARVEY (1980–)
■ **NBA: 2000–05** ■ *Power Forward*

COLLEGE: 1999–2000   6-8, 220 lbs.   5.6 / 4.0 / 0.8 / 0.4 /0.5

The 1999 Naismith Award winner as the country's top high school basketball player, Donnell Harvey was also on the *USA Today* All-USA first team and played in that year's McDonald's All-America Game. He arrived at Florida as a freshman and initially played for the team, but he left after appearing in only 37 games.

He was drafted in 2000 by the New York Knicks, then traded to the Dallas Mavericks, where he played 18 games in each of the 2000–01 and 2001–02 seasons as a power forward, none as a starter. Harvey was traded in February 2002 to the Denver Nuggets and finished the season with them, playing in 29 games, and the following season was primarily a small forward with the Nuggets, starting 27 of the 77 games in which he appeared.

The 2003–04 season began with Harvey on the Orlando Magic, but, just before Christmas, he was traded to the Phoenix Suns and played in a total of 70 games that year. At the beginning of the 2004–05 regular season, he signed with the Atlanta Hawks, who kept him only six days. He joined the Continental Basketball Association Sioux Falls Skyforce in December, and, the following February, he played three games for the New Jersey Nets during a pair of 10-day contracts, his last in the NBA.

He then moved to international play. In 2005–06, Harvey played for Panionios (Greece); in 2006–07, he was a member of Beşiktaş (Turkey) and then Rieti (Italy). The 2007–08 season was spent with Banvit B.K. (Turkey), and for the following season he was a Jiangsu Dragon (China). After a portion of 2009 with the Carolina Giants (Puerto Rico), he was back with Jiangsu to begin the 2010–11 season, moving to KK Igokea (Bosnia) in November.

For the 2011–12 season, Harvey was back in China on the Tianjin Ronggang team before switching to the Talk 'N Text Tropang Texters in the Philippines. After leading that team to the league championship game, he went back to Tianjin Ronggang. The year 2013 began with his second stint with Talk 'N Text, but Harvey left the team in mid-season to return to the United States to be with his children who had been injured in an auto accident. In September 2013, Harvey and his wife, Natischa, renewed their marriage vows in a ceremony that took place in Atlanta. They had gotten married during the busy 2001 basketball season and wanted to take advantage of his newly found free time to have an elablorate event.

UDONIS JOHNEAL HASLEM (1980–)
■ **NBA: 2003–14** ■ *Power Forward, Center*

COLLEGE: 1998–2002   6-8, 235 lbs.   8.6 / 7.5 / 0.9 / 0.3 / 0.5

Udonis Haslem began high school in Jacksonville, then moved to Miami where he was part of the state champion Miami High team in 1997 and 1998. An investigation showed that he actually lived in Broward County, making him ineligible to be a student at Miami High, which resulted in the school's forfeiting of its entire basketball schedule and the loss of its 1998 state title.

Miami Heat player Udonis Haslem in 2007

Haslem came to Gainesville, majored in leisure service management, and started at center all four years. He was part of the first Gator trip to the NCAA national final game, a loss to Michigan State University. His four years were also the Gators' first run of four consecutive years of NCAA tournament invitations. He led the Southeastern Conference in field goal percentage (.562) in 2000–01, and, as a senior, he was presented The Lieutenant Fred Koss Memorial Award by Gator alumnus Bill Koss, who established the award in memory of his brother, for leadership, sacrifice, integrity, and sportsmanship. In 2012, he was inducted into the University of Florida Athletic Hall of Fame.

In his first year out of college, Haslem played for a French team, Chalon-sur-Saône, and averaged 16.1 points per game. During his time there, he worked hard to lose 70 pounds, which he had put on after the end of his playing time for the Gators. In 2003, a stronger and leaner Haslem signed with the Miami Heat, where he continues to play. In his first year, he was named to the NBA All-Rookie second team, and he soon took over as starting power forward.

Haslem won the first of his three NBA championship rings in 2006 with a win over the Dallas Mavericks. For a time during the 2007–08 season, he switched to center after the trade of Shaquille O'Neal and an injury to Alonzo Mourning, but he returned to his usual power forward position after that season.

In 2010, Miami acquired Chris Bosh and LeBron James, and Haslem was faced with the choice of starting on another team and earning more money or remaining on the Heat and perhaps winning more championships. He chose the latter, and he was a member of an NBA championship team for the second time in 2011–12, the third time in 2012–13, and is the Heat's all-time rebounding leader. Haslem married Faith Rein, his long-time girlfriend from his Gator days, and they have two sons.

ALFRED JOEL HORFORD REYNOSO (1986–)
■ **NBA: 2007–14** ■ *Center*

COLLEGE: 2004–07   6-10, 245 lbs.   14.0 / 9.5 / 2.6 / 1.1 / 0.8

A native of the Dominican Republic, who moved with his family to Michigan in 2000, Al Horford played basketball for Grand Ledge High School in Grand Ledge, Michigan, and set school records, seven of which remain unbroken. He was named the Class A Player of the Year as a senior. As a freshman at the University of Florida, he started at center on the team that won the Southeastern Conference tournament, did it again in the 2005–06 season, and went on to win the school's first NCAA national championship.

Al Horford as a member of the Atlanta Hawks in 2008

As a junior, Horford reached the 1,000-point mark on the last day of the regular season and was again the center for the first team in 15 years to repeat as national champion. He led the SEC in defensive rebounds (6.95 per game) that year, his final season, and came back to UF after a year as a professional and finished his bachelor's degree.

The Atlanta Hawks selected Horford as the third pick in the 2007 draft. As a rookie, he started 77 games and averaged 10.1 points and 9.7 rebounds. He was named NBA Rookie of the Month four times, and was a unanimous choice for the All-Rookie team. In the All-Star Rookie Challenge, he scored 19 points and continued to improve his scoring in four of his next five seasons. Horford was named to the 2010 and 2011 NBA All-Star teams and is currently playing under a contract with the Hawks that runs through the end of the 2015–16 season.

Horford also plays for the national team of the Dominican Republic. In the 2008 Centrobasket tournament held in Mexico, he and his team won the bronze medal, which they repeated in the International Basketball Federation (FIBA) Americas Championship held in Argentina in 2011. In the 2012 tournament held in Puerto Rico, Horford helped the team win the gold medal.

GARY J. KELLER (1944–) ■ **NBA: 1967–69** ■ *Power Forward, Center*

COLLEGE: 1964–67   6-9, 220 lbs.   6.0 / 4.5 / 0.4 / n/a / n/a

After playing on the two-time state champion Dixie Hollins High School Rebels in St. Petersburg, Florida, Gary Keller came to UF. During his final season in 1966–67, the Gators posted their best win-loss record (21-4) to that point in their history. In addition to playing basketball, Keller was an Academic All-American and graduated in 1967 with a bachelor's degree in business administration. That year, he led the Southeastern Conference in rebounding (11.3 per game).

In the 1967 NBA draft, Keller was selected in the sixth round by the Los Angeles Lakers. He was also drafted by the American Basketball Association Denver Nuggets, who traded his rights to the Minnesota Muskies, and Keller opted to play for the Muskies instead of the Lakers. When the Minnesota team moved to Miami and changed its name to the Floridians, Keller moved with it and played for a year.

Keller is a member of the University of Florida Athletic Hall of Fame, and, in 2003, he was named by the Southeastern Conference as a Basketball Legend. He lives in St. Petersburg with his wife and has a son and a daughter.

DAVID LEE (1983–) ■ NBA: 2005–14 ■ *Power Forward, Center*
COLLEGE: 2001–05   6-9, 240 lbs.   15.2 / 9.8 / 2.4 / 0.4 / 0.8

David Lee was a high school basketball star in the St. Louis area and was named a first-team All-American by *Parade* magazine. He was also a McDonald's All-American and slam-dunk contest winner. As a freshman for UF, he was a member of the All-Southeastern Conference freshman team chosen by the SEC coaches.

Lee was selected late in the first round of the 2005 draft by the New York Knicks and played in 67 games in his rookie season, averaging 5.1 points and 4.5 rebounds per game. During the following season, he participated in the Rookie Challenge game during the All-Star break, and his 30 points earned him the game's MVP award. His playing time was cut short in 2007 after a severe ankle sprain in February.

David Lee in 2011 as a member of the Golden State Warriors

During the 2008–09 season, Lee became primarily a starter and was the first Knick to score at least 30 points and pull down at least 20 rebounds in a game since February 1997. In 2010, he became the first Knick to appear in an NBA All-Star game since 2001, and, in that same season, he became the first NBA player since 1976 to have at least 35 points, 20 rebounds, and 10 assists in a game. After the season, Lee was traded to the Golden State Warriors.

He was named to the 2013 NBA All-Star game, the first Warrior to be chosen in 16 years. An injury to his hip flexor at the beginning of the playoffs reduced his playing time, but he continued to play through the pain. He was honored as a third-team All-NBA player and is consistently ranked among the league leaders in rebounds. Lee injured his hamstring in March 2014 but was able to return for the playoffs. His current contract with Golden State goes through the end of the 2016 season.

Off the basketball court, Lee has made appearances on the television shows *Family Feud, Celebrity Apprentice, Lipstick Jungle,* and *The Electric Company,* and the movie *When in Rome*. In 2009, he was one of several NBA players who became involved with the Hoops for St. Jude charity to help raise funds for the St. Jude Children's Research Hospital.

VERNON LEON MACKLIN (1986–) ■ NBA: 2011–12 ■ *Center*
COLLEGE: 2009–11   6-10, 227 lbs.   2.0 / 1.5 / 0.2 / 0.2 / 0.2

In Virginia, Vernon Macklin played power forward for I.C. Norcom High School and Hargrave Military Academy, and he was honored as a McDonald's All-American. He was one of ten players throughout the country chosen for the USA Basketball Junior National Select Team in 2006, and he played in the Nike Hoop Summit.

Macklin started college at Georgetown University and, after two years, transferred to Florida. As a senior, he averaged 11.6 points and 5.4 rebounds per game. In the 2011 draft, he was selected by the Detroit Pistons, and, during the 2011–12 season, he had playing time with Detroit and the D-League Fort Wayne Mad Ants. His NBA experience lasted 23 games, all in a reserve center capacity.

Vernon Macklin as a student at Georgetown in 2006, before he transferred to Florida

From August to November 2012, he played for Royal Hali Gaziantep (Turkish Basketball League) then moved to the D-League Rio Grande Valley Vipers. In February 2013, Macklin signed with Barangay Genebra San Miguel in the Philippine Basketball Assocation. In December of that year, he moved to the Lianong Flying Dragons of the Chinese Basketball Association.

VERNON MAXWELL (1965–) ■ NBA: 1988–2001 ■ *Shooting Guard*
COLLEGE: 1984–88   6-4, 180 lbs.   12.8 / 2.6 / 3.4 / 0.2 / 1.1

Gainesville native Vernon Maxwell played for local Buchholz High School and was named Mr. Basketball (chosen by a panel of high school basketball coaches and media representatives) for the state during his senior year. He also played defensive back for the football team. Maxwell played for the Gators for four years and set the school record for the most career points (2,450). In Southeastern Conference history, the only player who exceeded that total (as of that time) was Pete Maravich. That number would still be the Florida record but for Maxwell's off-court activities. After he admitted snorting cocaine prior to a tournament game and accepting cash from coaches, his name was erased from the UF list of career leaders.

As a senior, Maxwell averaged 20.2 points per game. He had averaged more than 21 as a junior, but those years' records were also expunged. The record books still show him as the Gators' all-time leader for accomplishments in his sophomore season (field goals attempted 566, field goals made 262). If his junior and senior numbers were allowed to remain, he'd be listed as the school's all-time leader in about a dozen more categories.

In the 1988 draft, he was chosen by the Denver Nuggets in the second round and was immediately traded to the San Antonio Spurs. Maxwell played for about one and a half seasons for San Antonio, then went to the Houston Rockets. In 1991–92, he led the league in number of three-point field goals made, and, in 1992–93, he was the leader in both 3-point field goals attempted and made. Maxwell remained with the Rockets through the 1995 season and received two NBA championship rings (1994 and 1995), while earning the nickname "Mad Max" for his propensity to take shots from all over the court while being an aggressive defender with flashes of anger. In addition to his production on the court, he also exhibited troubling behavior, such as the February 1995 incident in which he was suspended and fined for going into the stands to punch a fan. During that same season, he faked an injury to protest a lack of playing time in the playoffs; he was later waived by the Rockets.

Vernon Maxwell as a member of the Houston Rockets

At the beginning of the 1995–96 season, Maxwell signed with the Philadelphia 76ers and, during his one year there, averaged 16.2 points per game. During that period, he also flirted with the idea of trying out for the Philadelphia Eagles football team, but the 76ers released him in 1996, and Maxwell went back to the Spurs for one season, mostly as a reserve player. He was released at the end of the season.

During the 1997–98 season, he played for the Orlando Magic (11 games) and Charlotte Hornets (31 games), then played 46 games the next season, all for the Sacramento Kings. Released by the Kings in August 1999, he signed with the Seattle SuperSonics, where he averaged 10.9 points over 47 games, starting none of them. Maxwell was traded to the New York Knicks in September 2000, was waived a week later, soon signed with the Philadelphia 76ers, and played 24 games before he was waived again. In February 2001, he became a Dallas Maverick and played his final 19 NBA games with that team. Maxwell now lives in Charlotte, North Carolina.

MICHAEL LLOYD MILLER (1980–)
■ **NBA: 2000–14** ■ *Small Forward, Shooting Guard*

COLLEGE: 1998–2000   6-8, 210 lbs.   11.8 / 4.6 / 2.8 / 0.2 / 0.6

South Dakota native Mike Miller was part of the gold-medal–winning USA National Team, which won the International Basketball Federation (FIBA) Americas U18 Championship in Puerto Plata in 1998. His two years with the Gators ended with

Mike Miller in 2009 when he played for the Washington Wizards

Florida's first trip to the finals of the NCAA national championship tournament in 2000. He made a last-second basket to get the team past Butler University in the first round, but the Gators fell to Michigan State University in the championship game.

The Orlando Magic drafted Miller in 2000; that season, he became the first rookie player to appear in all 82 games of his first regular season and was an obvious choice for NBA Rookie of the Year. Partway through the 2002–03 season, he was traded to the Memphis Grizzlies and finished the season (and five more) in Memphis. For the 2005–06 season, Miller was named the NBA Sixth Man of the Year. After a year with the Minnesota Timberwolves and another with the Washington Wizards, he signed a five-year contract as a free agent with the Miami Heat in July 2010.

In his first two seasons with the Heat, Miller was a reserve shooting guard who got into a total of 80 games. In his first championship series in 2012, he set an NBA Finals record by making seven three-point baskets in one game against the Oklahoma City Thunder, and his three-point shooting helped the Heat win the championship that year. For the 2012–13 season, Miller was predominantly a shooting guard and started 17 of the 59 games in which he played. He won his second championship with the Heat against the San Antonio Spurs, playing in the starting lineup in the final three games.

On July 16, 2013, Miller was waived by the Miami Heat; within two weeks, he was again a member of the Memphis Grizzlies, playing as a reserve in nearly every game of the 2013–14 season. Off the court, Miller is an entrepreneur and, in 2012, founded Let It Fly Energy, a line of energy drinks and shots that he developed as a healthier alternative to other energy drinks. He also once owned a Java macaque and tells the story about the time his monkey learned to unlock the house doors and escaped, which Miller didn't know until a neighbor called to say, "Your monkey is riding your dogs around the neighborhood."

JOAKIM SIMON NOAH (1985–) ■ NBA: 2007–14 ■ *Center*

COLLEGE: 2004–07   6-11, 232 lbs.   9.9 / 9.4 / 2.7 / 1.5 / 0.9

Joakim Noah played basketball for two high schools in New York and one in New Jersey before coming to Florida. In his freshman year, he averaged only 3.9 points and 2.7 rebounds per game, but he improved in his sophomore year to lead the Gators in points (14.2) and blocks (2.4) per game. In that year's NCAA Regional in Minneapolis, Noah scored 26 points and made 15 rebounds and five blocks in the game against

Where Did The Gators Go?

After their collegiate basketball careers, Gators went on to play for 28 different ABA and NBA franchises, plus many more around the world. Below is list of the U.S. teams they played for. Because many have played for multiple teams, the totals below exceed the number of individuals listed in this chapter.

Team	#	Team	#
Chicago Bulls	5	Sacramento Kings	3
New York Knicks	5	Cleveland Cavaliers	2
Orlando Magic	5	Indiana Pacers	2
San Antonio Spurs	5	Philadelphia 76ers	2
Dallas Mavericks	4	Washington Wizards	2
Miami Heat	4	Atlanta Hawks	1
Vancouver/Memphis Grizzlies	4	Charlotte Hornets	1
Boston Celtics	3	Detroit Pistons	1
Denver Nuggets	3	Los Angeles Clippers	1
Golden State Warriors	3	Minnesota Muskies/ Miami Floridians	1
Houston Rockets	3	New Orleans Jazz	1
Minnesota Timberwolves	3	Portland Trail Blazers	1
New Jersey Nets	3	Seattle SuperSonics	1
Phoenix Suns	3	Toronto Raptors	1

#1-seeded Villanova University. He was named the regional's Most Outstanding Player. In the Gators' victory over UCLA in the national title game, Noah set a championship game record with six blocks.

Rather than declare himself eligible for the NBA draft, he came back as a junior to try for a second championship. Florida did well in the regular season and made it to the final game against The Ohio State University led by center Greg Oden, who most figured would be the #1 draft pick (they were right). It was Noah's job to guard Oden, and he did it well, helping Florida secure its second NCAA championship in two years.

Noah was picked ninth by the Chicago Bulls in the 2007 draft, and with fellow Gators Corey Brewer (seventh) and Al Horford (third), were the highest-picked trio from the same school in the history of the NBA draft. Noah appeared in 74 games that year for the Bulls and soon moved into the starting center spot on a regular basis. In February 2012, he scored the first triple-double for a Chicago center since 1977.

He was named to the 2013 NBA All-Star Game, scored eight points, and made ten rebounds. That season, he became the sixth NBA player to record a triple-double

Joakim Noah, a member of the Chicago Bulls, in 2009

of 20 points, 20 rebounds, and 10 blocks (since blocks became an official statistic starting with the 1973–74 season). He was also named to the NBA All-Defensive team. In 2014, he was named to his second All-Star Game and again scored eight points. Since 2007, Noah has been a member of the French national team in international play.

The talented player had a little trouble off the court in May 2008 when he was arrested in Gainesville because he had an open container of alcohol and some marijuana in his possession; within a few hours, he was caught driving without his seat belt and with a suspended license. He was eventually placed on six months probation and paid separate fines for the possession/open container charges and the traffic offense. Noah and his mother, Cecilia Rodhe, a noted sculptor, started the Noah's Arc Foundation to help inner city children express themselves and feel empowered through sports and the arts.

CHANDLER PARSONS (1988–) ■ NBA: 2011–14 ■ *Small Forward*
COLLEGE: 2007–11   6-9, 227 lbs.   14.1 / 5.2 / 3.3 / 0.4 / 1.1

While playing for Lake Howell High School in Winter Park, Chandler Parsons helped his team to be the Florida state runner-up in 2005 and 2006, then the champion in 2007. In that championship game, he scored 30 points and grabbed 10 rebounds and was named the MVP. He arrived in Gainesville in 2007, an off-year, following a pair of NCAA national championships and the departure of the starting lineup.

As a freshman, Parsons played in 36 games and averaged 8.1 points and 4.0 rebounds. He improved those numbers as a sophomore, and again as a junior (12.4 points, 6.9 rebounds). After two years without an NCAA tournament appearance, the team made it to the first round in 2010. In 2011, he

Chandler Parsons in a 2012 game against the Thunder

became the first University of Florida player to be named the Southeastern Conference Player of the Year (as determined by the SEC coaches), and Florida improved and made it to the Elite Eight that year. Parsons received his bachelor's degree in 2011 in telecommunications.

In the 2011 draft, he was selected in the second round by the Houston Rockets. The season was delayed because of a lockout, so Parsons played three games with

Cholet Basket in France before returning to appear in 63 games for Houston and was named to the NBA All-Rookie second team. In 2012, Parsons started all 76 games in which he played, plus 74 in the following season.

CHRIS RICHARD (1984–)
■ **NBA: 2007–08, 2009–10** ■ *Center, Power Forward*

COLLEGE: 2003–07   6-9, 255 lbs.   1.9 / 2.8 / 0.4 / 0.2 / 0.3

A graduate of Lakeland's Kathleen High School, Chris Richard was the state's Mr. Basketball for 2002, as selected by high school coaches and media representatives. At Florida, he played in 141 games over his four years and averaged 4.9 points and 3.2 rebounds per game. As a senior, he was presented The Lieutenant Fred Koss Memorial Award for his leadership, sacrifice, integrity, and sportsmanship. That award was started by UF alumnus Bill Koss, in memory of his brother.

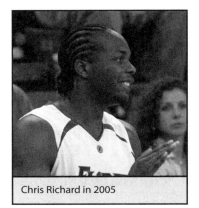

Chris Richard in 2005

In the 2007 NBA draft, Richard was selected in the second round by the Minnesota Timberwolves. He played for Minnesota in 2007–08 in 52 games as a reserve center, then moved to the D-League Sioux Falls Skyforce.

From 2008 to 2010, Richard played for another D-League team, the Tulsa 66ers. During a portion of the 2009–10 season, he also played power forward for 18 games for the Chicago Bulls before being waived after the season. He then traveled to China to play for the Liaoning Dinosaurs and retired from basketball in July 2012. Richard has since started a nonprofit organization called the Rich Kids Project, aimed at helping kids explore job opportunities outside of sports.

ANTHONY ROBERSON (1983–)
■ **NBA: 2005–07, 2008–09** ■ *Point Guard*

COLLEGE: 2002–05   6-2, 180 lbs.   4.1 / 0.8 / 0.5 / 0.0 / 0.4

Recognized as a *Parade* magazine All-American during his senior year with Saginaw High School in Michigan, Anthony Roberson played three years for Florida. In his first year in Gainesville, he was named the Southeastern Conference Freshman of the Year by the SEC coaches. He appeared in 93 games and averaged 29.4 minutes each and led the SEC in three-point percentage (.425) in 2003–04 and in free throw percentage (.900) in 2004–05. He scored 16.2 points per game and could have stayed another year at the university—if he had, he would have been a part of an NCAA championship team.

Instead, Roberson made himself eligible for the NBA draft but was not selected. As a free agent, he signed with the Memphis Grizzlies and spent his rookie year split between Memphis (16 games) and the D-League Arkansas RimRockers. Just before the 2006–07 season, he signed with the Golden State Warriors and played in 20 games before being waived in January 2007. For the 2007–08 season, he played for Hapoel Migdal Jerusalem (Israel) and TTNet Beykoz (Turkey).

Florida point guard Anthony Roberson

Roberson returned to the United States to play in 2008–09 for the New York Knicks (23 games) and the Chicago Bulls (six games). In 2009, he headed overseas again to play for Strasbourg IG (France 2009–10). For a brief period, he was a member of the Los Angeles Lakers but saw no playing time. Roberson went to Italy to play for Enel Brindisi (2010–11), then China for Fujian Xunzing (2011–12) and La union Formosa (2012), and back to France for Boulazac BD beginning in 2013.

DWAYNE KENNETH SCHINTZIUS (1968–2012)
■ NBA: 1990–97, 1998–99 ■ *Center*

COLLEGE: 1986–90   7-1, 260 lbs.   2.7 / 2.5 / 0.4 / 0.5 / 0.1

Gator center Dwayne Schintzius

Dwayne Schintzius was named as a high school All-American by McDonald's and *Parade* magazine as a senior at Brandon High School near Tampa. He came to Florida as a freshman and assumed the role of starting center. He was adept at blocking shots, and his first three seasons in Gainesville ranked as the top three all time for UF shot blockers. As a junior, he already held the school's all-time career blocks record.

With Schintzius as the center, the Gators made their first three appearances in the NCAA tournament, and won their first Southeastern Conference regular season title. As a junior, he was named first-team All-SEC by the conference coaches, and he led the SEC in blocks in 1986–88 and in rebounding in 1987–88. Off the court, however, he had behavior problems. He was suspended for four games for hitting another student with a tennis racket.

When head coach Norm Sloan was replaced by Don DeVoe, Schintzius protested by refusing to show up for practice. He then was allegedly involved in a fight at a fraternity house. He only played in 11 games during his senior year; after he left the team, it posted a record of 1-16.

Schintzius was drafted in the first round in 1990 by the San Antonio Spurs and played one season, during which he injured his back. He was traded to the Sacramento Kings, where he played 33 games during 1991–92, and was waived at season's end.

His next stop was the New Jersey Nets, and he played with them from 1992–95, before moving to the Indiana Pacers for a year. He spent the 1996–97 season with the Los Angeles Clippers (15 games). After taking the 1997–98 year off because of injury, Schintzius played his final season with the Boston Celtics in 1998–99, in which he appeared in 16 games. During 2001–02, he played with the D-League Mobile Revelers, then with the United States Basketball League Brevard Blue Ducks.

Schintzius was diagnosed with leukemia in 2009 and, after two bone marrow transplants, died on April 15, 2012, in Tampa.

MARREESE SPEIGHTS (1987–) ■ NBA: 2008–14 ■ *Center*
COLLEGE: 2006–08   6-10, 255 lbs.   7.5 / 4.3 / 0.5 / 0.5 / 0.3

Marreese Speights of St. Petersburg, Florida, played basketball at three high schools and spent his senior year at Hargrave Military Academy in Virginia. He arrived at Florida as a freshman while the university was attempting to win its second consecutive national championship, and the focus was on three other Gator big men who had received media attention the previous year. Speights' freshman numbers were about four points and two rebounds per game, in limited action.

Marreese Speights (right) guarding Washington's JaVale McGee

The following year, after another title and the departure of Al Horford, Joakim Noah, and Chris Richard, Speights had much more playing time and averaged 14.5 points, 8.1 rebounds, and 1.4 blocks per game. His sophomore year was his final one, after which he made himself eligible for the NBA draft. In 2008, he was selected in the first round by the Philadelphia 76ers. He played in 79 games in his rookie season.

Speights remained with the 76ers for the 2009–10 season, although he missed 14 games because of a torn medial collateral ligament. He was back for the 2010–11 season, but Philadelphia had a new coach, Doug Collins. The offense-focused Speights clashed with the defensive-minded Collins, and his playing time decreased.

He was traded to the Memphis Grizzlies in January 2012 and started 54 of the 60 games in which he appeared that season, mostly at power forward. He began the 2012–13 season with Memphis, but after starting only two of 40 games at center, he was traded to the Cleveland Cavaliers. He finished the year with Cleveland and played in 39 games there. After the season, Speights signed a three-year contract with the Golden State Warriors in July 2013 and played for them in a backup role in 2014.

NEAL EUGENE WALK (1948–) ■ NBA: 1970–77 ■ *Center*
COLLEGE: 1966–69   6-10, 220 lbs.   12.6 / 7.7 / 2.1 / 0.4 / 0.6

Neal Walk attended Miami Beach High School, then came to the University of Florida and played center for three years. He captained the Gators to their first postseason competition, the 1969 National Invitational Tournament. While at Florida, he set several school records that still stand: career rebounds (1,181), single game rebounds (31), and points per game (20.8). When he was named as a second-team All-American by the Associated Press (and third team by the National Association of Basketball Coaches and United Press International) in 1968, he became the Gators' first All-American in basketball.

Neal Walk (#41) on the Phoenix Suns

Walk led the SEC in rebounding in 1968 and 1969. When he graduated, he was also the all-time Florida leading scorer with 1,600 points in only three seasons.

After his final season, during which he led the nation in rebounding, Walk was drafted with the second pick in the first round in 1969 by the Phoenix Suns, who lost a coin toss with the Milwaukee Bucks for the first pick (they chose UCLA's Lew Alcindor, who later changed his name to Kareem Abdul-Jabbar). Walk played five seasons for the Suns, then was traded to the New Orleans Jazz, for whom he played in 37 games in 1974–75, and was again traded mid-season to the New York Knicks. He stayed with the Knicks for 1976–77 and was waived after playing 11 games the following season. That was the end of his NBA career, but he continued to play abroad, for Reyer Venezia Mestre (Italy) and Hapoel Ramat Gan (Israel).

During his NBA years, Walk began to explore his spirituality, which included him becoming a vegetarian and experimenting with drugs. This contributed to him losing weight and focus, which ultimately led to his being traded by the Suns. He was even arrested while in Europe for drug possession and spent three days in jail. Part of his spiritual quest included legally changing his name from Neal Walk to Joshua Hawk in 1980 to symbolize his separation from basketball.

Walk's life changed even more after his playing days were over when, in 1988, he was diagnosed with a benign tumor along his spine. He had surgery to correct it, but was left a paraplegic and was paralyzed from the chest down. After he recovered, he began to play in the National Wheelchair Basketball Association for the L.A.-Phoenix Samaritans and, in 1990, met with President George H.W. Bush at the White House and was honored as the Wheelchair Athlete of the Year.

He later worked for the Phoenix Suns in community relations from 1999 until 2012. Walk is a member of the University of Florida Athletic Hall of Fame, the Miami Beach Senior High School Hall of Fame, and the National Jewish Sports Hall of Fame, and is the only Gator basketball player to have his jersey number (#41) retired. Walk recently remarried and enjoys spending time with his granddaughter.

JAMES WILLIAM WHITE IV (1982–)
■ NBA: 2006–07, 2008–09, 2012–13   ■ *Small Forward*

COLLEGE: 2001–02   6-7, 215 lbs.   2.7 / 1.0 / 0.5 / 0.1 / 0.3

James White is one of several basketball players from Hargrave Military Academy in Chatham, Virginia, who went on to play at major universities and/or the NBA. Before coming to Florida, he participated in the 2001 McDonald's High School Slam Dunk Contest and finished second behind future Gator David Lee. White is best known for his between-the-legs dunk.

During his first year at Florida, he played in 29 of the team's 31 games and averaged 20.5 minutes while averaging 6.1 points and 2.9 rebounds. After his UF freshman year, he transferred to the University of Cincinnati, sat out the following season, and played three years for the Bearcats. White also lettered for the track and field team and qualified for the NCAA tournament in the high and triple jumps in 2004. As a senior, he led Cincinnati with a scoring average of 15.9 points per game and was named to the Las Vegas Holiday Classic all-tournament team. He also finished second in the 2006 NCAA College Slam Dunk Contest.

New York Knick James White in 2013

White was drafted in the second round in 2006 by the Portland Trail Blazers, who then traded him to the Indiana Pacers. He played in the preseason for Indiana, but was waived before seeing any action in the regular season. Within days, he signed with the San Antonio Spurs, and was sent to the D-League Austin Toros, where he played 15 games.

In March 2007, White saw his first NBA game action when the Spurs, in an attempt to rest the starters, brought him in for the upcoming playoffs. White appeared in six regular season games, earned an NBA championship ring, and was waived in July. He then signed with Fenerbahçe Ulker (Turkey) and played until 2008, also winning the Beko Allstar Slam Dunk Contest in Turkey.

For the 2008–09 season, he first played for the D-League Anaheim Arsenal, then signed with the Houston Rockets and played four games before his contract expired. In September 2009, White was drafted by the D-League Maine Red Claws; that same month, he played in the preseason for the Denver Nuggets, but was waived within three weeks before the regular season began. He returned to Europe and played for Spartak St. Petersburg (Russia 2009–10) and the Italian teams of Dinamo Sassari (2010–11) and Scavoline Pesaro (2011–12).

White had another trip to the NBA when he signed with the New York Knicks in July 2012. He played in their summer league team and was assigned more than once to their D-League affiliate, the Erie BayHawks. After playing 57 games for New York, starting 16 and posting a scoring average of 2.2 points per game, he was waived in June 2013. In September 2013, he signed a one-year contract with the Pallacanestro Reggiana in Italy.

JASON CHANDLER WILLIAMS (1975–)
■ **NBA: 1998–2008, 2009–11** ■ *Point Guard*

COLLEGE: 1997–98   6-1, 180 lbs.   12.8 / 2.8 / 7.2 / 0.1 / 1.4

Jason Williams was the first player at his high school in West Virginia to reach the 1,000-point and 500-assist level. For 1994, he was named the *USA Today* West Virginia Player of the Year. His first college team was Marshall University (1994–96), but when his head coach, Billy Donovan, moved from there to the University of Florida, he followed him to Gainesville and sat out one year so he could play his junior and senior seasons as a Gator.

During that year, Williams set a school record with 17 assists in one game. He averaged 17.1 points per game, but was suspended twice for marijuana use. In February 1998, he was suspended for the rest of the year for his third violation. He decided to skip his senior year and make himself eligible for the NBA draft, and he was chosen in 1998 in the first round by the Sacramento Kings. He started all 50 of the games in which he played and was named to the All-Rookie first team.

Jason Williams in 2007 when he was a member of the Miami Heat

Williams was suspended again in 2000 for the first five games by the NBA for not complying with his treatment obligations under their anti-drug program. In June 2001, he was traded to the Vancouver Grizzlies, which then moved to Memphis. He was the starting point guard for the next four years and then was traded to the Miami Heat, where he played in 2005–08. During 2005–06, he started in 56 of his 59 games. Williams won his first NBA championship ring when the Heat defeated the Dallas Mavericks in the finals.

He signed with the Los Angeles Clippers in August 2008 but did not play for them in a regular season game and retired from basketball in September 2008. Williams made a comeback in 2009 with the Orlando Magic and played 98 games for them, mostly in a reserve capacity, over the next two seasons. After being waived by Orlando, he signed with the Memphis Grizzlies once again and played his final 11 NBA games with that team before retiring for the second time in April 2011.

Early in his professional career, Williams developed an unusual "street" playing style, making amazing passes and incredible three-point shots, which led to one of his many nicknames, "White Chocolate." He was also known as "J-Will" and has a number of unusual tattoos, including "WHITEBOY" across his knuckles. His forearms are tattooed with his children's names. His playing style matured, but he continued to delight fans and be seen in highlight footage.

Williams and his wife have three children. He is a co-founder of the We Will Foundation, a Memphis charity, which benefits children who need treatment for craniofacial deformities. While he played for the Grizzlies, Williams often visited patients at St. Jude Children's Hospital. He continues to dazzle fans while playing in the NBA Legends Tour.

Other Florida Athletes Who Went Into Pro Basketball

NAME	POSITION	COLLEGE	PRO	TEAMS
Clifford Earl Lett	G	1985–89	1989–91	Chicago Bulls, San Antonio Spurs
Erik Murphy	PF	2009–13	2013–14	Chicago Bulls
Matthew Vincent Walsh	SG	2002–05	2005	Miami Heat

Matt Walsh (#55) in March 2013 on the Brose Baskets team

Erik Murphy cutting down the net after the Gators won the SEC championship in 2013

WOMEN

The Early Years

Women's basketball was played even before the University of Florida was formed through the consolidation of several previous institutions. With a few exceptions, notably football, the men's sports took years to be established, while women's sports other than basketball often took decades.

The passing of Title IX in 1972 established a federal mandate for the creation of athletic opportunities for collegiate women across the country. Intercollegiate basketball for Florida women began in 1973–74 with a club team, coached by graduate assistant Darlene Wyrnak, with a first-year record of 11-8. Following the season, UF hired its first real coach, Dr. Paula Welch, and the first official collegiate game took place in Alligator Alley on January 13, 1975. Their first win came five days later against Rollins College.

In March 1976, the team played in its first postseason tournament, the Association of Intercollegiate Athletics for Women regional in Cleveland, Mississippi. They won their first game against the University of Alabama, but they were eliminated in the second game by Mississippi College.

Florida's second coach, Cathy Davis, took over for the 1976–77 season. Previously, she had served as the team's trainer, and she continued in that position as well as being the head coach and working toward her master's degree. During that season, the Lady Gators added their first six-foot-tall player, Quientella Bonner. During her four years in Gainesville, Bonner had 1,321 rebounds, still the school's career record.

When the head coach position became a full-time job for the 1979–80 season, Davis stepped down after a career record of 38-40 and was replaced by Mickie DeMoss. The women's first assistant coach was also hired. In February 1980, Florida won its first game in the inaugural Southeastern Conference Women's Basketball Tournament. In the Florida Association of Intercollegiate Athletics for Women (FAIAW) Tournament, to decide the state championship, Florida defeated Florida State University twice. After the

1982–83 season, DeMoss left the team to coach at Auburn University and was replaced by Debbie Yow.

In the 1983–84 year, the Lady Gators were nationally ranked (19th) for the first time. The following year, Florida was the runner-up in the National Women's Invitational Tournament and finished with more than 20 wins for the first time. Yow resigned in 1985 to handle administrative work and was replaced by Carol Higginbottom-Whitmire. She coached well into the 1989–90 season but resigned, and Lea Henry coached the last six games.

The Carol Ross Era

Carol Ross became the sixth full-time head coach in April 1990 and led Florida to its best SEC season in 1991–92 by winning four games against conference opponents. Three years later, Florida received its first bid to the 48-team ESPN/NCAA Women's Basketball Championship tournament. The Gators won their first-round game, an upset of Bowling Green State University and also finished the season with six SEC wins, the most in their young history.

Coach Carol Ross in 2012

Their first undefeated home season (14-0) came in 1993–94, and the Gators were ranked (#25) for a time in the *USA Today* Coaches Poll. The team finished with an 8-3 SEC record and Ross was named the SEC Coach of the Year. Florida was seeded #4 in the NCAA Regional but lost in the first round to Texas A&M University. The season ended with UF ranked #20 in the Associated Press poll. The following year, the Lady Gators went back to the regional and won their first game but were eliminated in the second.

At the end of the 1995–96 season, Florida made its second trip to the SEC Tournament semifinals. The Gators made it to #16 in the final poll but fell in the first round of the NCAA tournament. In 1996–97, the team continued its rise in the AP poll, making it into the top 10 in February, and, for the first time, the Lady Gators made it to the finals of the SEC Tournament. UF was selected for the first time to host a portion of the NCAA Tournament. and the Lady Gators nearly advanced to the Final Four. The following November, the university made it to #5 in the AP and *USA Today* polls, the highest ranking ever to that point. Later in the season, Florida got to the NCAA Sweet Sixteen, and, in the 1999–2000 season, the team made it to the finals of the WNIT.

Ross resigned her position as head coach in March 2002. In 2008, she was the first (and still only) coach of a UF women's team to be named one of the All-Time SEC Greats.

The Carolyn Peck Era

In April 2002, Carolyn Peck became the new head coach, after having success as the head of the WNBA Orlando Miracle. One of her early decisions was to change the name of the team—no longer would they be known as the Lady Gators. Since then, they have been the Florida Gators.

Gator head coach Carolyn Peck

By winning their first-round game in the NCAA Tournament in March 2004, the Gators posted their largest turnaround in history, winning at least 10 more games than they did the previous year. During Peck's years in Gainesville, several individual players set records and received a variety of honors, but the team had trouble winning more than half its games. Midway through the 2006–07 season, it was announced by the school's athletic director that it would be Peck's last.

The team made it to the quarterfinals of the SEC Tournament but finished with a record of 9-22. Peck became an ESPN basketball analyst, and Amanda Butler was introduced as the new Gators head coach.

The Amanda Butler Era

Butler was no stranger to the campus, having previously played point guard for the University of Florida in 1990–94. In 1995, she received her bachelor's degree in exercise and sports sciences, and she earned a master's degree in the same major in 1997 while

Head coach Amanda Butler leading her team in 2011

serving as an assistant coach for the Gators. She was an assistant at Austin Peay State University (1997–2001) and an assistant, associate, and then head coach at the University of North Carolina-Charlotte (2001–07).

In her first six years as the head coach of the Gators, the team went to postseason play every year. The previous best for a Gator head coach at the beginning of her tenure was two years. In 2006–07 and 2010–11, the Gators made it to the WNIT round of 16, and in 2009–10, they made it to the WNIT second round. Their best finish in that tournament was in 2012–13, when they lost in the semifinals to Drexel University. They survived to the second round of the NCAA national championship tournament in 2008–09, 2011–12, and 2013–14.

Florida Coaching Records

Years	Head Coach	Seasons	Overall Wins	Overall Losses	Overall Pct.	SEC Wins	SEC Losses	SEC Pct.
1974–76	Paula Welch	2	29	14	.674	--	--	--
1976–79	Cathy Davis	3	36	39	.480	--	--	--
1979–83	Mickie DeMoss	4	45	68	.398	3	29	.094
1983–85	Debbie Yow	2	41	18	.695	6	10	.375
1985–90	Carol Whitmire	5	58	76	.433	5	38	.116
1990	Lea Henry	0	3	3	.500	0	2	.000
1990–2002	Carol Ross	12	247	121	.671	84	62	.575
2002–07	Carolyn Peck	5	72	76	.486	24	46	.343
2007–14	Amanda Butler	7	140	95	.596	51	57	.472
Totals		40	671	510	.568	171	222	.435

Southeastern Conference Teams
(All-time Wins through 2013-14 Season)

RECORD	TEAM	WINNING PCT.	SEASONS
1,247-279	Tennessee	.817	40
882-371	Georgia	.703	41
847-408	Auburn	.675	43
840-394	LSU	.681	39
765-480	Mississippi	.614	40

RECORD	TEAM	WINNING PCT.	SEASONS
740-343	Vanderbilt	.683	34
690-539	Texas A&M	.561	40
671-510	**Florida**	.568	40
667-503	Missouri	.570	39
635-379	Arkansas	.626	33
611-464	Alabama	.568	36
604-425	Kentucky	.587	34
564-590	Mississippi State	.489	40
551-404	South Carolina	.577	32

Southeastern Conference Championships

(Regular Season through 2013–14 Season)

18	Tennessee	1	Mississippi	0	Mississippi State
7	Georgia	1	South Carolina	0	Missouri
5	Auburn	0	Alabama	0	Texas A&M
3	LSU	0	Arkansas	0	Vanderbilt
2	Kentucky	0	**Florida**		

(Conference Tournament)

17	Tennessee	1	Kentucky	0	Mississippi
6	Vanderbilt	1	Texas A&M	0	Mississippi State
4	Auburn	0	Alabama	0	Missouri
4	Georgia	0	Arkansas	0	South Carolina
2	LSU	0	**Florida**		

Florida in the NCAA Tournament

(Regionals)

1993	Second Round	1998	Semifinals	2006	First Round
1994	First Round	1999	First Round	2009	Second Round
1995	Second Round	2001	Second Round	2012	Second Round
1996	First Round	2002	First Round	2014	Second Round
1997	Finals	2004	Second Round		

Florida In The Postseason NIT

1985	Finals	2008	Third Round	2011	Third Round
2000	Finals	2010	Second Round	2013	Semifinals
2005	First Round				

NCAA Championships
(Through 2014)

10	Connecticut	2	Stanford	1	Purdue
8	Tennessee	1	Maryland	1	Texas
2	Baylor	1	North Carolina	1	Texas A&M
2	Louisiana Tech	1	Notre Dame	1	Texas Tech
2	Southern California	1	Old Dominion		

Our Florida All-Stars: Basketball
(Based on their pro careers)

Guard:	Sophia Witherspoon
Guard:	Merlakia Jones
Center:	Aneika Henry
Forward:	DeLisha Milton-Jones
Forward:	Murriel Page
Best Overall:	DeLisha Milton-Jones

Athlete Bios

College years are those during which the athlete was awarded a letter for basketball. Pro years are those for which the athlete was active for at least one game.

Pro years are years actually played through 2013.

Statistics are pro career (per game) averages through the 2013 season:
Points / Rebounds / Assists / Blocks / Steals

VANESSA L'ASONYA HAYDEN-JOHNSON (1982–)
■ **WNBA: 2004-06, 2008-09** ■ *Center*

COLLEGE: 2000–04   6-4, 240 lbs.   5.6 / 3.6 / 0.5 / 1.2 / 0.3

After playing basketball for William R. Boone High School in Orlando, Vanessa Hayden enrolled at Florida and played for four years. In her senior year of 2003–04, she was named by the conference coaches as the Southeastern Conference Defensive Player of the Year and a member of the All-SEC team. She received her bachelor's degree in family, youth and community services in April 2005.

Hayden was picked in the first round of the 2004 WNBA draft by the Minnesota Lynx and played four seasons for them, taking off the 2007 season to give birth to her first child. As a rookie, she played in two playoff games for a total of 16 minutes. Hayden was usually a backup center, except for 2005 when she started 25 of the 31 games in which she played. In January 2009, she was traded to the Los Angeles Sparks and finished up her WNBA career with 25 games for that team.

Between WNBA seasons, Hayden played in Europe, for CB Halcón Viajes (Spain 2004–06), Beşiktaş Cola Turka (Turkey 2007–08), and Umana Reyer Venezia (Italy 2008–09).

ANEIKA HENRY (1986–) ■ WNBA: 2012 ■ *Center*

COLLEGE: 2007–09   6-3, 205 lbs.   4.8 / 4.1 / 0.4 / 0.9 / 0.5

Aneika Henry (#13) outjumping Shavonte Zelious in 2012

After four years at Coral Gables Senior High School, Aneika Henry attended Seminole Community College for three years and played basketball in 2005–07. Both seasons, she was named a second-team member of the Florida Community College Activities Association All-Conference team. She set her college's record for rebounds in a game (20) and blocked 108 shots during her two seasons.

After receiving her A.A. degree, Henry transferred to Florida and in her junior year played in all 33 games. Of the team's 105 blocked shots during the year, she was responsible for 63 of them while leading the Gators in field goal percentage. As a senior, she played in all 32 games and led the team in blocked shots (47).

Henry joined the Atlanta Dream of the WNBA in 2012 and played 34 games, blocking 30 shots and averaging 4.8 points per game. After the season ended, she played for the Spanish team Rivas Ecopolis and averaged 9.7 points per game (22 games) in the Spanish league and 11.4 points per game (15 games) in the Euroleague.

She was back in the U.S. for the 2013 WNBA season with the Dream and played in 13 games, scoring at a pace of 4.5 per game and blocking 10 shots. Since her entry into professional basketball, Henry has also played for Antakya (Turkey), BI SSA Lotos Gdynia (Poland), Mann Filter (Spain), and had been invited to training camp with the Seattle Storm (WNBA) in 2011 but did not make the team.

TAMMY ELOISE JACKSON (1962–) ■ WNBA: 1997–2002 ■ *Center*

COLLEGE: 1981–85   6-3, 190 lbs.   2.8 / 2.8 / 0.4 / 0.4 / 0.7
OLYMPICS: 1992 bronze medal

After playing basketball at Buchholz High School in Gainesville, Tammy Jackson played for the University of Florida Lady Gators for four years. Three times she was named to the All-Southeastern Conference first team, and, with 1,895 career points, she has the third-highest total in Florida women's basketball history. When she left the university, there was little opportunity to play basketball professionally in the United States, so Jackson got involved in international competition.

At the International Basketball Federation (FIBA) World Championship held in Malaysia in 1990, her U.S. team won the gold medal. Two years later in Barcelona, Jackson received a bronze medal when the U.S. team came in third in the Olympics. Over five games, she scored 36 points, grabbed 20 rebounds, and made five assists. In her ten years playing in other countries, one of her teams was the Chanson Cosmetics in Japan.

In the 1997 WNBA draft, Jackson was selected in the second round by the Houston Comets and played one full season (28 games). In 1998, she played two games for the Washington Mystics and 19 for the Comets; from 1999 through 2002, she continued with the Comets through the end of her WNBA career. She was one of the original players in the WNBA, and when she retired at the age of 39, she was the league's oldest player.

Jackson was inducted into the University of Florida Athletic Hall of Fame in 1995 and was named an SEC Great in 2003. In 2004, she became an assistant coach at nearby Santa Fe Community College. Jackson returned to UF in 2007 to receive her bachelor's degree in health and human performance.

MERLAKIA JONES (1973–) ■ WNBA: 1997–2004 ■ *Guard*

COLLEGE: 1991–95   5-11, 147 lbs.   9.4 / 3.8 / 1.4 / 0.1 / 1.0

Montgomery, Alabama, native Merlakia Jones played basketball for George Washington Carver High School, then came to the University of Florida and played for four more years. While there, she was a coaches' first-team All-Southeastern Conference selection as a sophomore, junior, and senior. In 2002, she was named one of the All-Time SEC Greats.

In the 1997 WNBA draft, Jones was chosen in the second round by the Cleveland Rockers. She played seven seasons there, starting 139 of the 218 games in which she appeared. Her best year was 2001, when she averaged 13.5 points and 5.5 rebounds per game and was an All-WNBA first team selection. Jones is the all-time leading scorer for Cleveland.

With the Rockers, Jones made it to the playoffs four times and, in 15 playoff games, averaged more than 10 points per game. Her final WNBA season was with the Detroit Shock in 2004, as a result of the demise of the Rockers and its players being picked up by other teams in a dispersal draft. Her year with Detroit consisted of 33 games (mostly in a reserve role) and three more in the playoffs. After her playing days, Jones was involved in coaching high school basketball at her alma mater in Montgomery.

BRANDI MCCAIN (1979–) ■ WNBA: 2002 ■ *Guard*
COLLEGE: 1998–2002   5-3, 135 lbs.   2.7 / 0.1 / 1.3 / 0.1 / 0.4

Brandi McCain playing for Maccabi Ashdod

Brandi McCain was a basketball standout at Silsbee High School in Silsbee, Texas. She was named a high school All-American by the WBCA (Women's Basketball Coaches Association), and she played in that organization's High School All-America Game in 1998. At the University of Florida, she was coaches' first-team All-Southeastern Conference in 1999 and 2001, second team in her senior year, and served as the team captain in 2000 and 2002. McCain graduated with a bachelor's degree in 2002.

She was a second-round draft pick for the WNBA in 2002 by the Cleveland Rockers. She remained with the team for her sole WNBA season, starting two of the 31 games in which she appeared. That same year, she was named by the conference as one of the All-Time SEC Greats.

In 2004–05, McCain began her international career with Maccabi Ashdod in Israel and played in nine games. The following season, she improved her scoring with 21.7 points per game as a starting guard. After the season, she moved to Mann Filter Zaragoza in Spain and played seven games, followed by summer camp with the WNBA Los Angeles Sparks. When the 2006–07 season began in Israel, she was back with Maccabi Ashdod and stayed with them until 2008, when she joined another Israeli team, Elitzu Maclaren Holon, but didn't play in any league games for them.

Where Did the Gators Go?

After their years at Florida, the Gators went on to play for 14 different WNBA franchises and one in the ABL, plus many more around the world. Below is a list of the teams they played for. Because many have played for multiple teams, the totals below exceed the number of individuals listed in this chapter.

Washington Mystics	5	Indiana Fever	1
Los Angeles Sparks	4	Minnesota Lynx	1
Cleveland Rockers	2	New York Liberty	1
Portland Fire	2	Phoenix Mercury	1
Atlanta Dream	1	Portland Power (ABL)	1
Charlotte Sting	1	San Antonio Silver Stars	1
Detroit Shock	1	Seattle Storm	1
Houston Comets	1		

DELISHA MILTON-JONES (1974–)
■ **ABL: 1997–98, WNBA: 1999–2014** ■ *Forward*

COLLEGE: 1993–97   6-1, 172 lbs.   12.0 / 5.5 / 1.9 / 0.7 / 1.3
OLYMPICS: 2000 gold medal; 2008 gold medal

After graduating from Bradwell Institute in Hinesville, Georgia, and there receiving the 1992 and 1993 Naismith High School Player of the Year Awards, DeLisha Milton began play for Florida in 1993. In each of her four seasons, the team made it to the NCAA Tournament. In her senior year, she was honored by the *Basketball Times*, Associated Press, and Kodak/WBCA as an All-American and, according to the conference coaches, was the 1997 Southeastern Conference Player of the Year. As the best female basketball player in Division I of the NCAA, Milton was presented with the State Farm Wade Trophy.

In addition to her athleticism, she was active in the community, visiting hospital patients and presenting motivational speeches, and was given the 1997 President's Recognition Award by the university. She received her bachelor's degree from UF in sports management.

DeLisha Milton-Jones at the 2007 WNBA All-Star Game

In addition to being tall, Milton has very long arms. Most people have a "wingspan" approximately equal to their height, but her outstretched fingertip-to-fingertip length is 11 inches longer than her height, giving her a reach advantage over many opponents. Her nickname is "Sunshine."

Before embarking on a professional career, Milton began representing the U.S. national team in international competition. In the International Basketball Federation (FIBA) World Championship held in 1998 in Germany, she came home with a gold medal. She and her team repeated that in the 2002 championship in China, and, in 2006 in Brazil, she and her American teammates won the bronze medal. Milton was on two gold-medal-winning Olympics teams, in Sydney in 2000 and in Beijing in 2008.

She was a member of the Portland Power of the American Basketball League (1997–98), and, with her at forward, the team won the Western Conference championship for the 1997–98 season and was leading the conference when the league folded on December 22, 1998. Milton was drafted in 1999 by the WNBA Los Angeles Sparks and played six seasons for them before being traded to the Washington Mystics for three. Then it was a trade back to the Sparks for four years and, in 2013, she became a member of the San Antonio Silver Stars. She was released by the Stars in August 2013 and was picked up on waivers by the New York Liberty just two days later. She has been named a WNBA All-Star three times (2000, 2004, and 2007), and has been on two WNBA championship teams (2001 and 2002).

Between WNBA seasons, Milton has played for European teams, including UMMC Ekaterinburg (Russia), Tarsus Bid (Turkey), USK Praha and Gambrinus Sika Brno (Czech Republic), Lavezzini Basket Parma (Italy), and Ros Casares Valencia (Spain). She is only the second woman to coach a professional men's basketball team (Los Angeles Stars of the American Basketball Association) and appeared as herself in a movie, *Love and Basketball*.

In 2001, Milton was designated by the conference as one of the All-Time SEC Greats, and she became a member of the University of Florida Athletic Hall of Fame in 2007.

LAMURRIEL PAGE (1975–) ■ WNBA: 1998–2009 ■ *Forward*

COLLEGE: 1994–98   6-2, 160 lbs.   6.1 / 4.5 / 1.2 / 0.5 / 0.6

A member of the two-time Mississippi state champion Bay Springs High School basketball team, Murriel Page played for Florida until 1998, when she received her bachelor's degree and went professional. At the time, she ranked second on the university's all-time list in field goal percentage (.550), points (1,915), rebounds (1,251), and free throws made (334). In 1998, she was the first female UF basketball player to be selected as a finalist for the Honda Award, to recognize athletic accomplishments, scholastics. and community involvement.

The Washington Mystics took her as the third pick in the 1998 WNBA draft. Page played for them for eight seasons (and served as team captain in 2000–05), then was traded to the Los Angeles Sparks for 2006–08. Between WNBA seasons, she also played for Spanish teams Ros Casares (2001–02 and 2004–05), Hondarribia (2003–04 and 2005–07), Baloncesto San Jose (2007–08), Soller (2008–10), and Mallorca; the Italian team Venezia (2002–03); and the Brazilian Mangueira (2000). An accurate shooter, she led the WNBA in field goal percentage in 1999 and 2000 and, because of that, received a pair of Bud Light Shooting Champions Awards.

Page had planned to continue to play and signed a contract with the Phoenix Mercury for the 2009 season, but she tore her Achilles tendon during training camp. After her professional playing days ended, she became an assistant coach in 2010 for the University of Florida and continues to work with the Gators. Page has been a member of the University of Florida Athletic Hall of Fame since 2009 and, in 2011, was recognized as one of the All-Time SEC Greats.

Forward Murriel Page on the Los Angeles Sparks

In July 2012, fans voted Page into the Washington Mystics All-Time Team. She became a member of the University of Florida Athletic Hall of Fame in 2009.

BRIDGET PETTIS (1971–) ■ WNBA: 1997-2003, 2006 ■ *Guard*
COLLEGE: 1991–93   5-9, 175 lbs.   6.2 / 2.0 / 1.4 / 0.1 / 0.8

Bridget Pettis played basketball for East Chicago Central High School in Illinois and began her collegiate career playing for the Vaqueras of Central Arizona College in Coolidge, Arizona. She transferred to the University of Florida in 1991. During her senior year in Gainesville, she set a school record by making eight three-point field goals in a game against the University of Georgia. In 1993, she received her bachelor's degree at UF.

The Phoenix Mercury chose Pettis in the first round of the 1997 WNBA draft. In her rookie season, she averaged 12.6 points and 3.8 rebounds per game. Over her eight-year WNBA career, she wound up with steadily decreasing numbers in most major categories, resulting in a per-game average of just 1.3 points in her final year.

Los Angeles Sparks assistant coach (left) with team mascot Sparky

After playing for the Mercury in 1997–2001, Pettis was a member of the Indiana Fever in 2002–03, and then was back in Phoenix for 2006, her final year. Over the course of her career, she started 71 of the 228 games in which she played. She became a coach for the Phoenix Mercury in 2006 and their operations direction in 2010.

That same year, she was named by the conference as one of the All-Time SEC Greats. Pettis became an assistant coach for the Los Angeles Sparks in 2013. In March 2014, she took on a new position as assistant coach of the Tulsa Shock (formerly known as the Detroit Shock).

TIFFANY TRAVIS (1978–) ■ WNBA: 2000 ■ *Guard, Forward*
COLLEGE: 1996–2000   5-10   5.4 / 2.5 / 0.8 / 0.1 / 1.0

Tiffany Travis played basketball for the Harrison Central High School Red Rebels in Gulfport, Mississippi. During that time, she was named Mississippi's Miss Basketball for 1996, and *USA Today* honored her as the Mississippi Player of the Year. She played four years for the University of Florida and, in her junior year, broke the school record for free-throw percentage (85.2%). That year, she was a State Farm Classic All-Tournament team member.

As a senior in 2000, Travis was a second-team selection for the All-Southeastern Conference team. She was a member of the *Oakland Tribune* Classic All-Tournament team and became the 13th Lady Gator to score more than 1,000 points in her career.

In the 2000 WNBA draft, Travis was selected in the second round with the 11th overall pick by the Charlotte Sting. She played one year for them, starting 12 of the scheduled 32 games in which she played. She missed the 2001 season because of a knee injury. On May 26, 2002, Travis was cut from the Charlotte roster, ending her brief WNBA career.

TONYA WASHINGTON (1977–) ■ WNBA: 2000–03 ■ *Forward*
COLLEGE: 1997–2000   6-0   2.6 / 1.2 / 0.4 / 0.0 / 0.1

Tonya Washington attended high school in Paxton, Florida, and over her final four years scored 4,489 points, setting a national high school record. In addition to those four years, she played two years on the varsity while she was still a middle school student. As a sophomore, she became the first Florida high school girl to score at least 1,000 points in a single year. In her junior and senior years, she led her team to Florida state championships. Washington was Florida's Miss Basketball for 2000.

She enrolled at the University of Florida in 1996 but did not play basketball that year. She played in a reserve capacity as a sophomore and, in her junior year, started 12 of her 28 games. She led the Gators in per-game scoring (16.7) and rebounding (8.3), and she made the All-Tournament teams for the Preseason Women's National Invitation Tournament, the Duke Classic and the State Farm Classic.

Washington was a starting forward in every Florida game during her senior year. The media named her second-team All-Southeastern Conference, but the coaches picked her for the first-team. She led UF in scoring at the WNIT and was named to the WNIT Final Four All-Tournament team. In 1999, she was named the MVP of the *Oakland Tribune* Classic Tournament hosted by the University of California. She was invited to try out for the World University Games team in 1999, but she had to decline because of an emergency appendectomy.

In 2000, the WNBA Washington Mystics drafted Washington in the second round. She played for the Mystics in 2000 through about half the 2003 season, then was traded to the Seattle Storm. Washington finished up her WNBA career with 11 games for the Storm in 2003.

SOPHIA L. WITHERSPOON (1969–)
■ WNBA: 1997–2003 ■ *Guard*

COLLEGE: 1988–91   5-10, 145 lbs.   10.7 / 2.2 / 1.5 / 0.1 / 1.0

Sophia Witherspoon starred on the Fort Pierce Central High School basketball team in Fort Pierce, Florida, and then moved to Gainesville and played for three years at Florida. As a senior, she was named a first-team All-Southeastern Conference player by the SEC coaches. She graduated with a bachelor's degree in health and human performance, with career statistics of 1,381 points and 445 rebounds.

Witherspoon was drafted in 1997 in the second round by the New York Liberty and played for them for three years. She moved to the Portland Fire for 2000–01 and finished up her WNBA career with the Los Angeles Sparks in 2002–03.

She became a member of the University of Florida Athletic Hall of Fame in 2005. Her name remains at the university on the Sophia Witherspoon Award. Each semester, the UF Office of Student Life selects two student athletes (one male and one female) for the Sophia Witherspoon Award, in recognition of their positive attitudes and strong work ethic shown on the playing field and in the classroom.

After her professional playing days, Witherspoon's activities included playing basketball for Athletes in Action, an Ohio-based organization that gives athletes the opportunity to both compete against Division I college programs and learn what it means to have a relationship with God. At the end of August 2013, Witherspoon was hired by Florida Atlantic University as the Director of Operations for its women's basketball program.

Other Florida Athletes Who Went Into Pro Basketball

NAME	POSITION	COLLEGE	PRO	TEAMS
Monique Cardenas	G	1998–2002	2002	Portland Fire
Tamara Stocks Lee	F/C	1997–2001	2001	Washington Mystics

GOLF
GOLF
GOLF

MEN

The first round of golf played as a team sport at Florida dates back to 1924 before the school had an actual coach. Golf was played for more than 20 years before it was an established intercollegiate sport with a regular full-time coach, some of whom had either never played golf or had played or coached a different sport. It took many more years for the school to record a well-documented history of the Gators' results. But it was worth the wait, as Florida has produced several national championship teams and is second on the list of SEC champions.

The Early Years

Intercollegiate golf began at the University of Florida during the 1924–25 academic year, and, for the first five years, there was no official coach. The Southeastern Conference hadn't yet been formed, so there was no championship tournament. In 1929–30, Joe Holsinger took over as the coach and remained for four seasons until he was succeeded by Edgar Jones, who led the Gators for just one year.

After he left in 1934, the team went back to playing without a coach for the next three years. Harry Smith took over for the 1937–38 season, was succeeded by M. Smith for the next year, and then, in 1939, Carlos Proctor became the head coach. He was later inducted into the University of Florida Athletic Hall of Fame, not for his involvement with golf, but as a boxer (see page 352). Proctor's coaching career ended in 1941 when the team was disbanded for the war years.

The Florida golf team reorganized in 1946 under head coach Paul Severin, who lasted a year, as did Archie Bagwell in 1947–48. The next head coach was Bill Dellastatious, who served from 1948 to 1952. During his final season, the Gators competed in their first NCAA national tournament and finished in ninth place. Dellastatious is probably better known for playing halfback for the University of Missouri and the Detroit Lions. After he left Florida, he went to Missouri State University to coach football.

Next came Andrew Bracken, who coached from 1952 to 1955. His final season included a tie for sixth place in the NCAA championship and the Gators' first win in the SEC tournament.

The Conrad Rehling Era

Conrad Rehling, who had played basketball at Taylor University, took over as a first-time head coach. He led the Gators to another SEC championship (1955–56), and they placed in the top 20 at the NCAA tournament in 1958–61, finishing fourth in 1959–60. He left Gainesville with a record of 66-26-1, moving on in 1963 to coach golf at the University of West Florida before finishing his distinguished coaching career at the University of Alabama (1972–88).

Rehling is credited with the development of the PGA Professional Special Olympics training sessions and the organization of the golf competition at the Special Olympics World Games. The Conrad Rehling Award is presented by Special Olympics to honor those who have contributed to the growth of Special Olympics golf.

The Buster Bishop Era

The Gators didn't have to go far to find their new head coach. Buster Bishop came aboard in 1963, following Rehling's departure, and remained in charge until 1978. He was a true local, having been born in Gainesville, graduated from Gainesville High School, and received his bachelor's and master's degrees in physical education in 1944 and 1955 from the University of Florida.

Bishop previously had taught at Gainesville's Buchholz High School and coached football at Gainesville High School before returning to UF to become a professor of physical education. When he took over as head coach of the golf team, he had never played a round of golf, but it didn't seem to hinder his coaching. Under Bishop's leadership, Florida won four SEC championships and was runner-up seven times, and they finished in the top three in the SEC for 14 out of the 15 years he coached. In 1966, Bob Murphy became the university's first individual national champion, and, in 1968, the Gators won their first NCAA championship, followed by a second in 1973. Throughout Bishop's tenure as the Gators' head coach, the team won 41 tournaments.

Although he did not compete as an athlete for Florida, Bishop was inducted into the University of Florida Athletic Hall of Fame as an honorary letter winner in 1996.

John Darr and Lynn Blevins

One of Bishop's students, John Darr, who had played on the Gators' 1968 national championship team, was their next coach from 1978–80. Under his leadership, the Gators came in 15th and 10th in the national championship tournament and second and third in the SEC.

For their next coach, the Gators looked beyond their alumni and found Lynn Blevins, a graduate and former golf coach of the University of Oklahoma, who coached the Gators from 1981 to 1987. During the 1984–85 season, Florida won the SEC championship and was the host team for the NCAA national championship tournament, finishing third. Blevins went on to coach at the University of Iowa (where he was the Big 10 Coach of the Year) and Rogers State University. He also served as the golf director for the city of Ocala, Florida.

The Buddy Alexander Era

In 1987, Buddy Alexander became the Florida head coach and still remains in that position. He previously played as an undergraduate (1972–75) and coached (1977–80) at Georgia Southern University, then was the head coach at LSU from 1983 to 1987. His honors include the SEC Coach of the Year (1989, 1991, 1992, 1993, 1994, 1999, 2003, and 2011), *Golf Week* National Coach of the Year (1993), and the Golf Coaches Association of America National Coach of the Year (1993, 2001, and 2004).

Florida golf coach Buddy Alexander (left)

In 26 seasons through the end of the 2012–13 year, Alexander's teams have earned a pair of national championships and eight SEC titles. In 2001, Nick Gilliam became the school's second individual national champion. In April 2014, Alexander announced that he would be retiring at the end of the season.

Head Coaching Records

YEARS	HEAD COACH	WINS	YEARS	HEAD COACH	WINS
1924–29	No Coach	n/a	1947–48	Archie Bagwell	n/a
1929–33	Joe Holsinger	n/a	1948–52	Bill Dellastatious	n/a
1933–34	Edgar Jones	n/a	1952–55	Andrew Bracken	n/a
1934–37	No Coach	n/a	1955–63	Conrad Rehling	n/a
1937–38	Harry Smith	n/a	1963–78	Buster Bishop	42
1938–39	M. Smith	n/a	1978–80	John Darr	5
1939–41	Carlos Proctor	n/a	1980–87	Lynn Blevins	18
1941–46	No Team		1987–2013	Buddy Alexander	80
1946–47	Paul Severin	n/a			

Gators in the NCAA Tournament

1951–52	9th	1978–79	15th	1996–97	15th
1954–55	T6th	1979–80	T10th	1997–98	14th
1960–61	17th	1980–81	14th	1998–99	12th
1961–62	4th	1982–83	16th	2000–01	1st
1962–63	15th	1983–84	11th	2001–00	T11th
1964–65	T4th	1984–85	3rd	2002–03	T4th
1965–66	T12th	1985–86	11th	2003–04	T6th
1966–67	2nd	1986–87	29th	2004–05	T18th
1967–68	1st	1987–88	5th	2005–06	2nd
1968–69	T5th	1988–89	11th	2006–07	T9th
1970–71	3rd	1989–90	2nd	2007–08	11th
1971–72	3rd	1990–91	20th	2008–09	19th
1972–73	1st	1991–92	7th	2009–10	T11th
1973–74	2nd	1992–93	1st	2010–11	23rd
1974–75	10th	1993–94	3rd	2011–12	T12th
1976–77	8th	1994–95	13th	2012–13	25th
1977–78	9th	1995–96	T6th		

Gators in the SEC Tournament

1954–55	1st	1966–67	2nd	1970–71	2nd
1955–56	1st	1967–68	1st	1971–72	2nd
1964–65	2nd	1968–69	2nd	1972–73	1st
1965–66	3rd	1969–70	3rd	1973–74	1st

1974–75	1st	1988–89	1st	2001–02	3rd
1975–76	5th	1989–90	2nd	2002–03	2nd
1976–77	2nd	1990–91	1st	2003–04	2nd
1977–78	2nd	1991–92	1st	2004–05	4th
1978–79	2nd	1992–93	1st	2005–06	2nd
1979–80	3rd	1993–94	1st	2006–07	5th
1980–81	6th	1994–95	3rd	2007–08	4th
1981–82	4th	1995–96	2nd	2008–09	3rd
1982–83	3rd	1996–97	1st	2009–10	T2nd
1983–84	4th	1997–98	1st	2010–11	1st
1984–85	1st	1998–99	1st	2011–12	3rd
1985–86	2nd	1999–2000	1st	2012–13	10th
1986–87	5th	2000–01	1st	2013–14	T12th
1987–88	T3rd				

National Championships
(Through 2013)

22	Yale	2	Arizona State	1	Dartmouth
16	Houston	2	Augusta State	1	Minnesota
12	Princeton	2	Georgia	1	Notre Dame
10	Oklahoma State	2	Michigan	1	Oklahoma
8	Stanford	2	Ohio State	1	Pepperdine
6	Harvard	2	UCLA	1	Purdue
4	**Florida**	1	Alabama	1	San Jose State
4	LSU	1	Arizona	1	SMU
4	North Texas	1	BYU	1	Texas A&M
3	Texas	1	California	1	UNLV
3	Wake Forest	1	Clemson		

SEC Championships
(Through April 2014)

17	Georgia	3	Tennessee	0	Missouri
15	**Florida**	2	Mississippi State	0	S. Carolina
5	Alabama	1	Arkansas	0	Texas A&M
4	LSU	1	Kentucky	0	Vanderbilt
3	Auburn	1	Mississippi		

Athlete Bios

College years are those during which the athlete was awarded a letter for golf. Pro year is the year the athlete turned pro. Dollar amounts are career winnings through the year indicated, as reported by www.pgatour.com for sums won on PGA (P), Champions (C), or total (T) events through the years indicated.

THOMAS DEAN AARON (1937–) ■ *Turned Pro:* **1960; C 1987**

COLLEGE: 1956–59   6-1, 180 lbs.   C $2,721,242; T $3,646,302 (2006)

Tommy Aaron was the individual Southeastern Conference champion while playing for the Gators in 1957 and 1958. He was the runner-up in the U.S. Amateur in 1958 and represented the United States in 1959 on the Walker Cup team. The year 1960 was a busy one, as he won the Western Amateur, received his bachelor's degree in business administration, and turned pro.

As a professional, Aaron won eight events, beginning with the 1969 Canadian Open, and the 1970 Atlantic Classic was the first of his three PGA wins. He represented the U.S. in the Ryder Cup competition in 1969 and 1973. He had his highest earnings in 1972, when he finished ninth on the PGA Tour list, followed by his biggest win in 1973, the Masters Tournament. Aaron's final professional win was the 1992 Kaanapali Classic, his only victory on the Champions Tour. When he made the 36-hole cut at the 2000 Masters Tournament at age 63, he became the oldest player to do so.

Aaron is a member of the University of Florida Athletic Hall of Fame, the Georgia Sports Hall of Fame, and the Georgia Golf Hall of Fame. He lives in Gainesville, Georgia.

PATRICK ALFRED BATES (1969–) ■ *Turned Pro:* **1991**

COLLEGE: 1988–90   6-3, 195 lbs.   T $924,432 (2010)

As a member of the Florida golf team, Pat Bates was named to the All-SEC first team for all three years. He received his bachelor's degree from UF in communications process and disorders.

Bates was a participant on the Nationwide Tour (1994, 1996–2001, and 2005–07) and the PGA Tour (1995 and 2002–04). He finished first in five events, three of which were on the Nationwide Tour in 2001, despite complications from neck surgery in 1999 that left him with nerve damage in one hand. His best result on the PGA Tour was a fifth-place tie on the 2003 Bank of America Colonial. Bates' first victory was at the 1994 Nike Dakota Dunes Open, and his last was at the 2001 Buy.com Tour Championship. He is married to the daughter of Doug Tewell, a Champions Tour golfer.

THOMAS ANDREW BEAN (1953–) ■ *Turned Pro:* 1975; C 2003
COLLEGE: 1972–75   6-4, 260 lbs.   C $6,711,480; T $10,246,108 (2014)

Raised among golf courses in Jekyll Island, Georgia, Andy Bean moved to Lakeland when he was 15, where his father bought a golf course. While a student at Florida, he earned All-SEC first-team honors twice (1973 and 1975) and, in 1973, was part of the team that won the conference and national titles. Bean also won the Eastern (1974), Falstaff (1974), Dixie (1975), and Western (1975) amateur tournaments as an undergraduate. He received his bachelor's degree in marketing in 1975 and is an inductee of the University of Florida Athletic Hall of Fame.

On the right is former Florida golfer Andy Bean

Bean became a professional in 1975, winning his first tournament in 1977, the Doral-Eastern Open, with his last victory on the PGA Tour in the 1986 Byron Nelson Classic. He was part of the U.S. Ryder Cup team in 1979 and 1987, and he had his best finishes in major tournaments as a runner-up in the 1980 and 1989 PGA Championships, plus the 1983 British Open.

At the age of 50, Bean won his first Champions Tour event in 2003 at the Greater Hickory Classic and his second at the Regions Charity Classic in 2008. That same year, he was victorious at the Charles Schwab Cup Championship. In 2000, Bean became a member of the Florida Sports Hall of Fame. He is married and lives in Lakeland, Florida.

JOSEPH FRANKLIN BEARD (1939–) ■ *Turned Pro:* 1962; C 1989
COLLEGE: 1959–61   6-0, 180 lbs.   C $779,684; T $1,798,127 (1993)

As a senior at St. Xavier High School in Louisville, Frank Beard won the Kentucky high school golf championship in 1957. He then competed for Florida for three years until his 1961 graduation with a bachelor's degree in accounting. He is a member of the University of Florida Athletic Hall of Fame.

The first of his 11 PGA Tour wins (of his 14 total) was the 1963 Frank Sinatra Open Invitational. His best finishes in major tournaments were third place in the 1965 and 1975 U.S. Opens, and he represented the U.S. on the Ryder Cup team in 1969 and 1971.

In 1969, Beard was first on the PGA Tour money list with $175,223. He wrote a book about that year called *Pro*, based on a diary he kept that gave readers an insider's view of life on the tour. It was described by sports commentators as "humorous and insightful" and revealed what professionals who are not at the top have to deal with every day.

Beard won one event on the Champions Tour, the 1990 Murata Reunion Pro-Am, after celebrating his 50th birthday, and has served as a golf commentator for ESPN. The Kentucky Athletic Hall of Fame inducted him in 1986.

WOODY T. BLACKBURN (1951–) ■ *Turned Pro:* 1975; C 2002

COLLEGE: 1972–73   6-2, 195 lbs.   C $1,959; T $312,190 (2007)

Woody Blackburn was a member of the Florida team that won the SEC and NCAA championships in 1973. That same year, he was named second-team All-SEC and received a bachelor's degree in journalism.

Blackburn turned professional in 1975 and won his first tournament the following year, the Walt Disney World Team Championship, and won the PGA Tour Qualifying Tournament. Ten years later, he won his second PGA event (and his only individual PGA victory), the Isuzu-Andy Williams San Diego Open. Blackburn's best finish at a major tournament was a tie for 40th place at the 1985 PGA Championship. He lives in Jacksonville, Florida.

WILLIAM TIMOTHY BRITTON (1955–) ■ *Turned Pro:* 1979; C 2005

COLLEGE: 1976–77   5-7, 140 lbs.   C $71,417; T $1,899,651 (2013)

After moving from New York City, Bill Britton began his college golf career at Miami Dade Community College where, in 1975, he won the National Junior College Championship. He transferred to the University of Florida, where he received a bachelor's degree in health and human performance in 1979.

He found success as an amateur, winning four tournaments: the 1975 and 1976 Metropolitan Amateurs, the 1975 National Junior College Championship, and the 1979 Azalea Invitational. Britton turned pro in 1979 and in 1980 joined the PGA Tour.

Bill Britton in the 2013 Trump National at Colts Neck

His first professional win was the 1979 Metropolitan Open, and his second the 1986 Westchester Open. Britton's sole PGA Tour win was the 1989 Centel Classic. Following that were his last two professional victories in the 2005 and 2006 New Jersey PGA Championship.

Following his touring days, he became a distinguished teaching pro in New Jersey and an author with articles published in *The Met Golfer*, *New Jersey Golfer*, and *Sports Illustrated*. *Golf Digest* named him one of the "Top Ten Teachers" in New Jersey, and he was the 2002 New Jersey Section PGA's Player of the Year. Britton has played on the Champions Tour and in 2006 was named the New Jersey Section PGA's Senior Player of the Year. He is currently the Director of Golf Instruction at the prestigious Trump National Golf Club in Colts Neck, New Jersey.

MARK JOHN CALCAVECCHIA (1960–) ■ *Turned Pro:* **1981; C 1997**
COLLEGE: 1978–80   6-0, 230 lbs.   C $4,932,238; T $29,117,888 (2014)

In 1977, Mark Calcavecchia won the Florida state high school golf championship while playing for North Shore High School in West Palm Beach. He attended the University of Florida and in 1979 was honored as a first-team All-Conference member.

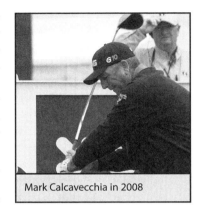

Mark Calcavecchia in 2008

He turned pro in 1981 and joined the PGA Tour the following year. His first professional victory was in the 1986 Southwest Golf Classic, and he had 12 other wins in PGA Tour events to go along with his other 13 wins, including the Phoenix Open (1989, 1992, and 2001) and the Honda Classic (1987 and 1998).

Calcavecchia's biggest win was in one of the four major tournaments, The Open Championship (a/k/a the British Open) in 1989, when he defeated Wayne Grady and Greg Norman in a four-hole playoff. He wasn't originally planning to play in the tournament because he and his wife were expecting their first child, but she convinced him to go. When handed the trophy known as the Claret Jug, Calcavecchia commented, "How's my name going to fit on that thing?" He won two other tournaments that year, his only multiple-win year, and spent the entire year, plus parts of 1988 and 1991 (109 consecutive weeks) in the top 10 of the Official World Golf Rankings. In the RBC Canadian Open in 2009, he set the PGA Tour record when he scored nine consecutive birdies.

Calcavecchia played on the Ryder Cup team in 1987, 1989, 1991, and 2002. His other appearances for the U.S. National Team were at the 1989 and 1990 Dunhill Cups and the 1998 Presidents Cup.

After his retirement from touring, his first victory on the Champions Tour was the 2011 Boeing Classic, followed by the 2012 Montreal Championship. Calcavecchia has a home in Palm Beach Gardens, Florida, and another in Phoenix, Arizona. He is a member of the Palm Beach County Sports Hall of Fame.

CHRISTIAN STRATTON COUCH (1973–) ■ *Turned Pro:* **1995**
COLLEGE: 1992–95   6-4, 225 lbs.   T $4,233,973 (2012)

Chris Couch played for the Gators when they won the NCAA national championship in 1993 and the Southeastern Conference in 1992–94. He was honored as the SEC Freshman of the Year in 1992 and made it to the All-SEC team in 1993, the second team in 1994, and in 1995 on the first team.

Couch went pro in 1995 and was a bit of a slow starter, but he won five Nationwide Tour events between 2001 and 2005, starting with the Buy.com Florida Classic in 2001. His first PGA win was the Zurich Classic of New Orleans in 2006, followed by an off year in 2007. A shoulder injury kept him off the tour in 2008, but he came back in 2009 and 2010 on a major medical extension that became unnecessary when his 2010 winnings qualified him for the tour.

In an interview in the spring of 2013 about his unexpected victory in the Zurich Classic, a reporter asked about unsubstantiated allegations Couch had made regarding his time in the city that had been ravaged by Hurricane Katrina just eight months earlier. Couch claimed that a few days before the tournament, after an evening on Bourbon Street, he was essentially mugged, but was asked to keep it quiet to avoid bad publicity for New Orleans while it was still recovering during its first post-hurricane sporting event. Police were notified, but no action was taken, and PGA officials deny his version of the story. Couch resides in Winter Garden, Florida.

Chris Couch in 2007

BENJAMIN GORDON DICKERSON (1981–) ■ *Turned Pro:* 2002

COLLEGE: 2000–01   6-0, 178 lbs.   T $731,711 (2013)

Bubba Dickerson practicing for the 2011 U.S. Open

While he was a member of the University of Florida golf team, Benjamin "Bubba" Dickerson came in second in the U.S. Amateur Public Links Championship in 2000. He and his Gator teammates won the NCAA national championship in 2001, and then Dickerson went to the Western Amateur and came in first. He was named second-team All-SEC in 2000 and first-team in 2001. Dickerson got his nickname from his older brother who couldn't say "brother" as a child.

In 2001, Dickerson won the Western Amateur and followed that with a win in the U.S. Amateur in the fall, which would have qualified him to play in the 2002 Masters, U.S. Open, and British Open as long as he kept his amateur status. He played in the Masters, but he then decided to leave school early, turn pro, and forfeit his automatic berths in the other two major tournaments.

He played on the European Challenge Tour in 2003, the next year on the NGA Hooters Tour. He was part of the Nationwide Tour in 2005 and qualified for the PGA Tour in 2006 and 2007. Dickerson went back to the Nationwide Tour in 2008 and 2009, and he won his first professional tournament, the Chitimacha Louisiana Open, in 2009. He lives in Hilliard, Florida.

CHRISTIAN DEAN DIMARCO (1968–) ■ *Turned Pro:* 1990
COLLEGE: 1987–90   6-0, 180 lbs.   T $22,656,443 (2014)

Chris DiMarco came from an athletic family—his father was a basketball player in college, his two older brothers played sports, and his nephew plays in the NFL. DiMarco played golf for Lake Brantley High School in Altamonte Springs, Florida, where he went to the prom with a girl he had known since middle school, who he eventually married. He then came to the University of Florida and won the 1988 Monroe Invitational as an amateur. In 1989, he won the Southeastern Conference individual championship and helped the Gators to the SEC team championship. DiMarco was a first-team All-SEC pick in 1989 and 1990, the SEC Player of the Year in 1990, and later was inducted into the University of Florida Athletic Hall of Fame.

Former Gator golfer Chris DiMarco

He turned pro in 1990 and played on the Canadian Tour, receiving its Order of Merit as the top tour money-winner in 1992, then earned his PGA Tour card in 1993 by finishing ninth on the Nike Tour. DiMarco struggled a bit to keep his place on the PGA tour but went on to win his first professional tournament while on the Nike Tour in 1997, the Nike Ozarks Open. His first PGA victory was at the 2000 SEI Pennsylvania Classic, his second was the 2001 Buick Challenge, and he had an interesting moment at his third victory at the 2002 Phoenix Open. As he was attempting a tense putt on the 16th hole, a fan yelled out "Noonan!" (a line from the movie *Caddyshack*). DiMarco calmly sank the putt and pointed out the fan to the tournament official, demanding his ejection.

DiMarco continued to improve his game and, by 2004, had finished as one of the top 20 money winners on the PGA Tour for five straight seasons. He was listed in the Official World Golf Rankings top 10 for 61 weeks between 2002 and 2006, reaching number six in 2005. On the European Tour, he won the Abu Dhabi Golf Championship in 2006. His highest finishes in a major tournament were second at the 2005 Masters (to Tiger Woods) and second at the British Open in 2006.

On the U.S. National Team, DiMarco competed for the Presidents Cup in 2003 and 2006, as well as the Ryder Cup in 2004 and 2006. Even though he had surgery in 2007 to correct a chronic shoulder injury, he still finished in the top 25 that year, playing in six tournaments in less than nine months. DiMarco hosts the annual "Norma DiMarco Tee Up For Life Golf Tournament" at his home course, the Country Club of Heathrow, in Heathrow, Florida. The tournament is in honor of his mother, who died in 2006, with proceeds given to R.O.C.K. (Reaching Out to Cancer Kids). DiMarco traditionally plays with every foursome on the 12th hole.

SCOTT MICHAEL DUNLAP (1963–) ■ *Turned Pro:* 1985
COLLEGE: 1982–85   5-11, 185 lbs.

As a senior, Scott Dunlap shared in the Gators' Southeastern Conference championship in 1985, which was quite a year for him—he was honored as a first-team All-SEC golfer, and *Golf Week* picked him as the Male Amateur of the Year. While playing for Florida, he won the 1984 Southern Amateur. He received his bachelor's degree in finance in 1986, while his sister, Page Dunlap, won the NCAA Women's Golf Championship as a Gator.

Dunlap's first professional victory was at the 1994 Manitoba Open on the Canadian Tour. On the Sunshine Tour, he won the 1995 Telekom South African Masters and the 1999 Dimension Data Pro-Am. He had two wins (out of 13 total) on the Nationwide Tour, the 2004 Mark Christopher Charity Classic, and the 2008 Panama Movistar Championship. Dunlap had his highest finish in 2000, as 44th on the PGA tour money list. He currently lives in Duluth, Georgia.

MATTHEW KING EVERY (1983–) ■ *Turned Pro:* 2006
COLLEGE: 2002–06   5-11, 190 lbs.   T $5,736,553 (2014)

Matt Every was a very good golfer in high school. For each of the four years he played for Mainland High School in Daytona Beach, he was named the Volusia County Golfer of the Year, and he was chosen for the All-State team in his junior and senior years. At the University of Florida, he was named All-SEC in 2004–06 and participated on the U.S. National Team. Every competed for the 2004 and 2005 Palmer Cups and the 2005 Walker Cup. In his senior year, he received the Ben Hogan Award as the best amateur golfer in the country.

In 2006, Every turned pro and competed on *The Big Break*, a television show on The Golf Channel. After playing in a few PGA Tour and Nationwide Tour tournaments, Every became a regular on the Nationwide Tour in 2008 and had his first professional win in the Nationwide Tour Championship in 2009. Every was arrested for drug possession, along with two other men in a hotel in Iowa during the summer of 2010. He denied the drug charge but issued an apology for showing poor judgment, and he was suspended from the Tour for ninety days.

Matt Every in January 2013

On March 23, 2014, Every won the Arnold Palmer Invitational by one stroke over Keegan Bradley. He currently lives in Jacksonville Beach, Florida.

JOSEPH BRIAN GAY (1971-) ■ *Turned Pro:* 1994
COLLEGE: 1991-94   5-10, 165 lbs.   T $17,741,437 (2014)

It was not unexpected when Brian Gay became a good golfer at a young age. His father, a non-commissioned officer in the U.S. Army, was a member of the All-Army golf team, and the youngster spent much of his youth on the Fort Rucker golf course in Alabama playing alongside military retirees. Gay played for four years for the University of Florida, and, in each year, the Gators won the Southeastern Conference championship and, in 1993, the NCAA national championship. Gay was honored as the SEC Freshman of the Year in 1991 and a first-team All-SEC choice in his other years. In 1992 and 1994, he was the SEC individual champion; in 1993, he played on the U.S. National Team for the Walker Cup.

Gay at the 2010 HP Byron Nelson Championship

Gay became a professional in 1994 and joined the PGA Tour in 1999. After 298 starts on the tour, he finally won his first PGA event in 2009 with the Mayakoba Golf Classic at Riviera Maya-Cancun. He quickly won two more in spring 2009 with the Verizon Heritage and St. Jude Classic. It took him four more years to get another victory, the January 2013 Humana Challenge, which earned him the title of PGA Tour Player of the Month. His best finish in a major tournament was a tie for 20th in the 2008 Masters. Gay is married and lives in Orlando, Florida.

KENNETH J. GREEN (1958-) ■ *Turned Pro:* 1979; C 2009
COLLEGE: 1977-79   5-10, 195 lbs.   C $177,622; T $4,077,136 (2014)

As a 12-year-old, Ken Green began playing golf in Honduras while his father was the principal of the American school there. At the age of 16, he quit school to attempt professional golf. Later, he attended Palm Beach Junior College before winding up at the University of Florida. During 1978, Green won the Azalea Invitational as an amateur, and, in 1979, he was named a second-team All-SEC player.

In 1979, he turned professional and the following year joined the PGA Tour. He won his first professional tournaments in 1985—the Buick Open (PGA), the King Hassan Open (in Morocco), and the Connecticut Open. His four other PGA Tour wins were The International (1986), the Canadian Open (1988), the Greater Milwaukee Open (1988), and the KMart Greater Greensboro Open (1989).

Green won four other non-PGA events, including the 1988 Dunlop Phoenix on the Japan Golf Tour. His best finish in one of the four major tournaments was a tie for seventh at the 1996 U.S. Open. He also played on the 1989 Ryder Cup team, representing the United States.

As a pro golfer, Green had a reputation for jokes and stunts, and he often refused to follow the rules of behavior. A few of his antics included drinking beer on the course during the 1997 Masters, sneaking friends into a major tournament in the trunk of his car, hitting golf balls through slightly open glass doors, criticizing officials, swearing on the course, and signing autographs while in the middle of playing, which resulted in several fines. Green was also known to play in tournaments dressed completely in green, including his shoes. Personal problems, such as divorce, gambling, and depression, affected his play and devastated him financially and likely were factors in his inability to maintain his PGA Tour status, dropping him to events on the Nationwide Tour.

Ken Green in 2010 at the Legends of Golf in Savannah

It was reported that, in 2003, Green jumped into a Palm Beach County, Florida, canal to rescue his dog, Nip, from an alligator's mouth. Green's life changed dramatically in 2009 when his motor home ran off the road on Interstate 20 in Mississippi while he was touring. The right front tire blew out, and the RV went down a steep embankment and ran into a tree. It killed his two passengers—his brother, William Green, and his girlfriend, Jeanne Hodgin—and his beloved dog, and required the amputation of Green's lower right leg. After less than a year, Green returned to play in a Champions Tour event in Savannah, Georgia, in April 2010, just a few months after the death of his son, Hunter, from a drug overdose. He has endured several surgeries on his leg to reduce his pain, but he continues to play in senior events and hopes to inspire others with disabilities.

Green lives in West Palm Beach, Florida, and has a renewed outlook on life. In 2011, he was inducted into the Palm Beach County Sports Hall of Fame.

PHILLIP RANSON HANCOCK (1953–) ■ *Turned Pro:* **1976; C 2003**

COLLEGE: 1973–76   5-10, 160 lbs.   T $437,163 (2002)

Phil Hancock was introduced to golf by his father, a dentist in Greenville, Alabama, and it wasn't unusual for the young man and his friends to play 45–54 holes a day during the summers. Hancock's first tournament win was the 1969 Alabama State Junior Championship when he was 16. He played for Florida and, as a freshman, was part of the squad that won the NCAA national title. He was a second-team All-Southeastern Conference player in his freshman and sophomore years, and he was named to the first team as a junior and senior. In those last two years, Hancock was also the SEC individual champion, and, as a senior, he was presented with the Fred

Haskins Award as the NCAA's best male college golfer of the year. He received a bachelor's degree in public relations at Florida in 1976.

After graduating, Hancock immediately turned pro and played for a time in Europe, having just missed qualifying for the PGA Tour by a single stroke. His first professional victory came in the 1977 Colombian Open, followed by first place in the 1977 PGA Tour Qualifying Tournament. He remained on the PGA Tour through 1985 but missed large chunks of touring time dealing with degenerative discs in his lower back. Hancock won one PGA event, the 1980 Hall of Fame Tournament, and his best finish in a major tournament was a tie for 16th in the 1978 PGA Championship.

After he stopped touring, he taught golf in Alabama and Florida, and he worked at the Indian Pines Golf Course in Auburn, Alabama, as a club and teaching pro. In 1992, he was inducted into the University of Florida Athletic Hall of Fame. Hancock is currently the senior vice president for International Golf Services in the Destin/Fort Walton Beach area in Florida.

HOWARD DUDLEY HART (1968–) ■ *Turned Pro:* 1990

COLLEGE: 1987–90   5-10, 190 lbs.   T $12,595,634 (2014)

Dudley Hart of Miami came to the University of Florida in 1987 to play golf and was named the Southeastern Conference Freshman of the Year. He was a first-team All-SEC player for three years and was part of the 1989 NCAA national championship team; in 2003, he became a member of the University of Florida Athletic Hall of Fame.

In 1990, Hart turned pro and became a part of the PGA Tour the next year. He won two tour events, the 1996 Bell Canadian Open and the 2000 Honda Classic. He also won four other events, including the 2002 CVS Charity Classic, in which he teamed up with fellow Gator alumnus Chris DiMarco. Despite having only won two PGA tournaments, Hart was one of the most consistent on the Tour for more than a decade with 55 top-ten finishes. His best finish in a major tournament was a tie for sixth in the 1993 PGA Championship.

Hart suffered a herniated disc in 2003 that limited his play for a time. That was followed by six months off in 2007 to care for his family, including six-year-old triplets, while his wife recovered from major lung surgery. He returned to the Tour in 2008 and was honored as the PGA Tour Comeback Player of the Year after having his best year, earning more than $2 million dollars without coming in first in any tournament.

In 2009, Hart had spinal fusion surgery, which wiped out any chance of playing in 2010. He tried to play in the 2011 Australian Open, but he dropped out early because of back pain similar to the pain that led to his surgery. Dudley was back on the PGA Tour in 2012 after receiving a major medical exemption. He lives in Clarence, New York, and is a part owner of the Lake Shore Golf Club in Rochester.

WILLIAM JOHN HORSCHEL (1986-) ■ *Turned Pro:* **2009**
COLLEGE: 2006-09   6-0, 175 lbs.   T $5,212,601 (2014)

Billy Horschel of Grant, Florida, won the 2006 U.S. Amateur tournament in Chaska, Minnesota. He then attended the University of Florida and was a four-time All-American (three times on the first team). In 2007 and 2009, he was the Southeastern Conference's Player of the Year. He received a bachelor's degree in sport management in 2009. As an amateur, he played for the U.S. Palmer Cup team in 2007 and 2008, as well as the Walker Cup team in 2008.

Horschel earned his PGA Tour card in December 2009 through the qualifying school but could only play in four events in 2010 because of a wrist injury. At his first PGA Tour start, the Mayakoba Golf Classic in 2011, he finished in a tie for 13th. The following year, he finished the True South Classic in third place.

The year 2013 was his best to date, with three top-ten finishes in a row, followed by a victory in the Zurich Classic of New Orleans, his 61st PGA Tour event. Horschel's best finish in a major (through March 2014) is a tie for fourth in the 2013 U.S. Open. He lives in Jacksonville Beach, Florida, with his wife, Brittany.

GARY D. KOCH (1952-) ■ *Turned Pro:* **1975; C 2002**
COLLEGE: 1971-74   5-11, 170 lbs.   C $1,528,599; T $3,196,773 (2014)

While a student at C. Leon King High School in Tampa, Gary Koch won the 1969 Florida Open at the age of 16. He was part of the squad from his school that won the Florida high school championship and set a scoring record that stood for three decades. Koch also won the 1970 U.S. Junior Amateur.

As a Gator, he was a four-year All-Southeastern Conference first-teamer, and he shared in SEC team championships in 1973 and 1974. He was part of the team that won the 1973 NCAA national title and was the runner-up to Ben Crenshaw for the individual trophy. That same year, he also won the Trans-Mississippi Amateur and was on the first of

Gary Koch in 2008

his two U.S. National Team winning Walker Cup teams (also 1975). In 1974, Koch was part of the U.S. National Team victory in the Eisenhower Trophy competition. He received his bachelor's degree from UF in journalism in 1976 and has been a member of the University of Florida Athletic Hall of Fame since 1978.

His first win as a professional was at the Tallahassee Open in 1976. Koch won five other PGA Tour events, concluding with the 1988 Panasonic Las Vegas Invitational. His best finish in a major tournament was a tie for fourth in the 1988 British Open.

In 2002, after his 50th birthday, he began play on the Champions Tour and won the Liberty Mutual Legends of Golf (Raphael Division) three times, all paired with Roger Maltbie, in 2003, 2008, and 2009.

Koch began his sportscasting career in 1990 with broadcasts of Champions Tour events on ESPN, later moving to NBC Sports by the end of the decade. He lives in the Tampa area and designed the front nine of the Forest Course at The Eagles Golf Course in nearby Odessa. Koch has been a member of the Florida Sports Hall of Fame since 2012.

STEVEN N. MELNYK (1947-) ■ *Turned Pro:* 1971; C 1997

COLLEGE: 1967–69   6-2, 225 lbs.   T $477,904 (1997)

As a high school student at the Glynn Academy in Brunswick, Georgia, Steve Melnyk won the 1965 Georgia Open as an Amateur and just kept on winning. He competed while a student at Florida and, in 1968, was the number one golfer on the team that captured the school's first NCAA national championship. In 1969, he received his bachelor's degree in industrial management and won the U.S. Amateur and the Western Amateur.

Melnyk played on the U.S. National Team that won the 1969 Walker Cup. In 1970, he won the Eastern Amateur and the following year won the British Amateur. His second Walker Cup competition was in 1971, the same year that he turned professional and joined the PGA Tour.

Steve Melnyk (with microphone) addressing other golfers

His winning ways did not continue as a pro. His best tournament finishes were second places in the 1973 Phoenix Open, the 1974 Houston Open, the 1979 First NBC New Orleans Open, and the 1981 Pensacola Open. In majors, his best finish was a tie for 12th at the 1972 Masters.

In 1982, Melnyk was again competing at the Phoenix Open when he slipped and broke his elbow. While it healed, he did on-course reporting for CBS Sports. He played again while he reported and, in 1984, retired as a player and shifted to reporting on a full-time basis. In 1992, he moved from CBS to ABC Sports and later did some work for ESPN. He retired from broadcasting in 2009 and that year was reinstated as an amateur and continues to compete.

Melnyk is a member of the University of Florida Athletic Hall of Fame, the Florida Sports Hall of Fame, the Georgia Golf Hall of Fame, and the Florida State Golf Association Hall of Fame. He has designed golf courses and for ten years was a member of the Gator Boosters board of directors. He resides in Jacksonville, Florida. The Melnyk Golf Practice Facility, named in his honor, is located adjacent to the 14th hole of the university's Mark Bostick Golf Course. It contains a state-of-the-art computerized video system used to analyze a player's swing.

ROBERT JOSEPH MURPHY JR. (1943–) ■ *Turned Pro:* **1967; C 1993**
COLLEGE: 1964–66   5-10, 205 lbs.   C $7,221,956; T $8,864,286 (2011)

As a result of a football injury in high school, Bob Murphy abandoned a promising career in baseball and took up golf, which was fortunate for the Gators. At the University of Florida, he won the U.S. Amateur Championship in 1965 and the NCAA individual national title in 1966. He received his bachelor's degree in 1966 in health and human performance. That year, Murphy also played on the U.S. National Team that competed for the Eisenhower Trophy and in 1967 won the Walker Cup.

Bob Murphy on the Champions Tour

He turned pro in 1967 and won the first of his five PGA Tour events the following year, the Philadelphia Golf Classic. He won three other professional tournaments before turning 50: the 1967 Florida Open, the 1970 Australian Masters, and the 1979 Jerry Ford Invitational. Murphy's highest finish at one of the four major tournaments was a tie for second in the 1970 PGA Championship. In 1975, he played on the U.S. National Team that won the Ryder Cup.

In 1993, Murphy began playing on the Champions Tour and quickly had success, winning the 1993 Bruno's Memorial Classic. He had 11 tour victories and two other senior wins to bring his total career professional wins to 21. He became a sportscaster with NBC Sports in 1999 as a tower announcer and covered the PGA Tour for ten years.

Murphy became a member of the University of Florida Athletic Hall of Fame in 1971 and a member of the Palm Beach County Sports Hall of Fame in 1983. Since 2011, he has been an inductee of the Florida Sports Hall of Fame. He was part of a team that developed a putter insert designed to improve putting in 2012. Murphy lives with his wife in Delray Beach, Florida.

ANDREW STEWARD NORTH (1950–) ■ *Turned Pro:* **1972; C 2000**
COLLEGE: 1969–72   6-4, 200 lbs.   C $1,880,533; T $3,246,063 (2013)

Andy North grew up in Wisconsin and was more interested in football and basketball, until a knee injury forced him to consider other sports. He took up golf and quickly excelled, winning the 1969 Wisconsin State Amateur Championship. At Florida, he was a three-year first-team All-Southeastern Conference player and won the 1971 Western Amateur during his college days. In 1972, North received his bachelor's degree in business administration and later became a member of the University of Florida Athletic Hall of Fame.

His professional career began in 1972, and he had his first pro victory at the PGA Tour American Express Westchester Classic in 1977. Although he had only two other PGA victories, both were in the U.S. Open in 1978 and 1985, and North was one of only 16 players to win the Open more than once. Other wins as a professional were the 1978 World Cup, the 1979 and 1990 PGA Grand Slams of Golf, and the 1980 Center Open in Argentina. He was part of the 1985 Ryder Cup team.

As a senior golfer, North won seven tournaments, concluding with the 2008 Liberty Mutual Legends of Golf, where he teamed up with Tom Watson. He began serving as a golf analyst for ESPN in 1993. North is a member of the Wisconsin Athletic Hall of Fame and lives in Madison, Wisconsin.

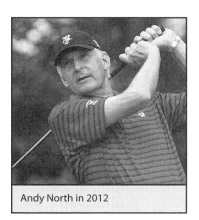
Andy North in 2012

DAVID ROY PEOPLES (1960–) ■ *Turned Pro:* 1981

COLLEGE: 1979–80   5-9, 170 lbs.   C $1,261,683; T $7,179,728 (2013)

David Peoples played golf for the Gators in 1979–80 and then went pro in 1981. His first two victories were the 1989 PGA Tour Qualifying Tournament and the 1990 Isuzu Kapalua International.

He won two PGA Tour events, the 1991 Buick Southern Open and the 1992 Anheuser-Busch Golf Classic. Peoples finished 25th on the money list, his best ranking, in 1992, and his best finish at one of the four major tournaments was a tie for 52nd at the 1993 Masters. In addition to the PGA, he has also competed on the Nationwide and the Champions Tours. Peoples lives in Orlando, Florida.

DAVID WILLIAM RAGAN JR. (1935–) ■ *Turned Pro:* 1956; C 1987

COLLEGE: 1954–56   5-11, 185 lbs.   C $6,991; T $179,247 (2013)

As a member of the Florida golf team, Dave Ragan participated in the NCAA tournament in 1955, when the Gators came in sixth. The team won its first two Southeastern Conference championships with Ragan on the team, in 1955 and 1956. He was the SEC individual champion in 1956 and is a member of the University of Florida Athletics Hall of Fame.

In 1956, he joined the PGA Tour and, three years later, had his first tour victory, the 1959 Eastern Open Invitational. His two other PGA wins were at the Beaumont Open Invitational and the West Palm Beach Open Invitational, both in 1962. Other professional wins were at the Waterloo Open Golf Classic in 1957 and the Haig & Haig Scotch Foursome in 1961 and 1963. Ragan's best finish in a major tournament was when he came in second to Jack Nicklaus at the 1963 PGA Championship. Beginning in 1987, he began playing occasionally on the Senior PGA Tour.

Ragan has coached golf at the college level, including stints at Tennessee Temple University in Chattanooga and the University of Southwestern Louisiana in Lafayette. In 1984–86, he worked at the Master's School of Golf. In 2007, he was named one of the top golf instructors in Alabama by *Golf Digest* magazine. These days, Ragan serves as a teaching pro at the Inverness Country Club in Birmingham, Alabama.

GEORGE DOUGLAS SANDERS (1933–) ■ *Turned Pro:* 1956; C 1983
COLLEGE: 1955   C $539,964; T $1,312,957 (2003)

Doug Sanders at Colonial Golf in 2009

Doug Sanders grew up in a dirt-poor family and picked cotton as a teenager. He taught himself to play golf and then received a scholarship to play at the University of Florida. During his one season playing for the university, he and his teammates won the Southeastern Conference championship and came in sixth in the NCAA national tournament, their best finish ever. In 1956, Sanders became the first (and only) amateur to win the Canadian Open.

Right after that victory, he turned pro in 1956 and won his first tournament in 1957, the Colombian Open. Nineteen of his professional wins were on the PGA Tour, and, during 1966, he finished in the top eight of all four majors. Although he never won any of the four major tournaments, Sanders was runner-up in the 1959 PGA Championship, the 1961 U.S. Open, and the 1966 and 1970 British Opens. The loss in 1970 was particularly difficult, as he was leading by four strokes on the final hole but, instead of winning, wound up in an 18-hole playoff that he lost to Jack Nicklaus . . . by one stroke.

A painful neck condition caused Sanders to have a very short and flat golf swing, but he finally had surgery that greatly reduced his pain. He was nicknamed the "Peacock of the Fairways" because of the stylish, bright-colored clothing he wore during tournaments, and, in 1973, he was named one of America's Ten Best Dressed Jocks by *Esquire* magazine. Sanders was flamboyant off the course as well, drinking, dating beautiful women, and hanging out with Evel Knievel and the Rat Pack, according to an interview in *Golf Digest* in 2003. And he didn't sleep much, but took little power naps, noting "I didn't want to sleep a third of my life away. For me, going to sleep was like ruining a good dream."

After his playing days, he sponsored the Doug Sanders Celebrity Classic and the Doug Sanders International Junior Golf Championship. He has also been active in his own golf entertainment company.

Sanders is a member of the Georgia Golf Hall of Fame, the Georgia Sports Hall of Fame, the Florida Sports Hall of Fame, and the University of Florida Athletic Hall of Fame. He lives in Houston, Texas.

DANIEL DAVID SIKES JR. (1929–87) ■ *Turned Pro:* **1960**
COLLEGE: 1951–53   C $488,632; T $1,308,233 (1987)

Dan Sikes graduated from Andrew Jackson High School in Jacksonville and came to the University of Florida where, in 1952, he was the school's first recognized All-American golfer. He received his bachelor's degree in business administration in 1953 and a law degree from Florida in 1960, and he later was chosen for the University of Florida Athletic Hall of Fame.

Sikes was known as the "Golfing Lawyer," but he never practiced law. While he was a law student, he won the 1958 U.S. Amateur Public Links Championship and then turned pro in 1960. The first of his nine professional victories was the 1963 Doral Country Club Open Invitational, giving him a total of six wins on the PGA Tour. His best finish in a major was a tie for third at the 1967 PGA Championship, and he was a member of the 1969 Ryder Cup team.

Sikes helped organize the Senior PGA Tour, now known as the Champions Tour, and then won three of its events, beginning with a tie for first with Miller Barber in the 1982 Hilton Head Seniors International. He died December 20, 1987, in Jacksonville, Florida, and the Jacksonville Sports Hall of Fame inducted him posthumously in 1988.

MICHAEL JAMES SULLIVAN (1955–) ■ *Turned Pro:* **1975; C 2005**
COLLEGE: 1974   6-2, 200 lbs.   C $316,029; T $2,811,486 (2006)

After playing for Forest High School in Ocala, Florida, Mike Sullivan came to Gainesville to be on the golf team. Just one season later, he turned pro and became a member of the PGA Tour in 1976.

The first of his three PGA victories came in 1980, when he won the Southern Open, which Sullivan considers to be one of the biggest thrills of his life because he was paired with the legendary Arnold Palmer. That was followed by wins in the 1989 Independent Insurance Agent Open and the 1994 B.C. Open. In a non-tour event, he partnered with Don January to win the 1984 Shootout at Jeremy Ranch.

Sullivan played in Nationwide Tour events, including the 1998 Nike Dominion Open and, in 2005–06, competed in Champions Tour tournaments, including the 2005 Blue Angels Classic. He resides in Ocala, Florida.

CAMILO VILLEGAS RESTREPO (1982-) ■ *Turned Pro:* 2004
COLLEGE: 2001–04   5-9, 160 lbs.   T $15,853,294 (2014)

Camilo Villegas of Colombia earned a reputation as a good golfer in his home country when he became that nation's first to win the Amateur's Grand Slam in one year. That consists of the National Junior Championship in both match and stroke play, the National Amateur Championship, and the Colombian Open. He was the second player to win the Colombian Open as an amateur, and the Colombian Golf Federation named him as its Player of the Decade.

In 2001, he was a part of the Florida NCAA national championship team as a freshman, and he individually was named the SEC Freshman of the Year. In his sophomore and senior years, he was the SEC Player of the Year. As an amateur, Villegas won the 2002 Mexican Open and the 2003 Players Amateur. During his junior and senior years, he was named to the Academic All-SEC list and in 2004, and he received his bachelor's degree in business administration.

Camilo Villegas in 2008

He went pro in 2004 and qualified for the PGA Tour just before the start of the 2006 season. That year, he was named by *Golf Digest* as the Sexiest Player on Tour, living up to his reputation for wearing flashy designer clothing.

Villegas won his first professional tournament on the Japan Golf Tour, the 2007 Coca-Cola Tokai Classic. In 2008, he won five tournaments, including the PGA Tour's BMW Championship and The Tour Championship. His best finish in the four major tournaments was a tie for fourth in the 2008 PGA Championship.

He represented Colombia in international play for the Eisenhower Trophy (1998, 2000, and 2002) and the World Cup (2006 and 2011), and he was on the International Team for the Presidents Cup in 2009. Villegas has homes in Gainesville and Jupiter, Florida.

Other Florida Athletes Who Went Into Pro Golf

NAME	COLLEGE	WENT PRO
Tyson Alexander	2006–10	c.2010
Terrence Anton	1978	1981
Walter Armstrong III	1965–67	1970
Jeff Barlow	1988–90	1991
Camilo Benedetti	1998–2002	2002
Mike Blackburn	1977–78	1979
John DeForest	c.1981	1982
Benjamin Duncan	1972–74	c.1982
Robert Floyd	1995–97	1997
Laurie Hammer	1962–65	1965
Bobby Heins	1970–72	1972
Guy Hill	1993	1994
David Jackson	1983–86	1986
Al Kelley	1956	n/a
Steve Lamontagne	1986–87	1987
Brad Lehmann	1993–94	c.1994
Josh McCumber	1995–98	c.1998
Rick Pearson	1978–80	1980
Lawrence Rentz	1980–81	c.1981
Larry Rinker	1976–78	n/a
Carlos Jose Rodiles	1996–97	1997
Ralph G. Schwab	1951–55	c.1955
Steve Scott	1996–99	c.1999
Richard Spears	1967–69	c.1969
Daniel Stone	1992–95	c.1995
Will Strickler	2005, 2007–09	2009
Dennis Sullivan	1974	n/a
Paul Tesari	1993	1995

WOMEN

Women stepped onto the links at Florida in 1969 to play golf as an intercollegiate club team. With a little help from Title IX, a federal law which established a mandate for the creation of athletic opportunities for collegiate women across the county, golf became a varsity sport for women in 1972, and the Gators have successfully competed in the NCAA and the Southeastern Conference, winning two NCAA championships and eight SEC championships.

The Mimi Ryan Era

The first women's golf coach at Florida was Mimi Ryan, who had earned degrees from Bouve College, Tufts University, and the University of North Carolina. Her first job coaching golf was at Penn State University in 1964. She left there in 1969 to become a physical education instructor at Florida, then took over as the first head golf coach and built the program from the ground up.

With the passing of Title IX, schools were required to supply equal opportunities for women in all areas, including sports programs, and UF athletic director Ray Graves, along with associate athletic director Ruth Alexander, decided to expand women's golf from a club sport to a varsity sport. When the team first played as a varsity program in 1971–72, it was as a member of the Association for Intercollegiate Athletics for Women (AIAW). During that year, the Gators finished seventh in the AIAW national championship tournament. For the next 18 years, Florida finished in the top 10 of the championship tournament (both AIAW and NCAA) every year.

During the 1981–82 season, the national championship process changed. It was the year of the last AIAW championship tournament and the first one sponsored by the NCAA. During that year, Florida finished third in the AIAW and fourth in the NCAA.

A good program got even better in the middle of the 1980s as the Lady Gators won the NCAA national championship two years in a row, 1985 and 1986. The five starters on the 1986 team were honored as All-Americans (an NCAA first), and the team had a couple of individual champions—sophomore Karen Davies won the SEC, and junior Page Dunlap won the NCAA title.

The Southeastern Conference added women's golf as a sport in 1980, and Florida immediately started winning titles. To date, the Gators have won eight conference titles (1981, 1982, 1984, 1986, 1987, 1991, 1995, and 2008). In 1986, Mimi Ryan was named the NCAA Coach of the Year and was later inducted as one of the charter members of the National Golf Coaches Association Coaches Hall of Fame. Ryan was inducted into the University of Florida Athletic Hall of Fame as an honorary letter winner in 1996, two years after she retired during the 1994 fall season.

More Recently

After Ryan's departure, former University of Arizona golf coach Kim Haddow was hired in October 1994. Under her leadership, Florida captured the SEC title in 1995, and its best finish in the NCAA tournament was runner-up in 1998, which was Haddow's last year as a Gator.

In 1998, Jill Briles-Hinton became the third coach of the Lady Gators golf team. She had graduated from the University of Miami in 1986, turned pro and played on the LPGA Tour for 12 years, earning $516,788. She remained the Florida head coach until May 2009 and had some success. During her 11 years in Gainesville, her teams made it to the NCAA championship tournament six times. Coach Briles-Hinton was honored as the SEC Coach of the Year in 2008. After leaving Florida, she was the head coach at the University of Richmond for three years.

Jan Dowling, previously an assistant coach at Kent State University (her alma mater) and Duke University, took over as the head coach at Florida in 2009. She had experience on the Canadian National Team and was the Canadian Women's Amateur champion in 2000. She led the Gators to a 10th place finish at the 2011 NCAA tournament and 12th place the following year. After leaving Florida, she took over as head coach of the University of Michigan.

She stepped down in May 2012 and was replaced by Michigan State University alumna Emily Bastel. With her as the head coach, the Gators finished 17th in the 2013 NCAA tournament and in 10th place in the SEC. In December 2012, Emily married Christian Glaser and is now known as Emily Glaser.

Gators in the AIAW Tournament

1970–71	4th	1974–75	3rd	1978–79	2nd
1971–72	7th	1975–76	4th	1979–80	7th
1972–73	7th	1976–77	5th	1980–81	8th
1973–74	5th	1977–78	2nd	1981–82	3rd

Gators in the NCAA Tournament

1982–83	4th	1989–90	3rd	2002–03	8th
1983–84	4th	1990–91	15th	2004–05	10th
1984–85	1st	1993–94	15th	2005–06	T6th
1985–86	1st	1995–96	9th	2007–08	9th
1986–87	3rd	1996–97	10th	2010–11	T10th
1987–88	4th	1997–98	2nd	2011–12	12th
1988–89	5th	1999–2000	18th	2012–13	17th
2001–02	T6th				

National Championships
(Through 2013)

7	Arizona State	2	Arizona	1	Georgia
5	Duke	2	**Florida**	1	Miami (Fla.)
3	San Jose State	2	Tulsa	1	Purdue
3	Southern Cal	1	Alabama	1	TCU
3	UCLA				

SEC Championships
(Through April 2014)

11	Georgia	1	LSU	0	Mississippi State
10	Auburn	1	South Carolina	0	Missouri
8	**Florida**	0	Arkansas	0	Tennessee
2	Vanderbilt	0	Kentucky	0	Texas A&M
1	Alabama	0	Mississippi		

Athlete Bios

College years are those during which the athlete was awarded a letter for golf. Pro year is the year the athlete turned pro. Dollar amounts are career winnings, as reported by **www.lpga.com** (as of the year indicated).

SANDRA GAL (1985–) ■ *Turned Pro:* **2007**
COLLEGE: 2004–07   6-0 $2,314,749.75 (2014)

Sandra Gal learned how to play golf in her home country of Germany and at age 17 became a member of the German National Team. She won the German National Girls Championship at age 18.

She enrolled at the University of Florida in 2004 and played for the Gators until 2007. While in Gainesville, she was the Southeastern Conference Co-Scholar-Athlete of the Year in 2007, and a member of the National Golf Coaches Association All-American Scholar Golf Team (2005–07). In 2006, Gal was named to the All-SEC second team and moved up to the first team the following year. As a Gator, she won the 2006 and 2007 SunTrust Lady Gator Invitationals and the 2007 Mercedes-Benz Collegiate Classic.

Sandra Gal at the 2009 Women's British Open

Gal set the Florida all-time record for top season stroke average (72.69). When she left the school, she had the second-best individual tournament average for 54 holes (217.6). Before turning pro late in 2007, she won the Ladies European Amateur. She qualified for the LPGA Tour at the 2007 Qualifying Tournament, and she immediately turned pro. She played on the LPGA Tour starting in 2008 while she was finishing up her bachelor's degree in advertising, which she received in August 2008.

Gal's single LPGA tournament win (as of March 2014) was the 2011 Kia Classic, which she won by one stroke over Jiyai Shin. Her highest finish in the major LPGA events was third place in the 2012 U.S. Women's Open. Gal participated in the 2011 Solheim Cup tournament, in which her European team defeated the U.S. National Team by a score of 15 to 13. She has often been photographed posing in glamorous clothing and, in 2012, was voted the winner of the GolfDigest.com Hottest Golfer competition.

LORI GARBACZ (1958–) ■ *Turned Pro:* **1979**
COLLEGE: 1977–78 $911,483 (2013)

Lori Garbacz played for the University of Florida women's golf team that came in second in the 1978 Association for Intercollegiate Athletics for Women national championship tournament. She also won the 1977 Tucker Invitational.

She turned professional in 1979 and played on the LPGA Tour for 16 years, retiring in 1995. Her sole LPGA victory was at the 1989 Circle K LPGA Tucson Open.

Garbacz's highest finishes in the major LPGA events were ties for third at the 1984 U.S. Women's Open and the 1985 LPGA Championship.

While playing as a pro, Garbacz was feisty and somewhat rebellious. During the Denver Pro-Am in 1987, a cameraman got too close to her after a poor shot, and she let loose a string of obscenities that was captured on a live ESPN broadcast. She was then called "the bad girl of the LPGA tour." What she is most famous for, however, is an incident that occurred at the 1991 U.S. Women's Open. Garbacz was upset at how slow the golfers ahead of her foursome were playing, so she protested by calling Domino's Pizza while she was at the 14th hole. A pepperoni and mushroom pizza was delivered to the 17th tee, and the message of her frustration reached the slow players. Garbacz followed her pro career as a volunteer in New York with New York Cares, an organization to help the disadvantaged in local communities.

DONNA HORTON WHITE (1954–) ■ *Turned Pro:* 1977
COLLEGE: 1975–76   5-2 $908,586 (1992)

Before arriving at the University of Florida, Donna Horton was an accomplished amateur golfer. In 1971, she was a semifinalist in the U.S. Girls' Junior tournament. She also was a semifinalist in the U.S. Women's Amateur in 1973 and, after heading to Florida, was the runner-up in 1975 and the winner in 1976. She began her college years at the University of North Carolina-Greensboro.

After she transferred to Florida, Horton was the medalist at four tournaments, beginning with the Tucker Invitational during her first year in Gainesville. She followed that in 1975 with wins at the WSIC, the Rollins Invitational, and the State Collegiate.

She graduated with a bachelor's degree in health and human performance in 1976. That same year, Horton won the Trans-National Amateur and competed on the victorious teams representing the United States for the Curtis Cup (against British and Irish golfers) and the Espirito Santo Trophy (edging out a team from France). She was also married that year and has since been known as Donna White. In 1978, she became a member of the University of Florida Athletic Hall of Fame. Eight years later, she was inducted into the Palm Beach County Sports Hall of Fame.

White played on the LPGA Tour for 16 years and had three victories—the 1980 Florida Lady Citrus, the 1980 Coca-Cola Classic, and the 1983 Sarasota Classic. Her best finish in the major LPGA events was a tie for second at the 1982 U.S. Women's Open. White continued to play through a pregnancy, hand issues, and back surgery with an easygoing attitude and an easy smile, which disguised her fierce competitiveness.

DEB RICHARD (1963–) ■ *Turned Pro:* 1986
COLLEGE: 1982–85   5-6 $2,779,041 (2005)

In Kansas, Deb Richard played golf for Manhattan High School in Manhattan, Kansas, during its three-year run as state champion (1979–81). She won the Kansas

Women's Amateur in 1982 and 1983, while beginning her college career with the 1982 season as a Gator.

At Florida, she won seven tournaments, including Southeastern Conference individual championships in 1982, 1983, and 1984. Richard was the U.S. Women's Amateur champion in 1984. She also competed for the victorious United States team in Espirito Santo Trophy play in Hong Kong and was the World Cup champion in 1985.

Richard was a first-team All-SEC golfer in each of her four years, and, as a senior, she was named the SEC Player of the Year. That year at the NCAA championship tournament, she finished in second place by just one stroke. She was awarded the Broderick Trophy in 1985 to honor her as the country's most outstanding female collegiate golfer. In 1989, she received her bachelor's degree in advertising. Six years later, she was inducted into the University of Florida Athletic Hall of Fame and was later inducted into the Kansas Golf Hall of Fame.

After turning pro, Richard won five tournaments on the LPGA Tour, beginning with the 1987 Rochester International and ending with the 1997 Friendly's Classic. Her highest finishes in major LPGA events were two ties for fourth in the 1988 and 1998 du Maurier Classic tournaments. In 1994, she was the recipient of the *Golf Digest* Founders Cup Award.

Richard is involved in charitable activities and was presented with the 1996 Samaritan Award for her work through the Deb Richard Foundation, providing college scholarships to physically challenged children. She endowed a scholarship program in 2003 and 2004 to help such students. In 2004, the University of Florida honored her with its Distinguished Alumnus Award.

LAURIE ANN RINKER (1962–) ■ *Turned Pro:* 1982
COLLEGE: 1980–82   5-6 $1,210,885 (2007)

Laurie Rinker played for the Lady Gators for three seasons, and she remained a student for one additional year because, after her junior year, she turned pro and qualified for the LPGA Tour. Although she could no longer participate in collegiate golf, she returned to Gainesville during off weeks to finish her bachelor's degree in finance, which she received in 1983.

In 1980, she won the U.S. Girls' Junior and two years later won the Doherty Challenge Cup. As a Gator, she won the 1981 South Florida Invitational and, in 1982, was named All-Southeastern Conference.

Rinker's most successful years as a touring pro were 1984 through 1986, during which all four of her tournament victories occurred. She won two events on the LPGA Tour, the 1984 Boston Five Classic, and the 1984 Nabisco Dinah Shore. In 1985, she won the J.C. Penney Classic with her partner, Larry Rinker, one of her two brothers who played on the PGA Tour. Her best finish in a major LPGA event was a tie for third in the 1987 LPGA Championship. Even though she won no tournaments in 1987, it was her best money year, with $158,916 in winnings. Rinker has continued to play in LPGA Legends Tour events and is active with charitable organizations.

Other Florida Athletes Who Went Into Pro Golf

NAME	COLLEGE	WENT PRO
Laura Alicia Brown	1998–91	c.1991
Jeanne-Marie Busuttil	1995–96	1998
Aimie Cho	2003–04	c.2004
Jeanne Cho-Hunicke	2000–03	c.2003
Lynn Connelly	1980–83	1984
Karen Davies	1985–88	1989
Beverly Davis	1976–79	1980
E. Page Dunlap	1984–87	1987
Lisa Ann Hackney Hall	1987–90	1991
Mary Hafeman	1978–79	c.1980
Riko Higashio	1996–98	1998
Amelia Lewis	2009	c.2009
Paula Martí	2000	2000
Cheryl Morley Pontious	1986–89	c.1989
Whitney Myers	2004–06	c.2006
Nancy Rubin-Scharff	1977	c.1980
Naree Song	2003	2004
Michelle Vinieratos	1989–91	1991
Jessica Yadloczky	2007–11	2011
Hannah Yun	2007	c.2007

TENNIS

MEN

The first intercollegiate tennis team at the University of Florida began competition in 1932, and men's tennis has remained a fixture on the campus sports scene ever since (other than the World War II years). The Gators have frequently contended (and occasionally won) the Southeastern Conference championship and, especially in recent years, have also had a presence at the NCAA national championships, with their best finishes to date being ties for third place in 2000 and 2005.

The first Gator tennis coach was D.K. "Dutch" Stanley, who also coached the football team from 1933 to 1935. He was the tennis coach from 1932 until 1940 and was followed by Frank Genovar, who led the team just for 1941. Genovar also coached the school's first swimming and diving team for 22 years, starting in 1930, and was inducted into the University of Florida Athletic Hall of Fame. The tennis team was then disbanded for the war years.

In 1947, there was a tennis team again, coached by Herman Schnell who, in 1946, had become one of the original faculty members of the Department of Physical Education. Schnell coached the tennis team for two years and was followed by Harry Fogelman, who coached the team for three years and, in 1950, led the Gators to their first Southeastern Conference regular season championship.

Florida's first long-term men's tennis coach was Bill Potter, who compiled a 415-122-2 dual match record over a 26-season career in Gainesville. His teams won the regular season SEC championship in 1961, 1968, and 1969, and tied for first in 1975. For 12 of Potter's seasons, Moses "M.B." Chafin was an assistant coach and, upon Potter's retirement, Chafin took over for seven years and was named the SEC Coach of the Year in 1984. Both men were memorialized through the William M. Potter/M.B. Chafin Scholarship

Fund for undergraduate students in UF's College of Health and Human Performance.

Steve Beeland was the next men's coach beginning in 1985, after serving as the Florida women's tennis coach in 1982–84. Beeland's four-year winning percentage was the lowest of all in the history of Florida men's tennis (.524), and his final season in 1988 had the team winding up with a record of 3-20.

Florida's eighth men's tennis coach was Ian Duvenhage, who had previously coached the women's team at the University of Miami (1982–88), where he received his bachelor's (1980) and master's (1983) degrees. He took over at Florida in 1989 and stayed until 2001, and his teams won the SEC regular season in 1994 and 2000. While at Florida, Duvenhage was named the SEC Coach of the Year in 1993, 1994, and 2000, and the Region 3 Coach of the Year in 1999 and 2000. After he left the University of Florida, he became the head coach of the men's tennis team at Vanderbilt University.

In 2002, the Gators welcomed another head coach, David Andrew "Andy" Jackson, who had played his collegiate tennis at the University of Kentucky and coached at Mississippi State University from 1985 through 2001. The Gators quickly reached the top of the SEC with an outright first place finish in 2003 and a tie for first in 2005, making Jackson the only men's head coach to win the SEC title at two different schools (won in 1993 at Mississippi State). The 2005 team finished in a tie for third in the NCAA national championship tournament, matching Florida's previous best NCAA finish in 2000 under Coach Duvenhage.

In May 2012, Andy Jackson resigned as head coach. In 2013, he was installed as the new head coach of the men's tennis team at the University of Arkansas. Jackson was succeeded by Bryan Shelton, who had coached the Georgia Tech women's tennis team for 13 years, winning a 2007 national title. In his first year at Florida, he led the team to a record of 15-11.

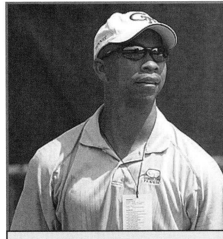

Coach Shelton in 2007 when he was with Georgia Tech

Florida Coaching Records

YEARS	WINNING SEASONS	HEAD COACH	WON	LOST	TIED	PCT.
1932–40	9	D.K. Stanley	54	12	0	.818
1941	1	Frank Genovar	10	2	1	.808
1947–48	2	Herman Schnell	12	11	1	.521
1949–51	3	Harry Fogelman	51	13	1	.792
1952–77	26	Bill Potter	415	122	2	.772
1978–84	7	M.B. Chafin	128	55	1	.698
1985–88	4	Steve Beeland	54	49	0	.524
1989–2001	13	Ian Duvenhage	221	126	0	.636
2001–12	11	Andy Jackson	208	84	0	.712
2013	1	Bryan Shelton	15	11	0	.577
Totals	77		1171	483	6	.709

Gators in the NCAA Tournament

1961	T10th	1976	16th	1998	T25th	2006	T9th
1963	18th	1991	T3rd	1999	T5th	2007	T9th
1967	7th	1992	5th	2000	T3rd	2008	T9th
1968	5th	1993	T9th	2001	T10th	2009	T17th
1969	6th	1994	T9th	2002	T9th	2010	T9th
1972	18th	1995	T9th	2003	T5th	2011	T9th
1973	22nd	1996	T17th	2004	T9th	2012	T9th
1974	T13th	1997	T9th	2005	T3rd	2013	T33rd
1975	T8th						

SEC Championships
(Through April 2014)

SCHOOL	REGULAR SEASON	TOURNAMENT
Georgia	28	9
Tulane	18	0
Tennessee	10	3
Florida	9	4
Mississippi	5	3

SCHOOL	REGULAR SEASON	TOURNAMENT
LSU	5	2
Mississippi State	3	1
Georgia Tech	3	0
Kentucky	2	1
Auburn	2	0
Alabama	1	0
Texas A&M	0	1
Vanderbilt	0	1
Arkansas	0	0
South Carolina	0	0

Athlete Bios

College years are those during which the athlete was awarded a letter for tennis. Pro year is the year the athlete turned pro.

MARK MERKLEIN (1972–) ■ *Turned Pro:* **1994**

COLLEGE: 1991–94   6-3, 181 lbs.   **OLYMPICS:** 2000; 2004

Mark Merklein, from the Bahamas, played for the University of Florida from 1991 to 1994 and, in 1993, was the NCAA individual singles champion. The following year, he teamed with fellow Gator David Blair to win the NCAA doubles title. Merklein was named to the All-SEC team three times and, as a senior, he was honored as the SEC Player of the Year. When he left UF, he ranked first in career wins, first in singles wins, and second in the number of doubles wins.

While touring as a professional, Merklein won no singles titles but did win four ATP doubles championships. The first two were in Orlando (1997) and Costa de Sauipe (2002) with partner James Blake, whom he coached for two years. Next was in Scottsdale (2003) with Scott Humphries. Merklein's last win was in Munich in 2004 with Vincent Spadea. His highest ranking as a doubles player was #35 on January 12, 2004, better than his best singles ranking of 160, which he reached on July 7, 1997. He played in tournaments until 2005; that same year, he became a member of the University of Florida Athletic Hall of Fame.

As a representative of the Bahamas, Merklein played in two Olympics in doubles competition, teaming up with Mark Knowles. In the 2000 Olympics, they came in with a tie for fifth. In 2004, they finished with a tie for 17th.

Merklein was a volunteer coach at UF (1998–2000) and for six years was a national coach with the United States Tennis Association Player Development Center. He then spent two years as an assistant coach at the University of Michigan. During May 2013, Merklein became an assistant tennis coach for his alma mater, the University of Florida, a goal of his dating back to his undergraduate days.

RYAN SWEETING (1987–) ■ *Turned Pro:* 2007
COLLEGE: 2006   6-5, 180 lbs.

Ryan Sweeting at the 2011 Aegon Championships

Before coming to the University of Florida, Ryan Sweeting was the 2005 U.S. Open Boys' Singles champion and that year reached a combined ranking of #2 junior in the world. He played one season at the University of Florida (2006) and turned professional later that year.

As a singles professional, Sweeting has won one tournament so far, the 2011 U.S. Men's Clay Court Championships in Houston. His highest ranking (through March 2014) was #116 on July 9, 2012. He played in each of the four Grand Slam events at least once, making it to the second round at the U.S. Open (2006), Wimbledon (2011 and 2012), and the Australian Open (2011 and 2012).

In doubles, his best finish has been runner-up (along with partner and fellow Gator Jesse Levine) in the 2009 ATP Houston. His highest doubles ranking was #139 on April 2 and November 2, 2008, and Sweeting's best Grand Slam finishes were in the second round of the U.S. Open (2009) and Wimbledon (2010).

Other Florida Athletes Who Went Into Pro Tennis

NAME	COLLEGE	WENT PRO
Jesse Levine	2007	2007
Jeff Morrison	1998–2000	2000

Jesse Levine at the 2009 U.S. Open

WOMEN

Tennis for women began at Florida in 1960, with a good intercollegiate club team coached by Alice Luthy Tym. Later, Tym also started the women's tennis program at the University of Tennessee-Chattanooga and won a pair of small-college national championships. With the expansion of women's collegiate sports as a result of Title IX, a federal law establishing a mandate for athletic opportunities for collegiate women across the county, the tennis program was elevated to a varsity sport beginning with the 1972–73 school year. Sue Whiddon became the head coach of the team in 1972 and stayed through 1975.

B.E. Palmer succeeded Whiddon, and, in 1978, Liz Broughton was named as the team's third official head coach. She left in 1981 to pursue her doctorate degree. Next came former Gator tennis player Steve Beeland, who served the women's team as head coach in 1982–84, then moved over to the men's team.

Florida played as part of the AIAW (Association for Intercollegiate Athletics), which sponsored a national championship tournament that usually included the Lady Gators among the top 10 finishers. Florida was the runner-up in the 1980 tournament. In 1981–82, the national championship began to be determined by a tournament sponsored by the NCAA, and Florida has been a frequent participant. Since tennis became a varsity sport at Florida, its women's team has failed to make it to the national championship tournament only three times (1973, 1986, and 2009).

The Southeastern Conference began offering championships in 1980, one for the school that has the best regular season record, and one for the school that wins the end-of-the-year conference tournament. Florida has, to date, won 25 regular season titles and 17 tournaments.

The Andy Brandi Era

In 1985, Andres V. "Andy" Brandi became the head coach of the Lady Gators. Born in Puerto Rico, he played his college tennis at Trinity University in San Antonio and earned a bachelor's degree in business administration in 1975.

After years as a touring pro and serving as the executive director of the IMG Bollettieri Tennis Academy in Bradenton, Florida, he took on the position of head coach of the Florida women's tennis team in August 1984.

In Brandi's fourth year as head coach (1988), the team made it to the finals of the NCAA tournament for the first time and was the top-seeded team. Florida wound up being the runner-up to Stanford University, but Shaun Stafford won the individual singles champion. Before the final match, Stafford was assured the Gators would bring home an individual title because Stafford's opponent was fellow Florida player Halle Cioffi. In 1990, UF hosted the tournament on its home courts and once again was defeated by Stanford.

The first national team championship for the Lady Gators came in 1992 with a victory over the University of Texas. UF's Lisa Raymond was the individual singles champion (as she was again in 1993). Texas got revenge in 1995, beating the Lady Gators in the finals.

Brandi coached the team to a second national championship in 1996 with its first post-season victory over Stanford in four tries. Florida players also won the individual singles (Jill Craybass) and doubles (Dawn Buth and Stephanie Nickitas) titles, and only once before had all three titles been won by the same school in a single season. Florida finished that season with a record of 31-0, and, against teams ranked in the top 25, they were 20-0.

Andy Brandi resigned as coach in 2001, and his winning percentage of .915 was the highest of any coach in the history of the NCAA. His 460 total wins ranked him #5 on the NCAA all-time list. In 2006, Brandi was inducted into the University of Florida Athletic Hall of Fame. He was a five-time SEC Coach of the Year (1987, 1988, 1993, 1996, and 1998), the 1996 and 1998 United States Professional Tennis Registry National Coach of the Year, the 1988 United States Professional Tennis Association National Coach of the Year, and the Intercollegiate Tennis Association National Coach of the Year in 1989 and 1996.

After leaving the University of Florida, Andy Brandi worked for the IMG Academy, the Chris Evert Tennis Academy, and the Harold Solomon Tennis Institute. He also served as a member of the player development staff and a national coach of the United States Tennis Association.

The Roland Thornqvist Era

The present coach of the Florida women's team is Roland Thornqvist, who was born in Sweden and played his college tennis at the University of North Carolina. He was a three-time All-Atlantic Coast Conference honoree and received his bachelor's degree in economics in 1996. He then went on to coach women's tennis at the University of Kansas (1997–98) and the University of North Carolina (1999–2001).

Thornqvist took over in Gainesville in 2002, bringing with him a coaching record of 75-50, and during his years with the Gators has had a winning percentage of nearly 90%. Each year that he has been the Gators' head coach, the team has made it to the NCAA national championship tournament.

Under Thornqvist, Florida has won the national championship three times (2003, 2011, and 2012), and was runner-up twice (2002 and 2010). For his accomplishments, the ITA named Thornqvist the National Coach of the Year in 2011.

Gators in the AIAW Tournament

1974	14th	1977	5th	1980	2nd
1975	7th	1978	4th	1981	4th
1976	11th	1979	6th		

Gators in the NCAA Tournament

1982	Round of 16	1994	Quarterfinals	2004	Round of 32
1983	Round of 16	1995	Runner-up	2005	Semifinals
1984	Quarterfinals	1996	Champion	2006	Semifinals
1985	Quarterfinals	1997	Runner-up	2007	Quarterfinals
1987	Semifinals	1998	Champion	2008	Semifinals
1988	Runner-up	1999	Runner-up	2009	Round of 16
1989	Semifinals	2000	Semifinals	2010	Runner-up
1990	Runner-up	2001	Semifinals	2011	Champion
1991	Semifinals	2002	Runner-up	2012	Champion
1992	Champion	2003	Champion	2013	Round of 16
1993	Semifinals				

National Championships
(Through 2013)

Stanford	17	S. California	2	Georgia Tech	1
Florida	**6**	Texas	2	UCLA	1
Georgia	2	Duke	1		

SEC Championships
(Through April 2014)

School	Regular Season	Tournament	School	Regular Season	Tournament
Florida	26	18	LSU	0	0
Georgia	9	8	Mississippi State	0	0
Alabama	1	0	Missouri	0	0
Kentucky	0	1	South Carolina	0	0
Mississippi	0	1	Tennessee	0	0
Arkansas	0	0	Texas A&M	0	0
Auburn	0	0	Vanderbilt	0	0

Athlete Bios

College years are those during which the athlete was awarded a letter for tennis. Pro year is the year the athlete turned pro.

NICOLE J. ARENDT (1969–) ■ *Turned Pro:* 1991
COLLEGE: 1988–91   5-9½, 150 lbs.

Nicole Arendt from New Jersey played for the Gators after graduating from the Hun School of Princeton. During 1989–90, she made it to the finals of the NCAA championships, and she was named first-team All-SEC for the three years she played for Florida. During the next year, she partnered with Jillian Alexander to win the NCAA doubles championship and the Rolex National Indoor Intercollegiate Championship (where Arendt also won the singles championship) in 1990. When Arendt left the university, she did so as its all-time singles winner with a record of 126-25.

In 1991, she turned professional and participated in both singles and doubles competition, having more success in the latter. In singles, Arendt had a record of 172-131 and did not win any tournaments. She attained her highest professional ranking on June 16, 1997, when she made it to #49. In the four Grand Slam tournaments, her best finish was the fourth round at the French Open in 1997.

In doubles competition, Arendt's record was 324-171. Her highest ranking as a doubles player was #3, reached on August 25, 1997. Arendt won 16 doubles titles with partners Kristine Kunce (two), Laura Golarsa (one), Manon Bollegraf (nine), Jana Novotná (one), Ai Sugiyama (two), and Liezel Huber (one). Her best finish in a Grand Slam doubles event was in the Wimbledon finals of 1997, when she and Bollegraf were defeated by Gigi Fernández and Natasha Zvereva by a score of 6-2, 3-6, 6-1.

Arendt has coached at City Community Tennis in Sydney, Australia.

DAWN ALEXIS BUTH (1976–) ■ *Turned Pro:* **1998**

COLLEGE: 1995–98   5-2½, 125 lbs.

In Kansas, Dawn Buth played singles and doubles for Wichita Southeast High School, which won the state championship during her freshman year of 1991. Buth won six national junior titles and won at both singles and doubles at the National Indoor Championships in 1991. She also was on the school track team and ran in multiple events, finishing fifth in the mile run at the state championships.

In her first tennis season at Florida, Buth was ranked as the number one college freshman in the U.S. In 1996 and 1998, she was an important member of the UF national championship team. She paired with Stephanie Nickitas to win the NCAA doubles title in both 1996 and 1997, and they were runners-up in 1998. They were the first to win the doubles title in consecutive years. Buth was honored as the Intercollegiate Tennis Association Rookie of the Year and was first-team All-Southeastern Conference during her four years as a Gator. She became a member of the University of Florida Athletic Hall of Fame in 2011.

In 1998, Buth turned pro and competed on the Women's Tennis Association Tour and the International Tennis Federation Women's Circuit until 2001, winning a pair of singles championships and a dozen doubles titles. In Grand Slam events, her best finish was making it to the second round in the 2000 U.S. Open in singles.

In 2002, Buth received her UF bachelor's degree in fine arts and became an assistant professional at the Gainesville Country Club. The following year, she moved to the University of Pennsylvania to be an assistant coach and helped guide the team to the highest national ranking in their history. In 2004, she took over as the head coach of the women's tennis team at George Washington University in Washington, DC. She led the Colonials to second place in its conference in 2009–10 and was named the Atlantic 10 Conference Coach of the Year. Buth left the university in the summer of 2013 to become the Associate Director of Leadership Development for the NCAA.

JILL N. CRAYBAS (1974–) ■ *Turned Pro:* **1996**

COLLEGE: 1993–96   5-3, 120 lbs.   **OLYMPICS:** 2008

Jill Craybas at the 2007 Acura Classic

Jill Craybas played tennis for Florida from 1993 through her senior year of 1996, when she was the NCAA singles champion. That year, she received her bachelor's degree in telecommunications with the intent to eventually get involved with television or film production.

Since turning pro in 1996, she has won four singles tournaments on the International Tennis Federation Women's Circuit and one Women's Tennis Association event, the 2002 Japan Open Tennis Championship. Her highest finish as a singles player in a Grand Slam event was reaching the fourth round of Wimbledon in 2005 by beating Serena Williams. Her highest ranking was #39 on April 17, 2006.

As a doubles player, Craybas has won one ITF title and five with the WTA, including the 2008 Istanbul Cup and the 2003 WTA Madrid Open. Her highest ranking as a doubles player was #41 on June 23, 2008. In Grand Slam events, her best doubles finish was the quarterfinals of the 2004 French Open.

Craybas became an Olympian when she replaced a pregnant U.S. team member. In the 2008 Beijing Olympics, Craybas played in the first round of the singles tournament and lost to Patty Schnyder of Switzerland, giving Craybas a final standing of a tie for 33rd place. She became a member of the University of Florida Athletic Hall of Fame in 2008.

JILL HETHERINGTON HULTQUIST (1964–) ■ *Turned Pro:* 1983
COLLEGE: 1984–87   5-10, 150 lbs.   **OLYMPICS:** 1984; 1988; 1996

A native of Ontario, Canada, Jill Hetherington played four years for Florida, winning the Southeastern Conference individual singles title each year. She was also half of the conference doubles championship pair in each of her last three years and was a four-time All-SEC first-team honoree.

Hetherington turned pro in 1983 and as a singles player won one International Tennis Federation tournament and one with the Women's Tennis Association, in Wellington, New Zealand. Her best finish in a Grand Slam tournament was in the third round of the 1988 U.S. Open. Her highest singles ranking was #64 on February 29, 1988.

As half of a doubles team, Hetherington won 14 WTA titles, playing with partners Helene Pelletier (one), Patty Fendick (seven), Elizabeth Smylie (one), Jo Durie (one), Kathy Rinaldi-Stunkel (two), Elna Reinach (one), and Kristine Kunce (one). Her best Grand Slam doubles results were with Patty Fendick in the 1989 finals of the Australian Open and the 1988 U.S. Open. In mixed doubles, she made it to the finals of the 1995 French Open with partner John-Laffnie de Jager. As a doubles player, her highest ranking was #6 on March 27, 1989.

Hetherington played for 13 straight years on the Canadian Fed Cup team, and, in 2001, she was inducted into the Canadian Tennis Hall of Fame. She represented Canada in the Olympics in 1984, 1988, and 1996. Her accolades include the WTA Sportsmanship Award, the Tennis Canada Sportsmanship Award, and the 1988 Player of the Year in Canada. She is considered a groundbreaker for Canadian women in tennis. Hetherington retired from the professional tour in 1997 and became a member of the University of Florida Athletic Hall of Fame in 1999.

After earning her bachelor's degree in psychology in 2000, Hetherington became an assistant coach of the women's tennis team for the University of Washington in Seattle. She worked with fellow coach Patty Fendick McCain, her frequent doubles partner since their junior year at the Nick Bollattieri Tennis Academy, and for several years, she has held the head coaching position. Hetherington coaches under her married name, Jill Hultquist, and lives with her husband and two children in Renton, Washington.

LISA RAYMOND (1973–) ■ *Turned Pro:* 1993

COLLEGE: 1992–93   5-5, 121 lbs.   **OLYMPICS:** 2004; 2012 1 bronze medal

In 1990, Lisa Raymond was ranked as the #1 Under-18 player in the country. As a member of the Florida tennis team, Raymond won the NCAA individual national championship singles title in 1992 and 1993, and she was a member of the team that won the school's first team title in 1992. That year, she became the first player to win all three collegiate Grand Slam titles in the same season.

Lisa Raymond in 2011

Raymond was the 1992 Volvo Rookie of the Year, the 1992 *Tennis Magazine* Collegiate Player of the Year, the 1992 and 1993 Broderick Award winner, and the 1993 recipient of the Honda Award. During her junior year at Florida, she won five U.S. national titles and became a member of the University of Florida Athletic Hall of Fame in 2003.

Her successes are mostly in doubles play, where she has won 79 Women's Tennis Association titles and one in the International Tennis Federation. Her first WTA win was in Tokyo in 1993, and her doubles partners have included Lindsay Davenport, Rennae Stubbs, Mary Joe Fernández, Jana Novotná, Samantha Stosur, Liezel Huber, and Martina Navratilova.

Raymond is one of the rare players to have accomplished the feat of a career Grand Slam in doubles. Her first win toward that distinction was at the 2000 Australian Open with partner Rennae Stubbs. She won at Wimbledon in 2001, also with Stubbs. Her U.S. Open victories came in 2001 (with Stubbs), 2005 (with Samantha Stosur), and 2011 (with Liezel Huber). Raymond completed her career slam with a win at the 2006 French Open (with Stosur).

When it comes to mixed doubles, Raymond has also had great success. She nearly has a career Grand Slam, with victories at the U.S. Open (1996 and 2002), Wimbledon (1999 and 2012), and the French Open (2003), and has made it to the semifinals at the Australian Open in 1996 and 2010. At the 2012 Olympics, she teamed with Mike Bryan to win the bronze medal.

At the same Olympics, Raymond and Liezel Huber just missed a medal, coming in fourth after losing a close match to a team from Japan. The Beijing Olympics were Lisa's second, after competing at the 2004 games and finishing in a tie for ninth in singles and a tie for fifth in doubles (with partner Martina Navratilova).

Other competitions in which she participated on behalf of the U.S. were the Fed Cup (1997, 1998, 2000, 2002, 2003, 2004, 2007, and 2008) and the Hopman Cup (2006).

She teamed with Bruno Soares of Brazil to finish second at the 2013 Wimbledon mixed doubles championships. In 2012, the indefatigable Raymond was at the top again as a doubles player and, at the age of 38, achieved the distinction of being the oldest man or woman to be ranked number one in professional tennis.

SHAUN STAFFORD BECKISH (1968–) ■ *Turned Pro:* **1989**
COLLEGE: 1987–88   5-11½

Shaun Stafford won the state singles championship in 1985 and 1986 while attending Gainesville's Buchholz High School. She attended the University of Florida and, at the NCAA national tournament, made it to the singles final match, winning the championship as a sophomore. Twice she was named All-Southeastern Conference, and, in 1988, she received the Honda Sports Award as the nation's top college women's tennis player.

In 1989, Stafford turned pro and had her only Women's Tennis Association tournament victory, the Taiwan Open. Her highest ranking as a singles player was #48 on January 22, 1990, and her best finish in Grand Slam events was the fourth round at the 1994 French Open.

Stafford also won one WTA event in doubles, the 1993 Internationaux de Strasbourg with partner Andrea Temesvári. She made it to #33 on the doubles ranking on May 16, 1994, and that year's Australian Open saw her best doubles Grand Slam finish, by making it into the quarterfinals. In mixed doubles, she did not win a tournament and her best finishes were in the second round of the French Open (1989, 1990, 1991, 1994, and 1995), Wimbledon (1990), and the U.S. Open (1994). She did win a gold medal in the 1995 Pan Am Games with Jack Waite.

After Stafford retired as a touring player in 1997, she became an assistant coach for Duke University from 1997 to 1998, where she helped lead the women's team to the finals of the NCAA national championship tournament. She became a member of the University of Florida Athletic Hall of Fame in 1999. Stafford, known for showing her emotions and her smile, married Michale Beckish in 1996, and they live in Williamston, South Carolina.

Other Florida Athletes Who Went Into Pro Tennis

NAME	COLLEGE	WENT PRO
Halle Cioffi Carroll	1988	1993
Andrea M. Farley	1990–93	c.1993
Jessica Lehnhoff	1999–2002	c.1993
Alice Luthy Tym	1960s	c.1972
Tammy Whittington	1984–87	c.1987

All 14 schools in the Southeastern Conference have teams participating in women's soccer, and each year two champions are determined—one for the regular season and one for the conference tournament held around Halloween. Florida has had tremendous success since it entered the program in 1995 because of its first—and still its only—head coach, Becky Burleigh.

Coach Becky Burleigh in November 2012

She formed the team in 1995 and led them to a 14-4-2 record and second place in the SEC's Eastern Division. The following year, the team improved to 22-3 and captured both the regular season and conference tournament championships, and they continued both streaks through 2001. In addition, in only its fourth year, the team won the NCAA national championship with a victory at the College Cup over the University of North Carolina.

Burleigh has been honored individually as the SEC Coach of the Year (1996, 2000, 2008, and 2010). In her national championship year of 1998 she was named National Coach of the Year by *College Soccer Weekly*, National Soccer Coaches Association of America/Adidas, and Soccer Buzz. She was only the second female coach to lead her team to the College Cup competition and the first one to win the championship. Before coming to Florida, Burleigh had already won a pair of National Association of Intercollegiate Athletics national championships as the coach of Georgia's Berry College in 1989–93.

Florida Women's Soccer Season Records

YEAR	WINS	LOSSES	TIES	PERCENTAGE
1995	14	4	2	.750
1996	22	3	0	.880
1997	20	3	1	.854
1998	26	1	0	.963
1999	21	2	0	.913
2000	16	8	0	.667
2001	21	4	1	.808
2002	10	10	2	.500
2003	19	4	2	.800
2004	16	4	3	.761
2005	13	6	1	.675
2006	14	6	5	.660
2007	17	5	3	.740
2008	19	4	1	.813
2009	16	6	2	.708
2010	19	2	3	.854
2011	18	8	0	.692
2012	20	5	1	.788
2013	18	5	1	.787
Total	339	90	28	.772

Southeastern Conference Championships
(Through 2013)

YEAR	REGULAR SEASON	TOURNAMENT
1993	Vanderbilt	Vanderbilt
1994	Vanderbilt	Vanderbilt
1995	Kentucky	Kentucky
1996	**Florida**	**Florida**
1997	**Florida**	**Florida**
1998	**Florida**	**Florida**
1999	**Florida**	**Florida**

YEAR	REGULAR SEASON	TOURNAMENT
2000	**Florida**	**Florida**
2001	**Florida**	**Florida**
2002	Auburn	Tennessee
2003	Tennessee	Tennessee
2004	Tennessee	**Florida**
2005	Tennessee	Tennessee
2006	**Florida**	Kentucky
2007	**Florida**	**Florida**
2008	**Florida**	Tennessee
2009	**Florida**	South Carolina
2010	**Florida**	**Florida**
2011	South Carolina	Auburn
2012	**Florida**	**Florida**
2013	**Florida** (co-champ)	Texas A&M

SEC Championships by Team
(Through 2013)

TEAM	REGULAR SEASON	TOURNAMENT
Florida	13	10
Tennessee	4	5
Vanderbilt	2	2
Kentucky	1	2
Auburn	1	1
South Carolina	1	1
Texas A&M	1	1
Alabama	0	0
Arkansas	0	0
Georgia	0	0
LSU	0	0
Mississippi	0	0
Mississippi State	0	0
Missouri	0	0

Athlete Bios

College years are those in which the athlete was awarded a letter for soccer. Pro years are those in which she played for one or more teams in Major League Soccer (MSL), National Women's Soccer League (NWSL), United Soccer Leagues (USL), Women's Premiere Soccer League (WPSL), Women's Professional Soccer (WPS), and Women's United Soccer Association (WUSA).

MELANIE LYNN BOOTH (1984–) ■ *Defender*

COLLEGE: 2003–05 5-8 **USL:** 2003–05; **WPSL:** 2008, 2009; **MSL:** 2010; **NWSL:** 2013; **OLYMPICS:** 2012 bronze medal

Born in Burlington, Ontario, Melanie Booth played on the Canadian national women's Under-19 team when it contested for the Nordic Cup in 2001 and the Algarve Cup in 2002, when the team finished second in the Fédération Internationale de Football Association U-19 World Championship.

Booth played for the Gators in 2003–05, the same time period she played for the Toronto Lady Lynx of the United Soccer Leagues. The following year, she began play for the Orlando Krush and the Canadian national women's team that earned the silver medal in the Peace Queen Cup, plus placed second in the Confederation of North, Central American, and Caribbean Association Gold Cup. In both competitions, Canada lost to the United States by a single goal. In 2007, Booth returned to the University of Florida to finish her bachelor's degree in applied physiology and kinesiology, which she received in 2008.

That same year, Booth was a member of the Tampa Bay Hellenic of the Women's Premier Soccer League. In 2009, she played for the Boston Renegades of the United Soccer Leagues W-League, moving to the Vancouver Whitecaps of Major League Soccer in 2010. The highlight of 2011 was her penalty kick goal after extra-time to beat Brazil in the Pan American Games held in Guadalajara, to help Canada to the gold medal.

For the 2012 Olympics, Booth was named to the Canadian team as an alternate and did not expect to play, but injuries to two other team members necessitated her promotion to an active team member just days before competition began in London. Although she saw no playing time on the field, she received a bronze medal for being a member of the third-place team.

In 2013, she was a member of New Jersey's Sky Blue FC, a team in the National Women's Soccer League. Booth retired from professional soccer on November 13, 2013.

JO DRAGOTTA (1989–) ■ *Defender-Midfielder*

COLLEGE: 2009–12 5-9 **NWSL:** 2013

During her years of high school soccer in Tampa, Jo Dragotta was becoming a star. She was named to three All-Sunshine Conference and All-Hillsborough County teams, and she also participated on the Florida state team of the Olympic Development Program. She attended the ODP national camp and, for five years, played on the Hillsborough County United Club Team that took first place in the 2009 Florida Youth Soccer Association State Cup (Under 19).

Dragotta was a midfielder for the Gators from 2009 through 2012 and majored in anthropology. As a freshman, she appeared in a dozen matches and still found time to study and was named to the 2010 Southeastern Conference Freshman Academic Honor Roll. The next season, she appeared in 21 matches and made her first start.

As a junior, she played in every game, starting 23 of them. In ten of those games, she was on the field the entire time. Dragotta was selected as SEC All-Tournament. In her final year, the National Soccer Coaches Association of America chose her for the All-South Region first team. She also was chosen for the second team for the SEC All-Tournament Team and was listed on the SEC Academic Honor Roll.

In January 2013, the new National Women's Soccer League held its first college draft, and the Boston Breakers selected Dragotta in the third round. She played in one match and, in September 2013, was released by the Breakers. Dragotta was one of the 11 players eligible, a few days later, to be picked by the NWSL Washington Spirit, but only one was chosen, and it wasn't her.

HOLLY KING (1991–) ■ *Midfielder*

COLLEGE: 2009–12   5-9   **NWSL:** 2013

Following a high school career filled with honors and titles, Holly King enrolled at the University of Florida. During her freshman year, she missed only the opening match and wound up starting 17 games that season. In two, she played every minute, even one that went into double overtime. King was named to the 2010 Southeastern Conference Freshman Academic Honor Roll.

She averaged 82.1 minutes per match as a sophomore and started 23 games. Her skills went beyond the playing field as she made the Southeastern Conference Academic Honor Roll and was named to the SEC Community Service Team. King was on the second team of the National Soccer Coaches Association of America All-South Region as a junior, and she was named to the All-SEC Tournament Team. Again, she was on the SEC Academic Honor Roll and was named an NSCAA Scholar All-American (third team).

During her senior year at Florida, she started every match and was on the field the entire time in 16 of them. King was a first-team All-SEC choice and a third-team for the NSCAA All-American team. During the summer, she attended classes at UF and played for D.C. United of the W-League. In May 2013, she graduated with her bachelor's degree, cum laude, in elementary education. She was also presented with the UF Alumni Association's Outstanding Leadership Award.

Four months earlier, King had been selected by the Washington Spirit in the third round of the inaugural season college draft of the National Women's Soccer League. After playing in 14 matches, she was waived by the Spirit and remains without a team.

HEATHER BLAINE MITTS FEELEY (1978–) ■ *Defender-Right Back*

COLLEGE: 1996–99   5-5   **WUSA:** 2000–03; **WPS:** 2009–11;
OLYMPICS: 2004 gold medal; 2008 gold medal; 2012 gold medal

After playing soccer in high school in Cincinnati, Heather Mitts came to the University of Florida. She formed part of the defensive line that, in 1998, was part of Florida's first NCAA national championship soccer team. During her years at Florida, she set the record for number of matches appeared in (95), number started (94), and minutes played (7,547). She received her bachelor's degree in advertising in 2000.

Philadelphia Independence player Heather Mitts in 2010

After college, Mitts played for the Tampa Bay Extreme of the W-League for a season, then was drafted by the Philadelphia Charge of the Women's United Soccer Association. In her first year with the Charge, Playboy Online named her the Sexiest Player in the WUSA. In her second year, she was named one of Philadelphia's sexiest singles and appeared on the cover of *Philadelphia* magazine. Mitts played from 2001 to 2003, making 51 appearances and had eight assists. For the 2003 season, she was named a WUSA All-Star, but, when the season ended, the league folded. Mitts served as a television commentator for the 2003 Fédération Internationale de Football Association Women's World Cup for ABC/ESPN and later did some commentary for Major League Soccer games and college football.

As a member of the national team, Mitts participated in the 2004 Olympics and received a gold medal. That same year, she was voted ESPN.com's Hottest Female Athlete and, in 2005, appeared in the swimsuit issue of *Sports Illustrated*. She went back to the W-League to play for the Central Florida Krush and the United States Women's National Team, and she helped the U.S. earn the silver medal in the 2006 Algarve Cup competition. In 2007, she tore her anterior cruciate ligament, causing her to miss the FIFA Women's World Cup tournament played later that year.

Mitts traveled to Beijing in 2008 on the U.S. national team and won her second Olympic gold medal. That same year also saw the creation of a new league, Women's Professional Soccer, and Mitts was allocated to the Boston Breakers. Play began in 2009, and she appeared in each of the Breakers' 19 games. After the season, she signed with the Philadelphia Independence. Early in 2011, she moved to the Atlanta Beat of the WPS, but the league soon went out of business. She played for the U.S. for the 2011 FIFA Women's World Cup and received a silver medal.

The 2012 Olympics gave her a third chance at a gold medal. She played the entire game against Columbia, and she and the team brought home the gold. For 2013, Mitts joined another Boston Breakers team in the new National Women's Soccer League, but she retired from professional soccer before the NWSL began. She is a member of the University of Florida Athletic Hall of Fame. In 2010, Mitts married NFL quarterback A.J. Feeley.

ERIKA TYMRAK (1991–) ■ *Midfielder-Forward*

COLLEGE: 2009–12   5-5   **NWSL:** 2013–14

Before starting college, Erika Tymrak played soccer for five years at the IMG Soccer Academy and made it to the Under 18 semifinal in 2008 and the Under 19 final in 2009. In both years, she was honored as the IMG Soccer Player of the Year. In her first three years (2005–07), she was named the IMG Most Valuable Player. During 2008, she also played in the Region III Olympic Development Program and on the Florida ODP team. Tymrak was named All-Region III and All-American by National Soccer Coaches Association of America/Adidas, and in 2009 was a *Parade* Magazine All-American.

As a Florida freshman, Tymrak played in all 20 games during the regular season and started 18 of them. Her pair of assists at the end of the season against the University of South Carolina helped the Gators to a 3-0 shutout and clinched the Southeastern Conference championship. Tymrak was a unanimous selection for the conference All-Freshman team. She was named to the NSCAA All-South Region third team and the Soccer American All-Freshman second team.

Tymrak opened the 2010 season as a member of the Coaches Preseason All-Southeastern Conference team. As a junior, she led the team in goals and points, and she was runner-up in assists. Again, she was All-SEC and moved up to the first team of the NSCAA All-South Region selections.

As a senior in 2012, the talented player led the Gators in goals, assists, and points. She made the NSCAA All-America, the NSCAA All-South Region, and All-SEC first teams. The SEC also named her its Offensive Player of the Year and Tournament MVP. Her fearless play earned her the nickname "Baby Samurai" amongst Gator fans.

In the inaugural National Women's Soccer League college draft, Tymrak was selected 11th overall and signed with FC Kansas City. She played in 21 of the team's 22 matches and was honored as the NWSL Rookie of the Year. Tymrak was then loaned to FC Bayern München for the rest of 2013.

MARY ABIGAIL WAMBACH (1980–) ■ *Forward*

COLLEGE: 1998–2001   5-11   **WUSA:** 2002–03; **WPS:** 2009–11;
NWSL: 2014; **OLYMPICS:** 2004 gold medal; 2012 gold medal

Abby Wambach began playing soccer at age 4, and was such a strong player that her first youth soccer league moved her from the girls' to the boys' team after she scored

27 goals in just three games. After high school, some of her many awards included National Soccer Coaches Association of America Player of the Year for the state of New York and the Gatorade Circle of Champions New York Player of the Year. She enrolled at the University of Florida, and, during each of her four years there, UF was the Southeastern Conference champion, winning the national championship in 1998. Wambach was twice the SEC Player of the Year (2000 and 2001), twice the SEC Tournament MVP, and four times a member of the All-SEC team. She left UF before receiving her degree so she could play professionally for the Washington Freedom of the Women's United Soccer Association in 2002, where she was the team's leading scorer and the league's Rookie of the Year.

Abby Wambach at a Washington Freedom game in 2004

In 2003, Wambach was named the MVP of the Founders Cup III, the league championship captured by her team, and she was presented the WUSA Goal of the Year Award for one of her diving headers. The WUSA folded after that year, and the team stayed together to play exhibitions as the Washington Freedom Soccer Club. Starting in 2006, the team was a member of the W-League and moved up to the WPS (Women's Professional Soccer) beginning with the 2009 season.

Because of financial problems, the team was sold and moved to Boca Raton, Florida, and continued play under the name of magicJack. For the 2011 season, Wambach served as a player-coach. In November of that year, the league terminated the franchise. Wambach was again on a professional team in 2013 with the formation of the National Women's Soccer League. She now plays for the Western New York Flash.

At the 2004 Olympics, her extra-time header goal against Brazil won the gold medal for the U.S. She was also named to the 2008 Olympic team, but she could not play because of a broken leg suffered in the final pre-Olympic match. During the 2012 Olympics, she scored against France, New Zealand, North Korea, Columbia, and Canada, and she received her second gold medal. Wambach led the U.S. team with five goals scored.

She is a member of the University of Florida Athletic Hall of Fame, a five-time honoree as the U.S. Soccer Federation's Athlete of the Year, the 2011 Associated Press Female Athlete of the Year, and the 2012 Fédération Internationale de Football Association World Player of the Year. On June 20, 2013, as a member of the U.S. National Team, Wambach broke the international record for goals previously held by former national teammate Mia Hamm.

KATHRYN WILLIAMSON (1989–) ■ *Defender*

COLLEGE: 2009–12   5-6   **NWSL:** 2013–14

Kathryn Williamson of McKinney, Texas, came to the University of Florida for her freshman year in 2008. Due to a torn anterior cruciate ligament, she sat out that year, but, for the rest of her college career, she played in 81 games (80 as a starter) for the Gators at the position of center back. She was the only player to start in all 24 matches in 2009, and, in 2010, Williamson was the Southeastern Conference Defensive Player of the year, leading the Gators with an average of 88.29 minutes played per match.

During 2011, she led the team with an average of 87.04 minutes per match and missed none of the team's 23 games. In her final year, she suffered a torn meniscus after five matches, but she returned to play in the NCAA tournament. In December 2012, Williamson graduated with a bachelor's degree in psychology.

During 2012, she played for the Ottawa Fury, a pro-am team that captured its first W-League championship that year. Williamson was honored as the Most Valuable Player of the Final Four of the championship tournament. In 2013, she was selected eighth overall in the National Women's Soccer League college draft by the Portland Thorns, the sister team of the men's Portland Timbers of Major League Soccer. Her rookie season included starting each of the 22 regular season matches, plus both of the Thorns' playoff matches. In her official Thorns biography, she is described as a "fast and technical defender." Williamson now plays for the Western New York Flash with fellow Gator alumna, Abby Wambach.

Kathryn Williamson (right) and her Portland Thorns teammates in a 2013 game against the Seattle Reign

Martial Arts

The spectrum of martial arts covers not only the basis of action movies (kung fu, karate, and the like), but also other "fighting" disciplines on a professional level, such as boxing and mixed martial arts. Many universities (not UF) participate in one of the oldest martial arts, wrestling, with collegiate champions often going on to the Olympics and other international competitions.

Years ago, there was another martial art popular at the college level—boxing. It was a fully recognized NCAA sport with official team championships awarded, beginning in 1932. Champions from 1924 to 1931 are considered to be unofficial, and competition in earlier years was under the auspices of other governing organizations.

The University of Florida, before the 1933 creation of the Southeastern Conference, had a boxing team that participated as a member of the Southern Intercollegiate Athletic Association and, starting in 1922, the Southern Conference. The first Gator conference championship was actually in boxing, won during the 1929–30 season.

Many considered boxing to be too brutal for college students, and the SEC dropped it as a sport in 1940. Several schools that continued to participate, including Florida, suspended their programs during World War II, and some afterwards resumed NCAA participation (Florida did not). That governing body eliminated the annual championship tournament after a University of Wisconsin boxer died within a week of being knocked out in the 1960 championship.

The number of schools with boxing teams began to decrease, but there were attempts to reinstate the sport on an intercollegiate level. The activities of the Florida Collegiate Boxing Conference and the United States Intercollegiate Boxing Association, as well as other organizations, may some day bring back this martial art as a full-fledged intercollegiate sport—for both men and women—at UF and other universities.

Two UF alumni went on to have brief careers as professional boxers. Three other Gator alumni also went on to have success in martial arts, one as a judoka and two as professional wrestlers.

Athlete Bios

College years are the years in which the athlete was on the team roster for UF, unless otherwise noted. Actual years of attendance as a student often included additional years. **DNC:** Did not compete (in that sport on behalf of the university)

THADDEUS MICHAEL BULLARD (1977–) ■ *Professional Wrestler*

COLLEGE: 1997–2000 (DNC)   6-4, 263 lbs.   **YEARS PRO:** 2010–2014

In 1997 as a redshirt freshman, Thaddeus Bullard began a four-year football career at Florida as a backup defensive end. That year, he made it into 11 regular season games and the Citrus Bowl. As a sophomore, he again played in 11 games in the regular season, plus the Orange Bowl. Because of his community involvement, he received the Goodwill Gator Award, which he was given again the next year.

Gator alum Thaddeus Bullard as Titus O'Neil in the ring in February 2013

As a junior, Bullard started two of the 12 regular season games, and played again in the Citrus Bowl. His senior year saw him start the Ball State University game and play as a backup in nine others. In the Southeastern Conference championship game against Auburn University, he made four tackles and was honored with the university's Most Improved Defensive Lineman Award. He was active off the football field as well, serving as the UF student body vice president in 2000.

Following his college years, Bullard played from 2003 to 2007 in the Arena Football League for the Utah Blaze, Tampa Bay Storm, Las Vegas Gladiators, and Carolina Cobras. For a time, he was an assistant football coach for Jesuit and Chamberlain High Schools in Tampa.

Bullard decided to switch sports in 2009, and, after years of watching Hulk Hogan and other wrestlers on TV, began training to be a professional wrestler with Florida Championship Wrestling, a branch of World Wrestling Entertainment. He made his pro television debut in a match on January 16, 2010, using the alias Titus O'Neil. Bullard chose the name Titus as a Biblical reference and O'Neil because he was a big Shaquille O'Neal fan in his younger days. In December 2011, he and partner Damien Sandow won the Florida Tag Team Championship. He also participated in WWE's television shows *NXT* and *NXT Redemption*.

In April 2012, O'Neil was promoted to the main roster of WWE wrestlers and appeared on its primetime shows *SmackDown* and *Raw*, usually in tag team bouts with partner Darren Young, appearing as the Prime Time Players. In addition to Titus O'Neil, Thaddeus Bullard has also appeared as Rufus "Pancake" Patterson and has the nickname of The Real/Big Deal. His signature moves and holds include the Clash of the Titus, the Three-Point Stance Body Avalanche, and the Ghetto Blaster.

Bullard remains active in charitable activities and enjoys handing out toys and T-shirts at community centers, bringing joy and excitement to underprivileged kids. Another of his activities has been the Tampa Gator Club's "Elves for the Elderly" program, where he visits and hands out gifts at nursing homes. The former Gator says, "I know I've been blessed by a lot of things, so it's my obligation to give back as best as I can."

PHILLIP D. O'CONNELL (1907-87) ■ *Boxer*

COLLEGE: 1930-31   **YEAR PRO:** 1931

Phil O'Connell served as the captain of the Gator boxing team and won 59 straight fights for the school. His 60th opponent broke O'Connell's jaw during the first round, but he made it through the entire ten rounds before losing on points. During 1931, he also served as the team's head coach. After leaving the UF law school, he embarked upon a career as a professional welterweight.

His boxing career lasted for nine bouts at Legion Arena in West Palm Beach, of which he won six and drew one. His sole knockout was of Johnny Meadows. By the end of 1931, he shifted his professional plans to courtrooms instead of boxing rings, but he did serve for a time as a boxing referee.

State's attorney O'Connell (right) in 1961

O'Connell was elected a municipal judge in West Palm Beach and served for two terms, then was a state attorney in Palm Beach County for about 25 years. He is a member of the University of Florida Athletic Hall of Fame and the Palm Beach County Sports Hall of Fame. He died in 1987.

CARLOS PROCTOR ■ *Boxer*

COLLEGE: unknown   **YEAR PRO:** 1931

As an undergraduate in Gainesville, Carlos Proctor was the heavyweight boxer on the university team and also played football in 1929 and 1930. Afterwards, he was the boxing team's head coach until the sport was suspended during World War II. During a period of five weeks in 1931, he had a brief professional boxing career consisting of three bouts.

Carlos Proctor on the beach

The first was a knockout of Cy Cason, a 175-pound heavyweight, at Benjamin Field Arena in Tampa. The next bout, against Jimmy Roundtree, was declared "no contest" by the referee because of stalling. Proctor wound up his pro career with another knockout, this time of Jim Austin, in Orlando on September 15. During 1939–1941, Proctor was the head coach of the Florida golf team. He was inducted into the University of Florida Athletic Hall of Fame.

COLLEEN ROSENSTEEL (1967–) ■ *Judoka*

COLLEGE: 1986–89 (DNC)   5-11, 229 lbs.   **OLYMPICS:** 1992; 1996; 2000

Born in Greensburg, Pennsylvania, Colleen Rosensteel was an accomplished track and field athlete at age 17, winning the silver medal for the discus throw in 1984 at the Pan American Junior Athletics Championships in Nassau. She attended the University of Florida and received her bachelor's and master's degrees in exercise and sports sciences in 1990 and 1994. As a Gator, she was a six-time Southeastern Conference champion—four times in shot put and twice in discus.

While studying in the classroom, Rosensteel also became a judoka (judo practitioner) and earned a place on the U.S. Judo Team. She participated in the 1992 Olympics and won the bronze medal in the heavyweight division (78kg or 172lb) at the 1995 Pan American Games in Mar del Plata. The following year, she was again a U.S. team member at the Olympics in Atlanta, and she won her next major medal—a silver—at the Pan Am Games in Winnipeg in 1999.

Rosensteel made her third Olympic appearance in 2000 in Sydney. There, she made her best Olympic showing, a tie for ninth place. She later became a staff member as a sports performance expert at the Center for Sports Performance at the University of Pittsburgh Medical Center. In 2014, Rosensteel was inducted into the University of Florida Athletic Hall of Fame in 2014 for her accomplishments as a member of the UF track and field team.

BERTON CASWELL WILLIAMS (1903–65) ■ *Professional Wrestler*

COLLEGE: DNC   **YEARS PRO:** 1928-48

The college and early professional football history of Cy Williams has already been covered in this book (see page 89), but there is more to his professional athletic activities. After leaving the Staten Island Stapletons, he went to Atlanta to try out professional wrestling. Williams stayed there until 1931, when he opted to leave for New York to get the appropriate training and make the "big time." A story of his departure in the *Atlanta Constitution* newspaper included a quote from a local wrestling promoter who claimed, "Any young man who is big and strong enough can't find a better profession if he has courage in addition to his other assets."

Williams wrestled in New York, which led to matches in Canada, California, Ohio, and Tennessee, where he was usually considered to be a "bad guy." On December 19, 1938, in the Montreal Forum, he defeated Yvon Robert and was thereafter recognized (at least in Montreal) as the Heavyweight Champion of the World. Nine months later, he was stripped of his title by the Montreal Athletic Commission for his failure to wrestle challenger Ernie Dusek. Williams claimed he was still the champ, at least until Dusek beat him in the ring two months later.

Sometimes billed as The Tennessee Terror or Giant Cy Williams, the 232-pound strongman traveled to Florida and won the NWA Southern and Florida titles, which he held for two months. By the 1950s, he married a woman from Florida named Margaret, and they moved to Hawaii, where she became a producer of recordings of Hawaiian music.

NASCAR

Gainesville, Florida, is not just the home of The Swamp; it is the home of the Gainesville Raceway, which was established in 1969 and has attracted some of the best racers in the world. They can be seen in a series of drag races, most prominently in The Gatornationals, a National Hot Rod Association event held every March since 1970, on one of the fastest tracks in the NHRA circuit. Record-breaking speeds attract large crowds, including cheering spring breakers, and they are treated to some of the best drag racing around.

So why have we included NASCAR in this book? There is no auto racing team at the University of Florida, and as best as we can tell, no records have been kept of who may have attended classes at UF and then gone on to race as a professional . . . with one notable exception.

Edward Glenn Roberts Jr. (1929–64) was born in Tavares, Florida, and grew up in Apopka, Florida, and was involved in both baseball and auto racing. As a pitcher on the Zellwood Mud Hens, his blazing fastball earned him the nickname of Fireball, a name he kept throughout his racing career. In 1945, he joined the Army Air Corps (now known as the U.S. Air Force) but had to leave after basic training because of his asthma. He then started classes in mechanical engineering at the University of Florida in 1947 but spent his weekends racing on dirt tracks.

Fireball Roberts in the driver's seat

When he was just 18, Roberts competed at the Daytona Beach Road Course and crashed on his ninth lap, but that didn't deter him. He continued racing and drove in his first NASCAR race on February 5, 1950, at Daytona Beach. A little more than six months later, the handsome, personable competitor scored the first of his 33 wins in Tampa. Roberts raced in 206

NASCAR Grand National events, finishing in the top 5 nearly half of the time, and became well-known and well-respected in and out of racing circles. In 1962, he won both the Daytona 500 and the Firecracker 250.

With all his acclaim, Roberts managed to keep his sense of humor. He was once pulled over by a police officer for speeding and was asked, "Who do you think you are, Fireball Roberts?" to which Roberts replied, "Yes. Yes I do."

Fireball Roberts raced for the final time on May 24, 1964, in the World 600 at Charlotte Motor Speedway. He was considering retiring from racing but wanted one more crack at Charlotte, the only major Southern track that he hadn't conquered. Unfortunately, he was involved in a horrific crash and suffered burns over 80 percent of his body. He was unable to recover and died on July 2, 1964, but he continued to influence the sport of racing. His death was a major catalyst in the creation of fire-retardant uniforms, which led to the mandatory racing suits worn by drivers today, as well as modifications to racecar engines to reduce the risk of fuel leakage.

The International Motorsports Hall of Fame inducted Roberts in 1990, followed by the Motorsports Hall of Fame of America in 1995. On January 29, 2014, he was inducted into the NASCAR Hall of Fame and was one of the first superstars in auto racing. His tombstone eloquently states, "He brought to stock car racing a freshness, distinction, a championship quality that surpassed the rewards collected by the checkered flag."

OLYMPIC SPORTS

Athletes who attended the University of Florida and continued competing as professionals have been included in this book, so why Olympians? Because many sports have no professional league. Competing in the Olympics is the equivalent of having *Gone Pro,* and those athletes deserve to be included in this book, whether or not they actually won a medal.

We've covered those who became Olympians and later enrolled as students at UF (while not always competing in the same, or any, sport), those who used their years of competition as a Gator to develop and hone skills that served them in international competition, and those who went on as athletes after their college years in Gainesville were over. Some of these athletes will be more recognizable than others—perhaps because they competed in more than one Olympics and/or returned as a network commentator. Some were lucky enough to negotiate lucrative product endorsement deals or even parlay their success into the entertainment world. And some may have made less-than-desirable choices during or after the Olympic Games that gave them additional media attention.

The University of Florida began its Olympic tradition in 1968 with a trio of athletes, but no one knew it at the time. That year, Marty Liquori ran the 1500 meters while a student at Villanova, and only later became a Gator when he enrolled in broadcasting courses. Jack Bacheler was a graduate student at UF and ran for the Florida Track Club, but his college eligibility had already been exhausted at another university before he ran in the Olympic 5000 meters. Catie Ball won a gold medal in the 4x100-meter medley relay but didn't become a Florida student until after the Olympics, and then she didn't join the school's women's swim team because there was no team. Sometimes it takes years for an individual to be able to say he or she is both a Gator and an Olympian, but those who can are listed here.

Gator Olympians cover a dozen sports, but the large majority participated in the swimming and diving pools. They have represented 39 nations' teams, with about half as members of the United States contingents. Three individuals have participated in the Winter Olympics, one in the Paralympics. The vast majority of Gator Olympians have been in one or more of a dozen Summer Olympic Games. If they had been considered as a separate team, the Gator Nation would outnumber the members of many of the competing countries.

The Modern Olympic Games

YEAR	SUMMER	WINTER
1896	Athens, Greece	
1900	Paris, France	
1904	St. Louis, USA	
1906	Athens (no longer recognized)	
1908	London, England	
1912	Stockholm, Sweden	
1916	Canceled (World War I)	
1920	Antwerp, Belgium	
1924	Paris, France	Chamonix, France
1928	Amsterdam, Netherlands	St. Moritz, Switzerland
1932	Los Angeles, USA	Lake Placid, USA
1936	Berlin, Germany	Garmisch-Partenkirchen, Germany
1940/1944	Canceled (World War II)	Canceled (World War II)
1948	London, England	St. Moritz, Switzerland
1952	Helsinki, Finland	Oslo, Norway
1956	Melbourne, Australia	Cortina d'Ampezzo, Italy
1960	Rome, Italy	Squaw Valley, USA
1964	Tokyo, Japan	Innsbruck, Austria
1968	Mexico City, Mexico	Grenoble, France
1972	Munich, West Germany	Sapporo, Japan
1976	Montreal, Canada	Innsbruck, Austria
1980	Moscow, USSR	Lake Placid, USA
1984	Los Angeles, USA	Sarajevo, Yugoslavia
1988	Seoul, South Korea	Calgary, Canada
1992	Barcelona, Spain	Albertville, France
1994		Lillehammer, Norway
1996	Atlanta, USA	
1998		Nagano, Japan
2000	Sydney, Australia	
2002		Salt Lake City, USA
2004	Athens, Greece	
2006		Torino, Italy
2008	Beijing, China	
2010		Vancouver, Canada
2012	London, England	
2014		Sochi, Russia
2016	Rio de Janeiro, Brazil	
2018		Pyeongchang, South Korea
2020	Tokyo, Japan	

Paralympics Games

YEAR	SUMMER	WINTER	YEAR	SUMMER	WINTER
1960	Rome, Italy		2000	Sydney, Australia	
1964	Tokyo, Japan		2002		Salt Lake City, USA
1968	Tel Aviv, Israel		2004	Athens, Greece	
1972	Heidelberg, West Germany		2006		Torino, Italy
1976	Toronto, Canada	Ornsköldsvik, Sweden	2008	Beijing, China	
1980	Arnheim, Netherlands	Geilo, Norway	2010		Vancouver, Canada
1984	Stoke Mandeville, England and New York, USA	Innsbruck, Austria	2012	London, England	
1988	Seoul, South Korea	Innsbruck, Austria	2014		Sochi, Russia
1992	Barcelona, Spain	Tignes-Albertville, France	2016	Rio de Janeiro, Brazil	
1996	Atlanta, USA		2018		Pyeongchang, South Korea
1998		Nagano, Japan	2020	Tokyo, Japan	

Florida Medal Winners
Gold

YEAR	ATHLETE	SPORT	EVENT
1968	Catie Ball	Swimming	4x100-meter medley relay
1972	Frank Shorter	Track and Field	Marathon
1984	Theresa Andrews	Swimming	100-meter backstroke, 4x100-meter medley relay
	Tracy Caulkins	Swimming	200-meter individual medley, 400-meter individual medley, 4x100-meter medley relay
	Geoff Gaberino	Swimming	4x200-meter freestyle relay
	Mike Heath	Swimming	4x100-meter freestyle relay, 4x200-meter freestyle relay, 4x100-meter medley relay
	David Larson	Swimming	4x200-meter freestyle relay
	Dara Torres	Swimming	4x100-meter freestyle relay
	Mary Wayte	Swimming	200-meter freestyle, 4x100-meter freestyle relay
1988	Duncan Armstrong	Swimming	200-meter freestyle
	Matt Cetlinski	Swimming	4x200-meter freestyle relay
	Troy Dalbey	Swimming	4x100-meter freestyle relay, 4x200-meter freestyle relay
1988	Anthony Nesty	Swimming	100-meter butterfly
1992	Nicole Haislett	Swimming	200-meter freestyle, 4x100-meter freestyle relay, 4x100-meter medley relay,

Olympic Sports

YEAR	ATHLETE	SPORT	EVENT
	Lea Loveless	Swimming	4x100-meter medley relay
	Dennis Mitchell	Track and Field	4x100-meter relay
	Ashley Tappin	Swimming	4x100-meter freestyle relay
	Dara Torres	Swimming	4x100-meter freestyle relay
	Janie Wagstaff	Swimming	4x100-meter medley relay
	Martin López-Zubero	Swimming	200-meter backstroke
1996	Whitney Hedgepeth	Swimming	4x100-meter medley relay
	Ashley Whitney	Swimming	4x200-meter freestyle relay
2000	Rob Evans	Track and Field	(Paralympics) 1500 meters, 5000 meters
	DeLisha Milton-Jones	Basketball	
	Ashley Tappin	Swimming	4x100-meter freestyle relay, 4x100-meter medley relay
	Dara Torres	Swimming	4x100-meter freestyle relay, 4x100-meter medley relay
	Brad Wilkerson	Baseball	
	Bernard Williams	Track and Field	4x100-meter relay
2004	Ryan Lochte	Swimming	4x200-meter freestyle relay
	Heather Mitts	Soccer	
	Darian Townsend	Swimming	4x100-meter freestyle relay
	Dana Vollmer	Swimming	4x200-meter freestyle relay
	Abby Wambach	Soccer	
2008	Kerron Clement	Track and Field	4x100-meter relay
	Ryan Lochte	Swimming	200-meter backstroke, 4x200-meter freestyle relay
	DeLisha Milton-Jones	Basketball	
	Heather Mitts	Soccer	
2010	Steve Mesler	Bobsled 4-man	
2012	Conor Dwyer	Swimming	4x200-meter freestyle relay
	Ryan Lochte	Swimming	400-meter individual medley, 4x200-meter freestyle relay
	Heather Mitts	Soccer	
	Christian Taylor	Track and Field	Triple jump
2012	Dana Vollmer	Swimming	100-meter butterfly, 4x100-meter medley relay, 4x200-meter freestyle relay
	Abby Wambach	Soccer	

Silver

YEAR	ATHLETE	SPORT	EVENT
1972	Tim McKee	Swimming	200-meter individual medley, 400-meter individual medley
1976	Tim McKee	Swimming	400-meter individual medley
	Frank Shorter	Track and Field	Marathon
1980	Frédéric Delcourt	Swimming	200-meter backstroke
1984	Sandy Goss	Swimming	4x100-meter medley relay
	Mike Heath	Swimming	200-meter freestyle
	Mark Stockwell	Swimming	100-meter freestyle, 4x100-meter freestyle relay
1988	Duncan Armstrong	Swimming	400-meter freestyle
	Sandy Goss	Swimming	4x100-meter medley relay
	Dara Torres	Swimming	4x100-meter medley relay
	Mary Wayte	Swimming	4x100-meter medley relay
1992	Greg Burgess	Swimming	200-meter individual medley
	Stephen Clarke	Swimming	4x100-meter medley relay
1996	Whitney Hedgepeth	Swimming	100-meter backstroke, 200-meter backstroke
	Dennis Mitchell	Track and Field	4x100-meter relay
	Allison Wagner	Swimming	400-meter individual medley
2004	Ryan Lochte	Swimming	200-meter individual medley
	Bernard Williams	Track and Field	200 meters
2008	Aaron Armstrong	Track and Field	4x100-meter relay
	Kerron Clement	Track and Field	400-meter hurdles
	Dara Torres	Swimming	50-meter freestyle, 4x100-meter freestyle relay, 4x100-meter relay
2012	Elizabeth Beisel	Swimming	400-meter relay
	Will Claye	Track and Field	Triple jump
	Jeff Demps	Track and Field	4x100-meter relay
	Ryan Lochte	Swimming	200-meter individual medley, 4x100-meter freestyle relay
	Tony McQuay	Track and Field	4x400-meter relay

Bronze

YEAR	ATHLETE	SPORT	EVENT
1980	David López-Zubero	Swimming	100-meter butterfly
1984	Mark Stockwell	Swimming	4x100-meter medley relay
	Rafael Vidal	Swimming	200-meter butterfly
	Andrew Weaver	Cycling	100-kilometer team time trial

1988	Jane Kerr	Swimming	4x100-meter medley relay
	Dara Torres	Swimming	4x100-meter freestyle relay
	Laura Walker	Swimming	4x100-meter freestyle relay
	Mary Wayte	Swimming	4x100-meter freestyle relay
	Paige Zemina	Swimming	4x100-meter freestyle relay
1992	Tammy Jackson	Basketball	
	Lea Loveless	Swimming	100-meter backstroke
	Dennis Mitchell	Track and Field	100 meters
	Anthony Nesty	Swimming	100-meter butterfly
1996	Michelle Freeman	Track and Field	4x100-meter relay
2000	Carlos Jayme	Swimming	4x100-meter freestyle relay
	Dara Torres	Swimming	50-meter freestyle, 100-meter freestyle, 100-meter butterfly
2004	Novlene Williams-Mills	Track and Field	4x400-meter relay
2008	Caroline Burckle	Swimming	4x200-meter freestyle relay
	Matt LaPorta	Baseball	
	Ryan Lochte	Swimming	200-meter individual medley, 400-meter individual medley
	Novlene Williams-Mills	Track and Field	4x400-meter relay
2012	Elizabeth Beisel	Swimming	200-meter backstroke
	Melanie Booth	Soccer	
	Will Claye	Track and Field	Long jump
	Ryan Lochte	Swimming	200-meter backstroke
	Lisa Raymond	Tennis	Mixed doubles
	Novlene Williams-Mills	Track and Field	4x400-meter relay

Florida Olympians, By Nations They Represented

United States	67	Brazil	3	Haiti	2
Canada	17	Hungary	3	Iceland	2
Great Britain	10	South Africa	3	Poland	2
Jamaica	7	Suriname	3	Belgium	1
Spain	6	Venezuela	3	Bermuda	1
Australia	5	Bahamas	2	Bosnia and Herzegovina	1
Puerto Rico	4	Cayman Islands	2	Estonia	1
Trinidad and Tobago	4	Columbia	2	Finland	1
Barbados	3	Germany	2	France	1

Florida Olympians, By Nations (cont'd.)

Georgia	1	Mexico	1	Portugal	1
Guam	1	Netherlands Antilles	1	Saint Kitts and Nevis	1
Ireland	1	Peru	1	South Korea	1
Libya	1	Philippines	1	Tunisia	1

Florida Olympians, By Sport

Swimming and Diving	105	Bobsled	3
Track and Field	41	Baseball	2
Gymnastics	4	Cycling	2
Soccer	4	Beach Volleyball	1
Tennis	4	Handball	1
Basketball	3	Judo	1

Florida Olympians, By Olympiad

1968 summer	3	1998 winter	2
1972 summer	4	2000 summer	24
1976 summer	12	2000 paralympics	1
1980 summer	13	2002 winter	1
1984 summer	26	2004 summer	31
1988 summer	20	2006 winter	1
1992 winter	2	2008 summer	39
1992 summer	28	2010 winter	1
1994 winter	2	2012 summer	38
1996 summer	33		

SWIMMING AND DIVING

Swimming is one of the five sports contested at each of the Summer Olympics, beginning in Athens in 1896. Diving has been an Olympic sport since 1904.

Intercollegiate swimming for men at the University of Florida began with a victory over Georgia Tech in 1930. The Gators' first year in the Southeastern Conference began with a championship in 1937, the first of five in a row. Other conference championships were won by UF in 1953-54, 1956-68, 1970-71, 1979-81, 1983-86, 1990-93, and 2013-14. National championships were won in 1983 and 1984 under head coach Randy Reese.

The women's team began competition in 1972, with an undefeated record under coach (and Olympic gold medal-winner) Catie Ball. They began in the SEC in 1981, also with a championship that first year. Their conference titles were won in 1981-84, 1986-96, 2002, and 2009. They won a national championship in 1982 under head coach Randy Reese and another in 2010, led by head coach Gregg Troy.

Men's Southeastern Conference Championships
(Through March 2014)

35	**Florida**	3	Georgia	0	Kentucky	0	Texas A&M
18	Auburn	2	Alabama	0	Missouri	0	South Carolina
10	Tennessee	2	Alabama	0	South Carolina	0	Texas A&M
4	Georgia Tech	1	LSU				

Women's Southeastern Conference Championships
(Through March 2014)

17	**Florida**	1	Alabama	0	LSU	0	Texas A&M
11	Georgia	0	Arkansas	0	South Carolina	0	Vanderbilt
5	Auburn	0	Kentucky	0	Tennessee		

Men's Swimming & Diving Head Coaching Dual Meet Records

YEARS	COACH	WON	LOST	TIED	PERCENTAGE
1930–51	Frank Genovar	81	23	0	.779
1952–59	Jack Ryan	51	22	3	.691
1960–62	Buddy Crone	28	7	0	.800
1963–76	Bill Harlan	105	29	0	.784
1976	Jimmy Dann	0	3	0	.000
1976–90	Randy Reese	100	21	0	.826
1990–92	Skip Foster	18	4	0	.818
1992–96	Chris Martin	26	10	0	.722
1996–99	Ron Ballatore	19	12	0	.619
1999–2014	Gregg Troy	127	35	1	.782
Total		565	166	4	.771

Women's Swimming & Diving Head Coaching Dual Meet Records

YEARS	COACH	WON	LOST	TIED	PERCENTAGE
1972–73	Catie Ball	4	0	0	1.000
1973–76	Sue Halfacre	11	5	0	.688
1976–90	Randy Reese	118	7	0	.944
1990–93	Mitch Ivey	27	2	0	.931
1993–96	Chris Martin	26	1	0	.963
1996–98	Kevin Thornton	11	9	0	.550
1998–2014	Gregg Troy	148	36	0	.804
Total		345	60	0	.851

TRACK AND FIELD

Track and field, often referred to internationally as athletics, was one of the original modern Olympic sports contested in 1896, and it has been a part of every Summer Games since then. It was also the original ancient sport when the Olympics consisted of a single sprint race for the length of a stadium.

The University of Florida formed its first track and field team in 1923 with J.L. Atkinson as its first head coach. At the time, it was a school for men, so there was only a men's team, but 50 years later, a women's team was created (again thanks to Title IX, a federal law intended to provide equal opportunities to women in intercollegiate athletics). Competition within the Southeastern Conference began in 1933.

Over the decades, the Gators have been competitive, although not dominating, until very recently. In 2012, the men won both NCAA championships (indoor and outdoor), and the women were the SEC indoor champs. Many Gator track stars have gone on to win medals in sports as far ranging as triple jump and bobsled, and several have used their speed and strength in other professional sports, especially football.

An important development in track and field in Gainesville happened in 1965 when head coach Jimmy Carnes saw a need for an active training program for undergraduates who were moving from other schools to Florida. Due

Former Florida track coach Jimmy Carnes (left) with Athletic Director Jeremy Foley in 2009

to NCAA rules, transfer students were required to sit out a year of eligibility. Carnes founded the Florida Track Club and staffed it with coaches and trainers who could work with the athletes so they didn't lose their skills during their year "off." As a team, they won their first national championship in 1970.

Other athletes were attracted to Gainesville to participate with the Florida Track Club, including Frank Shorter and Marty Liquori, who had used up their eligibility at other universities. They became students at the university and ran with a world-class track club and, although not actual members of the UF track team, focused international attention on the school, helping to draw others to Gainesville to compete and obtain an education.

Men's Track and Field Head Coaching Records
(Through March 2014)

YEARS	HEAD COACH	CHAMPIONSHIPS
1923	J.L. Atkinson	
1924	J.L. White, Jr.	
1925	Tom Sebring	
1926–27	A.C. Brown	
1928–33	Nash Higgins	
1934–36	Dutch Stanley	
1937–42, 1945–64	Percy Beard	SEC Outdoor (1953, 1956)
1965–76	Jimmy Carnes	SEC Indoor (1975, 1976)
1977–79	Roy Benson	
1980–85	John Randolph	
1986–88	Joe Walker	SEC Indoor (1987, 1988), Outdoor (1987)
1989–95	John Webb	
1996–2002	Doug Brown	
2003–14	Mike Holloway	NCAA Indoor (2010, 2011, 2012), Outdoor (2012, 2013 (tie)); SEC Indoor (2004, 2011), Outdoor (2010)

Women's Track and Field Head Coaching Records
(Through March 2014)

YEARS	HEAD COACH	CHAMPIONSHIPS
1973	Janice Thompson	
1974–75	Kate Pousos	

YEARS	HEAD COACH	CHAMPIONSHIPS
1976–77	Lacey O'Neal	
1978–79	Deanne Johnson	
1980–81	Carol Thompson	
1982–87	Lyle Knudson	
1988–92	Beverly Kearney	NCAA Indoor (1992); SEC Indoor (1990, 1992), Outdoor (1992)
1993–2007	Tom Jones	SEC Indoor (1997, 2002, 2004), Outdoor (1997, 1998, 2003)
2007	Steve Lemke	
2008–14	Mike Holloway	SEC Indoor (2010, 2012, 2014), Outdoor (2009)

GYMNASTICS

Gymnastics is one of the five Olympic sports that have been around since 1896. The University of Florida competes in women's gymnastics and won the Southeastern Conference championship in 1982–85, 1989, 2007, 2010, and 2012–13. In April 2013, the Gators won their first NCAA women's national gymnastics championship, moving up from the previous year's second-place finish. In 2014, they captured their second consecutive national championship, sharing it with co-champion University of Oklahoma.

Southeastern Conference Championships
(Through March 2014)

16	Georgia	8	Alabama	0	Arkansas	0	Kentucky
9	**Florida**	1	LSU	0	Auburn	0	Missouri

Gymnastics Head Coaching Records

YEARS	HEAD COACH	WON	LOST	TIED	PERCENTAGE
1973–75 & 1977–79	Sandy Phillips	39	18	0	.684
1976	Kay Hury	11	1	0	.917
1980–92	Ernestine Weaver	184	48	0	.793
1993–2002	Judi Markell	124	81	1	.604
2003–14	Rhonda Faehn	196	42	2	.904
Total		554	190	3	.744

SOCCER

Known to most of the world as football, the sport of soccer became a men's Olympic sport in 1900. Women's competition was added in 1996. The Gator women have been participating in the SEC since 1993 and have dominated, winning 13 regular season championships and 10 conference tournaments.

Florida has had three of its soccer players on Olympic teams, and each won at least one medal. They are:

NAME	COLLEGE	OLYMPICS	COUNTRY	MEDAL
Melanie Lynn Booth	2003–07	2012	Canada	Bronze (see page 344)
Heather Blaine Mitts Feeley	1996–99	2004	USA	Gold (see page 346)
		2008	USA	Gold
		2012	USA	Gold
Mary Abigail Wambach	1998–2001	2004	USA	Gold (see page 347)
		2012	USA	

All of Florida's soccer Olympians have also gone on to professional careers in the sport. Their biographies appear in the Soccer chapter of this book.

TENNIS

Tennis is both an old and a new Olympic sport. It was part of the Games from their modern start in 1896 but was eliminated after 1924. It was reintroduced in 1988. Tennis has been an intercollegiate sport at UF since 1932 for men and 1971 for women. The women have been very successful on the national scene, capturing NCAA championships in 1992, 1996, 1998, 2003, 2011, and 2012.

All four of Florida's tennis Olympians have gone on to play professional tennis. Their biographies can be found in the Tennis section of this book.

BASKETBALL

Basketball became an Olympic sport in 1936. The Gator men began intercollegiate play during the 1915–16 school year, took off the next three years because of World War I, and resumed their games in 1919. The university has been participating within the SEC since 1933. They were the national champs in 2006 and 2007. The Lady Gators began intercollegiate play in 1974–75, and three UF women have played on Olympic teams, two for the United States and one for Great Britain. Two (Tammy Jackson and DeLisha Milton-Jones) won at least one medal. They have each played professional basketball, so their biographies can be found in the Basketball chapter of this book.

BASEBALL

Baseball was briefly a sport played at the Summer Olympics, from 1992 through 2008. The University of Florida has participated in intercollegiate baseball since 1913 and as a part of the Southeastern Conference since 1933. Two of its players, Matt LaPorta and Brad Wilkerson, have represented the United States in the Olympics. Because they both made it to Major League Baseball, their biographies can be found in the Baseball chapter of this book.

HANDBALL

The team sport of handball was included at the 1936 Olympics but disappeared for more than three decades. It returned as an event for men in 1972 and women in 1976. The University of Florida does not field a handball team, but the school has one alumnus who participated on the U.S. Olympic handball team after becoming interested in the sport while in the military.

CYCLING

The road racing discipline of cycling has been an Olympic sport since the first modern Olympics in 1896. There is no intercollegiate cycling competition at the University of Florida, but two Gators have participated in the Olympics, one bringing home a bronze medal.

VOLLEYBALL

Played on a hard court, volleyball has been an Olympic sport since 1964. Beach volleyball, played by a team of two on an outdoor sand court, has been an event since 1996. The Gator women participate within the SEC, and their 19 regular-season championships (since the conference began recognizing such champions in 1983) is more than the other 12 participating universities' combined total. Although UF has not had an indoor volleyball Olympian, one member of its team went on to participate in beach volleyball for Germany in 2000.

BOBSLEDDING

Bobsledding, involving two or four individuals sliding down a frozen track on a sled, has been part of the Games since the first Winter Olympics in 1924. The University of Florida has no such facility and does not have a team, but three of its alumni (already collegiate stars in track and field) have participated in the sport, with one winning a gold medal.

Athlete Bios

College years are the years in which the athlete was on the team roster for UF, unless otherwise noted. Actual years of attendance as a student often included additional years. **DNC:** Did not compete (in that sport on behalf of the university)

SWIMMING AND DIVING

THERESA ANDREWS (1962–) ■ *United States*
COLLEGE: 1982–83   5-6, 137 lbs.   **OLYMPICS:** 1984 2 gold medals

A winner of six Big Ten swimming titles during her freshman year at Indiana University-Bloomington, Theresa Andrews transferred to the University of Florida. She was successful against Southeastern Conference competition, and in her two years at UF won the SEC titles in both the 50-yard and 100-yard backstroke, as well as sharing in six team relay titles. Andrews was the NCAA champion in the 4x100-yard medley relay (twice) and the 4x50-yard medley relay.

When the Gators won the national championship in 1982, Andrews was one-fourth of the 4x100-yard medley team that set a new American record. The following year, when the Gators finished in second place nationally, Andrews again swam on the winning 400-yard medley relay team. In her only Olympics in 1984, she won the gold medal in the 100-meter backstroke, and she won another as part of the winning 4x100-meter medley relay team.

Andrews received her bachelor's degree from UF in therapeutic recreation in 1986 and went on to earn a master's degree from The Ohio State University in clinical social work. After spending most of the 1990s as a clinical social worker in cancer treatment and clinical hematology, she went into consumer banking in Wilmington, Delaware, where she is a Senior Vice President in Customer Experience for Small Business and supervises 15 banking centers in Pennsylvania and Delaware.

Andrews also gives motivational speeches for organizations, including schools, and volunteers for the U.S. Olympic Committee. In 2008, the NCAA presented her with its Silver Anniversary Award, recognizing her as a former student-athlete who excelled in her later career.

DUNCAN JOHN D'ARCY ARMSTRONG (1968–) ■ *Australia*

COLLEGE: 1988–89   6-2, 163 lbs.
OLYMPICS: 1988 1 gold and 1 silver medal; 1992

Duncan Armstrong, previously a medalist at the 1986 Commonwealth Games as a freestyle swimmer, began competing for the University of Florida in 1988. His best distances in college were at 400 and 800 yards. In his first Olympics, he finished second in his qualifying heat in the 200-meter freestyle, then came back in the finals with an unexpected gold medal and world record time of 1:47:25, beating several record holders, including Matt Biondi. In the 400-meter freestyle, he finished third in his heat but second in the finals to win a silver medal. He also swam on the fourth-place 4x200-meter freestyle relay.

The year 1988 was also when Armstrong was honored as the Young Australian of the Year and began swimming for the University of Florida. He participated in intercollegiate competition for UF in 1988 and 1989, and he then intended to swim in the 1990 Commonwealth Games. However, a case of glandular fever kept him out of the competition and weakened him so that at the 1992 Olympics, he was no longer a favorite and in his only race, the 4x200-freestyle relay, his team finished in 8th place in the finals. He began training for a comeback for the 2000 Olympics but abandoned that after two months.

After the end of his competitive swimming days, Armstrong worked as a televised swimming commentator. Among his awards are the Medal of the Order of Australia and the Centenary Medal, both for his service to swimming. In addition, he is a spokesman for vitamins and fitness equipment. Armstrong has been a member of the International Swimming Hall of Fame since 1996 and is living in Australia with his wife and the two youngest of his four children.

CATHERINE NORTHCUTT BALL CONDON (1951–) ■ *United States*

COLLEGE: 1972–73 (DNC)   5-7, 128 lbs.   **OLYMPICS:** 1968 gold medal

Catie Ball became the first Gator Olympic medal winner by swimming the breaststroke leg of the 4x100-meter medley relay in Mexico City. In the summer of 1968, she held the world record in each of the four women's breaststroke distances and was favored to also win individual medals, but her endurance was greatly reduced as a result of the flu. She finished fifth in the 100-meter breaststroke and scratched from the 200-meter distance.

After the Olympics, Ball accepted a scholarship to attend UF and received her degree in education in 1973, but because women's swimming was not an intercollegiate sport, she did not compete for the university. When it became a sport in 1972, Ball (then a senior) was hired as its first head coach. During her only year at that position, the Lady Gators won every dual meet and came in second nationally.

Ball operates an interior decorating business in Pensacola called "Beside the Point," and she is a member of the International Swimming Hall of Fame and the Florida Sports Hall of Fame. She is married and has three children and one grandchild.

ELIZABETH LYON BEISEL (1992–) ■ *United States*

COLLEGE: 2010–14   5-7, 146 lbs.
OLYMPICS: 2008; 2012 1 silver and 1 bronze medal

Elizabeth Beisel, also known by the nicknames of Bekel and Diesel, began her international swimming career on the big stage with her participation in the 200-yard backstroke in the 2007 World Championships as a 14-year-old. In the 2008 Olympics, she finished fourth in the 400-meter individual medley and fifth in the 200-meter backstroke and was the youngest member of the U.S. swim team. The following year, Beisel won two gold medals in the national championships and successfully defended her title in the 200-meter backstroke in 2010. She graduated from high school in Rhode Island in 2010 and enrolled at the University of Florida.

Elizabeth Beisel at the 2011 Santa Clara Invitational

Through 2012, she won five Southeastern Conference individual championships. Beisel was named the SEC Female Swimmer of the Year for 2012. Her NCAA title in the 200-meter backstroke helped the Gators to third place in the NCAA national championship meet.

Beisel made her second trip to the Olympics in 2012. She competed in two events and posted personal best times in each. They were good enough for silver (400-meter individual medley) and bronze (200-meter backstroke) medals.

At the 2013 NCAA National Championship meet, she won the 400-yard individual medley. As a senior at UF, she was awarded the Commissioner's Trophy at the SEC championship meet, as the woman who scored the greatest number of points for her team. Beisel won her fourth consecutive gold medals in each of the 400-yard individual medley and the 200-yard backstroke, and she came in second in the

200-yard individual medley. At the 2014 NCAA National Championship, she helped the Gators to a sixth place finish by coming in second in the 400-yard individual medley, fifth in the 200-yard backstroke, fifteenth in the 200-yard butterfly, and was a member of the eighth place 800-yard freestyle relay squad.

CAROLINE BURCKLE (1986–) ■ *United States*

COLLEGE: 2004–05, 2007–08   5-9, 137 lbs.
OLYMPICS: 2008 bronze medal

Olympic medalist Caroline Burckle signs autographs in 2012

After graduating from Sacred Heart Academy in Louisville, Caroline Burckle swam for Florida, peaking in 2008. During that year, she won NCAA individual championships in the 200- and 500-yard freestyle events and was named the Southeastern Conference Female Swimmer of the Year. In SEC competition, Burckle won the individual 2005 title in the 200-yard freestyle, the 2005 and 2008 500-yard freestyle, the 2007 100-yard breaststroke, and the 2008 200-yard breaststroke, plus three relay championships. She received her bachelor's degree in sociology in 2009.

During 2005, Burckle represented the U.S. at the World Championships in Montreal, swimming in a preliminary heat of the 4x200-meter freestyle, and winning a gold medal. She won the individual gold in the 800-meter freestyle at the 2007 Pan American Games in Rio de Janeiro.

At the 2008 Olympics, Burckle swam in the 4x200-meter freestyle relay. In the prelims, she led off the first leg (and the team finished first in its heat), and in the final she handled the third leg. She and her teammates won the bronze medal.

In 2009, Burckle earned a degree in merchandise product development at the Fashion Institute of Design & Manufacturing and retired from competitive swimming. She worked in San Diego for Montiel USA, a women's clothing company, then came back home to Louisville in 2011 to open a health and wellness coaching business known as Stilwellness. Burckle is also seeking a degree from the Wellcoaches School of Coaching and is a member of the International Coaching Federation and the Ohio Valley Professional Coaching Alliance.

GREGORY STEWART BURGESS (1972–) ■ *United States*

COLLEGE: 1991–94   6-4, 205 lbs.   **OLYMPICS:** 1992 silver medal; 1996

While Greg Burgess swam for the University of Florida, he set four American records, two each in the 200- and 400-yard individual medleys and was the NCAA champion in both events in 1993 and 1994. Burgess received his bachelor's degree from UF in economics in 1994.

The first of his two trips to the Olympics was his most successful. He competed in one event, the 200-meter individual medley, and came in second in both his qualifying round and the finals, earning him a silver medal. Four years later, Burgess swam the same event and came in third in his qualifying round, but he finished sixth in the finals and out of the medals.

Other international competitions in which he won medals include the 1991 Summer Universiade in Sheffield (gold, 200-meter individual medley), 1993 Pan Pacific Championships in Kobe (gold, 4x200-meter freestyle), 1994 World Championships in Rome (silver, 200-meter individual medley), and the 1995 Pan American Games in Mar del Plata

Greg Burgess demonstrating the backstroke at the Marine Corps Base Camp in Pendleton, California, in 2012

(gold, 4x200-meter freestyle). In 1997, Burgess became a U.S. Marine. He was promoted to major and is most proud of never having lost a fellow Marine while serving three tours of duty, two of which were in Iraq. Burgess is a member of the U.S. Marine Corps Sports Hall of Fame.

TRACY ANN CAULKINS STOCKWELL (1963–) ■ *United States*
COLLEGE: 1981–84   5-9, 132 lbs.   **OLYMPICS:** 1984 3 gold medals

At age 14, Tracy Caulkins won her first of 63 national swimming titles and was named American Woman Swimmer of 1977 by *Swimming World*. The following year, she tied or set 27 American or world records and, just after reaching the age of 16, became the youngest person to receive the Sullivan Award, as the top U.S. amateur athlete in any sport. Caulkins seemed destined to star in the 1980 Olympics in Moscow, but her plans were delayed by the U.S. boycott of the games.

While she waited for the next Olympiad, she swam for the University of Florida, won a dozen SEC individual titles, 16 NCAA championships, and 21 All-American honors. In 1983 and 1984, she

Tracy Caulkins at a 1981 meet in Utrecht

received the Honda Broderick Cup as the country's outstanding female athlete. She is the only person to have set U.S. records in all four strokes.

Caulkins served as the captain of the U.S. swim team at the 1984 Olympics and showed her all-around excellence by winning three medley races, including the 400-meter medley relay. Individually, she won the 400-meter medley and, in winning the 200-meter medley, she set an Olympic record. After the Olympics, she retired from swimming and returned to UF, graduating with a degree in broadcast journalism in 1985.

Considered to be one of the best swimmers of all time, Caulkins is a member of several halls of fame, including those for Tennessee Sports, Women's Sports, International Swimming, and U.S. Olympics, and the University of Florida Athletic Hall of Fame. She married Australian Olympic (and UF) swimmer Mark Stockwell in 1991 and lives with him and their four children in Australia, where she has served as the chair of the Queensland Academy of Sport and helped to found Womensport Queensland, which aims to inspire and support women and girls in sport and physical activity. In 2008, Caulkins was awarded the Medal of the Order of Australia for her work in providing sporting opportunities for women.

MATTHEW J. CETLINSKI (1964–) ■ *United States*

COLLEGE: 1983–86   6-0, 161 lbs.   **OLYMPICS:** 1988 gold medal

Matt Cetlinski of West Palm Beach began swimming for the University of Florida in 1983. In his final season of 1986, he was an NCAA champion at the 500-yard freestyle, one of five individual national titles he held while at Florida. The following year, he received his bachelor's degree in religion from UF.

In 1986, he broke the school record in the 1,650-yard freestyle with a time of 14:47.26. That stood as the longest unbroken men's UF record for 28 years, until it was bested in 2014 by both Arthur Frayler and Mitch D'Arrigo.

In 1988, Cetlinski represented the United States at the Olympics in Seoul and participated in three events. In the 1,500-meter freestyle, he finished first in his qualifying round and fourth in the finals. He qualified for the finals of the 400-meter freestyle by finishing third in his heat, but he missed out on a medal by .35 second in the final race. In the 4x200-meter freestyle relay, he and teammates Doug Gjertsen, Troy Dalbey, and Matt Biondi finished first with a world record time of 7:12.51.

Cetlinski is currently an acupuncturist in Gainesville, Florida. He became a member of the University of Florida Athletic Hall of Fame in 1997.

STEPHEN CLARKE (1973–) ■ *Canada*

COLLEGE: 1993–97   6-5, 200 lbs.   **OLYMPICS:** 1992 bronze medal; 1996

Stephen Clarke was born in England and competed for Canada and, in 1991, was a member of the Canadian Youth Team for the Pan Am Games held in Havana, Cuba. He performed well and helped them win a silver medal in the men's 4x100-meter freestyle relay, and he earned the nickname of the "Brampton Bullet" from the Canadian Press. He attended school at the University of Florida, where he tied a four-year-old Gator record in the 50-yard freestyle and became the Gators' all-time All-American at that point (23 times). Clarke received a bachelor's degree in exercise and sport sciences from UF in 1997. Before coming to Florida, he swam at the Olympics in Barcelona in 1992 as the youngest member of the men's team. He swam in the individual events of the 50- and 100-meter freestyles (finishing 40th and tied for 18th, respectively), and he was a part of the bronze medal-winning team in the 4x100-meter medley relay.

In his second Olympics in 1996, he finished seventh in the 100-meter butterfly and also competed in the 100-meter freestyle (finishing 15th) and the 4x100-meter medley relay (12th). The following year, Clarke was a member of the Canadian squad that won the bronze medal in the 4x100-meter medley relay at the Pan Pacific Championships in Fukuoka.

TROY LANE DALBEY (1968–) ■ *United States*

COLLEGE: 1986–87   6-3, 170 lbs.   **OLYMPICS:** 1988 2 gold medals

Troy Dalbey swam for the Gators from 1986 to 1987 and was named to several All-American teams for numerous events: the 50-, 100-, and 200-yard freestyle, the 4x100-yard medley relay, and the 4x100- and 4x200-yard freestyle relays. At the 1987 Pan Pacific Championships in Brisbane, Dalbey won gold in both the 4x100- and 4x200-meter freestyle relays.

At the Olympics in 1988 in Seoul, Dalbey entered one individual event, the 200-meter freestyle, and finished third in his qualifying round but seventh in the finals. His two relay events turned out much better, both with gold medals in world record times, in the 4x100- and 4x200-meter freestyle relays. Later, he and a teammate were celebrating and saw a stone statue shaped like a mask in the lobby of the Hyatt Hotel. As a prank, the boys removed the statue (during an interview, Dalbey estimated it weighed about 50 pounds) and carried it into a nearby restaurant/bar to get something to eat. They were arrested, but, after a written apology, they were released without any formal criminal charges being brought. Dalbey claimed they never intended to keep it and were going to put it back, but he was suspended from competitive swimming for 18 months.

After returning to the states, Dalbey transferred to Arizona State University and swam for them through 1991. He also won a gold medal in the 4x200-meter freestyle relay in the Pan Pacific Championships in Edmonton and a silver in the 4x200-meter freestyle relay in the Pan Pacific Championships in Perth. Dalbey's later activities have included coaching swimming in Arizona and serving as a managing director of a global solar company named Upsolar America.

FRÉDÉRIC DELCOURT (1964–) ■ *France*

COLLEGE: 1984   5-11, 170 lbs.   **OLYMPICS:** 1980; 1984 silver medal

Frédéric Delcourt of France represented his home country in international competition at least as early as 1979, when he won a gold medal at the Mediterranean Games in Split, Croatia, in the 100-meter backstroke.

The following year, he swam in the Olympics in Moscow in three events, coming in fourth in the 100-meter medley relay. In 1981, he won the bronze medal in the 200-meter backstroke in the European Championships, also held in Split.

Delcourt was more successful at the 1984 Olympics, finishing second in both his qualifying round and the finals of the 200-meter backstroke, winning a silver medal. He also competed, but did not medal, in the 100-meter backstroke and the 4x100-meter medley relay. Delcourt was part of the swim team in 1984 while attending UF.

CONOR DWYER (1989–) ■ *United States*

COLLEGE: 2009–11   6-5, 196 lbs.   **OLYMPICS:** 2012 gold medal

Conor Dwyer swimming the 400 IM at the 2013 Santa Clara Grand Prix

Conor Dwyer of Illinois began college at the University of Iowa, where he was a member of the swim team in 2007–09. He transferred to UF for the 2009 season, and he remained through the spring of 2011. That year, he received a bachelor's degree in business administration.

Dwyer swam for the Gators at the 2010 NCAA national championships and came home with individual titles in the 200-yard and 500-yard freestyle events; he was named Swimmer of the Year in both the Southeastern Conference and the NCAA both in 2010 and 2011. At the long course world championships in Shanghai in 2011, he won gold in the 4x200-meter freestyle relay, and he received a gold medal in that same event at the Pan American Games that year in Guadalajara (along with silvers in the 200- and 400-meter individual medleys and the 4x100-meter freestyle relay).

At the 2012 Olympics, Dwyer finished fifth in the 400-meter freestyle and then swam the second leg of the 4x200-meter freestyle relay. With a time of 6:59.70, the team took first place and the gold medal. During the following year's world championships, Dwyer earned the gold medal in the 800-meter freestyle relay and silver in both the 200-meter freestyle and the 400-meter freestyle relay.

GEOFFREY STEVEN GABERINO (1962–) ■ *United States*

COLLEGE: 1980–84   6-3, 179 lbs.   **OLYMPICS:** 1984 gold medal

After a championship high school career in Chattanooga, Tennessee, Geoff Gaberino enrolled at the University of Florida and became a member of its swim team, focusing on freestyle relays. He won five Southeastern Conference titles and four NCAA titles as a member of UF's teams in the 4x100- and 4x200-yard freestyle relays. Gaberino served as team captain in 1983 and 1984, years in which the university was the overall national champion. He completed his bachelor's degree in business administration in 1984 and his master's in 1988.

During the 1984 Olympics, Gaberino swam one of the legs in the first heat of the 4x200-meter freestyle relay, and the U.S. team broke the world record time. In the finals held just hours later, the squad (which did not include Gaberino) broke the record again, and all who participated in any of the heats or the finals were awarded gold medals. As a consequence of his participation in a program known as "Olympic day in the Middle School," he was given the honor of being one of the eight Olympic flag bearers at the games held in Atlanta in 1996.

Gaberino is a member of the University of Florida Athletic Hall of Fame, the Tennessee Swimming Hall of Fame, the Baylor School Sports Hall of Fame, and the Greater Chattanooga Area Sports Hall of Fame. He and his wife, Susan, operate Gulf Shores Vacation Rentals, managing and renting properties in Gulf Shores, Alabama.

DONALD ALEXANDER GOSS (1966–) ■ *Canada*

COLLEGE: 1987–90   6-4, 196 lbs.
OLYMPICS: 1984 silver medal; 1988 silver medal

At the age of 17, Donald Alexander "Sandy" Goss caught the attention of the swimming world by setting a new short-course world record at the Canadian Nationals in the 200-meter backstroke event. He attended the University of Florida from 1987 through 1991 and, in his first year of competition, was a member of the NCAA championship relay team in the 4x200-yard freestyle relay. That same year, he also won Southeastern Conference titles in the 100- and 200-yard backstroke events. He successfully defended his 200-yard backstroke title in 1988.

Goss was a member of the Canadian 4x100-meter medley relay squads that won the silver medal at the 1984 and 1988 Olympics. He also participated, but did not medal in, the 4x100-meter freestyle relay (1984 and 1988), the 4x200-meter freestyle relay (1984 and 1988), the 100-meter backstroke (1984), and the 100-meter freestyle (1988).

In 1991, he completed his bachelor's degree in marketing at UF. Fifteen years later, he was inducted into the Swimming Canada Circle of Excellence Hall of Fame. Goss is an investment advisor at Mackie Research Investment Corporation in Toronto and a member of the Ontario Aquatic Hall of Fame.

NICOLE LEE HAISLETT-BACHER (1972–) ■ *United States*

COLLEGE: 1990–94   5-8, 141 lbs.   **OLYMPICS:** 1992 3 gold medals

At the age of six in St. Petersburg, Florida, Nicole Haislett began training with a swim team, and, by the time she graduated from Lakewood High School in that city, she had won four state high school titles. She continued her success as a Gator, and four

Nicole Haislett and some of her medals in 2010

years in a row she was the NCAA champion in the 200-yard freestyle. She also was the 200-yard individual medley champion in 1993 and the 500-yard freestyle champion in 1994. Haislett was part of the Gator national championship teams for the 4x100-yard freestyle relay (1993) and the 4x100-yard medley relay (1994).

She dominated her competition in the Southeastern Conference. For four seasons, she won every race in which she swam against SEC competition. That earned her four consecutive titles as the SEC Female Swimmer of the Year and as SEC Female Athlete of the Year. In 1996, Haislett received her bachelor's degree in telecommunications from UF.

In 1992, she participated in the Olympics and brought home three gold medals. Her individual one was in the 200-meter freestyle (and she set a U.S. record). Her relay medals were for swimming in a preliminary round of the 4x100-meter medley relay and in the world-record-setting final of the 4x100-meter freestyle relay. She just missed a fourth medal by coming in fourth in the 100-meter freestyle.

Haislett is a member of the University of Florida Athletic Hall of Fame and the Florida Sports Hall of Fame. She married executive chef Ricky Bacher in 2003, and they have a daughter. Haislett trained at the Florida Culinary Institute to become a chef, and she also serves as a physical therapist and activities counselor at a senior citizens' community in St. Petersburg.

MICHAEL STEWARD HEATH (1964−) ■ *United States*

COLLEGE: 1983–86   6-0, 170 lbs.
OLYMPICS: 1984 3 gold and 1 silver medal

Mike Heath's first year as a Gator swimmer was his first of two (along with 1986) as a member of an NCAA championship team. He held four national titles while he swam for the university and earned a bachelor's degree in exercise and sports science in 1988.

Heath came home from the 1984 Olympics with four medals, and he nearly got a fifth when he came in fourth in the 100-meter freestyle. In the 4x100-meter medley relay, he and his teammates came in second in heat three, but, in the finals (which he sat out), they finished first, and all squad members received a gold medal. Heath also received gold medals for swimming in the finals of the 4x100-meter and 4x200-meter freestyle relays, both of which set world records. In the 4x200-meter event, he swam the first leg in the final race, replacing fellow Gator Geoff Gaberino, who was in the preliminary round.

Heath became a member of the University of Florida Athletic Hall of Fame in 1966. After his career as a competitor, he coached at Jacksonville's Beaches Aquatic

Club and Orange Park's Spartan Aquatic Club. Heath is an officer with the Florida Fish and Wildlife Conservation Commission in Clay County, Florida, and is married with two children.

WHITNEY LYNN HEDGEPETH (1971-) ■ *United States*

COLLEGE: 1989–90   5-10, 141 lbs.
OLYMPICS: 1988; 1996 1 gold and 2 silver medals

Whitney Hedgepeth still holds some swimming records for the state of Virginia, where she swam with the Virginia Association for Competitive Swimming. Before college, she won a gold medal in the 4x200-meter freestyle and a silver medal in the 200-meter freestyle at the 1987 Pan American Games in Indianapolis, and she finished eighth in the 200-meter individual medley at the 1988 Olympics.

As a Gator, Hedgepeth won an individual NCAA national championship in the 200-yard freestyle and another title as a member of the national championship 4x100-yard relay squad. She only remained in Gainesville for one year before she transferred to the University of Texas, where she won three more national championships.

At the 1988 Olympics, Hedgepeth won silver medals in the 100- and 200-meter backstrokes and swam in a preliminary round of the gold medal 4x100-meter medley relay. She is a member of the University of Texas Longhorns Hall of Honor and is the Masters Swimming Coach at the University of Texas in Austin. In 2013, Hedgepeth was chosen as the Speedo/USMS Masters Coach of the Year for her work at Texas.

CARLOS ALBERTO BORGES JAYME (1980-) ■ *Brazil*

COLLEGE: 2000–04   6-3, 198 lbs.   **OLYMPICS:** 2000 bronze medal; 2004

After graduating from high school in Brazil, Carlos Jayme came to Jacksonville in 1999 to train for the upcoming 2000 Olympics. He was highly scouted after several weeks by colleges across the county, but Jayme chose the University of Florida and had success in freestyle individual and relay events. As a sophomore, he set a school record in the 100-yard freestyle at the Southeastern Conference championship. He also was part of the UF relay squads that won the SEC titles in the 200- and 400-yard freestyle relays.

In his junior year, Jayme won the SEC championship in the 100-yard freestyle. His times in that event, by the end of the year, included all ten of the top 10 UF times in history. When he graduated in 2004, in Florida's all-time ranking, he was first in the 50-yard freestyle, first in the 100-yard freestyle, and first as a member of the relay teams for the 200- and 400-yard freestyle and the 4x200-yard medley.

Prior to attending UF, Jayme participated at the Olympics in 2000, and he and his teammates from Brazil won the bronze medal in the 4x100-meter freestyle relay. He returned in 2004 to swim in the 4x100- and 4x200-meter freestyle relays, but he finished in 12th and 9th place, respectively. During his time swimming for Brazil and for the Gators, Jayme carried the nickname of "Cowboy," based on his hometown of Goias, considered to be out in the country. Jayme graduated from UF in 2005 with a bachelor's degree in Food and Resource Economics.

JANE LOUISE KERR THOMPSON (1968–) ■ *Canada*
COLLEGE: 1989–92   5-9, 140 lbs.   **OLYMPICS:** 1984; 1988 bronze medal

Jane Kerr made her first Olympic appearance at the young age of 16 in 1984. Individually, she finished in 14th place in each of the 100- and 200-meter freestyle events, and she was a member of the 4x100-meter freestyle relay that finished in fifth place. Two years later, at the 1986 Commonwealth Games, Kerr won gold medals in the 100-meter freestyle and the 4x100-meter freestyle relay. She also brought home the silver in the 200-meter freestyle and the 4x100-meter medley relay, as well as the bronze in the 200-meter individual medley and the 4x200-meter freestyle relay.

On her second trip to the Olympics in 1988, Kerr earned a bronze medal as a member of the 4x100-meter medley relay squad, while their 4x100-meter freestyle relay squad came in sixth. She also competed individually in the 200-meter freestyle (placed 28th), the 100-meter freestyle (20th), and the 100-meter butterfly (20th).

After the Olympics, Kerr began her collegiate swimming career at the University of Florida and won Southeastern Conference titles in the 200-yard freestyle (1989), 200-yard individual medley (1991 and 1992), 400-yard individual medley (1992), and seven relay events. Kerr received her UF bachelor's degree in business administration in 1992. She is married with two children and a partner in the consulting company Accenture in Toronto.

DAVID ERWIN LARSON (1959–) ■ *United States*
COLLEGE: 1977–81   6-3, 174 lbs.   **OLYMPICS:** 1984 gold medal

After graduating from Jacksonville's Bolles School, David Larson swam freestyle at the University of Florida. He was part of the UF squad that won NCAA national championships in the 4x200-yard freestyle relay in 1979 and 1981 and received his bachelor's degree in sociology in 1987. Larson is a member of the University of Florida Athletic Hall of Fame.

At the 1979 Pan American Games in San Juan, Larson won a silver in the 200-meter freestyle and a gold in the 4x200-meter freestyle relay (and repeated as part of the gold medal relay squad in 1983 in Caracas). He qualified for the 1980 Olympics but could not compete because of the U.S. boycott of the games, and he set his sights on training for the next four years.

During the 1984 Olympics, Larson swam a leg on the U.S. team in the 4x200-meter freestyle relay, which set a new world record time in the event. That time didn't remain the best for long, as the U.S. lowered it by more than three seconds in the final, taking the gold medal. Being a gold medalist opened doors for him, and he went into sports marketing for a decade, followed by working with NBC on the Olympics until he decided to spend more time with his family in 2005. Larson and his wife have a son.

RYAN STEVEN LOCHTE (1984–)   ■ *United States*

COLLEGE: 2002–05   6-2, 196 lbs.
OLYMPICS: 2004 gold and silver medal; 2008 2 gold and 2 bronze medals; 2012 2 gold, 2 silver, and 1 bronze medal

Ryan Lochte during the 2008 Olympic trials

As a child, Ryan Lochte and his family moved to Florida so his father could coach swimming. He was swimming by the time he was five and, a bit mischievous during swimming classes, was often sent to the showers by his father, who claimed, "He spent more time in the showers than he did in the pool." A loss in the Junior Olympics at age 14 changed Lochte, who was tired of losing and began to get serious about his swimming. That determination paid off when he came to UF. While competing for the Gators, he twice was named the NCAA Swimmer of the Year, received 24 All-American honors, and captured seven SEC championships. Lochte received his degree in sports management in 2007.

In 2004, at the Athens Olympics, he was part of the American 4x200-meter freestyle relay team that upset the Australians in the final to win the gold medal. In the 200-meter individual medley, he earned the silver by finishing behind Michael Phelps.

Four years later, Lochte won four medals, opening with a bronze in the 200-meter freestyle and closing with a bronze in the 400-meter individual medley. Sandwiched between those were two gold medal (and world record) performances, swimming the second leg of the 4x200-meter freestyle relay and winning his first individual gold in the 200-meter backstroke.

As a member of his third Olympic team in 2012, Lochte won an individual medal of each color—gold in the 400-meter individual medley, silver in the 200-meter individual medley, and bronze in the 200-meter backstroke. He was part of the gold medal 4x200-meter freestyle relay and received a silver for swimming a leg in the 4x100-meter freestyle relay.

Lochte's total of 11 Olympic medals has him tied for second on the all-time list of male swimmers, behind Michael Phelps. He is expected to compete in the 2016 Olympics in Rio de Janeiro. In the meantime, he is keeping his face before the public doing endorsements for several products, making cameo appearances on television, and for a time had his own reality show entitled *What Would Ryan Lochte Do?* The show had an eight-episode run before being canceled in September 2013. Lochte has also partnered with Yogurtology in Gainesville to promote two new flavors to raise money for two of his charities. He has also applied to the U.S. Patent & Technology Office to trademark his catchphrase "Jeah."

At the 2013 World Championships held in Barcelona, Lochte won three gold medals. He became the first swimmer to win two world championship medals (200-meter breaststroke and 4x200-meter freestyle relay) in one day on three separate occasions. That relay medal was the fifth one he earned in that same relay—no other swimmer has accomplished that feat. Only Michael Phelps has won five world championship golds in the same event, the 200-meter butterfly. The three gold medals brought Lochte's lifetime world championship total to 15.

Lochte serves as the spokesperson for a pair of charities, Parent Project Muscular Dystrophy and the Maq Crutchfield Foundation. They seek to raise funds for MD research and the prevention of drowning.

LEA E. LOVELESS MAURER (1971–) ■ *United States*

COLLEGE: 1989–90   5-6, 134 lbs.
OLYMPICS: 1992 gold and bronze medal

Lea Loveless of New York began her college career at the University of Florida in 1989, the same year she won gold medals in the Pan Pacific Championships in Tokyo in the 100-meter backstroke and the 4x100-meter medley relay. After one year, she transferred to Stanford University, where she became an NCAA champion in the 100-yard backstroke (three times) and the 200-yard backstroke (once).

At the 1992 Olympics, Loveless won a bronze medal in the 100-meter backstroke and barely finished off the medal stand in the 200-meter backstroke. She swam the backstroke leg of the 4x100-meter medley relay final on a squad that not only won the gold medal but also set a world record time in the event.

In 1993, she won gold medals in Kobe at the Pan Pacific Championships in the 100-meter backstroke and the 4x100-meter medley relay. The following year, Loveless won a silver in the same relay event at the World Championships in Rome. The Pan Pacific Championships in Fukuoka in 1997 saw her winning a gold in the same relay and silvers in the 100- and 200-meter backstroke events. Her last major international medals were both gold, won in Perth at the 1998 World Championships in both the 100-meter backstroke and the 4x100-meter medley relay.

Loveless coached swimming at Northwestern University and Lake Forest High School and, from 2005 to 2012, was the head coach of the women's team at Stanford University. She is an inductee of the Stanford Athletic Hall of Fame.

ALEXANDER TIMOTHY MCKEE (1953–) ■ *United States*

COLLEGE: 1972–74   5-8, 154 lbs.
OLYMPICS: 1972 2 silver medals; 1976 silver medal

Tim McKee of Pennsylvania participated in the 1972 Olympics in three events. He won the silver medal in the 200-meter individual medley and finished fifth in the 200-meter backstroke. In the 400-meter individual medley, he and Gunnar Larsson both finished with an Olympic record time of 4:31.98, according to the scoreboard. However, the official timing at those games was to the thousandth of a second, and Larsson won the gold medal with a time of 4:31.981, while McKee was awarded the silver with a time of 4:31.983, the closest margin between gold and silver in Olympic swimming history. As a result of this race, the rules were changed to deem a finish where times were identical to hundreths of a second to be a dead heat.

Olympian Tim McKee at a Swim Across America event

McKee swam for the Gators in 1972 through 1974 and won six NCAA titles. In 1987, he was inducted into the University of Florida Athletic Hall of Fame and is also a member of the International Swimming Hall of Fame.

In his second Olympics in 1976, McKee participated in just one event, the 400-meter individual medley. He won his preliminary heat but came in second in the finals.

McKee truly enjoyed his competitive years, was known to be a bit of a partier, and usually appeared much more relaxed and animated prior to entering the starting block. But it worked for him and added to his popularity. In later years, McKee has been a part of Swim Across America, raising money for cancer research.

ANTHONY CONRAD NESTY (1967–) ■ *Suriname*

COLLEGE: 1989–92   5-11, 172 lbs.
OLYMPICS: 1984; 1988 gold medal; 1992 bronze medal

Anthony Nesty was born in Trinidad and Tobago, but emigrated with his family to Suriname before he was a year old. There, he began swimming at the age of five and immediately showed promise. As he grew into a young man, he worked hard, trained and competed, and represented Suriname at the 1984 Olympics, coming in 21st in the 100-meter butterfly. He attended the Bolles School in Jacksonville, a high school that has produced many champions. At his second Olympics in 1988, Nesty won Suriname's first Olympic medal by placing first in the 100-meter butterfly. Suriname honored him by placing his likeness on coins and paper money and naming a stadium in the capital city after him. Nesty remained humble in the wake of all the accolades.

The following year, he enrolled as a student at UF and was a four-year member of the swim team. He was a three-time NCAA champion in the 100-yard butterfly, one at the 200-yard distance, and swam a leg on the 1991 national championship 400-yard medley relay team. Nesty was an 11-time SEC champion and a 16-time All-American.

After his third Olympics in 1992, in which he earned a bronze medal in the 100-meter butterfly, Nesty returned to UF and received his degree in 1994. He became a coach for his national team, as an assistant in 2004 and head coach in 2008. At the 2012 Olympics in Beijing, he not only served as the head coach but was also the Suriname flag bearer. He also was an assistant coach for the U.S. National Team at the 2011 World University Games, the Cayman Islands National Team in 2009-10, and has coached at the University of Florida since 1998.

Swimmer Brett Ringgold poses with coach Anthony Nesty in 2010 at the U.S. Olympic Training Center in Colorado Springs

Nesty is a member of the International Swimming Hall of Fame and the University of Florida Athletic Hall of Fame, and he was chosen in 2013 as a co-recipient of the Assistant Coach of the Year award by College.swimming.com.

MARCUS WILLIAM STOCKWELL (1963–) ■ *Australia*

COLLEGE: 1985   6-5, 190 lbs.
OLYMPICS: 1984 2 silver medals and 1 bronze medal

At the 1984 Olympics, Mark Stockwell won the silver medal as a member of the Australian squad in the 4x100-meter freestyle relay and another silver in the 100-meter freestyle. He also finished third in the 4x100-meter medley relay and out of the top three in the 100-meter butterfly. The following year, he also won the bronze medal in the 50-meter freestyle at the Pan Pacific Games in Tokyo.

Stockwell attended the University of Florida in 1985 and dated fellow Gator swimmer Tracy Caulkins, who he had met at the Olympics. They subsequently married and live with their five children in Australia, where he has coached at St. Laurence's College in Brisbane, and for which he serves as a trustee. Stockwell was instrumental in the successful bidding for the 2018 Commonwealth Games to be held in Gold Coast City, Queensland, Australia.

ASHLEY TARA TAPPIN-DOUSSAN (1974–) ■ *United States*

COLLEGE: 1993–94   5-10, 146 lbs.
OLYMPICS: 1992 gold medal; 2000 2 gold medals

In 1988, Ashley Tappin became the youngest swimmer (up to that time) to compete in the U.S. Olympic Trials at the age of 13. She continued to swim freestyle, winning three gold medals at the 1991 Pan American Games in Havana, in the 100-meter freestyle, the 4x100-meter freestyle relay, and the 4x100-meter medley relay. The following summer, she participated in her first Olympics in Barcelona as a member of the U.S. 4x100-meter freestyle relay squad. Tappin swam in the qualifying heat of the race, which the Americans won. She did not swim in the final, but the team won anyway, and she received a gold medal.

Tappin began swimming for the University of Florida in 1993 and, the following year, was part of the quartet that won the NCAA championship in the 4x100-yard medley relay. She spent the rest of her college career at the University of Arizona and won national titles in the 50-yard freestyle, the 200-yard freestyle, and the 4x50-yard freestyle relay.

In her second Olympics in 2000, Tappin participated in the preliminary heats of two relay events, the 4x100-meter freestyle and the 4x100-meter medley. The team came in first in the finals in both, giving Tappin her second and third gold medals in three attempts. In 2002, she was inducted into the University of Arizona Sports Hall of Fame.

She took some time during her competitive years to become a successful model, and, when she was finished competing, she coached swimming at the University of New Orleans (2004–07) and participated in events for Swim Across America, raising money to fight cancer. Tappin and her husband, Russell Doussan, have twins, a boy and girl, and began a foundation, Hartley's Hearts, named for their daughter, to help fund life-saving cardiac surgeries for children around the world.

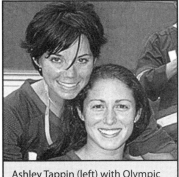

Ashley Tappin (left) with Olympic teammate Gabrielle Rose

DARA GRACE TORRES (1967–) ■ *United States*

COLLEGE: 1985–89   6-0, 150 lbs.
OLYMPICS: 1984 gold medal; 1988 1 silver and 1 bronze medal; 1992 gold medal; 2000 2 gold and 3 bronze medals; 2008 3 silver medals

Dara Torres earned the first of her 12 Olympic medals in 1984 by swimming a leg of the 4x100-meter freestyle relay at the age of 17. The only American swimmer to have participated in five Olympics, she was also the oldest at age 41 in 2008 when she won three silver medals. She missed qualifying for the U.S. team in 2012, in what would have been her sixth Olympics, by less than a tenth of a second in the trials for the 50-meter freestyle.

As a Gator, Torres was a nine-time SEC champion, mostly in freestyle distances. Her three individual NCAA national championships were in the 50- and 100-yard freestyle and 100-yard butterfly, plus she was a member of six UF national championship relay teams. A 28-time All-American (the maximum which can be awarded during a four-year career), Torres was the 1988 SEC Athlete of the Year and the

Dara Torres waves after winning the silver medal in the 2008 Olympic 50-meter freestyle

conference Female Swimmer of the Year in 1987 and 1989. Her bachelor's degree in communications was awarded in 1990.

In her second Olympics in 1988, Torres got a bronze for the 400-meter freestyle relay, plus a silver for swimming the freestyle leg of the 4x100-meter medley relay. She also swam, but did not medal in, the 100-meter freeestyle. In 1992, she was the second swimmer in the 4x100-meter freestyle relay, and she earned another gold.

After an eight-year layoff, Torres went to Sydney as the oldest member of the U.S. swim team and came home with more medals than any of her teammates. Individually, she received bronze for the 50- and 100-meter freestyle and the 100-meter butterfly. She won her two gold medals for that year by swimming relay legs on the winning 4x100-meter freestyle and 4x100-meter medley teams.

Another long layoff and the birth of her child preceded Torres' final Olympics appearance in 2008. In the finals of the 50-meter freestyle, in which she broke her own American record for that distance, she won the silver medal. She also received silver medals for two relays, the 4x100-meter freestyle and the 4x100-meter medley.

Torres has worked as a sports commentator for several television networks and has done some modeling work. She is the author of two books, *Age is Just a Number*, published in 2009, and *Gold Medal Fitness*, published in 2010, and has participated with Swim Across America, a charity raising funds for cancer research, as well as other charitable organizations. Torres is a member of the University of Florida Athletic Hall of Fame and the International Jewish Sports Hall of Fame, which she qualified for by converting to Judaism prior to her second marriage.

DARIAN ROY TOWNSEND (1984–) ■ *South Africa*

COLLEGE: 2004–05   6-5, 192 lbs.
OLYMPICS: 2004 gold medal; 2008; 2012

Born in Pinetown, KwaZulu-Natal, in South Africa, Darian Townsend participated in his first Olympics in 2004 as a freestyle swimmer. Although he finished well behind the medalists in the 200-meter individual medley, he earned a gold medal in a relay event. He and the rest of the South African 4x100-meter freestyle relay squad won their preliminary heat and, in the final race, not only won the gold medal but also set a world record.

Townsend then attended the University of Florida in 2004-05 and won Southeastern Conference titles in the 200-yard freestyle, the 4x100-yard freestyle relay, the

4x100-yard medley relay and the 4x200-yard freestyle relay. In the 4x200-yard distance, he was also part of the 2005 squad that won the NCAA national title.

In 2007, Townsend won the bronze medal at the 2007 All-Africa Games in Algiers in the 200-meter individual medley. He transferred to the University of Arizona and there won additional NCAA titles in the 200-yard freestyle (2007), 4x200-yard freestyle relay (2007 and 2008), 200-yard individual medley (2008), 4x100-yard freestyle relay (2008), and 4x200-yard medley relay (2008).

Darian Townsend after winning the bronze medal in the 4x100-meter individual medley at the FINA 2012 World Swimming World Cup meet in Berlin

His international medals also include bronzes in the 2010 Commonwealth Games in Delhi in the 4x100- and 4x200-meter freestyle relays and three golds and a silver at the 2011 All-Africa Games in Maputo in the 4x100- and 4x200-meter freestyle relays, the 4x100-meter medley relay, and the 200-meter freestyle.

Townsend coaches and continues training at Tucson Ford Aquatics with a sponsor, a rarity in the world of swimming, and hopes to compete in the 2016 Olympics. He made his debut in a masters swimming competition in November 2013.

RAFAEL ANTONIO VIDAL CASTRO (1964–2005) ■ *Venezuela*

COLLEGE: 1981–85   5-11, 160 lbs.
OLYMPICS: 1980; 1984 bronze medal

Rafael Vidal made his first Olympic appearance in 1980, swimming the 100- and 200-meter butterfly events for Venezuela and finishing fourth in his qualifying heat in each one. The following year, he came to the University of Florida and swam for the Gators while earning a bachelor's degree in computer and information sciences.

While he was still a student, Vidal represented his country in the 1983 Pan American Games in Caracas, where he was born. In both the 100- and 200-meter butterfly, he won the bronze medal. In 1984, he swam in the Olympics in the 100-meter butterfly (placed 4th), the 4x100- and 4x200-meter freestyle relays (12th and 10th), the 4x100-meter medley relay (13th), and the 200-meter butterfly. In the latter, Vidal's third-place finish made him the first Venezuelan man to win a medal in that event, and it made him a national celebrity in his home country at age 20.

He became a sports commentator in Venezuela and was well-known on television. In 2005, Vidal was killed when his car was hit by another driver racing on the street. The next year, a "Million Meter Swim" was held on the anniversary of his death, with swimmers from Venezuela and elsewhere swimming more than 14 million meters in countries around the globe, and the event has become an annual event to honor Vidal.

DANA WHITNEY VOLLMER (1987–) ■ *United States*

COLLEGE: 2005–06   6-1, 150 lbs.
OLYMPICS: 2004 gold medal; 2012 3 gold medals

Dana Vollmer won gold medals at two Olympics and in between was a student first at the University of Florida and then at the University of California-Berkeley. Despite only competing one year in Gainesville, she was honored as All-Southeastern Conference in the 50- and 100-yard freestyle; 100-yard butterfly; 200-, 400-, and 800-yard freestyle relays; and 200-yard medley relay. She was named an All-American for each of those four relay events.

Vollmer tried out for her first Olympics at age 12, making her the youngest swimmer at the 2000 U.S. Olympic Trials. She didn't make the team, but she did become the youngest competitor at the 2001 Goodwill Games. Two years later, she had heart surgery and, thereafter, upon her doctors' recommendation, her mother kept a defibrillator at poolside whenever she competed, but she thankfully never had to use it.

Gold medalist Dana Vollmer after the 2012 100-meter butterfly

At the 2004 Olympics, Vollmer won a gold medal as a member of the 4x200-meter freestyle relay team, which set a new world record in the event. She did not make the 2008 Olympic team, but she went to Beijing in 2012 and competed in three events. She set a new Olympic record in a qualifying heat of the 100-meter butterfly, then came back to win the gold medal in the final. Vollmer swam the second leg of the gold medal-winning 4x200-meter freestyle relay and, by swimming the butterfly leg of the 4x100-meter medley relay, not only won her fourth gold medal but also set a relay team world record.

Her own heart problems have resulted in her working hard for "Go Red for Women," a program of the American Heart Association. Vollmer continues to participate as a professional swimmer and train at Berkeley, California. She won a bronze medal in the 100-meter butterfly at the 2013 World Championships in Barcelona.

ALLISON MARIE WAGNER (1977–) ■ *United States*

COLLEGE: 1995–98   5-6, 117 lbs.   **OLYMPICS:** 1996 silver medal

Although Allison Wagner was born in Gainesville, she started competitive swimming at age 7 in Germany while her father served in the military. After he retired from the army, they returned to Gainesville, and she competed for Eastside High School. At the 1993 FINA (Fédération Internationale de Natation) Short Course World Championships in Palma, she won a silver medal in the 400-meter individual medley and gold in the 200-meter individual medley. Her time in the latter event stood as a world record for more than 14 years.

That same year, Wagner won the gold in the 200-meter individual medley at the Pan Pacific Championship in Kobe, and she followed that at the Long Course World Championships in Rome in 1994 with silvers in both individual medley events. *Swimming World* magazine named Wagner as its 1994 American Swimmer of the Year.

She stayed in Gainesville for college and began swimming for the University of Florida in 1995. In both that year and the next, she was named the Southeastern Conference Female Swimmer of the Year, and she wound up with seven conference titles and an NCAA national title in the 400-yard individual medley.

Wagner's Olympic experience consisted of two events in Atlanta in 1996. In the 200-meter individual medley, she finished second in her heat but sixth in the final. In the 400-meter individual medley, she qualified third in her heat and improved that to a silver medal finish in the final. Wagner is involved with Swim Across America and teaches Pilates.

ELIZABETH JANE WAGSTAFF (1974–) ■ *United States*
COLLEGE: 1992–94   5-11, 146 lbs.   **OLYMPICS:** 1992 gold medal

*Originally from Missou*ri, Elizabeth "Janie" Wagstaff caught international notice when she participated in the Long Course World Championships in Perth in 1991. She won the bronze medal in both the 100-meter and 200-meter backstroke events, and she was a member of the gold medal-winning squad in the 4x100-meter medley relay.

Wagstaff went to Barcelona for the Olympics in 1992 and participated in those same three events, where she did not medal as an individual but had success in the relay. Swimming in a preliminary heat, her team finished first to qualify for the finals. Although she watched from the sidelines, Wagstaff won a gold medal when the four U.S. swimmers finished ahead of all other teams in the final race.

After the Olympics, she enrolled at the University of Florida and joined the swim team. She was one of the four Gators who took home the NCAA title for the 1994 4x100-yard medley relay. In Southeastern Conference championship competition, Wagstaff won titles in five individual events and five relay events. She left the university in the fall of 1994 to train for a second trip to the Olympics, but she ultimately did not go to Atlanta in 1996 as a participant.

After her competitive swimming days, Wagstaff went back to school at Colorado State University and earned a degree in veterinary medicine and now practices at Mountainwood Pet Hospital in Windsor, Colorado.

LAURA ANNE WALKER (1970–) ■ *United States*
COLLEGE: 1988–92   5-6, 128 lbs.   **OLYMPICS:** 1988 bronze medal

In the summer of 1988, Laura Walker made her sole Olympic team, representing the United States in the 4x100-meter freestyle relay. She swam in the preliminary round, and the team wound up second, qualifying for the finals. There, Walker swam with teammates Mitzi Kremer and fellow Gators Mary Wayte and Dara Torres. They captured the bronze medal.

That fall, Laura started classes at the University of Florida and swam for the school for four years. She was part of four Southeastern Conference championship relay squads and the 1989 NCAA championship 4x200-yard freestyle relay squad. She completed her bachelor's degree in health science education in 1994.

MARY ALICE WAYTE BRADBURNE (1965–) ■ *United States*

COLLEGE: 1983–87   5-9, 128 lbs.
OLYMPICS: 1984 2 gold medals; 1988 2 bronze medals

At the age of 16 and a member of the Chinook Aquatic Club in Seattle, Washington, Mary Wayte won three gold medals at the 1981 National Sport Festival: 200-meter freestyle, 200-meter backstroke, and 4x200-meter freestyle relay. In 1983, she won a gold medal at the Pan American Games in Caracas in the 4x100-meter freestyle relay and a silver in the 200-meter freestyle.

She began swimming for the University of Florida in 1983 and became one of the school's most decorated athletes. Wayte was the NCAA champion twice in the 100-yard freestyle and once in the 400-yard individual medley. She was also a member of the championship squads that won the 4x100-yard and 4x200-yard freestyle relays in 1984, 1985, and 1986. She was named the Southeastern Conference Swimmer of the Year for 1985 and won 11 individual and 10 relay titles in SEC championship competition. In 1989, she received her bachelor's degree in telecommunications.

Wayte's first trip to the Olympics was in 1984, when she swam in the preliminary heat of the 4x100-meter freestyle relay and the prelims and final of the 200-meter freestyle, and she proceeded to win every race to take home two gold medals. In her second Olympics in 1988, she won silver medals in the 4x100-meter medley relay and the 4x100-meter freestyle relay, and she finished out of the medals in the 200-meter freestyle and the 200-meter individual medley.

In later years, Wayte promoted and endorsed the National Spa and Pool Institute, Speedo, Alamo Rent a Car, and the International Swimming Hall of Fame (of which she has been a member since 2000). She did color commentary and interviews for the Sports Channel network for swimming and basketball, for NBC at the 1992 Olympics, and for ESPN at the NCAA championships.

Wayte became a member of the University of Florida Athletic Hall of Fame in 1998 and the Pacific Northwest Swimming Hall of Fame in 2004. The Mercer Island, Washington, community pool where she trained as a child was named the "Mary Wayte Pool" in her honor. Wayte is married, has two daughters, is the senior manager of business communications at US Enterprise at Cisco, in Seattle, Washington, and has participated with Swim Across America.

ASHLEY ANN WHITNEY (1979–) ■ *United States*

COLLEGE: 1999–2000   5-7, 123 lbs.
OLYMPICS: 1996 gold medal

Ashley Whitney of Nashville swam on her high school team at the Bolles School in Jacksonville. In 1996, she represented the United States as a member of the swimming and diving team and competed in the 4x200-meter freestyle relay. She swam in the first round of the event and, in qualifying to go on, they also set an Olympic record in the event. Although she did not swim in the final race, the team won, so she brought home a gold medal. The following year, Whitney swam in the same event in the Pan Pacific Championships, held in Fukuoka, Japan. The result was another gold medal.

She began her college career at the University of Georgia in 1998–99. With her, Georgia captured its first NCAA swimming and diving national championship. Her next stop was the University of Florida, for which she swam in 1999–2000, and she ended her collegiate swimming years at the University of California-Berkeley.

Whitney's post-competitive activities have included Swim Across America, a charity that includes many notable swimmers who raise money and awareness in the fight against cancer. She is a swimming coach at the Seven Hills Swim and Tennis Club in Nashville.

KATHRYN PAIGE ZEMINA NORTHCUTT (1968–) ■ *United States*

COLLEGE: 1986–89   6-0, 154 lbs.
OLYMPICS: 1988 bronze medal

One summer when Paige Zemina was bored, her mother suggested she check out the local swim team—and the young girl loved it. As a high school student in Fort Lauderdale, she was a state champion in the 100-yard freestyle (three times) and the 200-yard freestyle (twice). In 1984, Zemina set the national high school record in the 200-yard freestyle. In 1985, she was part of a 4x50-meter freestyle relay that set a national record, and, at the 1986 Goodwill Games in Moscow, she earned a bronze medal in the 100-meter freestyle and gold medals in the 4x100- and 4x200-meter freestyle relays.

As a Gator, Zemina was a five-time national champion, all as part of relay squads—4x200-yard freestyle (1986, 1988, and 1989), 4x100-yard freestyle (1988), and 4x50-yard medley (1989). In 1988, she competed in the Olympics in Seoul by swimming in a preliminary heat of the 4x100-meter freestyle relay, and the squad finished second and qualified for the final. In the last race, the quartet (without Zemina) finished in third place and earned a bronze medal.

Zemina is working with the McMinnville Swim Team, a recreational summer league, in McMinnville, Tennessee.

DAVID LÓPEZ-ZUBERO PURCELL (1959–) ■ *Spain*

COLLEGE: 1977–81   5-10, 170 lbs.
OLYMPICS: 1976; 1980 bronze medal; 1984

David Zubero was born in Syracuse, New York, with dual U.S./Spanish citizenship, and he swam internationally for Spain, as did his sister Julie and brother Martín. Zubero's first Olympic appearance was in 1976, when he swam the 200- and 400-meter freestyle and the 4x200-meter freestyle relay. In none of those races was he or his relay squad able to advance past the first heat.

In 1977, Zubero became a student at Florida and a member of its swimming team. He was a member of the Gator squad that set an American record (and tied the NCAA record) in the 800-yard freestyle relay in 1979. His second NCAA national title came as a member of the 4x200-meter freestyle relay in 1981.

He represented Spain twice at the Mediterranean Games, in 1979 in Split, Yugoslavia, and in 1983 in Casablanca, Morocco, and both times he won a pair of gold medals. At the 1980 Olympics in Moscow, he won the 100-meter butterfly. He also competed, but did not medal, in the 100- and 200-meter freestyle, the 4x200-meter freestyle relay, and the 4x100-meter medley relay.

Zubero won the silver medal in the 100-meter butterfly in the 1983 European Championships. In his third Olympics in 1984, he swam the 100-meter butterfly (tied for 12th place) and the 4x200-meter freestyle relay (finished 11th).

In 1983, he received his bachelor's degree from Florida in microbiology and cell science. Later, he completed his master's degree in science education at Nova Southeastern University. Zubero became a member of the University of Florida Athletic Hall of Fame in 2002.

MARTÍN LÓPEZ-ZUBERO (1969–) ■ *Spain*

COLLEGE: 1988–91   6-2, 172 lbs.
OLYMPICS: 1988; 1992 gold medal; 1996

Martín López-Zubero was the youngest and most successful of three siblings who both swam for the University of Florida and made it onto Olympic teams for Spain (brother David and sister Julie). He was born in Jacksonville but held dual citizenship because of his father's Spanish birth. In his first Olympics in 1988, he swam in four individual events and one relay, but he did not make it into any finals races.

In college, Zubero held four NCAA titles: two in the 200-yard backstroke and one each in the 200- and 400-yard individual medleys, and he was named the NCAA Swimmer of the Year in 1991. He also was a European champion in the 100-meter backstroke (Bonn 1989, Athens 1991, Sheffield 1993, and Seville 1997), and in the 200-meter backstroke (1991). In the Goodwill Games of 1990 and 1994, he was the gold medalist in the 100- and 200-meter backstroke events.

At the 1992 Olympics, Zubero set an Olympic record in the 200-meter backstroke and won the gold medal; he swam in four other events but did not medal. He won the gold for the 200-meter backstroke and bronze for the 100-meter backstroke at the World Championships in 1991 in Perth; in 1994, when they were held in Rome, he won a silver and gold in each of the same two events.

A third trip to the Olympics in 1996 on behalf of the Spanish contingent had Zubero swimming in the 100- and 200-meter backstroke events. He came in second in the preliminary heats in both and qualified for the finals in each, but he finished fourth in the 100 and sixth in the 200. Two years later, he completed his bachelor's degree in health and human performance and recreation.

Zubero was an assistant head coach at his alma mater, The Bolles School in Jacksonville, and was named the Florida Age Group Coach of the Year in 1998, 1999, and 2002 by the American Swimming Coaches Association. He is a member of the International Swimming Hall of Fame and the University of Florida Athletic Hall of Fame. Zubero is married with a son and a daughter, and he is the head coach of the Spartan Aquatic Club in Orange Park, Florida.

TRACK AND FIELD

AARON NIGEL ARMSTRONG (1977–) ■ *Trinidad and Tobago*
COLLEGE: 2000–01   5-8, 154 lbs.
OLYMPICS: 2008 silver medal

Aaron Armstrong of Trinidad and Tobago competed as a sprinter for Barton Community College in Kansas and then the University of Florida. After leaving school, one of his first major international competitions was the 2005 Central American and Caribbean Championships. He won a silver medal in the 200 meters and won a gold medal as a member of the 4x100-meter relay squad, and, at the Commonwealth Games the following year, he finished fifth in the 200 meters.

In 2008, Armstrong again won a gold in the 4x100-meter relay at the Central American and Caribbean Championships, then went on to the Olympics in Beijing. He won his preliminary round in the 200 meters but finished out of the medals in fifth place in the quarterfinals. He ran in the preliminary heat of the 4x100-meter relay and won a silver medal when his teammates finished behind the Jamaican squad.

During 2009, Armstrong finished out of the medals in the 200 meters at the World Championships in Athletics held in Berlin, but, in that same event at the 2010 Commonwealth Games in Delhi, he received the bronze medal. Armstrong ran in the 4x100-meter relay in the Central American and Caribbean Championships in Mayaguez in 2011 and won a silver medal.

WILLIAM CLAYE (1991-) ■ *United States*

COLLEGE: 2011-12   5-11, 161 lbs.
OLYMPICS: 2012 1 silver and 1 bronze medal

Will Claye at the 2007 World Athletics Championships in Daegu

In high school, Will Claye starred in both the long jump and triple jump in Arizona, then enrolled at the University of Oklahoma where he was the 2009 NCAA national champion in the triple jump. After injuries limited his performance in the following track and field season, he transferred to the University of Florida to train with jumps coach Dick Booth. The jump in schools seemed to be a good choice. At the 2011 NCAA Indoor National Championship, Claye finished first in the triple jump and second in the long jump and was the Southeastern Conference champion in 2011 in both events.

In 2011, Claye finished third in the triple jump and ninth in the long jump at the World Championships in Daegu, and he left UF to prepare for the 2012 Olympics. In 2012, he won the triple jump at the Tyson Invitational and the USA Indoor Championships; at the latter, he was second in the long jump. He finished first at the IAAF World Indoor Championship in the triple jump and fourth in the long jump.

At the Olympics in 2012, Claye became the first man since 1936 to medal in both jumps at the same Olympics. He won the bronze in the long jump and silver in the triple jump. At the 2013 World Championships in Moscow, Claye won the bronze medal in the triple jump and is currently sponsored by Nike. He presently competes with a goal of making it to the 2016 Olympics, and, at the January 2014 New Balance Games, Claye won the triple jump with a distance of 55'11".

KERRON STEPHON CLEMENT (1985-) ■ *United States*

COLLEGE: 2004-06   6-2, 190 lbs.
OLYMPICS: 2008 1 gold and 1 silver medal; 2012

Kerron Clement was born in Trinidad and Tobago and moved to the U.S. in 1998 with his family. He was a track star in high school in Texas, winning the National Scholastic championship in the 110-meter high hurdles (2002) and the 400-meter hurdles (2003). As a freshman at the University of Florida in 2004, Clement won the NCAA championship in the 400-meter hurdles. That year, he became a U.S. citizen and although, he was eligible to try out for the Olympics, he opted instead to compete in that year's World Junior Championships in Athletics, where he won gold medals in the 400-meter hurdles and the 4x400-meter relay.

In 2005, as a UF sophomore, Clement broke the record in the 400 meters at the NCAA Indoor Championships. He won the 400-meter hurdles event later that year at the U.S. Outdoor Track and Field Championships and, as a professional, no longer competed for Florida. At the IAAF World Cup in 2006, he finished first in the 400-meter hurdles, and he did the same at the 2007 World Championship. Clement moved from Gainesville to California to prepare for the next Olympics under famed coach Bob Kersee.

That preparation earned him a spot on the U.S. team as a 400-meter hurdler. In Beijing, Clement won the silver medal in that event and, as one of the sprinters in the 4x400-meter relay, his participation in the first round qualified him for the gold medal his teammates won in the event final.

400-meter hurdles winner Kerron Clement at the 2007 World Athletics Championships in Osaka

Clement continued to compete internationally, winning the 400-meter hurdles at both the World Championships and the IAAF World Athletics Final, both held in 2009. He trained for the 2012 Olympics and made the U.S. team, but, in the finals of the 400-meter hurdles, Clement finished eighth.

JEFFREY DEMPS (1990–) ■ *United States*

COLLEGE: 2008–11   5-7, 175 lbs.   **OLYMPICS:** 2012 silver medal

As the only Gator athlete to win national championships in two sports, Jeff Demps was best known to football fans as one of the two main running backs for the 2008 team that beat the University of Oklahoma for the BCS championship. As a freshman, Demps rushed for 605 yards and seven touchdowns that season.

On the track as a high school senior, he ran the 100 meters in a time of 10.01 at the 2008 Olympic trials, breaking the American high school record and equaling the world junior record. The following year, Demps competed for the Gators in the Southeastern Conference championship and anchored the 4x100-meter squad that won the title. At the 2010 NCAA Indoor Track and Field Championships, he became the national champion in the 60 meters, and, later that year at the NCAA Outdoor Track and Field Championships, he took the title in the 100 meters. In 2012, he repeated as the 60-meter indoor champion.

Jeff Demps as a Gator running back

For the 2012 Olympics, Demps was added as a late replacement for an injured member of the 4x100-meter relay squad. He ran in a preliminary round, and the team set a new American record time. Although he did not run in the final, he received a silver medal because the team finished second in the event.

Following the Olympics, Demps signed a three-year contract with the New England Patriots, expecting to be a running back and kick return specialist. He was soon placed on the injured reserve list and sat out the rest of the season, but he was picked up by the Tampa Bay Buccaneers and placed on their active roster in September 2013. Demps played in two games and returned four kickoffs for a total of 93 yards.

ROBERT DEFRIESE EVANS (1977–) ■ *United States*
COLLEGE: 1997–2001 6-0, 140 lbs. **PARALYMPICS:** 2000 2 gold medals

Rob Evans was born without a right forearm, but he did not let that deter him from being active in athletics. In high school, he was All-State in soccer and undefeated in track during his junior and senior years. At UF, he ran cross country and indoor and outdoor track, at distances from 1,500 to 10,000 meters, and his college honors included All-Southeastern Conference and All-South Region in cross country, plus three times on the SEC Academic Honor Roll. Evans may have been able to qualify for the Honor Roll for 2000, but he left the team early to prepare for and compete in the Paralympic Games in Sydney.

The XIth Olympiad drew athletes from 123 nations, including about 400 from the U.S., but, unlike the Summer Olympics since 1968, there was only one Gator present. Evans ran in and won two individual events, setting world Paralympic records in the 1500 meters and the 5000 meters. After the longer race, he took a victory lap carrying both the U.S. and Australian flags, endearing him to the fans for more than just his athletic prowess. Evans also ran a leg of the 4x100-meter relay, but the U.S. squad did not make it to the medal stand.

MICHELLE FREEMAN (1969–) ■ *Jamaica*
COLLEGE: 1989–92 5-7, 139 lbs.
OLYMPICS: 1992; 1996 bronze medal; 2000

At the 1987 Under-20 CARIFTA Games in Port of Spain, Michelle Freeman won the bronze medal in the 100-meter hurdles. A year later, when those games were held in Kingston, she won gold in both the 100 meters and the 100-meter hurdles, and she was presented the Austin Sealy Trophy as the most outstanding athlete.

Freeman ran for Florida and won seven Southeastern Conference titles, and she ran one leg of the university's NCAA national championship 4x400-meter relay team. Freeman still holds the school's records in the 55-meter dash, 55-meter hurdles, 100-meters, and 100-meter hurdles. She became a member of the University of Florida Athletic Hall of Fame in 2011.

Freeman followed her beloved coach, Beverly Kearney, who left Florida to become the head coach at the University of Texas in Austin. In her first Olympics in

1992, Freeman ran in the preliminary round of the 4x100-meter relay. The Jamaican team won the preliminary but did not finish in the finals. Freeman also competed in the 100-meter hurdles and won her preliminary, but she finished 8th in her quarterfinal. She improved two years later at the Commonwealth Games and took home the gold medal in that event.

At the 1996 Olympics, Freeman ran a leg of the 4x100-meter relay and shared a bronze medal with her teammates. Individually, she ran the 100-meter hurdles and finished sixth. In that same event in 1997, she earned a bronze medal at the World Championships held in Athens, and she also won gold that year in the 60-meter hurdles at the World Indoor Championships in Paris.

Freeman earned a place on her third Olympic team in 2000, as a 100-meter hurdler. In the preliminary round, she finished third and moved on to the quarterfinals. There, she finished seventh, her last Olympic experience. She continued to compete in 2001 until she suffered a season-ending injury early in 2002, followed by a devastating car accident the day after Christmas that took the life of her mother and her dear friend, and injured Kearney. Freeman had a child and went back to competing in 2005 but did not achieve her former level of success. She spent a decade volunteering as an assistant coach at the University of Texas and became the interim assistant coach in January 2013.

TONY MCQUAY (1990–) ■ *United States*

COLLEGE: 2010–13   5-11, 154 lbs.   **OLYMPICS:** 2012 silver medal

In high school in Palm Beach, Tony McQuay ran the 100, 200 and 400 meters, and as a senior was the state champion in the 400 meters. He came to UF in 2010 and won the gold medal at that distance at the NCAA Indoor Track and Field Championships in 2011 and 2012, and at the NCAA 2012 Outdoor Track and Field Championships. Twice he was the Southeastern Conference outdoor champion. In the senior open division at 400 meters at the 2011 USA Outdoor Track and Field Championships, he posted a time of 44.68, giving him first place.

Tony McQuay (right) in the 4x400-meter relay at the 2012 Olympics

McQuay tried out for the U.S. Olympic team in 2012 at the 400-meter distance and finished second, good enough to participate in the individual event and the 4x400-meter relay. In London, he finished second in the 400 meters in the preliminary round and advanced to the semifinals, but there he came in fourth and missed out on qualifying for the finals. Things were different in the relay, where he ran both in the prelims and the final race, finishing second both times and being awarded a silver medal.

At the 2013 World Championships in Moscow, McQuay ran as part of the 4x400-meter relay team that won the gold medal, and he also won a silver medal in the men's 400 meters.

DENNIS ALLEN MITCHELL (1966–) ■ *United States*

COLLEGE: 1986–89 5-9, 154 lbs.
OLYMPICS: 1988; 1992 1 gold and 1 bronze medal; 1996 silver medal

Dennis Mitchell began competing for Florida in 1986 and, in 1988, competed in his first Olympics. He finished fourth in the 100 meters and was part of the U.S. team favored to win the gold medal in the 4x100-meter relay, but which wound up being disqualified because two of his teammates made an improper baton pass in a preliminary heat. In 1989, he became the NCAA national champion in the 200 meters.

During a meet in Zurich in 1991, Mitchell was part of the squad that broke the world record in the 4x100-meter relay and then, a month later at the world championships in Tokyo, set a new world record and received a gold medal. During the championships, he also won an individual silver medal in the 100 meters.

The following year, Mitchell became the U.S. national champion in the 100-meter distance, an accomplishment he repeated in 1994 and 1996. At the 1992 Olympics, he won the bronze medal in the 100 meters and was part of the team that set a new world record and won the gold medal in the 4x100-meter relay. In the 1993 world championships in Stuttgart, Mitchell won the bronze in the 100 meters and a gold in the 4x100-meter relay, a race in which the U.S. squad equaled their world record of 37.40.

In his third Olympics in 1996, he finished fourth in the 100 meters and won a silver as part of the 4x100-meter relay team. His track and field future looked bright, but, two years later, Mitchell was banned from track for two years by the International Association of Athletics Federations for unusually high levels of testosterone. He returned to international fame by being a part of the gold-medal team in the 4x100-meter relay at the 2001 world championships in Edmonton, but the U.S. later was disqualified because of a doping scandal involving one of the other members of the squad.

Currently, Mitchell coaches at the National Training Center in Clermont, Florida, and at his own club, Star Athletics, and has worked hard to be a good father and a good role model. He is married to Damu Cherry-Mitchell, also an Olympian, and they have three children. Mitchell became a member of the University of Florida Athletic Hall of Fame in 2005.

FRANK CHARLES SHORTER (1947–) ■ *United States*

COLLEGE: DNC 5-10, 134 lbs.
OLYMPICS: 1972 1 gold medal; 1976 1 silver medal

Marathoner Frank Shorter, who was born in Germany and grew up in New York, graduated from Yale University. He exhausted his college track eligibility there and, in 1969, was the NCAA national champion in the 10,000 meters. He had lots of running left in him, so he moved to Gainesville for the dual purpose of earning a law degree at Florida and competing on behalf of the Florida Track Club founded by UF track coach Jimmy Carnes.

Shorter was a national champion at 5,000 and 10,000 meters in 1970. He repeated at the longer distance in 1971, 1974, 1975, and 1977, and, was the national champion in cross-country for four consecutive years beginning in 1970. Twice (1972 and 1976) he qualified for the Olympics in both the 10,000 meters and the marathon. In 1972 in

Marathoner Frank Shorter in 2002

Munich, he finished fifth in the 10,000 meters and won Olympic gold in the marathon. He wasn't the first to cross the finish line, but the runner ahead of him was an imposter who hadn't run the whole race. Shorter was named the recipient of the James E. Sullivan Award that same year as the top amateur athlete in the country.

Going into the 1976 Olympic marathon, he was the favorite to repeat as gold medalist . . . so long as the weather remained dry. The announcers frequently reminded the television audience that Frank Shorter was not as effective in the rain, so a substantial part of the broadcast included weather reports of the skies over Montreal. Unfortunately, it did rain, and he faded to second place, behind Waldemar Cierpinski of East Germany. Shorter's winning a second Olympic medal in the marathon was the first (and only) time an American has accomplished that feat.

Shorter was a founder of the United States Anti-Doping Agency, which he chaired from 2000 to 2003. He is a member of the U.S. Olympic Hall of Fame, the USA National Track and Field Hall of Fame, and the Florida Sports Hall of Fame. He lives in Boulder, Colorado, where he was a co-founder of the Bolder Boulder 10K race that began honoring the U.S. Armed Forces in 1979. In 2010, the first annual Frank Shorter RACE4Kids' Health 5K race was held in Broomfield, Colorado, to benefit children.

CHRISTIAN TAYLOR (1990–) ■ *United States*

COLLEGE: 2009–13   6-2, 174 lbs.   **OLYMPICS:** 2012 gold medal

While a high school athlete in Georgia, Christian Taylor participated in the World Youth Championships in Ostrava and won the gold medal in the triple jump and the bronze in the long jump. At the 2008 National Scholastic Indoor Championships, he not only finished first in both of those events, he also won the gold in the 400 meters. During that same year, he made it to the finals of both the long and triple jumps at the World Junior Championships in Athletics.

As a freshman at Florida, Taylor won the Southeastern Conference Indoor Championships in both jumps and the 4x400-meter relay, and, at the NCAA Indoor

Championships, he won the triple jump and was part of the squad that came in third in the 4x400-meter relay. He then won the bronze medal in the triple jump at the NCAA Outdoor Championships. Taylor continued to medal in the jumps and relay during his years in college, and he earned gold medals in both jumps at the 2010 NACAC Under-23 Championships.

In 2011, Taylor won the gold in the triple jump at the world championships in Daegu. The following year, he came in second to fellow Gator Will Claye at the USA Indoor Championships and the International Association of Athletics Federations World Indoor Championships. He then beat Claye at the Prefontaine Classic. At the 2012 Olympics, Taylor won his first Olympic gold medal in his only event, the triple jump, and came in fourth in the 2013 World Championships in Moscow.

Christian Taylor lands during the 2012 IAAF World Championship in Istanbul

For the year 2014, Taylor and his coach decided to change their training regimen because there were no major meets, and instead look ahead toward the 2016 Olympics. Rather than focus on the jumps, he put more time into the 400 meters. At the Florida Relays held in April of that year, Taylor came in second in that event.

BERNARD ROLLEN WILLIAMS III (1978–) ■ *United States*

COLLEGE: 2000   6-0, 178 lbs.
OLYMPICS: 2000 gold medal; 2004 silver medal

At the Pan American Games in Winnipeg in 1999, Bernard Williams won the gold medal in the 100 meters. He enrolled at the University of Florida and, in 2000 as a Gator, won the NCAA national title in the 100 meters. At the 2000 Olympics, he ran the second leg of the 4x100-meter relay for the U.S. squad that took home the gold medal. During their celebratory lap, the four athletes got a little carried away with their celebration and faced some criticism, which Williams took personally and apologized in an interview, saying he had learned a great deal from the incident.

Sprinter Bernard Williams at a track meet in 2007

At the 2001 World Championships in Edmonton, Williams won a silver medal in the 100 meters and a gold in the 4x100-meter relay. However, the medals were voided after a teammate was found to have used illegal steroids.

Williams was the U.S. national champion in the 100 meters in 2003, and, that same year, he received a gold medal as a part of the U.S. squad that won the 2003 World Championships. During his second trip to the Olympics, in 2004 in Athens, he won the silver medal in the 200 meters.

Williams has coached sprinting at the high school level and is a stand-up comedian who performs under the name of "Hollywood." In 2008, he received his bachelor's degree from UF in sociology.

NOVLENE WILLIAMS-MILLS (1982–) ■ *Jamaica*

COLLEGE: 2003–04   5-6, 121 lbs.   **OLYMPICS:** 2004 bronze medal; 2008 bronze medal; 2012 bronze medal

Novlene Williams attended high school in Jamaica, then ran track for the University of Florida. She graduated with a bachelor's degree in 2004. That same year, she made her first Olympic appearance. She finished third in her preliminary heat in the 400 meters but did not move to the next round. In the 4x400-meter relay, her squad finished third, but that was good enough to move on to the finals, where they again finished third and received the bronze medal.

Novlene Williams running at the 2007 World Championships

With Williams, the Jamaican 4x400-meter relay team won the silver medal at the 2005 World Championships held in Helsinki, and again at the 2007 World Championships in Osaka. She won her own individual bronze in the 400 meters at the 2006 Commonwealth Games. At the 2008 Olympics, her 4x400-meter relay squad wound up with the bronze medal, and Williams won her first heat in the 100-meter hurdles but finished third in the semifinals.

In 2009, her relay team won another silver in the World Championships in Berlin, and she repeated that feat in 2011 in Daegu. On June 25, 2012, prior to the Olympics, Williams was diagnosed with breast cancer but withheld that news from the public for a year. Despite her diagnosis, she ran her familiar races and finished 5th in the 400 meters and won her third bronze medal as a member of the 4x400-meter relay team.

Three days after the games, she had her first surgery to remove a lump. She had a double mastectomy, followed by reconstructive surgery in January 2013, and, less than seven months later, made it into the finals of the 2013 World Championships in Moscow. Williams finished last in the race but first in the hearts of all who knew her story and her courage.

BOBSLEDDING

JOHN C. AMABILE (1962-) and
LISTON BOCHETTE III (1957-) ■ *Puerto Rico*

COLLEGE: DNC   **OLYMPICS:** 1992; 1994; 1998

Not unexpectedly, Gators rarely have participated in the Winter Olympics, and UF has no official team sports that compete at those games. The exceptions are three men who have participated in bobsled, the first two during the 1990s. John Amabile was on the UF track and field team in 1982–84 and was the SEC javelin champion in 1983. Liston Bochette was a Gator student in 1977–80 and served as captain of the UF track team and the decathlon champion of Puerto Rico. He received his bachelor's degree in humanities from UF and went on to get a master's degree in humanities from Inter American University and his Ph.D. in education from Pacific Western University.

They each teamed up with other Puerto Rican athletes to participate in three Olympiads. Three times, Amabile raced in the two-man bobsled event. Bochette did the two-man in 1992, then switched to the four-man in 1994 and 1998. They never were serious contenders to win a medal, but they were crowd favorites because Puerto Rico and Florida are not traditional winter sports regions.

After their Olympic participation as athletes, Dr. Bochette continued his strong affiliation with the games by serving as secretary general of the International Olympic Committee's Athletes Commission, a member of the United States President's Panel on Olympic Affairs, the founding president of the Puerto Rico National Olympians Association, and a director of the Art of the Olympians Al Oerter Center for Excellence.

Optometrist Amabile was indicted in 1999 for defrauding 27 insurance carriers and, in 2002, was sentenced to seven years imprisonment for insurance fraud. Joseph Keosseian, the third athlete and Amabile's brakeman in the bobsled during the 1998 Olympics, was sentenced to three years in 1998, also for health insurance fraud.

STEVEN MICHAEL MESLER (1978-)
■ *United States*

COLLEGE: DNC   6-2, 192 lbs.
OLYMPICS: 2002; 2006; 2010 gold medal

The first (and still only) Gator to win a Winter Olympics medal of any color is Steven Mesler, who was a student at UF from 1997 to 2000. Mesler was a member of the track and field team as a decathlete, and he received a degree in exercise and sports science. As a member of a four-man bobsled team representing the

Steve Mesler (center) and teammates enjoy their 2010 gold medals

United States, he won the bronze medal at the 2004 world championships in Königssee and the gold in 2009 in Lake Placid.

In 2010, he served as a pusher for the four-man sled driven by Steve Holcomb, which won the Olympic gold medal for the U.S. Mesler lives in Calgary, Alberta, and is a motivational speaker, television host, and consultant. He is a member of the Greater Buffalo Sports Hall of Fame and the National Jewish Sports Hall of Fame.

CYCLING

ANDREW WEAVER (1959–) ■ *United States*

COLLEGE: DNC
OLYMPICS: 1980 (DNC, national boycott); 1984 bronze medal

Andrew Weaver began as a student at the University of Florida in 1977 and received a bachelor's degree in architecture before enrolling at the Massachusetts Institute of Technology, where he received his master's degree in the same subject. While at Florida, he trained for a sport not contested at the university, cycling.

Weaver was a member of the U.S. team that went to the 1979 Pan American Games, and he won a gold medal at the 1983 games. For the 1984 Olympics, he teamed with Clarence Knickman, Ron Kiefel, and Davis Phinney, and they won the bronze medal in the 100-kilometer team time trial. Weaver was a national cycling champion nine times.

In 1994, Weaver founded an architectural firm and designs projects in the Northeast for private institutions, resorts and golf developments, sports facilities, and multifamily housing.

Andrew Weaver (right) and teammates during the 1984 Olympic 100k team time trial

Other Florida Olympians— Non-Medal Winners
(All Summer Olympics, through 2012)
DNC: Did not compete (in that sport on behalf of the university)

Swimming and Diving

NAME	COLLEGE	OLYMPICS	COUNTRY	EVENT
Bradley Kevin Ally	2005–08	2004	Barbados	100- and 200-meter breaststroke, 200- and 400-meter individual medley
		2008		200- and 400-meter individual medley
		2012		100-meter backstroke, 200- and 400-meter individual medley
Janelle Anya Monique Atkinson-Wignall	2000–03	2000	Jamaica	400- and 800-meter freestyle
		2004		200- and 400-meter freestyle
José Luis Ballester	1991	1988	Spain	100- and 200-meter butterfly, 4x100-meter medley relay
		1992		200-meter butterfly
		1996		200-meter butterfly
Sarah Blake Bateman	2008–12	2008	Iceland	100-meter backstroke
		2012		50-meter freestyle, 100-meter butterfly, 4x100-meter medley relay
Vipa Bernhardt	2002–05	2004	Germany	100-meter breaststroke
Rosemary Edith Brown Fydler	1979–83	1980	Australia	100-, 200-, 400- and 800-meter freestyle, 4x100-meter freestyle relay, 4x100-meter medley relay
Tami Lee Bruce	1986–89	1988	USA	400- and 800-meter freestyle
Thomas Carlton Bruner	1991-94	1996	USA	1500-meter freestyle
Christopher Clarke Burckle Jr.	2006–08	2012	USA	200-meter breaststroke
Marcin Cieślak	2010–14	2012	Poland	200-meter butterfly, 200-meter individual medley
Melaniá Felicitas Costa-Schmid	2008–10	2008	Spain	200-meter freestyle, 4x200-meter freestyle relay
		2012		200- and 400-meter freestyle, 4x100-meter medley relay, 4x100-meter freestyle relay
Jose Emmanuel Crescimbeni	2008–09	2008	Peru	200-meter butterfly
Rodion Davelaar	2008–12	2008	Netherlands Antilles	50-meter freestyle
Nicole Dryden	1993–96	1992	Canada	4x100-meter freestyle relay, 4x100-meter medley relay, 100- and 200-meter backstroke, 200-meter freestyle
		1996		800-meter freestyle

NAME	COLLEGE	OLYMPICS	COUNTRY	EVENT
Renate Magdaleen du Plessis	2001–03	2000	South Africa	100-meter butterfly
Asmahan (Mercedes) Farhat	2008–12	2008	Libya	100-meter breaststroke
Elizabeth Marie Forrest	1982–83	1980	Australia	100- and 200-meter backstroke, 4x100-meter medley relay
Bárbara Franco	1992–96	1992	Spain	100-meter butterfly
		1996		200-meter butterfly
Claudia Maria Franco Solana	1993–94	1992	Spain	50- and 100-meter freestyle, 4x100-meter medley relay
		1996		50- and 100-meter freestyle, 4x100-meter freestyle relay, 4x100-meter medley relay
Brett Michael Fraser	2007–11	2008	Cayman Islands	200-meter backstroke
		2012		50-, 100- and 200-meter freestyle
Shaune David Fraser	2006–10	2004	Cayman Islands	200-meter freestyle
		2008		100- and 200-meter freestyle, 100-meter butterfly
		2012		100- and 200-meter freestyle
Deborah Lynne Fuller	1984–87	1984	Canada	Springboard and platform diving
		1988		Springboard and platform diving
Balázs Gercsák	2007–11	2008	Hungary	400-meter freestyle, 4x200-meter freestyle relay
Csaba Gercsák	DNC	2008	Hungary	10,000-meter open water
		2012		10,000-meter open water
Cerian Gibbes	2000–02	1996	Trinidad and Tobago	100- and 200-meter breaststroke
Chantal Gibney	2000–04	2000	Ireland	50-, 100-, 200- and 400-meter freestyle
Jesús Francisco González Cisneros	1996–97	1996	Mexico	100-meter butterfly
Elizabeth Merryn Hazel	1991–95	1992	Canada	200-meter backstroke
Jill Horstead	1986–90	1984	Canada	200-meter butterfly
Patrick David Kennedy	1983–86	1984	USA	200-meter butterfly
Bang-Hyun Kim	1997–2001	1996	South Korea	200- and 400-meter individual medley
		2000		400-meter individual medley
		2004		200- and 400-meter individual medley
Sarra Lajnef	2009–13	2012	Tunisia	200-meter breaststroke
Renee A. Laravie	1977–79	1976	USA	100-meter breaststroke
Nuno Filipe Gomes Laurentino	1997	1996	Portugal	100- and 200-meter backstroke
		2000		100-meter backstroke, 4x100-meter medley relay

NAME	COLLEGE	OLYMPICS	COUNTRY	EVENT
Eva Lehtonen	2009–10	2008	Finland	400- and 800-meter freestyle
Tom Lemaire	1978–82	1984	Belgium	Springboard and platform diving
		1988		Springboard and platform diving
Enrico Gustavo Linscheer	1993–94	1992	Suriname	50- and 100-meter freestyle
		1996		50-meter freestyle
Giovanni Rodolfo Linscheer	1991–94	1992	Suriname	100-meter freestyle, 100-meter butterfly
		1996		100-meter freestyle, 100-meter butterfly
Arsenio Alexander Lopez	1997–2001	1996	Puerto Rico	200- and 400-meter individual medley, 4x100-meter freestyle relay
		2000		100-meter breaststroke, 200-meter individual medley
		2004		100-meter breaststroke
Marco Antonio Loughren	2009–11	2012	Great Britain	200-meter backstroke
Jemma Louise Lowe	2009–10	2008	Great Britain	100- and 200-meter butterfly, 4x100-meter medley relay
		2012		200-meter butterfly, 4x100-meter medley relay
Hrafnhildur Luthersdótir	2010–14	2012	Iceland	200-meter breaststroke, 4x100-meter medley relay
Gabriel Mangabeira	2001–04	2004	Brazil	100-meter butterfly
		2008		100-meter butterfly
Leah Simone Martindale-Stancil	1998–2002	1996	Barbados	50- and 100-meter freestyle
		2000		50- and 100-meter freesyle
Raúl Martinez Colomer	2008–10	2012	Puerto Rico	200-meter freestyle
Steven Mellor	1994	1992	Great Britain	4x200-meter freestyle relay
Alberto Eugenio Mestre-Sosa	1983–86	1980	Venezuela	100- and 200-meter freestyle
		1984		100- and 200-meter freestyle, 4x100- and 4x200-meter freestyle relay, 4x100-meter medley relay
Whitney Beth Metzler	1996–98	1996	USA	400-meter individual medley
Ricardo Andres Monasterio Guimaraes	1997–98, 2000–01	1996	Venezuela	400- and 1500-meter freestyle
		2000		400- and 1500-meter freestyle
		2004		400- and 1500-meter freestyle
		2008		1500-meter freestyle
Victor Mauricio Moreno Castillo	1998–2000	1996	Colombia	100-meter breaststroke
Melisa A. Moses	1992–93	1996	USA	Springboard diving

NAME	COLLEGE	OLYMPICS	COUNTRY	EVENT
Omar Andrés Pinzón Garcia	2006–10	2004	Colombia	200-meter backstroke
		2008		100- and 200-meter backstroke, 200- and 400-meter individual medley, 200-meter butterfly
		2012		100- and 200-meter backstroke, 200-meter butterfly
Anna-Liisa Põld	2008–12	2008	Estonia	400-meter individual medley
Stephanie Mary Proud	2007–09	2012	Great Britain	200-meter backstroke
Wendy Quirk	1977–78	1976	Canada	100- and 200-meter butterfly, 400- and 800-meter freestyle
Stephanie Richardson	1996–97	1996	Canada	800-meter freestyle
Andrew James Allan Ritchie	1970s	1976	Canada	400-meter individual medley
Sebastien Daniel Rousseau	2009–11, 2012–14	2008	South Africa	4x200-meter freestyle relay
		2012		4x200-meter freestyle relay
Roland Rudolf	2006–10	2008	Hungary	100- and 200-meter backstroke
Sinéad Russell	2012–14	2012	Canada	100- and 200-meter backstroke
Jonathan Dehe Sakovich	1989–92	1988	Guam	100-, 200-, 400- and 1500-meter freestyle, 200- and 400-meter individual relay
Lucas Vinicius Yokoo Salatta	2005–07	2004	Brazil	400-meter individual medley, 200-meter backstroke, 4x200-meter freestyle relay
William Sawchuk	1979, 1981–82	1976	Canada	200- and 400-meter freestyle, 4x200-meter freestyle relay
		1980		Made team, but national boycott
Adam Sioui	2001–02, 2004–05	2008	Canada	100- and 200-meter butterfly, 4x200-meter freestyle relay
Christopher Snode	1977–80	1976	Great Britain	Springboard diving
		1980		Springboard and platform diving
		1984		Springboard and platform diving
Gemma Mary Spofforth	2006–10	2008	Great Britain	100- and 200-meter backstroke, 4x100-meter medley relay
		2012		100-meter backstroke, 4x100-meter medley relay
James Bernard Walsh	2004–05, 2007–08	2004	Philippines	200-meter butterfly
		2008		200-meter butterfly

Track and Field

NAME	COLLEGE	OLYMPICS	COUNTRY	EVENT
Jack Bacheler	DNC	1968	USA	5,000 meters
		1972		Marathon
Kimberly Barrett	2001–04	2004	Jamaica	Shot put
Keith Alan Brantly	1980–83	1996	USA	Marathon
John Capel Jr.	1999–2000	2000	USA	200 meters
Hazel Mae Clark-Riley	1996–99	2000	USA	800 meters
		2004		800 meters
		2008		800 meters
Gerald Clervil	1994–98	2000	Haiti	400 meters
David Mark Everett	1987–90	1988	USA	800 meters
		1992		800 meters
		2000		800 meters
Erin Gilreath	2002–03	2004	USA	Hammer throw
Kenneth Gray	1979–83	1984	Jamaica	400-meter hurdles
Kristin L. Heaston	1995–98	2004	USA	Shot put
		2008		Shot put
Stephen Jones	2000–01	2004	Barbados	110-meter hurdles
Moise Joseph	2001–04	2004	Haiti	800 meters
		2012		800 meters
Ronald Lee Jourdan	1967–70	1972	USA	High jump
Mariam Kevkhishvili Machavariani	2007–08	2004	Georgia	Shot put
		2008		Shot put
Genevieve LaCaze	2009–13	2012	Australia	3000-meter steeplechase
Fletcher Lewis	1975–76	1976	Bahamas	Long jump
Martin William Liquori	DNC	1968	USA	1500 meters
Kemal Mesić	2009–12	2012	Bosnia and Herzegovina	Shot put
Dan Middleman	1987–92	1996	USA	10,000 meters
Tiandra Ponteen	2004–05	2004	Saint Kitts and Nevis	400 meters
		2008		400 meters
Shara Proctor	2007–11	2012	Great Britain	Long jump
Thomas Paul Pukstys	1987–89	1992	USA	Javelin throw
		1996		Javelin throw
Leroy Reid	1983–84	1984	Jamaica	200 meters

NAME	COLLEGE	OLYMPICS	COUNTRY	EVENT
Dionne Marie Rose-Henley	1991–92	1992	Jamaica	100-meter hurdles, Long jump
		1996		100-meter hurdles
Candice Henrietta Scott	2001–05	2004	Trinidad and Tobago	Hammer throw
		2008		Hammer throw
Michael Sharpe	1974–75	1976	Bermuda	100 meters, 4x100-meter relay
Anne Rochelle Steely Ramirez	1982–85	1992	USA	3000 meters
Dariusz Trafas	1993–96	2000	Poland	Javelin throw
Horace Tuitt	1975–77	1976	Trinidad and Tobago	800 meters, 4x400-meter relay

Gymnastics

NAME	COLLEGE	OLYMPICS	COUNTRY	EVENT
Anita Botnen-Fisher	1985–88	1984	Canada	Gymnastics
Marissa Petra King	2010–13	2008	Great Britain	Gymnastics
Christina Anne McDonald Fritz	1989–92	1988	Canada	Gymnastics
Nicola Willis	2005–08	2004	Great Britain	Gymnastics

Tennis

NAME	COLLEGE	OLYMPICS	COUNTRY	EVENT
Jill N. Craybas	1994–96	2008	USA	Singles tennis (see page 336)
Jill Hetherington Hultquist	1984–87	1984	Canada	Demonstration event (see page 337)
		1988		Singles and doubles tennis
		1996		Doubles tennis
Mark Merklein	1991–94	2000	Bahamas	Doubles tennis (see page 330)
		2004		Doubles tennis
Lisa Raymond	1992–93	2004	USA	Singles and doubles tennis (see page 338)
		2012		Singles and mixed doubles

Women's Basketball

NAME	COLLEGE	OLYMPICS	COUNTRY	POSITION
Azania Jocelyn D. Stewart	2008–12	2012	Great Britain	Center

Judo

NAME	COLLEGE	OLYMPICS	COUNTRY	SPORT
Colleen Rosensteel	DNC	1992	USA	Judo (see page 353)
		1996		Judo
		2000		Judo

Handball

NAME	COLLEGE	OLYMPICS	COUNTRY	SPORT
Harry William Winkler, Jr	DNC	1976	USA	Handball

Cycling

NAME	COLLEGE	OLYMPICS	COUNTRY	EVENT
Jeanne Golay	DNC	1992	USA	Individual road race
	1996			Individual road race, individual time trial, Points race

Volleyball

NAME	COLLEGE	OLYMPICS	COUNTRY	SPORT
Gudula Staub	1991–92	2000	Germany	Beach Volleyball

APPENDIX

Gator Players and Head Coaches in Halls of Fame

Baylor School Sports Hall of Fame CHATTANOOGA, TENNESSEE
Geoffrey Steven Gaberino (Swimming) 1992

Broward County Sports Hall of Fame FORT LAUDERDALE, FLORIDA Louis Oliver III (Football) 2011
Errict Rhett (Football) 2007 | Robert Michael Stanley (Baseball) 2003

Bubby LaRosa High School Sports Hall of Fame CINCINNATI, OHIO
Andrea Farley (Tennis) 2000 | Heather Blaine Mitts Feeley (Soccer) 2009

Canadian Football Hall of Fame HAMILTON, ONTARIO John B. Barrow 1976

Capital One Academic All-America Hall of Fame
Cris Collinsworth (Football) 2001 | Tracy Caulkins Stockwell (Swimming) 1997

Cleveland Indians Hall of Fame CLEVELAND, OHIO Albert Leonard Rosen 2006

College Football Hall of Fame SOUTH BEND, INDIANA Wilbur Buddyhia Marshall 2008 | Emmitt James Smith III 2006 | Steven Orr Spurrier 1986 | Daniel Carl Wuerffel 2013

Colorado Sports Hall of Fame DENVER, COLORADO Frank Charles Shorter 2008

Columbus Athletic Hall of Fame MIAMI, FLORIDA Robert Albert Murphy (Baseball)

Dallas Cowboys Ring of Honor IRVING, TEXAS Emmitt James Smith III 2005

Florida Sports Hall of Fame AUBURNDALE, FLORIDA

Catherine Ball Condon (Swimming) 2010	Steven N. Melnyk (Golf) 2000
Walter Lanier Barber (Broadcasting) 1979	Nathaniel Moore (Football) 1998
Thomas Andrew Bean (Golf) 2000	Robert Joseph Murphy Jr. (Golf) 2011
Otis Boggs (Broadcasting) 1990	Edward Glenn Roberts Jr. (NASCAR) 1961
Scot Eugene Brantley (Football) 1996	Albert Leonard Rosen (Baseball) 1967
Ricardo Jose Casares (Football) 1972	George Douglas Sanders (Golf) 1972
Tracy Caulkins Stockwell (Swimming) 1988	Frank Charles Shorter (Track and Field) 1993
Wesley Sandy Chandler (Football) 1992	Emmitt James Smith III (Football) 2006
Anthony Cris Collinsworth (Football) 1990	Steven Orr Spurrier (Football) 1970
Donald Denver Fleming (Football) 1963	Daniel Carl Wuerffel (Football) 2005
Nicole Lee Haislett Bacher (Swimming) 2005	Herbert Jackson Youngblood III (Football) 1975
Gary D. Koch (Golf) 2012	

Florida State Golf Association Hall of Fame TAMPA, FLORIDA
Gary D. Koch 2006 | Robert Joseph Murphy Jr. 2005 | Steven N. Melnyk 2008

Appendix 415

Florida-Georgia Hall of Fame JACKSONVILLE, FLORIDA

Reidel Clarence Anthony 2004	Wilber Buddyhia Marshall 2010
Kerwin Douglas Bell 1996	Michael Shane Matthews 1996
Scot Eugene Brantley 2010	Nathaniel Moore 2001
Kevin Louis Carter 2011	Ricky Rennard Nattiel 2002
Ricardo Jose Casares 1998	Thomas Johnson Reaves 2001
Wesley Sandy Chandler 2004	Errict Undra Rhett 2003
Christopher Paul Doering 2001	Steven Orr Spurrier 1996
Rex Daniel Grossman III 2009	Frederick Antwon Taylor 2008
Isaac Jason Hilliard 2006	Richard Earl Trapp 1998
Charles Ray Hunsinger 1998	John L. Williams 2012
Willie Bernard Jackson Jr. 2008	Lawrence D. Wright III 2009
Doug Johnson Jr. 2007	Daniel Carl Wuerffel 1997
Buford Eugene Long 2003	Herbert Jackson Youngblood III 1997

Gator Football Ring of Honor GAINESVILLE, FLORIDA

Wilber Buddyhia Marshall 2007 | Emmitt James Smith III 2006 | Steven Orr Spurrier 2006 | Daniel Carl Wuerffel 2006 | Herbert Jackson Youngblood III 2006

Georgia Golf Hall of Fame MARIETTA, GEORGIA
Thomas Dean Aaron 1989 | Steven N. Melnyk 1992 | George Douglas Sanders 1989

Georgia Sports Hall of Fame MACON, GEORGIA
Thomas Dean Aaron (Golf) 1980 | George Douglas Sanders (Golf) 1975

Georgia Tech Hall of Fame ATLANTA, GEORGIA Bryan Shelton (Tennis) 1993

Georgia Tennis Hall of Fame ATLANTA, GEORGIA Bryan Shelton 2002

Golf Coaches Association of America Hall of Fame NORMAN, OKLAHOMA
Buddy Alexander 2001 | Buster Bishop 1982 | Conrad Rehling 1980

Greater Buffalo Sports Hall of Fame BUFFALO, NEW YORK Steven Michael Mesler (Bobsledding)

Greater Chattanooga Area Sports Hall of Fame CHATTANOOGA, TENNESSEE
Geoffrey Steven Gaberino (Swimming)

Greater Peoria Sports Hall of Fame PEORIA HEIGHTS, ILLINOIS Alice Luthy Tym (Golf)

Green Bay Packers Hall of Fame GREEN BAY, WISCONSIN Donald Gene Chandler 1975

Huntsville-Madison County Athletic Hall of Fame HUNTSVILLE, ALABAMA
Bryan Shelton (Tennis) 2007

Intercollegiate Tennis Association Hall of Fame WILLIAMSBURG, VIRGINIA
Andy Brandi 2012 | Lisa Raymond 2012 | Alice Luthy Tym 2008

International Motorsports Hall of Fame TALLADEGA, ALABAMA Edward Glenn Roberts Jr. 1990

International Swimming Hall of Fame FORT LAUDERDALE, FLORIDA Duncan John D'Arcy Armstrong 1996 | Tracy Anne Caulkins Stockwell 1990 | Catherine Northcutt Ball Condon 1976 | Alexander Timothy McKee 1998 | Anthony Conrad Nesty 1998 | Mary Alice Wayte-Bradburne 2000 | Martin López-Zubero 2004

International Women's Sports Hall of Fame NEW YORK, NEW YORK	
Tracy Anne Caulkins Stockwell (Swimming) | Carolyn Peck (Basketball) | Dara Grace Torres (Swimming)	
Jewish Sports Hall of Fame NETANYA, ISRAEL Al Rosen (Baseball) 1980	
Kansas Golf Hall of Fame LAWRENCE, KANSAS Deb Richard 2006	
Kent State University Varsity "K" Hall of Fame KENT, OHIO Jan Dowling (Golf) 2008	
Kentucky Athletic Hall of Fame LOUISVILLE, KENTUCKY Joseph Franklin Beard 1985	
Lakeland High School Hall of Fame LAKELAND, FLORIDA David Wayne Williams 1993	
Michigan State Athletics Hall of Fame EAST LANSING, MICHIGAN Emily Bastel (Golf) 2012	
Missouri Sports Hall of Fame SPRINGFIELD, MISSOURI David Mark Eckstein (Baseball) 2013	
Motorsports Hall of Fame of America DETROIT, MICHIGAN Edward Glenn Roberts Jr. 1995	
NASCAR Hall of Fame CHARLOTTE, NORTH CAROLINA Edward Glenn Roberts Jr. 2014	
Nashville Aquatic Club Hall of Fame NASHVILLE, TENNESSEE	
Tracy Caulkins Stockwell | William Sawchuk | Ashley Ann Whitney	
National Distance Running Hall of Fame UTICA, NEW YORK	
Martin William Liquori 2006 | Frank Charles Shorter 1998	
National Golf Coaches Association Coaches Hall of Fame CORAL SPRINGS, FLORIDA Mimi Ryan 1986	
National Golf Coaches Association Players Hall of Fame CORAL SPRINGS, FLORIDA E. Page Dunlap-Halpin 2002 | Donna Horton White 1987 | Cheryl Morley Pontious 2000 | Deb Richard 2002	
National Italian American Sports Hall of Fame CHICAGO, ILLINOIS Ricardo Jose Casares (Football) 2010 Martin William Liquori (Track and Field) 1990	
National Jewish Sports Hall of Fame and Museum COMMACK, NEW YORK	
Steven Michael Mesler (Bobsled) 2011 | Albert Leonard Rosen (Baseball) 1998 Dara Grace Torres (Swimming) 2009 | Neal Eugene Walk (Basketball) 2006	
National Sportscasters and Sportswriters Association Hall of Fame SALISBURY, NORTH CAROLINA	
Walter Lanier Barber 1973	
National Track and Field Hall of Fame WASHINGTON HEIGHTS, NEW YORK	
Martin William Liquori 1995 | Frank Charles Shorter 1989	
Ohio Valley Athletic Conference Hall of Fame BRENTWOOD, TENNESSEE	
Donald Denver Fleming (Football) 2007	
Oklahoma Sports Hall of Fame OKLAHOMA CITY, OKLAHOMA Donald Gene Chandler (Football) 2004	
Ontario Aquatic Hall of Fame NORTH YORK, ONTARIO Stephen Clarke 2003 | Donald Alexander Goss 1996 | Jane Louise Kerr Thompson 1996 | William Sawchuk 1991	
Orange County Sports Hall of Fame ANAHEIM, CALIFORNIA Herbert Jackson Youngblood III (Football)	

Palm Beach County Sports Hall of Fame WEST PALM BEACH, FLORIDA

Clarence Reidel Anthony (Football) 2014	John B. Barrow (Football) 1991
James Edward Beaver (Football) 1989	Mark John Calcavecchia (Golf) 2009
Kenneth J. Green (Golf) 2011	Donna Horton White (Golf) 1986
Robert Joseph Murphy Jr. (Golf) 1983	Phillip D. O'Connell (Boxing) 1979
James Arthur Spencer (Football) 2012	Frederick Antwon Taylor (Football) 2010
Harry William Winkler Jr. (Basketball, Track and Team Handball) 1981	

Peoria High School Alumni Association Athletic Hall of Fame   PEORIA, ILLINOIS   Alice Luthy Tym (Golf)

Pro Football Hall of Fame   CANTON, OHIO
Emmitt James Smith III 2010 | Herbert Jackson Youngblood III 2001

St. Louis Football Ring of Fame   ST. LOUIS, MISSOURI   Herbert Jackson Youngblood III 2001

San Diego Chargers Hall of Fame   SAN DIEGO, CALIFORNIA   Wesley Sandy Chandler (Football) 2001

South Florida PGA Hall of Fame   ATLANTIS, FLORIDA
Laurie Hammer 2003 | Robert Joseph Murphy Jr. 2011

Space Coast Sports Hall of Fame   MELBOURNE, FLORIDA
Anthony Cris Collinsworth (Football) 2013 | Calvert Roy Dixon III (Football) 2014 | William John Horschel (Golf) 2014 | Wilber Buddyha Marshall (Football) 2012

Sports Hall of Fame of New Jersey   EAST RUTHERFORD, NEW JERSEY
Martin William Liquori (Track and Field) 1997

State of Tennessee Swimming Hall of Fame   KNOXVILLE, TENNESSEE   Geoffrey Steven Gaberino

Swimming Canada Circle of Excellence Hall of Fame   TORONTO, CANADA
Donald Alexander Goss | Jane Louise Kerr Thompson

Sydney and Theodore Rosenberg Hall of Fame   STANFORD, CALIFORNIA
Lea E. Loveless Maurer (Swimming) 1994

Tennessee Sports Hall of Fame   NASHVILLE, TENNESSEE
Tracy Anne Stockwell Caulkins (Swimming) 1996

Texas Golf Hall of Fame   SAN ANTONIO, TEXAS   George Douglas Sanders 1987

Texas League Hall of Fame   SAN ANTONIO, TEXAS   Allen Leonard Rosen (Football) 2005

Texas Sports Hall of Fame   WACO, TEXAS   Emmitt James Smith III (Football) 2005

United States Marine Corps Sports Hall of Fame   QUANTICO, VIRGINIA
Gregory Stewart Burgess (Swimming) 2010

United States Olympic Hall of Fame   COLORADO SPRINGS, COLORADO
Tracy Caulkins Stockwell (Swimming) | Frank Charles Shorter (Track and Field)

University of Arizona Sports Hall of Fame   TUCSON, ARIZONA
Ashley Tara Tappin-Doussan (Swimming) 2002

University of Florida Athletic Hall of Fame   GAINESVILLE, FLORIDA

Thomas Dean Aaron (Golf)	Douglas Ray Belden Sr. (Football, Basketball, Baseball)
Frederic M. Abbott (Football)	Kerwin Douglas Bell (Football)
Charles Neal Anderson (Football)	Lamar Bruce Bennett Jr. (Football)
Reidel Clarence Anthony (Football)	Otis Boggs (Broadcasting)
Nicole J. Arendt (Tennis)	Scot Eugene Brantley (Football)
Raymond L. Armstrong III (Football)	Keith Alan Brantly (Track and Field)
John B. Barrow (Football)	Alex James Brown (Football)
Thomas Andrew Bean (Golf)	Lomas Brown Jr. (Football)
Joseph Franklin Beard (Golf)	Tami Lee Bruce (Swimming)
James Edward Beaver (Football)	Carl Lowry Brumbaugh (Football)

Dawn Alexis Buth (Tennis)	Samuel Lee Green (Football)
Glenn Scott Cameron (Football)	Rex Daniel Grossman III (Football)
Kevin Louis Carter (Football)	Nicole Lee Haislett Bacher (Swimming)
Ricardo Jose Casares (Football, Basketball)	Malcolm Eugene Hammack (Football)
Tracy Anne Caulkins Stockwell (Swimming)	Phillip Ranson Hancock (Golf)
Mathew J. Cetlinski (Swimming)	Howard Dudley Hart (Golf)
Donald Gene Chandler (Football)	Udonis Johneal Haslem (Basketball)
Wesley Sandy Chandler (Football)	Michael Steward Heath (Swimming)
Hazel Mae Clark-Riley (Track and Field)	Charles Kimberlin Helton (Football)
Hagood Clarke III (Football)	Jill Hetherington Hultquist (Tennis)
Anthony Cris Collinsworth (Football)	Riko Higashio (Golf)
Douglas Michael Corbett (Baseball)	Isaac Jason Hilliard (Football)
Clyde Crabtree (Football, Basketball)	Donna Horton White (Golf)
Jill N. Craybas (Tennis)	Charles Ray Hunsinger (Football)
John Broward Culpepper (Football)	Gelindo Infante (Football)
Karen Davies (Golf)	Randall Belford Jackson (Football)
James Franklin Dempsey (Football)	Tammy Eloise Jackson (Basketball)
Guy Dorell Dennis Jr. (Football)	Willie Bernard Jackson Jr. (Football)
Christian Dean DiMarco (Golf)	John Wilbur James Jr. (Football)
Dwayne Keith Dixon (Football)	Alonzo Johnson (Football)
Christopher Paul Doering (Football)	Ellis Bernard Johnson (Football)
Jimmy DuWayne DuBose (Football)	James Roosevelt Jones (Football)
E. Page Dunlap-Halpin (Golf)	Ronald Lee Jourdan (Track and Field)
Thomas L. Durrance (Football)	Gary J. Keller (Basketball)
David Mark Eckstein (Baseball)	Patrick David Kennedy (Swimming)
George Edmondson Jr. (Cheerleading)	Gary D. Koch (Golf)
David Mark Everett (Track and Field)	James W. Kynes (Football)
Andrea M. Farley (Tennis)	Renee A. Laravie (Swimming)
J. Rex Farrior Sr. (Football, Basketball)	David Erwin Larson (Swimming)
Donald Denver Fleming (Football, Baseball)	Richard Burton Lawless (Football)
Joshua Smith Fogg (Baseball)	David Lamar Little Sr. (Football)
Michelle Freeman (Track and Field)	Buford Eugene Long (Football)
Geoffrey Steven Gaberino (Swimming)	Wilber Buddyia Marshall (Football)
Lawrence Joseph Gagner (Football)	Michael Shane Matthews (Football)
David Lawrence Galloway Sr. (Football)	Lee Colson McGriff (Football)
Joseph Brian Gay (Golf)	Alexander Timothy McKee (Swimming)
Erving Max Goldstein (Football)	Steven N. Melnyk (Golf)
Bobby Joe Green (Football, Track and Field)	Mark Merklein (Tennis)

Alberto Eugenio Mestre-Sosa (Swimming)	Emmitt James Smith III (Football)
DeLisha Milton-Jones (Basketball)	William Lawrence Smith (Football)
Dennis Alan Mitchell (Track and Field)	Christopher Snode (Diving)
Heather Mitts Feeley (Soccer)	Steven Orr Spurrier (Football)
Nathaniel Moore (Football)	Shaun Stafford Beckish (Tennis)
Jeffrey Alan Morrison (Tennis)	Robert Michael Stanley (Baseball)
Alvin Dennis Murphy (Football)	Gudula Staub (Volleyball)
Robert Joseph Murphy Jr. (Golf)	Anne Rochelle Steely Ramirez (Track and Field)
Ricky Rennard Nattiel (Football)	Haywood Cooper Sullivan (Football, Baseball)
Anthony Conrad Nesty (Swimming)	John Richard Symank (Football)
Robert D. Newton (Football, Basketball)	Steven Olson Tannen (Football)
Andrew S. North (Golf)	Frederick Antwon Taylor (Football)
Phillip D. O'Connell (Boxing)	Dara Grace Torres (Swimming)
Jason Brian Odom (Football)	Allen Raymond Trammel Jr. (Football)
Louis Oliver III (Football)	Richard Earl Trapp (Football)
Ralph Ortega (Football)	Alice Luthy Tym (Tennis)
Murriel Page (Basketball)	Neal Eugene Walk (Basketball)
Bernard Paul Parrish (Football, Baseball)	Mary Abigail Wambach (Soccer)
Porter Michael Peterson (Football)	Mary Alice Wayte Bradburne (Swimming)
Carlos R. Proctor (Boxing)	Stephen Bradley Wilkerson (Baseball)
David William Ragan Jr. (Golf)	David Wayne Williams (Football)
Kiewan Jevar Ratliff (Football)	Jarvis Eric Williams Sr. (Football)
Lisa Raymond (Tennis)	John L. Williams (Football)
Thomas Johnson Reaves (Football)	Dale Jerome Willis (Baseball)
Errict Undra Rhett (Football)	Sophia L. Witherspoon (Basketball)
Deb Richard (Golf)	Lawrence D. Wright III (Football)
Huey L. Richardson Jr. (Football)	Daniel Carl Wuerffel (Football)
Colleen Rosensteel (Track and Field)	James Kelley Yarbrough (Football)
James W. Rountree (Football)	Herbert Jackson Youngblood III (Football)
George Douglas Sanders (Golf)	David López-Zubero (Swimming)
Daniel David Sikes Jr. (Golf)	Martin López-Zubero (Swimming)
John Marlin Simpson (Football)	

University of Texas Women's Hall of Honor AUSTIN, TEXAS   Whitney Lynn Hedgepeth (Swimming) 2007
UTC Athletics Hall of Fame CHATTANOOGA, TENNESSEE   Alice Luthy Tym (Golf) 2011
Virginia Sports Hall of Fame PORTSMOUTH, VIRGINIA   Whitney Lynn Hedgepeth (Swimming) 2010
Wisconsin Golf Hall of Fame WEST ALLIS, WISCONSIN   Andrew Steward North 1990
WRUF Hall of Fame GAINESVILLE, FLORIDA   Walter Lanier Barber | Otis Boggs

BIBLIOGRAPHY

Aaseng, Nathan. *African-American Athletes.* New York, NY: Facts On File, Inc., 2003.

Alexander, Ruth Hammack and Wesch, Paula D. *Lady Gators—Simply the Best.* Gainesville, FL: Klane Publishing, 1981.

Barkow, Al. *The History of the PGA Tour.* New York, NY: Doubleday, 1989.

Barnhart, Tony. *Southern Fried Football: The History, Passion, and Glory of the Great Southern Game.* Chicago, IL: Triumph Books, 2000.

Boxerman, Burton A. and Boxerman, Benita W. *Jews and Baseball: Volume 2 The Post-Greenberg Years, 1949–2008.* Jefferson, NC: McFarland & Co., Inc., 2009.

Carlson, Norm. *University of Florida Football Vault: The History of the Florida Gators.* Atlanta, GA: Whitman Publishing, LLC, 2007.

Clarkson, Julian Derieux. *Let No Man Put Asunder.* Fort Myers, FL: Julian D. Clarkson, 1968.

Cobb, Arthur E. *Go Gators! Official History, University of Florida Football, 1889–1966.* Pensacola, FL: Sunshine Publishing Company, 1967.

Cohen, Marty. *Gator Tales: Stories, Stats and Stuff About Florida Football.* Wichita, KS: The Wichita Eagle and Beacon Publishing Co., 1995.

Dooley, Pat. *Game of My Life Florida: Memorable Stories of Gators Football.* Champaign, IL: Sports Publishing L.L.C., 2007.

Edelstein, Robert. *NASCAR Legends: Memorable Men, Moments, and Machines in Racing History.* New York, NY: The Overlook Press, 2011.

Editors of ESPN. *College Basketball Encyclopedia: The Complete History of the Men's Game.* New York, NY: ESPN Books, 2009.

Edwards, Bob. *Fridays with Red: A Radio Friendship.* New York, NY: Simon & Schuster, 1993.

Ernsberger Jr., Richard. *Bragging Rights: A Season Inside the SEC, Football's Toughest Conference.* New York, NY: M. Evans and Company, Inc., 2000.

Golenbock, Peter. *Go Gators!: An Oral History of Florida's Pursuit of Gridiron Glory.* Danbury, CT: Legends Publishing Company, LLC, 2002.

Hairston, Jack. *Tales from the Gator Swamp: A Collection of the Greatest Gator Stories Ever Told.* Champaign, IL: Sports Publishing, L.L.C., 2002.

Horrigan, Joe, ed. *The Pro Football Hall of Fame 50th Anniversary Book: Where Greatness Lives*. New York, NY: Grand Central Publishing, 2012.

Hunt, Chris, ed. *The Complete Book of Soccer*. Buffalo, NY: Firefly Books Ltd., 2012.

James, Craig. *Game Day: A Rollicking Journey to the Heart of College Football*. Hoboken, NJ: John Wiley & Sons, Inc., 2009.

Jones, James P. and McCarthy, Kevin M. *The Gators and the Seminoles: Honor, Guts and Glory*. Gainesville, FL: Maupin House, 1993.

Kerasotis, Peter. *Stadium Stories: Florida Gators*. Guilford, CT: The Globe Pequot Press, 2005.

Koss, Bill. *Pond Birds: Gator Basketball—the Whole Story from the Inside*. Gainesville, FL: Fast Break Press, 1996.

Lahman, Sean. *The Pro Football Historical Abstract: A Hardcore Fan's Guide to All-time Player Rankings*. Guilford, CT: Lyons Press, 2008.

Layden, Joseph. *Women in Sports: The Complete Book on the World's Greatest Female Athletes*. Los Angeles, CA: General Publishing Group, 1997.

Lea, Bud. *Magnificent Seven: The Championship Games that Built the Lombardi Dynasty*. Chicago, IL: Triumph Books, 2002.

Light, Jonathan Fraser. *The Cultural Encyclopedia of Baseball*. Jefferson, NC: McFarland & Company, Inc., 1997.

Martin, Buddy. *The Boys from Old Florida: Inside Gator Nation*. Champaign, IL: Sports Publishing, L.L.C., 2006.

Martin, Buddy. *Down Where the Old Gators Play: How Steve Spurrier Brought Glory Home to Florida Football*. Dubuque, IA: Kendall/Hunt Publishing Company, 1995.

Martin, Buddy. *Urban's Way: Urban Meyer, the Florida Gators, and His Plan to Win*. New York, NY: St. Martin's Press, 2008.

McCambridge, Michael, ed. *Southeastern Conference Football Encyclopedia: The Complete History*. New York, NY: ESPN Books, 2009.

McCarthy, Kevin. *Baseball in Florida*. Sarasota, FL: Pineapple Press, Inc., 1996.

McCarthy, Kevin. *Fightin' Gators: A History of University of Florida Football*. Charleston, SC: Arcadia Publishing, 2000.

McCarthy, Kevin and Laurie, Murray D. *Guide to the University of Florida and Gainesville*. Sarasota, FL: Pineapple Press, Inc., 1997.

McCarthy, Kevin. *Historic Photos of University of Florida Football.* Nashville, TN: Turner Publishing Company, 2009.

McEwan, Tom. *The Gators: A Story of Florida Football.* Huntsville, AL: The Strode Publishers, 1974.

McGinn, Bob. *The Ultimate Super Bowl Book.* Minneapolis, MN: MVP Books, 2009.

Miller, Ernestine Gichner. *Making Her Mark: Firsts and Milestones in Women's Sports.* Chicago, IL: Contemporary Books, 2002.

Miller, Jeff. *Sunshine Shootouts: The Greatest Games Between Florida-Florida State, Florida State-Miami, Miami-Florida.* Atlanta, GA: Longstreet Press, 1992.

Patoski, Joe Nick. *The Dallas Cowboys: The Outrageous History of the Biggest, Loudest, Most Hated, Best Loved Football Team in America.* New York, NY: Little, Brown and Company, 2012.

Pleasants, Julian M. *Gator Tales: An Oral History of the University of Florida.* Gainesville, FL: University of Florida, 2006.

Pluto, Terry. *When All the World was Browns Town: Cleveland Browns and the Championship Season of '64.* New York, NY: Simon & Schuster, 1997.

Proctor, Samuel and Langley, Wright. *Gator History: A Pictorial History of the University of Florida.* Gainesville, FL: South Star Publishing Company, 1986.

Rajtar, Steve. *A Guide to Historic Gainesville.* Charleston, SC: The History Press, 2007.

Rajtar, Steve. *Historic Photos of Gainesville.* Nashville, TN: Turner Publishing Company, 2008.

Rajtar, Steve. *Historic Photos of the University of Florida.* Nashville, TN: Turner Publishing Company, 2009.

Schlabach, Mark. *What It Means to Be a Gator.* Chicago, IL: Triumph Books, 2008.

Scott, Richard. *SEC Football: 75 Years of Pride and Passion.* Minneapolis, MN: Voyageur Press, 2008.

Sharpe, Wilton. *Gators Glory: Great Eras in Florida Football.* Nashville, TN: Cumberland House, 2007.

Shatzkin, Mike, ed. *The Ballplayers.* New York, NY: Arbor House, 1990.

Shorter, Frank and Bloom, Marc. *Olympic Gold: A Runner's Life and Times.* Boston, MA: Houghton Mifflin Company, 1984.

Slater, Robert. *Great Jews in Sports.* Middle Village, NY: Jonathan David Publishers, Inc., 1983.

Smith, Derek. *Glory Yards.* Nashville, TN: Rutledge Hill Press, 1993.

Smith, Emmitt, and Delsohn, Steve. *The Emmitt Zone.* New York, NY: Crown Publishers, Inc., 1994.

Snook, Jeff. *Year of the Gator: Florida's 1993 SEC Championship Season.* Nashville, TN: Rutledge Hill Press, 1994.

Spurrier, Steve. *It's Always too Soon to Quit: The Steve Spurrier Story, as Told to Mel Larson.* Grand Rapids, MI: Zondervan Publishing House, 1968.

Spurrier, Steve and Carlson, Norm. *Gators: The Inside Story of Florida's First SEC Title.* Orlando, FL: Tribune Publishing, 1992.

Tebow, Tim and Whitaker, Nathan. *Through My Eyes.* New York, NY: HarperCollins, 2011.

Wallechinsky, David and Loucky, Jaime. *The Complete Book of the Olympics.* London, UK: Aurum Press Ltd., 2008.

Walsh, Christopher J. *Who's #1? 100-Plus Years of Controversial National Champions in College Football.* Lanham, MD: Taylor Trade Publishing, 2007.

Wells, Lawrence, Ed. *Football Powers of the South.* Oxford, MS: Sports Yearbook Company, 1983.

Whittingham, Richard. *Rites of Autumn: The Story of College Football.* New York, NY: The Free Press, 2001.

Youngblood, Jack and Engel, Joel. *Blood.* Chicago, IL: Contemporary Books, 1988.

www.baseball-almanac.com   Professional baseball players.

www.basketball.usbasket.com   Women's professional basketball.

www.commons.wikimedia.org   Photos posted by various photographers.

www.databasefootball.com   College football players who went pro.

www.databasegolf.com   Men's professional golfers.

www.espnmediazone.com   Professional football player biographies.

www.fanbase.com   Rosters for professional football, basketball, and baseball teams, Gator football teams.

www.flickr.com   Photos posted by various photographers.

www.floridamemory.com   Photos from the State of Florida Archives.

www.gatorsports.com   News of Gator athletes.

www.gatorzone.com Official Gator media guides for each sport, rosters, biographies, statistics, and news.

www.loc.gov/pictures Photos from the National Archives.

www.lpga.com Womens' professional golfers.

www.ncaa.com College sports championships.

www.oldestlivingprofootball.com Old professional football players.

www.pgatour.com Men's professional golfers.

www.photobucket.com Photos posted by various people.

www.profootballresearchers.org Early professional football players.

www.rci.rutgers.edu Early professional football team rosters.

www.sports-reference.com Statistics and rosters for professional football, baseball, and basketball and Olympics.

www.tennisexplorer.com Professional tennis players.

www.ufdc.ufl.edu Photos from the University of Florida archives.

www.usabasketball.com Women's professional basketball.

Plus websites for each of the professional leagues and teams, the halls of fame, and many of the individual athletes.

ABOUT THE PHOTOGRAPHS

These notes, listed by page number, provide information about the photographs included in this book. The photos come from a variety of sources: the Florida Photographic Collection pursuit to Florida Statute §257.35 (FPC), the University of Florida Archives (UFA), the Library of Congress (LOC), the athletes themselves, the photographers, or those who own the rights to the photos, or have been made available by them by posting on internet sites including Photobucket (PB), Flicker (FL), and Wikimedia Commons (WC).

The owner of the rights to each photo herein has either made it available for use in this type of publication, as is or as it may be adapted, either without limitation (often as a matter being placed in the public domain) or under a license, the details of which may be found on the respective websites: Creative Commons Attribution 2.5 Generic (2.5), Creative Commons Attribution-Share Alike 2.0 (2.0), Creative Commons Attribution-Share Alike 3.0 (3.0), or GNU Free Documentation License, Version 1.2 (1.2). The provisions of the licenses are hereby incorporated herein by reference. The photos have not been modified other than cropping to fit the subject into the size and shape.

PAGE	SUBJECT	SOURCE (LICENSE)	PHOTOGRAPHER AND/OR LICENSOR (IF KNOWN)
INTRODUCTION			
11	Ben Hill Griffin Stadium	FL (2.0)	Douglas Green
13	O'Connell Center	WC (2.0)	Douglas Green
15	James G. Pressly Stadium	WC	Porsche997SBS
15	Bostic Golf Course	WC (3.0)	Ebyabe
16	Ring Tennis Complex	WC	Porsche997SBS
17	Alfred A. McKethan Stadium	FL (2.0)	arctic_whirlwind
18	Katie Seashole Pressly Stadium	WC	Ocdmuch
FOOTBALL			
21	Swamp Sign	WC	Hatmatbbat
24	1902 Football Team	UFA	
25	1904 Postcard	FPC	
26	1907 Football Team	UFA	
27	Florida vs. Riverside A.C.	UFA	

PAGE	SUBJECT	SOURCE (LICENSE)	PHOTOGRAPHER AND/OR LICENSOR (IF KNOWN)
28	G.E. Pyle	WC	
30	James Van Fleet	FPC	
30	Tom Sebring	WC	
31	Dennis K. Stanley	UFA	
32	1939 Football Team	UFA	
32	Thomas Lieb	UFA	
33	Haywood Sullivan	UFA	
34	Bob Woodruff	UFA	
36	Governors Cup	FPC	
37	Ray Graves	UFA	
38	Robert Cade	UFA	
39	Doug Dickey	PB	DMEvans photos
41	Charley Pell	PB	DMEvans photos
42	Galen Hall	PB	DMEvans photos
44	Steve Spurrier	WC (3.0)	Zeng8r
47	Ron Zook	PF	JSeverin0
48	Urban Meyer	WC (3.0)	Harrison Diamond
50	Will Muschamp	FL	Dennis Adair
58	Neal Anderson	UFA	
58	Reidel Anthony	PB	DMEvans photos
59	Trace Armstrong	PB	Stephen Warnock
60	John Barrow	PB	DMEvans photos
61	Kerwin Bell	PB	DMEvans photos
62	Ahmad Black	FL	Dennis Adair
63	Scot Brantley	UFA	
65	Gator Growl	FL (2.0)	Chris Bohn
66	Lomas Brown	FL	United Way for Southeastern Michigan
67	Carl Brumbaugh	PB	DMEvans photos
68	Andre Caldwell	WC (3.0)	Jeffrey Beall
68	Reche Caldwell	PB	numba2393
70	Kevin Carter	FL	M.Shawn Hennessy
71	Rick Casares	PB	DMEvans photos
72	Don Chandler	OSHOF	Oklahoma Sports Hall of Fame
73	Wes Chandler	PB	DMEvans photos
74	Auburn War Eagle	LOC	Carol M. Highsmith

About the Photographs 427

PAGE	SUBJECT	SOURCE (LICENSE)	PHOTOGRAPHER AND/OR LICENSOR (IF KNOWN)
76	Riley Cooper	WC (3.0)	Matthew Straubmuller
77	Channing Crowder	WC (3.0)	
78	Brad Culpepper	PB	DMEvans photos
78	Andra Davis	WC (3.0)	Jeffrey Beall
79	Frank Dempsey	PB	DMEvans photos
81	Chris Doering	PB	DMEvans photos
81	Jimmy DuBose	PB	DMEvans photos
83	Gator Walk	FL (2.0)	Photo-gator
83	Don Fleming	OVACHOF	Ohio Valley Athletic Conf. Hall of Fame
84	Derrick Gaffney	PB	DMEvans photos
85	Jabar Gaffney	WC (2.0)	Keith Allison
86	Chan Gailey	PB	imageslibrary
88	Earnest Graham	PB	newsteenfan 2007
91	Jacquez Green	PB	motleygator
92	Rex Grossman	WC	Keith Allison
94	Albert and Alberta	WC	Tampa Gator
95	Lorenzo Hampton	UFA	
96	Derrick Harvey	WC (3.0)	
97	Percy Harvin	WC (2.0)	Mike Morbeck
98	Kim Helton	WC	University of Houston
98	Aaron Hernandez	WC (2.0)	Jack Newton
99	Reynaldo Hill	PB	numba2393
100	Ike Hilliard	PB	roundpuff
100	Chuck Hunsinger	PB	DMEvans photos
101	Work 'em Silly	FL (2.0)	Bryan McDonald
103	Lindy Infante	UFA	
104	Chad Jackson	PB	justbeingdodds
104	Darrell Jackson	WC (2.0)	John Pavliga
105	Randy Jackson	FPC	Associated Press
105	Taylor Jacobs	PB	DMEvans photos
106	Willie Jackson Sr.	UFA	
108	Doug Johnson	PB	nfl Mitchell
109	Todd Johnson	Todd Johnson	Todd Johnson
110	James Jones	PB	DMEvans photos

PAGE	SUBJECT	SOURCE (LICENSE)	PHOTOGRAPHER AND/OR LICENSOR (IF KNOWN)
111	Jevon Kearse	WC	Sgt. Gaelen Lowers
112	Crawford Ker	Crawford Ker	
112	Erron Kinney	PB	captainsexy
113	Burton Lawless	PB	DMEvans photos
114	Terry LeCount	UFA	
116	Buford Long	PB	DMEvans photos
116	Marquand Manuel	WC (2.0)	James Healy
117	Wilber Marshall	UFA	
118	Shane Matthews	PB	cbear4610
119	Tony McCoy	PB	DMEvans photos
120	Bobby McCray	PB	gomblin305
120	Ray McDonald	PB	Ambivalent1
121	Reggie McGrew	PB	DMEvans photos
121	Travis McGriff	PB	DMEvans photos
122	Otis Boggs	UFA	
124	Ernie Mills	FL	Jacksonville University
126	Jeff Mitchell	PB	DMEvans photos
126	Alonzo Mitz	PB	DMEvans photos
127	Nat Moore	PB	DMEvans photos
128	Jarvis Moss	WC (2.0)	Mstern3 at en.wikipedia
129	Mike Mularkey	WC	Seaman Rob Alward
129	Louis Murphy	WC (3.0)	Jeffrey Beall
132	Godfrey Myles	PB	timcodaville
133	Ricky Nattiel	PB	milehimojoe
133	David Nelson	WC (3.0)	Denverjeffrey
134	Reggie Nelson	WC (2.0)	Craig O'Neal
135	Cam Newton	WC	Pantherfan11
135	Tim Newton	PB	DMEvans photos
136	Jason Odom	PB	thegeniustpa
137	Louis Oliver	PB	DMEvans photos
138	Bernie Parrish	PB	montblanc67
140	Mike Peterson	PB	tazfreak89
140	Zach Piller	Zach Piller	
141	Keiwan Ratliff	PB	devils13 07
142	Pouncey Twins	FL	Dennis Adair

About the Photographs

PAGE	SUBJECT	SOURCE (LICENSE)	PHOTOGRAPHER AND/OR LICENSOR (IF KNOWN)
144	John Reaves	FPC	United Press International
145	Errict Rhett	PB	DMEvans photos
146	Ian Scott	PB	DMEvans photos
147	Coaches' Trophy	PB	nmw0917
148	Lito Sheppard	WC	Monica Halman, USN
149	Brandon Siler	WC (3.0)	Jeffrey Beall
150	Jackie Simpson	PB	DMEvans photos
151	Emmitt Smith	FPC	Mark T. Foley
153	Brandon Spikes	FL	Dennis Adair
156	Steve Spurrier	UFA	
158	Max Starks	WC	Theo Wilkerson, USN
160	Steve Tannen	PB	DMEvans photos
161	Fred Taylor	WC	JollyOldStNick08
162	Travis Taylor	PB	numba2393
162	Tim Tebow	WC (3.0)	Jeffrey Beall
165	Marcus Thomas	WC (3.0)	Jeffrey Beall
166	Ben Troupe	PB	motleygator
167	Aaron Walker	PB	gogators200405
168	Gerard Warren	WC (2.0)	Michael Dorausch
169	Dale Waters	UFA	
170	Fred Weary	PB	DMEvans photos
171	Elijah Williams	PB	FLChams
173	Jarvis Williams	PB	bretbaxley
189	Mr. Two Bits	FL	flattop341
BASEBALL AND SOFTBALL			
191	1914 Baseball Team	FPC	
195	Rex Farrior	UFA	
195	Ben Clemons	UFA	
196	Bob Pittman	UFA	
197	Dave Fuller	UFA	
198	Andy Lopez	WC	D. Myles Cullen
200	Kevin O'Sullivan	FL	Dennis Adair
203	Ross Baumgarten	PB	Ross Baumgarten/killingdream
205	Johnny Burnett	FL	Courtesy of the Boston Public Library, Leslie Jones Collection
205	Tiny Chaplain	PB	brettw1971

PAGE	SUBJECT	SOURCE (LICENSE)	PHOTOGRAPHER AND/OR LICENSOR (IF KNOWN)
207	David Eckstein	WC (3.0)	Djh57
208	Dave Eiland	WC (2.0)	Keith Allison
209	Mark Ellis	WC (2.0)	Keith Allison
209	Josh Fogg	WC (2.0)	jkonrath
210	Red Barber	FPC	
212	Matt LaPorta	WC (2.0)	jiazi
213	Steve Lombardozzi	PB	imageslibrary
214	Nick Maronde	FL	Dennis Adair
215	Rob Murphy	Rob Murphy	Boston Red Sox 1989
216	Darren O'Day	WC (2.0)	Keith Allison
218	Tim Olson	PB	DBackBrat22
221	Ryan Raburn	WC (2.0)	Keith Allison
222	Bill Ramsey	PB	jcrmoon42
222	Lance Richbourg	PB	Dto7
224	Al Rosen	WC	Bowman Gum
226	David Ross	WC (2.0)	LWY
227	Russ Scarritt	PB	gatorcollector
228	Ryan Shealy	WC (2.0)	tracie7779
228	Mike Stanley	PB	lc481
229	Haywood Sullivan	PB	DMEvans photos
231	Robby Thompson	PB	ronfromfresno
232	Brad Wilkerson	WC (2.0)	UCinternational
234	Mike Zunino	FL	Dennis Adair
237	Tim Walton	PB	GreatToBeAGator
240	Kelsey Bruder	PB	GreatToBeAGator
242	Kristen Butler	FL (2.0)	navy.outreach
243	Francesca Enea	PB	GreatToBeAGator
244	Aja Paculba	PB	GreatToBeAGator
BASKETBALL			
248	Ben Clemons	UFA	
249	Sam McAllister	UFA	
250	Norm Sloan	UFA	
251	Don DeVoe	PB	gogators200405
252	Lon Kruger	PB	BigGinDaHouse
253	Billy Donovan	FL	Dennis Adair

About the Photographs

PAGE	SUBJECT	SOURCE (LICENSE)	PHOTOGRAPHER AND/OR LICENSOR (IF KNOWN)
258	Bradley Beal	FL (2.0)	Keith Allison
259	Matt Bonner	WC (3.0)	Zereshk
260	Corey Brewer	WC (2.0)	Frog Brother
260	Nick Calathes	WC (2.0)	Klearchos Kapoutsis
261	Ben Davis	PB	thevirtualgaragesale
262	Andrew DeClerq	FL	Dennis Adair
263	Taurean Green	FL	Dennis Adair
264	Orien Greene	WC (2.0)	Jeff Egnaczyk
266	Udonis Haslem	WC (2.0)	Keith Allison
267	Al Horford	WC (3.0)	Chris Nelson
268	David Lee	WC (2.0)	Keith Allison
269	Vernon Macklin	WC (2.0)	Keith Alliso
270	Vernon Maxwell	PB	nbacardDOThat
271	Mike Miller	WC (3.0)	
273	Joakim Noah	WC (2.0)	Keith Allison
273	Chandler Parsons	WC (2.0)	Norma Gonzalez
274	Chris Richard	FL	Dennis Adair
275	Anthony Roberson	PB	motleygator
275	Dwayne Schintzius	FL	Dennis Adair
276	Marreese Speights	WC (2.0)	Keith Allison
276	Neal Walk	PB	gogators200405
278	James White	WC (3.0)	Keith Allison
279	Jason Williams	WC (2.0)	Keith Allison
280	Matt Walsh	FL	Dennis Adair
280	Erik Murphy	FL	Dennis Adair
282	Carol Ross	PB	theyreplayingbasketball
283	Carolyn Peck	FL (2.0)	Cheryl Coward
283	Amanda Butler	FL	Dennis Adair
289	Brandi McCain	Brandi McCain	
290	DeLisha Milton-Jones	WC	Gerry J. Gilmore
292	Murriel Page	PB	tguest5
292	Bridget Pettis	PB	theyreplayingbasketball
GOLF			
298	Buddy Alexander	PB	KGA 1908

PAGE	SUBJECT	SOURCE (LICENSE)	PHOTOGRAPHER AND/OR LICENSOR (IF KNOWN)
302	Andy Bean	PB (2.0)	Highdraw
303	Bill Britton	FL	Michael Moretti
304	Mark Calcavecchia	WC (2.0)	Steven Newton
305	Chris Couch	PB	jimmyv99
305	Bubba Dickerson	FL (2.0)	Keith Allison
306	Chris DiMarco	PB	koerkev
307	Matt Every	WC (1.2)	Orrios
308	Brian Gay	PB	jbx35
309	Ken Green	FL (2.0)	Keith Allison
311	Gary Koch	FL (2.0)	Keith Allison
312	Steve Melnyk	FPC	Karl E. Holland
313	Bob Murphy	Bob Murphy	Rob Valashinas, Double RL Enterprises
314	Andy North	FL (2.0)	UW Health
315	Doug Sanders	FL	Richard Wayne
317	Camilo Villegas	WC (2.0)	Steven Newton
322	Sandra Gal	WC (3.0)	Wojciech Migda
TENNIS			
328	Bryan Shelton	WC (2.5)	Jamie Howell
331	Ryan Sweeting	WC (2.0)	Kate
331	Jesse Levine	WC (2.0)	Robbie Mendelson
336	Jill Craybas	WC	Markabq
338	Lisa Raymond	WC (2.0)	paddynapper
SOCCER			
341	Becky Burleigh	FL	Dennis Adair
346	Heather Mitts	WC	Johnmaxmena2
348	Abby Wambach	WC (3.0)	Pat Gunn
349	Kathryn Williamson	WC (3.0)	Hmlarson
MARTIAL ARTS			
351	Thaddeus Bullard	WC (2.0)	Matt Brink
352	Phillip O'Connell	FPC	Associated Press
353	Carlos Proctor	UFA	
MASCAR			
355	Fireball Roberts	FPC	
367	Jimmy Carnes	FL	Dennis Adair

About the Photographs

PAGE	SUBJECT	SOURCE (LICENSE)	PHOTOGRAPHER AND/OR LICENSOR (IF KNOWN)
374	Elizabeth Beisel	FL	J.D. Lasica
375	Caroline Burckle	PB	Chris Chimes
376	Greg Burgess	FL	Daniel Wetzel
376	Tracy Caulkins	WC (3.0)	Marcel Antonisse
379	Conor Dwyer	FL	J.D. Lasica
381	Nicole Haislett	Nicole Haislett	Nicole Haislett/Debbie Townshend
384	Ryan Lochte	FL (2.0)	Toby and Tai Shan
386	Tim McKee	PB	knoonepics
387	Anthony Nesty	FL	Andy Ringgold
388	Ashley Tappin	PB (2.0)	Scott Goldblatt
389	Dara Torres	WC (2.0)	Bryan Allison
390	Darian Townsend	FL (2.0)	morshus
391	Dana Vollmer	WC (2.0)	Matt Churchill
397	Will Claye	WC (1.2)	Erik van Leeuwen
398	Kerron Clement	WC (2.5)	Eckhard Pecher
398	Jeff Demps	PB	mattyboi4crunkinit
400	Tony McQuay	WC (2.0)	Neil Thompson
402	Frank Shorter	WC (3.0)	Dpbush
403	Christian Taylor	WC (1.2)	Erik van Leeuwen
403	Bernard Williams	WC (1.2)	Erik van Leeuwen
404	Novlene Williams	WC (1.2)	Erik van Leeuwen
405	Steve Mesler	FL (2.0)	familymwr
406	Andrew Weaver	WC (3.0)	Jamie53x12
AUTHORS			
446	Steve & Gayle Rajtar	The Authors	The Authors

INDEX

A

Aaron, Thomas Dean, 301
Abdul-Jabbar, Kareem, 277
Adams, Bud, 172
Albert the Alligator, 94
Alexander, Buddy, 298
Alexander, Jillian, 335
Alfred A. McKethan Stadium at Perry Field, 16–17
"All-American," 9–10
Allen, Mel, 211
all-star teams
    baseball (table), 202
    football (table), 56
    men's basketball (table), 257
    selections, 10
    women's basketball (table), 286
Alvarez, Carlos, 10, 19, 38, 39, 144
Amabile, John C., 405
Anderson, Charles Neal, 57–58, 71, 95, 112, 173, 181
Andrews, Theresa, 372–373
Anthony, Reidel Clarence, 58, 99
Arendt, Nicole J., 335
Armstrong, Aaron Nigel, 396
Armstrong, Duncan John D'Arcy, 373
Armstrong, Raymond L. "Trace," 59
Arnold, Joe, 197–198
Arnsparger, Bill, 159
athlete biographies
    baseball, 203–234
    cycling, 406
    football, 57–189
    martial arts, 351–354
    men's basketball, 258–280
    men's golf, 301–318
    men's tennis, 330–331
    softball, 240–245
    swimming and diving, 372–396
    track and field, 396–404
    women's basketball, 287–294
    women's golf, 322–325
    women's soccer, 344–349
    women's tennis, 335–339
Atkinson, J.L., 367
Auburn's eagle, 74
Austin, Jim, 353
authors, contacting the, vii

B

Bacheler, Jack, 358
Bachman, Charlie, 169
Bachman Jr., Charles W., 30–31
Bagwell, Archie, 296
Ball, Catie, 358, 365, 373
Barber, Miller, 316
Barber, Walter Lanier "Red," 210–211
Barnes, Bobby, 197
Barrow, John B., 59–60
Bartlett, Tommy, 250
baseball
    2013 Division I college home attendance leaders (table), 193
    athlete biographies, 203–234
    early coaches, 194–196
    Florida athletes who went into professional (tables), 235–236
    head coaching records (table), 201
    major league players by school (table), 202
    nicknames of Gators, 233
    Olympic sports, 371
    overview, 191
    professional teams where Gators have gone (table), 217
    season, 2
    softball. See softball
    Southeastern Conference championships (table), 194
    stadiums in Southeastern Conference, 17–18
    top 30 all-time college teams (table), 192–193
basketball, men's
    arenas in Southeastern Conference, 13–14
    athlete biographies, 258–280
    early coaches, 247–249
    Florida coaching records (table), 255
    Florida in NCAA Tournament (table), 256
    Florida in postseason NIT (table), 257
    Florida non-medal winners (table), 412
    Lon Kruger, Billy Donovan eras, 252–254
    NCAA championships (table), 257
    nicknames of Gators players and coaches, 263
    Norm Sloan eras, 250–252
    Olympic sports, 370–371
    our Florida all-stars (table), 257
    overview, 247
    season, 2–3
    SEC teams, championships (tables), 255–256
    teams Gators have played for (table), 272
basketball, women's
    arenas in Southeastern Conference, 13–14
    athlete biographies, 287–294
    early years, 281–282
    Florida coaching records (table), 284
    Florida in NCAA Tournament (table), 285

434

Florida in postseason NIT (table), 286
NCAA championships (table), 286
Olympic sports, 370–371
our Florida all-stars (table), 286
overview, 247
Ross, Peck, and Butler eras, 282–284
season, 2–3
SEC teams, championships (tables), 284–285
teams Gators have played for (table), 290
Bates, Patrick Alfred, 301
Baumgarten, Ross, 203
Beal, Bradley Emmanuel, 258
Bean, Thomas Andrew "Andy," 302
Beard, Joseph Franklin, 302–303
Beard, Percy, 18
Beckish, Shuan Stafford, 339
Beeland, Steve, 328, 332
Beisel, Elizabeth Lyon, 374–375
Bell, Kerwin Douglas, 42, 60–61, 112, 125, 132
Ben Hill Griffin Stadium at Florida Field, 11, 83, 101
Bennett Jr., Lamar Bruce, 61–62
Bergman, Jay, 197
bibliography, 420–424
biographies. *See* athlete biographies
Biondi, Matt, 373
Bishop, Butler, 297–298
Black, Ahmad, 62
Blackburn, Woody T., 303
Blaine, Dan, 89
Blair, David, 330
Blake, James, 330
Bleier, Rocky, 161
Blevins, Lynn, 298
Bo Gator Club, 27
bobsledding, Olympic sports, 372, 405–406
Bochette III, Liston, 405
Boggs, Otis, 101, 122–123
Bollegraf, Manon, 335
Bonner, Matthew Robert, 258–259
Bonner, Quientella, 281
Booth, Dick, 397
Booth, Melanie Lynn, 342
Bosh, Chris, 266
Bostick, Mark, 15
Bostick Golf Course, 15
bowls
  all-time Florida game records (table), 54–55
  Florida history at (table), 52–54
  top 20 schools by bowl wins (table), 55–56
boxing, 350
Bracken, Andrew, 297
Bradburne, Mary Alice Wayte, 393
Brandi, Andres V. "Andy," 332–333
Brantley, John, 134
Brantley, Scot Eugene, 40, 62–63
Brantley III, John, 39

Branyan, Russell, 212
Brewer, Corey Wayne, 259–260
Brewer, Rodney Lee, 203
Bridges, M. O., 25
Brinson, Lawrence Sylvesta, 63
Britton, William Timothy, 303
Bromley, Phil, 112
Brown, Alex James, 63–64
Brown, Joseph Barry, 64
Brown, Lomas, 112
Brown, Mack, 50
Brown Jr., Lomas, 64, 66
Bruder, Kelsey, 240–241
Brumbaugh, Carl Lowry, 31, 66–67
Bryan, Dr. Robert, 43, 157
Bryant, Bear, 36
Bullard, Thaddeus Michael, 351–352
Burckle, Caroline, 375
Burgess, Gregory Stewart, 375–376
Burke, John Chandler, 204
Burleigh, Becky, 341
Burnett, John Henderson, 204–205
Buser, Al L., 29
Bush, Megan, 241–242
Bush, President George H.W., 277
Buth, Dawn Alexis, 333, 336
Butler, Amanda, 283–284
Butler, Kristen, 242–243

C

Cade, Dr. Robert, 37, 38
Calamore, Pete, 101
Calathes, Nicholas William, 260–261
Calcavecchia, Mark John, 304
Caldwell, Andre Jerome "Bubba," 67–68
Caldwell Jr., Donald Reche, 68–69
Cameron, Glenn Scott, 69
Cameron, Lindsey, 243
Capital One Cup, 5–6
Carlisle, Cooper Morrison, 69–70
Carnes, Jimmy, 367, 368
Carter, Kevin Louis, 70
Casares, Ricardo "Rick" Jose, 34, 71
Cason, Cy, 353
Castro, Rafael Antonio Vidal, 390
Caulkins, Tracy, 376–377
Cetlinski, Matthew J., 377
Chafin, Moses "M.B.," 327
Chandler, Donald Gene, 71–72
Chandler, Jeffrey Robin, 72–73
Chandler, Wesley Sandy "Wes," 40, 73–74, 74
Chaplin, James "Tiny" Bailey, 205
Chapman, Kevin Allen, 205–206
Charles, Orson, 147
Charles R. and Nancy V. Perry Indoor Facility, 15
Cherry, Spurgeon, 249
Cherry-Mitchell, Damu, 401

Cioffi, Halle, 333
Clarke, Stephen, 377–378
Clarke III, Hagood, 74–75
Claye, William, 397
Clement, Kerron Stephon, 397
Clemons, Ben, 195–196, 248–249
coaches
    See also specific sport
    in Halls of Fame, 414–419
Coaches' Trophy, 147
Cody, Josh, 31, 249
Collins, Doug, 276
Collinsworth, Anthony Cris, 75–76, 84
Condon, Catherine Northcutt Ball, 359, 365, 373
Cooper, Riley Thomas, 76
Corbett, Douglas Mitchell, 206
Corso, Lee, 48
Costner, Kevin, 208
Couch, Christian Stratton, 304–305
Cowell, Brady, 195, 248
Cox, N. H., 24
Coxe, C.A., 248
Crabtree, Clyde "Cannonball," 30–31
Craybas, Jill, 333, 336–337
cross-country season, 3
Crowder, Randolph Channing, 76–77
Cruiser, Marshall, 42
Culpepper II, John Broward "Brad," 44, 77–78
Culverhouse, Hugh, 189
cycling, Olympic sports, 371, 413

D

Dalbey, Troy Lane, 378
Darnell, Gary, 43
Darr, John, 298
D'Arrigo, Mitch, 377
Davenport, Lindsay, 338
Davis, Andra Raynard, 78–79
Davis, Ben Jerome, 261–262
Davis, Cathy, 281
Dean, Terry, 174
DeClerq, Andrew Donald, 262
Delcourt, Frédéric, 378–379
Dellastatious, Bill, 296
DeMoss, Mickie, 281
Demps, Jeffrey, 398–399
Dempsey, Frank, 101
Dempsey, James Franklin "Frank," 79
Dennis Jr., Guy Durell, 79–80
deQuesada, A. M., 37
DeVoe, Don, 251–252, 275
Dickerson, Benjamin "Bubba" Gordon, 305
Dickey, Doug, 34, 39–40, 73, 81, 86, 92, 95, 97, 102, 114, 116
DiMarco, Christian Dean, 306

diving. *See* swimming and diving
Dixon, Dwayne, 132
Dixon III, Calvert Roy, 80
Doering, Christopher Paul, 0–81
Donald R. Disney Stadium at Florida Lacrosse Facility, 16
Donovan, Billy, 48, 252–254, 279
Douglas, Dwayne, 37
Dragotta, Jo, 342–343
DuBose, Jimmy Duwayne, 39, 81–82
Dunlap, Scott Michael, 307
Dunn, Jimmy, 81
Durie, Jo, 337
Durrance, Tommy, 38
Dusek, Ernie, 354
Duvenhage, Ian, 328
Dwyer, Conor, 379

E

Eckstein, David Mark, 206–207
Edmonson Jr., George, 188–189
Educational Amendments Act of 1972, Title IX, 4–5
Edwards, Bob, 211
Eiland, David William, 207–208
Ellenson, Gene, 35, 36
Ellis, Mark William, 208–209
Enea, Francesca, 243–244
Evans, Robert Deffriese, 399
Every, Matthew King, 307

F

facilities, sports, 11–16
Farr, James M., 25
Feeley, Heather Blaine Mitts, 346–347
Fendick, Patty, 337
Fernández, Gigi, 335
Fernández, Joe, 338
Fike Jr., Dan Clement, 82
Finney-Smith, Dorian, 254
Fisher, Jimmy, 74
Fisk, Carlton, 230
Fleming, Donald Denver, 35, 82–84
Fleming Field, 83
Florida A&M University, 24
Florida Agricultural College, 23, 24, 25, 191
Florida Blue Key, 65
Florida club sports, 9
Florida Field (football), 11, 83
Fogelman, Harry, 327
Fogg, Joshua Smith, 209
Foley, Jeremy, 46, 47, 51, 123, 157, 367
football
    all-time Florida bowl game records (table), 54–55

Index 437

athlete biographies, 57–189
coaches and eras, 25–52
Florida bowl history (table), 52–54
head coaching records (table), 51–52
major college leaders since 1990 (table), 52
national titles since 1990 (table), 52
nicknames of players, head coaches (table), 178–179
other Florida athletes who went into pro (tables), 181–187
our Florida all-stars (table), 56
overview and history, 21–25
season, 3
SEC championship game records (table), 56
stadiums in Southeastern Conference, 12–13
teams Gators have played for (table), 130–131
top 20 schools by bowl wins (table), 55–56
top 20 schools by bowls played (table), 55
Forsythe Jr., James A., 26
Frayler, Arthur, 377
Free, Jim, 37
Freeman, Michelle, 399–400
Fuller, Dave, 196–197

G

Gaberino, Geoffrey Steven, 379–380
Gaffney, Derrick Jabar, 84–85
Gaffney, Derrick Tyrone, 84
Gaffney, Don, 39, 84, 114
Gaffney, Jabar, 149
Gagner, Lawrence Joseph, 85–86
Gailey Jr., Thomas Chandler, 86–87
Gaines, William Albert, 87
Gal, Sandra, 322
Galloway Sr., David Lawrence, 87
Garbacz, Lori, 322–323
Gator Bowl, 50, 65
Gator Walk, 83
Gatorade, 37, 38
"Gators," 26–28
Gay, Joseph Brian, 308
Genovar, Frank, 327
George, Leonard, 39
Golarsa, Laura, 335
Golden, Timothy George, 88
Goldstein, Erving Max, 89
golf, men's
athlete biographies, 301–318
Bostick Golf Course, 15
Darr, Blevins, and Alexander eras, 298
early years, 296–297
Gators in NCAA Tournament (table), 299
Gators in SEC Tournament (table), 299–300
head coaching records (table), 299
national championships (table), 300
Rehling and Bishop eras, 297–298
season, 3
SEC championships (table), 300
golf, women's
athlete biographies, 322–325
Bostick Golf Course, 15
Florida athletes who went pro (tables), 325
Gators in AIAW, NCAA Tournaments (tables), 321
national championships (table), 321
Ryan, and other coaches, 319–320
season, 3
SEC championships (table), 321
Gone Pro
series, website, vi–vii
who's included, 1–2
Goss, Donald Alexander "Sandy," 380
Graham Jr., Earnest, 88, 90
Grandholm, James Thomas, 262–263
Grange, Red, 67, 89
Grasso, Mickey, 225
Graves, Ray, 36–38, 61, 64, 156
Green, Anthony "Tony" Edward, 90
Green, Bobby Joe, 90–91
Green, D'Tanyian Jacquez, 91
Green, Kenneth J., 308–309
Green, Samuel Lee, 92
Green, Taurean, 263–264
Green III, Orien Randolph, 264–265
Griese, Brian, 93
Griffin, Ben Hill, 11
Griffin III, Robert, 93
Gronkowski, Rob, 99
Grossman III, Rex Daniel, 92–93, 157
Groves, Tim, 114–115
Guy Bostick Clubhouse, 15
gymnastics
Florida non-medal winners (table), 412
Olympic sports, 369
season, 3

H

Haden, Joe, 51, 164
Haislett-Bacher, Nicole, 380–381
Halas, George, 67, 71
Hall, Galen, 42–43, 80, 123, 124, 126, 170
Hall, J. "Papa," 34
halls of fame, 19, 414–419
Hambrick, Darren, 93–94
Hammack, Malcolm "Mal" Eugene, 94–95
Hampton, Lorenzo, 41
Hampton, Lorenzo Timothy, 95
Hancock, Phillip Ranson, 309–310
handball, Olympic sports, 371, 413
Hanifan, Jim, 180

Hanratty, Terry, 161
Hardage, Lew, 196
Harrell Jr., James Clarence, 95–96
Hart, Howard Dudley, 310
Harvey, Derrick, 96
Harvey, Donnell Eugene, 265
Harvin, Percy, 51
Harvin III, William Percy, 96–97
Haslem, Udonis Johneal, 266
Hayden-Johnson, Vanessa L'Asonya, 287
Heath, Michael "Mike" Steward, 381–382
Heckman, Vel, 35
Hedgepeth, Whitney Lynn, 382
Heisman Trophy, 154–155
Helton, Charles Kimberlin, 97–98
Henry, Aneika, 287–288
Hernandez, Aaron Michael, 98–99
Hetherington, Jill, 337–338
Hill, Reynaldo Romel, 99
Hilliard, Isaac "Ike" Jason, 99–100
Hinson, Billy, 112
Hoffman, R.P., 194
Holsinger, Joe, 296
Holtz, Lou, 157
Horford, Al, 276
Hornung, Paul, 72
Horschel, William John, 311
Horton, Donna, 323
Huber, Liezel, 335, 338
Hultquist, Jill Hetherington, 337–338
Humphries, Scott, 330
Hunsinger, Charles Ray, 100–102
Hutchinson, Scott Rawls, 102

I

Infante, Gelindo "Lindy," 102–103

J

Jackson, Andy, 328
Jackson, Bo, 43
Jackson, Chad W., 103–104
Jackson, Darrell Lamont, 104–105
Jackson, David Andrew "Andy," 328
Jackson, Mark, 133
Jackson, Randall Belford, 105
Jackson, Tammy Eloise, 288, 371
Jackson, Terrance "Terry" Bernard, 106–107
Jackson Jr., Willie Bernard, 106–107
Jackson Sr., Willie Bernard, 106–107
Jacobs, Taylor Houser, 105, 107
Jager, John-Laffnie de, 337
James, Garry, 110
James, LeBron, 266
James Sr., John Wilbur, 108
Jayme, Carlos Alberto Borges, 382–383

Jeffrey, J. D., 25
Johns, Karen, 237
Johnson, Ellis Bernard, 109
Johnson, Todd Edward, 109–110
Johnson, Vance, 133
Johnson Jr., Doug, 108–109
Jones, Edgar, 296
Jones, James Roosevelt, 110
Jones, Merlakia, 288–289
Jones, Ralph, 67
judo, 413

K

Katie Seashole Pressly Softball Stadium, 18
Kearney, Beverly, 399, 400
Kearse, Jevon, 111
Keller, Gary J., 267–268
Kelly, Jim, 41
Keosseian, Joseph, 405
Ker, Crawford Francis, 112
Kerr, Jane, 383
King, Holly, 345–346
Kinney, Erron Quincy, 112–113
Kline, William G., 29, 194, 248
Knotts, Doug, 63
Knowles, Mark, 330
Knox, Chuck, 158
Koch, Gary D., 311–312
Koss, Bill, 266, 274
Kramer, Jerry, 72
Kruger, Lon, 252
Kunce, Kristine, 335, 337
Kynes, Jimmy, 32, 79

L

lacrosse season, 3
Lake Alice, 28
LaPorta, Matthew Vincent, 210–212, 371
Larson, David Erwin, 383–384
Laudner, Tim, 213
Lawless, Richard Burton, 113–114
Leach, Bob, 122
Leak, Chris, 48, 49, 147, 157
LeCount, Terry Jerome, 114
Ledman, Gary, 122
Lee, David, 268–269, 278
Levine, Jess, 331
Lieb, Thomas J., 31–32
Lilly, Robert Anthony, 114–115
Linder Stadium at Ring Tennis Complex, 15–16
Liquori, Marty, 358, 368
Little, Floyd, 102
Little Sr., David Lamar, 115
Lloyd, Odin, 99
Lochte, Ryan Steven, 384–385

Index

Lombardi, Vince, 159
Lombardozzi, Steve, 213
Lombardozzi Sr., Stephen Paul, 212–213
Long, Buford, 34
Long, Buford Eugene, 115–116
Long, Jeff, 23
Lopez, Andy, 198–199
López-Zubero, Martin, 395
Lott, Anthony, 170
Lotz, John, 250–251, 262
Loveless, Lea, 385
Luckman, Sid, 66
Lusader, Scott Edward, 213–214

M

Macklin, Vernon Leon, 269
Madden, John, 180
Manning, Peyton, 45
Manuel, Marquand Alexander, 116–117
Maronde, John Nicholas, 214
Marshall, Wilber, 41
Marshall, Wilber Buddyhia, 117–118
Marston, Dr. Robert, 40
martial arts
    athlete biographies, 351–354
    overview, 350
mascots Albert and Alberta the Alligators, 94
Matthews, Michael Shane, 44, 118–119, 124
Mauer, John, 249
Maurer, Lea E. Loveless, 385
Maxwell, Vernon, 269–270
McAllister, Sam, 196, 249
McAndrew, James "Jamie" Brian, 214–215
McCain, Brandi, 289
McCain, Patty Fendick, 337
McCoy, Anthony "Tony" Bernard, 119
McCoy, Charles J., 29
McCoy, C.J., 247–248
McCray Jr., Bobby L., 119–120
McDonald, Raymondo Antoine, 120
McDonald Sr., Ray, 120
McGee, JaVale, 276
McGrew, Reginald Gerald, 121
McGriff, William Travis, 121, 123
McKee, Alexander Timothy, 386
McKethan, Alfred A., 16
McKethan Stadium at Perry Field, 16–17
McLeod, H.D., 194
McMahon, Pat, 199
McNabb, Denter Eugene, 123
McQuay, Tony, 400–401
Melnyk, Steven N., 312
Merklein, Mark, 330–331
Mesler, Steven Michael, 405–406
Meyer, Urban, 47–50, 76, 83, 120, 128, 153

Mickell, Darren, 123–124
Miller, Austin and Phillip, 26–27
Miller, J. Hillis, 33
Miller, Michael Lloyd, 270–271
Mills III, Ernest "Ernie" Lee, 124–125
Milton-Jones, DeLisha, 290–291, 371
Mincey, Jeremy Lamar, 51, 125
Mitchell, Dennis Allen, 401
Mitchell, Jeffrey Clay, 125–126
Mitts, Heather, 346–347
Mitz, Alonzo Loqwone, 126
Moore, Nathaniel, 39, 126–127
Moss, Jarvis Jaray, 127–128
Mourning, Alonzo, 266
Mularkey, Michael Rene, 128–129
Murphree, Albert A., 29
Murphy, Bob, 297
Murphy, Erik, 280
Murphy, Robert "Rob" Albert, 215–216
Murphy Jr., Louis Morris, 129, 131
Murphy Jr., Robert Murphy, 313
Muschamp, William "Will," 50–51, 83, 189
Myles, Godfrey Clarence, 132

N

NACDA Learfield Sports Director's Cup, 5–6
Nagurski, Bronko, 67
Namath, Joe, 36
NASCAR racing, 355–356
Nattiel, Ricky Rennard, 132–133, 174
Navratilova, Martina, 338
Nelson, David Alan, 133
Nelson, Reggie, 134
Nesty, Anthony Conrad, 386–387
Newton, Cam, 51
Newton, Cameron Jerrell, 134–135, 155
Newton, R. D., 29
Newton, Timothy Reginald, 135
Newton Robert D. "Ark," 89
Neyer, Megan, 19
Neyland, Robert, 33
Nickey, Donnie, 141
Nickitas, Stephanie, 333, 336
Nicklaus, Jack, 314, 315
Noah, Joakim Simon, 271–273, 276
North, Andrew "Andy" Steward, 313–314
Northcutt, Kathryn Page Zemina, 394
Novotná, Jana, 335, 338

O

O'Brien, Bill, 150
O'Brien, Jack Edward, 136
O'Connell, Phillip D., 352
O'Connell, Stephen C., 39
O'Connell Center, 12–13

O'Day, Darren Christopher, 216–218
Oden, Greg, 272
Odom, Jason Brian, 136
Oliver III, Louis, 137
Olson, Lute, 261
Olson, Timothy Lane, 218
Olympic sports
    baseball, 371
    bobsled, 405–406
    bobsledding, 372
    cycling, 371, 406
    Florida medal winners, 360–363
    Florida non-medal winners (table), 407–413
    Florida Olympians (table), 363–364
    gymnastics, 369
    handball, 371
    modern Olympic Games (table), 359
    overview, 358
    Paralympic Games (table), 360
    soccer, 370
    swimming and diving, 365–366, 372–396
    tennis, 370
    track and field, 367–369
    volleyball, 371–372
O'Neal, Randall Jeffrey, 218–219
O'Neal, Shaquille, 266, 351
O'Neil, Titus, 352
Ortega, Michael "Mike" Irvin Pérez, 219–220
Ortega, Ralph, 137–138
Ortiz, Javier Victor, 219
Orton, Kyle, 93, 164
O'Sullivan, Kevin, 199–200
Outback Bowl, 49

P

Paculba, Aja, 244–245
Page, LaMurriel "Murriel," 290–291
Paralympic Games (table), 360
Parrish, Bernard "Bernie" Paul, 138–139, 196
Parrish, Bernie, 35
Parson, Chandler, 273–274
Peace, Wayne, 41
Pearson, Michael Wayne, 139
Peck, Carolyn, 283
Pell, Charles, 40–42, 126, 132
Pelletier, Helene, 337
Peoples, David Roy, 314
Percy Beard Track and Field Complex, 14, 18–19
Perry, Carl "Tootie," 16, 29
Perry, Chan, 220
Perry, Charles R. and Nancy V., 15
Perry, Herbert Edward, 220
Perry Field, McKathan Stadium at, 16
Pestrak, Stacie, 245
Peterson, Bill, 35

Peterson, Porter Michael, 139–140
Pettis, Bridget, 292–293
Phelps, Michael, 384, 385
Piller, Zachary Paul, 140–141
Pittman, Bob, 196
Polcovich, Kevin Michael, 220–221
Potter, Bill, 327
Pouncey, James Michael "Mike," 142–143
Pouncey, Leshawn Maurkice, 142–143
Pouncey, Mike, 51
Pressly, James G., 14
Pressly, Jamie and Katie, 18
Proctor, Carlos, 296, 352–353
Purcell, David López-Zubero, 395
Pyle, G. E., 28–29

R

Raburn, Ryan Neil, 221–222
Ragan Jr., David William, 314–315
Rajtar, Gayle Prince, 446
Rajtar, Steve, 446
Ramsey, William Thrace, 222
Ratliff, Keiwan Jevar, 141
Ray, Larry, 237
Raymond, Lisa, 333, 338–339
Reaves, John, 38, 39
Reaves, Thomas Johnson, 143–144
Reese, Randy, 365
Rehling, Conrad, 297
Reinach, Elna, 337
Restrepo, Camilo Villegas, 317
Reynoso, Alfred Joel Horford, 267
Rhett, Errict Undra, 57, 144–145, 189
Rhine, Jack, 197
Richard, Chris, 274, 276
Richard, Deb, 323–324
Richbourg, Lance, 1, 194–195
Richbourg, Lance Clayton, 222–223
Rigdon, Paul David, 223
Riggins, Anthony, 93
Rinaldi-Stunkel, Kathy, 337
Ring, Dr. Alfred A., 15
Ring Tennis Complex, 15–16
Ringgold, Brett, 387
Rinker, Larry, 324
Rinker, Laurie Ann, 324–325
Rob Gidel Family Practice Field, 16
Roberson, Anthony, 274–275
Robert, Yvon, 354
Roberts Jr., Edward Glenn "Fireball," 355–356
Rockne, Knute, 30
Rodhe, Cecilia, 273
Rodriguez, Steven "Paco," 223
Rose, Gabrielle, 388
Rosen, Albert "Al" Leonard, 10, 224–225

Rosenberg, Steven Allen, 226
Rosensteel, Colleen, 353
Ross, Carol, 282–283
Ross, David Wade, 226
Ross, Donald, 15
Roundtree, James W., 145–146, 353
Ruskin, Scott Drew, 227
Rutledge III, Johnny Boykins, 146

S

Sanders, Barry, 66
Sanders, George Douglas, 315–316
Sankford, Sam, 35
Scarritt, Stephen Russell "Russ" Mallory, 227
Schintzius, Dwayne Kenneth, 275–276
Schnell, Herman, 327
Scott, Josef Ian, 146, 148
Seagle, Georgia, 11
seasons of sports, 2–4
Sebring, H. L. "Tom," 30
Severin, Paul, 296
Shanahan, Mike, 46
Shannon, Tom, 37
Shealy, Ryan Nelson, 228
Shelton, Bryon, 328
Sheppard, Lito Decorian, 84, 148–149
Shires, Dana, 37
Shorter, Frank, 368
Shorter, Frank Charles, 401–402
Sikes Jr., Daniel David, 316
Siler, Brandon T., 149
Simpson, John Marlin, 149–150
Sloan, Norm, 250–252, 262, 275
Smith, Cedric Delon, 150
Smith, Emmitt, 164
Smith, M., 296
Smith, Troy, 49
Smith, William Lawrence "Larry," 150–152
Smith III, Emmitt James, 19, 43, 57, 144, 150–152
Smylie, Elizabeth, 337
Soares, Bruno, 339
soccer
    athlete biographies, 344–349
    Florida women's season records (table), 342
    James G. Pressly Stadium at Percy Beard Track, 14
    Olympic sports, 370
    overview, 341
    season, 3
    Southeastern Conference championships (tables), 342–343
softball
    athlete biographies, 240–245
    Florida coaching records (table), 238
    overview, 237

Seashole Pressly Softball Stadium, 18
season, 4
SEC championships by team (table), 239–240
Southeastern Conference championships (table), 239
women's college World Series appearances (table), 238–239
Southern Intercollegiate Athletic Association, 21
Spadea, Vincent, 330
Speights, Marreese, 276
Spencer, James "Jimmy" Arthur, 152–153
Spikes, Brandon, 153, 156
sports
    See also specific sport
    facilities described, 11–16
    Florida club, 9
    Olympic. See Olympic sports
    and seasons, 2–4
    success in, 5–8
Spurrier, Jeri, 101
Spurrier, Steve Orr, 11, 21, 22, 37, 38, 43–46, 68, 80, 87, 93, 98, 118, 123, 124, 144, 146, 155, 156–157, 166, 176
Stafford, Shaun, 333
Stanley, Dennis K. "Dutch," 31
Stanley, D.K. "Dutch," 327
Stanley, Robert Michael, 228–229
Starks IV, Maximillian Weisner, 157–158
Steele, David, 122
Steinbrenner, George, 16
Stephen C. O'Connell Student Activity Center, 12
Stephenson, George Kay, 158–159
Stevens, Kent, 33
Stockwell, Marcus William, 387
Stockwell, Tracy Ann Caulkins, 376–377
Stoops, Bob, 45, 46
Storter, Neal "Bo Gator," 27
Stosur, Samantha, 338
Strong, Charlie, 47
Stubbs, Rennae, 338
success in sports, 5–8
Sugar Bowl, 49, 50
Sugiyama, Ai, 335
Sullivan, Haywood Cooper, 33, 34, 229–230
Sullivan, Marc Cooper, 230
Sullivan, Michael James, 316
"Swamp, The," 21, 44
Swanson, Bob, 29
Sweeting, Ryan, 331
swimming and diving
    athlete biographies, 372–396
    Florida non-medal winners (table), 407–410
    men's head coaching dual meet records (table), 366
    Olympic sports, 365–366, 372–396

season, 4
Southeastern Conference championships (table), 365
women's head coaching dual meet records (table), 366
Symank, John Richard, 159–160

T
Tannen, Steve Olsen, 38, 160–161
Tappin-Doussan, Ashley Tara, 387–388
Taylor, Christian, 402–403
Taylor, Earle "Dummy," 26, 28
Taylor, Frederick Antwon, 161–162
Taylor, Travis Lamont, 162–163
teams, all-star, 10
Tebow, Timothy "Tim" Richard, 48, 49, 50, 133, 134, 155, 163–165
Temesvári, Andrea, 339
tennis, men's
    athlete biographies, 330–331
    Florida coaching records (table), 329
    Florida non-medal winners (table), 412
    Gators in NCAA Tournament (table), 329
    Linder Stadium at Ring Tennis Complex, 15–16
    Olympic sports, 370
    overview, 327–328
    season, 4
    SEC championships (table), 329–330
tennis, women's
    athlete biographies, 335–339
    Brandi and Thornqvist eras, 333–334
    Florida non-medal winners (table), 412
    Gators in AIAW, NCAA Tournaments (tables), 334
    Linder Stadium at Ring Tennis Complex, 15–16
    national championships (table), 334
    Olympic sports, 370
    overview, 332
    season, 4
    SEC championships (table), 335
Tewell, Doug, 301
Thomas, Kite, 225
Thomas, Marcus, 165–166
Thompson, Jane Louis Kerr, 383
Thompson, Robert "Robby" Randall, 230–231
Thornqvist, Roland, 333–334
Tigert, John J., 21, 31
Title IX, Educational Amendments Act of 1972, 4–5, 281
Torres, Dara Grace, 388–389
Townsend, Darian Roy, 389–390
track and field
    athlete biographies, 396–404

Florida non-medal winners (table), 411–412
men's head coaching records (table), 368
Olympic sports, 367–369
season, 4
women's head coaching records (table), 368–369
Trammell, Allen, 37–38
Travis, Lee, 123
Travis, Tiffany, 293
Troupe, Benjamin Lashaun, 166
Troy, Gregg, 365
Tym, Alice Luthy, 332
Tymrak, Erika, 347

U
Unitas, Johnny, 159
University of Florida, 25, 191, 414–417

V
Valdes, Marc Christopher, 231–232
Van Fleet, James A., 29–30
Van Sickel, Dale, 31
Vernon, Mickey, 225
Vidal, Rafael, 390
Visscher, Ed, 251
volleyball
    Olympic sports, 371–372, 413
    season, 4
Vollmer, Dana Whitney, 391

W
Wages, Harmon Leon, 166–167
Wagner, Allison Marie, 391–392
Wagstaff, Elizabeth Jane, 392
Wahlberg, Mark, 123
Waite, Jack, 339
Walk, Neal Eugene, 277–278
Walker, Aaron Scott, 167
Walker, Herschel, 164
Walker, Idrees Kenyatta, 167–168
Walker, Laura Anne, 392–393
Walker, Sullivan, 92
Walsh, Matt, 280
Walton, Tim, 237
Wambach, Mary Abigail, 347–348, 349
Warren, Gerard Thurston, 168–169
Washington, Tonya, 293–294
Waters, Dale Barnard, 169
Wayte, Mary Alice, 393
Weary, Joseph Frederick, 170
Weaver, Andrew, 406
websites, Gone Pro, vi–vii
Welch, Dr. Paula, 281
Whiddon, Sue, 332
White, Adrian Darnell, 170–171

White, Donna Horton, 323
White, James L., 195, 248
White IV, James William, 278–279
Whitney, Ashley Ann, 394
Wilbekin, Scottie, 254
Wilkerson, Stephen Bradley, 232–233, 371
Williams, Angus, 33
Williams, Berton Caswell "Cy," 89, 353–354
Williams, Charles, 63
Williams, David Wayne, 171–172
Williams, Ejijah Elgebra, 172
Williams, Jason Chandler, 279–280
Williams, John L., 95, 112, 173–174, 180
Williams III, Bernard Rollen, 403
Williams Sr., Jarvis Eric, 172–173
Williams-Mills, Novlene, 404
Williamson, Kathryn, 349
Wise, Kendall Cole "Casey," 233–234
Witherspoon, Sophia L., 294
Wolf, Frank, 79
Wolf, Raymond B. "Bear," 32–33
women's sports
    See also specific sport
    generally, 4–5
Woodruff, Bob, 33–35, 82, 90, 115, 136, 145, 149, 159

Wright, Major, 174
Wuerffel, Daniel "Danny" Carl, 174–176
Wuerffel, Danny, 44, 45, 48, 155
Wynn, DeShawn, 176–177
Wyrnak, Darlene, 281

Y

Yarbrough, James Kelley, 177
Yost, Eddie, 225
Young, Darren, 352
Young, Patric, 254
Youngblood, Jack, 19, 38, 39
Youngblood III, Herbert Jackson "Jack," 177–180
Yow, Debbie, 281–282

Z

Zemina, Paige, 394
Zimmerman, Jeffrey "Jeff" Alan, 112, 180–181
Zook, Ron, 46–47, 120, 128, 146, 157, 166
Zubero, David, 395
Zubero, Martin, 395
Zunino, Michael Accorsi, 234
Zvereva, Natasha, 335

ABOUT THE AUTHORS

Steve Rajtar grew up near Cleveland, Ohio, came to Florida to go to college, met his future wife, and decided to stay. After earning degrees in Mathematics and Anthropology from what is now the University of Central Florida, he attended the University of Florida and earned two law degrees, a J.D. and an LL.M. in Taxation. He has been involved with the Boy Scouts for more than 35 years and has been an activity leader with the Florida Trail Association, leading historical walking tours through the communities of Central Florida. He has had 25 books published so far, including *Historical Photos of Gainesville, Historical Photos of the University of Florida, A Guide to Historic Gainesville, Remembering the University of Florida,* and *Remembering Gainesville.*

Three gators relaxing in the sun

Gayle Prince Rajtar is a native Floridian whose family came to Orlando in 1908. She earned a degree from what is now the University of Central Florida in Communications while working as a professional singer and drummer. In Gainesville, she worked at a pair of radio stations and spent more time in the stadium on campus than many Gator athletes. She worked for the UF College of Journalism while its offices were in the west side of the stadium, adjacent to a field where she listened to the Gator marching band practicing (now the location of the O'Connell Center). She is the co-author (with Steve) of *A Guide to Historic Winter Park, Florida* and *Winter Park Chronicles,* as well as more than three dozen articles in *Winter Park Magazine* on local historical subjects.

They have a son, Jason, married to Karen, with three children, twins Jax and Alex and daughter, Elleri; and a daughter, Kelly, married to Will, with two children, Nate and Gillian. They join their parents and grandparents in cheering on the Gators . . . they never were really given any other option.